CORPORATE FINANCE

CFA Institute is the premier association for investment professionals around the world, with over 95,000 members in 133 countries. Since 1963 the organization has developed and administered the renowned Chartered Financial Analyst® Program. With a rich history of leading the investment profession, CFA Institute has set the highest standards in ethics, education, and professional excellence within the global investment community, and is the foremost authority on investment profession conduct and practice.

Each book in the CFA Institute Investment Series is geared toward industry practitioners along with graduate-level finance students and covers the most important topics in the industry. The authors of these cutting-edge books are themselves industry professionals and academics and bring their wealth of knowledge and expertise to this series.

CORPORATE FINANCE

A Practical Approach

Michelle R. Clayman, CFA

Martin S. Fridson, CFA

George H. Troughton, CFA

WILEY

John Wiley & Sons, Inc.

Published by John Wiley & Sons, Inc., Hoboken, New Jersey.
Published simultaneously in Canada.

For general information on our other products and services or for technical support, please contact our Customer
Care Department within the United States at (800) 762-2974, outside the United States at (317) 572-3993 or fax
(317) 572-4002.

Wiley also publishes its books in a variety of electronic formats. Some content that appears in print may not be
available in electronic books. For more information about Wiley products, visit our web site at www.wiley.com.

Library of Congress Cataloging-in-Publication Data:

Clayman, Michelle R.
    Corporate finance : a practical approach / Michelle R. Clayman, Martin S. Fridson, George H. Troughton.
      p.   cm.
    Includes index.
    ISBN 978-0-470-19768-4 (cloth)
      1. Corporations—Finance.   I. Fridson, Martin S.   II. Troughton, George H.   III. Title.
  HG4026.C5274 2008
  658.15—dc22

                                                                                          2008002759

Printed in the United States of America

10 9 8 7 6 5 4 3 2 1

CONTENTS

CHAPTER 6
Working Capital Management   263

CHAPTER 7
Financial Statement Analysis   **311**

CHAPTER 8
Mergers and Acquisitions   367

FOREWORD

I am delighted that CFA Institute is publishing a book on corporate finance. Having worked and taught in the corporate finance area, I believe that a fundamental grounding in corporate finance concepts is crucial in all areas of business enterprise. Whether working in finance, in marketing, as an engineer, as an entrepreneur, or in another activity of a business enterprise, professionals must be able to evaluate the financial implications of their activities and decisions. That evaluation is what the concepts of corporate finance help one do.

The concepts developed in this book are particularly important for investment professionals. The value of a financial security is ultimately determined by the value of the cash flows that the owner of the security can expect to receive in the future. Corporate finance helps investors, analysts, and portfolio managers evaluate how changes in capital or product/market conditions, as well as corporate managers' decisions, affect the value of the cash flows underlying security holder claims. The need for this information is a key reason that corporate finance was added to the CFA curriculum in the mid-1990s.

The first corporate finance material in the CFA curriculum consisted mainly of chapters selected from undergraduate textbooks. Because these chapters were designed for use in formal university courses, they were not ideal readings for professionals studying corporate finance on the conceptual level or for purposes of practical application. The coverage of some topical areas was limited, and relatively little attention was paid to institutional details and practical applications. Over the years, CFA Institute has worked to develop materials that have a scope, depth of coverage, and a practical emphasis that are better suited for professionals. *Corporate Finance: A Practical Approach* is a key product of this effort.

Written by corporate finance experts who bring both industry and academic perspectives to the topic, *Corporate Finance* does an exceptional job of presenting key corporate finance concepts clearly and concisely. It is, moreover, a highly readable book that is practical yet rigorous. Each chapter begins with a list of learning outcomes, so that the reader knows from the beginning the key lessons of the chapter. The authors then discuss specific fundamental concepts in a way that provides the reader with a strong intuitive understanding. Analytical tools are introduced, and their applications are demonstrated in ways that facilitate understanding and nurture an ability to apply the concepts immediately in practice.

Corporate finance involves (1) identifying investments in real (nonfinancial) assets that create value for the owners of a business, (2) financing those investments at the lowest possible cost, and (3) managing working capital investments. The analysis of real asset investment opportunities requires knowledge of fundamental valuation concepts. These concepts are the same when used to determine whether an individual project creates value for the owners of a business as when used to estimate the value of an entire business enterprise. After all, a business enterprise is nothing more than a collection of related projects. Capital structure and dividend policies concern how the permanent assets of the firm are financed to create the highest possible value for stockholders. The key in this area is to finance the assets at the lowest possible cost. Finally, working capital management concerns the efficiency with which current assets and liabilities—such as cash, receivables, inventory, and payables—are managed. The objective of working capital management is to get the most out of the liquid assets of the firm.

This book starts off the discussion of these topics with a comprehensive chapter on corporate governance. Placing this chapter first underscores the important relationship between the quality of corporate governance and value creation at a firm. The incentives of managers and directors often are not well aligned with the objectives of the stockholders, which can lead to investment and financing decisions that benefit managers or directors at the expense of stockholders. Effective corporate governance helps align these incentives and objectives so that decisions reflect the principal stockholder objective of maximizing shareholder wealth.

Chapters 2 and 3 focus on the capital budgeting process and the costs of financing investments in real assets. Chapter 2 does an exceptional job of covering the methods used to evaluate projects and the advantages and disadvantages of each. These discussions include practical introductions to preparing cash flow projections and to spreadsheet modeling. Chapter 2 also includes an accessible treatment of *real options*. Traditional project analysis does not adequately capture the effect on the value of a project of real options, such as the option to delay an investment or, once an investment in a project is made, to change the nature of the project or abandon it. Chapter 3 follows with a discussion of how to estimate the costs of the various components of the financing used by a firm and the cost of capital used in project analysis.

Chapters 4 and 5 present the theory and practical issues associated with a company's financing and dividend policies. Chapter 4 focuses on capital structure decisions, and Chapter 5, on dividend decisions. Chapter 4 provides insights concerning the factors that determine the appropriate mix of debt and equity for financing a company's real assets. Empirical evidence suggests that these financing decisions can increase the total value of a business enterprise by as much as 10 percent. Chapter 5 examines the alternative ways in which a firm can distribute value to its stockholders and the reasons that a firm might or might not want to adopt a particular method of distribution.

Chapter 6 covers key concepts associated with working capital management. Effective management of working capital can be crucial to the success of a business. Many businesses fail because their managers do not adequately forecast and monitor short-term liquidity needs. This chapter describes how cash flows (requirements and surpluses) are forecast and how the balances in various current asset accounts are monitored and managed. Finally, Chapter 6 supplies an extensive, practical discussion of sources of short-term financing and how they are managed.

Chapters 7 and 8 complete the book with in-depth discussions of financial statement analysis (Chapter 7) and mergers and acquisitions (Chapter 8). A solid understanding of financial statement analysis helps analysts, whether within or outside a firm, to interpret the organization's financial statements. The analytical tools and applications covered in Chapter 7 are useful in evaluating the past performance of a business and thereby in promoting an understanding of its future prospects. This chapter covers concepts related to all of the areas addressed in previous chapters.

Chapter 8 is a comprehensive presentation of mergers and acquisitions—the concepts related to these activities, their objectives, and the techniques used in business valuation. A discussion of mergers and acquisitions is a fitting ending for this book because mergers and acquisitions are in fact simply large projects that should be analyzed by application of the key concepts explained in the previous chapters. This concept is apparent in the discussion of target company valuation, which provides a clear summary of business valuation techniques. By the time readers reach this point in the book, they will have been treated to a very accessible and practical discussion of corporate finance concepts and applications.

Robert Parrino, PhD, CFA
University of Texas at Austin

ACKNOWLEDGMENTS

We would like to thank the many individuals who played important roles in producing this book.

Robert R. Johnson, CFA, managing director of the Education Division at CFA Institute, originally saw the need for specialized curriculum materials and initiated their development. We appreciate his support. Dennis W. McLeavey, CFA, initiated this project during his term as head of Curriculum Development. Christopher B. Wiese, CFA, had primary responsibility for the delivery of chapters, taking over that role from Jerald E. Pinto, CFA, at the beginning of 2006. Mr. Wiese oversaw the final organization, writing, and editing of the chapters for the CFA curriculum.

Individual manuscript reviews were provided by Jean-Francois Bureau, CFA, Sean D. Carr, Rosita P. Chang, CFA, Jacques R. Gagné, CFA, Gene C. Lai, Asjeet S. Lamba, CFA, Piman Limpaphayom, CFA, and Zhiyi Song, CFA. Chapter author Pamela Peterson Drake, CFA, and John D. Stowe, CFA—now head of Curriculum Development at CFA Institute—provided notable assistance at critical junctures. We thank all of them for their excellent and detailed work.

Ellen Barber provided copyediting that substantially contributed to the book's readability. MaryAnn Dupes and Christine Kemper of CFA Institute also contributed to the book's copyediting. Wanda Lauziere of CFA Institute expertly served as project manager for the book's production.

INTRODUCTION

CFA Institute is pleased to provide you with this Investment Series covering major areas in the field of investments. These texts are thoroughly grounded in the highly regarded CFA Program Candidate Body of Knowledge that serves as the anchor for the three levels of the CFA Program. Currently, nearly 200,000 aspiring investment professionals are devoting hundreds of hours each to master this material, as well as other elements of the Candidate Body of Knowledge, to obtain the coveted CFA charter. We provide these materials for the same reason we have been chartering investment professionals for over 40 years: to lead the investment profession globally by setting the highest standards of ethics, education, and professional excellence.

HISTORY

This book series draws on the rich history and origins of CFA Institute. In the 1940s, a handful of societies for investment professionals developed around common interests in the evolving investment industry. At that time, the idea of purchasing common stock as an investment—as opposed to pure speculation—was still a relatively new concept for the general public. Just ten years before, the U.S. Securities and Exchange Commission had been formed to help referee a playing field marked by robber barons and stock market panics.

In January 1945, a fundamentally driven professor and practitioner from Columbia University and Graham-Newman Corporation wrote an article in the precursor of today's CFA Institute *Financial Analysts Journal*, making the case that people who research and manage portfolios should have some sort of credential to demonstrate competence and ethical behavior. This person was none other than Benjamin Graham, the father of security analysis and future mentor to well-known modern investor Warren Buffett.

Creating such a credential took 16 years. By 1963, 284 brave souls—all over the age of 45—took an exam and successfully launched the CFA credential. What many do not fully understand is that this effort was driven by a desire to create a profession whose practitioners were professionals providing investing services to individuals in need. In so doing, a fairer and more productive capital market would result.

Most professions—including medicine, law, or accounting—have certain hallmark characteristics that help to attract serious individuals and motivate them to devote energy to their life's work. First, there must be a body of knowledge. Second, there need to be entry requirements, such as those required to achieve the CFA credential. Third, there must be a commitment to continuing education. Finally, a profession must serve a purpose beyond one's individual interests. By properly conducting one's affairs and putting client interests first, the investment professional encourages general participation in the incredibly productive global capital markets. This encourages the investing public to part with their hard-earned savings for redeployment in the fair and productive pursuit of appropriate returns.

As C. Stewart Sheppard, founding executive director of the Institute of Chartered Financial Analysts, said,

Society demands more from a profession and its members than it does from a professional crafts-man in trade, arts, or business. In return for status, prestige, and autonomy, a profession extends a public warranty that it has established and maintains conditions of entry, standards of fair practice, disciplinary procedures, and continuing education for its particular constituency. Much is expected from members of a profession, but over time, more is given.

"The Standards for Educational and Psychological Testing," put forth by the American Psychological Association, the American Educational Research Association, and the National Council on Measurement in Education, state that the validity of professional credentialing examinations should be demonstrated primarily by verifying that the content of the examination accurately represents professional practice. In addition, a practice analysis study, which confirms the knowledge and skills required for the competent professional, should be the basis for establishing content validity.

For more than 40 years, hundreds upon hundreds of practitioners and academics have served on CFA Institute curriculum committees, sifting through and winnowing out all the many investment concepts and ideas to create a body of investment knowledge and the CFA curriculum. One of the hallmarks of curriculum development at CFA Institute is its extensive use of practitioners in all phases of the process. CFA Institute has followed a formal practice analysis process since 1995. The effort involves special practice analysis forums held, most recently, at 20 locations around the world. Results of the forums were put forth to 70,000 CFA charterholders for verification and confirmation of the body of knowledge so derived. In 2007, CFA Institute moved to implement a continuous practice analysis by making use of a collaborative web-based site and "wiki" technology. This will open the process to thousands more charterholders and significantly reduce the lag effect of concepts and techniques moving from practice to the CBOK.

What this means for the reader is that the concepts highlighted in these texts were selected by practitioners who fully understand the skills and knowledge necessary for success. We are pleased to put this extensive effort to work for the benefit of the readers of the Investment Series.

BENEFITS

This series will prove useful to those contemplating entry into the extremely competitive field of investment management, as well as those seeking a means of keeping one's knowledge fresh and up-to-date. Regardless of its use, this series was designed to be both user-friendly and highly relevant. Each chapter within the series includes extensive references for those who would like to dig deeper into a given concept. The workbooks provide a summary of each chapter's key points to help organize your thoughts, as well as sample questions and answers to test yourself on your progress.

For those new to the industry, the essential concepts that any investment professional needs to master are presented in a time-tested fashion. This material will help you better understand the investment field. I believe that the general public seriously underestimates the disciplined processes needed for the best investment firms and individuals to prosper. These texts lay the basic groundwork for many of the processes that successful firms use on a day-to-day basis. Without this base level of understanding and an appreciation for how the capital markets work, it becomes challenging to find competitive success. Furthermore, the concepts herein provide a true sense of the kind of work that is to be found managing portfolios, doing research, or pursuing related endeavors.

The investment profession, despite its relatively lucrative compensation, is not for everyone. It takes a special kind of individual to fundamentally understand and absorb the teachings from this body of work and then apply it in practice. In fact, most individuals who enter the field do not survive in the long run. The aspiring professional should think long and hard about whether this is the right field. There is no better way to make such a critical decision than by reading and evaluating the classic works of the profession.

The more experienced professional understands that the nature of the capital markets requires a commitment to continuous learning. Markets evolve as quickly as smart minds can find new ways to create exposure, attract capital, or manage risk. A number of the concepts in these pages did not exist a decade or two ago when many were starting out in the business. Hedge funds, derivatives, alternative investment concepts, and behavioral finance are just a few examples of the new applications and concepts that have altered the capital markets in recent years.

As markets invent and reinvent themselves, a best-in-class foundation investment series is of great value. Investment professionals must continuously hone their skills and knowledge if they are to compete with the young talent that constantly emerges. In fact, as we talk to major employers about their training needs, we are often told that one of the biggest challenges they face is how to help the experienced professional keep up with the recent graduates. This series can be part of that answer.

CONVENTIONAL WISDOM

It doesn't take long for the astute investment professional to realize two common characteristics of markets. First, prices are set by conventional wisdom, as a function of the many variables in the market. Truth in markets is, at its essence, what the market believes it is and how it assesses pricing credits or debits based on those beliefs. Second, inasmuch as conventional wisdom is a product of the evolution of general theory and learning, by definition conventional wisdom is often wrong or at the least subject to material change.

When I first entered this industry in the mid-1970s, conventional wisdom held that the concepts examined in these texts were a bit too academic for use in the competitive marketplace. What were considered to be the best investment firms of the time were led by men who had an eclectic style, an intuitive sense of markets, and a great track record. In the rough-and-tumble world of the practitioner, some of these concepts were considered to be of no use. Could conventional wisdom have been more wrong?

During the years of my tenure in the profession, the practitioner investment management firms that evolved successfully were full of determined, intelligent, intellectually curious investment professionals who endeavored to apply these concepts in a serious and disciplined manner. Today, the best firms are run by those who carefully form investment hypotheses and test them rigorously in the marketplace, whether it be in a quant strategy, comparative shopping for stocks within an industry, or hedge fund strategies. Their goal is to create investment processes that can be replicated with some statistical reliability. I believe those who embraced the so-called academic side of the learning equation have been much more successful as real-world investment managers.

THE TEXTS

A significant portion of the Candidate Body of Knowledge is represented in the initial five texts of the series. A text on international financial statement analysis is in development, and more texts may be forthcoming.

One of the most prominent texts over the years in the investment management industry has been Maginn and Tuttle's *Managing Investment Portfolios: A Dynamic Process.* The third edition updates key concepts from the 1990 second edition. Some of the more experienced members of our community own the prior two editions and will add the third edition to their library. Not only does this seminal work take the concepts from the other readings and put them in a portfolio context, but it also updates the concepts of alternative investments, performance presentation standards, portfolio execution and, very importantly, managing individual investor portfolios. Focusing attention away from institutional portfolios, and toward the individual investor, makes this edition an important and timely work.

Quantitative Investment Analysis focuses on some key tools that are needed for today's professional investor. In addition to classic time value of money, discounted cash flow applications, and probability material, there are two aspects that can be of value over traditional thinking.

The first involves the chapters dealing with correlation and regression that ultimately figure into the formation of hypotheses for purposes of testing. This gets to a critical skill that many professionals are challenged by: the ability to distinguish useful information from the overwhelming quantity of available data. For most investment researchers and managers, their analysis is not solely the result of newly created data and tests that they perform. Rather, they synthesize and analyze primary research done by others. Without a rigorous manner by which to understand quality research, you can not understand good research, nor do you have a basis to evaluate less rigorous research. What is often put forth in the applied world as good quantitative research frequently lacks rigor and validity.

Second, the last chapter of *Quantitative Investment Analysis* on portfolio concepts takes the reader beyond the traditional capital asset pricing model (CAPM) type of tools and into the more practical world of multifactor models and arbitrage pricing theory. This chapter also helps address the concerns of those who thought the text had a CAPM bias.

Equity Asset Valuation is a particularly cogent and important resource for anyone involved in estimating the value of securities and understanding security pricing. A well-informed professional knows that the common forms of equity valuation—dividend discount modeling, free cash flow modeling, price/earnings models, and residual income models—can all be reconciled to one another under certain assumptions. With a deep understanding of the underlying assumptions, the professional investor can better understand what other investors assume when calculating their valuation estimates. In my prior life as the head of an equity investment team, this knowledge gave us an edge over other investors.

Fixed Income Analysis has been at the forefront of new concepts in recent years, and this particular text offers some of the most recent material for the seasoned professional who is not a fixed-income specialist. The application of option and derivative technology to the once staid province of fixed income has helped contribute to an explosion of thought in this area.

Not only are professionals challenged to stay up to speed with credit derivatives, swaptions, collateralized mortgage securities, mortgage backed securities, and other vehicles, but this explosion of thought also puts a strain on the world's central banks to provide sufficient oversight. Armed with a thorough grasp of the new exposures, the professional investor is much better able to anticipate and understand the challenges our central bankers and markets face.

Corporate Finance: A Practical Approach is a solid foundation for those looking to achieve lasting business growth. In today's competitive business environment, companies must find innovative ways to enable rapid and sustainable growth. This text equips readers with the foundational knowledge and tools for making smart business decisions and formulating strategies to maximize company value. It covers everything from managing relationships between stakeholders to evaluating mergers and acquisitions bids as well as the companies behind them.

Through extensive use of real-world examples, readers will gain critical perspective into interpreting corporate financial data, evaluating projects, and allocating funds in ways that increase corporate value. Readers will gain insights into the tools and strategies employed in modern corporate financial management.

I hope you find this new series helpful in your efforts to grow your investment knowledge, whether you are a relatively new entrant or an experienced veteran ethically bound to keep up-to-date in the ever changing market environment. CFA Institute, as a long-term committed participant of the investment profession and a not-for-profit association, is pleased to give you this opportunity.

Jeff Diermeier, CFA
President and Chief Executive Officer
CFA Institute
January 2008

CORPORATE FINANCE

CHAPTER 1

CORPORATE GOVERNANCE

Rebecca Todd McEnally, CFA

CFA Institute
Charlottesville, Virginia

Kenneth Kim

State University of New York at Buffalo
Buffalo, New York

LEARNING OUTCOMES

After completing this chapter, you will be able to do the following:

- Define corporate governance and explain its importance.
- List and explain the objectives of an effective corporate governance system.
- Describe the core attributes of an effective corporate governance system, and evaluate whether a company's corporate governance has those attributes.
- Compare and contrast the three major business forms and the conflicts of interest problems in each.
- Explain the types of principal–agent problems.
- Compare and contrast agency relationships between (1) managers and shareholders, and (2) directors and shareholders.
- Describe the responsibilities of the board of directors, and list and explain the attributes of the board that an investor or investment analyst must assess.
- Illustrate effective corporate governance practice as it relates to attributes of the board of directors, and evaluate the strengths and weaknesses of a company's corporate governance practice.
- Describe the elements of a company's statement of corporate governance policies that investors and analysts should assess.
- Discuss the valuation implications of corporate governance.

1. INTRODUCTION

The modern corporation is a very efficient and effective means of raising capital, obtaining needed resources, and generating products and services. These and other advantages have caused the corporate form of business to become the dominant one in many countries. The corporate form, in contrast to other business forms, frequently involves the separation of ownership and control of the assets of the business. The ownership of the modern public corporation is typically diffuse; it has many owners, most with proportionally small stakes in the company, who are distant from, and often play no role in, corporate decisions. Professional managers control and deploy the assets of the corporation. This separation of ownership (shareholders) and control (managers) may result in a number of conflicts of interest between managers and shareholders. Conflicts of interest can also arise that affect creditors as well as other stakeholders, such as employees and suppliers. To remove or at least to minimize such conflicts of interest, corporate governance structures have been developed and implemented in corporations. Specifically, **corporate governance** is the system of principles, policies, procedures, and clearly defined responsibilities and accountabilities used by stakeholders to overcome the conflicts of interest inherent in the corporate form.

The failure of a company to establish an effective system of corporate governance represents a major operational risk to the company and its investors.[1] Corporate governance deficiencies may even imperil the continued existence of a company. Consequently, to understand the risks inherent in an investment in a company, it is essential to understand the quality of the company's corporate governance practices. It is also necessary to continually monitor a company's practices because companies are affected in important ways by changes in management, the composition of its board of directors, the company's competitive and market conditions, or mergers and acquisitions.

A series of major corporate collapses in North America, Europe, and Asia, nearly all of which involved the failure or direct override by managers of corporate governance systems, have made it clear that strong corporate governance structures are essential to the efficient and effective functioning of companies and to the financial markets in which they operate. Investors lost great amounts of money in the failed companies. The collapses weakened the trust and confidence essential to the efficient functioning of financial markets worldwide.

Legislators and regulators responded to the erosion of trust by introducing strong new regulatory frameworks. These measures are intended to restore the faith of investors in companies and the markets, and, very importantly, to help prevent future collapses. Nevertheless, the new regulations did not address all outstanding corporate governance problems and were not uniform across capital markets. Thus, we may expect corporate governance-related laws and regulations to further evolve.

The chapter is organized as follows: Section 2 presents the objectives of corporate governance systems and the key attributes of effective ones. Section 3 addresses forms of business and conflicts of interest, and Section 4 discusses two major sources of governance problems. In Section 5 we discuss standards and principles of corporate governance, providing three representative sets of principles from current practice. Section 6 touches on the valuation implications of the quality of corporate governance, and Section 7 summarizes the chapter.

---

[1]An **operational risk** is the risk of loss from failures in a company's systems and procedures or from external events.

2. CORPORATE GOVERNANCE: OBJECTIVES AND GUIDING PRINCIPLES

The modern corporation is subject to a variety of conflicts of interest. This fact leads to the following two major objectives of corporate governance:

- To eliminate or mitigate conflicts of interest, particularly those between managers and shareholders; and
- To ensure that the assets of the company are used efficiently and productively and in the best interests of its investors and other stakeholders.

How can a company go about achieving those objectives? It should have a set of principles and procedures sufficiently comprehensive to be called a corporate governance system. No single system of effective corporate governance applies to all firms in all industries worldwide. Different industries and economic systems, legal and regulatory environments, and cultural differences may affect the characteristics of an effective corporate governance system for a particular company. However, certain characteristics are common to all sound corporate governance structures. The core attributes of an effective corporate governance system are

- Delineation of the *rights* of shareholders and other core stakeholders;
- Clearly defined manager and director governance *responsibilities* to stakeholders;
- Identifiable and measurable *accountabilities* for the performance of the responsibilities;
- *Fairness* and equitable treatment in all dealings between managers, directors, and shareholders; and
- Complete *transparency* and accuracy in disclosures regarding operations, performance, risk, and financial position.

These core attributes form the foundation for systems of good governance, as well as for the individual principles embodied in such systems. Investors and analysts should determine whether companies in which they may be interested have these core attributes.

3. FORMS OF BUSINESS AND CONFLICTS OF INTEREST

The goal of for-profit businesses in any society is simple and straightforward: to maximize their owners' wealth. This can be achieved through strategies that result in long-term growth in sales and profits. However, pursuing wealth maximization involves taking risks. A business itself is risky for a variety of reasons. For example, there may be demand uncertainty for its products and/or services, economic uncertainty, and competitive pressures. Financial risk is present when a business must use debt to finance operations. Thus, continued access to sufficient capital is an important consideration and risk for businesses. These risks, and the inherent conflicts of interests in businesses, increase the need for strong corporate governance.

A firm's ability to obtain capital and to control risk is perhaps most influenced by how it is organized. Three of the predominant forms of business globally are the sole proprietorship, the partnership, and the corporation. Hybrids of these three primary business forms also exist, but we do not discuss them here because they are simply combinations of the three main business forms. Each of the three primary forms has its advantages and disadvantages.

EXHIBIT 1-1   Comparison of Characteristics of Business Forms

Characteristic	Sole Proprietorship	Partnership	Corporation
Ownership	Sole owner	Multiple owners	Unlimited ownership
Legal requirements and regulation	Few; entity easily formed	Few; entity easily formed	Numerous legal requirements
Legal distinction between owner and business	None	None	Legal separation between owners and business
Liability	Unlimited	Unlimited but shared among partners	Limited
Ability to raise capital	Very limited	Limited	Nearly unlimited
Transferability of ownership	Nontransferable (except by sale of entire business)	Nontransferable	Easily transferable
Owner expertise in business	Essential	Essential	Unnecessary

We will discuss each of them, the conflicts of interest that can arise in each, and the relative need for strong corporate governance associated with each form. However, a summary of the characteristics is provided in Exhibit 1-1.

3.1. Sole Proprietorships

The **sole proprietorship** is a business *owned and operated* by a single person. The owner of the local cleaner, restaurant, beauty salon, or fruit stand is typically a sole proprietor. Generally, few, if any, legal formalities are involved in establishing a sole proprietorship, and such businesses are relatively easy to start. In many jurisdictions, there are few, if any, legal distinctions between the sole proprietor and the business. For example, tax liabilities and related filing requirements for sole proprietorships are frequently based on the level of the sole proprietor. Legitimate business expenses are simply deducted from the sole proprietor's taxable income.

Sole proprietorships are the most numerous form of business worldwide, representing, for example, approximately 70 percent of all businesses in the United States by number.[2] However, because they are usually small-scale operations, they represent the lowest amount of market capitalization in many markets. Indeed, the difficulties of the sole proprietor in raising large amounts of capital, coupled with unlimited liability and lack of transferability of ownership, are serious impediments to the growth of a sole proprietorship.

From the point of view of corporate governance, the sole proprietorship presents fewer risks than the corporation because the manager and the owner are one and the same. Indeed, the major corporate governance risks are those faced by creditors and suppliers of goods and services to the business. These stakeholders are in a position to be able to demand the types and quality of information that they need to evaluate risks before lending money

---
[2]Megginson (1997), p. 40.

to the business or providing goods and services to it. In addition, because they typically maintain direct, recurring business relations with the companies, they are better able to monitor the condition and risks of the business, as well as control their own exposure to risk. Consequently, we will not consider sole proprietorships further.

3.2. Partnerships

A **partnership**, which is composed of more than one owner/manager, is similar to a sole proprietorship. For the most part, partnerships share many of the same advantages and disadvantages as the sole proprietorship. Two obvious advantages of a partnership over a sole proprietorship are the pooling of financial capital of the partners and the sharing of business risk among them. However, even these advantages may not be as important as the pooling of the partners' service-oriented expertise and skill, especially in large partnerships. Some very large international partnerships operate in such fields as real estate, law, investment banking, architecture, engineering, advertising, and accounting. Note also that large partnerships may enjoy competitive and economy-of-scale benefits over sole proprietorships.

Partners typically overcome conflicts of interest internally by engaging in partnership contracts specifying the rights and responsibilities of each partner. Conflicts of interest with entities outside the partnership are similar to those for the sole proprietorship and are dealt with in the same way. Hence, we will not consider these conflicts further.

3.3. Corporations

Corporations represent less than 20 percent of all businesses in the United States but generate approximately 90 percent of the country's business revenue.[3] The percentage is lower elsewhere, but growing. The **corporation** is a legal entity, and has rights similar to those of a person. For example, a corporation is permitted to enter into contracts. The chief officers of the corporation, the executives or top managers, act as agents for the firm and are legally entitled to authorize corporate activities and to enter into contracts on behalf of the business.

There are several important and striking advantages of the corporate form of business. First, corporations can raise very large amounts of capital by issuing either stocks or bonds to the investing public. A corporation can grant ownership stakes (i.e., common stock) to individual investors in exchange for cash or other assets. Similarly, it can borrow money (e.g., bonds or other debt) from individual or institutional investors, in exchange for interest payments and a promise to pay back the principal of the loan. Shareholders are the owners of the corporation, and any profits that the corporation generates accrue to the shareholders.

A second advantage is that corporate owners need not be experts in the industry or management of the business, unlike the owners of sole proprietorships and partnerships where business expertise is essential to success. Any individual with sufficient money can own stock. This has benefits to both the business and the owners. The business can seek capital from millions of investors, not only in domestic markets but worldwide.

Among the most important advantages of the corporate form is that stock ownership is easily transferable. Transferability of shares allows corporations to have unlimited life. A final and extremely important advantage is that shareholders have limited liability. That is, they can lose only the money they have invested, nothing more.

---

[3]Megginson (1997).

The corporate form of business has a number of disadvantages, however. For example, because many corporations have thousands or even millions of nonmanager owners, they are subject to more regulation than are partnerships or sole proprietorships. While regulation serves to protect shareholders, it can also be costly to shareholders as well. For example, the corporation must hire accountants and lawyers to deal with the accounting and other legal documents needed to comply with regulations. Perhaps the most significant disadvantage with the corporation (and the one most critical to corporate governance) is the difficulty that shareholders have in monitoring management and the firm's operations. As a sole proprietor of a small business, the owner is able to directly oversee such day-to-day business concerns as inventory levels, product quality, expenses, and employees. However, it is impossible for a shareholder of a large corporation such as General Motors or International Business Machines to monitor business activities and personnel, and to exert any control rights over the firm. In fact, a shareholder of a large firm may not even feel like an owner in the usual sense, especially because corporations are owned by so many other shareholders and because most owners of a large public corporation hold only a relatively small stake in it.

Agency relationships arise when someone, an agent, acts on behalf of another person, the principal. In a corporation, managers are the agents who act on behalf of the owners, the shareholders. If a corporation has in place a diligent management team that works in the best interests of its shareholders and other stakeholders, then the problem of passive shareholders and bondholders becomes a nonissue. In real life, unfortunately, management may not always work in the stakeholders' best interests. Managers may be tempted to see to their own well-being and wealth at the expense of their shareholders and others to whom they owe a fiduciary duty. This is known as an **agency problem,** or **principal–agent problem**. The money of shareholders, the principals, is used and managed by agents, the managers, who promise that the firm will pursue wealth-maximizing business activities. However, there are potential problems with these relationships, which we will discuss next.

4. SPECIFIC SOURCES OF CONFLICT: AGENCY RELATIONSHIPS

Conflicts among the various constituencies in corporations have the potential to cause problems in the relationships among managers, directors, shareholders, creditors, employees, and suppliers. However, we will concentrate here on the relationships between (1) managers and shareholders and (2) directors and shareholders. These two relationships are the primary focus of most systems of corporate governance. However, to the extent that strong corporate governance structures are in place and effective in companies, the agency conflicts among other stakeholders are mitigated as well. For example, managers are responsible for maximizing the wealth of the shareholders and minimizing waste (including excessive compensation and perquisite consumption). To the extent that managers do so, the interests of employees and suppliers are more likely to be met because the probability increases that sufficient funds will be available for payment of salaries and benefits, as well as for goods and services. In this section, we will describe these agency relationships, discuss the problems inherent in each, and we will illustrate these agency problems with real-world examples. An understanding of the nature of the conflicts in each relationship is essential to a full understanding of the importance of the provisions in codes of corporate governance.

4.1. Manager–Shareholder Conflicts

For investors, the manager–shareholder relationship is the most critical of agency relationships. It is important to recognize that firms and their managers, the shareholders' agents, obtain operating and investing capital from the shareholders, the owners, in two ways. First, although shareholders have a 100 percent claim on the firm's net income, the undistributed net income (the earnings remaining after the payment of dividends) is reinvested in the company. We normally term this reinvested income *retained earnings*. Second, the firm can issue stock to obtain the capital, either through an initial public offering (IPO) if the firm is currently privately owned, or through a seasoned equity offering (SEO) if the firm already has shares outstanding. By whatever means the firm obtains equity capital, shareholders entrust management to use the funds efficiently and effectively to generate profits and maximize investors' wealth.

However, although the manager is responsible for advancing the shareholders' best interests, this may not happen. For example, management may use funds to try to expand the size of the business to increase their job security, power, and salaries without consideration of the shareholders' interests. In addition, managers may also grant themselves numerous and expensive perquisites, which are treated as ordinary business expenses. Managers enjoy these benefits, and shareholders bear the costs. This is a serious agency problem, and unfortunately there are a number of recent real-world examples of their occurrence in corporations.

Managers also may make other business decisions, such as investing in highly risky ventures, that benefit themselves but that may not well serve the company's investors. For example, managers who hold substantial amounts of executive stock options will receive large benefits if risky ventures pay off, but will not suffer losses if the ventures fail. By contrast, managers whose wealth is closely tied to the company and who are therefore not well diversified may choose to not invest in projects with a positive expected net present value because of excessive risk aversion. The checks and balances in effective corporate governance systems are designed to reduce the probability of such practices.

The cases of Enron Corporation (bankruptcy filing: 2001, in the United States) and Tyco International Ltd. (resignation of CEO: 2002, in the United States) make clear that, in the absence of the checks and balances of strong and effective corporate governance systems, investors and others cannot necessarily rely on managers to serve as stewards of the resources entrusted to them. Example 1-1, dealing with Enron, illustrates the problems that can ensue from a lack of commitment to a corporate governance system. Example 1-2, dealing with Tyco, illustrates a case in which there were inadequate checks and balances to the power of a CEO.

EXAMPLE 1-1 Corporate Governance Failure (1)

Enron Corporation was one of the world's largest energy, commodities, and services companies. However, it is better known today as a classic example of how the conflicts of interest between shareholders and managers can harm even major corporations and their shareholders. Enron's executives, with the approval of members of the board of directors, overrode provisions in the company's code of ethics and corporate governance system that forbade any practices involving self-dealing by executives. Specifically, Enron's chief financial officer (CFO) set up offshore partnerships in which he served as general partner. As an Enron executive, he was able to make deals with these partnerships on behalf of Enron. As a general partner of the partnerships, he received the enormous fees that the deals generated.[4]

The partnerships served other useful purposes. For example, they made it possible to hide billions of dollars in Enron debt off the company's balance sheet, as well as to generate artificial profits for Enron. Thus, disclosure of the company's rapidly deteriorating financial condition was delayed, preventing investors and creditors from obtaining information critical to the valuation and riskiness of their securities. At the same time, Enron executives were selling their own stock in the company.

These egregious breaches of good governance harmed both Enron's outside shareholders and their creditors. The bonds were becoming riskier, but the creditors were not informed of the deteriorating prospects. The exorbitant fees the executives paid themselves came out of the shareholders' earnings, earnings that were already overstated by the artificial profits. Investors did not receive full information about the problems in the company until well after the collapse and the company's bankruptcy filing, by which time their stock had lost essentially all of its value.

Most, if not all, of the core attributes of good governance were violated by Enron's managers, but especially the responsibility to deal fairly with all stakeholders, including investors and creditors, and to provide full transparency of all material information on a timely basis.

EXAMPLE 1-2   Corporate Governance Failure (2)

Tyco International Ltd. provides another well-known example of a corporate governance failure. The chief executive officer (CEO) of Tyco used corporate funds to buy home decorating items, including a $17,000 traveling toilette box, a $445 pin cushion, and a $15,000 umbrella stand. He also borrowed money from the company's employee loan program to buy $270 million worth of yachts, art, jewelry, and vacation estates. Then, in his capacity as CEO, he forgave the loan. All told, the CEO may have looted the firm, and thereby its shareholders, of over $600 million.[5]

It is instructive that, in the Tyco case court proceedings, the CEO and his representatives have not argued that he did not do these things, but rather that it was not illegal for him to do so.

Tyco is a striking example of excessive perquisite consumption by a CEO.

The role of complete transparency in sound corporate governance, including understandable and accurate financial statements, cannot be overestimated. Without full information, investors and other stakeholders are unable to evaluate the company's financial position

---

[4]Powers, Troubh, and Winokur (2002).
[5]Maremont and Cohen (2002), p. A1.

and riskiness, whether the condition is improving or deteriorating, and whether insiders are aggrandizing themselves or just making poor business decisions to the detriment of long-term investors.

Two additional cases illustrate how false, misleading, or incomplete corporate disclosure may harm investors and other stakeholders.

EXAMPLE 1-3   Corporate Governance Failure (3)

The Italian firm, Parmalat SpA, was one of the world's largest dairy foods suppliers. The founders and top executives of Parmalat were accused of fictitiously reporting the existence of a $4.9 billion bank account so that the company's enormous liabilities would appear less daunting.[6] By hiding the true financial condition of the firm, the executives were able to continue borrowing from creditors. The fraud perpetrated by Parmalat's largest shareholders and executives hurt Parmalat's creditors as well as the shareholders. Parmalat eventually defaulted on a $185 million bond payment in November 2003 and the company collapsed shortly thereafter.

EXAMPLE 1-4   Corporate Governance Failure (4)

During the late 1990s, Adelphia, the fifth-largest provider of cable entertainment in the United States, and the company's founders embarked on an aggressive acquisition campaign to increase the size of the company. During this time, the size of Adelphia's debt more than tripled from $3.5 billion to $12.6 billion. However, the founders also arranged a $2.3 billion personal loan, which Adelphia guaranteed, but this arrangement was not fully disclosed to Adelphia's other stakeholders.[7] In addition, it is alleged that fictitious transactions were recorded to boost accounting profits.[8] These actions by Adelphia's owners were harmful to all of Adelphia's nonfounder stakeholders, including investors and creditors. The company collapsed in bankruptcy in 2002.

The severity of the agency problems of the companies discussed in Examples 1-1 through 1-4 does not represent the norm, although the potential for serious conflicts of interest between shareholders and managers is inherent in the modern corporation. Strong corporate governance systems provide mechanisms for monitoring managers' activities, rewarding good performance, and disciplining those in a position of responsibility for the company to make sure they act in the interests of the company's stakeholders.

---

[6]Edmondson (2004).
[7]Nofsinger and Kim (2003), pp. 60–61.
[8]Markon and Frank (2002), p. A3.

4.2. Director–Shareholder Conflicts

Corporate governance systems rely on a system of checks and balances between the managers and investors in which the board of directors plays a critical role. The purpose of boards of directors in modern corporations is to provide an intermediary between managers and the owners, the shareholders. Members of the board of directors act as agents for the owners/shareholders, a mechanism designed to represent the investors and to ensure that their interests are being well served. This intermediary generally is responsible for monitoring the activities of managers, approving strategies and policies, and making certain that these serve investors' interests. The board is also responsible for approving mergers and acquisitions, approving audit contracts and reviewing the audit and financial statements, setting managers' compensation including any incentive or performance awards, and disciplining or replacing poorly performing managers.

The conflict between directors and shareholders arises when directors come to identify with the managers' interests rather than with those of the shareholders. This can occur when the board is not independent, for example, or when the members of the board have business or personal relationships with the managers that bias their judgment or compromise their duties to the shareholders. If members of the board have consulting agreements with the company, serve as major lenders to the firm, are members of the manager's family, or are from the same circle of close friends, their objectivity may be called into question. Many corporations have been found to have interlinked boards. For example, one or more senior managers from one firm may serve as directors in the companies of their own board members, frequently on compensation committees.

Another ever present problem is the frequently overly generous compensation paid to directors for their services. Excessive compensation may incline directors to accommodate the wishes of management rather than attend to the concerns of investors.

All of the examples cited in this section involve compliant or less than independent board members. In Section 5 we formulate the most important points to check in evaluating a company's corporate governance system.

5. CORPORATE GOVERNANCE EVALUATION

An essential component of the analysis of a company and its risk is a review of the quality of its corporate governance system. This evaluation requires an assessment of issues relating to the board of directors, managers, and shareholders. Ultimately, the long-term performance of a company is dependent on the quality of managers' decisions and their commitment to applying sound management practice. However, as one group concerned with the issues observes, "by analyzing the state of corporate governance for a given company, an analyst or shareholder may ascertain whether the company is governed in a manner that produces better management practices, promotes higher returns on shareholder capital, or if there is a governance and/or management problem which may impair company performance."[9]

In the following sections we provide a set of guidelines for evaluating the quality of corporate governance in a company. We reiterate that there is no single system of governance that is appropriate for all companies in all industries worldwide. However, this core

[9]New York Society of Securities Analysts (2003), p. 1.

set of global best practices is being applied in financial markets in Europe, Asia, and North America. They represent a standard by which corporate practices may be evaluated.

The information and corporate disclosure available in a specific jurisdiction will vary widely. However, most large financial markets and, increasingly, smaller ones require a substantial amount of information be provided about companies' governance structures and practices. In addition, a few regulatory jurisdictions will require a subset of the criteria we will give as part of registration, exchange listing, or other requirements.

The analyst should begin by carefully reviewing the requirements in effect for the company. Information is generally available in the company's required filings with regulators. For example, in the United States, such information is provided in the 10-K report, the annual report, and the Proxy Statement (SEC Form DEF 14A). All of these are filed with the U.S. Securities and Exchange Commission (U.S. SEC), are available on the U.S. SEC web site, usually are available on the company's web site, and are provided by the company to current investors as well as on request. In Europe, the company's annual report provides some information. However, in an increasing number of European Union (EU) countries, companies are required to provide a report on corporate governance. This report typically will provide information on board activities and decisions, state whether the company has abided by its relevant national code, and explain why it departed from the code, if it has. In addition, the announcement of the company's annual general meeting should disclose the issues on the agenda that are subject to shareholder vote. The specific sources of information will differ by jurisdiction and company.

5.1. The Board of Directors

Boards of directors are a critical part of the system of checks and balances that lie at the heart of corporate governance systems. Board members, both individually and as a group, have the responsibility to

- Establish corporate values and governance structures for the company to ensure that the business is conducted in an ethical, competent, fair, and professional manner;
- Ensure that all legal and regulatory requirements are met and complied with fully and in a timely fashion;
- Establish long-term strategic objectives for the company with a goal of ensuring that the best interests of shareholders come first and that the company's obligations to others are met in a timely and complete manner;
- Establish clear lines of responsibility and a strong system of accountability and performance measurement in all phases of a company's operations;
- Hire the chief executive officer, determine the compensation package, and periodically evaluate the officer's performance;
- Ensure that management has supplied the board with sufficient information for it to be fully informed and prepared to make the decisions that are its responsibility, and to be able to adequately monitor and oversee the company's management;
- Meet regularly, and in extraordinary session as required by events, to perform its duties;
- Acquire training so that members are able to adequately perform their duties.

Depending on the nature of the company and the industries within which the company operates, these responsibilities will vary; however, these general obligations are common to all companies.

In summarizing the duties and needs of boards of directors, *The Corporate Governance of Listed Companies: A Manual for Investors*[10] states:

> *Board members owe a duty to make decisions based on what ultimately is best for the long-term interests of shareowners. In order to do this effectively, board members need a combination of three things: independence, experience and resources.*
>
> ***First**, a board should be composed of at least a majority of independent board members with the autonomy to act independently from management. Board members should bring with them a commitment to take an unbiased approach in making decisions that will benefit the company and long-term shareowners, rather than simply voting with management. **Second**, board members who have appropriate experience and expertise relevant to the Company's business are best able to evaluate what is in the best interests of shareowners. Depending on the nature of the business, this may require specialized expertise by at least some board members. **Third**, there need to be internal mechanisms to support the independent work of the board, including the authority to hire outside consultants without management's intervention or approval. This mechanism alone provides the board with the ability to obtain expert help in specialized areas, to circumvent potential areas of conflict with management, and to preserve the integrity of the board's independent oversight function.* [Emphasis added]

In the following sections we detail the attributes of the board that an investor or investment analyst must assess.

5.1.1. Board Composition and Independence

The board of directors of a corporation is established for the primary purpose of serving the best interests of the outside shareholders in the company. Other stakeholders, including employees, creditors, and suppliers, are usually in a more powerful position to oversee their interests in the company than are shareholders. The millions of outside investors cannot, individually or collectively, monitor, oversee, and approve management's strategies and policies, performance, and compensation and consumption of perquisites.

The objectives of the board are to see that company assets are used in the best long-term interests of shareholders and that management strategies, plans, policies, and practices are designed to achieve this objective. In a recent amendment to the *Investment Company Act of 1940* rules, the U.S. SEC argues that a board must be "an independent force in [company] affairs rather than a passive affiliate of management. Its independent directors must bring to the boardroom a high degree of rigor and skeptical objectivity to the evaluation of [company] managements and its plans and proposals, particularly when evaluating conflicts of interest."[11]

Similarly, the *Corporate Governance Handbook*[12] observes:

> *Board independence is essential to a sound governance structure. Without independence there can be little accountability. In the words of Professor Jeffrey Sonnenfeld of Yale University, "The highest performing companies have extremely contentious boards that regard dissent as an obligation and that treat no subject as undiscussable."*

---

[10] *The Corporate Governance of Listed Companies: A Manual for Investors* (2005), p. 11.

[11] Amendments to Rules Governing the Investment Company Act of 1940, 17 CFR Part 270, July 2004, p. 3.

[12] New York Society of Securities Analysts (2003), p. 3.

Clearly, for members who are appointed to the board to be in a position to best perform their fiduciary responsibilities to shareholders, at a minimum a majority of the members must be independent of management. However, global best practice now recommends that *at least three-quarters* of the board members should be independent.

Some experts in corporate governance have argued that all members of the board should be independent, eliminating the possibility of any senior executives serving on the board. Those who hold this position argue that the presence of managers in board deliberations may work to the detriment of the best interests of investors and other shareholders by intimidating the board or otherwise limiting debate and full discussion of important matters. Others argue that, with appropriate additional safeguards, such potential problems can be overcome to the benefit of all stakeholders.

Independence is difficult to evaluate. Factors that often indicate a lack of independence include

- Former employment with the company, including founders, executives, or other employees;
- Business relationships, such as prior or current service as outside counsel, auditors, or consultants, or business interests involving contractual commitments and obligations;
- Personal relationships, whether familial, friendship, or other affiliations;
- Interlocking directorships, a director of another company whose independence might be impaired by the relationship with the other board or company, particularly if the director serves on interlocking compensation committees; and
- Ongoing banking or other creditor relationships.

Information on the business and other relationships of board members as well as nominees for the board may be obtained from regulatory filings in most jurisdictions. For example, in the United States, such information is required to be provided in the Proxy Statement, SEC Form DEF 14A, sent to shareholders and filed with the SEC prior to shareholder meetings.

5.1.2. Independent Chair of the Board   Many, if not most, corporate boards now permit a senior executive of a corporation to serve as the chair of the board of directors. However, corporate governance experts do not regard such an arrangement to be in the best interests of the shareholders of the company. As the U.S. SEC observes:

> *This practice may contribute to the [company's] ability to dominate the actions of the board of directors. The chairman of a . . . board can largely control the board's agenda, which may include matters not welcomed by the [company's management] . . . Perhaps more important, the chairman of the board can have a substantial influence on the . . . boardroom's culture. The boardroom culture can foster (or suppress) the type of meaningful dialogue between . . . management and independent directors that is critical for healthy . . . governance. It can support (or diminish) the role of the independent directors in the continuous, active engagement of . . . management necessary for them to fulfill their duties. A boardroom culture conducive to decisions favoring the long-term interest of . . . shareholders may be more likely to prevail when the chairman does not have the conflicts of interest inherent in his role as an executive of the [company]. Moreover, a . . . board may be more effective when negotiating with the [company] over matters such as the [compensation] if it were not at the same time led by an executive of the [company] with whom it is negotiating.*[13]

---

[13]Amendments to Rules Governing the Investment Company Act of 1940, 17 CFR Part 270, July 2004, p. 4.

Not all market participants agree with this view. Many corporate managers argue that it is essential for efficient and effective board functioning that the chairman be the senior executive in the company. They base their arguments on the proposition that only such an executive has the knowledge and experience necessary to provide needed information to the board on questions affecting the company's strategy, policy, and operations. Critics of this position counter that it is incumbent upon corporate management to provide all such necessary information to the board. Indeed, many argue that this obligation is the sole reason that one or more corporate managers serve as members of the board.

Whether the company has separate positions for the chief executive and chairman of the board can be determined readily from regulatory filings of the company. If the positions are not separate, an investor may doubt that the board is operating efficiently and effectively in its monitoring and oversight of corporate operations and that the decisions made are necessarily in the best interests of investors and other stakeholders.

Tradition and practice in many countries prescribe a so-called "unitary" board system, a single board of directors. However, some countries, notably Germany, have developed a formal system whose intent is to overcome such difficulties as a lack of independence of board members and of the chair of the board from company management. The German approach requires a tiered hierarchy of boards; a management board responsible for overseeing management's strategy, planning, and similar functions; and an independent supervisory board charged with monitoring and reviewing decisions of the management board, as well as with making decisions in which conflicts of interest in the management board may impair their independence, for example, in determining managerial compensation.

Clearly, independence of the chairman of the board does not guarantee that the board will function properly. However, independence should be regarded as a necessary condition, even if it is not sufficient of itself to eliminate conflicts of interest.

5.1.3. Qualifications of Directors

In addition to independence, directors need to bring sufficient skill and experience to the position to ensure that they will be able to fulfill their fiduciary responsibilities to investors and other stakeholders. Information on directors' prior business experience and other biographical material, including current and past business affiliations, can generally be found in regulatory filings.

Boards of directors require a variety of skills and experience to function properly. These skills will vary by industry, but such core skills as knowledge of finance, accounting, and legal matters are required by all boards. Evaluation of the members should include an assessment of whether needed skills are available among the board members. Among the qualifications and core competencies that an investor should look for in the board as a group, and in individual members or candidates for the board, are

- Independence (see factors to consider in Section 5.1.1);
- Relevant expertise in the industry, including the principal technologies used in the business and in financial operations, legal matters, accounting and auditing; and managerial considerations such as the success of companies with which the director has been associated in the past;
- Indications of ethical soundness, including public statements or writings of the director, problems in companies with which the director has been associated in the past, such as legal or other regulatory violations involving ethical lapses;
- Experience in strategic planning and risk management;

- Other board experience with companies that are regarded as having sound governance practices and as being effective stewards of investors' capital as compared to serving management's interests;
- Dedication and commitment to serving the board and investors' interests (e.g., not serving on more than a few boards, having an excellent record of attendance at board meetings, and limiting other business commitments that require large amounts of time); and
- Commitment to the needs of investors as shown, for example, by significant personal investments in this or other companies for which he or she serves as a director, and by an absence of conflicts of interest.

Such attributes are essential to the sound functioning of a board of directors and should be carefully considered in any investment decision. Board members may be selected as much for their general stature and name recognition as for the specialized expertise they bring to their responsibilities. However, the skills, knowledge, and experience we have described are essential to effective corporate governance, oversight, and monitoring on behalf of shareholders.

5.1.4. Annual Election of Directors   Members of boards of directors may be elected on either an annual or a staggered basis. In annual votes, every member of the board stands for reelection every year. Such an approach ensures that shareholders are able to express their views on individual members' performance during the year and to exercise their right to control who will represent them in corporate governance and oversight of the company. Opponents argue that subjecting members to annual reelection is disruptive to effective board oversight over the company.

Those who support the election of board members on a staggered basis with reelection of only a portion of the board each year, argue that such a scheme is necessary to ensure the continuity of the knowledge and experience in the company essential for good corporate governance. Critics express the view that such a practice diminishes the limited power that shareholders have to control who will serve on the board and to ensure the responsiveness of board members to investor concerns, such as poor management performance and practices. They also argue that staggered boards better serve the interests of entrenched managers by making the board less responsive to the needs of shareholders, more likely to align their interests with those of managers, and more likely to resist takeover attempts that would benefit shareholders to the detriment of managers.

Corporate governance best practice generally supports the annual election of directors, which is viewed as being in the best interests of investors. When shareholders can express their views annually, either by casting a positive vote or by withholding their votes for poorly performing directors, directors are thought to be more likely to weigh their decisions carefully, to be better prepared and more attentive to the needs of investors, and to be more effective in their oversight of management.

Information on directors' terms and the frequency of elections may be obtained by examining the term structure of the board members in regulatory filings.

5.1.5. Annual Board Self-Assessment   Board members have a fiduciary duty to shareholders to oversee management's use of assets; to monitor and review strategies, policies, and practices; and to take the actions necessary to fulfill their responsibilities to stakeholders. It is essential that a process be in place for periodically reviewing and evaluating their performance and making recommendations for improvement. Generally, this evaluation should occur at least annually. The review should include

- An assessment of the board's effectiveness as a whole;
- Evaluations of the performance of individual board members, including assessments of the participation of each member, with regard to both attendance and the number and relevance of contributions made, and an assessment of the member's willingness to think independently of management and address challenging or controversial issues;
- A review of board committee activities;
- An assessment of the board's effectiveness in monitoring and overseeing their specific functions;
- An evaluation of the qualities the company will need in its board in the future, along with a comparison of the qualities of current board members;
- A report of the board self-assessment, typically prepared by the nominations committee, and included in the proxy in the United States and in the corporate governance report in Europe.

The process of periodic self-assessment by directors can improve board and company performance by reminding directors of their role and responsibilities, improving their understanding of the role, improving communications among board members, and enhancing the cohesiveness of the board. Self-assessment allows directors to improve not only their own performance but to make needed changes in corporate governance structures. All of these measures will lead to greater efficiency and effectiveness in serving investors' and other stakeholders' interests.

The process of self-assessment should focus on board responsibilities and individual members' accountability for fulfilling these responsibilities. It should consider both substantive matters and procedural issues, for example, evaluations of the adequacy and effectiveness of the committee structure. The committees regarded as essential by corporate governance experts include the auditing, nominations, and compensation committees, all of which should be staffed by independent directors who are experts in the relevant areas. (The specific functions of these committees will be considered in later sections.)

The company, however, may need to establish additional committees. For example, for a mutual fund company, these might include a securities valuation committee responsible for setting policies for the pricing of securities and for monitoring the application of the policies by management. For a high-technology company, the committees might include one tasked with the valuation of intellectual property or perhaps of management's success in creating new intellectual property through its investments in research and development.

In evaluating the effectiveness of the corporate governance system and specifically of the board of directors, an investment professional should consider the critical functions unique to a company and evaluate whether the board's structure and membership provides adequate oversight and control over management's strategic business decision making and policy making.

5.1.6. **Separate Sessions of Independent Directors**   Corporate governance best practice requires that independent directors of the board meet at least annually, and preferably quarterly, in separate sessions—that is, in meetings without the presence of the management, other representatives, or interested persons (for example, retired founders of the company). The purpose of these sessions is to provide an opportunity for those entrusted with the best interests of the shareholders to engage in candid and frank discussions and debate regarding the management of the company, its strategies and policies, strengths and weaknesses, and other matters of concern. Such regular sessions would avoid the appearance that directors are concerned with specific problems or threats to the company's well-being. Separate sessions could also enhance the board's effectiveness by improving the cooperation among board members, and their cohesiveness as a board, attributes that can strengthen the board in the fulfillment of its responsibilities to shareholders.

Regulatory filings should indicate how often boards have met and which meetings were separate sessions of the independent directors. The investment professional should be concerned if such meetings appeared to be nonexistent, infrequent, or irregular in occurrence. These could suggest a variety of negative conclusions, including the presence of a "captive," that is, a nonindependent board, inattention or disinterest among board members, a lack of cohesion and sense of purpose, or other conditions that can be detrimental to the interests of investors.

5.1.7. Audit Committee and Audit Oversight The audit committee of the board is established to provide independent oversight of the company's financial reporting, nonfinancial corporate disclosure, and internal control systems. This function is essential for effective corporate governance and for seeing that their responsibilities to shareholders are fulfilled.

The primary responsibility for overseeing the design, maintenance, and continuing development of the control and compliance systems rests with this committee. At a minimum the audit committee must

- Include only independent directors;
- Have sufficient expertise in financial, accounting, auditing, and legal matters to be able to adequately oversee and evaluate the control, risk management, and compliance systems, as well as the quality of the company's financial disclosure to shareholders and others (it is advisable for at least two members of the committee to have relevant accounting and auditing expertise);
- Oversee the internal audit function, with the internal audit staff reporting directly and routinely to this committee of the board and, when necessary, reporting any concerns regarding the quality of controls or compliance issues;
- Have sufficient resources to be able to properly fulfill their responsibilities;
- Have full access to and the cooperation of management;
- Have authority to investigate fully any matters within its purview;
- Have the authority for the hiring of auditors, including the setting of contractual provisions; for review of the cost-effectiveness of the audit; for approving nonaudit services provided by the auditor; and for assessing the auditors' independence;
- Meet with auditors independently of management or other company interest parties periodically but at least once annually; and
- Have the full authority to review the audit and financial statements, to question auditors regarding audit findings, including the review of the system of internal controls, and to determine the quality and transparency of financial reporting choices.

Strong internal controls, risk management, and compliance systems are critical to a company's long-term success, the meeting of its business objectives, and enhancing the best interests of shareholders. Nearly all of the major corporate collapses have involved an absence of effective control systems or the overriding of the systems by management to achieve their own interests and objectives to the detriment of those of investors.

The internal audit function should be entirely independent and separate from any of the activities being audited. Internal auditors should report directly to the chairman of the audit committee of the board of directors. The board should regularly meet with the internal audit supervisor and review the activities and address any concerns.

In evaluating the effectiveness of the board of directors, an investor should review the qualifications of the members of the audit committee, being alert to any conflicts of interest that individual members might have, for example, having previously been employed or otherwise associated with the current auditor or the company. The investor should also determine the number of meetings held by the committee during the year and whether the meetings were held independent of management. A report on the activities of the audit committee, including a statement on whether the committee met independently and without the presence of management, should be included in the proxy in the United States and in the corporate governance report in Europe.

The audit committee should discuss in the regulatory filings the responsibilities and authority it has to evaluate and assess these functions, any findings or concerns the committee has with regard to the audit, internal control and compliance systems, and corrective action taken.

5.1.8. Nominating Committee   In most corporations, currently, nominations for members of the board of directors and for executive officers of the company are made by members of the board, most often at the recommendation of, or in consultation with, the management of the company. In such circumstances, the criteria for the selection of nominees may favor management's best interests at the expense of the interests of shareholders. This is all the more important because, in the usual case, shareholders have no authority to nominate slates of directors who might best represent them. Consequently, corporate governance best practice requires that nominees to the board be selected by a nominating committee comprised only of independent directors. The responsibilities of the nominating committee are to

- Establish criteria for evaluating candidates for the board of directors;
- Identify candidates for the general board and for all committees of the board;
- Review the qualifications of the nominees to the board and for members of individual committees;
- Establish criteria for evaluating nominees for senior management positions in the company;
- Identify candidates for management positions;
- Review the qualifications of the nominees for management positions; and
- Document the reasons for the selection of candidates recommended to the board as a whole for consideration.

Given the pivotal role that the members of the nominating committee have in representing and protecting the interests of investors and other stakeholders, it is essential that the qualifications of these members be carefully reviewed in assessing the long-term investment prospects of a company. Particular attention should be paid to evaluating their independence, the qualities of those selected for senior management positions, and the success of businesses with which they've been associated. This information is available in the regulatory filings of the company.

5.1.9. Compensation Committee Ideally, compensation should be a tool used by directors, acting on behalf of shareholders, to attract, retain, and motivate the highest-quality and most experienced managers for the company. The compensation should include incentives to meet and exceed corporate *long-term* goals, rather than short-term performance targets.

Decisions regarding the amounts and types of compensation to be awarded to senior executives and directors of a company are thought by many corporate governance experts to be the most important decisions to be made by those in a position of trust. Reports abound of compensation that is excessive relative to corporate performance and that is awarded to executives by compliant boards. The problem has been particularly acute in the United States, but examples are found worldwide.

In recent years, a practice has developed of gauging levels of compensation awards based not on company objectives and goals but rather by comparison to the highest levels of compensation awarded in other companies. This practice occurs whether the reference companies are relevant benchmarks or not, and it has caused compensation packages in many cases to be unrelated to the performance of the company. Needless to say, such excessive compensation is highly detrimental to the interests of shareholders.

In one well-known case, that of the New York Stock Exchange, the compensation of the chief executive was a substantial proportion of the net earnings of the Exchange and considerably higher than the compensation awarded to senior executives of comparable companies. The facts that have come to light in the case suggest that the compensation committee of the board was not independent as measured by the usual criteria, was not expert in compensation matters, did not seek outside counsel, was not well-informed on the details of the compensation package, and acquiesced in management's proposal of its own compensation.[14] This case is currently the subject of extensive legal and regulatory action.

Several different types of compensation awards in common use today are

- Salary, generally set by contractual commitments between the company and the executive or director;
- Perquisites, additional compensation in the form of benefits, such as insurance; use of company planes, cars, and apartments; services, ranging from investment advice, tax assistance, and financial planning advice to household services;
- Bonus awards, normally based on performance as compared to company goals and objectives;
- Stock options, options on future awards of company stock; and
- Stock awards or restricted stock.

In general, shareholders would prefer that salary and perquisite awards constitute a relatively small portion of the total compensation award. That is, the fixed, nonperformance-based portion of the award should be adequate but not excessive. Because these fixed costs must be borne by shareholders regardless of corporate performance, executives should not be automatically rewarded by poor performance. Information on salaries and some perquisites can be found in regulatory filings of companies. For example, in the United States, this information is found in the tables and accompanying text of the Proxy Statement. The investor should be alert to the fact that significant amounts of perquisites may not be fully disclosed,

---

[14]Thomas (2004a and 2004b).

as has been shown to be the case in a number of corporate scandals recently in Europe and the United States.

Bonuses should be awarded based solely on exceeding expected performance. They should provide an incentive to motivate managers to achieve the highest and most stable long-term performance, rather than to reward short-term nonsustainable "growth" at the expense of the best interests of shareholders. To the extent that management controls the operations of the company as well as corporate disclosure, incentive-based awards require the most diligent monitoring by the members of the compensation committee. Directors must ascertain that management is not manipulating variables within its control, for example, accounting disclosure choices, to artificially achieve performance targets. The investor should examine the bonus awards carefully, evaluating the performance targets for reasonableness, and make certain that the awards are consistent with investors' best interests.

Stock options and stock awards have been argued to better align the interests of managers with those of shareholders by making a portion of the manager's compensation dependent on the value of the stock. Unfortunately, as recent events have made clear, stock options do not always result in such an alignment of interests. Indeed, until recently, the lack of appropriate accounting recognition of the expense of stock option awards has led to widespread abuse of this form of compensation. Large grants of stock options dilute shareholders' positions in the company and diminish the value of their holdings.

Appropriate accounting for stock options, that is, expensing in the income statement with assumed conversion to stock in the earnings-per-share calculation, has come to be seen as a litmus test for high-quality financial reporting and transparency.[15] Nevertheless, abusive practices involving information manipulation related to stock option grants and option exercise still occur.

In theory, grants of stock options to executives and other employees should be subject to shareholder approval. As a practical matter, however, there are loopholes that permit managers and directors to bypass such approval, although some jurisdictions have closed some of these loopholes recently.

Stock options' potential dilutive effect on shareholders can be assessed by a measure known as the "share overhang." The overhang is simply the number of shares represented by the options, relative to the total amount of stock outstanding. Both of these numbers are readily available in company regulatory filings in most jurisdictions.

In addition, investors should be alert to any provisions permitting the so-called "repricing" of stock options. Repricing means that the company can, with approval of the board of directors, adjust the exercise price of outstanding option grants downward to the current price of the stock. This is done by some companies when the price of the stock has declined significantly and the options are out-of-the-money. As is readily apparent, such repricing is inconsistent with the argument that options should serve the interests of managers and shareholders and provide an incentive for managers to strive for excellent long-term corporate performance. The managers may have at-the-money options following repricing, but investors cannot recoup their losses so easily. Abuse in this area has been stemmed somewhat by accounting rule changes that now require that such repriced options be expensed in the income statement, although companies can still cancel the options and reissue them later at a time consistent with the rules, usually six months.

---

[15]In 2003, the International Accounting Standards Board (IASB) issued a standard requiring the fair value expensing of stock options for all companies that use IASB standards. Some ninety countries worldwide adhere to IASB standards.

Stock grants by companies to executives can be an effective means of motivating them to achieve sustainable, long-term performance objectives. Restricted stock grants, that is, stock awards that cannot be sold or otherwise disposed of for a period of time or that are contingent on reaching certain performance goals, can be subject to the same abusive practices as stock option awards, depending on the terms of the awards. Well-designed restricted stock awards are increasingly used by companies to reward executives for their performance as well as to remunerate lower-level employees. Most jurisdictions require companies to disclose such grants in regulatory filings.

5.1.10. Board's Independent Legal and Expert Counsel   The board of directors should have the ability and sufficient resources to hire such legal and other expert counsel as they require to fulfill their fiduciary duties. In most companies, for example, the corporate counsel also has the responsibility to advise the board of directors. Because the board of directors is charged with overseeing management on behalf of the shareholders, this represents a direct conflict of interest. That is, the corporate counsel cannot be wholly independent with regard to the advice provided to the directors if it also serves and is paid by corporate management.

Legal counsel will be needed to help the board assess the company's compliance with legal and regulatory requirements. Outside counsel becomes increasingly important for companies with global operations. Similarly, for example, in high-technology companies, the members of the board will likely require the assistance of experts in the particular specialized technologies employed or developed by the company. However, all boards, regardless of the industry, are likely to require additional counsel and should be able to obtain such services when they require it.

The investor should review regulatory filings carefully to determine whether the board makes use of independent outside counsel. If the filings are silent on the issue, the analyst or investor should specifically inquire about the board's use of independent counsel. The absence of satisfactory answers should reflect negatively on the board's independence as well as on its ability to perform its fiduciary duties.

5.1.11. Statement of Governance Policies   Companies that have a strong commitment to corporate governance frequently supply a statement of their corporate governance policies, variously in their regulatory filings, on their web sites, or as part other investor information packets. Investors and investment analysts should assess the following elements of a statement of corporate governance policies:

- Codes of ethics;
- Statements of the oversight, monitoring, and review responsibilities of directors, including internal control, risk management, audit and accounting and disclosure policy, compliance assessment, nominations, compensation awards, and other responsibilities;
- Statements of management's responsibilities to provide complete and timely information to the board members prior to board meetings, and to provide directors with free and unfettered access to control and compliance functions within the company;
- Reports of directors' examinations, evaluations, and findings in their oversight and review function;
- Board and committee performance self-assessments;
- Management performance assessments; and
- Training provided to directors prior to joining the board and periodically thereafter.

Obviously, one cannot rely solely on the corporate governance statement for assurance that the company has a sound corporate governance structure. Nevertheless, such disclosures provide investors with a comparison for evaluating company and director performance over time. For example, such disclosures should not be "boilerplate" statements that do not change over time and that provide no real content or information.

5.1.12. Disclosure and Transparency The purpose of accounting and disclosure is to tell the company's economic story as it is, not as some might want it to be in order to achieve personal objectives. Investors depend critically on the quality, clarity, timeliness, and completeness of financial information in valuing securities and assessing risk. Attempts to hide or otherwise obfuscate essential information can result in the mispricing of securities and the misallocation of capital, reducing the efficiency and effectiveness of markets.

It is worth observing that nearly all of the major corporate collapses in recent years have involved equally massive attempts to hide, obfuscate, or falsify information that could have alerted investors to the seriousness of the financial problems and the impending implosions. Enron attempted to hide its massive and growing debt by moving it off the balance sheet and into "partnerships," run by insiders, for which no information was available. Tyco failed to report billions in "loans" to insiders. WorldCom not only hid $11 billion in operating expenses by recording them as assets in the balance sheet, but also failed to disclose hundreds of billions of dollars in loans to the chief executive. Parmalat staved off collapse for some time by reporting falsely that the company had nearly $5 billion in a corporate account with a major international financial institution.

The crisis of the loss of confidence and trust in the broad financial markets globally, rather than just the companies involved, signals the depths of the concern that investors have had about the quality and completeness of the disclosure they are receiving. Not surprisingly, the response has been a major overhaul of legislative, regulatory, and related criminal code provisions in countries in North America and Europe, as well as elsewhere. Such provisions as the requirements in the United States that the chief executive officer and chief financial officer certify the accuracy of financial statements and develop rigorous new systems of internal controls, backed up by new audit attestation requirements and stiffer criminal penalties, make clear the seriousness of the offenses and the public's response to such malfeasance.

However, such changes do not guarantee that those in a position of trust will not again willingly mislead and misinform their investors and others, particularly when they are faced with serious financial difficulties. Consequently, an evaluation of the quality and extent of financial information provided to investors is a crucial element in evaluating the corporate governance structure of a company and the risk borne by an investor in the company's securities. In assessing the quality of disclosure, some indicators of good quality financial reporting are[16]

- Conservative assumptions used for employee benefit plans;
- Adequate provisions for lawsuits and other loss contingencies;
- Minimal use of off-balance-sheet financing techniques and full disclosure of assets, liabilities, revenues, and expenses associated with such activities;
- Absence of nonrecurring gains;
- Absence of noncash earnings;
- Clear and adequate disclosure;

---

[16]White, Sondhi, and Fried (2003), p. 637 ff.

- Conservative revenue and expense recognition methods;
- Use of last-in/first-out (LIFO) inventory accounting (during periods of generally rising prices);
- Bad debt reserves that are high relative to receivables and past credit losses;
- Use of accelerated depreciation methods and short lives;
- Rapid write-off of acquisition-related intangible assets;
- Minimal capitalization of interest and overhead;
- Minimal capitalization of computer software costs;
- Expensing of start-up costs of new operations; and
- Use of the completed contract method of accounting for contracts.

One area of concern in recent years is the reporting by companies of so-called pro forma earnings numbers, earnings before noncash or nonrecurring charges. Pro forma earnings have occasionally been dubbed "earnings-before-the-bad-stuff." Such misleading disclosures have been widely used by companies with poor performance and poor prospects. Unfortunately, some analysts and investors have been willing to accept the deception as reflective of economic reality, frequently to their regret. To survive and flourish in the long term, companies must be able to cover all of their costs.

In addition to high-quality financial disclosure, the company should make readily available in its regulatory filings clear and complete information on such items as:

- Governance policies and procedures;
- Reporting lines and organizational structure;
- Corporate strategy, goals, and objectives;
- Competitive threats and other risks and contingencies faced by the company and the potential effect of these on the company's operations;
- Insider transactions involving executives or other senior employees, and directors;
- Compensation policies and amounts of compensation awarded, including perquisites, for key executives and directors; and
- Changes to governance structures, including the corporate charter and by-laws.

The investor should be alert particularly to references to off-balance-sheet or insider transactions that are not accompanied by full disclosure of the effects of the items on the company. The investor should also consider the implications of a lack of disclosure. For example, many large companies maintain fleets of corporate jets for the use of executives and other employees. They routinely make such planes available to executives for their private use on holidays. A failure to mention such perquisites should raise questions, not only about this item but about other possible compensation that has not been disclosed.

5.1.13.   Insider or Related-Party Transactions   The corporate collapse cases cited earlier involve egregious insider transactions by senior executives, frequently with the acquiescence of a compliant board of directors. The executives' objective was self-aggrandizement at the expense of shareholders and other stakeholders in the company. This is not a new problem. Indeed, audit standards have required for decades that auditors investigate such items and flag them for users of the statements. However, both the frequency and extent of the theft and fraud, along with the losses incurred by investors, employees, and others recently, have dismayed even the most seasoned professionals in the financial markets.

The analyst should assess the company's policies concerning related-party transactions, whether the company has entered into any such transactions, and, if so, what the effects are on the company's financial statements. Any related-party transaction should require the prior approval of the board of directors and a statement that such transactions are consistent with company policy. Financial disclosures and related notes in regulatory filings are a source for analysts in researching such transactions.

5.1.14. Responsiveness of Board of Directors to Shareholder Proxy Votes

A clear indicator of the extent to which directors and executives take seriously their fiduciary responsibility to shareholders is the response of the company to shareholder votes on proxy matters. A recent example involves the issue of expensing stock options, which has been put to proxy vote in a sizable number of companies. Shareholders in many of the companies have voted in the majority that the company begin expensing stock options. Very few company managers and directors have responded positively to the votes.

Directors cannot be expected to respond to trivial or frivolous shareholder initiatives, but few such issues carry a large portion of the vote of shareholders. However, when matters related to governance, executive compensation, mergers and acquisitions, or other matters of great importance to investors are put to a vote of the shareholders, and the results of the vote are ignored, the implications are abundantly clear: Management and the board are not concerned for or motivated by the best interests of the company's shareholders. An analyst should review all such proxies put to the shareholders, determine the shareholders' consensus as reflected in the relative size of the affirmative vote, and determine the directors' response to the vote as reflected in the actions taken by the board and management. The responsiveness is a clear signal of the board's willingness to act in the best interests of the owners of the company.

5.2. Examples of Codes of Corporate Governance

We provide examples of three codes of corporate governance, one from General Electric, one from the Monetary Authority of Singapore, and a third from an international organization, the Organisation for Economic Co-Operation and Development. The first code provides an example for one of the largest globally diversified corporations. The second addresses corporate governance issues for financial institutions, specifically commercial banks and insurers operating in Singapore. The third has a much broader scope, addressing corporate governance issues in any type of firm in any industry, operating in a variety of countries that are members of the organization. Taken together, these three codes indicate the varying approaches to corporate governance worldwide while also illustrating how the core conflicts of interest between managers and owners are addressed.

5.2.1. General Electric: Governance Principles

General Electric's *Governance Principles* are a particularly good example of a company code of corporate governance. GE established the code not only to guide its managers and board of directors in their activities and decision making, but to serve as a benchmark by which their performance may be evaluated. The company publishes their *Principles* in a prominent place on their web site. A review of these principles will show that many of the major governance concerns just discussed are reflected here. The principles also explicitly address issues such as the company's policy on the adoption of poison pills and director education.

EXAMPLE 1-5   General Electric's *Governance Principles*

1. Role of Board and Management

GE's business is conducted by its employees, managers and officers, under the direction of the chief executive officer (CEO) and the oversight of the board, to enhance the long-term value of the company for its shareowners. The board of directors is elected by the shareowners to oversee management and to assure that the long-term interests of the shareowners are being served. Both the board of directors and management recognize that the long-term interests of shareowners are advanced by responsibly addressing the concerns of other stakeholders and interested parties including employees, recruits, customers, suppliers, GE communities, government officials and the public at large.

2. Functions of Board

The board of directors has eight scheduled meetings a year at which it reviews and discusses reports by management on the performance of the company, its plans and prospects, as well as immediate issues facing the company. Directors are expected to attend all scheduled board and committee meetings. In addition to its general oversight of management, the board also performs a number of specific functions, including:

- selecting, evaluating and compensating the CEO and overseeing CEO succession planning;
- providing counsel and oversight on the selection, evaluation, development and compensation of senior management;
- reviewing, monitoring and, where appropriate, approving fundamental financial and business strategies and major corporate actions;
- assessing major risks facing the company – and reviewing options for their mitigation; and
- ensuring processes are in place for maintaining the integrity of the company – the integrity of the financial statements, the integrity of compliance with law and ethics, the integrity of relationships with customers and suppliers, and the integrity of relationships with other stakeholders.

3. Qualifications

Directors should possess the highest personal and professional ethics, integrity and values, and be committed to representing the long-term interests of the shareowners. They must also have an inquisitive and objective perspective, practical wisdom and mature judgment. We endeavor to have a board representing diverse experience at policy-making levels in business, government, education and technology, and in areas that are relevant to the company's global activities.

Directors must be willing to devote sufficient time to carrying out their duties and responsibilities effectively, and should be committed to serve on the board for an extended period of time. Directors should offer their resignation in the event of any significant change in their personal circumstances, including a change in their principal job responsibilities.

Directors who also serve as CEOs or in equivalent positions should not serve on more than two boards of public companies in addition to the GE board, and other directors should not serve on more than four other boards of public companies in addition to the GE board. Current positions in excess of these limits may be maintained unless the board determines that doing so would impair the director's service on the GE board.

The board does not believe that arbitrary term limits on directors' service are appropriate, nor does it believe that directors should expect to be renominated annually until they reach the mandatory retirement age. The board self-evaluation process described below will be an important determinant for board tenure. Directors will not be nominated for election to the board after their 73rd birthday, although the full board may nominate candidates over 73 for special circumstances.

4. Independence of Directors

A majority of the directors will be independent directors, as independence is determined by the board, based on the guidelines set forth below.

All future non-employee directors will be independent. GE seeks to have a minimum of ten independent directors at all times, and it is the board's goal that at least two-thirds of the directors will be independent. Directors who do not satisfy GE's independence guidelines also make valuable contributions to the board and to the company by reason of their experience and wisdom.

For a director to be considered independent, the board must determine that the director does not have any direct or indirect material relationship with GE. The board has established guidelines to assist it in determining director independence, which conform to or are more exacting than the independence requirements in the New York Stock Exchange listing requirements (NYSE rules). In addition to applying these guidelines, the board will consider all relevant facts and circumstances in making an independence determination, and not merely from the standpoint of the director, but also from that of persons or organizations with which the director has an affiliation.

The board will make and publicly disclose its independence determination for each director when the director is first elected to the board and annually thereafter for all nominees for election as directors. If the board determines that a director who satisfies the NYSE rules is independent even though he or she does not satisfy all of GE's independence guidelines, this determination will be disclosed and explained in the next proxy statement.

In accordance with the revised NYSE rules, independence determinations under the guidelines in section (a) below will be based upon a director's relationships with GE during the 36 months preceding the determination. Similarly, independence determinations under the guidelines in section (b) below will be based upon the extent of commercial relationships during the three completed fiscal years preceding the determination.

a. A director will not be independent if:
  • the director is employed by GE, or an immediate family member is an executive officer of GE;

- the director receives any direct compensation from GE, other than director and committee fees and pension or other forms of deferred compensation for prior service (provided such compensation is not contingent in any way on continued service);
- an immediate family member who is a GE executive officer receives more than $100,000 per year in direct compensation from GE;
- the director is affiliated with or employed by GE's independent auditor, or an immediate family member is affiliated with or employed in a professional capacity by GE's independent auditor; or
- a GE executive officer is on the compensation committee of the board of directors of a company which employs the GE director or an immediate family member as an executive officer.

b. A director will not be independent if, at the time of the independence determination, the director is an executive officer or employee, or if an immediate family member is an executive officer, of another company that does business with GE and the sales by that company to GE or purchases by that company from GE, in any single fiscal year during the evaluation period, are more than the greater of one percent of the annual revenues of that company or $1 million.

c. A director will not be independent if, at the time of the independence determination, the director is an executive officer or employee, or an immediate family member is an executive officer, of another company which is indebted to GE, or to which GE is indebted, and the total amount of either company's indebtedness to the other at the end of the last completed fiscal year is more than one percent of the other company's total consolidated assets.

d. A director will not be independent if, at the time of the independence determination, the director serves as an officer, director or trustee of a charitable organization, and GE's discretionary charitable contributions to the organization are more than one percent of that organization's total annual charitable receipts during its last completed fiscal year. (GE's automatic matching of employee charitable contributions will not be included in the amount of GE's contributions for this purpose.)

5. Size of Board and Selection Process

The directors are elected each year by the shareowners at the annual meeting of shareowners. Shareowners may propose nominees for consideration by the nominating and corporate governance committee by submitting the names and supporting information to: Secretary, General Electric Company, 3135 Easton Turnpike, Fairfield, CT 06828. The board proposes a slate of nominees to the shareowners for election to the board. The board also determines the number of directors on the board provided that there are at least 10. Between annual shareowner meetings, the board may elect directors to serve until the next annual meeting. The board believes that, given the size and breadth of GE and the need for diversity of board views, the size of the board should be in the range of 13 to 17 directors.

6. Board Committees

The board has established the following committees to assist the board in discharging its responsibilities: (i) audit; (ii) management development and compensation;

(iii) nominating and corporate governance; and (iv) public responsibilities. The current charters and key practices of these committees are published on the GE website, and will be mailed to shareowners on written request. The committee chairs report the highlights of their meetings to the full board following each meeting of the respective committees. The committees occasionally hold meetings in conjunction with the full board. For example, it is the practice of the audit committee to meet in conjunction with the full board in February so that all directors may participate in the review of the annual financial statements and Management's Discussion and Analysis of Financial Condition and Results of Operations for the prior year and financial plans for the current year.

7. Independence of Committee Members

In addition to the requirement that a majority of the board satisfy the independence standards discussed in section 4 above, members of the audit committee must also satisfy an additional NYSE independence requirement. Specifically, they may not accept directly or indirectly any consulting, advisory or other compensatory fee from GE or any of its subsidiaries other than their directors' compensation. As a matter of policy, the board will also apply a separate and heightened independence standard to members of both the management development and compensation committee and the nominating and corporate governance committee. No member of either committee may be a partner, member or principal of a law firm, accounting firm or investment banking firm that accepts consulting or advisory fees from GE or any of its subsidiaries.

8. Meetings of Non-Employee Directors

The board will have at least three regularly scheduled meetings a year for the non-employee directors without management present. The directors have determined that the chairman of the management development and compensation committee will preside at such meetings, and will serve as the presiding director in performing such other functions as the board may direct, including advising on the selection of committee chairs and advising management on the agenda for board meetings. The non-employee directors may meet without management present at such other times as determined by the presiding director.

9. Self-Evaluation

As described more fully in the key practices of the nominating and corporate governance committee, the board and each of the committees will perform an annual self-evaluation. Each November, each director will provide to an independent governance expert his or her assessment of the effectiveness of the board and its committees, as well as director performance and board dynamics. The individual assessments will be organized and summarized by this independent governance expert for discussion with the board and the committees in December.

10. Setting Board Agenda

The board shall be responsible for its agenda. At the December board meeting, the CEO and the presiding director will propose for the board's approval key issues of strategy, risk and integrity to be scheduled and discussed during the course of the next calendar year. Before that meeting, the board will be invited to offer its suggestions. As a result of this process, a schedule of major discussion items for the following year will be established. Prior to each board meeting, the CEO will discuss the other specific agenda items for the meeting with the presiding director, who shall have authority to approve the agenda for the meeting. The CEO and the presiding director, or committee chair as appropriate, shall determine the nature and extent of information that shall be provided regularly to the directors before each scheduled board or committee meeting. Directors are urged to make suggestions for agenda items, or additional pre-meeting materials, to the CEO, the presiding director, or appropriate committee chair at any time.

11. Ethics and Conflicts of Interest

The board expects GE directors, as well as officers and employees, to act ethically at all times and to acknowledge their adherence to the policies comprising GE's code of conduct set forth in the company's integrity manual, "Integrity: The Spirit and the Letter of Our Commitment". GE will not make any personal loans or extensions of credit to directors or executive officers, other than consumer loans or credit card services on terms offered to the general public. No non-employee director may provide personal services for compensation to GE, other than in connection with serving as a GE director. The board will not permit any waiver of any ethics policy for any director or executive officer. If an actual or potential conflict of interest arises for a director, the director shall promptly inform the CEO and the presiding director. If a significant conflict exists and cannot be resolved, the director should resign. All directors will recuse themselves from any discussion or decision affecting their personal, business or professional interests. The board shall resolve any conflict of interest question involving the CEO, a vice chairman or a senior vice president, and the CEO shall resolve any conflict of interest issue involving any other officer of the company.

12. Reporting of Concerns to Non-Employee Directors or the Audit Committee

The audit committee and the non-employee directors have established the following procedures to enable anyone who has a concern about GE's conduct, or any employee who has a complaint about the company's accounting, internal accounting controls or auditing matters, to communicate that concern directly to the presiding director, to the non-employee directors or to the audit committee. Such communications may be confidential or anonymous, and may be e-mailed, submitted in writing or reported by phone to special addresses and a toll-free phone number that are published on the company's website. All such communications shall be promptly reviewed by GE's ombudsman, and any concerns relating to accounting, internal controls, auditing or officer conduct shall be sent immediately to the presiding director and to the chair of the audit committee. All concerns will be reviewed and addressed by GE's ombudsman in the same way that other concerns are addressed by the company. The status of all outstanding concerns addressed to the non-employee directors, the presiding director or the audit committee will be reported to the presiding director and the chair of the audit committee on a quarterly basis. The presiding director or the audit committee chair may direct that certain matters be presented to the audit committee or the full board and may direct special treatment, including the retention of outside advisors or counsel, for any concern addressed to them. The company's integrity manual prohibits any employee from retaliating or taking any adverse action against anyone for raising or helping to resolve an integrity concern.

13. Compensation of the Board

The nominating and corporate governance committee shall have the responsibility for recommending to the board compensation and benefits for non-employee directors. In discharging this duty, the committee shall be guided by three goals: compensation should fairly pay directors for work required in a company of GE's size and scope; compensation should align directors' interests with the long-term interests of shareowners; and the structure of the compensation should be simple, transparent and easy for shareowners to understand. As discussed more fully in the key practices of the nominating and corporate governance committee, the committee believes these goals will be served by providing 40% of non-employee director compensation in cash and 60% in deferred stock units. At the end of each year, the nominating and corporate governance committee shall review non-employee director compensation and benefits.

14. Succession Plan

The board shall approve and maintain a succession plan for the CEO and senior executives, based upon recommendations from the management development and compensation committee.

15. Annual Compensation Review of Senior Management

The management development and compensation committee shall annually approve the goals and objectives for compensating the CEO. That committee shall evaluate the CEO's performance in light of these goals before setting the CEO's salary, bonus and other incentive and equity compensation. The committee shall also annually approve the compensation structure for the company's officers, and shall evaluate the performance of the company's senior executive officers before approving their salary, bonus and other incentive and equity compensation.

16. Access to Senior Management

Non-employee directors are encouraged to contact senior managers of the company without senior corporate management present. To facilitate such contact, non-employee directors are expected to make two regularly scheduled visits to GE businesses a year without corporate management being present.

17. Access to Independent Advisors

The board and its committees shall have the right at any time to retain independent outside auditors and financial, legal or other advisors, and the company shall provide appropriate funding, as determined by the board or any committee, to compensate such independent outside auditors or advisors, as well as to cover the ordinary administrative expenses incurred by the board and its committees in carrying out their duties.

18. Director Education

The general counsel and the chief financial officer shall be responsible for providing an orientation for new directors. Each new director shall, within three months of election to the board, spend a day at corporate headquarters for personal briefing by senior management on the company's strategic plans, its financial statements, and its key policies and practices. In addition, directors shall be provided with continuing education on subjects that would assist them in discharging their duties, including regular programs on GE's financial planning and analysis, compliance and corporate governance developments; business-specific learning opportunities through site visits and Board meetings; and briefing sessions on topics that present special risks and opportunities to the company.

19. Policy on Poison Pills

The term "poison pill" refers to the type of shareowner rights plan that some companies adopt to make a hostile takeover of the company more difficult. GE does not have a poison pill and has no intention of adopting a poison pill because a hostile takeover of a company of our size is impractical and unrealistic. However, if GE were ever to adopt a poison pill, the board would seek prior shareowner approval unless, due to timing constraints or other reasons, a committee consisting solely of independent directors determines that it would be in the best interests of shareowners to adopt a poison pill before obtaining shareowner approval. If the GE board of directors were ever to adopt a poison pill without prior shareowner approval, the board would either submit the poison pill to shareowners for ratification, or would cause the poison pill to expire, without being renewed or replaced, within one year.

5.2.2. Monetary Authority of Singapore: Guidelines and Regulations on Corporate Governance In February 2003, the Monetary Authority of Singapore (MAS) established principles of corporate governance for the banks and insurers that fall within its regulatory purview. The code, *Guidelines and Regulations on Corporate Governance*,[17] defines and explains corporate governance as:

> . . . *The processes and structures by which the business and affairs of an Institution are directed, managed and controlled. [p. 6]*

The MAS makes clear that the key element in an effective system of corporate governance rests with the board of directors and that its primary duties are to shareholders and depositors or, in the case of an insurer, to the policyholders:

> *The board of directors is responsible for directing the management of the Institution. Besides its obligations to the shareholders, the board of directors of an Institution has a duty to act in the best interest of the Institution and to ensure that the Institution has sufficient resources to meet its obligations to other stakeholders, in particular a bank's depositors or an insurer's policyholders*

---

[17]These guidelines expand and build on the *Code of Corporate Governance*, issued in 2001 by the Corporate Governance Committee, established by the Ministry of Finance, the Authority, and the Attorney-General's Chambers.

The Monetary Authority of Singapore has the following 13 principles to guide the banks and insurers within its regulatory authority in compliance with the corporate governance standards in its *Guidelines and Regulations on Corporate Governance*:

Principle 1:   Every Institution should be headed by an effective Board.

Principle 2:   There should be a strong and independent element on the Board which is able to exercise objective judgment on corporate affairs independently from management and substantial shareholders.

Principle 3:   The Board should set and enforce clear lines of responsibility and accountability throughout the Institution.

Principle 4:   There should be a formal and transparent process for the appointment of new directors to the Board.

Principle 5:   There should be a formal assessment of the effectiveness of the Board as a whole and the contribution by each director to the effectiveness of the Board.

Principle 6:   In order to fulfill their responsibilities, Board members should be provided with complete, adequate and timely information prior to board meetings and on an on-going basis by the management.

Principle 7:   There should be a formal and transparent procedure for fixing the remuneration packages of individual directors. No director should be involved in deciding his own remuneration.

Principle 8:   The level and composition of remuneration should be appropriate to attract, retain and motivate the directors to perform their roles and carry out their responsibilities.

Principle 9:   The Board should establish an Audit Committee with a set of written terms of reference that clearly sets out its authority and duties.

Principle 10:   The Board should ensure that there is an adequate risk management system and sound internal controls.

Principle 11:   The Board should ensure that an internal audit function that is independent of the activities audited is established.

Principle 12:   The Board should ensure that management formulates policies to ensure dealings with the public, the Institution's policyholders and claimants, depositors and other customers are conducted fairly, responsibly and professionally.

Principle 13:   The Board should ensure that related party transactions with the Institution are made on an arm's length basis.

These principles are supported by requirements for extensive disclosures regarding companies' implementation and of the standards and their procedures for continuous monitoring of compliance. It is notable that the Monetary Authority does not require that a majority of the board members be independent, but only that one-third meet such a test.

5.2.3. Organisation for Economic Co-Operation and Development: *OECD Principles of Corporate Governance*

The Organisation for Economic Co-Operation and Development (OECD)[18] issued its code, *OECD Principles of Corporate Governance* (*OECD*

---

[18]Issued in 1999 and subsequently revised, the *OECD Principles* are intended to be adopted by each of the OECD member countries, which include Australia, Austria, Belgium, Canada, the Czech Republic, Denmark, Finland, France, Germany, Greece, Hungary, Iceland, Ireland, Italy, Japan, Korea, Luxembourg, Mexico, the Netherlands, New Zealand, Norway, Poland, Portugal, Spain, Sweden, Switzerland, Turkey, the United Kingdom, and the United States.

Principles), which applies to all Member countries. These countries comprise a number of different legislative, regulatory, and market systems.

The OECD observes that its *Principles* "represent the first initiative by an inter-governmental organisation to develop the core elements of a good corporate governance regime. As such, the Principles can be used as a benchmark by governments as they evaluate and improve their laws and regulations." The Preface to the *OECD Principles* states:

> *A good corporate governance regime helps to assure that corporations use their capital efficiently. Good corporate governance helps, too, to ensure that corporations take into account the interests of a wide range of constituencies as well as of the communities within which they operate, and that their boards are accountable to the company and the shareholders. This, in turn, helps to assure that corporations operate for the benefit of society as a whole. It helps to maintain the confidence of investors—both foreign and domestic—and to attract more "patient", long-term capital . . . **Common to all good corporate governance regimes, however, is a high degree of priority placed on the interests of shareholders, who place their trust in corporations to use their investment funds wisely and effectively.** [Emphasis added]*

Despite the application of the *OECD Principles* to a wide variety of regimes, the OECD provides a special emphasis on the rights and fair treatment of shareholders. This characteristic, although considered to be a fundamental requirement for good systems of corporate governance, is not frequently found in either corporate codes or those of other business organizations. For example, the General Electric code is silent on shareholder rights although it acknowledges in the first principle that managers and the directors have an obligation to attend to the interests of shareholders. The Monetary Authority of Singapore's code takes a similar approach.

EXAMPLE 1-6 *OECD Principles of Corporate Governance*

I. The Rights of Shareholders
The corporate governance framework should protect shareholders' rights.

A. Basic shareholder rights include the right to: 1) secure methods of ownership registration; 2) convey or transfer shares; 3) obtain relevant information on the corporation on a timely and regular basis; 4) participate and vote in general shareholder meetings; 5) elect members of the board; and 6) share in the profits of the corporation.
B. Shareholders have the right to participate in, and to be sufficiently informed on, decisions concerning fundamental corporate changes such as:
   1. Amendments to the statutes, or articles of incorporation or similar governing documents of the company;
   2. The authorisation of additional shares; and
   3. Extraordinary transactions that in effect result in the sale of the company.
C. Shareholders should have the opportunity to participate effectively and vote in general shareholder meetings and should be informed of the rules, including voting procedures that govern general shareholder meetings:

1. Shareholders should be furnished with sufficient and timely information concerning the date, location and agenda of general meetings, as well as full and timely information regarding the issues to be decided at the meeting.
2. Opportunity should be provided for shareholders to ask questions of the board and to place items on the agenda at general meetings, subject to reasonable limitations.
3. Shareholders should be able to vote in person or in absentia, and equal effect should be given to votes whether cast in person or in absentia.

D. Capital structures and arrangements that enable certain shareholders to obtain a degree of control disproportionate to their equity ownership should be disclosed.

E. Markets for corporate control should be allowed to function in an efficient and transparent manner.

1. The rules and procedures governing the acquisition of corporate control in the capital markets, and extraordinary transactions such as mergers, and sales of substantial portions of corporate assets, should be clearly articulated and disclosed so that investors understand their rights and recourse. Transactions should occur at transparent prices and under fair conditions that protect the rights of all shareholders according to their class.
2. Anti-take-over devices should not be used to shield management from accountability.

F. Shareholders, including institutional investors, should consider the costs and benefits of exercising their voting rights.

II.   The Equitable Treatment of Shareholders

The corporate governance framework should ensure the equitable treatment of all shareholders, including minority and foreign shareholders. All shareholders should have the opportunity to obtain effective redress for violation of their rights.

A. All shareholders of the same class should be treated equally.

1. Within any class, all shareholders should have the same voting rights. All investors should be able to obtain information about the voting rights attached to all classes of shares before they purchase. Any changes in voting rights should be subject to shareholder vote.
2. Votes should be cast by custodians or nominees in a manner agreed upon with the beneficial owner of the shares.
3. Processes and procedures for general shareholder meetings should allow for equitable treatment of all shareholders. Company procedures should not make it unduly difficult or expensive to cast votes.

B. Insider trading and abusive self-dealing should be prohibited.
C. Members of the board and managers should be required to disclose any material interests in transactions or matters affecting the corporation.

III.   The Role of Stakeholders in Corporate Governance

The corporate governance framework should recognise the rights of stakeholders as established by law and encourage active co-operation between corporations and stakeholders in creating wealth, jobs, and the sustainability of financially sound enterprises.

A. The corporate governance framework should assure that the rights of stakeholders that are protected by law are respected.

B. Where stakeholder interests are protected by law, stakeholders should have the opportunity to obtain effective redress for violation of their rights.

C. The corporate governance framework should permit performance-enhancing mechanisms for stakeholder participation.

D. Where stakeholders participate in the corporate governance process, they should have access to relevant information.

IV. Disclosure and Transparency

The corporate governance framework should ensure that timely and accurate disclosure is made on all material matters regarding the corporation, including the financial situation, performance, ownership, and governance of the company.

A. Disclosure should include, but not be limited to, material information on:

   1. The financial and operating results of the company.
   2. Company objectives.
   3. Major share ownership and voting rights.
   4. Members of the board and key executives, and their remuneration.
   5. Material foreseeable risk factors.
   6. Material issues regarding employees and other stakeholders.
   7. Governance structures and policies.

B. Information should be prepared, audited, and disclosed in accordance with high quality standards of accounting, financial and non-financial disclosure, and audit.

C. An annual audit should be conducted by an independent auditor in order to provide an external and objective assurance on the way in which financial statements have been prepared and presented.

D. Channels for disseminating information should provide for fair, timely and cost-efficient access to relevant information by users.

V. The Responsibilities of the Board

The corporate governance framework should ensure the strategic guidance of the company, the effective monitoring of management by the board, and the board's accountability to the company and the shareholders.

A. Board members should act on a fully informed basis, in good faith, with due diligence and care, and in the best interest of the company and the shareholders.

B. Where board decisions may affect different shareholder groups differently, the board should treat all shareholders fairly.

C. The board should ensure compliance with applicable law and take into account the interests of stakeholders.

D. The board should fulfill certain key functions, including:

   1. Reviewing and guiding corporate strategy, major plans of action, risk policy, annual budgets and business plans; setting performance objectives; monitoring implementation and corporate performance; and overseeing major capital expenditures, acquisitions and divestitures.

2. Selecting, compensating, monitoring and, when necessary, replacing key executives and overseeing succession planning.

3. Reviewing key executive and board remuneration, and ensuring a formal and transparent board nomination process.

4. Monitoring and managing potential conflicts of interest of management, board members and shareholders, including misuse of corporate assets and abuse in related party transactions.

5. Ensuring the integrity of the corporation's accounting and financial reporting systems, including the independent audit, and that appropriate systems of control are in place, in particular, systems for monitoring risk, financial control, and compliance with the law.

6. Monitoring the effectiveness of the governance practices under which it operates and making changes as needed.

7. Overseeing the process of disclosure and communications.

E. The board should be able to exercise objective judgement on corporate affairs independent, in particular, from management.

1. Boards should consider assigning a sufficient number of non-executive board members capable of exercising independent judgement to tasks where there is a potential for conflict of interest. Examples of such key responsibilities are financial reporting, nomination and executive and board remuneration.

2. Board members should devote sufficient time to their responsibilities.

F. In order to fulfill their responsibilities, board members should have access to accurate, relevant and timely information.

This code, and its predecessor variants, is not only among the earliest efforts to establish guidelines for good governance, but with its global reach has had wide influence on the development of other codes and regulatory frameworks.

6. ENVIRONMENTAL, SOCIAL, AND GOVERNANCE FACTORS

Investors now understand that nontraditional business factors—specifically, a company's environmental, social, and governance (ESG) risk exposures—may be as critical to the company's long-term sustainability as more traditional concerns. Indeed, many major financial institutions and portfolio managers routinely integrate ESG analyses into their equity valuations and other investment decisions.[19] Those analysts who fail to consider ESG factors in their valuations may well be assuming far greater long-term risks than they or their clients realize.[20]

ESG factors range from those associated with climate change (for example, carbon-based greenhouse gas emissions resulting from a company's operations) to labor rights, public and occupational health issues, and the soundness of the company's governance structures.[21]

---

[19]See, for example, Anderson and Gardiner (2006).
[20]United Nations Environmental Programme Finance Initiative (2004).
[21]Ibid.

The risks resulting from exposure to these various issues will now be discussed.

1. **Legislative and regulatory risk**: The risk that governmental laws and regulations directly or indirectly affecting a company's operations will change, with potentially severe adverse effects on the company's continued profitability and even its long-term sustainability.

For example, in the United States, a law enacted in California in 2004 requires a 30 percent reduction in carbon dioxide emissions by 2016 for all new automobiles sold in the state. Other states, including Connecticut, Maine, Massachusetts, New Jersey, New York, Oregon, Pennsylvania, Rhode Island, Vermont, and Washington, are following California's example.[22] These states currently represent more than half of all U.S. automobile sales. Consequently, manufacturers that fail to meet the standards can expect to suffer a reduction in revenues and earnings as well as in market power. Given strong industry competition, the effects of the changes in the laws on companies operating in the industry could be severe.

Other national and global efforts have brought rapid changes in operations for companies in affected countries. For example, the Kyoto Protocol is a 1997 amendment to the United Nations Framework Convention on Climate Change (UNFCCC). The Protocol now covers more than 160 countries, not including the United States and Australia, and over 60 percent of greenhouse gas emissions. The agreement calls for staged reductions in emissions of carbon dioxide and five other greenhouse gases for the countries that have ratified the agreement. The Protocol also provides for emissions credit trading for those signatories, principally in emerging countries, that could not otherwise afford the investment.

Companies in most industries are likely to be affected to at least some degree by these mandated changes, although the effects will vary widely across industries. Even in industries with the greatest exposures, companies that have invested in new, up-to-date technologies are likely to be affected less by the changes than their competitors. Thus, investors who consider ESG factors and who monitor regulatory and legislative developments for the companies they follow will be better equipped to make sound investment decisions.

2. **Legal risk**: The risk that failures by company managers to effectively manage ESG factors will lead to lawsuits and other judicial remedies, resulting in potentially catastrophic losses for the company.

All areas of ESG can, and sometimes do, lead to such lawsuits. The actions can be brought by employees for workplace issues and contractual defaults, by shareholders for management or director governance or other lapses that impair shareholder value, or by government attorneys for abridgement of federal or state laws.

An investor can begin to analyze the potential for such risks in a particular company by reviewing regulatory filings for the particular jurisdictions in which the company operates. Many such filings, such as the U.S. SEC–required disclosures in the Form 10-K Business, Risks, and Legal Proceedings sections, as well as the Management Discussion and Analysis of Financial Condition and Results of Operations, require substantial discussion of possible legal risk exposures. For the companies that provide them, the GRI reports may include useful insights.[23] However, an analyst should make an independent assessment of the company

---

[22]Anderson et al., p. 7.

[23]The Global Reporting Initiative (GRI) promotes systematic reporting of economic, environmental, and social performance. The web site for the GRI is www.globalreporting.org.

and carefully consider the nature of a company's operations to evaluate the possible scope of such exposures and their potential effects. The business press may also be a good source of information regarding such risks for both the company of immediate interest as well as for other companies in the same industry.

3. **Reputational risk**: The risk that failure by company managers to effectively manage ESG factors will result in diminished respect and status of the company in the eyes of customers and stakeholders.

This particular source of risk has risen in importance as ESG factors are increasingly recognized as a potentially major source of risk. Specifically, companies whose managers have demonstrated a lack of concern for managing ESG factors in the past, so as to eliminate or otherwise mitigate risk exposures, will suffer a diminution in market value relative to other companies in the same industry that may persist for a long period of time.

4. **Operating risk**: The risk that a company's operations may be severely affected by ESG factors, even to the requirement that one or more product lines or possibly all operations might be shut down.

An example of such a risk is that deriving from the industrial use of benzene, a powerful carcinogen and one of the most toxic chemicals known. Because of its use as both a building block in the plastics and rubber industry, as well as its more general use as an industrial solvent, benzene had been widely used in industry and was dispersed into the air, drinking water, and soil. Billions of pounds of the chemical were produced and used annually.

Once studies confirmed the harmful effects of the chemical, the U.S. Environmental Protection Agency (EPA) moved, for example, under the 1974 Safe Drinking Water Act to set targets for acceptable levels in water. The EPA Maximum Contaminant Level for benzene in drinking water was set at five parts per billion. Thus, companies that had previously relied on the extensive use of benzene in their operations had either to modify their operations to ensure that no benzene escaped into the environment or to cease the operations that used benzene altogether.

5. **Financial risk**: The risk that ESG factors will result in significant costs or other losses to the company and its shareholders.

Any of these sources of risk can affect a company and its financial health, sometimes severely.

In summary, investors are well advised to consider the potential effects of ESG factors on companies in which they invest and to carefully analyze all sources of information relevant to such risk exposures. These analyses may alert the analyst to risk factors that should be incorporated into company valuations.

7. VALUATION IMPLICATIONS OF CORPORATE GOVERNANCE

The relative quality, strength, and reliability of a company's corporate governance system have direct and profound implications for investors' assessments of investments and their valuations. As we have seen in the massive corporate collapses in recent years, most or all of an investor's capital can be lost suddenly if a company fails to establish an effective corporate governance system with the appropriate checks and balances.

Weak corporate governance systems pose the following risks to the value of investments in the company:

- *Accounting risk*: The risk that a company's financial statement recognition and related disclosures, upon which investors base their financial decisions, are incomplete, misleading, or materially misstated.
- *Asset risk*: The risk that the firm's assets, which belong to investors, will be misappropriated by managers or directors in the form of excessive compensation or other perquisites.
- *Liability risk*: The risk that management will enter into excessive obligations, committed to on behalf of shareholders, that effectively destroy the value of shareholders' equity; these frequently take the form of off-balance-sheet obligations.
- *Strategic policy risk*: The risk that managers may enter into transactions, such as mergers and acquisitions, or incur other business risks that may not be in the best long-term interest of shareholders, but that may result in large payoffs for management or directors.

Not surprisingly, a growing body of evidence indicates that companies with sound corporate governance systems show higher profitability and investment performance measures, including returns, relative to those assessed to have weaker structures. For example, a joint study of Institutional Shareholder Services (ISS) and Georgia State University[24] found that the best governed companies, as measured by the ISS Corporate Governance Quotient, generated returns on investment and equity over the period under study that were 18.7 percent and 23.8 percent, respectively, better than those of companies with poor governance. Similarly, a study of U.S. markets, conducted by researchers at Harvard University and the University of Pennsylvania[25] found that portfolios of companies with strong shareholder rights protections outperformed portfolios of companies with weaker protections by 8.5 percent per year. A study of European firms found annual mean return differences of 3.0 percent.[26]

This phenomenon is not limited to developed markets. Even before the collapse of Enron, a Malaysia-based analyst found that investors in emerging markets overwhelmingly preferred companies with good governance.[27] Of the 100 largest emerging markets companies his firm followed, those with the best governance, based on management discipline, transparency, independence, accountability, responsibility, fairness and social responsibility, generated three-year U.S. dollar returns of 267 percent, compared with average returns of 127 percent. The disparity in five-year returns was even greater, at 930 percent versus an average of 388 percent.

The conclusion from these and other studies is that good corporate governance leads to better results, both for companies and for investors. Therefore, investors and analysts should carefully evaluate the corporate governance structures of companies they are considering as investments and should continue to monitor the systems once the investments are made.

---

[24]Brown and Caylor (2004).

[25]Gompers, Ishii, and Metrick (2003), pp. 107–155. The authors compared the investment performance of some 1,500 U.S.-listed companies against a corporate governance index the authors constructed from 24 distinct governance rules.

[26]Bauer and Guenster (2003). This study used Deminor Ratings as the basis for determining companies' relative corporate governance quality (www.deminor.org).

[27]Gill (2001) points out that CLSA assigned corporate governance ratings to 495 companies in 25 markets.

8. SUMMARY

Corporate governance is an essential concern for investors and investment analysts. This chapter has presented the attributes of an effective corporate governance system and the types of practices that should raise investors' concerns. This chapter has made the following points:

- Corporate governance is the system of principles, policies, procedures, and clearly defined responsibilities and accountabilities, used by stakeholders to eliminate or minimize conflicts of interest.
- The objectives of a corporate governance system are (1) to eliminate or mitigate conflicts of interest among stakeholders, particularly between managers and shareholders, and (2) to ensure that the assets of the company are used efficiently and productively and in the best interests of the investors and other stakeholders.
- The failure of a company to establish an effective system of corporate governance represents a major operational risk to the company and its investors. To understand the risks inherent in an investment in a company, it is essential to understand the quality of the company's corporate governance practices.
- The core attributes of an effective corporate governance system are
  - Delineation of the rights of shareholders and other core stakeholders;
  - Clearly defined manager and director governance responsibilities to the stakeholders;
  - Identifiable and measurable accountabilities for the performance of the responsibilities;
  - Fairness and equitable treatment in all dealings between managers, directors, and shareholders; and
  - Complete transparency and accuracy in disclosures regarding operations, performance, risk, and financial position.
- The specific sources of conflict in corporate agency relationships are
  - Manager–shareholder conflicts: Managers may, for example,
    - Use funds to try to expand the size of a business even when this is not in the best interests of shareholders; and
    - Grant themselves numerous expensive perquisites, which are treated as ordinary business expenses.
  - Director–Shareholder Conflicts: Directors may, for example, identify with the managers' interests rather than with those of the shareholders as a result of personal or business relationships with the manager.
- The responsibilities of board members, both individually and as a group, are to
  - Establish corporate values and governance structures for the company to ensure that the business is conducted in an ethical, competent, fair, and professional manner;
  - Ensure that all legal and regulatory requirements are met and complied with fully and in a timely fashion;
  - Establish long-term strategic objectives for the company with a goal of ensuring that the best interests of shareholders come first and that the company's obligations to others are met in a timely and complete manner;
  - Establish clear lines of responsibility and a strong system of accountability and performance measurement in all phases of a company's operations;
  - Hire the chief executive officer, determine the compensation package, and periodically evaluate the officer's performance;

- Ensure that management has supplied the board with sufficient information for it to be fully informed and prepared to make the decisions that are its responsibility, in addition to being able to adequately monitor and oversee the company's management;
- Meet regularly to perform its duties and in extraordinary session as required by events;
- Acquire training so that members are able to adequately perform their duties.

- An investor or investment analyst must assess

  - Board composition and independence;
  - Whether the chairman of the board is independent;
  - The qualifications of the directors;
  - Whether the board is elected on an annual or staggered basis;
  - Board self-assessment practices;
  - The frequency of separate sessions of independent directors;
  - The audit committee and audit oversight;
  - The nominating committee;
  - The compensation committee and compensation awards to management; and
  - The use (or nonuse) of independent legal and expert counsel.

- Companies committed to corporate governance often provide a statement of corporate governance policies. Analysts should assess:

  - The code of ethics.
  - Statements of the oversight, monitoring, and review responsibilities of directors.
  - Statements of management's responsibilities with respect to information and access of directors to internal company functions.
  - Reports of directors' examinations, evaluations, and findings.
  - Board and committee self-assessments.
  - Management self-assessments; and
  - Training policies for directors.

- Weak corporate governance systems give rise to risks, including accounting risk, asset risk, liability risk, and strategic policy risk. Such risks may compromise the value of investments in the company.

PRACTICE PROBLEMS

1. Which of the following *best* defines the concept of corporate governance?
   A. A system for monitoring managers' activities, rewarding performance, and disciplining misbehavior.
   B. Identifiable and measurable accountabilities for all stakeholders.
   C. Corporate values and governance structures that ensure the business is conducted in an ethical, competent, fair, and professional manner.
   D. A system of principles, policies, and procedures used to manage and control the activities of a corporation so as to overcome conflicts of interest inherent in the corporate form.

2. Which of the following is an example of a conflict of interest that an effective corporate governance system would mitigate or eliminate?
   A. A majority of the board who are independent of management.
   B. Directors who have come to identify with the managers' interests rather than with those of the shareholders.

C. Directors who have board experience with companies regarded as having sound governance practices.
D. The process of performing a periodic self-assessment by directors.

3. Which of the following *best* describes the corporate governance responsibilities of members of the board of directors?
   A. Establishing long-term strategic objectives for the company.
   B. Establishing global best practice standards for proxy voting.
   C. Ensuring at board meetings that no subject is undiscussable and that dissent is regarded as an obligation.
   D. Ensuring that the board negotiates with the company over all matters such as compensation.

4. Which of the following is *least likely* to be useful in evaluating a company's corporate governance system for investment analysis purposes?
   A. Assessing issues related to the board, managers, and shareholders.
   B. Reviewing the company's regulatory filings and financial information provided to shareholders.
   C. Identifying any off-balance-sheet or insider transactions and determining the company's policies with regard to related party transactions.
   D. Flagging items such as the egregious use of insider transactions for users of the financial statements.

5. The objectives of an effective system of corporate governance include *all* of the following *except*
   A. Ensuring that the assets of the company are used efficiently and productively.
   B. Eliminating or mitigating conflicts of interest among stakeholders.
   C. Ensuring that the assets of the company are used in the best interests of investors and other stakeholders.
   D. Ensuring complete transparency in disclosures regarding operations, performance, risk, and financial position.

6. *All* of the following are core attributes of an effective corporate governance system *except*
   A. Fairness and accuracy in identifying inherent conflicts of interest.
   B. Clearly defined governance responsibilities for managers and directors.
   C. Identifiable and measurable accountabilities for the performance of responsibilities.
   D. Delineation of shareholders' and other core stakeholders' rights.

7. *All* of the following are examples of conflicts of interest that an effective corporate governance system should address *except* relationships between
   A. Managers and shareholders.
   B. Directors and shareholders.
   C. Managers and directors.
   D. Managers and institutional analysts.

8. *All* of the following are true of an effective system of corporate governance *except*
   A. The system must be continually monitored, especially with changes in management and the board.
   B. A single system of effective corporate governance applies to all firms worldwide.

    C. The failure to establish an effective system of corporate governance to overcome inherent conflicts of interest represents a major operational risk.

    D. There are a number of common characteristics of all sound corporate governance structures.

The following information relates to Questions 9 through 14.

Jane Smith, CFA, has recently joined Zero Asset Management, Inc. (Zero) as a board member. Since Smith is also outside council for Zero Asset Management, she is already very familiar with Zero's operations and expects to begin contributing good ideas right away. Zero is a publicly traded investment management firm that has historically focused on mutual fund management. Although there is current market opportunity to add a new type of mutual fund, the board recently decided against adding the fund. Instead, the board decided to expand its business to include a hedge fund operation within the existing corporation.

    Bill Week, CEO of Zero, has publicly stated that he is willing to bet the company's future on hedge fund management. Week is the founder of Zero, as well as chairman of the board, and maintains a controlling interest in the company.

    Like the rest of Zero, the firm's new hedge fund is quantitatively driven and index based. The fund has been set up in a separate office with new systems so that the analysts and managers can create a unique hedge fund culture. Trading and execution are the only operations that remain with Zero. The fund is run by one of Zero's most successful portfolio managers.

    Smith learns that, although none of the board members sit on other companies' boards, most have at one point or another worked at Zero and so they are very familiar with Zero's operations. A board member has attempted to make the health insurance and retirement concerns of the board members an agenda item, without success to date. Smith eagerly anticipates the next board meeting because they are always in a luxurious setting.

    The board becomes concerned by Smith's questions and decides to hire an independent consultant to review their corporate governance responsibilities. The consultant starts his analysis by stating that a corporate governance system relies on checks and balances among managers, directors, and investors. Smith asks whether Zero has the proper systems in place. The consultant says that he has looked at conflicts of interest and has one more area to review in order to verify that the board is meeting its major objectives. Concerned about the company's stock price, Smith asks the consultant what work he has done concerning Zero's corporate disclosures for investment professionals. The consultant indicates that he has reviewed Zero's regulatory filings for clear and complete information, as well as the company's policies regarding related-party transactions.

  9. *All* of the following indicate Zero's board's lack of independence *except*

    A. Former employment with the company.

    B. Personal relationships.

    C. Service of the outside counsel as a board member.

    D. Lack of interlocking directorships.

10. Which of the following is the *most effective* action for the board to take to address their oversight responsibilities concerning the hedge fund's proxy voting?
    A. Establishing corporate values and a governance structure for the company.
    B. Establishing long-term strategic objectives that are met and fully complied with.
    C. Performing adequate training so that employees are able to perform their duties.
    D. Monitoring and overseeing the company's operations on a daily basis to ensure that all legal and regulatory requirements are met and complied with in a timely manner.

11. Which of the following omissions *best* describes a corporate governance shortcoming of Zero's board of directors?
    A. The board's failure to address the potential conflicts of interest between managing the firm's hedge fund and its mutual fund business.
    B. The board's failure to make the health insurance and retirement concerns of board members an agenda item.
    C. The board's failure to meet the market opportunity for a new kind of mutual fund.
    D. The board's failure to establish the hedge fund operation in a separate corporation.

12. Given that Zero's directors all previously worked at the company, which of the following would you recommend for a more effective system of corporate governance?
    A. Ensuring that assets are used efficiently and productively and in the best interests of investors and stakeholders.
    B. Eliminating or mitigating conflicts of interest among stakeholders, particularly between managers and shareholders.
    C. Identifying and measuring accountabilities for the performance of the board's responsibilities.
    D. Providing complete transparency and accuracy regarding operations, performance, and financial position.

13. Which of the following *best* describes the objectives of Zero's board that the consultant has not yet reviewed?
    A. Where board decisions may affect shareholder groups differently, the board should treat all shareholders fairly.
    B. The board should ensure that the assets of the company are used efficiently and productively and in the best interests of the investors and other stakeholders.
    C. The board should ensure that material foreseeable risk factors are addressed and considered.
    D. The board should ensure compliance with applicable laws and take into account the interest of stakeholders.

14. Which of the following is the *most* critical activity that an analyst can engage in to assess the quality of the corporate governance system at Zero, among those that the consultant did not review?
    A. Looking for vague references to off-balance-sheet or insider information.
    B. Identifying the responsiveness of the board to shareholder proxy votes.
    C. Clearly identifying reporting lines and organizational structure.
    D. Evaluating the quality and extent of financial information provided to investors.

The following information relates to Questions 15 through 19.

Shelley Newcome is the new CEO for a publicly traded financial services company, Asset Management Co. (AMC). Newcome is new to the corporate governance requirements of a publicly traded company; she previously worked for a family office that invested in private equity.

At her first board meeting, the company's first in six months, she asks a director what the objectives of corporate governance should be. The director tells her that the most important objective he can think of is to eliminate or mitigate conflicts of interest among stakeholders.

One of Newcome's first steps as CEO is to fly to New York City to address a group of Wall Street analysts. Newcome is happy to discover that AMC provides her, and other senior management, with a company jet to attend such meetings.

At the opening of the meeting, Newcome is surprised to hear that most of the analysts are extremely interested in learning about AMC's corporate governance system. One analyst indicates that he has studied several of AMC's competitors and found that they share a set of critical and core attributes. The analyst goes on to note that, like its competitors, AMC has included in its corporate governance system the following attributes: the rights of shareholders and other core stakeholders are clearly delineated; there is complete transparency and accuracy in disclosures regarding operations, performance, risk, and financial position; and identifiable and measurable accountabilities for the performance of responsibilities are in place. The analyst also says that, to verify that the board is meeting its major objectives, he has looked at AMC's conflicts of interest and has one more area to review.

Newcome then asks the analyst why his corporate governance evaluation of AMC is so important. The analyst responds by saying that his decision whether to invest in AMC and ultimately the long-term performance of the company are dependent on the quality of AMC's managers' decisions and the skill they use in applying sound management practices.

Closing the meeting, Newcome is delayed by one analyst who complains about the difficulties of flying these days and how he has to get to the airport hours ahead of time. The analyst goes on to say that he reviewed AMC's regulatory filings and was happy to see that the company does not spend its money on frivolous perquisites like executive jets.

15. Which of the following would *best* complete the objectives of corporate governance for the CEO?
    A. Ensuring that assets of the company are used efficiently and productively and in the best interests of investors and other stakeholders.
    B. Clearly defining governance responsibilities for both managers and directors.
    C. Evaluating the quality of corporate governance of a company prior to investing in or working for it.
    D. Establishing clear lines of responsibility and a strong system of accountability and performance measurement in all phases of a company's operations.

16. On the basis of the Wall Street analyst's comments about AMC's corporate governance system, which of the following would be *most* effective for AMC to attract investors' interest?

    A. Implementing a corporate governance system in which business activity is encouraged and rewarded and that leads to innovation.

    B. Establishing a corporate governance system that overcomes inherent conflicts of interest since they represent a major operational risk to investors and to the continued existence of the company.

    C. Providing full transparency of all material information on a timely basis to all investment analysts.

    D. Dealing fairly with all stakeholders, including investors and creditors.

17. Which of the following is a core attribute that the Wall Street analyst left out of his analysis of AMC?

    A. Corporate governance systems rely on checks and balances among managers, directors, and investors.

    B. Fairness in all dealings between managers, directors, and shareholders.

    C. Governance responsibilities for the managers and directors are clearly defined.

    D. Both B and C.

18. Based on the information provided in the case, which of the following corporate disclosures could investment professionals use to evaluate the quality of the corporate governance system at AMC?

    A. Inclusion of all vague references to off-balance-sheet or insider transactions in board minutes.

    B. Failure to disclose executive perquisites such as the use of corporate jets by senior management.

    C. Providing other compensation that has not been disclosed to investment analysts.

    D. Prior approval by the board of directors of all transactions and a statement that such transactions are consistent with company policy.

19. Which of the following is an example of a corporate governance responsibility that AMC's board of directors has failed to meet?

    A. Ensuring that the board adequately monitors and oversees the company's management.

    B. Ensuring that management has supplied the board with sufficient information for it to be fully informed.

    C. Meeting regularly to perform its duties.

    D. Requiring training so that members will be able to adequately perform their duties.

CHAPTER 2

CAPITAL BUDGETING

John D. Stowe, CFA

CFA Institute
Charlottesville, Virginia

Jacques R. Gagné, CFA

La Société de l'assurance automobile du Québec
Quebec City, Canada

LEARNING OUTCOMES

After completing this chapter, you will be able to do the following:

- Define the capital budgeting process, explain the administrative steps of the process, and categorize the capital projects that can be evaluated.
- Summarize and explain the principles of capital budgeting, including the choice of the proper cash flows and the identification of the proper discount rate.
- Explain how the following project interactions affect the evaluation of a capital project: (1) independent versus mutually exclusive projects, (2) project sequencing, and (3) unlimited funds versus capital rationing.
- Calculate and interpret the results produced by each of the following methods when evaluating a single capital project: net present value (NPV), internal rate of return (IRR), payback period, discounted payback period, average accounting rate of return (AAR), and profitability index (PI).
- Explain the NPV profile, compare and contrast the NPV and IRR methods when evaluating more than one capital project, and describe the multiple IRR and no IRR problems that can arise when calculating an IRR.
- Describe the relative popularity of the various capital budgeting methods and explain the effects of the NPV on a stock price.
- Compute the yearly cash flows of an expansion capital project and of a replacement capital project, and show how the depreciation method affects those cash flows.
- Discuss the effects of inflation on capital budgeting analysis.

- Select the optimal capital project in situations of (1) mutually exclusive projects with unequal lives, using either the least common multiple of lives approach or the equivalent annual annuity approach, and (2) capital rationing.
- Explain how sensitivity analysis, scenario analysis, and Monte Carlo simulation can be used to estimate the standalone risk of a capital project.
- Discuss the procedure for determining the discount rate to be used in valuing a capital project and illustrate the procedure based on the CAPM.
- Discuss the types of real options and evaluate the profitability of investments with real options.
- Describe several capital budgeting pitfalls.
- Calculate and interpret accounting income and economic income in the context of capital budgeting.
- Describe and contrast the following valuation models of a capital project: economic profit (EP), residual income, and claims valuation.

1. INTRODUCTION

Capital budgeting is the process that companies use for decision making on capital projects—projects with a life of a year or more. This is a fundamental area of knowledge for financial analysts for many reasons.

- First, capital budgeting is very important for corporations. Capital projects, which make up the long-term asset portion of the balance sheet, can be so large that sound capital budgeting decisions ultimately decide the future of many corporations. Capital decisions cannot be reversed at a low cost, so mistakes are very costly. Indeed, the real capital investments of a company describe a company better than its working capital or capital structures, which are intangible and tend to be similar for many corporations.
- Second, the principles of capital budgeting have been adapted for many other corporate decisions, such as investments in working capital, leasing, mergers and acquisitions, and bond refunding.
- Third, the valuation principles used in capital budgeting are similar to the valuation principles used in security analysis and portfolio management. Many of the methods used by security analysts and portfolio managers are based on capital budgeting methods. Conversely, there have been innovations in security analysis and portfolio management that have also been adapted to capital budgeting.
- Finally, although analysts have a vantage point outside the company, their interest in valuation coincides with the capital budgeting focus of maximizing shareholder value. Because capital budgeting information is not ordinarily available outside the company, the analyst may attempt to estimate the process, within reason, at least for companies that are not too complex. Further, analysts may be able to appraise the quality of the company's capital budgeting process, for example, on the basis of whether the company has an accounting focus or an economic focus.

This chapter is organized as follows: Section 2 presents the steps in a typical capital budgeting process. After introducing the basic principles of capital budgeting in Section 3, in Section 4 we discuss the criteria by which a decision to invest in a project may be made.

Section 5 presents a crucial element of the capital budgeting process: organizing the cash flow information that is the raw material of the analysis. Section 6 looks further at cash flow analysis. Section 7 demonstrates methods to extend the basic investment criteria to address economic alternatives and risk. Finally, Section 8 compares other income measures and valuation models that analysts use to the basic capital budgeting model.

2. THE CAPITAL BUDGETING PROCESS

The specific capital budgeting procedures that managers use depend on their level in the organization, the size and complexity of the project being evaluated, and the size of the organization. The typical steps in the capital budgeting process are as follows:

- *Step one, generating ideas:* Investment ideas can come from anywhere, from the top or the bottom of the organization, from any department or functional area, or from outside the company. Generating good investment ideas to consider is the most important step in the process.
- *Step two, analyzing individual proposals:* This step involves gathering the information to forecast cash flows for each project and then evaluating the project's profitability.
- *Step three, planning the capital budget:* The company must organize the profitable proposals into a coordinated whole that fits within the company's overall strategies, and it also must consider the projects' timing. Some projects that look good when considered in isolation may be undesirable strategically. Because of financial and real resource issues, scheduling and prioritizing projects are important.
- *Step four, monitoring and postauditing:* In a postaudit, actual results are compared to planned or predicted results, and any differences must be explained. For example, how do the revenues, expenses, and cash flows realized from an investment compare to the predictions? Postauditing capital projects is important for several reasons. First, it helps monitor the forecasts and analysis that underlie the capital budgeting process. Systematic errors, such as overly optimistic forecasts, become apparent. Second, it helps improve business operations. If sales or costs are out of line, it will focus attention on bringing performance closer to expectations if at all possible. Finally, monitoring and postauditing recent capital investments will produce concrete ideas for future investments. Managers can decide to invest more heavily in profitable areas and scale down or cancel investments in areas that are disappointing.

   Planning for capital investments can be very complex, often involving many persons inside and outside the company. Information about marketing, science, engineering, regulation, taxation, finance, production, and behavioral issues must be systematically gathered and evaluated. The authority to make capital decisions depends on the size and complexity of the project. Lower-level managers may have discretion to make decisions that involve less than a given amount of money or that do not exceed a given capital budget. Larger and more complex decisions are reserved for top management, and some are so significant that the company's board of directors ultimately has the decision-making authority.

   Like everything else, capital budgeting is a cost–benefit exercise. At the margin, the benefits from the improved decision making should exceed the costs of the capital budgeting efforts.

Companies often put capital budgeting projects into rough categories for analysis. One such classification is as follows:

1. *Replacement projects:* These are among the easier capital budgeting decisions. If a piece of equipment breaks down or wears out, whether to replace it may not require careful analysis. If the expenditure is modest and if not investing has significant implications for production, operations, or sales, it would be a waste of resources to overanalyze the decision. Just make the replacement. Other replacement decisions involve replacing existing equipment with newer, more efficient equipment or perhaps choosing one type of equipment over another. These replacement decisions are often amenable to very detailed analysis, and you might have a lot of confidence in the final decision.

2. *Expansion projects:* Instead of merely maintaining a company's existing business activities, expansion projects increase the size of the business. These expansion decisions may involve more uncertainties than replacement decisions, and they should be more carefully considered.

3. *New products and services:* These investments expose the company to even more uncertainties than expansion projects. These decisions are more complex and will involve more people in the decision-making process.

4. *Regulatory, safety, and environmental projects:* These projects are frequently required by a governmental agency, an insurance company, or some other external party. They may generate no revenue and might not be undertaken by a company maximizing its own private interests. Often, the company will accept the required investment and continue to operate. Occasionally, however, the cost of the regulatory, safety, or environmental project is sufficiently high that the company would do better to cease operating altogether or to shut down any part of the business that is related to the project.

5. *Other:* The preceding projects are all susceptible to capital budgeting analysis, and they can be accepted or rejected using the net present value (NPV) or some other criterion. Some projects escape such analysis. These are either pet projects of someone in the company (such as the CEO buying a new aircraft) or so risky that they are difficult to analyze by the usual methods (such as some research and development decisions).

3. BASIC PRINCIPLES OF CAPITAL BUDGETING

Capital budgeting has a rich history and sometimes employs some sophisticated procedures. Fortunately, capital budgeting relies on just a few basic principles and typically uses the following assumptions:

1. *Decisions are based on cash flows:* The decisions are not based on accounting concepts, such as net income. Furthermore, intangible costs and benefits are often ignored because, if they are real, they should result in cash flows at some other time.

2. *Timing of cash flows is crucial:* Analysts make an extraordinary effort to detail precisely when cash flows occur.

3. *Cash flows are based on opportunity costs:* What are the incremental cash flows that occur with an investment, compared to what they would have been without the investment?

4. *Cash flows are analyzed on an after-tax basis:* Taxes must be fully reflected in all capital budgeting decisions.

5. *Financing costs are ignored:* This may seem unrealistic, but it is not. Most of the time, analysts want to know the after-tax operating cash flows that result from a capital investment. Then these after-tax cash flows and the investment outlays are discounted at the required rate of return to find the net present value (NPV). Financing costs are reflected in the required rate of return. If we included financing costs in the cash flows and in the discount rate, we would be double-counting the financing costs. So. even though a project may be financed with some combination of debt and equity, we ignore these costs, focusing on the operating cash flows and capturing the costs of debt (and other capital) in the discount rate.

Capital budgeting cash flows are not accounting net income. Accounting net income is reduced by noncash charges such as accounting depreciation. Furthermore, to reflect the cost of debt financing, interest expenses are also subtracted from accounting net income. (No subtraction is made for the cost of equity financing in arriving at accounting net income.) Accounting net income also differs from economic income, which is the cash inflow plus the change in the market value of the company. Economic income does not subtract the cost of debt financing, and it is based on the changes in the market value of the company, not on changes in its book value (accounting depreciation). We will further consider cash flows, accounting income, economic income, and other income measures at the end of this chapter.

In assumption 5, we referred to the rate used in discounting the cash flows as the required rate of return, which is the discount rate that investors should require given the riskiness of the project. This discount rate is frequently called the opportunity cost of funds or the cost of capital. If the company can invest elsewhere and earn a return of r, or if the company can repay its sources of capital and save a cost of r, then r is the company's opportunity cost of funds. If the company cannot earn more than its opportunity cost of funds on an investment, it should not undertake that investment. Unless an investment earns more than the cost of funds from its suppliers of capital, the investment should not be undertaken. The cost-of-capital concept is discussed more extensively elsewhere. Regardless of what it is called, an economically sound discount rate is essential for making capital budgeting decisions.

Although the principles of capital budgeting are simple, they are easily confused in practice, leading to unfortunate decisions. Some important capital budgeting concepts that managers find very useful are as follows:

- A **sunk cost** is one that has already been incurred. You cannot change a sunk cost. Today's decisions, on the other hand, should be based on current and future cash flows and should not be affected by prior, or sunk, costs.
- An **opportunity cost** is what a resource is worth in its next best use. For example, if a company uses idle property, what should it record as the investment outlay: the purchase price several years ago, the current market value, or nothing? If you replace an old machine with a new one, what is the opportunity cost? If you invest $10 million, what is the opportunity cost? The answers to these three questions are, respectively: the current market value, the cash flows that the old machine would generate, and $10 million (which you could invest elsewhere).
- An **incremental cash flow** is the cash flow that is realized because of a decision: the cash flow *with* a decision minus the cash flow *without* that decision. If opportunity costs are correctly assessed, the incremental cash flows provide a sound basis for capital budgeting.
- An **externality** is the effect of an investment on other things besides the investment itself. Frequently, an investment affects the cash flows of other parts of the company, and these

externalities can be positive or negative. If possible, these should be part of the investment decision. Sometimes externalities occur outside the company. An investment might benefit (or harm) other companies or society at large; yet the company is not compensated for these benefits (or charged for the costs). **Cannibalization** is one externality. Cannibalization occurs when an investment takes customers and sales away from another part of the company.

- A **conventional cash flow** pattern is one with an initial outflow followed by a series of inflows. In a **nonconventional cash flow** pattern, the initial outflow is not followed by inflows only, but the cash flows can flip from positive to negative again (or even change signs several times). An investment that involved outlays (negative cash flows) for the first couple of years that were then followed by positive cash flows would be considered to have a conventional pattern. If cash flows change signs once, the pattern is conventional. If cash flows change signs two or more times, the pattern is nonconventional.

Several types of project interactions make the incremental cash flow analysis challenging. The following are some of these interactions:

- **Independent projects** versus **mutually exclusive projects:** Independent projects are projects whose cash flows are independent of each other. Mutually exclusive projects compete directly with each other. For example, if Projects A and B are mutually exclusive, you can choose A or B, but you cannot choose both. Sometimes there are several mutually exclusive projects, and you can choose only one from the group.
- **Project sequencing:** Many projects are sequenced through time so that investing in a project creates the option to invest in future projects. For example, you might invest in a project today and then in one year invest in a second project if the financial results of the first project or new economic conditions are favorable. If the results of the first project or new economic conditions are not favorable, you do not invest in the second project.
- **Unlimited funds** versus **capital rationing:** An unlimited funds environment assumes that the company can raise the funds it wants for all profitable projects simply by paying the required rate of return. Capital rationing exists when the company has a fixed amount of funds to invest. If the company has more profitable projects than it has funds for, it must allocate the funds to achieve the maximum shareholder value subject to the funding constraints.

4. INVESTMENT DECISION CRITERIA

Analysts use several important criteria to evaluate capital investments. The two most comprehensive measures of whether a project is profitable or unprofitable are the net present value (NPV) and internal rate of return (IRR). In addition to these, we present four other criteria that are frequently used: the payback period, discounted payback period, average accounting rate of return (AAR), and profitability index (PI). An analyst must fully understand the economic logic behind each of these investment decision criteria, as well as its strengths and limitations in practice.

4.1. Net Present Value

For a project with one investment outlay, made initially, the net present value (NPV) is the present value of the future after-tax cash flows minus the investment outlay, or

$$NPV = \sum_{t=1}^{n} \frac{CF_t}{(1+r)^t} - Outlay \qquad (2\text{-}1)$$

where

CF_t = after-tax cash flow at time t

r = required rate of return for the investment

Outlay = investment cash flow at time 0

To illustrate the net present value criterion, we will take a look at a simple example. Assume that Gerhardt Corporation is considering an investment of €50 million in a capital project that will return after-tax cash flows of €16 million per year for the next four years plus another €20 million in year 5. The required rate of return is 10 percent.

For the Gerhardt example, the NPV would be

$$NPV = \frac{16}{1.10^1} + \frac{16}{1.10^2} + \frac{16}{1.10^3} + \frac{16}{1.10^4} + \frac{20}{1.10^5} - 50$$

$$= 14.545 + 13.223 + 12.021 + 10.928 + 12.418 - 50$$

$$= 63.136 - 50 = €13.136 \text{ million.}[1]$$

The investment has a total value, or present value of future cash flows, of €63.136 million. Since this investment can be acquired at a cost of €50 million, the investing company is giving up €50 million of its wealth in exchange for an investment worth €63.136 million. The investor's wealth increases by a net of €13.136 million.

Because the NPV is the amount by which the investor's wealth increases as a result of the investment, the decision rule for the NPV is as follows:

Invest if   NPV > 0

Do not invest if   NPV < 0

Positive NPV investments are wealth increasing, and negative NPV investments are wealth decreasing.

Many investments have cash flow patterns in which outflows may occur not only at time 0, but also at future dates. It is useful to consider the NPV to be the present value of all cash flows:

$$NPV = CF_0 + \frac{CF_1}{(1+r)^1} + \frac{CF_2}{(1+r)^2} + \dots + \frac{CF_n}{(1+r)^n}$$

or

$$NPV = \sum_{t=0}^{n} \frac{CF_t}{(1+r)^t} \qquad (2\text{-}2)$$

In Equation 2-2, the investment outlay, CF_0, is simply a negative cash flow. Future cash flows can also be negative.

---

[1]Occasionally, you will notice some rounding errors in our examples. In this case, the present values of the cash flows, as rounded, add up to 63.135. Without rounding, they add up to 63.13627, or 63.136. We will usually report the more accurate result, the one that you would get from your calculator or computer without rounding intermediate results.

4.2. Internal Rate of Return

The internal rate of return (IRR) is one of the most frequently used concepts in capital budgeting and in security analysis. The IRR definition is one that all analysts know by heart. For a project with one investment outlay, made initially, the IRR is the discount rate that makes the present value of the future after-tax cash flows equal that investment outlay. Written out in equation form, the IRR solves this equation:

$$\sum_{t=1}^{n} \frac{CF_t}{(1 + IRR)^t} = \text{Outlay}$$

where IRR is the internal rate of return. The left-hand side of this equation is the present value of the project's future cash flows, which, discounted at the IRR, equals the investment outlay. This equation will also be seen rearranged as

$$\sum_{t=1}^{n} \frac{CF_t}{(1 + IRR)^t} - \text{Outlay} = 0 \tag{2-3}$$

In this form, Equation 2-3 looks like the NPV equation, Equation 2-1, except that the discount rate is the IRR instead of r (the required rate of return). Discounted at the IRR, the NPV is equal to 0.

In the Gerhardt Corporation example, we want to find a discount rate that makes the total present value of all cash flows, the NPV, equal 0. In equation form, the IRR is the discount rate that solves this equation:

$$-50 + \frac{16}{(1 + IRR)^1} + \frac{16}{(1 + IRR)^2} + \frac{16}{(1 + IRR)^3} + \frac{16}{(1 + IRR)^4} + \frac{20}{(1 + IRR)^5} = 0$$

Algebraically, this equation would be very difficult to solve. We normally resort to trial and error, systematically choosing various discount rates until we find one, the IRR, that satisfies the equation. We previously discounted these cash flows at 10 percent and found the NPV to be €13.136 million. Since the NPV is positive, the IRR is probably greater than 10 percent. If we use 20 percent as the discount rate, the NPV is −€0.543 million; so 20 percent is a little high. One might try several other discount rates until the NPV is equal to 0; this approach is illustrated in Exhibit 2-1.

EXHIBIT 2-1   Trial-and-Error Process for Finding IRR

Discount Rate	NPV
10%	13.136
20%	−0.543
19%	0.598
19.5%	0.022
19.51%	0.011
19.52%	0.000

The IRR is 19.52 percent. Financial calculators and spreadsheet software have routines that calculate the IRR for us, so that we do not have to go through this trial-and-error procedure ourselves. The IRR, computed more precisely, is 19.5197 percent.

The decision rule for the IRR is to invest if the IRR exceeds the required rate of return for a project:

Invest if $\text{IRR} > r$

Do not invest if $\text{IRR} < r$

In the Gerhardt example, since the IRR of 19.52 percent exceeds the project's required rate of return of 10 percent, Gerhardt should invest.

Many investments have cash flow patterns in which the outlays occur at time 0 and at future dates. Thus it is common to define the IRR as the discount rate that makes the present values of all cash flows sum to 0:

$$\sum_{t=0}^{n} \frac{CF_t}{(1 + \text{IRR})^t} = 0 \qquad (2\text{-}4)$$

Equation 2-4 is a more general version of Equation 2-3.

4.3. Payback Period

The payback period is the number of years required to recover the original investment in a project. The payback is based on cash flows. For example, if you invest $10 thousand in a project, how long will it be until you recover the full original investment? Exhibit 2-2 illustrates the calculation of the payback period by following an investment's cash flows and cumulative cash flows.

In the first year, the company recovers $2,500 of the original investment, with $7,500 still unrecovered. You can see that the company recoups its original investment between year 3 and year 4. After three years, $2,000 is still unrecovered. Since the year 4 cash flow is $3,000, it would take two-thirds of the year 4 cash flow to bring the cumulative cash flow to 0. So the payback period is three years plus two-thirds of the year 4 cash flow, or 3.67 years.

The drawbacks of the payback period are transparent. Since the cash flows are not discounted at the project's required rate of return, the payback period ignores the time value of money and the risk of the project. Additionally, the payback period ignores cash flows after the payback period is reached. In Exhibit 2-2, for example, the year 5 cash flow is completely ignored in the payback computation!

Example 2-1 on page 56 is designed to illustrate some of the implications of these drawbacks of the payback period.

The payback period has many drawbacks—it is a measure of payback and not a measure of profitability. By itself, the payback period would be a dangerous criterion for evaluating capital projects. Its simplicity, however, is an advantage. The payback period is very easy to

EXHIBIT 2-2   Payback Period Example ($)

Year	0	1	2	3	4	5
Cash flow	−10,000	2,500	2,500	3,000	3,000	3,000
Cumulative cash flow	−10,000	−7,500	−5,000	−2,000	1,000	4,000

EXAMPLE 2-1 Drawbacks of the Payback Period

The cash flows, payback periods, and NPVs for Projects A through F are given in Exhibit 2-3. For all of the projects, the required rate of return is 10 percent.

EXHIBIT 2-3   Examples of Drawbacks of the Payback Period

	Cash Flows					
Year	Project A	Project B	Project C	Project D	Project E	Project F
0	−1,000	−1,000	−1,000	−1,000	−1,000	−1,000
1	1,000	100	400	500	400	500
2		200	300	500	400	500
3		300	200	500	400	10,000
4		400	100		400	
5		500	500		400	
Payback period	1.0	4.0	4.0	2.0	2.5	2.0
NPV	−90.91	65.26	140.60	243.43	516.31	7,380.92

Comment on why the payback period provides misleading information about the following:

1. Project A.
2. Project B versus Project C.
3. Project D versus Project E.
4. Project D versus Project F.

Solutions

1. Project A does indeed pay itself back in one year. However, this result is misleading because the investment is unprofitable, with a negative NPV.
2. Although Projects B and C have the same payback period and the same cash flow after the payback period, the payback period does not detect the fact that Project C's cash flows within the payback period occur earlier and result in a higher NPV.
3. Projects D and E illustrate a common situation. The project with the shorter payback period is the less profitable project. Project E has a longer payback and higher NPV.
4. Projects D and F illustrate an important flaw of the payback period: The payback period ignores cash flows after the payback period is reached. In this case, Project F has a much larger cash flow in Year 3, but the payback period does not recognize its value.

calculate and to explain. The payback period may also be used as an indicator of project liquidity. A project with a two-year payback may be more liquid than another project with a longer payback.

Because it is not economically sound, the payback period has no decision rule like that of the NPV or IRR. If the payback period is being used (perhaps as a measure of liquidity), analysts should also use an NPV or IRR to ensure that their decisions also reflect the profitability of the projects being considered.

4.4. Discounted Payback Period

The discounted payback period is the number of years it takes for the cumulative discounted cash flows from a project to equal the original investment. The discounted payback period partially addresses the weaknesses of the payback period. Exhibit 2-4 gives an example of calculating the payback period and discounted payback period. The example assumes a discount rate of 10 percent.

EXHIBIT 2-4   Payback Period and Discounted Payback Period

Year	0	1	2	3	4	5
Cash flow (CF)	5,000	1,500.00	1,500.00	1,500.00	1,500.00	1,500.00
Cumulative CF	−5,000	−3,500.00	−2,000.00	−500.00	1,000.00	2,500.00
Discounted CF	−5,000	1,363.64	1,239.67	1,126.97	1,024.52	931.38
Cumulative discounted CF	−5,000	−3,636.36	−2,396.69	−1,269.72	−245.20	686.18

The payback period is three years plus $500/1,500 = 1/3$ of the fourth year's cash flow, or 3.33 years. The discounted payback period is between four and five years. The discounted payback period is four years plus $245.20/931.38 = 0.26$ of the fifth year's discounted cash flow, or 4.26 years.

The discounted payback period relies on discounted cash flows, much as the NPV criterion does. If a project has a negative NPV, it will usually not have a discounted payback period since it never recovers the initial investment.

The discounted payback does account for the time value of money and risk within the discounted payback period, but it ignores cash flows after the discounted payback period is reached. This drawback has two consequences. First, the discounted payback period is not a good measure of profitability (like the NPV or IRR) because it ignores these cash flows. A second idiosyncrasy of the discounted payback period comes from the possibility of negative cash flows after the discounted payback period is reached. It is possible for a project to have a negative NPV but to have a positive cumulative discounted cash flow in the middle of its life and thus a reasonable discounted payback period. The NPV and IRR, which consider all of a project's cash flows, do not suffer from this problem.

4.5. Average Accounting Rate of Return

The average accounting rate of return (AAR) can be defined as

$$AAR = \frac{\text{Average net income}}{\text{Average book value}}$$

To understand this measure of return, we will use a numerical example.

EXHIBIT 2-5   Net Income for Calculating an Average Accounting Rate of Return ($)

	Year 1	Year 2	Year 3	Year 4	Year 5
Sales	100,000	150,000	240,000	130,000	80,000
Cash expenses	50,000	70,000	120,000	60,000	50,000
Depreciation	40,000	40,000	40,000	40,000	40,000
Earnings before taxes	10,000	40,000	80,000	30,000	−10,000
Taxes (at 40%)	4,000	16,000	32,000	12,000	−4,000*
Net income	6,000	24,000	48,000	18,000	−6,000

*Negative taxes occur in Year 5 because the earnings before taxes of –$10,000 can be deducted against earnings on other projects, thus reducing the tax bill by $4,000.

Assume a company invests $200,000 in a project that is depreciated straight-line over a five-year life to a 0 salvage value. Sales revenues and cash operating expenses for each year are as shown in Exhibit 2-5. The table also shows the annual income taxes (at a 40 percent tax rate) and the net income.

For the five-year period, the average net income is $18,000. The initial book value is $200,000, declining by $40,000 per year until the final book value is $0. The average book value for this asset is ($200,000 – $0)/2 = $100,000. The average accounting rate of return is

$$AAR = \frac{\text{Average net income}}{\text{Average book value}} = \frac{18,000}{100,000} = 18\%$$

The advantages of the AAR are that it is easy to understand and easy to calculate. The AAR has some important disadvantages, however. Unlike the other capital budgeting criteria discussed here, the AAR is based on accounting numbers, not on cash flows. This is an important conceptual and practical limitation. The AAR also does not account for the time value of money, and there is no conceptually sound cutoff for the AAR that distinguishes between profitable and unprofitable investments. The AAR is frequently calculated in different ways, so the analyst should verify the formula behind any AAR numbers that are supplied by someone else. Analysts should know the AAR and its potential limitations in practice, but they should rely on more economically sound methods like the NPV and IRR.

4.6. Profitability Index

The profitability index (PI) is the present value of a project's future cash flows divided by the initial investment. It can be expressed as

$$PI = \frac{\text{PV of future cash flows}}{\text{Initial investment}} = 1 + \frac{\text{NPV}}{\text{Initial investment}} \qquad (2\text{-}5)$$

You can see that the PI is closely related to the NPV. The PI is the ratio of the PV of future cash flows to the initial investment, while an NPV is the difference between the PV of future cash flows and the initial investment. Whenever the NPV is positive, the PI will be greater than 1.0, and conversely, whenever the NPV is negative, the PI will be less than 1.0. The investment decision rule for the PI is as follows:

Invest if $PI > 1.0$

Do not invest if $PI < 1.0$

Because the PV of future cash flows equals the initial investment plus the NPV, the PI can also be expressed as 1.0 plus the ratio of the NPV to the initial investment, as shown in Equation 2-5. Example 2-2 illustrates the PI calculation.

EXAMPLE 2-2   Example of a PI Calculation

The Gerhardt Corporation investment discussed earlier had an outlay of €50 million, a present value of future cash flows of €63.136 million, and an NPV of €13.136 million. The profitability index is

$$PI = \frac{PV \text{ of future cash flows}}{\text{Initial investment}} = \frac{63.136}{50.000} = 1.26$$

The PI can also be calculated as

$$PI = 1 + \frac{NPV}{\text{Initial investment}} = 1 + \frac{13.136}{50.000} = 1.\ddot{.}$$

Because PI > 1.0, this is a profitable investment.

The PI indicates the value you are receiving in exchange for one unit of currency invested. Although the PI is used less frequently than the NPV and IRR, it is sometimes used as a guide in capital rationing, which we will discuss later. The PI is usually called the profitability index in corporations, but it is commonly referred to as a benefit–cost ratio in governmental and not-for-profit organizations.

4.7. NPV Profile

The NPV profile shows a project's NPV graphed as a function of various discount rates. Typically, the NPV is graphed vertically (on the *y*-axis) and the discount rates are graphed horizontally (on the *x*-axis). The NPV profile for the Gerhardt capital budgeting project is shown in Example 2-3.

EXAMPLE 2-3   NPV Profile

For the Gerhardt example, we have already calculated several NPVs for different discount rates. At 10 percent the NPV is €13.136 million; at 20 percent the NPV is –€0.543 million; and at 19.52 percent (the IRR), the NPV is 0. What is the NPV if the discount rate is 0 percent? The NPV, discounted at 0 percent, is €34 million, which is simply the sum of all of the undiscounted cash flows. Exhibits 2-6 and 2-7 show the NPV profile for the Gerhardt example for discount rates between 0 percent and 30 percent.

EXHIBIT 2-6   Gerhardt NPV Profile

Discount Rate (%)	NPV (€ millions)
0	34.000
5.00	22.406
10.00	13.136
15.00	5.623
19.52	0.000
20.00	−0.543
25.00	−5.661
30.00	−9.954

EXHIBIT 2-7   Gerhardt NPV Profile

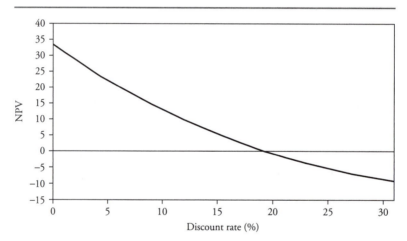

Three interesting points on this NPV profile are where the profile goes through the vertical axis (the NPV when the discount rate is 0), where the profile goes through the horizontal axis (where the discount rate is the IRR), and the NPV for the required rate of return (NPV is €13.136 million when the discount rate is the 10 percent required rate of return).

The NPV profile in Exhibit 2-7 is very well behaved. The NPV declines at a decreasing rate as the discount rate increases. The profile is convex from the origin (convex from below). You will shortly see some examples in which the NPV profile is more complicated.

4.8. Ranking Conflicts Between NPV and IRR

For a single conventional project, the NPV and IRR will agree on whether to invest or not to invest. For independent, conventional projects, no conflict exists between the decision rules for the NPV and IRR. However, in the case of two mutually exclusive projects, the two criteria will sometimes disagree. For example, Project A might have a larger NPV than Project B, but Project B has a higher IRR than Project A. In this case, should you invest in Project A or in Project B?

Differing cash flow patterns can cause two projects to rank differently with the NPV and IRR. For example, suppose Project A has shorter-term payoffs than Project B. This situation is presented in Example 2-4.

EXAMPLE 2-4   Ranking Conflict Due to Differing Cash Flow Patterns

Projects A and B have similar outlays but different patterns of future cash flows. Project A realizes most of its cash payoffs earlier than Project B. The cash flows, along with the NPV and IRR for the two projects, are shown in Exhibit 2-8. For both projects, the required rate of return is 10 percent.

EXHIBIT 2-8   Cash Flows, NPV, and IRR for Two Projects with Different Cash Flow Patterns

	Cash Flows						
Year	0	1	2	3	4	NPV	IRR
Project A	−200	80	80	80	80	53.59	21.86%
Project B	−200	0	0	0	400	73.21	18.92%

If the two projects were not mutually exclusive, you would invest in both because they are both profitable. However, you can choose either A (which has the higher IRR) or B (which has the higher NPV).

Exhibits 2-9 and 2-10 show the NPVs for Project A and Project B for various discount rates between 0 percent and 30 percent.

EXHIBIT 2-9   NPV Profiles for Two Projects with Different Cash Flow Patterns

Discount Rate	NPV for Project A	NPV for Project B
0%	120.00	200.00
5.00%	83.68	129.08
10.00%	53.59	73.21
15.00%	28.40	28.70
15.09%	27.98	27.98
18.92%	11.41	0.00
20.00%	7.10	−7.10
21.86%	0.00	−18.62
25.00%	−11.07	−36.16
30.00%	−26.70	−59.95

EXHIBIT 2-10   NPV Profiles for Two Projects with Different Cash Flow Patterns

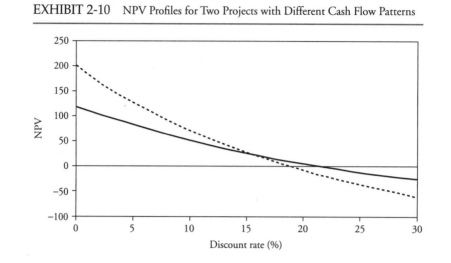

Note that Project B has the higher NPV for discount rates between 0 percent and 15.09 percent. Project A has the higher NPV for discount rates exceeding 15.09 percent. The crossover point of 15.09 percent in Exhibit 2-10 corresponds to the discount rate at which both projects have the same NPV (of 27.98). Project B has the higher NPV below the crossover point, and Project A has the higher NPV above it.

Whenever the NPV and IRR rank two mutually exclusive projects differently, as they do in the preceding example, you should choose the project based on the NPV. Project B, with the higher NPV, is the better project because of the reinvestment assumption. Mathematically, whenever you discount a cash flow at a particular discount rate, you are implicitly assuming that you can reinvest a cash flow at that same discount rate.[2] In the NPV calculation, you use a discount rate of 10 percent for both projects. In the IRR calculation, you use a discount rate equal to the IRR of 21.86 percent for Project A and 18.92 percent for Project B.

Can you reinvest the cash inflows from the projects at 10 percent, or 21.86 percent, or 18.92 percent? When you assume that the required rate of return is 10 percent, you are assuming an opportunity cost of 10 percent; you are assuming that you can either find other

---

[2]For example, assume that you are receiving $100 in one year discounted at 10 percent. The present value is $100/1.10 = $90.91. Instead of receiving the $100 in one year, invest it for one additional year at 10 percent, and it grows to $110. What is the present value of $110 received in two years discounted at 10 percent? It is the same $90.91. Because both future cash flows are worth the same, you are implicitly assuming that reinvesting the earlier cash flow at the discount rate of 10 percent has no effect on its value.

projects that pay a 10 percent return or pay back your sources of capital that cost you 10 percent. The fact that you earned 21.86 percent in Project A or 18.92 percent in Project B does not mean that you can reinvest future cash flows at those rates. (In fact, if you can reinvest future cash flows at 21.86 percent or 18.92 percent, these should have been used as your required rate of return instead of 10 percent.) Because the NPV criterion uses the most realistic discount rate—the opportunity cost of funds—the NPV criterion should be used for evaluating mutually exclusive projects.

Another circumstance that frequently causes mutually exclusive projects to be ranked differently by NPV and IRR criteria is project scale—the sizes of the projects. Would you rather have a small project with a higher rate of return or a large project with a lower rate of return? Sometimes, the larger, low rate of return project has the better NPV. This case is developed in Example 2-5.

The good news is that the NPV and IRR criteria will usually indicate the same investment decision for a given project. They will usually both recommend acceptance or rejection of the project. When the choice is between two mutually exclusive projects and the NPV and IRR rank the two projects differently, the NPV criterion is strongly preferred. There are good reasons for this preference. The NPV shows the amount of gain, or wealth increase, as a currency amount. The reinvestment assumption of the NPV is the more economically realistic. The IRR does give you a rate of return, but the IRR could be for a small investment or for only a short period of time. As a practical matter, once a corporation has the data to calculate the NPV, it is fairly trivial to go ahead and calculate the IRR and other capital budgeting criteria. However, the most appropriate and theoretically sound criterion is the NPV.

EXAMPLE 2-5   Ranking Conflicts Due to Differing Project Scale

Project A has a much smaller outlay than Project B, although they have similar future cash flow patterns. The cash flows as well as the NPVs and IRRs for the two projects are shown in Exhibit 2-11. For both projects, the required rate of return is 10 percent.

EXHIBIT 2-11   Cash Flows, NPV, and IRR for Two Projects of Differing Scale

| | Cash Flows | | | | | | |
Year	0	1	2	3	4	NPV	IRR
Project A	−100	50	50	50	50	58.49	34.90%
Project B	−400	170	170	170	170	138.88	25.21%

If they were not mutually exclusive, you would invest in both projects because they are both profitable. However, you can choose either Project A (which has the higher IRR) or Project B (which has the higher NPV).

Exhibits 2-12 and 2-13 show the NPVs for Project A and Project B for various discount rates between 0 percent and 30 percent.

EXHIBIT 2-12   NPV Profiles for Two Projects of Differing Scale

Discount Rate (%)	NPV for Project A	NPV for Project B
0	100.00	280.00
5.00	77.30	202.81
10.00	58.49	138.88
15.00	42.75	85.35
20.00	29.44	40.08
21.86	25.00	25.00
25.00	18.08	1.47
25.21	17.65	0.00
30.00	8.31	−31.74
34.90	0.00	−60.00
35.00	−0.15	−60.52

EXHIBIT 2-13   NPV Profiles for Two Projects of Differing Scale

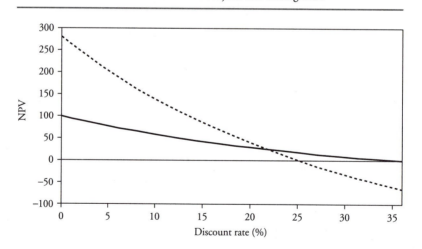

Note that Project B has the higher NPV for discount rates between 0 percent and 21.86 percent. Project A has the higher NPV for discount rates exceeding 21.86 percent. The crossover point of 21.86 percent in Exhibit 2-13 corresponds to the discount rate at which both projects have the same NPV (of 25.00). Below the crossover point, Project B has the higher NPV, and above it, Project A has the higher NPV. When cash flows are discounted at the 10 percent required rate of return, the choice is clear: Project B, the larger project, which has the superior NPV.

4.9. The Multiple IRR Problem and the No IRR Problem

The IRR criterion can give rise to multiple solutions. This is often referred to as the *multiple IRR problem*. We can illustrate this problem with the following nonconventional cash flow pattern:[3]

Time	0	1	2
Cash Flow	−1,000	5,000	−6,000

The IRR for these cash flows satisfies this equation:

$$-1,000 + \frac{5,000}{(1+\text{IRR})^1} + \frac{-6,000}{(1+\text{IRR})^2} = 0$$

It turns out that two values of IRR satisfy the equation: IRR = 1 = 100% and IRR = 2 = 200%. To further understand this problem, consider the NPV profile for this investment, shown in Exhibits 2-14 and 2-15.

EXHIBIT 2-14   NPV Profile for a Multiple IRR Example

Discount Rate (%)	NPV
0	−2,000.00
25	−840.00
50	−333.33
75	−102.04
100	0.00
125	37.04
140	41.67
150	40.00
175	24.79
200	0.00
225	−29.59
250	−61.22
300	−125.00
350	−185.19
400	−240.00
500	−333.33
1,000	−595.04
2,000	−775.51
3,000	−844.95
4,000	−881.62
10,000	−951.08
1,000,000	−999.50

---

[3]This example is adapted from Hirschleifer (1958).

EXHIBIT 2-15   NPV Profile for a Multiple IRR Example

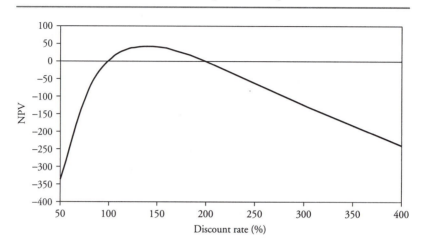

As you can see in the NPV profile, the NPV is equal to 0 at IRR = 100% and IRR = 200%. The NPV is negative for discount rates below 100 percent, positive between 100 percent and 200 percent, and then negative above 200 percent. The NPV reaches its highest value when the discount rate is 140 percent.

It is also possible to have an investment project with no IRR. The *no-IRR problem* occurs with this cash flow pattern:[4]

Time	0	1	2
Cash Flow	100	−300	250

The IRR for these cash flows satisfies this equation:

$$100 + \frac{-300}{(1+\text{IRR})^1} + \frac{250}{(1+\text{IRR})^2} = 0$$

For these cash flows, no discount rate exists that results in a zero NPV. Does that mean this project is a bad investment? In this case, the project is actually a good investment. As Exhibits 2-16 and 2-17 show, the NPV is positive for all discount rates. The lowest NPV, of 10, occurs for a discount rate of 66.67 percent, and the NPV is always greater than 0. Consequently, no IRR exists.

For conventional projects that have outlays followed by inflows—negative cash flows followed by positive cash flows—the multiple IRR problem cannot occur. However, for non-conventional projects, as in the preceding example, the multiple IRR problem can occur. The IRR equation is essentially an *n*th degree polynomial. An *n*th degree polynomial can have up to *n* solutions, although it will have no more real solutions than the number of cash flow sign changes. For example, a project with two sign changes could have zero, one, or two IRRs. Having two sign changes does not mean that you *will* have multiple IRRs; it just means that you *might*. Fortunately, most capital budgeting projects have only one IRR. Analysts should always be aware of the unusual cash flow patterns that can generate the multiple IRR problem.

---

[4]This example is also adapted from Hirschleifer.

EXHIBIT 2-16   NPV Profile for a Project with No IRR

Discount Rate (%)	NPV
0	50.00
25	20.00
50	11.11
66.67	10.00
75	10.20
100	12.50
125	16.05
150	20.00
175	23.97
200	27.78
225	31.36
250	34.69
275	37.78
300	40.63
325	43.25
350	45.68
375	47.92
400	50.00

EXHIBIT 2-17   NPV Profile for a Project with No IRR

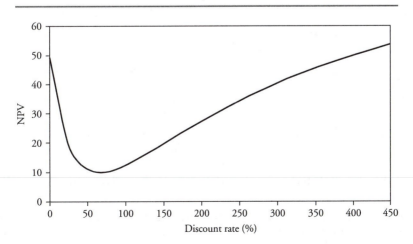

4.10. Popularity and Usage of the Capital Budgeting Methods

Analysts need to know the basic logic of the various capital budgeting criteria as well as the practicalities involved in using them in real corporations. Before delving into the many issues involved in applying these models, we will present some feedback on their popularity.

The usefulness of any analytical tool always depends on the specific application. Corporations generally find these capital budgeting criteria useful. Two recent surveys by Graham and Harvey (2001) and Brounen, De Jong, and Koedijk (2004) report on the frequency of their use by U.S. and European corporations. Exhibit 2-18 gives the mean responses of executives in five countries to the question "How frequently does your company use the following techniques when deciding which projects or acquisitions to pursue?"

Although financial textbooks preach the superiority of the NPV and IRR techniques, it is clear that several other methods are heavily used.[5] In the four European countries, the payback period is used as often as, or even slightly more often than, the NPV and IRR. In these two studies, larger companies tended to prefer the NPV and IRR over the payback period. The fact that the U.S. companies were larger, on average, partially explains the greater U.S. preference for the NPV and IRR. Other factors influence the choice of capital budgeting techniques. Private corporations used the payback period more frequently than did public corporations. Companies managed by an MBA had a stronger preference for the discounted cash flow techniques. Of course, any survey research also has some limitations. In this case, the persons in these large corporations responding to the surveys may not have been aware of all of the applications of these techniques.

EXHIBIT 2-18   Mean Responses About Frequency of Use of Capital Budgeting Techniques

	U.S.	U.K.	Netherlands	Germany	France
Internal rate of return*	3.09	2.31	2.36	2.15	2.27
Net present value*	3.08	2.32	2.76	2.26	1.86
Payback period*	2.53	2.77	2.53	2.29	2.46
Hurdle rate	2.13	1.35	1.98	1.61	0.73
Sensitivity analysis	2.31	2.21	1.84	1.65	0.79
Earnings multiple approach	1.89	1.81	1.61	1.25	1.70
Discounted payback period*	1.56	1.49	1.25	1.59	0.87
Real options approach	1.47	1.65	1.49	2.24	2.20
Accounting rate of return*	1.34	1.79	1.40	1.63	1.11
Value at risk	0.95	0.85	0.51	1.45	1.68
Adjusted present value	0.85	0.78	0.78	0.71	1.11
Profitability index*	0.85	1.00	0.78	1.04	1.64

Respondents used a scale ranging from 0 (never) to 4 (always).

*These techniques were described in this section of the chapter. You will encounter the others elsewhere.

---

[5]Analysts often refer to the NPV and IRR as discounted cash flow techniques because they accurately account for the timing of all cash flows when they are discounted.

EXAMPLE 2-6   NPVs and Stock Prices.

Freitag Corporation is investing €600 million in distribution facilities. The present value of the future after-tax cash flows is estimated to be €850 million. Freitag has 200 million outstanding shares with a current market price of €32.00 per share. This investment is new information, and it is independent of other expectations about the company. What should be the effect of the project on the value of the company and the stock price?

Solution

The NPV of the project is €850 million − €600 million = €250 million. The total market value of the company prior to the investment is €32.00 × 200 million shares = €6,400 million. The value of the company should increase by €250 million to €6,650 million. The price per share should increase by the NPV per share, or €250 million/200 million shares = €1.25 per share. The share price should increase from €32.00 to €33.25.

These capital budgeting techniques are essential tools for corporate managers. Capital budgeting is also relevant to external analysts. Because a corporation's investing decisions ultimately determine the value of its financial obligations, the corporation's investing processes are vital. The NPV criterion is the criterion most directly related to stock prices. If a corporation invests in positive NPV projects, these should add to the wealth of its shareholders. Example 2-6 illustrates this scenario.

The effect of a capital budgeting project's positive or negative NPV on share price is more complicated than Example 2-6, in which the value of the stock increased by the project's NPV. The value of a company is the value of its existing investments plus the net present values of all of its future investments. If an analyst learns of an investment, the impact of that investment on the stock price will depend on whether the investment's profitability is more or less than expected. For example, an analyst could learn of a positive NPV project, but if the project's profitability is less than expected, this stock might drop in price on the news. Alternatively, news of a particular capital project might be considered as a signal about other capital projects underway or in the future. A project that by itself might add, say, €0.25 to the value of the stock might signal the existence of other profitable projects. News of this project might increase the stock price by far more than €0.25.

The integrity of a corporation's capital budgeting processes is important to analysts. Management's capital budgeting processes can demonstrate two things about the quality of management: the degree to which management embraces the goal of shareholder wealth maximization, and its effectiveness in pursuing that goal. Both of these factors are important to shareholders.

5. CASH FLOW PROJECTIONS

In Section 4, we presented the basic capital budgeting models that managers use to accept or reject capital budgeting proposals. In that section, we assumed the cash flows were given, and we used them as inputs to the analysis. In this section, we detail how these cash flows are found for an expansion project, which is an independent investment that does not affect the cash flows for the rest of the company. In Section 6, we will deal with a replacement project, in which the cash flow analysis is more complicated. A replacement project must deal with the differences between the cash flows that occur with the new investment and the cash flows that would have occurred for the investment being replaced.

5.1. Table Format with Cash Flows Collected by Year

The cash flows for a conventional expansion project can be grouped into (1) the investment outlays, (2) after-tax operating cash flows over the project's life, and (3) terminal year after-tax nonoperating cash flows. Exhibit 2-19 gives an example of the cash flows for a capital project where all of the cash flows are collected by year.

EXHIBIT 2-19   Capital Budgeting Cash Flows Example (Cash Flows Collected by Year, $)

Year	0	1	2	3	4	5
Investment outlays:						
Fixed capital	−200,000					
Net working capital	−30,000					
Total	−230,000					
Annual after-tax operating cash flows:						
Sales		220,000	220,000	220,000	220,000	220,000
Cash operating expenses		90,000	90,000	90,000	90,000	90,000
Depreciation		35,000	35,000	35,000	35,000	35,000
Operating income before taxes		95,000	95,000	95,000	95,000	95,000
Taxes on operating income		38,000	38,000	38,000	38,000	38,000
Operating income after taxes		57,000	57,000	57,000	57,000	57,000
Add back: Depreciation		35,000	35,000	35,000	35,000	35,000
After-tax operating cash flow		92,000	92,000	92,000	92,000	92,000
Terminal year after-tax nonoperating cash flows:						
After-tax salvage value						40,000
Return of net working capital						30,000
Total						70,000
Total after-tax cash flow	−230,000	92,000	92,000	92,000	92,000	162,000
Net present value at 10% required rate of return	162,217					
Internal rate of return	32.70%					

The investment outlays include a $200,000 outlay for fixed capital items. This outlay includes $25,000 for nondepreciable land, plus $175,000 for equipment that will be depreciated straight-line to 0 over five years. The investment in net working capital is the net investment in short-term assets required for the investment. This is the investment in receivables and inventory needed, less the short-term payables generated by the project. In this case, the project required $50,000 of current assets but generated $20,000 in current liabilities, resulting in a total investment in net working capital of $30,000. The total investment outlay at time 0 is $230,000.

Each year, sales will be $220,000 and cash operating expenses will be $90,000. Annual depreciation for the $175,000 depreciable equipment is $35,000 (one-fifth of the cost). The result is an operating income before taxes of $95,000. Income taxes at a 40 percent rate are $0.40 \times \$95,000 = \$38,000$. This leaves operating income after taxes of $57,000. Adding back the depreciation charge of $35,000 gives the annual after-tax operating cash flow of $92,000.[6]

At the end of year 5, the company will sell off the fixed capital assets. In this case, the fixed capital assets (including the land) are sold for $50,000, which represents a gain of $25,000 over the remaining book value of $25,000. The gain of $25,000 is taxed at 40 percent, resulting in a tax of $10,000. This leaves $40,000 for the fixed capital assets after taxes. Additionally, the net working capital investment of $30,000 is recovered, because the short-term assets (such as inventory and receivables) and short-term liabilities (such as payables) are no longer needed for the project. Total terminal year nonoperating cash flows are then $70,000.

The investment project has a required rate of return of 10 percent. Discounting the future cash flows at 10 percent and subtracting the investment outlay gives an NPV of $162,217. The internal rate of return is 32.70 percent. Because the investment has a positive NPV, this project should be accepted. The IRR investment decision criterion would also recommend accepting the project because the IRR is greater than the required rate of return.

5.2.   Table Format with Cash Flows Collected by Type

In the layout in Exhibit 2-19, we essentially collected the cash flows in the columns by *year* and then found the NPV by summing the present values of the annual cash flows (at the bottom of each column). There is another way of organizing the same information. We could also find the NPV by finding the present values of the cash flows in Exhibit 2-19 by rows, which are the *types* of cash flows. This approach is shown in Exhibit 2-20 on page 72.

As Exhibit 2-20 shows, the outlays in fixed capital and in net working capital at time 0 total $230,000. For years 1 though 5, the company realizes an after-tax cash flow for sales minus cash expenses of $78,000, which has a present value of $295,681. The depreciation charge results in a tax savings of $14,000 per year, which has a present value of $53,071. The present values of the after-tax salvage and of the return of net working capital are also shown in the table. The present value of all cash flows is an NPV of $162,217. Obviously, collecting the after-tax cash flows by year, as in Exhibit 2-19, or by type, as in Exhibit 2-20, results in the same NPV.

---

[6]Examining the operating cash flows in Exhibit 2-19, we have a $220,000 inflow from sales, a $90,000 outflow for cash operating expenses, and a $38,000 outflow for taxes. This is an after-tax cash flow of $92,000.

EXHIBIT 2-20   Capital Budgeting Cash Flows Example (Cash Flows Collected by Type)

Time	Type of Cash Flow	Before-Tax Cash Flow ($)	After-Tax Cash Flow ($)	PV at 10% ($)
0	Fixed capital	−200,000	−200,000	−200,000
0	Net working capital	−30,000	−30,000	−30,000
1–5	Sales minus cash expenses	220,000 − 90,000 = 130,000	130,000(1 − 0.40) = 78,000	295,681
1–5	Depreciation tax savings	None	0.40(35,000) = 14,000	53,071
5	After-tax salvage value	50,000	50,000 − 0.40(50,000 − 25,000) = 40,000	24,837
5	Return of net working capital	30,000	30,000	18,628
			NPV =	162,217

5.3. Equation Format for Organizing Cash Flows

The capital budgeting cash flows in the preceding example project were laid out in one of two alternative tabular formats. Analysts may wish to take even another approach. Instead of producing a table, you can also look at the cash flows using equations such as the following:

1. *Initial outlay:* For a new investment

$$\text{Outlay} = \text{FCInv} + \text{NWCInv}$$

where

FCInv = investment in new fixed capital

NWCInv = investment in net working capital

This equation can be generalized for a replacement project (covered in Section 6.2), in which existing fixed capital is sold and provides some of the funding for the new fixed capital purchased. The outlay is then

$$\text{Outlay} = \text{FCInv} + \text{NWCInv} - \text{Sal}_0 + T(\text{Sal}_0 - B_0) \tag{2-6}$$

where

Sal_0 = cash proceeds (salvage value) from sale of old fixed capital

T = tax rate

B_0 = book value of old fixed capital

2. *Annual after-tax operating cash flow:*

$$CF = (S - C - D)(1 - T) + D \tag{2-7}$$

or

$$CF = (S - C)(1 - T) + T_D \tag{2-8}$$

where

S = Sales

C = cash operating expenses

D = depreciation charge

3. *Terminal year after-tax nonoperating cash flow:*

$$\text{TNOCF} = \text{Sal}_T + \text{NWCInv} - T(\text{Sal}_T - B_T) \tag{2-9}$$

where

Sal_T = cash proceeds (salvage value) from sale of fixed capital on termination date

B_T = book value of fixed capital on termination date

The outlay in the example is found with Equation 2-6:

$$\text{Outlay} = 200,000 + 30,000 - 0 + 0 = \$230,000$$

For a replacement project, the old fixed capital would be sold for cash (Sal_0) and then there would be taxes paid on the gain (if $\text{Sal}_0 - B_0$ were positive) or a tax saving (if $\text{Sal}_0 - B_0$ were negative). In this example, Sal_0 and $T(\text{Sal}_0 - B_0)$ are 0 because no existing fixed capital is sold at time 0.

Using Equation 2-7, we find that the annual after-tax operating cash flow is

$$\begin{aligned}
\text{CF} &= (S - C - D)(1 - T) + D \\
&= (220,000 - 90,000 - 35,000)(1 - 0.40) + 35,000 \\
&= 95,000(0.60) + 35,000 = 57,000 + 35,000 = \$92,000
\end{aligned}$$

Equation 2-7 is the project's net income plus depreciation. An identical cash flow results if we use Equation 2-8:

$$\begin{aligned}
\text{CF} &= (S - C)(1 - T) + T_D \\
&= (220,000 - 90,000)(1 - 0.40) + 0.40(35,000) \\
&= 130,000(0.60) + 0.40(35,000) = 78,000 + 14,000 = \$92,000
\end{aligned}$$

Equation 2-8 is the after-tax sales and cash expenses plus the depreciation tax savings. The analyst can use either equation.

Equation 2-9 provides the terminal year nonoperating cash flow:

$$\begin{aligned}
\text{TNOCF} &= \text{Sal}_T + \text{NWCInv} - T(\text{Sal}_T - B_T) \\
&= 50,000 + 30,000 - 0.40(50,000 - 25,000) \\
&= 50,000 + 30,000 - 10,000 = \$70,000
\end{aligned}$$

The old fixed capital (including land) is sold for $50,000, but $10,000 of taxes must be paid on the gain. Including the $30,000 return of net working capital gives a terminal year non-operating cash flow of $70,000.

The NPV of the project is the present value of the cash flows—an outlay of $230,000 at time 0, an annuity of $92,000 for five years, plus a single payment of $70,000 in five years:

$$\begin{aligned}
\text{NPV} &= -230,000 + \sum_{t=1}^{5} \frac{92,000}{(1.10)^t} + \frac{70,000}{(1.10)^5} \\
&= -230,000 + 348,752 + 43,465 = \$162,217
\end{aligned}$$

We obtain an identical NPV of $162,217 whether we use a tabular format collecting cash flows by year, a tabular format collecting cash flows by type, or an equation format using Equations 2-6 through 2-9. The analyst usually has some flexibility in choosing how to solve a problem. Furthermore, the analysis that an analyst receives from someone else could be in varying formats. The analyst must interpret this information correctly regardless of format. An analyst may need to present information in alternative formats, depending on what the client or user of the information wishes to see. All that is important is that the cash flows are complete (with no cash flows omitted and none double-counted), that their timing is recognized, and that the discounting is done correctly.

6. MORE ON CASH FLOW PROJECTIONS

Cash flow analysis can become fairly complicated. This section extends the analysis of the previous section to include more details on depreciation methods, replacement projects (as opposed to simple expansion projects), the use of spreadsheets, and the effects of inflation.

6.1. Straight-Line and Accelerated Depreciation Methods

Before going on to more complicated investment decisions, we should mention the variety of depreciation methods that are in use. The example in Section 5.1 assumed straight-line depreciation down to a zero salvage value. Most accounting texts give a good description of the straight-line method, the sum-of-years digits method, the double declining balance method (and the 150 percent declining balance method), and the units-of-production and service hours method.[7]

Many countries specify the depreciation methods that are acceptable for tax purposes in their jurisdictions. For example, in the United States, corporations use the MACRS (modified accelerated cost recovery system) for tax purposes. Under MACRS, real property (real estate) is usually depreciated straight-line over a 27.5- or 39-year life, and other capital assets are usually grouped into MACRS asset classes and subject to a special depreciation schedule in each class. These MACRS classes and the depreciation rates for each class are shown in Exhibit 2-21.

For the first four MACRS classes (3-year, 5-year, 7-year, and 10-year), the depreciation is double declining balance with a switch to straight-line when optimal and with a half-year convention. For the last two classes (15-year and 20-year), the depreciation is 150 percent declining balance with a switch to straight-line when optimal and with a half-year convention. Take 5-year property in Exhibit 2-21 as an example. With double declining balance, the depreciation each year is 2/5 = 40% of the beginning-of-year book value. However, with a half-year convention, the asset is assumed to be in service for only 6 months during the first year, and only one-half of the depreciation is allowed the first year. After the first year, the depreciation rate is 40 percent of the beginning balance until year 4, when straight-line depreciation would be at least as large; so we switch to straight-line. In year 6, we have one-half of a year of the straight-line depreciation remaining because we assumed the asset was placed in service halfway through the first year.

Accelerated depreciation generally improves the NPV of a capital project compared to straight-line depreciation. For an example of this effect, we will assume the same capital project as in Exhibit 2-19, except that the depreciation is MACRS three-year property. When using straight-line, the depreciation was 20 percent per year ($35,000). The depreciation

---

[7]White, Sondhi, and Fried (2003) is a good example. Consult their Chapter 8, "Analysis of Long-Lived Assets: Part II—Analysis of Depreciation and Impairment" for review and examples.

EXHIBIT 2-21   Depreciation Rates under U.S. MACRS

	Recovery Period Class (%)					
Year	3-Year	5-Year	7-Year	10-Year	15-Year	20-Year
1	33.33	20.00	14.29	10.00	5.00	3.75
2	44.45	32.00	24.49	18.00	9.50	7.22
3	14.81	19.20	17.49	14.40	8.55	6.68
4	7.41	11.52	12.49	11.52	7.70	6.18
5		11.52	8.93	9.22	6.93	5.71
6		5.76	8.93	7.37	6.23	5.28
7			8.93	6.55	5.90	4.89
8			4.45	6.55	5.90	4.52
9				6.55	5.90	4.46
10				6.55	5.90	4.46
11				3.29	5.90	4.46
12					5.90	4.46
13					5.90	4.46
14					5.90	4.46
15					5.90	4.46
16					2.99	4.46
17						4.46
18						4.46
19						4.46
20						4.46
21						2.25

percentages for MACRS three-year property are given in Exhibit 2-21. The first-year depreciation is $0.3333 \times \$175,000 = \$58,327.50$, second-year depreciation is $0.4445 \times \$175,000 = \$77,787.50$, third-year depreciation is $0.1481 \times \$175,000 = \$25,917.50$, fourth-year depreciation is $0.0741 \times \$175,000 = \$12,967.50$, and fifth-year depreciation is 0. The impact on the NPV and IRR of the project is shown in Exhibit 2-22 on page 76.

As Exhibit 2-22 shows, the depreciation charges still sum to $175,000 (except for $2 of rounding), but they are larger in years 1 and 2 and smaller in years 3, 4, and 5. Although this method reduces operating income after taxes in years 1 and 2 (and increases it in years 3, 4, and 5), it reduces tax outflows in years 1 and 2 and increases them later. Consequently, the after-tax operating cash flows (which were $92,000 per year) increase in early years and decrease in later years. This increases the NPV from $162,217 to $167,403, a difference of $5,186. The IRR also increases from 32.70 percent to 34.74 percent.[8]

---

[8]This example assumes that the investment occurs on the first day of the tax year. If the outlay occurs later in the tax year, the depreciation tax savings for the tax years are unchanged, which means that the cash savings occur sooner, increasing their present values. The result is a higher NPV and IRR.

EXHIBIT 2-22   Capital Budgeting Example with MACRS ($)

Year	0	1	2	3	4	5
Investment outlays:						
Fixed capital	−200,000					
Net working capital	−30,000					
Total	−230,000					
Annual after-tax operating cash flows:						
Sales		220,000	220,000	220,000	220,000	220,000
Cash operating expenses		90,000	90,000	90,000	90,000	90,000
Depreciation		58,328	77,788	25,918	12,968	0
Operating income before taxes		71,673	52,213	104,083	117,033	130,000
Taxes on operating income (40%)		28,669	20,885	41,633	46,813	52,000
Operating income after taxes		43,004	31,328	62,450	70,220	78,000
Add back: Depreciation		58,328	77,788	25,918	12,968	0
After-tax operating cash flow		101,331	109,115	88,367	83,187	78,000
Terminal year after-tax nonoperating cash flows:						
After-tax salvage value						40,000
Return of net working capital						30,000
Total						70,000
Total after-tax cash flows	−230,000	101,331	109,115	88,367	83,187	148,000
Net present value at 10% required rate of return	$167,403					
Internal rate of return	34.74%					

The impact of accelerated depreciation can be seen without going through the complete analysis in Exhibit 2-22. We previously showed in Exhibit 2-20 that the present value of the depreciation tax savings (which was an annuity of 0.40 × $35,000 = $14,000 a year for five years) was $53,071. The present value of the tax savings from accelerated depreciation is shown in Exhibit 2-23.

By using the accelerated depreciation schedule, we increase the present value of the tax savings from $53,071 (from Exhibit 2-20) to $58,257, an increase of $5,186. The tax deferral associated with the accelerated depreciation (compared to straight-line) adds $5,186 to the NPV of the project.

Myriad tax and depreciation schedules apply to investment projects around the world. These tax and depreciation schedules are also subject to change from year to year. To accurately assess the profitability of a particular capital project, it is vital to identify and apply the schedules that are relevant to the capital budgeting decision at hand.

EXHIBIT 2-23   Present Value of Tax Savings from Accelerated Depreciation

Year	Depreciation ($)	Tax Savings	PV at 10% ($)
1	58,327.50	0.40 × $58,327.50 = $23,331	21,210
2	77,787.50	0.40 × $77,787.50 = $31,115	25,715
3	25,917.50	0.40 × $25,917.50 = $10,367	7,789
4	12,967.50	0.40 × $12,967.50 = $5,187	3,543
5	0	0.40 × $0 = $0	0
Total present value			58,257

6.2. Cash Flows for a Replacement Project

In Section 5.1, we evaluated the cash flows for an expansion project, basing our after-tax cash flows on the outlays, annual operating cash flows after tax, and salvage value for the project by itself. In many cases, however, investing in a project is more complicated. Investing could affect many of the company's cash flows. In principle, the cash flows relevant to an investing decision are the incremental cash flows: the cash flows the company realizes *with* the investment compared to the cash flows the company would realize *without* the investment. For example, suppose we are investing in a new project with an outlay of $100,000 and we sell off existing assets that the project replaces for $30,000. The incremental outlay is $70,000.

A very common investment decision is a replacement decision, in which you replace old equipment with new equipment. This decision requires very careful analysis of the cash flows. The skills required to detail the replacement decision cash flows are also useful for other decisions in which an investment affects other cash flows in the company. We use the term "replacement" loosely, primarily to indicate that the cash flow analysis is more complicated than it was for the simpler expansion decision.

Assume we are considering the replacement of old equipment with new equipment that has more capacity and that is less costly to operate. The characteristics of the old and new equipment follow:

Old Equipment		New Equipment	
Current book value	$400,000		
Current market value	$600,000	Acquisition cost	$1,000,000
Remaining life	10 years	Life	10 years
Annual sales	$300,000	Annual sales	$450,000
Cash operating expenses	$120,000	Cash operating expenses	$150,000
Annual depreciation	$40,000	Annual depreciation	$100,000
Accounting salvage value	$0	Accounting salvage value	$0
Expected salvage value	$100,000	Expected salvage value	$200,000

If the new equipment replaces the old equipment, an additional investment of $80,000 in net working capital will be required. The tax rate is 30 percent, and the required rate of return is 8 percent.

The cash flows can be found by carefully constructing tables like Exhibit 2-19 or by using Equations 2-6 through 2-9. The initial outlay is the investment in the new equipment plus the additional investment in net working capital less the after-tax proceeds from selling the old equipment:

$$\text{Outlay} = \text{FCInv} + \text{NWCInv} - \text{Sal}_0 + T(\text{Sal}_0 - B_0)$$
$$= 1,000,000 + 80,000 - 600,000 + 0.3(600,000 - 400,000)$$
$$= \$540,000$$

In this case, the outlay of $540,000 is $1,080,000 for new equipment and net working capital minus the after-tax proceeds of $540,000 the company receives from selling the old equipment. The incremental operating cash flows are

$$CF = [S - C - D](1 - T) + D$$
$$= [(450,000 - 300,000) - (150,000 - 120,000) -$$
$$(100,000 - 40,000)](1 - 0.30) + (100,000 - 40,000)$$
$$= (150,000 - 30,000 - 60,000)(1 - 0.30) + 60,000$$
$$= \$102,000$$

The incremental sales are $150,000, incremental cash operating expenses are $30,000, and incremental depreciation is $60,000. The incremental after-tax operating cash flow is $102,000 per year.

At the project termination, the new equipment is expected to be sold for $200,000, which constitutes an incremental cash flow of $100,000 over the $100,000 expected salvage price of the old equipment. Since the accounting salvage values for both the new and old equipment were 0, this gain is taxable at 30 percent. The company also recaptures its investment in net working capital. The terminal year after-tax nonoperating cash flow is

$$\text{TNOCF} = \text{Sal}_T + \text{NWCInv} - T(\text{Sal}_T - B_T)$$
$$= (200,000 - 100,000) + 80,000 - 0.30[(200,000 - 100,000) - (0 - 0)]$$
$$= \$150,000$$

Once the cash flows are identified, the NPV and IRR are readily found. The NPV, found by discounting the cash flows at the 8 percent required rate of return, is

$$\text{NPV} = -540,000 + \sum_{t=1}^{10} \frac{102,000}{1.08^t} + \frac{150,000}{1.08^{10}} = \$213,907$$

The IRR, found with a financial calculator, is 15.40 percent. Because the NPV is positive, this equipment replacement decision is attractive. The fact that the IRR exceeds the 8 percent required rate of return leads to the same conclusion.

The key to estimating the incremental cash flows for the replacement is to compare the cash flows that occur with the new investment to the cash flows that would have occurred without the new investment. The analyst is comparing the cash flows with a particular course of action to the cash flows with an alternative course of action.

6.3. Spreadsheet Modeling

Although the examples in this book can be readily solved with a financial calculator, capital budgeting is usually done with the assistance of personal computers and spreadsheets such as Microsoft Excel®. Spreadsheets are heavily used for several reasons. They provide a very effective way of building even complex models. Built-in spreadsheet functions (such as those for finding rates of return) are easy to use. The model's assumptions can be changed and solved easily. Models can be shared with other analysts, and they also help in presenting the results of the analysis. Example 2-7 shows how a spreadsheet can be used to solve a capital budgeting problem.

6.4. Effects of Inflation on Capital Budgeting Analysis

Inflation affects capital budgeting analysis in several ways. The first decision the analyst must make is whether to do the analysis in nominal terms or in real terms. Nominal cash flows

---

EXAMPLE 2-7   Capital Budgeting with a Spreadsheet

Lawton Enterprises is evaluating a project with the following characteristics:

- Fixed capital investment is $2,000,000.
- The project has an expected six-year life.
- The initial investment in net working capital is $200,000. At the end of each year, net working capital must be increased so that the cumulative investment in net working capital is one-sixth of the next year's projected sales.
- The fixed capital is depreciated 30 percent in year 1, 35 percent in year 2, 20 percent in year 3, 10 percent in year 4, 5 percent in year 5, and 0 percent in year 6.
- Sales are $1,200,000 in year 1. They grow at a 25 percent annual rate for the next two years, and then grow at a 10 percent annual rate for the last three years.
- Fixed cash operating expenses are $150,000 for years 1–3 and $130,000 for years 4–6.
- Variable cash operating expenses are 40 percent of sales in year 1, 39 percent of sales in year 2, and 38 percent in years 3–6.
- Lawton's marginal tax rate is 30 percent.
- Lawton will sell its fixed capital investments for $150,000 when the project terminates and recapture its cumulative investment in net working capital. Income taxes will be paid on any gains.
- The project's required rate of return is 12 percent.
- If taxable income on the project is negative in any year, the loss will offset gains elsewhere in the corporation, resulting in a tax savings.

1. Determine whether this is a profitable investment using the NPV and IRR.
2. If the tax rate increases to 40 percent and the required rate of return increases to 14 percent, is the project still profitable?

Solution to 1

EXHIBIT 2-24   Cash Flows for Lawton Investment (Rounded to Nearest $1,000)

Year	0	1	2	3	4	5	6
Fixed capital investment	−2,000						
NWC investments	−200	−50	−63	−31	−34	−38	
Sales		1,200	1,500	1,875	2,063	2,269	2,496
Fixed cash expenses		150	150	150	130	130	130
Variable cash expenses		480	585	713	784	862	948
Depreciation		600	700	400	200	100	0
Operating income before taxes		−30	65	613	949	1177	1417
Taxes on operating income		−9	20	184	285	353	425
Operating income after taxes		−21	45	429	664	824	992
Add back: Depreciation		600	700	400	200	100	0
After-tax operating cash flow		579	745	829	864	924	992
Salvage value							150
Taxes on salvage value							−45
Return of NWC							416
Total after-tax cash flows	−2,200	529	682	798	830	886	1,513
NPV (at $r = 12\%$)	1,181						
IRR	26.60%						

Because the NPV of $1,181,000 is positive, the project is profitable for Lawton to undertake. The IRR investment decision rule also indicates that the project is profitable because the IRR of 26.60 percent exceeds the 12 percent required rate of return.

Solution to 2

The tax rate and required return can be changed in the spreadsheet model. When these changes are made, the NPV becomes $736,000 and the IRR becomes 24.02 percent. (The revised spreadsheet is not printed here.) Although profitability is lower, the higher tax rate and required rate of return do not change the investment decision.

include the effects of inflation, whereas real cash flows are adjusted downward to remove the effects of inflation. It is perfectly acceptable to do the analysis in either nominal or real terms, and sound decisions can be made either way. However, inflation creates some issues regardless of the approach.

The cash flows and discount rate used should both be nominal or both be real. In other words, nominal cash flows should be discounted at a nominal discount rate, and real cash flows should be discounted at a real rate. The real rate, just like real cash flows, has had the effect of inflation taken out. In general, the relationship between real and nominal rates is

$$(1 + \text{Nominal rate}) = (1 + \text{Real rate})(1 + \text{Inflation rate})$$

Inflation reduces the value of depreciation tax savings (unless the tax system adjusts depreciation for inflation). The effect of expected inflation is captured in the discounted cash flow analysis. If inflation is higher than expected, the profitability of the investment is correspondingly lower than expected. Inflation essentially shifts wealth from the taxpayer to the government. Higher-than-expected inflation increases the corporation's real taxes because it reduces the value of the depreciation tax shelter. Conversely, lower-than-expected inflation reduces real taxes (the depreciation tax shelters are more valuable than expected).

Inflation also reduces the value of fixed payments to bondholders. When bonds are originally issued, bondholders pay a price for the bonds reflecting their inflationary expectations. If inflation is higher than expected, the real payments to bondholders are lower than expected. Higher-than-expected inflation shifts wealth from bondholders to the issuing corporations. Conversely, if inflation is lower than expected, the real interest expenses of the corporation increase, shifting wealth from the issuing corporation to its bondholders.

Finally, inflation does not affect all revenues and costs uniformly. The company's after-tax cash flows will be better or worse than expected depending on how particular sales outputs or cost inputs are affected. Furthermore, contracting with customers, suppliers, employees, and sources of capital can be complicated as inflation rises.

The capital budgeting model accommodates the effects of inflation, although inflation complicates the capital budgeting process (and the operations of a business in general).

7. PROJECT ANALYSIS AND EVALUATION

Assessing the opportunity costs and analyzing the risks of capital investments becomes more complex and sophisticated as you examine real cases. The first project interaction we examine in this section is that of comparing mutually exclusive projects with unequal lives. We will briefly describe other project interactions, but will not examine them in detail. We also examine the process of capital budgeting under capital rationing.

Up to this point, we have largely ignored the issue of accounting for risk. We will introduce risk analysis in two ways. The first is accounting for risk on a stand-alone basis. The second is accounting for risk on a systematic basis.

7.1. Mutually Exclusive Projects with Unequal Lives

We have previously looked at mutually exclusive projects and decided that the best project is the one with the greatest NPV. However, if the mutually exclusive projects have differing lives and the projects will be replaced (or replicated) repeatedly when they wear out, the analysis is more complicated. The analysis of a one-shot (one-time-only) investment differs from that of an investment chain (in which the asset is replaced regularly in the future).

For example, assume we have two projects with unequal lives of two and three years, with the following after-tax cash flows:

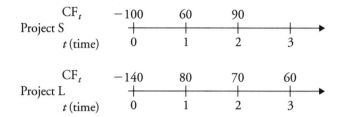

Both projects have a 10 percent required rate of return. The NPV of Project S is $28.93 and the NPV of Project L is $35.66. Given that the two projects are mutually exclusive, Project L, with the greater NPV, should be chosen.

However, let us now assume that these are not one-shot investments, but investments in assets that the company will need to replace when they wear out. Project S would be replaced every two years and Project L every three years. This situation is often referred to as a replacement chain. In this type of problem, you should examine the entire chain, not just the first link. If the projects are part of a replacement chain, examining the cash flows for only the initial investment for Projects S and L is improper because Project L provides cash flows during year 3, when Project S provides none.

There are two logically equivalent ways of comparing mutually exclusive projects in a replacement chain. They are the least common multiple of lives approach and the equivalent annual annuity approach.

7.1.1. Least Common Multiple of Lives Approach

For the least common multiple of lives approach, the analyst extends the time horizon of analysis so that the lives of both projects will divide exactly into the horizon. For Projects S and L, the least common multiple of 2 and 3 is 6: The two-year project would be replicated three times over the six-year horizon and the three-year project would be replicated two times over the six-year horizon.[9] The cash flows for replicating Projects S and L over a six-year horizon follow:

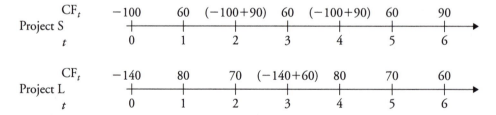

Discounting the cash flows for the six-year horizon results in an NPV for Project S of $72.59 and an NPV for Project L of $62.45. Apparently, investing in Project S and replicating the investment over time has a greater NPV than choosing Project L and replicating it. This decision is the reverse of the one we made when looking solely at the NPVs of the initial investments!

---

[9]The least common multiple of lives is not necessarily the product of the two lives, as in the case of Projects S and L. For example, if two projects have lives of 8 and 10 years, the least common multiple of lives is 40 years, not 80. Both 8 and 10 are exactly divisible into 40.

Because the NPV of a single investment represents the present values of its cash flows, you can also visualize the NPV of a replacement chain as the present value of the NPVs of each investment (or link) in the chain. For Projects S and L, the NPVs of each investment are shown on the following timelines:

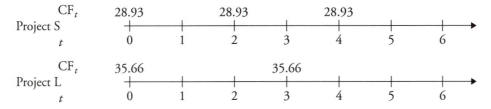

Investing in Project S is equivalent to receiving values of $28.93 at times 0, 2, and 4, while investing in Project L is equivalent to receiving values of $35.66 at times 0 and 3. The present values of these cash flow patterns are $72.59 for Project S and $62.45 for Project L. Discounting the NPVs of each investment in the chain is equivalent to discounting all of the individual cash flows in the chain.

7.1.2. Equivalent Annual Annuity Approach

The other method for properly evaluating a replacement chain is called the equivalent annual annuity (EAA) approach. The name for this approach is very descriptive. For an investment project with an outlay and variable cash flows in the future, the project NPV summarizes the equivalent value at time 0. For this same project, the EAA is the annuity payment (series of equal annual payments over the project's life) that is equivalent in value to the NPV.

Analysts can use a simple two-step procedure to find the EAA. The first step is to find the present value of all of the cash flows for an investment: the investment's NPV. The second step is to calculate an annuity payment that has a value equivalent to the NPV. For Project S, we already calculated the NPV of the project over its two-year life to be $28.93. The second step is to find an annuity payment for the two-year life that is equivalent. For a two-year life and a 10 percent discount rate, a payment of $16.66 is the equivalent annuity.

The EAA for Project L is found by annuitizing its $35.66 NPV over three years; so the EAA for Project L is $14.34.

The decision rule for the EAA approach is to choose the investment chain that has the highest EAA, which in this case is Project S.

Given these two approaches to comparing replacement chains, which one should the analyst use? As a practical matter, the two approaches are logically equivalent and will result in the same decision.[10] Consequently, the analyst can choose one approach over the other based on personal preference. Or, if the audience for the analyst's work prefers to see the analysis using one approach, the analyst can simply produce the analysis in that format.

7.2. Capital Rationing

Capital rationing applies when the company's capital budget has a size constraint. For example, the capital budget is a fixed money amount. A fixed capital budget can place the

---

[10]For Projects S and L, the NPVs of a replacement chain over the least common multiple of lives (6 years) were $72.59 for Project S and $62.45 for Project L. If we discount the EAA for Project S ($16.66) and the EAA for Project L ($14.34) for six years (treating each as a 6-year annuity), we have the same NPVs. Hence, the least common multiple of lives and EAA approaches are consistent with each other.

EXHIBIT 2-25   First Capital Rationing Example

	Investment Outlay ($)	NPV ($)	PI	IRR (%)
Project 1	600	220	1.37	15
Project 2	200	70	1.35	16
Project 3	200	−60	0.70	10
Project 4	400	−100	0.75	8

EXHIBIT 2-26   Second Capital Rationing Example

	Investment Outlay ($)	NPV ($)	PI	IRR (%)
Project 5	600	300	1.50	16
Project 6	200	80	1.40	18
Project 7	200	60	1.30	12
Project 8	200	40	1.20	14

company in several interesting situations. To illustrate these, we will assume that the company has a fixed $1,000 capital budget and has the opportunity to invest in four projects. The projects are of variable profitability.

In the first situation, the budget is adequate to invest in all profitable projects. Consider the four projects in Exhibit 2-25.

In this case, the company has two positive-NPV projects, Projects 1 and 2, which involve a total outlay of $800. Their total NPV is $290. The company should choose these projects, and it will have $200 in its capital budget left over. These excess funds can be used elsewhere in the company (moved to someone else's budget, used to pay dividends or repurchase shares, or used to pay down debt). The manager who is afraid to return the excess funds and chooses to invest in Project 3 will consume the whole capital budget but reduce the total NPV to $230, essentially destroying $60 of wealth for the company.

A second case exists in which the company has more profitable projects than it can choose, but it is able to invest in the most profitable ones available. Continuing with the $1,000 capital budget, this second case is illustrated in Exhibit 2-26.

When the analyst has a fixed budget, the PI is especially useful because it shows the profitability of each investment per currency unit invested. If we rank these projects by their PIs, Projects 5, 6, and 7 are the best projects and we are able to select them. This selection results in a total NPV of $440. The IRRs, shown in the last column, are not a reliable guide to choosing projects under capital rationing because a high-IRR project may have a low NPV. Wealth maximization is best guided by the NPV criterion.

A third case exists in which the company has more profitable projects than it can choose, but it is not able to invest in the most profitable ones available. Assume the company cannot invest in fractional projects: It must take all or none of each project it chooses. Continuing with the $1,000 capital budget, this case is illustrated in Exhibit 2-27.

In this example, an unlimited budget of $1,800 would generate a total NPV of $750. However, when the budget constraint is imposed, the highest NPV results from choosing Projects 9 and 12. The company is forced to choose its best project and its fourth best

EXHIBIT 2-27   Third Capital Rationing Example

	Investment Outlay ($)	NPV ($)	PI	IRR
Project 9	600	300	1.50	15%
Project 10	600	270	1.45	16%
Project 11	200	80	1.40	12%
Project 12	400	100	1.25	11%

project, as indicated by their relative PIs. Any other combination of projects either violates the budget or has a lower total NPV.

Capital rationing has the potential to misallocate resources. Capital markets are supposed to allocate funds to their highest and best uses, with the opportunity cost of funds (used as the discount rate for NPVs or the hurdle rate for IRRs) guiding this allocation process. Capital rationing violates market efficiency if society's resources are not allocated where they will generate the best returns. Companies that use capital rationing may be doing either hard or soft capital rationing. Under hard capital rationing, the budget is fixed and the managers cannot go beyond it. Under soft capital rationing, managers may be allowed to overspend their budgets if they argue effectively that the additional funds will be deployed profitably.

In the case of hard rationing, choosing the optimal projects that fit within the budget and maximize the NPV of the company can be computationally intensive. Sometimes, managers use estimates and trial and error to find the optimal set of projects. The PI can be used as a guide in this trial-and-error process. Other times, the number of possibilities is so daunting that mathematical programming algorithms are used.

7.3. Risk Analysis of Capital Investments—Stand-Alone Methods

So far, we have evaluated projects by calculating a single NPV to decide whether a project is profitable. We took a single value, or point estimate, of each input into the model and combined the values to calculate the NPV.

Risk is usually measured as a dispersion of outcomes. In the case of stand-alone risk, we typically measure the riskiness of a project by the dispersion of its NPVs or the dispersion of its IRRs. Sensitivity analysis, scenario analysis, and simulation analysis are very popular stand-alone risk analysis methods. These risk measures depend on the variation of the project's cash flows.

To illustrate the stand-alone risk tools, we will use the following base case capital project:

Unit price	$5.00
Annual unit sales	40,000
Variable cost per unit	$1.50
Investment in fixed capital	$300,000
Investment in working capital	$50,000
Project life	6 years
Depreciation (straight-line)	$50,000
Expected salvage value	$60,000
Tax rate	40 percent
Required rate of return	12 percent

The outlay, from Equation 2-6, is $300,000 plus $50,000, or $350,000. The annual after-tax operating cash flow, from Equation 2-7, is

$$
\begin{aligned}
CF &= (S - C - D)(1 - T) + D \\
&= [(5 \times 40,000) - (1.50 \times 40,000) - (50,000)](1 - 0.40) + 50,000 \\
&= \$104,000
\end{aligned}
$$

The terminal year's after-tax nonoperating cash flow, from Equation 2-9, is

$$
\begin{aligned}
TNOCF &= Sal_6 + NWCInv - T(Sal_6 - B_6) \\
&= 60,000 + 50,000 - 0.40(60,000 - 0) \\
&= \$86,000
\end{aligned}
$$

The project NPV is

$$
\begin{aligned}
NPV &= -350,000 + \sum_{t=1}^{6} \frac{104,000}{1.12^t} + \frac{86,000}{1.12^6} \\
&= -350,000 + 471,157 \\
&= \$121,157
\end{aligned}
$$

7.3.1. Sensitivity Analysis Sensitivity analysis calculates the effect on the NPV of changes in one input variable at a time. The preceding base case has several input variables. If we wish to do a sensitivity analysis of several of them, we must specify the changes in each that we wish to evaluate. Suppose we want to consider the following:

	Base Value	Low Value	High Value
Unit price	$5.00	$4.50	$5.50
Annual unit sales	40,000	35,000	45,000
Variable cost per unit	$1.50	$1.40	$1.60
Expected salvage value	$60,000	$30,000	$80,000
Tax rate	40%	38%	42%
Required rate of return	12%	10%	14%

We have changed each of six input variables. Exhibit 2-28 shows the NPV calculated for the base case. Then the NPV is recalculated by changing one variable from its base case value to its high or low value.

As Exhibit 2-28 shows, the project's NPV is most sensitive to changes in the unit price variable. The project's NPV is least sensitive to changes in the salvage value. Roughly speaking, the project's NPV is most sensitive to changes in unit price and in unit sales. It is least affected by changes in cost per unit, salvage value, and the tax rate. Changes in the required rate of return also have a substantial effect, but not as much as changes in price or unit sales.

In a sensitivity analysis, the manager can choose which variables to change and by how much. Many companies have access to software that can be instructed to change a particular variable by a certain amount—for example, to increase or decrease unit price, unit sales, and cost per unit by 10 percent. The software then produces the changes in NPV for each of these changes. Sensitivity analysis can be used to establish which variables are most influential on the success or failure of a project.

EXHIBIT 2-28 Sensitivity of Project NPV to Changes in a Variable ($)

Variable	Project NPV			
	Base Case	With Low Estimate	With High Estimate	Range of Estimates
Unit price	121,157	71,820	170,494	98,674
Annual unit sales	121,157	77,987	164,326	86,339
Cost per unit	121,157	131,024	111,289	19,735
Salvage value	121,157	112,037	127,236	15,199
Tax rate	121,157	129,165	113,148	16,017
Required return	121,157	151,492	93,602	57,890

EXHIBIT 2-29 Input Variables and NPV for Scenario Analysis

Variable	Scenario		
	Pessimistic	Most Likely	Optimistic
Unit price	$4.50	$5.00	$5.50
Annual unit sales	35,000	40,000	45,000
Variable cost per unit	$1.60	$1.50	$1.40
Investment in fixed capital	$320,000	$300,000	$280,000
Investment in working capital	$50,000	$50,000	$50,000
Project life	6 years	6 years	6 years
Depreciation (straight-line)	$53,333	$50,000	$46,667
Salvage value	$40,000	$60,000	$80,000
Tax rate	40%	40%	40%
Required rate of return	13%	12%	11%
NPV	−$5,725	$121,157	$269,685
IRR	12.49%	22.60%	34.24%

7.3.2. Scenario Analysis Sensitivity analysis calculates the effect on the NPV of changes in one variable at a time. In contrast, scenario analysis creates scenarios that consist of changes in several of the input variables and calculates the NPV for each scenario. Although corporations could do a large number of scenarios, in practice they usually do only three. They can be labeled variously, but we will present an example with pessimistic, most likely, and optimistic scenarios. Continuing with the basic example from the preceding section, the values of the input variables for the three scenarios are given in Exhibit 2-29.

The most likely scenario is the same as the base case for sensitivity analysis, and the NPV for the most likely scenario is $121,157. To form the pessimistic and optimistic scenarios, managers change several of the assumptions for each scenario. For the pessimistic scenario, several of the input variables are changed to reflect higher costs, lower revenues, and a higher required rate of return. As the table shows, the result is a negative NPV for the pessimistic scenario and an IRR that is less than the pessimistic scenario's 13 percent required rate of return. For the optimistic scenario, the more favorable revenues, costs, and required rate of return result in very good NPV and IRR.

For this example, the scenario analysis reveals the possibility of an unprofitable invest-ment, with a negative NPV and with an IRR less than the cost of capital. The range for the NPV is fairly large compared to the size of the initial investment, which indicates that the investment is fairly risky. This example included three scenarios for which management wants to know the profitability of the investment for each set of assumptions. Other scenarios can be investigated if management chooses to do so.

7.3.3. Simulation (Monte Carlo) Analysis   Simulation analysis is a procedure for estimating a probability distribution of outcomes, such as for the NPV or IRR for a capital investment project. Instead of assuming a single value (a point estimate) for the input variables in a capital budgeting spreadsheet, the analyst can assume several variables to be stochastic, following their own probability distributions. By simulating the results hundreds or thousands of times, the analyst can build a good estimate of the distributions for the NPV or IRR. Because of the volume of computations, analysts and corporate managers rely heavily on their personal computers and specialized simulation software such as @RISK.[11] Example 2-8 presents a simple simulation analysis.

This capital budgeting simulation example is not very complex, with only five stochastic variables. The example's five input variables were assumed to be normally distributed; in reality, many other distributions can be employed. Finally, the randomly chosen values for each vari-able were assumed to be independent. They can be selected jointly instead of independently. Simulation techniques have proved to be a boon for addressing capital budgeting problems.

Sensitivity analysis, scenario analysis, and simulation analysis are well developed stand-alone risk analysis methods. These risk measures depend on the variation of the project's cash flows. Market risk measures, presented in the next section, depend not only on the variation of a project's cash flows, but also on how those cash flows covary (or correlate) with market returns.

EXAMPLE 2-8   Capital Budgeting Simulation

Gouhua Zhang has made the following assumptions for a capital budgeting project:

- Fixed capital investment is 20,000; no investment in net working capital is required.
- The project has an expected five-year life.
- The fixed capital is depreciated straight-line to 0 over a five-year life. The salvage value is normally distributed with an expected value of 2,000 and a standard deviation of 500.
- Unit sales in year 1 are normally distributed with a mean of 2,000 and a standard deviation of 200.

---

[11]@RISK is a popular and powerful risk analysis tool sold by Palisade Corporation. It is an add-in for Microsoft Excel that allows simulation techniques to be incorporated into spreadsheet models.

- Unit sales growth after year 1 is normally distributed with a mean of 6 percent and standard deviation of 4 percent. Assume the same sales growth rate for years 2–5.
- The sales price is 5.00 per unit, normally distributed with a standard deviation of 0.25 per unit. The same price holds for all five years.
- Cash operating expenses as a percentage of total revenue are normally distributed with a mean and standard deviation of 30 percent and 3 percent, respectively.
- The discount rate is 12 percent and the tax rate is 40 percent.

1. What are the NPV and IRR using the expected values of all input variables?
2. Perform a simulation analysis and provide probability distributions for the NPV and IRR.

Solution to 1

EXHIBIT 2-30   Expected Cash Flows for Simulation Example

Time	0	1	2	3	4	5
Fixed capital	−20,000					
After-tax salvage value						1,200
Price		5.00	5.00	5.00	5.00	5.00
Output		2,000	2,120	2,247	2,382	2,525
Revenue		10,000	10,600	11,236	11,910	12,625
Cash operating expenses		3,000	3,180	3,371	3,573	3,787
Depreciation		4,000	4,000	4,000	4,000	4,000
Operating income before taxes		3,000	3,420	3,865	4,337	4,837
Taxes on operating income		1,200	1,368	1,546	1,735	1,935
Operating income after taxes		1,800	2,052	2,319	2,602	2,902
Depreciation		4,000	4,000	4,000	4,000	4,000
Total after-tax cash flow	−20,000	5,800	6,052	6,319	6,602	8,102
NPV (at $r = 12\%$)	3,294					
IRR	18.11%					

Based on the point estimates for each variable (the mean values for each), which are shown in Exhibit 2-30, Zhang should find the NPV to be 3,294 and the IRR to be 18.11 percent.

Solution to 2

Zhang performs a simulation using @RISK with 10,000 iterations. For each iteration, values for the five stochastic variables (price, output, output growth rate, cash expense percentage, and salvage value) are selected from their assumed distributions and the NPV and IRR are calculated. After the 10,000 iterations, the resulting information about the probability distributions for the NPV and IRR is shown in Exhibits 2-31 and 2-32.

EXHIBIT 2-31   Probability Distributions for NPV and IRR

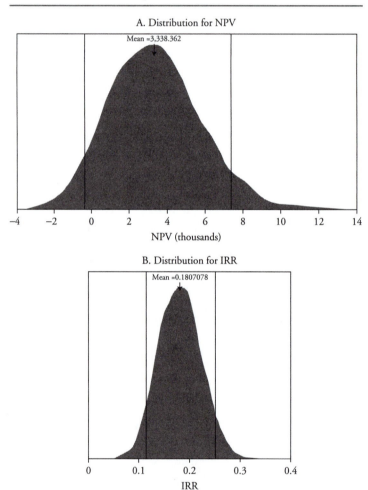

As shown, the distributions for the NPV and IRR are somewhat normal looking. The means and standard deviations for each are given in Exhibit 2-32. Both distributions have a slight positive skewness, which means the distributions are skewed to the right. The two kurtosis values are fairly close to 3.0, which means that the distributions

EXHIBIT 2-32   Summary Statistics for NPV and IRR

Statistic	NPV	IRR
Mean	3,338	18.07%
Standard deviation	2,364	4.18%
Skewness	0.2909	0.1130
Kurtosis	3.146	2.996
Median	3,236	18.01%
90% confidence interval	–3,779 to 7,413	11.38% to 25.13%

Correlations Between Input Variables and NPV and IRR

Input Variable	NPV	IRR
Output	0.71	0.72
Output growth rate	0.49	0.47
Price	0.34	0.34
Cash expense proportion	–0.28	–0.29
Salvage value	0.06	0.05

are not peaked or fat-tailed compared to the standard normal distribution. The median is the value at which 50 percent of the 10,000 outcomes fall on either side. The 90 percent confidence intervals show that 90 percent of the observations fall between –3,779 and 7,413 for the NPV and between 11.38 percent and 25.13 percent for the IRR. Although not shown in the table, 7.04 percent of the observations had a negative NPV and an IRR less than the 12 percent discount rate.

The means of the NPV and IRR from the simulation (in Exhibit 2-32) are fairly close to their values calculated using point estimates for all of the input variables (in Exhibit 2-30). This is not always the case, but it is here. The additional information from a simulation is the dispersions of the NPV and IRR. Given these assumptions and model, the simulation results show Zhang the distributions of NPV and IRR outcomes that should be expected. Managers and analysts often prefer to know these total distributions rather than just their mean values.

The correlations in Exhibit 2-32 can be interpreted as sensitivity measures. Changes in the output variable have the highest correlation with NPV and IRR outcomes. The salvage value has the lowest (absolute value) correlation.

7.4. Risk Analysis of Capital Investments—Market Risk Methods

When using market risk methods, the discount rate to be used in evaluating a capital project is the rate of return required on the project by a diversified investor. The discount rate should thus be a risk-adjusted discount rate, which includes a premium to compensate investors for risk.[12] This risk premium should reflect factors that are priced or valued in the marketplace. The two equilibrium models for estimating this risk premium are the capital asset pricing model (CAPM) and arbitrage pricing theory (APT). We will discuss the CAPM as a way of finding risk-adjusted discount rates, although you should be aware that other methods can be used.

In the CAPM, total risk can be broken into two components: systematic risk and unsystematic risk. Systematic risk is the portion of risk that is related to the market and that cannot be diversified away. Unsystematic risk is nonmarket risk, which is idiosyncratic and can be diversified away. Diversified investors can demand a risk premium for taking systematic risk, but not for unsystematic risk.[13] Hence, the stand-alone risk measures—total risk measured by the dispersion of the NPV or the IRR—are inappropriate when the corporation is diversified or, as is more likely, when the corporation's investors are themselves diversified.

In the capital asset pricing model, a project's or asset's beta (β) is generally used as a measure of systematic risk. The security market line (SML) expresses the asset's required rate of return as a function of β:

$$r_i = R_F + \beta_i[E(R_M) - R_F] \tag{2-10}$$

where

r_i = required return for project or asset i

R_F = risk-free rate of return

β_i = beta of project or asset i

$[E(R_M) - R_F]$ = market risk premium, the difference between the expected market return and the risk-free rate of return

The project's required rate of return is equal to the risk-free rate plus a risk premium, where the risk premium is the product of the project beta and the market risk premium.

Here the required rate of return (sometimes called a hurdle rate) is specific to the risk of the project. There is no one hurdle rate appropriate for all projects.

The security market line (SML) is graphed in Exhibit 2-33. This line indicates the required rate of return for a project, given its beta. The required rate of return can be used in two ways:

1. The SML is used to find the required rate of return. The required rate of return is then used to find the NPV. Positive NPV projects are accepted and negative NPV projects are rejected.
2. The SML is used to find the required rate of return. The project's IRR is compared to the required rate of return. If the IRR is greater than the required return, the project is accepted (this point would plot above the SML in Exhibit 2-33). If the IRR is less than the required rate of return (below the SML), the project is rejected.

Example 2-9 illustrates how the capital asset pricing model and the security market line are used as part of the capital budgeting process.

---

[12]Our approach to capital budgeting is to discount expected cash flows at a risk-adjusted cost of capital. An alternative approach, which is also conceptually sound, is the "certainty-equivalent method." In this method, certainty-equivalent cash flows (expected cash flows that are reduced to certainty equivalents) are valued by discounting them at a risk-free discount rate. The use of risk-adjusted discount rates is more intuitive and much more popular.

[13]The capital asset pricing model uses this intuition to show how risky assets should be priced relative to the market. While the CAPM assigns a single market risk premium for each security, the APT develops a set of risk premia. The CAPM and APT are developed in detail elsewhere in the CFA curriculum.

EXHIBIT 2-33   SML for Capital Budgeting Projects

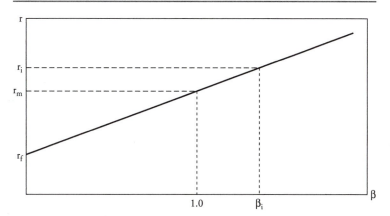

EXAMPLE 2-9   Using the SML to Find the Project Required Rate of Return

Premont Systems is evaluating a capital project with the following characteristics:

- The initial outlay is €150,000.
- Annual after-tax operating cash flows are €28,000.
- After-tax salvage value at project termination is €20,000.
- Project life is 10 years.
- The project beta is 1.20.
- The risk-free rate is 4.2 percent and the expected market return is 9.4 percent.

1. Compute the project NPV. Should the project be accepted?
2. Compute the project IRR. Should the project be accepted?

Solution to 1

The project required rate of return is

$$r_i = R_F + \beta_i[E(R_M) - R_F]$$
$$= 4.2\% + 1.20(9.4\% - 4.2\%)$$
$$= 4.2\% + 6.24\%$$
$$= 10.44\%$$

The cash flows discounted at 10.44 percent give an NPV of

$$NPV = -150,000 + \sum_{t=1}^{10} \frac{28,000}{1.1044^t} + \frac{20,000}{1.1044^{10}}$$

$$= €26,252$$

The project should be accepted because it has a positive NPV.

Solution to 2

The IRR, found with a financial calculator, is 14.24 percent. The required rate of return, established with the SML as in solution 1, is 10.44 percent. Since the IRR exceeds the required rate of return, the project should be accepted. For a beta of 1.20, the IRR of 14.24 percent would plot above the SML.

Using project betas to establish required rates of return for capital projects is especially important when a project's risk differs from that of the company. The cost of capital for a company is estimated for the company as a whole; it is based on the average riskiness of the company's assets as well as on its financial structure. The required rates of return of debt and equity are used to estimate the weighted (overall) average cost of capital (WACC) for the company. When a project under consideration involves more risk or less risk than the company as a whole, the WACC should not be used as the project required rate of return.

For example, assume that the risk-free rate of return is 3 percent, the market return is 8 percent, and the company beta is 0.9. Assume also that the company is considering three projects: Project A with a 0.5 beta, Project B with a 0.9 beta, and Project C with a 1.1 beta. The required rates of return for the company and for each project are as follows:

$$\text{Company:} \quad 3\% + 0.9(8\% - 3\%) = 7.5\%$$

$$\text{Project A:} \quad 3\% + 0.5(8\% - 3\%) = 5.5\%$$

$$\text{Project B:} \quad 3\% + 0.9(8\% - 3\%) = 7.5\%$$

$$\text{Project C:} \quad 3\% + 1.1(8\% - 3\%) = 8.5\%$$

If management uses the company WACC as the required return for all projects, this rate is too high for Project A, making it less likely that Project A would be accepted. Project B has the same risk as the company, so it would be evaluated fairly. Using the WACC for Project C leads to the error of using a discount rate that is too low, which would make it more likely that this high-risk project would be accepted. Whenever possible, it is desirable to use project-specific required rates of return instead of the company's overall required rate of return.

Market returns are readily available for publicly traded companies. The stock betas of these companies can then be calculated, and this calculation assists in estimating the companies' betas and WACC. Unfortunately, however, the returns for specific capital projects are not directly observable, and we have to use proxies for their betas. Frequently, we can employ the pure-play method, in which the analyst identifies other publicly traded stocks in the same business as the project being considered. The betas for the stocks of these companies are used to estimate a project beta. In the pure-play method, these proxy companies need to be relatively focused in the same line of business as the project. When the pure-play method is not possible, other methods, such as estimating accounting betas or cross-sectional regression analysis, are used.

7.5. Real Options

Real options are capital budgeting options that allow managers to make decisions in the future that alter the value of capital budgeting investment decisions made today. Instead of making all capital budgeting decisions now, at time 0, managers can wait and make additional decisions at future dates when these future decisions are contingent upon future economic events or information. These sequential decisions, in which future decisions depend on the decisions made today as well as on future economic events, are very realistic capital budgeting applications.

Real options are like financial options; they just deal with real assets instead of financial assets. A simple financial option could be a call option on a share of stock. Suppose the stock is selling for $50, the exercise (strike) price is $50, and the option expires in one year. If the stock goes up to $60, you exercise the option and have a gain of $10 in one year. If the stock goes down to $40, you do not exercise, and you have no gain. However, no gain is better than the $10 loss you would have had if you had purchased the stock at the beginning of the year. Real options, like financial options, entail the right to make a decision, but not the obligation. The corporation should exercise a real option only if it is value-enhancing.

Just as financial options are contingent on an underlying asset, real options are contingent on future events. The flexibility that real options give to managers can greatly enhance the NPV of the company's capital investments. The following are several types of these real options:

1. *Timing options:* Instead of investing now, the company can delay investing. Delaying an investment and basing the decision on hopefully improved information that you might have in, say, a year could help improve the NPV of the projects selected.
2. *Sizing options:* If after investing, the company can abandon the project when the financial results are disappointing, it has an abandonment option. At some future date, if the cash flow from abandoning a project exceeds the present value of the cash flows from continuing the project, managers should exercise the abandonment option. Conversely, if the company can make additional investments when future financial results are strong, the company has a growth option or an expansion option.
3. *Flexibility options:* Once an investment is made, other operational flexibilities may be available besides abandonment or expansion. For example, suppose demand exceeds capacity. Management may be able to exercise a price-setting option. By increasing prices, the company could benefit from the excess demand, which it cannot do by increasing production. There are also production-flexibility options. Even though doing so is expensive, the company can profit from working overtime or from adding additional shifts. The company can also work with customers and suppliers for their mutual benefit whenever a demand–supply mismatch occurs. This type of option also includes the possibility of using different inputs or producing different outputs.
4. *Fundamental options:* In cases like those in the first three entries, there are options embedded in a project that can raise its value. In other cases, the whole investment is essentially an option. The payoffs from the investment are contingent on an underlying asset, just like most financial options. For example, the value of an oil well or refinery investment is contingent on the price of oil. The value of a gold mine is contingent on the price of gold. If oil prices are low, you may not drill a well. If oil prices are high, you go ahead and drill. Many R&D (research and development) projects also look like options.

There are several approaches to evaluating capital budgeting projects with real options. One of the difficulties with real options is that the analysis can be very complicated. Although some of the problems are simple and can be readily solved, many of them are so complex that they are expensive to evaluate or you may not have much confidence in the analysis. Four commonsense approaches to real options analysis follow.

1. *Use DCF analysis without considering options:* If the NPV is positive without considering real options, and the project has real options that would simply add more value, it is unnecessary to evaluate the options. Just go ahead and make the investment.
2. *Consider the Project NPV = NPV (based on DCF alone) − Cost of options + Value of options:* Go ahead and calculate the NPV based on expected cash flows. Then simply add the value associated with real options. For example, if a project has a negative NPV based on DCF alone of $50 million, will the options add at least that much to its value?
3. *Use decision trees:* Although they are not as conceptually sound as option pricing models, decision trees can capture the essence of many sequential decision-making problems.
4. *Use option pricing models:* Except for simple options, the technical requirements for solving these models may require you to hire special consultants or "quants." Some large companies have their own specialists.

The analyst is confronted with (1) a variety of real options that investment projects may possess and (2) a decision about how to reasonably value these options. Example 2-10 deals with production flexibility; in this case, an additional investment outlay gives the company an option to use alternative fuel sources.

Two of the most valuable options are to abandon or expand a project at some point after the original investment. Example 2-11 illustrates the abandonment option.

EXAMPLE 2-10   Production-Flexibility Option

Sackley AquaFarms estimated the NPV of the expected cash flows from a new processing plant to be −$0.40 million. Sackley is evaluating an incremental investment of $0.30 million that would give management the flexibility to switch between coal, natural gas, and oil as an energy source. The original plant relied only on coal. The option to switch to cheaper sources of energy when they are available has an estimated value of $1.20 million. What is the value of the new processing plant, including this real option to use alternative energy sources?

Solution

The NPV, including the real option, should be

$$\text{Project NPV} = \text{NPV(based on DCF alone)} - \text{Cost of options} + \text{Value of options}$$
$$= -0.40 \text{ million} - 0.30 \text{ million} + 1.20 \text{ million}$$
$$= \$0.50 \text{ million}$$

Without the flexibility offered by the real option, the plant is unprofitable. The real option to adapt to cheaper energy sources adds enough to the value of this investment to give it a positive NPV.

EXAMPLE 2-11   Abandonment Option

Nyberg Systems is considering a capital project with the following characteristics:

- The initial outlay is €200,000.
- Project life is four years.
- Annual after-tax operating cash flows have a 50 percent probability of being €40,000 for the four years and a 50 percent probability of being €80,000.
- Salvage value at project termination is 0.
- The required rate of return is 10 percent.
- In one year, after realizing the first-year cash flow, the company has the option to abandon the project and receive the salvage value of €150,000.

1. Compute the project NPV assuming no abandonment.
2. What is the optimal abandonment strategy? Compute the project NPV using that strategy.

Solution to 1

The expected annual after-tax operating cash flow is $0.50(40,000) + 0.50(80,000) =$ €60,000.

The cash flows discounted at 10 percent give an NPV of

$$NPV = -200,000 + \sum_{t=1}^{4} \frac{60,000}{1.10^t}$$

$$= -€9,808$$

The project should be rejected because it has a negative NPV.

Solution to 2

The optimal abandonment strategy would be to abandon the project in one year if the subsequent cash flows are worth less than the abandonment value. If at the end of the first year the low cash flow occurs, you can abandon for €150,000 and give up €40,000 for the following three years. The €40,000 annual cash flow, discounted for three years at 10 percent, has a present value of only €99,474; so you should abandon. Three years of the higher €80,000 cash flow has a present value of €198,948; so you should not abandon. After the first year, abandon if the low cash flow occurs, and do not abandon if the high cash flow occurs.

If the high cash flow occurs and you do not abandon, the NPV is

$$NPV = -200,000 + \sum_{t=1}^{4} \frac{80,000}{1.10^t}$$

$$= €53,589$$

If you abandon when the low cash flow occurs, you receive the first-year cash flow and the abandonment value and then no further cash flows. In that case, the NPV is

$$NPV = -200,000 + \frac{40,000 + 150,000}{1.10}$$
$$= -€27,273$$

The expected NPV is then

$$NPV = 0.50(53,589) + 0.50(-27,273)$$
$$= €13,158$$

Optimal abandonment raises the NPV by $13,158 - (-€9,808) = €22,966$.

A fundamental real option could be a gold mine or an oil well. Example 2-12 looks at the possibility of purchasing the rights to a gold mining property.

EXAMPLE 2-12   Erichmann Gold Mine

The Erichmann family has offered a five-year option on one of its small gold mining properties for $10 million. The current price of gold is $400 per ounce. The mine holds an estimated 500,000 ounces that could be mined at an average cost of $450 per ounce. The maximum production rate is 200,000 ounces per year. How would you assess the Erichmann family's offer?

Solution

A binomial option model can be built for the underlying price of gold. These binomial models are very common in assessing the value of financial options such as puts and calls on stocks, callable bonds, or mortgages with prepayment options. Whenever the price path for gold is more than $450 per ounce, it might be attractive to commence mining. Of course, you would cease mining whenever the price is lower. With additional information about the volatility of gold prices and the risk-free interest rate, an expert could build this binomial model and value the real option. Comparing the value of this real option to its $10 million cost would enable you to make an investment decision.

A critical assumption of many applications of traditional capital budgeting tools is that the investment decision is made now, with no flexibility considered in future decisions. A more reasonable approach is to assume that the corporation is making sequential decisions, some now and some in the future. A combination of optimal current and future decisions is what will maximize company value. Real options analysis tries to incorporate rational future

EXHIBIT 2-34   Common Capital Budgeting Pitfalls

Not incorporating economic responses into the investment analysis

Misusing capital budgeting templates

Engaging in pet projects

Basing investment decisions on EPS, net income, or return on equity

Using IRR to make investment decisions

Bad accounting for cash flows

Overhead costs

Not using the appropriate risk-adjusted discount rate

Spending all of the investment budget just because it is available

Failure to consider investment alternatives

Handling sunk costs and opportunity costs incorrectly

decisions into the assessment of current investment decision making. This future flexibility, exercised intelligently, enhances the value of capital investments. Some real options can be valued with readily available option pricing models, such as the binomial model or the Black–Scholes–Merton option pricing model.[14] Unfortunately, many real options are very complex and hard to value, which poses a challenge as the analyst tries to lay out the economic contingencies of an investment and assess their values. A real option, with the future flexibility it provides, can be an important piece of the value of many projects.

7.6. Common Capital Budgeting Pitfalls

Although the principles of capital budgeting may be easy to learn, applying the principles to real-world investment opportunities can be challenging. Some of the common mistakes that managers make are listed in Exhibit 2-34 above and discussed in the following:

- *Economic responses:* Economic responses to an investment often affect its profitability, and these responses have to be correctly anticipated. For example, in response to a successful investment, competitors can enter and reduce the investment's profitability. Similarly, vendors, suppliers, and employees may want to gain from a profitable enterprise. Companies that make highly profitable investments often find that a competitive marketplace eventually causes profitability to revert to normal levels.
- *Template errors:* Because hundreds or even thousands of projects need to be analyzed over time, corporations have standardized capital budgeting templates for managers to use in evaluating projects. This situation creates risks in that the template model may not match the project or employees may input inappropriate information.
- *Pet projects:* Pet projects are projects that influential managers want the corporation to invest in. Ideally, pet projects will receive the normal scrutiny that other investments receive and will be selected on the strength of their own merits. Often, unfortunately, pet projects are selected without undergoing normal capital budgeting analysis. Or the pet project receives the analysis, but overly optimistic projections are used to inflate the project's profitability.

---

[14]Chapter 4 of Chance (2003) gives an excellent overview of option pricing models.

- *Earnings per share (EPS), net income, or return on equity (ROE):* Managers sometimes have incentives to boost EPS, net income, or ROE. Many investments, even those with strong NPVs, do not boost these accounting numbers in the short run and may even reduce them. Paying attention to short-run accounting numbers can result in choosing projects that are not in the long-run economic interests of the business.
- *Basing decisions on the IRR:* The NPV criterion is economically sound. The IRR criterion is also sound for independent projects (with conventional cash flow patterns). If projects are mutually exclusive or competitive with each other, investing in projects based on the IRR will tend to result in choosing smaller, short-term projects with high IRRs at the expense of larger, longer-term, high-NPV projects. Basing decisions on paybacks or accounting rates of return is even more dangerous. These measures can be economically unsound.
- *Bad accounting for cash flows:* In analyzing a complicated project, it is easy to omit relevant cash flows, to double-count cash flows, and to mishandle taxes.
- *Overhead costs:* In large companies, the cost of a project must include the overhead it generates for such things as management time, information technology support, financial systems, and other support. Although these items are hard to estimate, over- or underestimating these overhead costs can lead to poor investment decisions.
- *Discount rate errors:* The required rate of return for a project should be based on its risk. If a project is being financed with debt (or with equity), you should still use the project's required rate of return and not the cost of debt (or the cost of equity). Similarly, a high-risk project should not be discounted at the company's overall cost of capital, but at the project's required rate of return. Discount rate errors have a huge impact on the computed NPVs of long-lived projects.
- *Overspending and underspending the capital budget:* Politically, many managers will spend all of their budget and argue that their budget is too small. In a well run company, managers will return excess funds whenever their profitable projects cost less than their budget, and they will make a sound case for extra funds if their budget is too small.
- *Failure to consider investment alternatives:* Generating good investment ideas is the most basic step in the capital budgeting process, and many good alternatives are never even considered.
- *Sunk costs and opportunity costs:* Ignoring sunk costs is difficult for managers to do. Furthermore, not identifying the economic alternatives (real and financial) that are the opportunity costs is probably the biggest failure in much analysis. Only costs that change with the decision are relevant.

8. OTHER INCOME MEASURES AND VALUATION MODELS

Capital budgeting was one of the first widespread applications of discounted cash flow analysis. In the basic capital budgeting model, the analyst values an investment by discounting future after-tax cash flows at the rate of return required by investors. Subtracting the initial investment results in the project's NPV. The future cash flows consist of after-tax operating cash flows plus returns of investment (such as salvage value and sale of working capital).

Analysts will employ and encounter other concepts of income and other valuation approaches besides this basic capital budgeting model. Because some of these other approaches are economically sound and widely employed, we will briefly describe some of them here. By considering these approaches, you can see the distinguishing features of each approach and that they should result in consistent valuations (if they are used correctly).

To facilitate the comparison of income measures and valuation models, we will employ as an example a simple company (the Granite Corporation) that invests in one project. The company goes out of business when that project expires. After evaluating that project with the NPV and IRR capital budgeting models, we will examine that same project using the following alternative methods:

- Economic income and accounting income.
- Economic profit valuation.
- Residual income valuation.
- Claims valuation.

Our purpose is to show how the various income measures and valuation methods are related to each other.

8.1.   The Basic Capital Budgeting Model

The basic capital budgeting model (presented earlier) identifies the after-tax operating cash flows from an investment as well as nonoperating cash flows (such as the initial investment or future recovery of invested capital or net working capital). Then these cash flows are discounted at the required rate of return for the asset to establish the NPV.

The base-case capital budgeting project is the following (see Exhibit 2-35). The company is going to invest $150,000 and generate sales for the next five years, as shown in Exhibit 2-35. Variable cash operating expenses will be 50 percent of sales each year, and fixed cash operating

EXHIBIT 2-35   Basic Capital Budgeting Example for Granite Corporation ($)

Year	0	1	2	3	4	5
Fixed capital investment	−150,000					
Sales		150,000	200,000	250,000	200,000	150,000
Variable cash expenses		75,000	100,000	125,000	100,000	75,000
Fixed cash expenses		20,000	20,000	20,000	20,000	20,000
Depreciation		30,000	30,000	30,000	30,000	30,000
Operating income before taxes		25,000	50,000	75,000	50,000	25,000
Taxes at 40%		10,000	20,000	30,000	20,000	10,000
Operating income after taxes		15,000	30,000	45,000	30,000	15,000
After-tax operating cash flow		45,000	60,000	75,000	60,000	45,000
Salvage value						10,000
Taxes on salvage value						4,000
After-tax salvage value						6,000
Total after-tax cash flow	−150,000	45,000	60,000	75,000	60,000	51,000
NPV (at $r = 10\%$)	69,492					
IRR	26.27%					

expenses are $20,000. Depreciation is straight-line to 0, $30,000 per year with a zero book value at the end of five years. The income tax rate is 40 percent. Salvage value is $10,000, which is taxable at 40 percent, leaving an after-tax salvage value of $6,000 at the end of five years. The required rate of return is 10 percent.

The present value of the after-tax cash flows for years 1–5 is $219,492. Subtracting the investment of $150,000 results in the NPV of $69,492. The IRR for the investment is 26.27 percent.

8.2. Economic and Accounting Income

Economic income and accounting income differ from the after-tax operating cash flows used in the basic capital budgeting model.

Economic income is the profit realized from an investment. For a given year, economic income is the investment's after-tax cash flow plus the change in the market value:

$$\text{Economic income} = \text{Cash flow} + \text{Change in market value}$$

$$= \text{Cash flow} + (\text{Ending market value} - \text{Beginning market value})$$

$$\text{or} \tag{2-11}$$

$$\text{Economic income} = \text{Cash flow} - (\text{Beginning market value} - \text{Ending market value})$$

$$= \text{Cash flow} - \text{Economic depreciation}[15]$$

For the Granite Corporation, the cash flows are already calculated in Exhibit 2-35. The beginning market value at time 0 is the present value of the future after-tax cash flows at the 10 percent required rate of return, or $219,492. The market value at any future date is the present value of subsequent cash flows discounted back to that date. For the Granite Corporation, the cash flows, changes in market value, and economic incomes are shown in Exhibit 2-36.

EXHIBIT 2-36   Economic Income for Granite Corporation ($)

Year	1	2	3	4	5
Beginning market value	219,492	196,441	156,086	96,694	46,364
Ending market value	196,441	156,086	96,694	46,364	0
Change in market value	−23,051	−40,356	−59,391	−50,331	−46,364
After-tax cash flow	45,000	60,000	75,000	60,000	51,000
Economic income	21,949	19,644	15,609	9,669	4,636
Economic rate of return	10%	10%	10%	10%	10%

---

[15]These equations are conceptually identical because economic depreciation is the negative of the change in market value. For example, assume the cash flow is 10, the beginning market value is 30, and the ending market value is 25. Cash flow + Change in market value = Cash flow + (Ending market value − Beginning market value) = 10 + (25 − 30) = 5. Or, Cash flow − Economic depreciation = Cash flow − (Beginning market value − Ending market value) = 10 − (30 − 25) = 5.

In year 1, the beginning value is $219,492 and the ending value is $196,441; so the change in value is $-$23,051. The economic income is the cash flow plus the change in value, or $45,000 + (-$23,051) = $21,949. The economic income for years 2–5 is found similarly. The economic rate of return is the year's economic income divided by its beginning market value. Notice that the economic rate of return is precisely 10 percent each year, which was the required rate of return on the project.

Accounting income for this company will differ from the economic income for two reasons. First, the accounting depreciation is based on the original cost of the investment (not on the market value of the investment). Consequently, the accounting depreciation schedule does not follow the declines in the market value of an asset. Besides being based on accounting depreciation instead of economic depreciation, accounting net income is the after-tax income remaining after paying interest expenses on the company's debt obligations. In contrast, interest expenses are ignored when computing the economic income for an asset or the after-tax operating cash flows in the basic capital budgeting model. As explained in Section 3, the effects of financing costs are captured in the discount rate, not in the cash flows. In the capital budgeting model, if we included interest expenses in the cash flows, we would be double-counting them.

To illustrate these differences, we will assume that the company borrows an amount equal to one-half of the value of the company, which is 50 percent of $219,492, or $109,746, and that it pays 8⅓ percent interest each year on the beginning balance. With a 40 percent tax rate, the after-tax interest cost is 8⅓%(1 − 0.40) = 5.0%. Because the Granite Corporation has a five-year life, it does not need to borrow or retain earnings for the future, and all cash flows will be distributed to bondholders and stockholders. Granite will maintain a 50 percent debt-to-value ratio on the company's debt; so bondholders will receive 8⅓ percent interest on their beginning bond balance and the debt will also be amortized (paid down) whenever the value of the company goes down. Furthermore, after all operating costs, interest expenses, and taxes are paid, stockholders will receive all remaining cash flows each year as a cash dividend or share repurchase.[16]

The financial statements for the Granite Corporation are shown in Exhibit 2-37.

The income statement for financial reporting purposes differs from that used in the capital budgeting model because the interest on debt obligations is now taken out as an expense before arriving at net income. The book value of the company's assets is based on the original accounting cost minus accumulated accounting depreciation. Note that the liabilities and net worth are also declining in the balance sheet. The liabilities decline each year, reflecting the amounts that were paid annually to reduce the principal of the loan. Notice, also, that the net worth is declining. Normally, the net worth of a company increases because beginning equity is increased by net retentions—the excess of net income over dividends paid. In this case, the company is shrinking and going out of business in five years; so the distributions to shareholders (which can be either cash dividends or share repurchases) exceed net income and net worth declines. The amounts that are paid each year to reduce debt and for dividends or share repurchases are shown in the financing section of the statement of cash flows.

Accounting measures of performance also can differ from economic measures of performance. Exhibit 2-38 repeats the economic income and accounting income from Exhibits 2-36 and 2-37. The table also shows the economic rate of return each year and two popular

---

[16]The assumptions may be unrealistic, but this is a very simple corporation.

EXHIBIT 2-37   Condensed Financial Statements for Granite Corporation ($)

Year	0	1	2	3	4	5
Balance Sheets:						
Assets	150,000	120,000	90,000	60,000	30,000	0
Liabilities	109,746	98,221	78,043	48,347	23,182	0
Net worth	40,254	21,779	11,957	11,653	6,818	0
Income Statements:						
Sales		150,000	200,000	250,000	200,000	150,000
Variable cash expenses		75,000	100,000	125,000	100,000	75,000
Fixed cash expenses		20,000	20,000	20,000	20,000	20,000
Depreciation		30,000	30,000	30,000	30,000	30,000
EBIT (earnings before interest and taxes)		25,000	50,000	75,000	50,000	25,000
Interest expense		9,146	8,185	6,504	4,029	1,932
EBT (earnings before taxes)		15,854	41,815	68,496	45,971	23,068
Taxes at 40%		6,342	16,726	27,399	18,388	9,227
Net income before salvage		9,513	25,089	41,098	27,583	13,841
After-tax salvage value						6,000
Net income		9,513	25,089	41,098	27,583	19,841
Statements of Cash Flows:						
Operating cash flows:						
Net income		9,513	25,089	41,098	27,583	19,841
Depreciation		30,000	30,000	30,000	30,000	30,000
Total		39,513	55,089	71,098	57,583	49,841
Financing cash flows:						
Debt repayment		−11,525	−20,178	−29,696	−25,165	−23,182
Dividends/repurchases		−27,987	−34,911	−41,402	−32,417	−26,659
Total		−39,513	−55,089	−71,098	−57,583	−49,841
Investing cash flows		0	0	0	0	0
Total cash flows		0	0	0	0	0

accounting measures of performance: the return on equity (ROE = net income divided by beginning equity) and return on assets (ROA = EBIT divided by beginning assets).

As Exhibit 2-38 illustrates, economic and accounting incomes differ substantially. Over the five years, economic income is much less than accounting income, and the patterns certainly differ. In addition, the accounting rates of return, the ROE and ROA, for this admittedly unusual company are quite different from the economic rate of return.

EXHIBIT 2-38   Economic Income, Accounting Income, and Rates of Return for Granite Corporation

Year	1	2	3	4	5
Economic income ($)	21,949	19,644	15,609	9,669	4,636
Accounting income ($)	9,513	25,089	41,098	27,583	19,841
Economic rate of return	10.00%	10.00%	10.00%	10.00%	10.00%
Return on equity (ROE)	23.63%	115.20%	343.71%	236.70%	291.00%
Return on assets (ROA)	16.67%	41.67%	83.33%	83.33%	83.33%

8.3. Economic Profit, Residual Income, and Claims Valuation

Although the capital budgeting model is widely employed, analysts have used other procedures to divide up the cash flows from a company or project and then value them using discounted cash flow methods. We present three of these alternative models here: the economic profit model, the residual income model, and the claims valuation model. Used correctly, they are all consistent with the basic capital budgeting model and with each other.

8.3.1. Economic Profit   The first alternative method for measuring income and valuing assets is based on economic profit (EP).[17] Economic profit has been used in asset valuation as well as in performance measurement and management compensation. Its calculation is loosely as follows:

$$EP = NOPAT - \$WACC \qquad (2\text{-}12)$$

where

> EP = economic profit
>
> NOPAT = net operating profit after tax = EBIT(1 − Tax rate)
>
> EBIT = operating income before taxes, or Earnings before interest and taxes
>
> $WACC = dollar cost of capital = WACC × Capital
>
> WACC = weighted average (or overall) cost of capital
>
> Capital = investment

EP is a periodic measure of profit above and beyond the dollar cost of the capital invested in the project. The dollar cost of capital is the dollar return that the company must make on the project to pay the debt holders and the equity holders their respective required rates of return.[18]

---

[17]Economic Value Added® (EVA), trademarked by the consulting firm Stern Stewart & Company, is a well-known commercial application of the economic profit approach. See Stewart (1991) and Peterson and Peterson (1996) for complete discussion.

[18]In the chapter on cost of capital, we will explain the relationship between the required rate of return on the project or WACC (here 10 percent), the rate of return required by debt holders (here 8⅓ percent), and the rate of return required by equity holders (here 15 percent).

EXHIBIT 2-39   EP for Granite Corporation ($)

Year	1	2	3	4	5**
Capital*	150,000	120,000	90,000	60,000	30,000
NOPAT	15,000	30,000	45,000	30,000	21,000
$WACC	15,000	12,000	9,000	6,000	3,000
EP	0	18,000	36,000	24,000	18,000

*Depreciation is $30,000 per year.
**The $6,000 after-tax gain from salvage is included in NOPAT in year 5.

For the Granite Corporation, for the first year, we have the following:

$$NOPAT = EBIT(1 - Tax\ rate) = 25,000(1 - 0.40) = \$15,000$$
$$\$WACC = WACC \times Capital = 10\% \times 150,000 = \$15,000$$
$$EP = NOPAT - \$WACC = 15,000 - 15,000 = \$0$$

Exhibit 2-39 shows the EP for all five years for the Granite Corporation.

EP is readily applied to the valuation of an asset or security. The NPV found by discounted cash flow analysis in the basic capital budgeting model will be equal to the present value of future EP discounted at the weighted average cost of capital.

$$NPV = \sum_{t=1}^{\infty} \frac{EP_t}{(1 + WACC)^t} \tag{2-13}$$

This NPV is also called the market value added (MVA).[19] So we have

$$NPV = MVA = \sum_{t=1}^{\infty} \frac{EP_t}{(1 + WACC)^t} \tag{2-14}$$

Discounting the five years of EP for the Granite Corporation at the 10 percent WACC gives an NPV (and MVA) of $69,492. The total value of the company (of the asset) is the original investment of $150,000 plus the NPV of $69,492, or $219,492. The valuation using EP is the same as that found with the basic capital budgeting model.

8.3.2. Residual Income   Another method for estimating income and valuing an asset is the residual income method.[20] This method focuses on the returns to equity, where

$$Residual\ income = Net\ income - Equity\ charge$$

[19]Peterson and Peterson (1996) define MVA as the market value of the company minus the capital invested, which is an NPV.
[20]See Chapter 5 in Stowe, Robinson, Pinto, and McLeavey (2002) and Edwards and Bell (1961) for treatments of residual income analysis.

or

$$RI_t = NI_t = r_e B_{t-1} \qquad (2\text{-}15)$$

where

   RI_t = residual income during period t

   NI_t = net income during period t

   $r_e B_{t-1}$ = equity charge for period t, which is the required rate of return on equity, r_e, times the beginning-of-period book value of equity, B_{t-1}

For the first year for the Granite Corporation, the net income is \$9,513. The beginning book value of equity is \$40,254 (from the balance sheet in Exhibit 2-37), and the required rate of return on equity is 15 percent. Consequently, the residual income for year 1 is:

$$
\begin{aligned}
RI_t &= NI_t - r_e B_{t-1} \\
&= 9{,}513 - 0.15(40{,}254) \\
&= 9{,}513 - 6{,}038 \\
&= \$3{,}475
\end{aligned}
$$

The residual income for all five years for Granite is shown in Exhibit 2-40.

   Residual income, like EP, can also be applied to valuation of an asset or security. The NPV of an investment is the present value of future residual income discounted at the required rate of return on equity.

$$NPV = \sum_{t=1}^{\infty} \frac{RI_t}{(1+r_e)^t} \qquad (2\text{-}16)$$

   Discounting the residual income for the Granite Corporation at the 15 percent required rate of return on equity gives an NPV of \$69,492. The total value of the company (of the asset) is the present value of the residual income, the original equity investment, plus the original debt investment:

PV of residual income	\$ 69,492
Equity investment	40,254
Debt investment	109,746
Total value	\$219,492

   The value of the company is the original book value of its debt and equity plus the present value of the residual income (which is the project's NPV). Again, this is the same value we found with the basic capital budgeting model and with the EP model.

EXHIBIT 2-40   Residual Income for Granite Corporation (\$)

Year	1	2	3	4	5*
NI_t	9,513	25,089	41,098	27,583	19,841
$r_e B_{t-1}$	6,038	3,267	1,794	1,748	1,023
RI_t	3,475	21,822	39,304	25,835	18,818

*The \$6,000 after-tax gain from salvage is included in NI in year 5.

8.3.3. Claims Valuation   To value a company, the EP valuation approach essentially adds the present value of EP to the original investment. The residual income approach adds the present value of residual income to the original debt and equity investments in the company. Since the EP approach is from the perspective of all suppliers of capital, EP is discounted at the overall WACC. The residual income approach takes the perspective of equity investors; so residual income is discounted at the cost of equity.

The third and final alternative valuation approach that we present is to divide the operating cash flows between security holder classes (in this example, debt and equity) and then value the debt and equity cash flows separately.

Balance Sheet

Assets	Liabilities
	Equity

The basic capital budgeting approach is to value the asset, which is on the left-hand side of the balance sheet above. The claims valuation approach values the liabilities and equity, the claims against the assets, which are on the right-hand side of the balance sheet. The value of the claims should equal the value of the assets.

For the Granite Corporation, the cash flows to debt holders are the interest payments and principal payments. These are valued by discounting them at the cost of debt, which is 8⅓ percent. The cash flows to stockholders are the dividends and share repurchases, which are valued by discounting them at the 15 percent cost of equity. Exhibit 2-41 lists the future cash flows for debt and equity.

The present value of the total debt payments, discounted at the cost of debt, is $109,746. The value of the equity distributions, discounted at the cost of equity, is $109,746. The total value of the company is the combined value of debt and equity, which is $219,492.

In our example, the basic capital budgeting model, the economic profit model, the residual income model, and the claims valuation model all result in the same valuation of the company. In the real world, analysts must deal with many accounting complications. Some of these complications may include pension liability adjustments, valuations of marketable securities held, exchange rate gains and losses, and adjustments for leases, inventories, goodwill, deferred taxes, etc. In theory, all of the valuation models are equivalent. In practice, even with due diligence and care, analysts may prefer one approach over others and disagree about valuations.

There are other approaches to valuation that analysts use and run across. Two common ones are the free cash flow to the firm and free cash flow to equity approaches.[21] The free cash

EXHIBIT 2-41   Payments to Bondholders and Stockholders of Granite Corporation ($)

Year	1	2	3	4	5
Interest payments	9,146	8,185	6,504	4,029	1,932
Principal payments	11,525	20,178	29,696	25,165	23,182
Total debt payments	20,671	28,363	36,199	29,194	25,114
Equity distributions	27,987	34,911	41,402	32,417	26,659

---

[21]The free cash flow to the firm and free cash flow to equity approaches are developed in Chapter 3 of Stowe, Robinson, Pinto, and McLeavey (2002).

flow to the firm approach is fundamentally the same as the basic capital budgeting approach. The free cash flow to equity approach is related to the claims valuation approach. In corporate finance, corporate managers usually value an asset by valuing its total after-tax cash flows. Security analysts typically value equity by valuing the cash flows to stockholders. Real estate investors often evaluate real estate investments by valuing the cash flows to the equity investor after payments to creditors, which is like the claims valuation approach.

9. SUMMARY

Capital budgeting is the process that companies use for decision making on capital projects—projects with a life of a year or more. This chapter developed the principles behind the basic capital budgeting model, the cash flows that go into the model, and several extensions of the basic model.

- Capital budgeting undergirds the most critical investments for many corporations: their investments in long-term assets. The principles of capital budgeting have been applied to other corporate investing and financing decisions and to security analysis and portfolio management.
- The typical steps in the capital budgeting process are (1) generating ideas, (2) analyzing individual proposals, (3) planning the capital budget, and (4) monitoring and postauditing.
- Projects susceptible to capital budgeting process can be categorized as (1) replacement, (2) expansion, (3) new products and services, and (4) regulatory, safety, and environmental.
- Capital budgeting decisions are based on incremental after-tax cash flows discounted at the opportunity cost of funds. Financing costs are ignored because both the cost of debt and the cost of other capital are captured in the discount rate.
- The net present value (NPV) is the present value of all after-tax cash flows, or

$$\text{NPV} = \sum_{t=0}^{n} \frac{\text{CF}_t}{(1+r)^t}$$

where the investment outlays are negative cash flows included in the CF_ts and r is the required rate of return for the investment.
- The IRR is the discount rate that makes the present value of all future cash flows sum to 0. This equation can be solved for the IRR:

$$\sum_{t=0}^{n} \frac{\text{CF}_t}{(1+\text{IRR})^t} = 0$$

- The payback period is the number of years required to recover the original investment in a project. The payback is based on cash flows.
- The discounted payback period is the number of years it takes for the cumulative discounted cash flows from a project to equal the original investment.
- The average accounting rate of return (AAR) can be defined as follows:

$$\text{AAR} = \frac{\text{Average net income}}{\text{Average book value}}$$

- The profitability index (PI) is the present value of a project's future cash flows divided by the initial investment:

$$PI = \frac{\text{PV of future cash flows}}{\text{Initial investment}}$$
$$= 1 + \frac{\text{NPV}}{\text{Initial investment}}$$

- The capital budgeting decision rules are to invest if the NPV > 0, if the IRR $> r$, or if the PI > 1.0. There are no decision rules for the payback period, discounted payback period, and AAR because they are not always sound measures.
- The NPV profile is a graph that shows a project's NPV graphed as a function of various discount rates.
- For mutually exclusive projects that are ranked differently by the NPV and IRR, it is economically sound to choose the project with the higher NPV.
- The multiple IRR problem and the no IRR problem can arise for a project with nonconventional cash flows—cash flows that change signs more than once during the project's life.
- The fact that projects with positive NPVs theoretically increase the value of the company and the value of its stock could explain the popularity of NPV as an evaluation method.
- Analysts often organize the cash flows for capital budgeting in tables, summing all of the cash flows occurring at each point in time. These totals are then used to find an NPV or IRR. Alternatively, tables collecting cash flows by type can be used. Equations for the capital budgeting cash flows are as follows:

Initial outlay:

$$\text{Outlay} = \text{FCInv} + \text{NWCInv} - \text{Sal}_0 + \text{T}(\text{Sal}_0 - \text{B}_0)$$

Annual after-tax operating cash flow:

$$\text{CF} = (\text{S} - \text{C} - \text{D})(1 - \text{T}) + \text{D}$$

or

$$\text{CF} = (\text{S} - \text{C})(1 - \text{T}) + \text{T}_\text{D}$$

Terminal year after-tax nonoperating cash flow:

$$\text{TNOCF} = \text{Sal}_\text{T} + \text{NWCInv} - \text{T}(\text{Sal}_\text{T} - \text{B}_\text{T})$$

- Depreciation schedules affect taxable income, taxes paid, and after-tax cash flows, and therefore capital budgeting valuations.
- Spreadsheets are heavily used for capital budgeting valuation.
- When inflation exists, the analyst should perform capital budgeting analysis in nominal terms if cash flows are nominal and in real terms if cash flows are real.
- Inflation reduces the value of depreciation tax savings (unless the tax system adjusts depreciation for inflation). Inflation reduces the value of fixed payments to bondholders. Inflation usually does not affect all revenues and costs uniformly. Contracting with customers, suppliers, employees, and sources of capital can be complicated as inflation rises.
- Two ways of comparing mutually exclusive projects in a replacement chain are the least common multiple of lives approach and the equivalent annual annuity approach.
- For the least common multiple of lives approach, the analyst extends the time horizon of analysis so that the lives of both projects will divide exactly into the horizon. The projects

are replicated over this horizon, and the NPV for the total cash flows over the least common multiple of lives is used to evaluate the investments.

- The equivalent annual annuity is the annuity payment (series of equal annual payments over the project's life) that is equivalent in value to the project's actual cash flows. Analysts find the present value of all of the cash flows for an investment (the NPV) and then calculate an annuity payment that has a value equivalent to the NPV.
- With capital rationing, the company's capital budget has a size constraint. Under hard capital rationing, the budget is fixed. In the case of hard rationing, managers use trial and error and sometimes mathematical programming to find the optimal set of projects. In that situation, it is best to use the NPV or PI valuation methods.
- Sensitivity analysis calculates the effect on the NPV of changes in one input variable at a time.
- Scenario analysis creates scenarios that consist of changes in several of the input variables and calculates the NPV for each scenario.
- Simulation (Monte Carlo) analysis is used to estimate probability distributions for the NPV or IRR of a capital project. Simulations randomly select values for stochastic input variables and then repeatedly calculate the project NPV and IRR to find their distributions.
- Risk-adjusted discount rates based on market risk measures should be used as the required rate of return for projects when the investors are diversified. The capital asset pricing model (CAPM) and arbitrage pricing theory (APT) are common approaches for finding market-based risk-adjusted rates.
- In the CAPM, a project's or asset's beta (β) is used as a measure of systematic risk. The security market line (SML) estimates the asset's required rate of return as $r_i = R_F + \beta_i[E(R_M) - R_F]$.
- Project-specific betas should be used instead of company betas whenever the risk of the project differs from that of the company.
- Real options can be classified as (1) timing options; (2) sizing options, which can be abandonment options or growth (expansion) options; (3) flexibility options, which can be price-setting options or production-flexibility options; and (4) fundamental options. Simple options can be evaluated with decision trees; for more complex options, the analyst should use option pricing models.
- Economic income is the investment's after-tax cash flow plus the change in the market value. Accounting income is revenues minus expenses. Accounting depreciation, based on the original cost of the investment, is the decrease in the book (accounting) value, and economic depreciation is the decrease in the market value of the investment. Accounting net income is net of the after-tax interest expenses on the company's debt obligations. In computing economic income, financing costs are ignored.
- Economic profit is

$$EP = NOPAT - \$WACC$$

where NOPAT = Net operating profit after tax = EBIT(1 − Tax rate) and $WACC = Dollar cost of capital = WACC × Capital. When applied to the valuation of an asset or security, the NPV of an investment (and its market value added) is the present value of future EP discounted at the weighted average cost of capital.

$$NPV = MVA = \sum_{t=1}^{\infty} \frac{EP_t}{(1 + WACC)^t}$$

- The total value of the company (of the asset) is the original investment plus the NPV.

- Residual income = Net income − Equity charge, or $RI_t = NI_t - r_e B_{t-1}$ where RI_t = Residual income during period t, NI_t = Net income during period t, r_e = the cost of equity, and B_{t-1} = the beginning-of-period book value of equity. The NPV of an investment is the present value of future residual income discounted at the required rate of return on equity:

$$NPV = \sum_{t=1}^{\infty} \frac{RI_t}{(1+r_e)^t}$$

- The total value of the company (of the asset) is the NPV plus the original equity investment plus the original debt investment.
- The claims valuation approach values an asset by valuing the claims against the asset. For example, an asset financed with debt and equity has a value equal to the value of the debt plus the value of the equity.

PRACTICE PROBLEMS

1. Given the following cash flows for a capital project and a required rate of return of 8 percent, calculate the NPV and IRR.

Year	0	1	2	3	4	5
Cash flow ($)	−50,000	15,000	15,000	20,000	10,000	5,000

	NPV	IRR
A.	$1,905	10.9%
B.	$1,905	26.0%
C.	$3,379	10.9%
D.	$3,379	26.0%

2. Given the following cash flows for a capital project, calculate its payback period and discounted payback period. The required rate of return is 8 percent. The discounted payback period is

Year	0	1	2	3	4	5
Cash flow ($)	−50,000	15,000	15,000	20,000	10,000	5,000

A. 0.16 years longer than the payback period.
B. 0.80 years longer than the payback period.
C. 1.01 years longer than the payback period.
D. 1.85 years longer than the payback period.

3. An investment of $100 generates after-tax cash flows of $40 in year 1, $80 in year 2, and $120 in year 3. The required rate of return is 20 percent. The net present value is closest to
A. $42.22.
B. $58.33.
C. $68.52.
D. $98.95.

4. An investment of $150,000 is expected to generate an after-tax cash flow of $100,000 in one year and another $120,000 in two years. The cost of capital is 10 percent. What is the internal rate of return?
   A. 28.19 percent.
   B. 28.39 percent.
   C. 28.59 percent.
   D. 28.79 percent.

5. Kim Corporation is considering an investment of 750 million won with expected after-tax cash inflows of 175 million won per year for seven years. The required rate of return is 10 percent. What are the project's NPV and IRR?

	NPV	IRR
A.	102 million won	14.0 percent
B.	102 million won	23.3 percent
C.	193 million won	14.0 percent
D.	193 million won	23.3 percent

6. Kim Corporation is considering an investment of 750 million won with expected after-tax cash inflows of 175 million won per year for seven years. The required rate of return is 10 percent. Expressed in years, what are the project's payback and discounted payback periods?

	Payback Period	Discounted Payback Period
A.	4.3	5.4
B.	4.3	5.9
C.	4.8	5.4
D.	4.8	5.9

7. An investment of $20,000 will create a perpetual after-tax cash flow of $2,000. The required rate of return is 8 percent. What is the investment's profitability index?
   A. 1.00.
   B. 1.08.
   C. 1.16.
   D. 1.25.

8. Hermann Corporation is considering an investment of €375 million with expected after-tax cash inflows of €115 million per year for seven years and an additional after-tax salvage value of €50 million in year 7. The required rate of return is 10 percent. What is the investment's PI?
   A. 1.19.
   B. 1.33.
   C. 1.56.
   D. 1.75.

9. Erin Chou is reviewing a profitable investment project that has a conventional cash flow pattern. If the cash flows for the project, initial outlay, and future after-tax cash flows all double, Chou would predict that the IRR would
   A. Increase and the NPV would increase.
   B. Increase and the NPV would stay the same.
   C. Stay the same and the NPV would increase.
   D. Stay the same and the NPV would stay the same.

10. Shirley Shea has evaluated an investment proposal and found that its payback period is one year, that it has a negative NPV, and that it has a positive IRR. Is this combination of results possible?
   A. Yes.
   B. No, because a project with a positive IRR has a positive NPV.
   C. No, because a project with a negative NPV has a negative payback period.
   D. No, because a project with such a rapid payback period has a positive NPV.

11. An investment has an outlay of 100 and after-tax cash flows of 40 annually for four years. A project enhancement increases the outlay by 15 and the annual after-tax cash flows by 5. As a result, the vertical intercept of the NPV profile of the enhanced project shifts
   A. Up and the horizontal intercept shifts left.
   B. Up and the horizontal intercept shifts right.
   C. Down and the horizontal intercept shifts left.
   D. Down and the horizontal intercept shifts right.

12. Projects 1 and 2 have similar outlays, although the patterns of future cash flows are different. The cash flows, along with the NPV and IRR for the two projects, are shown in the following table. For both projects, the required rate of return is 10 percent. The two projects are mutually exclusive. What is the appropriate investment decision?

	Cash Flows					NPV	IRR
Year	0	1	2	3	4		
Project 1	−50	20	20	20	20	13.40	21.86%
Project 2	−50	0	0	0	100	18.30	18.92%

   A. Invest in Project 1 because it has the higher IRR.
   B. Invest in Project 2 because it has the higher NPV.
   C. Invest half in each project.
   D. Invest in both projects.

13. Consider the following two projects, for which the cash flows, the NPV, and IRR are given. For both projects, the required rate of return is 10 percent. What discount rate would result in the same NPV for both projects?

	Cash Flows					NPV	IRR
Year	0	1	2	3	4		
Project 1	−100	36	36	36	36	14.12	16.37%
Project 2	−100	0	0	0	175	19.53	15.02%

   A. A rate between 0.00 percent and 10.00 percent.
   B. A rate between 10.00 percent and 15.02 percent.
   C. A rate between 15.02 percent and 16.37 percent.
   D. A rate above 16.37 percent.

14. Wilson Flannery is concerned that this project has multiple IRRs. How many discount rates produce a zero NPV for this project?

Year	0	1	2	3
Cash flows	−50	100	0	−50

   A. One, a discount rate of 0 percent.
   B. Two, discount rates of 0 percent and 32 percent.
   C. Two, discount rates of 0 percent and 62 percent.
   D. Two, discount rates of 0 percent and 92 percent.

15. FITCO is considering the purchase of new equipment. The equipment costs $350,000, and an additional $110,000 is needed to install it. The equipment will be depreciated straight-line to 0 over a five-year life. The equipment will generate additional annual revenues of $265,000, and it will have annual cash operating expenses of $83,000. The equipment will be sold for $85,000 after five years. An inventory investment of $73,000 is required during the life of the investment. FITCO is in the 40 percent tax bracket and its cost of capital is 10 percent. What is the project NPV?
   A. $47,818.
   B. $63,658.
   C. $80,189.
   D. $97,449.

16. After estimating a project's NPV, the analyst is advised that the fixed capital outlay will be revised upward by $100,000. The fixed capital outlay is depreciated straight-line over an eight-year life. The tax rate is 40 percent and the required rate of return is 10 percent. No changes in cash operating revenues, cash operating expenses, or salvage value are expected. What is the effect on the project NPV?
   A. A $100,000 decrease.
   B. A $73,325 decrease.
   C. A $59,988 decrease.
   D. No change.

17. When assembling the cash flows to calculate an NPV or IRR, the project's after-tax interest expenses should be subtracted from the cash flows for
   A. The NPV calculation, but not the IRR calculation.
   B. The IRR calculation, but not the NPV calculation.
   C. Both the NPV calculation and the IRR calculation.
   D. Neither the NPV calculation nor the IRR calculation.

18. Standard Corporation is investing $400,000 of fixed capital in a project that will be depreciated straight-line to 0 over its ten-year life. Annual sales are expected to be $240,000, and annual cash operating expenses are expected to be $110,000. An investment of $40,000 in net working capital is required over the project's life. The corporate income tax rate is 30 percent. What is the after-tax operating cash flow expected in year 1?
   A. $63,000.
   B. $92,000.
   C. $103,000.
   D. $130,000.

19. Five years ago, Frater Zahn's Company invested £38 million—£30 million in fixed capital and another £8 million in working capital—in a bakery. Today, Frater Zahn's is selling the fixed assets for £21 million and liquidating the investment in working capital. The book value of the fixed assets is £15 million, and the marginal tax rate is 40 percent. The fifth year's after-tax nonoperating cash flow to Frater Zahn's is closest to
    A. £20.6 million.
    B. £23.0 million.
    C. £26.6 million.
    D. £29.0 million.

The following information is used for Questions 20, 21, and 22.

McConachie Company is considering the purchase of a new 400-ton stamping press. The press costs $360,000, and an additional $40,000 is needed to install it. The press will be depreciated straight-line to 0 over a five-year life. The press will generate no additional revenues, but it will reduce cash operating expenses by $140,000 annually. The press will be sold for $120,000 after five years. An inventory investment of $60,000 is required during the life of the investment. McConachie is in the 40 percent tax bracket.

20. What is McConachie's net investment outlay?
    A. $360,000.
    B. $400,000.
    C. $420,000.
    D. $460,000.

21. McConachie's annual after-tax operating cash flow is closest to
    A. $116,000.
    B. $124,000.
    C. $140,000.
    D. $164,000.

22. What is the terminal year's after-tax nonoperating cash flow at the end of year 5?
    A. $108,000.
    B. $129,000.
    C. $132,000.
    D. $180,000.

The following information relates to Questions 23 through 28.

Linda Pyle is head of analyst recruiting for PPA Securities. She has been very frustrated by the number of job applicants who, in spite of their stellar pedigrees, seem to have little understanding of basic financial concepts. Pyle has written a set of conceptual questions and simple problems for the human resources department to use to screen for the better candidates in the applicant pool. A few of her corporate finance questions and problems follow.

> *Concept 1:* "A company invests in depreciable assets, financed partly by issuing fixed-rate bonds. If inflation is lower than expected, the value of the real tax savings from depreciation and the value of the real after-tax interest expense are both reduced."

Concept 2: "Sensitivity analysis and scenario analysis are useful tools for estimating the impact on a project's NPV of changing the value of one capital budgeting input variable at a time."

Concept 3: "When comparing two mutually exclusive projects with unequal lives, the IRR is a good approach for choosing the better project because it does not require equal lives."

Concept 4: "Project-specific betas should be used instead of company betas whenever the risk of the project differs from that of the company."

Problem: "Fontenot Company is investing €100 in a project that is being depreciated straight-line to 0 over a two-year life with no salvage value. The project will generate earnings before interest and taxes of €50 each year for two years. Fontenot's weighted average cost of capital and required rate of return for the project are both 12 percent, and its tax rate is 30 percent."

23. For Concept 1, the statement is correct regarding the effects on
    A. The real tax savings from depreciation, but incorrect regarding the real after-tax interest expense.
    B. The real after-tax interest expense, but incorrect regarding the real tax savings from depreciation.
    C. Both the real tax savings from depreciation and the real after-tax interest expense.
    D. Neither the real tax savings from depreciation nor the real after-tax interest expense.

24. For Concept 2, the statement is correct regarding
    A. Sensitivity analysis, but not correct regarding scenario analysis.
    B. Scenario analysis, but not correct regarding sensitivity analysis.
    C. Both sensitivity analysis and scenario analysis.
    D. Neither sensitivity analysis nor scenario analysis.

25. Are the statements identified as Concept 3 and Concept 4 correct?

	Concept 3	Concept 4
A.	No	No
B.	No	Yes
C.	Yes	No
D.	Yes	Yes

26. What are the after-tax operating cash flows in euros for the Fontenot Company?
    A. 70 in year 1 and 70 in year 2.
    B. 70 in year 1 and 85 in year 2.
    C. 85 in year 1 and 70 in year 2.
    D. 85 in year 1 and 85 in year 2.

27. What are the economic incomes in euros for the Fontenot Company?
    A. 9.11 in year 1 and 17.24 in year 2.
    B. 17.24 in year 1 and 9.11 in year 2.
    C. 17.76 in year 1 and 24.89 in year 2.
    D. 24.89 in year 1 and 17.76 in year 2.

28. The market value added (MVA) in euros for the Fontenot Company is closest to
    A. 38.87.
    B. 39.92.
    C. 43.65.
    D. 44.88.

The following information relates to Questions 29 through 34.

The capital budgeting committee for Laroche Industries is meeting. Laroche is a North American conglomerate that has several divisions. One of these divisions, Laroche Livery, operates a large fleet of vans. Laroche's management is evaluating whether it is optimal to operate new vans for two, three, or four years before replacing them. The managers have estimated the investment outlay, annual after-tax operating expenses, and after-tax salvage cash flows for each of the service lives. Because revenues and some operating costs are unaffected by the choice of service life, they were ignored in the analysis. Laroche Livery's opportunity cost of funds is 10 percent. The following table gives the cash flows in thousands of Canadian dollars (C$).

Service Life	Investment	Year 1	Year 2	Year 3	Year 4	Salvage
2 years	−40,000	−12,000	−15,000			20,000
3 years	−40,000	−12,000	−15,000	−20,000		17,000
4 years	−40,000	−12,000	−15,000	−20,000	−25,000	12,000

Schoeman Products, another division of Laroche, has evaluated several investment projects and now must choose the subset of them that fits within its C$40 million capital budget. The outlays and NPVs for the six projects follow. Schoeman cannot buy fractional projects and must buy all or none of a project. The currency amounts are in millions of Canadian dollars.

Project	Outlay	PV of Future Cash Flows	NPV
1	31	44	13
2	15	21	6
3	12	16.5	4.5
4	10	13	3
5	8	11	3
6	6	8	2

Schoeman wants to determine which subset of the six projects is optimal.

A final proposal comes from the division Society Services, which has an investment opportunity with a real option to invest further if conditions warrant. The crucial details are as follows:

The original project:

An outlay of C$190 million at time 0.

Cash flows of C$40 million per year for years 1–10 if demand is high.

Cash flows of C$20 million per year for years 1–10 if demand is low.

The optional expansion project:

An outlay of C$190 million at time 1.

Cash flows of C$40 million per year for years 2–10 if demand is high.

Cash flows of C$20 million per year for years 2–10 if demand is low.

Whether demand is high or low in years 1–10 will be revealed during the first year. The probability of high demand is 0.50, and the probability of low demand is 0.50.

The option to make the expansion investment depends on making the initial investment. If the initial investment is not made, the option to expand does not exist.

The required rate of return is 10 percent.

Society Services wants to evaluate its investment alternatives.

The internal auditor for Laroche Industries has made several suggestions for improving capital budgeting processes at the company. The internal auditor's suggestions are as follows:

Suggestion 1: "In order to put all capital budgeting proposals on an equal footing, the projects should all use the risk-free rate for the required rate of return."

Suggestion 2: "Because you cannot exercise both of them, you should not permit a given project to have both an abandonment option and an expansion/growth option."

Suggestion 3: "When rationing capital, it is better to choose the portfolio of investments that maximizes the company NPV than the portfolio that maximizes the company IRR."

Suggestion 4: "Project betas should be used for establishing the required rate of return whenever the project's beta is different from the company's beta."

29. What is the optimal service life for Laroche Livery's fleet of vans?
    A. Two years.
    B. Three years.
    C. Four years.
    D. Three and four years are equally attractive.

30. The optimal subset of the six projects that Schoeman is considering consists of which projects?
    A. 1 and 5.
    B. 2, 3, and 4.
    C. 2, 3, and 5.
    D. 2, 4, 5, and 6.

31. What is the NPV (C$ millions) of the original project for Society Services without considering the expansion option?
    A. −6.11.
    B. −5.66.
    C. 2.33.
    D. 5.58.

32. What is the NPV (C$ millions) of the optimal set of investment decisions for Society Services including the expansion option?
    A. 1.83.
    B. 6.34.
    C. 9.17.
    D. 12.68.

33. Should the capital budgeting committee accept the internal auditor's first and second suggestions?

	Suggestion 1	Suggestion 2
A.	No	No
B.	No	Yes
C.	Yes	No
D.	Yes	Yes

34. Should the capital budgeting committee accept the internal auditor's third and fourth suggestions?

	Suggestion 3	Suggestion 4
A.	No	No
B.	No	Yes
C.	Yes	No
D.	Yes	Yes

The following information relates to Questions 35 through 40.

Maximilian Böhm is reviewing several capital budgeting proposals from subsidiaries of his company. Although his reviews deal with several details that may seem like minutiae, the company places a premium on the care it exercises in making its investment decisions.

The first proposal is a project for Richie Express, which is investing $500,000, all in fixed capital, in a project that will have depreciation and operating income after taxes, respectively, of $40,000 and $20,000 each year for the next three years. Richie Express will sell the asset in three years, paying 30 percent taxes on any excess of the selling price over book value. The proposal indicates that a $647,500 terminal selling price will enable the company to earn a 15 percent internal rate of return on the investment. Böhm doubts that this terminal value estimate is correct.

Another proposal concerns Gasup Company, which does natural gas exploration. A new investment has been identified by the Gasup finance department with the following projected cash flows:

Investment outlays are $6 million immediately and $1 million at the end of the first year.

After-tax operating cash flows are $0.5 million at the end of the first year and $4 million at the end of each of the second, third, fourth, and fifth years. In addition, an after-tax outflow occurs at the end of the five-year project that has not been included in the operating cash flows: $5 million required for environmental cleanup.

The required rate of return on natural gas exploration is 18 percent.

The Gasup analyst is unsure about the calculation of the NPV and the IRR because the outlay is staged over two years.

Finally, Dominion Company is evaluating two mutually exclusive projects: The Pinto grinder involves an outlay of $100,000, annual after-tax operating cash flows of $45,000, an after-tax salvage value of $25,000, and a three-year life. The Bolten grinder has an outlay of $125,000, annual after-tax operating cash flows of $47,000, an after-tax salvage value of $20,000, and a four-year life. The required rate of return is 10 percent. The net present value (NPV) and equivalent annual annuity (EAA) of the Pinto grinder are $30,691 and $12,341, respectively. Whichever grinder is chosen, it will have to be replaced at the end of its service life. The analyst is unsure about which grinder should be chosen.

Böhm and his colleague Beth Goldberg have an extended conversation about capital budgeting issues. Goldberg makes two comments about real options:

1. "The abandonment option is valuable, but it should be exercised only when the abandonment value is above the amount of the original investment."

2. "If the cost of a real option is less than its value, this will increase the NPV of the investment project in which the real option is embedded."

Böhm also makes several comments about specific projects under consideration:

A. "The land and building were purchased five years ago for $10 million. This is the amount that should now be included in the fixed capital investment."

B. "We can improve the project's NPV by using the after-tax cost of debt as the discount rate. If we finance the project with 100 percent debt, this discount rate would be appropriate."

C. "It is generally safer to use the NPV than the IRR in making capital budgeting decisions. However, when evaluating mutually exclusive projects, if the projects have conventional cash flow patterns and the same investment outlays, it is acceptable to use either the NPV or IRR."

D. "You should not base a capital budgeting decision on its immediate impact on earnings per share (EPS)."

35. What terminal selling price is required for a 15 percent internal rate of return on the Richie project?
    A. $552,087.
    B. $588,028.
    C. $593,771.
    D. $625,839.

36. The NPV and IRR, respectively, of the Gasup Company investment are closest to

	NPV	IRR
A.	$509,600	21.4%.
B.	$509,600	31.3%.
C.	$946,700	21.4%.
D.	$946,700	31.3%.

37. Of the two grinders that the Dominion Company is evaluating, Böhm should recommend the
    A. Bolten grinder because its NPV is higher than the Pinto grinder NPV.
    B. Bolten grinder because its EAA is higher than the Pinto grinder EAA.
    C. Pinto grinder because its NPV is higher than the Bolten grinder NPV.
    D. Pinto grinder because its EAA is higher than the Bolten grinder EAA.

38. Are Goldberg's comments about real options correct?

	Comment 1: Abandonment Value	Comment 2: Increasing the NPV of the Investment Project
A.	No	No
B.	No	Yes
C.	Yes	No
D.	Yes	Yes

39. Is Böhm most likely correct regarding his

	Comment A: $10 million Capital Investment?	Comment B: Using the After-Tax Cost of Debt?
A.	No	No
B.	No	Yes
C.	Yes	No
D.	Yes	Yes

40. Is Böhm most likely correct regarding his

	Comment C: Acceptability of Using Either NPV or IRR?	Comment D: Immediate Impact on EPS?
A.	No	No
B.	No	Yes
C.	Yes	No
D.	Yes	Yes

The following information relates to Questions 41 through 46.

Barbara Simpson is a sell-side analyst with Smith Riccardi Securities. Simpson covers the pharmaceutical industry. One of the companies she follows, Bayonne Pharma, is evaluating a regional distribution center. The financial predictions for the project are as follows:

Fixed capital outlay is €1.50 billion.

Investment in net working capital is €0.40 billion.

Straight-line depreciation is over a six-year period with zero salvage value.

Project life is 12 years.

Additional annual revenues are €0.10 billion.

Annual cash operating expenses are reduced by €0.25 billion.

The capital equipment is sold for €0.50 billion in 12 years.

Tax rate is 40 percent.

Required rate of return is 12 percent.

Simpson is evaluating this investment to see whether it has the potential to affect Bayonne Pharma's stock price. Simpson estimates the NPV of the project to be €0.41 billion, which should increase the value of the company.

Simpson is evaluating the effects of other changes to her capital budgeting assumptions. She wants to know the effect of a switch from straight-line to accelerated depreciation on the company's operating income and the project's NPV. She also believes that the initial outlay might be much smaller than initially assumed. Specifically, she thinks the outlay for fixed capital might be €0.24 billion lower, with no change in salvage value.

When reviewing her work, Simpson's supervisor provides the following comments. "I note that you are relying heavily on the NPV approach to valuing the investment decision. I don't think you should use an IRR because of the multiple IRR problem that is likely to arise with the Bayonne Pharma project. However, the equivalent annual annuity would be a more appropriate measure to use for the project than the NPV. I suggest that you compute an EAA."

41. Simpson should estimate the after-tax operating cash flow for years 1–6 and 7–12, respectively, to be closest to

	Years 1–6	Years 7–12
A.	€0.31 billion	€0.21 billion.
B.	€0.31 billion	€0.25 billion.
C.	€0.35 billion	€0.21 billion.
D.	€0.35 billion	€0.25 billion.

42. Simpson should estimate the initial outlay and the terminal year non-operating cash flow, respectively, to be closest to

	Initial Outlay	Terminal Year Nonoperating Cash Flow
A.	€1.50 billion	€0.70 billion.
B.	€1.50 billion	€0.90 billion.
C.	€1.90 billion	€0.70 billion.
D.	€1.90 billion	€0.90 billion.

43. Is Simpson's estimate of the NPV of the project correct?
    A. Yes.
    B. No. The NPV is –€0.01 billion.
    C. No. The NPV is €0.34 billion.
    D. No. The NPV is €0.78 billion.

44. What effect would a switch from straight-line to accelerated depreciation have?
    A. Increase the NPV and decrease the first-year operating income after taxes.
    B. Increase the first-year operating income after taxes and decrease the NPV.
    C. Increase both the NPV and first-year operating income after taxes.
    D. Decrease both the NPV and first-year operating income after taxes.

45. If the outlay is lower by the amount that Simpson suggests, the project NPV should increase by an amount closest to which of the following figures?
    A. €0.09 billion.
    B. €0.14 billion.
    C. €0.17 billion.
    D. €0.24 billion.

46. How would you evaluate the comments by Simpson's supervisor about not using the IRR and about using the EAA?

	Comment about IRR	Comment about EAA
A.	Correct	Correct
B.	Correct	Incorrect
C.	Incorrect	Correct
D.	Incorrect	Incorrect

The following information relates to Questions 47 through 52.

Mun Hoe Yip is valuing Pure Corporation. Pure is a simple corporation that is going out of business in five years, distributing its income to creditors and bondholders as planned in the following financial statements. Pure has a 19 percent cost of equity, 8⅓ percent before-tax cost of debt, 12 percent weighted average cost of capital, and 40 percent tax rate; it maintains a 50 percent debt-to-value ratio.

Yip is valuing the company using the basic capital budgeting method as well as other methods, such as EP, residual income, and claims valuation. Yip's research assistant, Linda Robinson, makes three observations about the analysis.

Observation 1: "The present value of the company's economic income should be equal to the present value of the discounted cash flows in the basic capital budgeting approach."

Observation 2: "The economic income each year is equal to the cash flow minus the economic depreciation."

Observation 3: "The market value added is the present value of the company's economic profit (EP), which equals the net worth of 77,973."

Year	0	1	2	3	4	5
Balance Sheets:						
Assets	200,000	160,000	120,000	80,000	40,000	0
Liabilities	122,027	107,671	88,591	64,222	33,929	0
Net worth	77,973	52,329	31,409	15,778	6,071	0
Income Statements:						
Sales		180,000	200,000	220,000	240,000	200,000
Variable cash expenses		90,000	100,000	110,000	120,000	100,000
Fixed cash expenses		20,000	20,000	20,000	20,000	20,000
Depreciation		40,000	40,000	40,000	40,000	40,000

Year	0	1	2	3	4	5
EBIT		30,000	40,000	50,000	60,000	40,000
Interest expense		10,169	8,973	7,383	5,352	2,827
EBT		19,831	31,027	42,617	54,648	37,173
Taxes at 40%		7,932	12,411	17,047	21,859	14,869
Net income before salvage		11,899	18,616	25,570	32,789	22,304
After-tax salvage value						12,000
Net income		11,899	18,616	25,570	32,789	34,304
Statements of Cash Flows:						
Operating cash flows						
Net income		11,899	18,616	25,570	32,789	34,304
Depreciation		40,000	40,000	40,000	40,000	40,000
Total		51,899	58,616	65,570	72,789	74,304
Financing cash flows:						
Debt repayment		14,357	19,080	24,369	30,293	33,929
Dividends/repurchases		37,542	39,536	41,201	42,496	40,375
Total		−51,899	−58,616	−65,570	−72,789	−74,304
Investing cash flows:	0	0	0	0	0	0
Total cash flows:	0	0	0	0	0	0

47. Economic income during year one is closest to
    A. 23,186.
    B. 29,287.
    C. 46,101.
    D. 51,899.

48. What is EP during year 1?
    A. −12,101.
    B. −6,000.
    C. 6,000.
    D. 13,542.

49. What is residual income during year 1?
    A. −2,916.
    B. 2,542.
    C. 8,653.
    D. 14,815.

50. What is the value of equity at time 0?
    A. 29,287.
    B. 44,055.
    C. 77,973.
    D. 122,027.

51. Are Robinson's first two observations correct?

	Observation 1	Observation 2
A.	No	No
B.	No	Yes
C.	Yes	No
D.	Yes	Yes

52. Which of the following would be Yip's most appropriate response to Robinson's third observation?
   A. "Your observation is correct."
   B. "The market value added is not equal to the present value of EP, although the market value of equity is equal to 77,973."
   C. "The market value added is equal to the present value of EP, which in this case is 44,055."
   D. "The market value added is not equal to the present value of EP, and market value added is equal to 44,055."

CHAPTER 3

COST OF CAPITAL

Yves Courtois, CFA

KPMG Corporate Finance
Luxembourg

Gene C. Lai

Washington State University
Pullman, Washington

Pamela Peterson Drake, CFA

James Madison University
Harrisonburg, Virginia

LEARNING OUTCOMES

After completing this chapter, you will be able to do the following:

- Determine and interpret the weighted average cost of capital (WACC) of a company, and explain the adjustments to it that an analyst should make in developing a cost of capital for a specific project.
- Describe the role of taxes in the cost of capital from the different capital sources.
- Describe alternative methods of calculating the weights used in the WACC, including the use of the company's target capital structure.
- Explain the analyst's concern with the marginal cost of capital in evaluating investment projects, and explain the use of the marginal cost of capital and the investment opportunity schedule in determining the optimal capital budget for a company.
- Explain the marginal cost of capital's role in determining the net present value of a project.
- Calculate and analyze the cost of fixed-rate debt capital using the yield-to-maturity approach and the debt-rating approach.
- Calculate the cost of noncallable, nonconvertible preferred stock.

- Calculate and analyze the cost of equity capital using the capital asset pricing model approach, the dividend discount approach, and the bond yield plus risk premium approach.
- Calculate an unlevered beta using the pure-play method and use this unlevered beta to estimate a levered beta for a project or company.
- Explain the country risk premium in the estimation of the cost of equity for a company situated in a developing market.
- Describe the marginal cost of capital schedule, explain why it may be upward sloping with respect to additional capital, and calculate and interpret its break points.
- Explain and demonstrate the correct treatment of flotation costs.

1. INTRODUCTION

A company grows by making investments that are expected to increase revenues and profits. The company acquires the capital or funds necessary to make such investments by borrowing or using funds from owners. By applying this capital to investments with long-term benefits, the company is producing value today, but how much value? The answer depends not only on the investments' expected future cash flows but also on the cost of the funds. Borrowing is not costless. Neither is using owners' funds.

The cost of this capital is an important ingredient both in investment decision making by the company's management and in the valuation of the company by investors. If a company invests in projects that produce a return in excess of the cost of capital, the company has created value; in contrast, if the company invests in projects whose returns are less than the cost of capital, the company has actually destroyed value. Therefore, the estimation of the cost of capital is a central issue in corporate financial management. For the analyst seeking to evaluate a company's investment program and its competitive position, an accurate estimate of a company's cost of capital is important as well.

Cost of capital estimation is a challenging task. As we have already implied, the cost of capital is not observable but rather must be estimated. Arriving at a cost of capital estimate requires a host of assumptions and estimates. Another challenge is that the cost of capital that is appropriately applied to a specific investment depends on the characteristics of that investment: The riskier the investment's cash flows, the greater its cost of capital will be. In reality, a company must estimate project-specific costs of capital. What is often done, however, is to estimate the cost of capital for the company as a whole and then adjust this overall corporate cost of capital upward or downward to reflect the risk of the contemplated project relative to the company's average project.

This chapter is organized as follows: In the next section, we introduce the cost of capital and its basic computation. Section 3 presents a selection of methods for estimating the costs of the various sources of capital, and Section 4 discusses issues an analyst faces in using the cost of capital. Section 5 summarizes the chapter.

2. COST OF CAPITAL

The **cost of capital** is the rate of return that the suppliers of capital—bondholders and owners—require as compensation for their contribution of capital. Another way of looking at the cost of capital is that it is the opportunity cost of funds for the suppliers of capital: A potential supplier of capital will not voluntarily invest in a company unless its return meets or exceeds what the supplier could earn elsewhere in an investment of comparable risk.

A company typically has several alternatives for raising capital, including issuing equity, debt, and instruments that share the characteristics of debt and equity. Each source selected becomes a component of the company's funding and has a cost (required rate of return) that may be called a **component cost of capital**. Because we are using the cost of capital in the evaluation of investment opportunities, we are dealing with a *marginal* cost—what it would cost to raise additional funds for the potential investment project. Therefore, the cost of capital that the investment analyst is concerned with is a marginal cost.

Let us focus on the cost of capital for the entire company (later we will address how to adjust that for a specific project). The cost of capital of a company is the required rate of return that investors demand for the average-risk investment of a company. The most common way to estimate this required rate of return is to calculate the marginal cost of each of the various sources of capital and then calculate a weighted average of these costs. This weighted average is referred to as the **weighted average cost of capital (WACC)**. The WACC is also referred to as the **marginal cost of capital** (**MCC**) because it is the cost that a company incurs for additional capital. The weights in this weighted average are the proportions of the various sources of capital that the company uses to support its investment program. Therefore, the WACC, in its most general terms, is

$$\text{WACC} = w_d r_d (1 - t) + w_p r_p + w_e r_e \tag{3-1}$$

where

w_d = proportion of debt that the company uses when it raises new funds

r_d = before-tax marginal cost of debt

t = company's marginal tax rate

w_p = proportion of preferred stock the company uses when it raises new funds

r_p = marginal cost of preferred stock

w_e = proportion of equity that the company uses when it raises new funds

r_e = marginal cost of equity

EXAMPLE 3-1   Computing the Weighted Average Cost of Capital

Assume that ABC Corporation has the following capital structure: 30 percent debt, 10 percent preferred stock, and 60 percent common stock. ABC Corporation wishes to maintain these proportions as it raises new funds. Its before-tax cost of debt is 8 percent, its cost of preferred stock is 10 percent, and its cost of equity is 15 percent. If the company's marginal tax rate is 40 percent, what is ABC's weighted average cost of capital?

Solution

The weighed average cost of capital is

$$\text{WACC} = (0.3)(0.08)(1 - 0.40) + (0.1)(0.1) + (0.6)(0.15)$$
$$= 11.44 \text{ percent}$$

There are important points concerning the calculation of the WACC, as shown in Equation 3-1, that the analyst must be familiar with. The next two sections address two key issues: taxes and the selection of weights.

2.1. Taxes and the Cost of Capital

Notice that in Equation 3-1 we adjust the expected before-tax cost on new debt financing, r_d, by a factor of $(1 - t)$. In the United States and many other tax jurisdictions, the interest on debt financing is a deduction to arrive at taxable income. Taking the tax deductibility of interest as the base case, we adjust the pretax cost of debt for this tax shield. Multiplying r_d by $(1 - t)$ results in an estimate of the after-tax cost of debt.

For example, suppose a company pays €1 million in interest on its €10 million of debt. The cost of this debt is not €1 million because this interest expense reduces taxable income by €1 million, resulting in a lower tax. If the company is subject to a tax rate of 40 percent, this €1 million of interest costs the company (€1 million)$(1 - 0.4)$ = €0.6 million because the interest reduces the company's tax bill by €0.4 million. In this case, the before-tax cost of debt is 10 percent, whereas the after-tax cost of debt is (€0.6 million)/(€10 million) = 6 percent.

Estimating the cost of common equity capital is more challenging than estimating the cost of debt capital. Debt capital involves a stated legal obligation on the part of the company to pay interest and to repay the principal on the borrowing. Equity entails no such obligation. Estimating the cost of conventional preferred equity is rather straightforward because the dividend is generally stated and fixed, but estimating the cost of common equity is challenging. There are several methods available for estimating the cost of common equity, and we discuss two in this chapter. The first method uses the capital asset pricing model (CAPM), and the second method uses the dividend discount model, which is based on discounted cash flows. No matter the method, there is no need to make any adjustment in the cost of equity for taxes because the payments to owners, whether in the form of dividends or the return on capital, are not tax deductible for the company.

EXAMPLE 3-2   Incorporating the Effect of Taxes on the Costs of Capital

Jorge Ricard, a financial analyst, is estimating the costs of capital for the Zeale Corporation. In the process of this estimation, Ricard has estimated the before-tax costs of capital for Zeale's debt and equity as 4 percent and 6 percent, respectively. What are the after-tax costs of debt and equity if Zeale's marginal tax rate is

1. 30 percent?
2. 48 percent?

Solutions

	Marginal Tax Rate	After-Tax Cost of Debt	After-Tax Cost of Equity
1.	30 percent	$0.04(1 - 0.30) = 2.80$ percent	6 percent
2.	48 percent	$0.04(1 - 0.48) = 2.08$ percent	6 percent

Note: There is no adjustment for taxes in the case of equity; the before-tax cost of equity is equal to the after-tax cost of equity.

2.2. Weights of the Weighted Average

How do we determine what weights to use? Ideally, we want to use the proportion of each source of capital that the company would use in the project or company. If we assume that a company has a target capital structure and raises capital consistent with this target, we should use this target capital structure. The **target capital structure** is the capital structure that a company is striving to obtain.[1] If we know the company's target capital structure, then, of course, we should use this in our analysis. Someone outside the company, however, such as an analyst, typically does not know the target capital structure and must estimate it using one of several approaches:

1. *Method 1:* Assume the company's current capital structure, at market value weights for the components, represents the company's target capital structure.
2. *Method 2:* Examine trends in the company's capital structure or statements by management regarding capital structure policy to infer the target capital structure.
3. *Method 3:* Use averages of comparable companies' capital structures as the target capital structure.

In the absence of knowledge of a company's target capital structure, we may take Method 1 as the baseline. Note that in applying Method 3, we use unweighted, arithmetic average, as is often done for simplicity. An alternative is to calculate a weighted average, which would give more weight to larger companies.

Suppose we are using the company's current capital structure as a proxy for the target capital structure. In this case, we use the market value of the different capital sources in the calculation of these proportions. For example, assume a company has the following market values for its capital:

Bonds outstanding	$ 5 million
Preferred stock	1 million
Common stock	14 million
Total capital	$20 million

The weights that we apply would be

$$w_d = 0.25$$
$$w_p = 0.05$$
$$w_e = 0.70$$

Example 3-3 illustrates the estimation of weights. Note that a simple way of transforming a debt-to-equity ratio (D/E) into a weight—that is, $D/(D+E)$—is to divide D/E by $(1 + D/E)$.

---

[1]In the chapter on capital structure and leverage, we will discuss the capital structure decision in greater detail, including a look at how it relates to the value of the company.

EXAMPLE 3-3   Estimating the Proportions of Capital

Fin Anziell is a financial analyst with Analytiker Firma. Anziell is in the process of esti-mating the cost of capital of Gewicht GmbH. The following information is provided:

Gewicht GmbH
Market value of debt   €50 million
Market value of equity   €60 million

Primary competitors and their capital structures (in millions):

Competitor	Market Value of Debt	Market Value of Equity
A	€25	€50
B	€101	€190
C	£40	£60

What are Gewicht's proportions of debt and equity that Anziell would use if esti-mating these proportions using the company's

1. Current capital structure?
2. Competitors' capital structure?

Suppose Gewicht announces that a debt-to-equity ratio of 0.7 reflects its target capital structure.

3. What weights should Anziell use in the cost-of-capital calculations?

Solution to 1

Current capital structure

$$w_d = \frac{€50 \text{ million}}{€50 \text{ million} + €60 \text{ million}} = 0.4545$$

$$w_e = \frac{€60 \text{ million}}{€50 \text{ million} + €60 \text{ million}} = 0.5454$$

Solution to 2

Competitors' capital structure[2]

$$w_d = \frac{\left(\frac{€25}{€25 + €50}\right) + \left(\frac{€101}{€101 + €190}\right) + \left(\frac{£40}{£40 + £60}\right)}{3} = 0.3601$$

---

[2]These weights represent the arithmetic average of the three companies' debt proportion and equity pro-portion, respectively. If instead we chose to use a weighted average, we would calculate the debt propor-tion as the sum of the debt for all three companies, divided by the sum of the total capital for all three; we would calculate the equity proportion in the same manner. The weighted average proportions are 0.3562 and 0.6438, respectively.

$$w_e = \frac{\left(\dfrac{€50}{€25 + €50}\right) + \left(\dfrac{€190}{€101 + €190}\right) + \left(\dfrac{£60}{£40 + £60}\right)}{3} = 0.6399$$

Solution to 3

A debt-to-equity ratio of 0.7 represents a weight on debt of $0.7/1.7 = 0.4118$ so that $w_d = 0.4118$ and $w_e = 1 - 0.4118 = 0.5882$. These would be the preferred weights to use in a cost-of-capital calculation.

2.3. Applying the Cost of Capital to Capital Budgeting and Security Valuation

With some insight now into the calculation of the cost of capital, let us continue to improve our understanding of the roles it plays in financial analysis. A chief use of the marginal cost of capital estimate is in capital budgeting decision making. What role does the marginal cost of capital play in a company's investment program, and how do we adapt it when we need to evaluate a specific investment project?

A company's marginal cost of capital (MCC) may increase as additional capital is raised, whereas returns to a company's investment opportunities are generally believed to decrease as the company makes additional investments, as represented by the **investment opportunity schedule (IOS)**.[3] We show this relation in Exhibit 3-1, graphing the upward-sloping marginal cost of capital schedule against the downward-sloping investment opportunity schedule. In the context of a company's investment decision, the optimal capital budget is the amount of capital raised and invested at which the marginal cost of capital is equal to the marginal return from investing. In other words, the optimal capital budget occurs when the marginal cost of capital intersects with the investment opportunity schedule as seen in Exhibit 3-1.

EXHIBIT 3-1   Optimal Investment Decision

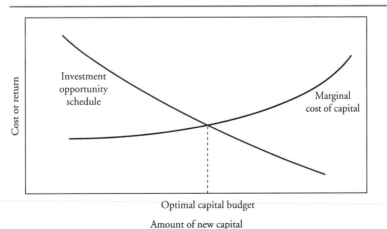

---

[3]The investment opportunity schedule originates with Fisher's production opportunities (Fisher, 1930) and was adapted to capital budgeting by John Hirshleifer (1958).

The relation between the MCC and the IOS provides a broad picture of the basic decision-making problem of a company. However, we are often interested in valuing an individual project or even a portion of a company, such as a division or product line. In these applications, we are interested in the cost of capital for the project, product, or division as opposed to the cost of capital for the company overall. The cost of capital in these applications should reflect the riskiness of the future cash flows of the project, product, or division. For an average-risk project, the opportunity cost of capital is the company's WACC. If the systematic risk of the project is above or below average relative to the company's current portfolio of projects, an upward or downward adjustment, respectively, is made to the company's WACC. Companies may take an ad hoc or a systematic approach to making such adjustments. The discussion of a systematic approach is a somewhat advanced topic that we defer to Section 4.1.

The WACC or MCC corresponding to the average risk of the company, adjusted appropriately for the risk of a given project, plays a role in capital budgeting decision making based on the **net present value (NPV)** of that project. Recall from the capital budgeting chapter that the NPV is the present value of all the project cash flows. It is useful to think of it as the difference between the present value of the cash inflows, discounted at the opportunity cost of capital applicable to the specific project, and the present value of the cash outflows, discounted using that same opportunity cost of capital:

$$NPV = \text{Present value of inflows} - \text{Present value of outflows}$$

If an investment's NPV is positive, the company should undertake the project. If we choose to use the company's WACC in the calculation of the NPV of a project, we are assuming that the project

- Has the same risk as the average-risk project of the company, and
- Will have a constant target capital structure throughout its useful life.[4]

These may not be realistic or appropriate assumptions and are potential drawbacks to using the company's WACC in valuing projects. However, alternative approaches are subject to drawbacks as well, and the approach outlined has wide acceptance.[5]

For the analyst, the second key use of the marginal cost of capital is in security valuation using any one of several discounted cash flow valuation models available.[6] For a particular valuation model, if these cash flows are cash flows to the company's suppliers of capital (that is, free cash flow to the firm), the analyst uses the weighted average cost of capital of the company in the valuation.[7] If these cash flows are strictly those belonging to the company's

---

[4]WACC is estimated using fixed proportions of equity and debt. The NPV method assumes a constant required rate of return, whereas a fluctuating capital structure would cause WACC to fluctuate. The importance of this issue is demonstrated by Miles and Ezzell (1980).

[5]See the chapter on capital budgeting for a discussion.

[6]See Stowe, Robinson, Pinto, and McLeavey (2002) for a presentation of such models.

[7]**Free cash flow to the firm (FCFF)** is the cash flow available to the company's suppliers of capital after all operating expenses (including taxes) have been paid and necessary investments in working capital (e.g., inventory) and fixed capital (e.g., plant and equipment) have been made.

owners, such as the free cash flow to equity, or dividends, the analyst uses the cost of equity capital to find the present value of these flows.[8]

In the next section, we discuss how an analyst may approach the calculation of the component costs of capital, focusing on debt, preferred stock, and common equity.

3. COSTS OF THE DIFFERENT SOURCES OF CAPITAL

Each source of capital has a different cost because of the differences among the sources, such as seniority, contractual commitments, and potential value as a tax shield. We focus on the costs of three primary sources of capital: debt, preferred equity, and common equity.

3.1. Cost of Debt

The **cost of debt** is the cost of debt financing to a company when it issues a bond or takes out a bank loan. We discuss two methods to estimate the before-tax cost of debt, r_d: the yield-to-maturity approach and debt-rating approach.

3.1.1. Yield-to-Maturity Approach

The **yield to maturity (YTM)** is the annual return that an investor earns on a bond if the investor purchases the bond today and holds it until maturity. In other words, it is the yield, r_d, that equates the present value of the bond's promised payments to its market price:

$$P_0 = \frac{PMT_1}{\left(1 + \frac{r_d}{2}\right)} + \ldots + \frac{PMT_n}{\left(1 + \frac{r_d}{2}\right)^n} + \frac{FV}{\left(1 + \frac{r_d}{2}\right)^n} = \left(\sum_{t=1}^{n} \frac{PMT_i}{\left(1 + \frac{r_d}{2}\right)^t}\right) + \frac{FV}{\left(1 + \frac{r_d}{2}\right)^n} \quad (3\text{-}2)$$

where

P_0 = current market price of the bond

PMT_t = interest payment in period t

r_d = yield to maturity[9]

n = number of periods remaining to maturity

FV = maturity value of the bond

This valuation equation assumes that the bond pays semiannual interest and that any intermediate cash flows (in this case, the interest prior to maturity) are reinvested at the rate $r_d/2$.

Example 3-4 illustrates the calculation of the after-tax cost of debt.

---

[8]**Free cash flow to equity (FCFE)** is the cash flow available to holders of the company's common equity after all operating expenses, interest, and principal payments have been paid and necessary investments in working capital and fixed capital have been made. See Stowe, et al. for more details on FCFF and FCFE and valuation models based on those concepts.

[9]r_d is expressed as an annual rate and is divided by the number of payment periods per year. Because most corporate bonds pay semiannual interest, we divide r_d by 2 in this calculation. The interest payment for each period thus corresponds with the bond's semiannual coupon payment.

EXAMPLE 3-4   Calculating the After-Tax Cost of Debt

Valence Industries issues a bond to finance a new project. It offers a 10-year, 5 percent semiannual coupon bond. Upon issue, the bond sells at $1,025. What is Valence's before-tax cost of debt? If Valence's marginal tax rate is 35 percent, what is Valence's after-tax cost of debt?

Solution

Given:

$PV = \$1,025$

$FV = \$1,000$

$PMT = 5$ percent of $1,000 \div 2 = \$25$

$n = 10 \times 2 = 20$

$$\$1,025 = \left(\sum_{t=1}^{20} \frac{\$25}{(1 + i)} \right) + \frac{\$1,000}{(1 + i)^{20}}$$

Use a financial calculator to solve for i, the six-month yield. Because $i = 2.342$ percent, the before-tax cost of debt is $r_d = 2.342$ percent $\times 2 = 4.684$ percent, and Valence's after-tax cost of debt is $r_d (1 - t) = 0.04684 (1 - 0.35) = 0.03045$, or 3.045 percent.

3.1.2. Debt-Rating Approach   When a reliable current market price for a company's debt is not available, the **debt-rating approach** can be used to estimate the before-tax cost of debt. Based on a company's debt rating, we estimate the before-tax cost of debt by using the yield on comparably rated bonds for maturities that closely match that of the company's existing debt.

Suppose a company's capital structure includes debt with an average maturity (or duration) of 10 years and the company's marginal tax rate is 35 percent. If the company's rating is AAA and the yield on debt with the same debt rating and similar maturity (or duration) is 4 percent, the company's after-tax cost of debt is[10]

$$r_d(1 - t) = 4 \text{ percent}(1 - 0.35)$$
$$= 2.6 \text{ percent}$$

A consideration when using this approach is that debt ratings are ratings of the debt issue itself, with the issuer being only one of the considerations. Other factors, such as debt seniority and security, also affect ratings and yields; so care must be taken to consider the likely type of debt to be issued by the company in determining the comparable debt rating and yield. The debt-rating approach is a simple example of pricing on the basis of valuation-relevant characteristics, which in bond markets has been known as evaluated pricing or **matrix pricing**.

---

[10]Duration is a more precise measure of a bond's interest rate sensitivity than maturity.

3.1.3. Issues in Estimating the Cost of Debt

3.1.3.1. Fixed-Rate Debt Versus Floating-Rate Debt Up to now, we have assumed that the interest on debt is a fixed amount each period. We can observe market yields of the company's existing debt or market yields of debt of similar risk in estimating the before-tax cost of debt. However, the company may also issue floating-rate debt in which the interest rate adjusts periodically according to a prescribed index, such as the prime rate or LIBOR, over the life of the instrument.

Estimating the cost of a floating-rate security is difficult because the cost of this form of capital over the long term depends not only on the current yields but also on the future yields. The analyst may use the current term structure of interest rates and term structure theory to assign an average cost to such instruments.

3.1.3.2. Debt with Optionlike Features How should an analyst determine the cost of debt when the company uses debt with optionlike features, such as call, conversion, or put provisions? Clearly, options affect the value of debt. For example, a callable bond would have a yield greater than a similar noncallable bond of the same issuer because bondholders want to be compensated for the call risk associated with the bond. In a similar manner, the put feature of a bond, which provides the investor with an option to sell the bond back to the issuer at a predetermined price, has the effect of lowering the yield on a bond below that of a similar nonputable bond.

If the company already has outstanding debt that incorporates optionlike features that the analyst believes are representative of the future debt issuance of the company, the analyst may simply use the yield to maturity on such debt in estimating the cost of debt.

If the analyst believes that the company will add or remove option features in future debt issuance, the analyst can make market value adjustments to the current YTM to reflect the value of such additions and/or deletions. The technology for such adjustments is an advanced topic that is outside the scope of this chapter.[11]

3.1.3.3. Nonrated Debt If a company does not have any debt outstanding or if the yields on the company's existing debt are not available, the analyst may not always be able to use the yield on similarly rated debt securities. It may be the case that the company does not have rated bonds. Though researchers offer approaches for estimating a company's "synthetic" debt rating based on financial ratios, these methods are imprecise because debt ratings incorporate not only financial ratios but also information about the particular bond issue and the issuer that are not captured in financial ratios.

3.1.3.4. Leases A lease is a contractual obligation that can substitute for other forms of borrowing. This is true whether the lease is an operating lease or a capital lease, though only the capital lease is represented as a liability on the company's balance sheet.[12] If the company uses leasing as a source of capital, the cost of these leases should be included in the cost of capital. The cost of this form of borrowing is similar to that of the company's other long-term borrowing.

---

[11]See, for example, Fabozzi (2004), for an introduction. Fabozzi discusses the estimation of an option-adjusted spread (OAS) to price the call option feature of a callable bond.

[12]In the United States, an operating lease is distinguished from a capital lease in Statement of Financial Accounting Standards No. 13, *Accounting for Leases* (FASB, November 1976). (IAS No. 17 similarly

3.2. Cost of Preferred Stock

The **cost of preferred stock** is the cost that a company has committed to pay preferred stockholders as a preferred dividend when it issues preferred stock. In the case of nonconvertible, noncallable preferred stock that has a fixed dividend rate and no maturity date (**fixed rate perpetual preferred stock**), we can use the formula for the value of a preferred stock:

$$P_p = \frac{D_p}{r_p}$$

where

P_p = current preferred stock price per share

D_p = preferred stock dividend per share

r_P = cost of preferred stock

We can rearrange this equation to solve for the cost of preferred stock:

$$r_p = \frac{D_p}{P_p} \tag{3-3}$$

Therefore, the cost of preferred stock is the preferred stock's dividend per share divided by the current preferred stock's price per share. Unlike interest on debt, the dividend on preferred stock is not tax deductible by the company; therefore, there is no adjustment to the cost for taxes.[13]

A preferred stock may have a number of features that affect the yield and hence the cost of preferred stock. These features include a call option, cumulative dividends, participating dividends, adjustable-rate dividends, or convertibility into common stock. When estimating a yield based on current yields of the company's preferred stock, we must make appropriate adjustments for the effects of these features on the yield of an issue. For example, if the company has callable, convertible preferred stock outstanding, yet it is expected that the company will issue only noncallable, nonconvertible preferred stock in the future, we would have to either use the current yields on comparable companies' noncallable, nonconvertible preferred stock or estimate the yield on preferred equity using methods outside the scope of this chapter.[14]

---

distinguishes between operating and finance leases, another term for capital-type leases.) These two forms of leases are distinguished on the basis of ownership transference, the existence of a bargain purchase option, the term of the lease relative to the economic life of the asset, and the present value of the lease payments relative to the value of the asset. In either case, however, the lease obligation is a form of borrowing, even though it is only in the case of a capital lease that the obligation appears as a liability on the company's balance sheet. The discount rate applied in the valuation of a capital lease is the rate of borrowing at the time of the lease commencement; therefore, it is reasonable to apply the company's long-term borrowing rate when estimating the cost of capital for leasing.

[13]This is not to be confused, however, with the dividends received deduction, which reduces the effective tax on intercorporate preferred dividends received.

[14]A method for estimating this yield involves first estimating the option-adjusted spread (OAS). For further information on the OAS, see, for example, Fabozzi (2004).

EXAMPLE 3-5   Calculating the Cost of Preferred Equity

Alcoa, Inc. has one class of preferred stock outstanding, a $3.75 cumulative preferred stock, for which there are 546,024 shares outstanding.[15] If the price of this stock is $72, what is the estimate of Alcoa's cost of preferred equity?

Solution

The cost of Alcoa's preferred stock = $3.75/$72.00 = 5.21 percent.

EXAMPLE 3-6   Choosing the Best Estimate of the Cost of Preferred Equity

Wim Vanistendael is finance director of De Gouden Tulip N.V., a leading Dutch flower producer and distributor. He has been asked by the CEO to calculate the cost of preferred equity and has recently obtained the following information:

- The issue price of preferred stock was €3.5 million and the preferred dividend is 5 percent.
- If the company issued new preferred stock today, the preferred coupon rate would be 6.5 percent.
- The company's marginal tax rate is 30.5 percent.

What is the cost of preferred equity for De Gouden Tulip N.V.?

Solution

If De Gouden Tulip were to issue new preferred stock today, the coupon rate would be close to 6.5 percent. The current terms thus prevail over the past terms when evaluating the actual cost of preferred stock. The cost of preferred stock for De Gouden Tulip is therefore 6.5 percent. Because preferred dividends offer no tax shield, there is no adjustment made based on the marginal tax rate.

3.3. Cost of Common Equity

The cost of common equity, r_e, usually referred to simply as the cost of equity, is the rate of return required by a company's common shareholders. A company may increase common equity through the reinvestment of earnings—that is, retained earnings—or through the issuance of new shares of stock.

---

[15]Alcoa Annual Report 2004, footnote R, p. 56.

As discussed earlier, the estimation of the cost of equity is challenging because of the uncertain nature of the future cash flows in terms of the amount and timing. Commonly used approaches for estimating the cost of equity include the capital asset pricing model, the dividend discount model, and the bond yield plus risk premium method.

3.3.1. Capital Asset Pricing Model Approach   In the capital asset pricing model (CAPM) approach, we use the basic relationship from the capital asset pricing model theory that the expected return on a stock, $E(R_i)$, is the sum of the risk-free rate of interest, R_F, and a premium for bearing the stock's market risk, $\beta_i(R_M - R_F)$:

$$E(R_i) = R_F + \beta_i\left[E(R_M) - R_F\right] \tag{3-4}$$

where

β_i = return sensitivity of stock i to changes in the market return

$E(R_M)$ = expected return on the market

$E(R_M) - R_F$ = expected market risk premium

A risk-free asset is defined here as an asset that has no default risk. A common proxy for the risk-free rate is the yield on a default-free government debt instrument. In general, the selection of the appropriate risk-free rate should be guided by the duration of projected cash flows. If we are evaluating a project with an estimated useful life of 10 years, we may want to use the rate on the 10-year Treasury bond.

EXAMPLE 3-7   Using the CAPM to Estimate the Cost of Equity

Valence Industries wants to know its cost of equity. Its chief financial officer (CFO) believes the risk-free rate is 5 percent, equity risk premium is 7 percent, and Valence's equity beta is 1.5. What is Valence's cost of equity using the CAPM approach?

Solution

$$\text{Cost of common stock} = 5 \text{ percent} + 1.5(7 \text{ percent})$$
$$= 15.5 \text{ percent}$$

The expected market risk premium, $E(R_M - R_F)$, is the premium that investors demand for investing in a market portfolio relative to the risk-free rate. When using the CAPM to estimate the cost of equity, in practice we typically estimate beta relative to an equity market index. In that case, the market premium estimate we are using is actually an estimate of the **equity risk premium (ERP)**.

An alternative to the CAPM to accommodate risks that may not be captured by the market portfolio alone is a multifactor model that incorporates factors that may be other sources of **priced risk** (risk for which investors demand compensation for bearing), including macroeconomic factors and company-specific factors. In general

$$E(R_i) = R_F + \beta_{i1}(\text{Factor risk premium})_1 + \beta_{i2}(\text{Factor risk premium})_2$$
$$+ \ldots + \beta_{ij}(\text{Factor risk premium})_j \tag{3-5}$$

where

β_{ij} = stock i's sensitivity to changes in the jth factor

(Factor risk premium)$_j$ = expected risk premium for the jth factor

The basic idea behind these multifactor models is that the CAPM beta may not capture all the risks, especially in a global context, which include inflation, business cycle, interest rate, exchange rate, and default risks.[16,17]

There are several ways to estimate the equity risk premium, though there is no general agreement as to the best approach. The three we discuss are the historical equity risk premium approach, the dividend discount model approach, and the survey approach.

The **historical equity risk premium approach** is a well-established approach based on the assumption that the realized equity risk premium observed over a long period of time is a good indicator of the expected equity risk premium. This approach requires compiling historical data to find the average rate of return of a country's market portfolio and the average rate of return for the risk-free rate in that country. For example, an analyst might use the historical returns to the TOPIX Index to estimate the risk premium for Japanese equities. The exceptional bull market observed during the second half of the 1990s and the bursting of the technology bubble that followed during the years 2000–2002 remind us that the time period for such estimates should cover complete market cycles.

Elroy Dimson, Paul Marsh, and Mike Staunton conducted an analysis of the equity risk premiums observed in markets located in 16 countries, including the United States, over the period 1900–2002.[18] These researchers found that the annualized U.S. equity risk premium relative to U.S. Treasury bills was 5.3 percent (geometric mean) and 7.2 percent (arithmetic mean). They also found that the annualized U.S. equity risk premium relative to bonds was 4.4 percent (geometric mean) and 6.4 percent (arithmetic mean).[19] Note that the arithmetic mean is greater than the geometric mean as a result of the significant volatility of the observed market rate of return and of the observed risk-free rate. Under the assumption of an unchanging distribution of returns through time, the arithmetic mean is the unbiased estimate of the expected single-period equity risk premium, but the geometric mean better reflects growth rate over multiple periods.[20] In Exhibit 3-2 we provide historical estimates of the equity risk premium for 16 developed markets from Dimson, Marsh, and Staunton's study.

To illustrate the historical method as applied in the CAPM, suppose that we use the historical geometric mean for U.S. equity of 4.8 percent to value Citibank Inc. (NYSE: C) as

---

[16]An example of the multifactor model is the three-factor Fama and French model [Fama and French (1992)], which includes factors for the market, equity capitalization, and the ratio of book value of equity to the market value of equity.

[17]These models are discussed in more detail by Bruner, Conroy, Li, O'Halloran, and Palacios Lleras (2003) and by Fama and French (2004).

[18]Dimson, Marsh, and Staunton (2003).

[19]Siegel (2005) presents a longer time series of market returns, covering the period from 1802 through 2004, and observes an equity return of 6.82 percent and an equity risk premium in the range of 3.31 to 5.36 percent. The range depends on the method of calculation (compounded or arithmetic) and the benchmark (bonds or bills).

[20]Aside from the method of averaging (geometric versus arithmetic), estimates of the historical equity risk premium differ depending on the assumed investment horizon (short versus intermediate versus long), whether conditional on some variable or unconditional, whether U.S. or global markets are examined, the source of the data, the period observed, and whether nominal or real returns are estimated.

EXHIBIT 3-2   Equity Risk Premiums Relative to Bonds (1900–2001)

Country	Mean (%)	
	Geometric	Arithmetic
Australia	6.3	7.9
Belgium	2.8	4.7
Canada	4.2	5.7
Denmark	1.8	3.1
France	4.6	6.7
Germany	6.3	9.6
Ireland	3.1	4.5
Italy	4.6	8.0
Japan	5.9	10.0
The Netherlands	4.4	6.4
South Africa	5.4	7.1
Spain	2.2	4.1
Sweden	4.9	7.1
Switzerland	2.4	3.9
United Kingdom	4.2	5.5
United States	4.8	6.7
World	4.3	5.4

Source: Dimson, Marsh, and Staunton (2003).
Note: Germany excludes 1922–1923. Switzerland commences in 1911.

of early January 2006. According to Standard & Poor's, Citibank had a beta of 1.32 at that time. Using the 10-year U.S. Treasury bond yield of 4.38 percent to represent the risk-free rate, the estimate of the cost of equity for Citibank is 4.38 percent + 1.32(4.8 percent) = 10.72 percent.

The historical premium approach has several limitations. One is that the level of risk of the stock index may change over time. Another is that the risk aversion of investors may change over time. And still another limitation is that the estimates are sensitive to the method of estimation and the historical period covered.

EXAMPLE 3-8   Estimating the Equity Risk Premium Using Historical Rates of Return

Suppose that the arithmetic average T-bond rate observed over the last 100 years is an unbiased estimator for the risk-free rate and amounts to 5.4 percent. Likewise, suppose the arithmetic average of return on the market observed over the last 100 years is an unbiased estimator for the expected return for the market. The average rate of return of the market was 9.3 percent. Calculate the equity risk premium.

Solution

$$\text{ERP} = \overline{R}_M - \overline{R}_F = 9.3 \text{ percent} - 5.4 \text{ percent}$$
$$= 3.9 \text{ percent}$$

A second approach for estimating the equity risk premium is the **dividend discount model based approach** or **implied risk premium approach**, which is implemented using the Gordon growth model (also known as the constant-growth dividend discount model). For developed markets, corporate earnings often meet, at least approximately, the model's assumption of a long-run trend growth rate. We extract the premium by analyzing how the market prices an index. That is, we use the relationship between the value of an index and expected dividends, assuming a constant growth in dividends:

$$P_0 = \frac{D_1}{r_e - g}$$

where

P_0 = current market value of the equity market index

D_1 = dividends expected next period on the index

r_e = required rate of return on the market

g = expected growth rate of dividends

We solve for the required rate of return on the market as

$$r_e = \frac{D_1}{P_0} + g \tag{3-6}$$

Therefore, the expected return on the market is the sum of the dividend yield and the growth rate in dividends.[21] The equity risk premium thus is the difference between the expected return on the equity market and the risk-free rate.

Suppose the expected dividend yield on an equity index is 5 percent and the expected growth rate of dividends on the index is 2 percent. The expected return on the market according to the Gordon growth model is

$$E(R_M) = 5 \text{ percent} + 2 \text{ percent}$$
$$= 7 \text{ percent}$$

A risk-free rate of interest of 3.8 percent implies an equity risk premium of 3.2 percent (= 7 percent − 3.8 percent).

---

[21]We explain Equation 3-6 in more detail in Section 3.3.2.

Another approach to estimate the equity risk premium is quite direct: Ask a panel of finance experts for their estimates and take the mean response. This is the **survey approach**. For example, one set of U.S. surveys found that the expected U.S. equity risk premium over the next 30 years was 5.5 percent to 7 percent, forecasting from 2001 as the baseline year, and 7.1 percent, using 1998 as the baseline year.

Once we have an estimate of the equity risk premium, we fine-tune this estimate for the particular company or project by adjusting it for the specific systematic risk of the project. We adjust for the specific systematic risk by multiplying the market risk premium by beta to arrive at the company's or project's risk premium, which we then add to the risk-free rate to determine the cost of equity within the framework of the CAPM.[22]

3.3.2. Dividend Discount Model Approach

Earlier we used the Gordon growth model to develop an estimate of the equity risk premium for use in the CAPM. We can also use the Gordon growth model directly to obtain an estimate of the cost of equity. To review, the dividend discount model in general states that the intrinsic value of a share of stock is the present value of the share's expected future dividends:

$$V_0 = \sum_{t=1}^{\infty} \left(\frac{D_t}{(1 + r_e)^t} \right) = \frac{D_1}{(1 + r_e)} + \frac{D_2}{(1 + r_e)^2} + \dots$$

where

V_0 = intrinsic value of a share

D_t = share's dividend at the end of period t

r_e = cost of equity

Based on Gordon's constant growth formulation, we assume dividends are expected to grow at a constant rate, g.[23] Therefore, if we assume that price reflects intrinsic value ($V_0 = P_0$), we can rewrite the valuation of the stock as

$$P_0 = \frac{D_1}{r_e - g}$$

We can then rewrite this equation and estimate the cost of equity as we did for Equation 3-6 in Section 3.3.1:

$$r_e = \frac{D_1}{P_0} + g$$

Therefore, to estimate r_e, we need to estimate the dividend in the next period and the assumed constant dividend growth rate. The current stock price, P_0, is known, and the dividend of the next period, D_1, can be predicted if the company has a stable dividend policy.

---

[22]Some researchers argue that the equity risk premium should reflect a country risk premium. For example, a multinational company or project may have a higher cost of capital than a comparable domestic company because of political risk, foreign exchange risk, or higher agency costs. In most cases, this risk is unsystematic and hence does not affect the cost of capital estimate.

[23]Gordon (1962).

(The ratio D_1/P_0 may be called the forward annual dividend yield.) The challenge is estimating the growth rate.

There are at least two ways to estimate the growth rate. The first is to use a forecasted growth rate from a published source or vendor. A second is to use a relationship between the growth rate, the retention rate, and the return on equity. In this context, this is often referred to as the **sustainable growth rate** and is interpretable as the rate of dividend (and earnings) growth that can be sustained over time for a given level of return on equity, keeping the capital structure constant and without issuing additional common stock. The relationship is given in Equation 3-7:

$$g = \left(1 - \frac{D}{EPS}\right) ROE \qquad (3\text{-}7)$$

where

D/EPS = assumed stable dividend payout ratio

ROE = historical return on equity

The term $(1 - D/\text{EPS})$ is the company's earnings retention rate.

Consider Citigroup, Inc. Citigroup has an earnings retention rate of 59 percent. As of early January 2006, Citigroup had a forward annual dividend yield of 3.9 percent, a trailing return on equity of approximately 20 percent, but an estimated average return on equity going forward of approximately 16.6 percent. According to Equation 3-7, Citigroup's sustainable growth rate is 0.59(16.6 percent) = 9.79 percent. The dividend discount model estimate of the cost of equity is therefore 9.79 percent + 3.9 percent = 13.69 percent.

3.3.3. Bond Yield Plus Risk Premium Approach   The **bond yield plus risk premium approach** is based on the fundamental tenet in financial theory that the cost of capital of riskier cash flows is higher than that of less risky cash flows. In this approach, we sum the before-tax cost of debt, r_d, and a risk premium that captures the additional yield on a company's stock relative to its bonds. The estimate is, therefore,

$$r_e = r_d + \text{Risk premium} \qquad (3\text{-}8)$$

The risk premium compensates for the additional risk of equity compared with debt.[24] Ideally, this risk premium is forward looking, representing the additional risk associated with the stock of the company as compared with the bonds of the same company. However, we often estimate this premium using historical spreads between bond yields and stock yields. In developed country markets, a typical risk premium added is in the range of 3 to 5 percent.

Looking again at Citigroup, as of early January 2006, the yield to maturity of the Citigroup 5.3s bonds maturing in 2016 was approximately 4.95 percent. Adding an arbitrary risk premium of 3.5 percent produces an estimate of the cost of equity of 4.95 + 3.5 = 8.45 percent. This estimate contrasts with the higher estimates of 10.72 percent under the CAPM approach and with 13.69 percent under the dividend discount model approach. Such disparities are not uncommon and reflect the difficulty of cost of equity estimation.

---

[24]This risk premium is not to be confused with the equity risk premium. The equity risk premium is the difference between the cost of equity and the *risk-free rate of interest*. The risk premium in the bond yield plus risk premium approach is the difference between the cost of equity and the *company's cost of debt*.

4. TOPICS IN COST OF CAPITAL ESTIMATION

When calculating a company's weighted average cost of capital (WACC), it is essential to understand the risk factors that have been considered in determining the risk-free rate, the equity risk premium, and beta to ensure a consistent calculation of WACC and to avoid the double-counting or omission of pertinent risk factors.

4.1. Estimating Beta and Determining a Project Beta

When using the CAPM to estimate the cost of equity, the analyst must estimate beta. The estimation of beta presents many choices as well as challenges.

One common method of estimating the company's stock beta is to use a market model regression of the company's stock returns (R_i) against market returns (R_m) over T periods:[25]

$$R_{it} = \hat{a} + \hat{b}\,R_{mt} \qquad t = 1, 2, \ldots T$$

where

$\hat{a}$ = estimated intercept

$\hat{b}$ = estimated slope of the regression that is used as an estimate of beta

However, beta estimates are sensitive to the method of estimation and data used. Consider some of the issues:

- *Estimation period:* The estimated beta is sensitive to the length of the estimation period, with beta commonly estimated using data over two to nine years. Selection of the estimation period is a trade-off between data richness captured by longer estimation periods and company-specific changes that are better reflected with shorter estimation periods. In general, longer estimation periods are applied to companies with a long and stable operating history, and shorter estimation periods are used for companies that have undergone significant structural changes in the recent past (such as restructuring, recent acquisition, or divestiture) or changes in financial and operating leverage.
- *Periodicity of the return interval* (e.g., daily, weekly, or monthly): Researchers have observed smaller standard error in beta estimated using smaller return intervals, such as daily returns.[26]
- *Selection of an appropriate market index:* The choice of market index affects the estimate of beta.
- *Use of a smoothing technique:* Some analysts adjust historical betas to reflect the tendency of betas to revert to 1.[27] As an example, the expression $\beta_{i,adj} = 0.333 + 0.667\beta_i$ adjusts betas above and below 1.0 toward 1.0.
- *Adjustments for small-capitalization stocks:* Small-capitalization stocks have generally exhibited greater risks and greater returns than large-capitalization stocks over the long run. Roger Ibbotson, Paul Kaplan, and James Peterson argue that betas for small-capitalization companies be adjusted upward.[28]

---

[25]This equation is commonly referred to as the *market model* and was first introduced by Jensen (1969).
[26]Daves, Ehrhardt, and Kunkel (2000).
[27]Blume (1971).
[28]Ibbotson, Kaplan, and Peterson (1997).

Arriving at an estimated beta for publicly traded companies is generally not a problem because of the accessibility of stock return data, the ease of use of estimating beta using simple regression, and the availability of estimated betas on publicly traded companies from financial analysis vendors, such as Barra, Bloomberg, Thomson Financial's Datastream, Reuters, and Value Line. The challenge is to estimate a beta for a company that is not publicly traded or to estimate a beta for a project that is not the average or typical project of a publicly traded company. Estimating a beta in these cases requires proxying for the beta by using the information on the project or company combined with a beta of a publicly traded company.

The beta of a company or project is affected by the systematic components of business risk and by financial risk. Both of these factors affect the uncertainty of the cash flows of the company or project. The **business risk** of a company or project is the risk related to the uncertainty of revenues, referred to as **sales risk**, and to **operating risk**, which is the risk attributed to the company's operating cost structure. Sales risk is affected by the elasticity of the demand of the product, the cyclicality of the revenues, and the structure of competition in the industry. Operating risk is affected by the relative mix of fixed and variable operating costs: The greater the fixed operating costs, relative to variable operating costs, the greater the uncertainty of income and cash flows from operations will be.

Financial risk is the uncertainty of net income and net cash flows attributed to the use of financing that has a fixed cost, such as debt and leases. The greater the use of fixed-financing sources of capital, relative to variable sources, the greater the financial risk. In other words, a company that relies heavily on debt financing instead of equity financing is assuming a great deal of financial risk.

How does a financial analyst estimate a beta for a company or project that is not publicly traded? One common method is the **pure-play method**, which requires using a comparable publicly traded company's beta and adjusting it for financial leverage differences.

A **comparable company** is a company that has similar business risk. The reason for the name "pure-play" is that one of the easiest ways of identifying a comparable for a project is to find a company in the same industry that is in that *single* line of business. For example, if the analyst is examining a project that involves drugstores, appropriate comparables in the United States may be Walgreens, CVS Corporation, and Rite Aid Corporation.

In estimating a beta in this way, the analyst must make adjustments to account for differing degrees of financial leverage. This requires a process of "unlevering" and "levering" the beta. The beta of the comparable is first "unlevered" by removing the effects of its financial leverage.[29] The unlevered beta is often referred to as the **asset beta** because it reflects the business risk of the assets. Once we determine the unlevered beta, we adjust it for the capital structure of the company or project that is the focus of our analysis. In other words, we "lever" the asset beta to arrive at an estimate of the equity beta for the project or company of interest.

For a given company, we can unlever its equity beta to estimate its asset beta. To do this, we must determine the relationship between a company's asset beta and its equity beta. Because the company's risk is shared between creditors and owners, we can represent the company's risk, β_{asset}, as the weighted average of the company's creditors' market risk, β_{debt}, and the market risk of the owners, β_{equity}:

$$\beta_{asset} = \beta_{debt}\, w_d + \beta_{equity}\, w_e$$

---

[29]The process of unlevering and levering a beta was developed by Hamada (1972) and is based on the capital structure theories of Franco Modigliani and Merton Miller.

or

$$\beta_{asset} = \beta_{debt}\left(\frac{D}{D+E}\right) + \beta_{equity}\left(\frac{E}{D+E}\right)$$

where

E = market value of equity

D = market value of debt

w_d = proportion of debt = $D/(D+E)$

w_e = proportion of equity = $E/(D+E)$

But interest on debt is deducted by the company to arrive at taxable income, so that the claim that creditors have on the company's assets does not cost the company the full amount but rather the after-tax claim; the burden of debt financing is actually less due to interest deductibility. We can represent the asset beta of a company as the weighted average of the betas of debt and equity after considering the effects of the tax deductibility of interest:

$$\beta_{asset} = \beta_{debt}\frac{(1-t)D}{(1-t)D+E} + \beta_{equity}\frac{E}{(1-t)D+E}$$

where t is the marginal tax rate.

We generally assume that a company's debt does not have market risk; so $\beta_{debt} = 0$. This means that the returns on debt do not vary with the returns on the market, which we generally assume to be true for most large companies. If $\beta_{debt} = 0$, then[30]

$$\beta_{asset} = \beta_{equity}\left[\frac{1}{1 + \left((1-t)\dfrac{D}{E}\right)}\right] \qquad (3\text{-}9)$$

Therefore, the market risk of a company's equity is affected by both the asset's market risk, β_{asset}, and a factor representing the nondiversifiable portion of the company's financial risk, $[1 + (1-t)\,^{D}/_{E})]$:

$$\beta_{equity} = \beta_{asset}\left[1 + \left((1-t)\frac{D}{E}\right)\right] \qquad (3\text{-}10)$$

Suppose a company has an equity beta of 1.5, a debt-to-equity ratio of 0.4, and a marginal tax rate of 30 percent. Using Equation 3-9, the company's asset beta is 1.1719:

$$\beta_{asset} = 1.5\left[\frac{1}{1 + ((1-0.3)(0.4))}\right]$$

$$= 1.5\,(0.7813)$$

$$= 1.1719$$

In other words, if the company did not have any debt financing, its $\beta_{asset} = \beta_{equity} = 1.1719$; however, the use of debt financing increases its β_{equity} from 1.1719 to 1.5. What would the

---

[30]The first step is $\beta_{asset} = \beta_{equity}\left[\dfrac{E}{(1-t)D+E}\right]$, which we simplify to arrive at Equation 3-9.

company's equity beta be if the company's debt-to-equity ratio were 0.5 instead of 0.4? In this case, we apply Equation 10, using the debt-to-equity ratio of 0.5:

$$\beta_{equity} = 1.1719 \{1 + [(1 - 0.3)(0.5)]\} = 1.5821$$

Therefore, the unlevering calculation produces a measure of market risk for the assets of the company—ignoring the company's capital structure. We use the levering calculation in Equation 3-10 to estimate the market risk of a company given a specific asset risk, marginal tax rate, and capital structure.

We can use the same unlevering and levering calculations to estimate the asset risk and equity risk for a project. We start with the equity beta of the comparable company, which is the levered beta, $\beta_{L,comparable}$, and then convert it into the equivalent asset beta for the unlevered company, $\beta_{U,comparable}$. Once we have the estimate of the unlevered beta, which is the company's asset risk, we then can use the project's capital structure and marginal tax rate to convert this asset beta into an equity beta for the project, $\beta_{L,project}$.

Estimating a Beta Using the Pure-Play Method

Step 1: Select the comparable.

Determine comparable company or companies (companies with similar business risk).

⇩

Step 2: Estimate comparable's beta.

Estimate the equity beta of the comparable company or companies.

⇩

Step 3: Unlever the comparable's beta.

Unlever the beta of the comparable company or companies, removing the financial risk component of the equity beta, leaving the business risk component of the beta.

⇩

Step 4: Lever the beta for the project's financial risk.

Lever the beta of the project by adjusting the asset beta for the financial risk of the project.

We begin by estimating the levered beta of the comparable company, $\beta_{L,comparable}$. Using the capital structure and tax rate of the levered company, we estimate the asset beta for the comparable company, $\beta_{U,comparable}$:

$$\beta_{U,comparable} = \frac{\beta_{L,comparable}}{\left[1 + \left((1 - t_{comparable})\dfrac{D_{comparable}}{E_{comparable}}\right)\right]} \tag{3-11}$$

We then consider the financial leverage of the project or company and calculate its equity risk, $\beta_{L,project}$:

$$\beta_{L,project} = \beta_{U,comparable}\left[1 + \left((1 - t_{project})\frac{D_{project}}{E_{project}}\right)\right] \quad (3\text{-}12)$$

To illustrate the use of these equations, suppose we want to evaluate a project that will be financed with debt and equity in a ratio of 0.4:1 [a debt-to-equity ratio of 0.4, corresponding to approximately 0.4/(0.4 + 1.0) = €0.286 for each euro of capital needed]. We find a comparable company operating in the same line of business as the project. The marginal tax rate for the company sponsoring the project and the comparable company is 35 percent. The comparable company has a beta of 1.2 and a debt-to-equity ratio of 0.125. The unlevered beta of the comparable is 1.1098:

$$\beta_{U,comparable} = \frac{1.2}{\left[1 + \left((1 - 0.35)\,0.125\right)\right]}$$
$$= 1.1098$$

The levered beta for the project is 1.3983:

$$\beta_{L,project} = 1.1098\left[1 + \left((1 - 0.35)\,0.4\right)\right]$$
$$= 1.3983$$

We then use the 1.3983 as the beta in our CAPM estimate of the component cost of equity for the project and, combined with the cost of debt in a weighted average, provide an estimate of the cost of capital for the project.[31]

EXAMPLE 3-9   Inferring an Asset Beta

Suppose that the beta of a publicly traded company's stock is 1.3 and that the market value of equity and debt are, respectively, C$540 million and C$720 million. If the marginal tax rate of this company is 40 percent, what is the asset beta of this company?

Solution

$$\beta_U = \frac{1.3}{\left[1 + \left((1 - 0.4)\frac{720}{540}\right)\right]}$$
$$= 0.72$$

---

[31]In this example, the weights are $w_d = 0.4/1.4 = 0.2857$ and $w_e = 1/1.4 = 0.7143$.

EXAMPLE 3-10   Calculating a Beta Using the Pure-Play Method

Raymond Cordier is the business development manager of Aerotechnique S.A., a private Belgian subcontractor of aerospace parts. Although Aerotechnique is not listed on the Belgian stock exchange, Cordier needs to evaluate the levered beta for the company. He has access to the following information:

- The average levered and average unlevered betas for the group of comparable companies operating in different European countries are 1.6 and 1.0, respectively.
- Aerotechnique's debt-to-equity ratio, based on market values, is 1.4.
- Aerotechnique's corporate tax rate is 34 percent.

Solution

The beta for Aerotechnique is estimated on the basis of the average unlevered beta extracted from the group of comparable companies. On that basis, and applying the financing structure of Aerotechnique, the estimated beta for Aerotechnique is

$$\beta_{\text{Aerotechnique}} = 1.0\left[1 + \left((1 - 0.34)(1.4)\right)\right]$$
$$= 1.924$$

EXAMPLE 3-11   Estimating the Weighted Average Cost of Capital

Georg Schrempp is the CFO of Bayern Chemicals KgaA, a large German manufacturer of industrial, commercial, and consumer chemical products. Bayern Chemicals is privately owned, and its shares are not listed on an exchange. The CFO has appointed Markus Meier, CFA, of Crystal Clear Valuation Advisors, a third-party valuator, to perform a stand-alone valuation of Bayern Chemicals. Meier had access to the following information to calculate Bayern Chemicals' weighted average cost of capital:

- The nominal risk-free rate is represented by the yield on the long-term 10-year German bund, which at the valuation date was 4.5 percent.
- The average long-term historical equity risk premium in Germany is assumed at 5.7 percent.[32]
- Bayern Chemicals' corporate tax rate is 38 percent.
- Bayern Chemicals' target debt-to-equity ratio is 0.7. Bayern is operating at its target debt-to-equity ratio.

---

[32]Dimson, Marsh, and Staunton, ibid.

- Bayern Chemicals' cost of debt has an estimated spread of 225 basis points over the 10-year bund.
- Exhibit 3-3 supplies additional information on comparables for Bayern Chemicals.

EXHIBIT 3-3   Information on Comparables

Comparable Companies	Country	Tax Rate (%)	Market Capitalization (in millions)	Net Debt (in millions)	D/E	Beta
British Chemicals Ltd.	U.K.	30.0	4,500	6,000	1.33	1.45
Compagnie Petrochimique S.A.	France	30.3	9,300	8,700	0.94	0.75
Rotterdam Chemie N.V.	Netherlands	30.5	7,000	7,900	1.13	1.05
Average					1.13	1.08

Based only on the information given, calculate Bayern Chemicals' WACC.

Solution

To calculate the cost of equity, the first step is to unlever the betas of the comparable companies and calculate an average for a company with business risk similar to the average of these companies:

Comparable Companies	Unlevered Beta
British Chemicals Ltd.	0.75
Compagnie Petrochimique S.A.	0.45
Rotterdam Chemie N.V.	0.59
Average[33]	0.60

Levering the average unlevered beta for the peer group average, applying Bayern Chemicals' target debt-to-equity ratio and marginal tax rate, results in a beta of 0.86:

$$\beta_{\text{Bayern Chemical}} = 0.60 \{1 + [(1 - 0.38)\, 0.7]\}$$
$$= 0.86$$

The cost of equity of Bayern Chemicals, r_e, can be calculated as follows:

$$r_e = 4.5 \text{ percent} + (0.86)(5.7 \text{ percent})$$
$$= 9.4 \text{ percent}$$

---

[33]An analyst must apply judgment and experience to determine a representative average for the comparable companies. This example uses a simple average, but in some situations a weighted average based on some factor such as market capitalization may be more appropriate.

The weights for the cost of equity and cost of debt may be calculated as follows:

$$w_d = \frac{D/E}{\left(\dfrac{D}{E} + 1\right)}$$

$$= \frac{0.7}{1.7}$$

$$= 0.41$$

$$w_e = 1 - w_d$$

$$= 1 - 0.41$$

$$= 0.59$$

The before-tax cost of debt of Bayern Chemicals, r_d, is 6.75 percent:

$$r_d = 4.5 \text{ percent} + 2.25 \text{ percent}$$

$$= 6.75 \text{ percent}$$

As a result, Bayern Chemicals' WACC is 7.27 percent:

$$\text{WACC} = [(0.41)(0.0675)(1 - 0.38)] + [(0.59)(0.094)]$$

$$= 0.0726 \text{ or } 7.26 \text{ percent}$$

4.2. Country Risk

The use of a stock's beta to capture the country risks of a project is well supported in empirical studies that examine developed nations. However, beta does not appear to adequately capture country risk for companies in developing nations.[34] A common approach for dealing with this problem is to adjust the cost of equity estimated using the CAPM by adding a **country spread** to the market risk premium.[35] The country spread is also referred to as a **country equity premium**.

Perhaps the simplest estimate of the country spread is the **sovereign yield spread**, which is the difference between the government bond yield in that country, denominated in the currency of a developed country, and the Treasury bond yield on a similar maturity bond in the developed country.[36] However, this approach may be too coarse for the purposes of equity risk premium estimation.

---

[34]Harvey (2001).

[35]Adding the country spread to the market risk premium for a developing country and then multiplying this sum by the market risk of the project is making the assumption that the country risk premium varies according to market risk. An alternative method calculates the cost of equity as the sum of three terms: (1) the risk-free rate of interest, (2) the product of the beta and the developed market risk premium, and (3) the country risk premium. This latter method assumes that the country risk premium is the same, regardless of the project's market risk.

[36]Mariscal and Lee (1993).

Another approach is to calculate the country equity premium as the product of the sovereign yield spread and the ratio of the volatility of the developing country equity market to that of the sovereign bond market denominated in terms of the currency of a developed country:[37]

$$\text{Country equity premium} = \text{Sovereign yield spread} \left(\frac{\substack{\text{Annualized standard deviation} \\ \text{of equity index}}}{\substack{\text{Annualized standard deviation} \\ \text{of the sovereign bond market} \\ \text{in terms of the developed} \\ \text{market currency}}} \right) \qquad (3\text{-}13)$$

The logic of this calculation is that the sovereign yield spread captures the general risk of the country, which is then adjusted for the volatility of the stock market relative to the bond market. This country equity premium is then used in addition to the equity premium estimated for a project in a developed country. Therefore, if the equity risk premium for a project in a developed country is 4.5 percent and the country risk premium is 3 percent, the total equity risk premium used in the CAPM estimation is 7.5 percent. If the appropriate beta is 1.2 and the risk-free rate of interest is 4 percent, the cost of equity is

Equity risk premium $= 0.04 + 1.2(0.045 + 0.03) = 0.13$ or 13 percent

---

EXAMPLE 3-12   Estimating the Country Equity Premium

Miles Avenaugh, an analyst with the Global Company, is estimating a country equity premium to include in his estimate of the cost of equity capital for Global's investment in Argentina. Avenaugh has researched yields in Argentina and observed that the Argentinean government's 10-year bond is 9.5 percent. A similar maturity U.S. Treasury bond has a yield of 4.5 percent. The annualized standard deviation of the Argentina Merval stock index, a market value index of stocks listed on the Buenos Aires Stock Exchange, during the most recent year is 40 percent. The annualized standard deviation of the Argentina dollar-denominated 10-year government bond over the recent period was 28 percent.

What is the estimated country equity premium for Argentina based on Avenaugh's research?

Solution

$$\text{Country risk premium} = 0.05 \left(\frac{0.40}{0.28} \right)$$

$$= 0.05(1.4286)$$

$$= 0.0714, \text{ or } 7.14 \text{ percent}$$

---

[37]Damodaran (1999 and 2003).

Still another approach is to use country credit ratings to estimate the expected rates of returns for countries that have credit ratings but no equity markets.[38] This method requires estimating reward to credit risk measures for a large sample of countries for which there are both credit ratings and equity markets, then applying this ratio to those countries without equity markets based on the country's credit rating.

4.3.   Marginal Cost of Capital Schedule

As we noted in Section 2.3, as a company raises more funds, the costs of the different sources of capital may change, resulting in a change in the weighted average cost of capital for different levels of financing. The result is the marginal cost of capital (MCC) schedule, which we often depict in graphical form as the weighted average cost of capital for different amounts of capital raised, as we showed earlier in Exhibit 3-1.[39]

Why would the cost of capital change as more capital is raised? One source of a difference in cost depending on the amount of capital raised is that a company may have existing debt with a bond covenant that restricts the company from issuing debt with similar seniority as existing debt. Or a **debt incurrence test** may restrict a company's ability to incur additional debt at the same seniority based on one or more financial tests or conditions. For example, if a company issues senior debt such that any additional debt at that seniority violates the debt incurrence test of an existing bond covenant, the company may have to issue less senior debt or even equity, which would have a higher cost.

Another source of increasing marginal costs of capital is a deviation from the target capital structure. In the ideal, theoretical world, a company has a target capital structure, goes to the market each period, and raises capital in these proportions. However, as a practical matter, companies do not necessarily tap the market in these ideal proportions because of considerations for economies of scale in raising new capital and market conditions. Because of such perceived economies of scale, companies tend to issue new securities such that, in any given period, it may deviate from the proportions dictated by any target or optimal capital structure. In other words, these short-run deviations are due to the "lumpiness" of security issuance. As the company experiences deviations from the target capital structure, the marginal cost of capital may increase, reflecting these deviations.

The amount of capital at which the weighted average cost of capital changes—which means that the cost of one of the sources of capital changes—is referred to as a **break point**. The reality of raising capital is that the marginal cost of capital schedule is not as smooth as we depicted in Exhibit 3-1 but rather is a step-up cost schedule, as shown in Exhibit 3-4.

Consider the case of a company facing the costs of capital given in Exhibit 3-5.

---

[38]Erb, Harvey, and Viskanta (1996).

[39]In the section on capital structure and leverage, we will discuss cases where a company's WACC may actually decrease as additional capital is raised. For example, if a company financed solely with common equity raises additional capital via debt, the tax advantages provided by debt will result in a lower WACC under the new capital structure. For this discussion, we are assuming that the company is already operating at or near its optimum balance of debt versus equity.

EXHIBIT 3-4   Marginal Cost of Capital Schedule

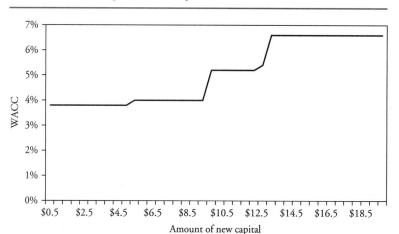

EXHIBIT 3-5   Schedule of the Costs of Debt and Equity

Amount of New Debt (in millions)	After-tax Cost of Debt (%)	Amount of New Equity (in millions)	Cost of Equity (%)
New debt ≤ €2	2.0	New equity ≤ €6	5.0
€2 < New debt ≤ €5	2.5	€6 < New equity ≤ €8	7.0
€5 < New debt	3.0	€8 < New equity	9.0

If the company raises capital according to its target capital structure proportions of 40 percent debt and 60 percent equity, this company faces a marginal cost of capital schedule that is upward sloping, with break points at €5 million, €10 million, €12.5 million, and €13.3 million, as depicted in Exhibit 3-4. These break points are determined from the amounts of capital at which the cost changes, calculated as

$$\text{Break point} = \frac{\text{Amount of capital at which the source's cost of capital changes}}{\text{Proportion of new capital raised from the source}} \qquad (3\text{-}14)$$

For example, the first break point for debt financing is reached with €2 million/0.4 = €5 million of new capital raised. The first break point attributed to a change in equity cost occurs at €6 million/0.6 = €10 million. Example 3-13 illustrates a marginal cost of capital schedule with break points and also how the WACC figures in the choice of an optimal capital structure.

EXAMPLE 3-13   Marginal Cost of Capital Schedule

Alan Conlon is the CFO of Allied Canadian Breweries Ltd. He wants to determine the capital structure that will result in the lowest cost of capital for Allied. He has access to the following information:

- The minimum rate at which the company can borrow for 12 months is the 12-month LIBOR + 200 basis points until it reaches a debt-to-total-capital ratio of 30 percent. For debt-to-total-capital ratios above 30 percent, the spread over 12-month LIBOR increases according to the schedule given in Exhibit 3-6.

EXHIBIT 3-6   Spreads over LIBOR for Alternative Debt-to-Equity Ratios

$\dfrac{D}{D + E}$	Spread (BPS)
0.4	300
0.5	400
0.6	600
0.7	800
0.8	1,000

- The current 12-month LIBOR is 4.5 percent.
- The market risk premium is 4 percent, the risk-free rate is 4.25 percent, and unleveraged beta is 0.9.
- The company's tax rate is 36 percent.

1. Determine the WACC for levels of the debt-to-equity ratio given in Exhibit 3-6.
2. Recommend a target capital structure, given that the company is concerned with achieving the lowest possible cost of capital.

Solution to 1

The WACC expressed as a function of the capital structure is shown in Exhibit 3-7.

EXHIBIT 3-7   WACC for Alternative Capital Structures

$\dfrac{D}{D + E}$	β	R_D (%)	R_E (%)	WACC (%)
0.1	0.96	6.5	8.1	7.7
0.2	1.04	6.5	8.4	7.6
0.3	1.15	6.5	8.8	7.4
0.4	1.28	7.5	9.4	7.6
0.5	1.48	8.5	10.2	7.8
0.6	1.76	10.5	11.3	8.6
0.7	2.24	12.5	13.2	9.6
0.8	3.20	14.5	17.1	10.8
0.9	6.08	16.5	28.6	12.4

Solution to 2

The optimal capital structure is 30 percent debt, which corresponds to an optimal D/E of 0.43.

4.4. Flotation Costs

When a company raises new capital, it generally seeks the assistance of investment bankers. Investment bankers charge the company a fee based on the size and type of offering. This fee is referred to as the **flotation cost**. In the case of debt and preferred stock, we do not usually incorporate flotation costs into the estimated cost of capital because the amount of these costs is quite small, often less than 1 percent.[40]

However, with equity issuance, the flotation costs may be substantial; so we should consider these when estimating the cost of external equity capital. For example, Inmoo Lee, Scott Lochhead, Jay Ritter, and Quanshui Zhao observe average flotation costs for new equity in the United States of 7.11 percent.[41] The flotation costs in other countries differ from the U.S. experience: Thomas Bühner and Christoph Kaserer observe flotation costs around 1.65 percent in Germany, Seth Armitage estimates an average issuance cost of 5.78 percent in the United Kingdom, and Christoph Kaserer and Fabian Steiner observe an average cost of 4.53 for Swiss capital offerings.[42] A large part of the differences in costs among these studies is likely attributed to the type of offering; cash underwritten offers, typical in the United States, are generally more expensive than rights offerings, which are common in Europe.

Should we incorporate flotation costs into the cost of capital? There are two views on this topic. One view, which you can find often in textbooks, is to incorporate the flotation costs into the cost of capital. The other view is that flotation costs should not be included in the cost of capital but rather incorporated into any valuation analysis as an additional cost of the project.

Consistent with the first view, we can specify flotation costs in monetary terms, as an amount per share or as a percentage of the share price. With flotation costs in monetary terms on a per-share basis, F, the cost of external equity is

$$r_e = \left(\frac{D_1}{P_0 - F} \right) + g \qquad (3\text{-}15)$$

As a percentage applied against the price per share, the cost of external equity is

$$r_e = \left(\frac{D_1}{P_0 (1 - f)} \right) + g \qquad (3\text{-}16)$$

where f is the flotation cost as a percentage of the issue price.

---

[40]We can incorporate them for these sources by simply treating the flotation costs as an outlay, hence reducing proceeds from the source.

[41]Lee, Lochhead, Ritter, and Zhao (1996).

[42]Bühner and Kaserer (2002); Armitage (2000); and Kaserer and Steiner (2004).

Suppose a company has a current dividend of $2 per share, a current price of $40 per share, and an expected growth rate of 5 percent. The cost of internally generated equity would be 10.25 percent:

$$r_e = \left(\frac{\$2\,(1 + 0.05)}{\$40} \right) + 0.05$$

$$= 0.0525 + 0.05$$

$$= 0.1025 \text{ or } 10.25 \text{ percent}$$

If the flotation costs are 4 percent of the issuance, the cost of externally generated equity would be slightly higher at 10.469 percent:

$$r_e = \left(\frac{\$2\,(1 + 0.05)}{\$40(1 - 0.04)} \right) + 0.05$$

$$= 0.05469 + 0.05$$

$$= 0.1047, \text{ or } 10.47 \text{ percent}$$

The problem with this approach is that the flotation costs are a cash flow at the initiation of the project and affect the value of any project by reducing the initial cash flow. Adjusting the cost of capital for flotation costs is incorrect because by doing so we are adjusting the present value of the future cash flows by a fixed percentage—in the preceding example, a difference of 22 basis points, which does not necessarily equate to the present value of the flotation costs.[43]

The alternative and recommended approach is to make the adjustment to the cash flows in the valuation computation. For example, consider a project that requires a €60,000 initial cash outlay and is expected to produce cash flows of €10,000 each year for 10 years. Suppose the company's marginal tax rate is 40 percent and that the before-tax cost of debt is 5 percent. Furthermore, suppose that the company's dividend next period is €1, the current price of the stock is €20, and the expected growth rate is 5 percent, so that the cost of equity using the dividend discount model is (€1/€20) + 0.05 = 0.10, or 10 percent. Assume the company will finance the project with 40 percent debt and 60 percent equity. Exhibit 3-8 summarizes the information on the component costs of capital.

The weighted average cost of capital is 7.2 percent, calculated as 0.40(3 percent) + 0.60(10 percent). Ignoring flotation costs for the moment, the net present value (NPV) of this project is

$$\text{NPV} = €69,591 - €60,000$$

$$= €9,591$$

EXHIBIT 3-8   After-Tax Costs of Debt and Equity

Source of Capital	Amount Raised (€)	Proportion	Marginal After-Tax Cost
Debt	24,000	0.40	0.05(1 − 0.4) = 0.03
Equity	36,000	0.60	0.10

---

[43]This argument is made by Ezzell and Porter (1976). They argue that the correct treatment is to deduct flotation costs as part of the valuation as one of the initial-period cash flows.

If the flotation costs are, say, 5 percent of the new equity capital, the amount is €1,800. The net present value considering flotation costs is

$$NPV = €69,591 - €60,000 - €1,800$$
$$= €7,791$$

If, instead of considering the flotation costs as part of the cash flows, we adjust the cost of equity, the cost of capital is 7.3578 percent and the NPV is

$$NPV = €69,089 - €60,000$$
$$= €9,089$$

As you can see, we arrive at different assessments of value using these two methods.

So, if it is preferred to deduct the flotation costs as part of the net present value calculation, why do we see the adjustment in the cost of capital so often in textbooks? The first reason is that it is often difficult to identify particular financing associated with a project. Using the adjustment for the flotation costs in the cost of capital may be useful if specific project financing cannot be identified. Second, by adjusting the cost of capital for the flotation costs, it is easier to demonstrate how costs of financing a company change as a company exhausts internally generated equity (i.e., retained earnings) and switches to externally generated equity (i.e., a new stock issue).

4.5. What Do Chief Financial Officers Do?

In this chapter, we have introduced you to methods that may be used to estimate the cost of capital for a company or a project. What do companies actually use when making investment decisions? In a survey of a large number of U.S. company CFOs, John Graham and Campbell Harvey asked about the methods that companies actually use.[44] Their survey revealed the following:

- The most popular method for estimating the cost of equity is the capital asset pricing model.
- Few companies use the dividend cash flow model to estimate a cost of equity.
- Publicly traded companies are more likely to use the capital asset pricing model than are private companies.
- In evaluating projects, the majority use a single-company cost of capital, but a large portion apply some type of risk adjustment for individual projects.

The survey also reveals that the single-factor capital asset pricing model is the most popular method for estimating the cost of equity, though the next most popular methods, respectively, are average stock returns and multifactor return models. The lack of popularity of the dividend discount model indicates that this approach, which was once favored, has lost its following in practice.[45]

---

[44]Graham and Harvey (2002).

[45]A survey published by Gitman and Mercurio (1982) indicated that fewer than 30 percent used the CAPM model in the estimation of the cost of equity.

In a survey of publicly traded multinational European companies, Franck Bancel and Usha Mittoo provide evidence consistent with the Graham and Harvey survey.[46] They find that over 70 percent of companies use the CAPM to determine the cost of equity; this compares with the 73.5 percent of U.S. companies that use the CAPM. In a survey of both publicly traded and private European companies, Dirk Brounen, Abe de Jong, and Kees Koedijk confirm the result of Graham and Harvey that larger companies are more likely to use the more sophisticated methods, such as CAPM, in estimating the cost of equity.[47] Brounen, Jong, and Koedijk find that the popularity of the use of CAPM is less for their sample (ranging from 34 percent to 55.6 percent, depending on the country) than for the other two surveys, which may reflect the inclusion of smaller, private companies in the latter sample.

We learn from the survey evidence that the CAPM is a popular method for estimating the cost of equity capital and that it is used less by smaller, private companies. This latter result is not surprising because of the difficulty in estimating systematic risk in cases in which the company's equity is not publicly traded.

5. SUMMARY

In this chapter, we provided an overview of the techniques used to calculate the cost of capital for companies and projects. We examined the weighted average cost of capital, discussing the methods commonly used to estimate the component costs of capital and the weights applied to these components. The international dimension of the cost of capital, as well as key factors influencing the cost of capital, were also analyzed.

- The weighted average cost of capital is a weighted average of the after-tax marginal costs of each source of capital: $\text{WACC} = w_d r_d (1 - t) + w_p r_p + w_e r_e$.
- An analyst uses the WACC in valuation. For example, the WACC is used to value a project using the net present value method:
  $\text{NPV} = \text{Present value of inflows} - \text{Present value of the outflows}$
- The before-tax cost of debt is generally estimated by means of one of the two methods: yield to maturity or bond rating.
- The yield-to-maturity method of estimating the before-tax cost of debt uses the familiar bond valuation equation. Assuming semiannual coupon payments, the equation is

$$P_0 = \frac{PMT_1}{\left(1 + \frac{r_d}{2}\right)} + \ldots + \frac{PMT_n}{\left(1 + \frac{r_d}{2}\right)^n} + \frac{FV}{\left(1 + \frac{r_d}{2}\right)^n}$$

$$= \left[\sum_{t=1}^{n} \frac{PMT_i}{\left(1 + \frac{r_d}{2}\right)^t}\right] + \frac{FV}{\left(1 + \frac{r_d}{2}\right)^n}$$

We solve for the six-month yield ($r_d/2$) and then annualize it to arrive at the before-tax cost of debt, r_d.

---

[46]Bancel and Mittoo (2004).
[47]Brounen, de Jong, and Koedijk (2004).

- Because interest payments are generally tax deductible, the after-tax cost is the true, effective cost of debt to the company. If a current yield or bond rating is not available, such as in the case of a private company without rated debt or a project, the estimate of the cost of debt becomes more challenging.
- The cost of preferred stock is the preferred stock dividend divided by the current preferred stock price:

$$r_p = \frac{D_p}{P_p}$$

- The cost of equity is the rate of return required by a company's common stockholders. We estimate this cost using the CAPM (or its variants) or the dividend discount method.
- The CAPM is the approach most commonly used to calculate the cost of common stock. The three components needed to calculate the cost of common stock are the risk-free rate, the equity risk premium, and beta:

$$E(R_i) = R_F + \beta_i \left[E(R_M) - R_F \right]$$

- When estimating the cost of equity capital using the CAPM when we do not have publicly traded equity, we may be able to use the pure-play method in which we estimate the unlevered beta for a company with similar business risk, β_U,

$$\beta_{U,comparable} = \frac{\beta_{L,comparable}}{\left[1 + \left((1 - t_{comparable}) \frac{D_{comparable}}{E_{comparable}} \right) \right]}$$

and then lever this beta to reflect the financial risk of the project or company:

$$\beta_{L,project} = \beta_{U,comparable} \left[1 + \left((1 - t_{project}) \frac{D_{project}}{E_{project}} \right) \right]$$

- It is often the case that country and foreign exchange risk are diversified so that we can use the estimated β in the CAPM analysis. However, in the case in which these risks cannot be diversified away, we can adjust our measure of systematic risk by a country equity premium to reflect this nondiversified risk:

$$\text{Country equity premium} = \text{Sovereign yield spread} \left(\frac{\text{Annualized standard deviation of equity index}}{\begin{array}{c} \text{Annualized standard deviation} \\ \text{of the sovereign bond market} \\ \text{in terms of the developed} \\ \text{market currency} \end{array}} \right)$$

- The dividend discount model approach is an alternative approach to calculating the cost of equity, whereby the cost of equity is estimated as follows:

$$r_e = \frac{D_1}{P_0} + g$$

- We can estimate the growth rate in the dividend discount model by using published forecasts of analysts or by estimating the sustainable growth rate:

$$g = \left(1 - \frac{D}{EPS}\right) ROE$$

- In estimating the cost of equity, an alternative to the CAPM and dividend discount approaches is the bond yield plus risk premium approach. In this approach, we estimate the before-tax cost of debt and add a risk premium that reflects the additional risk associated with the company's equity.
- The marginal cost of capital schedule is a graph plotting the new funds raised by a company on the *x*-axis and the cost of capital on the *y*-axis. The cost of capital is level to the point at which one of the costs of capital changes, such as when the company bumps up against a debt covenant, requiring it to use another form of capital. We calculate a break point using information on when the different sources' costs change and the proportions that the company uses when it raises additional capital:

$$\text{Break point} = \frac{\text{Amount of capital at which the source's cost of capital changes}}{\text{Proportion of new capital raised from the source}}$$

- Flotation costs are costs incurred in the process of raising additional capital. The preferred method of including these costs in the analysis is as an initial cash flow in the valuation analysis.
- Survey evidence tells us that the CAPM method is the most popular method used by companies in estimating the cost of equity. The CAPM is more popular with larger, publicly traded companies, which is understandable considering the additional analyses and assumptions required in estimating systematic risk for a private company or project.

PRACTICE PROBLEMS

1. The cost of equity is equal to the
   A. Expected market return.
   B. Rate of return required by stockholders.
   C. Cost of retained earnings plus dividends.
   D. Risk the company incurs when financing.

2. Which of the following statements is correct?
   A. The appropriate tax rate to use in the adjustment of the before-tax cost of debt to determine the after-tax cost of debt is the average tax rate because interest is deductible against the company's entire taxable income.
   B. For a given company, the after-tax cost of debt is less than both the cost of preferred equity and the cost of common equity.
   C. For a given company, the investment opportunity schedule is upward sloping because, as a company invests more in capital projects, the returns from investing increase.
   D. The target capital structure is the average ratio of debt to equity for the most recent fiscal years.

3. Using the dividend discount model, what is the cost of equity capital for Zeller Mining if the company will pay a dividend of C$2.30 next year, has a payout ratio of 30 percent, a return on equity of 15 percent, and a stock price of C$45?
   A. 5.11 percent.
   B. 9.61 percent.
   C. 10.50 percent.
   D. 15.61 percent.

4. Dot.Com has determined that it could issue $1,000 face value bonds with an 8 percent coupon paid semiannually and a five-year maturity at $900 per bond. If Dot.Com's marginal tax rate is 38 percent, its after-tax cost of debt is *closest* to
   A. 6.2 percent.
   B. 6.4 percent.
   C. 6.6 percent.
   D. 6.8 percent.

5. The cost of debt can be determined using the yield-to-maturity and the bond rating approaches. If the bond rating approach is used, the
   A. Coupon is the yield.
   B. Yield is based on the interest coverage ratio.
   C. Company is rated and the rating can be used to assess the credit default spread of the company's debt.
   D. After-tax cost of the debt is not known.

6. Morgan Insurance Ltd. issued a fixed-rate perpetual preferred stock three years ago and placed it privately with institutional investors. The stock was issued at $25 per share with a $1.75 dividend. If the company were to issue preferred stock today, the yield would be 6.5 percent. The stock's current value is
   A. $25.00.
   B. $26.92.
   C. $37.31.
   D. $40.18.

7. A financial analyst at Buckco Ltd. wants to compute the company's weighted average cost of capital (WACC) using the dividend discount model. The analyst has gathered the following data:

Before-tax cost of new debt	8 percent
Tax rate	40 percent
Target debt-to-equity ratio	0.8033
Stock price	$30
Next year's dividend	$1.50
Estimated growth rate	7 percent

Buckco's WACC is *closest* to
A. 8 percent.
B. 9 percent.
C. 12 percent.
D. 20 percent.

8. The Gearing Company has an after-tax cost of debt capital of 4 percent, a cost of preferred stock of 8 percent, a cost of equity capital of 10 percent, and a weighted average cost of capital of 7 percent. Gearing intends to maintain its current capital structure as it raises additional capital. In making its capital budgeting decisions for the average-risk project, the relevant cost of capital is
    A. 4 percent.
    B. 7 percent.
    C. 8 percent.
    D. 10 percent.

9. Fran McClure of Alba Advisers is estimating the cost of capital of Frontier Corporation as part of her valuation analysis of Frontier. McClure will be using this estimate, along with projected cash flows from Frontier's new projects, to estimate the effect of these new projects on the value of Frontier. McClure has gathered the following information on Frontier Corporation:

	Current Year	Forecasted for Next Year
Book value of debt	$50	$50
Market value of debt	$62	$63
Book value of shareholders' equity	$55	$58
Market value of shareholders' equity	$210	$220

The weights that McClure should apply in estimating Frontier's cost of capital for debt and equity are, respectively,
    A. $w_d = 0.200$; $w_e = 0.800$.
    B. $w_d = 0.185$; $w_e = 0.815$.
    C. $w_d = 0.223$; $w_e = 0.777$.
    D. $w_d = 0.228$; $w_e = 0.772$.

10. Wang Securities had a long-term stable debt-to-equity ratio of 0.65. Recent bank borrowing for expansion into South America raised the ratio to 0.75. The increased leverage has what effect on the asset beta and equity beta of the company?

	Asset Beta	Equity Beta
A.	Same	Higher
B.	Same	Lower
C.	Lower	Higher
D.	Lower	Lower

11. Brandon Wiene is a financial analyst covering the beverage industry. He is evaluating the impact of DEF Beverage's new product line of flavored waters. DEF currently has a debt-to-equity ratio of 0.6. The new product line would be financed with $50 million of debt and $100 million of equity. In estimating the valuation impact of this new product line on DEF's value, Wiene has estimated the equity beta and asset beta

of comparable companies. In calculating the equity beta for the product line, Wiene is
intending to use DEF's existing capital structure when converting the asset beta into a
project beta. Which of the following statements is correct?

A. Using DEF's debt-to-equity ratio of 0.6 is appropriate in calculating the new product
line's equity beta.

B. Using DEF's debt-to-equity ratio of 0.6 is not appropriate; rather, the debt-to-equity
ratio of the new product, 0.5, is appropriate to use in calculating the new product
line's equity beta.

C. Wiene should use the new debt-to-equity ratio of DEF that would result from the
additional $50 million debt and $100 million equity in calculating the new product
line's equity beta.

D. Wiene should use the asset beta determined from the analysis of comparables as the
equity beta in evaluating the new product line.

12. Trumpit Resorts Company currently has 1.2 million common shares of stock
outstanding and the stock has a beta of 2.2. It also has $10 million face value of bonds
that have five years remaining to maturity and 8 percent coupon with semiannual
payments, and they are priced to yield 13.65 percent. Trumpit has learned that it
can issue new common stock at $10 a share. The current risk-free rate of interest
is 3 percent and the expected market return is 10 percent. If Trumpit issues up
to $2.5 million of new bonds, the bonds will be priced at par and have a yield of
13.65 percent; if it issues bonds beyond $2.5 million, the expected yield will be
16 percent. Trumpit's marginal tax rate is 30 percent. If Trumpit raises $7.5 million of
new capital while maintaining the same debt-to-equity ratio, its weighted average cost
of capital is *closest* to

A. 14.5 percent.

B. 15.5 percent.

C. 16.5 percent.

D. 17.5 percent.

The following information relates to Questions 13 through 18.

Jurgen Knudsen has been hired to provide industry expertise to Henrik Sandell, CFA, an
analyst for a pension plan managing a global large-cap fund internally. Sandell is concerned
about one of the fund's larger holdings, auto parts manufacturer Kruspa AB. Kruspa currently operates in 80 countries, with the previous year's global revenues at €5.6 billion.
Recently, Kruspa's CFO announced plans for expansion into China. Sandell worries that this
expansion will change the company's risk profile and wonders if he should recommend a sale
of the position.

Sandell provides Knudsen with the basic information. Kruspa's global annual free cash flow
to the firm is €500 million and earnings are €400 million. Sandell estimates that cash flow will
level off at a 2 percent rate of growth. Sandell also estimates that Kruspa's after-tax free cash flow
to the firm on the China project for next three years is, respectively, €48 million, €52 million,
and €54.4 million. Kruspa recently announced a dividend of €4.00 per share of stock. For the
initial analysis, Sandell requests that Knudsen ignore possible currency fluctuations. He expects
the Chinese plant to sell only to customers within China for the first three years. Knudsen is
asked to evaluate Kruspa's planned financing of the required €100 million with a €80 public
offering of 10-year debt in Sweden and the remainder with an equity offering.

Additional information:

Equity risk premium, Sweden	4.82 percent
Risk-free rate of interest, Sweden	4.25 percent
Industry debt-to-equity ratio	0.3
Market value of Kruspa's debt	€900 million
Market value of Kruspa's equity	€2.4 billion
Kruspa's equity beta	1.3
Kruspa's before-tax cost of debt	9.25 percent
China credit A2 country risk premium	1.88 percent
Corporate tax rate	37.5 percent
Interest payments each year	Level

13. Using the capital asset pricing model, Kruspa's cost of equity capital for its typical project is *closest* to
    A. 7.62 percent.
    B. 10.52 percent.
    C. 12.40 percent.
    D. 14.84 percent.

14. Sandell is interested in the weighted average cost of capital of Kruspa AB prior to its investing in the China project. This weighted average cost of capital (WACC) is *closest* to
    A. 7.65 percent.
    B. 9.23 percent.
    C. 10.17 percent.
    D. 10.52 percent.

15. In his estimation of the project's cost of capital, Sandell would like to use the asset beta of Kruspa as a base in his calculations. The estimated asset beta of Kruspa prior to the China project is *closest* to
    A. 1.053.
    B. 1.110.
    C. 1.140.
    D. 1.327.

16. Sandell is performing a sensitivity analysis of the effect of the new project on the company's cost of capital. If the China project has the same asset risk as Kruspa, then the estimated project beta for the China project, if it is financed 80 percent with debt, is *closest* to
    A. 1.053.
    B. 1.300.
    C. 2.635.
    D. 3.686.

17. As part of the sensitivity analysis of the effect of the new project on the company's cost of capital, Sandell is estimating the cost of equity of the China project considering that the China project requires a country equity premium to capture the risk of the project. The cost of equity for the project in this case is *closest* to
    A. 9.23 percent.
    B. 10.52 percent.
    C. 19.91 percent.
    D. 28.95 percent.

18. In his report, Sandell would like to discuss the sensitivity of the project's net present value to the estimation of the cost of equity. The China project's net present values, calculated using the equity beta without and with the country risk premium, are, respectively
    A. €26 million and €24 million.
    B. €28 million and €25 million.
    C. €30 million and €27 million.
    D. €32 million and €31 million.

The following information relates to Questions 19 through 22.

Boris Duarte, CFA, covers initial public offerings for Zellweger Analytics, an independent research firm specializing in global small-cap equities. He has been asked to evaluate the upcoming new issue of TagOn, a U.S.-based business intelligence software company. The industry has grown at 26 percent per year for the previous three years. Large companies dominate the market, but sizable "pure-play" companies such as Relevant, Ltd., ABJ, Inc., and Opus Software Pvt. Ltd. also compete. Each of these competitors is domiciled in a different country, but they all have shares of stock that trade on the U.S. NASDAQ. The debt ratio of the industry has risen slightly in recent years.

Company	Sales in Millions	Market value equity in Billions	Market value debt in Millions	Equity Beta	Tax Rate	Share Price
Relevant Ltd.	$752	$3.8	$0.0	1.702	23 percent	$42
ABJ, Inc.	$843	$2.15	$6.5	2.800	23 percent	$24
Opus Software Pvt. Ltd.	$211	$0.972	$13.0	3.400	23 percent	$13

Duarte uses the information from the preliminary prospectus for TagOn's initial offering. The company intends to issue 1 million new shares. In his conversation with the investment bankers for the deal, he concludes the offering price will be between $7 and $12. The current capital structure of TagOn consists of a $2.4 million five-year noncallable bond issue and 1 million common shares. Other information that Duarte has gathered:

Currently outstanding bonds	$2.4 million five-year bonds, coupon of 12.5 percent, with a market value of $2.156 million
Risk-free rate of interest	5.25 percent
Estimated equity risk premium	7 percent
Tax rate	23 percent

19. The asset betas for Relevant, ABJ, and Opus, respectively, are
    A. 1.70, 2.52, 2.73.
    B. 1.70, 2.79, 3.37.
    C. 1.70, 2.81, 3.44.
    D. 2.634 for each.

20. The weighted average asset beta for the pure players in this industry—Relevant, ABJ, and Opus—weighted by market value, is *closest* to
    A. 1.37.
    B. 1.67.
    C. 1.97.
    D. 2.27.

21. Using the capital asset pricing model, the cost of equity capital for a company in this industry, with a debt-to-equity ratio of 0.01 and a marginal tax rate of 23 percent, is *closest* to
    A. 17 percent.
    B. 21 percent.
    C. 24 percent.
    D. 31 percent.

22. The marginal cost of capital for TagOn, based on the average asset beta for the industry and assuming that new stock can be issued at $8 per share, is *closest* to
    A. 20.0 percent.
    B. 20.5 percent.
    C. 21.0 percent.
    D. 21.5 percent.

CHAPTER 4

CAPITAL STRUCTURE AND LEVERAGE

Raj Aggarwal, CFA
University of Akron
Akron, Ohio

Cynthia Harrington, CFA
Harrington Capital Management Ltd.
Los Angeles, California

Adam Kobor, CFA
The World Bank
Washington, D.C.

Pamela Peterson Drake, CFA
James Madison University
Harrisonburg, Virginia

LEARNING OUTCOMES

After completing this chapter, you will be able to do the following:

- Define and explain leverage, business risk, sales risk, operating risk, and financial risk, and classify a risk, given a description.
- Calculate and interpret the degree of operating leverage, the degree of financial leverage, and the degree of total leverage.

- Characterize the operating leverage, financial leverage, and total leverage of a company given a description of it.
- Calculate the breakeven quantity of sales and determine the company's net income at various sales levels.
- Describe the effect of financial leverage on a company's net income and return on equity.
- Compare and contrast the risks of creditors and owners.
- Describe the objective of the capital structure decision.
- Characterize the Modigliani and Miller capital structure irrelevance proposition and their proposition concerning the relationship between the cost of equity and financial leverage.
- Identify and explain the costs of financial distress, the agency costs of equity, and the costs of asymmetric information, as well as the potential effect of these costs on a company's optimal capital structure.
- Compare the implications for managers' decisions regarding capital structure from the perspective of (1) the Modigliani and Miller capital structure theory, (2) the pecking order theory, and (3) the static trade-off theory.
- Describe and interpret the effects of expanding the Modigliani and Miller capital structure theory to account for both the tax shield provided by debt and the cost of financial distress (the static trade-off theory).
- Explain and diagram the static trade-off of the optimal capital structure.
- Explain the target capital structure and why the actual capital structure may fluctuate around the target.
- Review the role of debt ratings in capital structure policy.
- Explain the factors an analyst should consider in evaluating the impact of capital structure policy on valuation.
- Review international differences in financial leverage and discuss the implications for investment analysis.

1. INTRODUCTION

This chapter presents capital structure and leverage. **Leverage** is the use of fixed costs in a company's cost structure. The fixed costs that are operating costs (such as depreciation or rent) create operating leverage. Fixed costs that are financial costs (such as interest expense) create financial leverage. Analysts need to understand a company's use of leverage for three main reasons:

- First, the degree of leverage is an important component in assessing a company's risk and return characteristics.
- Second, analysts may be able to discern a company's prospects from management's decisions about financing choices. Knowing how to interpret these signals also helps the analyst evaluate the quality of management's decisions.
- Third, the valuation of a company requires forecasting future cash flows and assessing the risk associated with those cash flows.

The cost structure of a company affects its risk: The greater the company's fixed costs relative to its variable costs, the greater the potential volatility there is in its future earnings and hence cash flows. We refer to the use of fixed costs as leverage because these fixed costs act as a fulcrum for the company's earnings. Leverage can magnify earnings both up and down. The profits of highly leveraged companies might soar with small upturns in sales. But the reverse is also true: Small drops in revenue can rapidly lead to losses.

This chapter also discusses the choice about how to finance (i.e., raise money for) a company's operations, which is the capital structure decision made by senior management. The capital structure that is chosen will very often include the use of debt, which will affect the company's financial leverage. Thus, it is natural to discuss capital structure and leverage together. In this chapter, therefore, we will

- Discuss and illustrate the business risk and financial risk of a company;
- Show how to quantify these risks for a company or division using degrees of leverage;
- View how leverage affects a company's value; and
- Learn how to evaluate a company's capital structure.

The chapter is organized as follows: In Section 2, we introduce the concept of leverage. In Section 3, we discuss the sources of earnings volatility, including sales risk, operating risk, and financial risk, and explain quantitative measures of leverage. In Section 4, we discuss the company's capital structure decision and the choice of alternative sources of financing. In Section 5, we present important issues for the analyst, such as the role of debt rating in the capital structure decision and international differences in capital structure policies. We summarize the chapter in Section 6.

2. LEVERAGE

Leverage increases the potential volatility of a company's earnings and cash flows and increases the risk of lending to or owning a company. Additionally, the valuation of a company and its equity is affected by the degree of leverage: The greater the leverage is, the greater the risk will be and hence the greater the discount rate applied in its valuation. Further, highly leveraged companies have a heightened chance of incurring significant losses during downturns, thus accelerating conditions that lead to financial distress and bankruptcy.

Consider the simple example of two companies, Impulse Robotics, Inc., and Malvey Aerospace, Inc. Exhibit 4-1 displays these companies' performance for the period of study.[1]

These companies have the same net income, but are they identical in terms of financial characteristics? Would we appraise these two companies at the same value? Not necessarily.

EXHIBIT 4-1   Impulse Robotics and Malvey Aerospace

	Impulse Robotics	Malvey Aerospace
Revenues	$1,000,000	$1,000,000
Operating costs	700,000	750,000
Operating income	$300,000	$250,000
Financing expense	100,000	50,000
Net income	$200,000	$200,000

---

[1] We are ignoring taxes for this example, but when taxes are included, the general conclusions remain the same.

EXHIBIT 4-2   Impulse Robotics and Malvey Aerospace

	Impulse Robotics	Malvey Aerospace
Number of units produced and sold	100,000	100,000
Sales price per unit	$10	$10
Variable cost per unit	$2	$6
Fixed operating cost	$500,000	$150,000
Fixed financing expense	$100,000	$50,000

The risk associated with future earnings and cash flows of a company is affected by the company's cost structure. The **cost structure** of a company is the mix of variable and fixed costs. **Variable costs** fluctuate with the level of production and sales. Some examples of variable costs are the cost of goods purchased for resale, costs of materials or supplies, shipping charges, delivery charges, wages for hourly employees, sales commissions, and sales or production bonuses. **Fixed costs** are expenses that are the same regardless of the production and sales of the company. These costs include depreciation, rent, interest on debt, insurance, and wages for salaried employees.

Suppose that the cost structures of the companies differ in the manner shown in Exhibit 4-2. The risk associated with these companies is different, although, as we saw in Exhibit 4-1, they have the same net income. They have different operating and financing cost structures, resulting in differing potential volatility of net income.

For example, if the number of units produced and sold is different from 100,000, the net income of the two companies diverges. If 50,000 units are produced and sold, Impulse Robotics has a loss of $200,000 and Malvey Aerospace has $0 earnings. If, on the other hand, the number of units produced and sold is 200,000, Impulse Robotics earns $1 million, whereas Malvey Aerospace earns $600,000. In other words, the swing in net income is greater for Impulse Robotics, which has higher fixed costs in terms of both fixed operating costs and fixed financing costs.

EXHIBIT 4-3   Net Income for Different Numbers of Units Produced and Sold

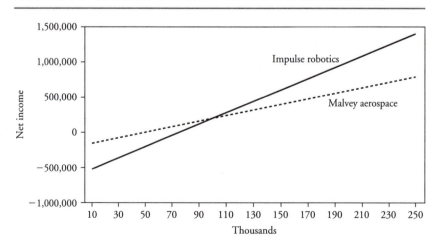

Impulse Robotics' cost structure results in more leverage than that of Malvey Aerospace. We can see this effect when we plot the net income of each company against the number of units produced and sold, as in Exhibit 4-3. The greater leverage of Impulse Robotics is reflected in the greater slope of the line representing net income. This means that as the number of units sold changes, Impulse Robotics experiences a greater change in net income than does Malvey Aerospace for the same change in units sold.

Companies that have more fixed costs relative to variable costs in their cost structures have greater variation in net income as revenues fluctuate and hence more risk.

3. BUSINESS RISK AND FINANCIAL RISK

Risk arises from both the operating and financing activities of a company. In the following, we address how that happens and the measures available to the analyst to gauge the risk in each case.

3.1. Business Risk and Its Components

Business risk is the risk associated with operating earnings. Operating earnings are uncertain because total revenues and many of the expenditures contributed to produce those revenues are uncertain. Revenues are affected by a large number of factors, including economic conditions, the actions of competitors, governmental regulation, and demographics. Therefore, prices of the company's goods or services or the quantity of sales may be different from what is expected. We refer to the uncertainty with respect to the price and quantity of goods and services as **sales risk**.

Operating risk is the risk attributed to the operating cost structure, in particular the use of fixed costs in operations. The greater the fixed operating costs relative to variable operating costs, the greater the operating risk will be. Business risk is therefore the combined risk of sales and operations. Companies that operate in the same line of business generally have similar business risk.

3.2. Sales Risk

Consider Impulse Robotics once again. Suppose that the forecasted number of units produced and sold in the next period is 100,000 but that the standard deviation of the number of units sold is 20,000. And suppose the price that the units sell for is expected to be $10 per unit but the standard deviation is $2. Contrast this situation with that of a company named Tolley Aerospace, Inc., which has the same cost structure but a standard deviation of units sold of 40,000 and a price standard deviation of $4.

If we assume, for simplicity's sake, that the fixed operating costs are known with certainty and that the units sold and price per unit follow a normal distribution, we can see the impact of the different risks on the operating income of the two companies through a simulation; the results are shown in Exhibit 4-4. In the exhibit we see the differing distributions of operating income that result from the distributions of units sold and price per unit. So, even if the companies have the same cost structure, differing *sales risk* affects the potential variability of the company's profitability. In our example, Tolley Aerospace has a wider distribution of likely outcomes in terms of operating profit. This greater potential volatility in operating earnings means that Tolley Aerospace has more sales risk than Impulse Robotics.

EXHIBIT 4-4   Operation Income Simulation for Impulse Robotics and Tolley Aerospace

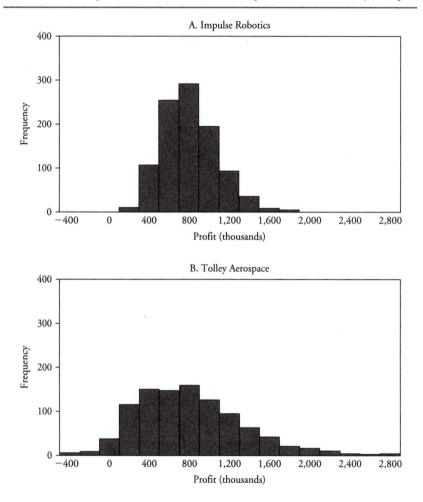

3.3. Operating Risk

The greater the fixed component of costs, the more difficult it is for a company to adjust its operating costs to changes in sales. The mixture of fixed and variable costs depends largely on the type of business. Even within the same line of business, companies can vary their fixed and variable costs to some degree. We refer to the risk arising from the mix of fixed and variable costs as operating risk. The greater the fixed operating costs relative to variable operating costs, the greater the operating risk will be.

Next, we will look at how operating risk affects the variability of cash flows. A concept taught in microeconomics is **elasticity**, which is simply a measure of the sensitivity of changes in one item to changes in another. We can apply this concept to examine how sensitive a company's operating income is to changes in demand, as measured by unit sales. We will calculate the operating income elasticity, which we refer to as the **degree of operating leverage (DOL)**.

The degree of operating leverage is the ratio of the percentage change in operating income to the percentage change in units sold. We will simplify things and assume that the company sells all that it produces in the same period. Then,

$$\text{DOL} = \frac{\text{Percentage change in operating income}}{\text{Percentage change in units sold}} \tag{4-1}$$

Returning to Impulse Robotics, the price per unit is $10, the variable cost per unit is $2, and the total fixed costs are $500,000. If Impulse Robotics' output changes from 100,000 units to 110,000 units—an increase of 10 percent in the number of units sold—operating income changes from $300,000 to $380,000 (see Exhibit 4-5).[2]

Operating income increases by 26.67 percent when units sold increases by 10 percent. What if the number of units *decreases* by 10 percent, from 100,000 to 90,000? Operating income is $220,000, representing a *decline* of 26.67 percent.

What is happening is that, for a 1 percent change in units sold, the operating income changes by 2.67 times that percentage, in the same direction. If units sold increases by 10 percent, operating income increases by 26.7 percent; if units sold decreases by 20 percent, operating income would decrease by 53.3 percent.

We can represent the degree of operating leverage as given in Equation 4-1 in terms of the basic elements of the price per unit, variable cost per unit, number of units sold, and fixed operating costs. Operating income is

$$\begin{array}{l}\text{Operating} \\ \text{income}\end{array} = \left[\left(\begin{array}{c}\text{Price} \\ \text{per unit}\end{array}\right)\left(\begin{array}{c}\text{Number of} \\ \text{units sold}\end{array}\right)\right] - \left[\left(\begin{array}{c}\text{Variable cost} \\ \text{per unit}\end{array}\right)\left(\begin{array}{c}\text{Number of} \\ \text{units sold}\end{array}\right)\right]$$

$$- \left[\left(\begin{array}{c}\text{Fixed operating} \\ \text{costs}\end{array}\right)\right]$$

or

$$\begin{array}{l}\text{Operating} \\ \text{income}\end{array} = \underbrace{\left(\begin{array}{c}\text{Number of} \\ \text{units sold}\end{array}\right)\left[\left(\begin{array}{c}\text{Price} \\ \text{per unit}\end{array}\right) - \left(\begin{array}{c}\text{Variable cost} \\ \text{per unit}\end{array}\right)\right]}_{\text{Contribution margin}} - \left[\begin{array}{c}\text{Fixed operating} \\ \text{costs}\end{array}\right]$$

EXHIBIT 4-5   Operating Leverage of Impulse Robotics

Item	Selling 100,000 Units ($)	Selling 110,000 Units ($)	Percentage Change (%)
Revenues	1,000,000	1,100,000	+10.00
Less variable costs	200,000	220,000	+10.00
Less fixed costs	500,000	500,000	0.00
Operating income	300,000	380,000	+26.67

[2]We provide the variable and fixed operating costs for our sample companies used in this chapter to illustrate the leverage and breakeven concepts. In reality, however, the financial analyst does not have these breakdowns but rather is faced with interpreting reported account values that often combine variable and fixed costs and costs for different product lines.

The **per-unit contribution margin** is the amount that each unit sold contributes to covering fixed costs—that is, the difference between the price per unit and the variable cost per unit. That difference multiplied by the quantity sold is the **contribution margin**, which equals revenue minus variable costs.

How much does operating income change when the number of units sold changes? Fixed costs do not change; therefore, operating income changes by the contribution margin. The percentage change in operating income for a given change in units sold simplifies to

$$\text{DOL} = \frac{Q(P-V)}{Q(P-V)-F} \qquad (4\text{-}2)$$

where

Q = number of units

P = price per unit

V = variable operating cost per unit

F = fixed operating cost.

Therefore, $P - V$ is the per unit contribution margin, and $Q(P - V)$ is the contribution margin.

Applying the formula for DOL using the data for Impulse Robotics, we can calculate the sensitivity to change in units sold from 100,000 units:

$$\underset{100,000 \text{ units}}{\text{DOL @}} = \frac{100,000\,(\$10 - \$2)}{100,000(\$10 - \$2) - \$500,000}$$

$$= 2.67$$

A DOL of 2.67 means that a 1 percent change in units sold results in a 1 percent $\times$ 2.67 = 2.67 percent change in operating income; a DOL of 5 means that a 1 percent change in units sold results in a 5 percent change in operating income, and so on.

Why do we specify that the DOL is at a particular quantity sold (in this case, 100,000 units)? Because the DOL is different at different numbers of units produced and sold. For example, at 200,000 units,

$$\underset{200,000 \text{ units}}{\text{DOL @}} = \frac{200,000(\$10 - \$2)}{200,000(\$10 - \$2) - \$500,000}$$

$$= 1.45$$

In Exhibit 4-6, we can see the sensitivity of the DOL for different numbers of units produced and sold. When operating profit is negative, the DOL is negative. At positions just below and just above the point where operating income is $0, operating income is at its most sensitive on a percentage basis to changes in units produced and sold. At the point at which operating income is $0 (at 62,500 units produced and sold in this example), the DOL is undefined because the denominator in the DOL calculation is $0. After this point, the DOL gradually declines as more units are produced and sold.

We will now look at a similar situation in which the company has shifted some of the operating costs away from fixed costs and into variable costs. Malvey Aerospace has a unit sales price of $10, a variable cost of $6 a unit, and $150,000 in fixed costs. A change in units

EXHIBIT 4-6   Impulse Robotics' Degree of Operating Leverage for Different
Number of Units Produced and Sold ($P = \$10$; $V = \$2$; $F = \$500,000$)

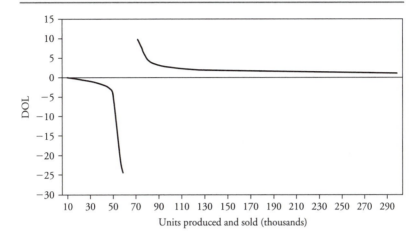

sold from 100,000 to 110,000 (a 10 percent change) changes operating profit from $250,000
to $290,000, or 16 percent. The DOL in this case is 1.6:

$$\begin{array}{c} \text{DOL @} \\ \text{100,000 units} \end{array} = \frac{100,000\,(\$10 - \$6)}{100,000\,(\$10 - \$6) - \$150,000}$$

$$= 1.6$$

and the change in operating income is 16 percent:

$$\begin{array}{c} \text{Percentage change} \\ \text{in operating income} \end{array} = \text{DOL}\left(\begin{array}{c} \text{Percentage change} \\ \text{in units sold} \end{array}\right)$$

$$= 1.6\,(10\%)$$

$$= 16\%$$

We can see the difference in leverage in the case of Impulse Robotics and Malvey
Aerospace companies in Exhibit 4-7. In Panel A, we see that Impulse Robotics has higher
operating income than Malvey Aerospace when both companies produce and sell more than
87,500 units, but lower operating income than Malvey when both companies produce and
sell fewer than 87,500 units.[3]

This example confirms what we saw earlier in our reasoning of fixed and variable costs:
The greater the use of fixed, relative to variable, operating costs, the more sensitive operat-
ing income is to changes in units sold and therefore the greater the operating risk. Impulse
Robotics has more operating risk because it has more operating leverage. However, as Panel B

---

[3]We can calculate the number of units that produce the same operating income for these two companies by equating the operating incomes and solving for the number of units. Let X be the number of
units. The X at which Malvey Aerospace and Impulse Robotics generate the same operating income is
the X that solves the following: $10X - 2X - 500,000 = 10X - 6X - 150,000$; that is, $X = 87,500$.

EXHIBIT 4-7   Profitability and the DOL for Impulse Robotics and Malvey Aerospace
(Impulse Robotics: $P = \$10$; $V = \$2$; $F = \$500,000$; Malvey Aerospace: $P = \$10$;
$V = \$6$; $F = \$150,000$)

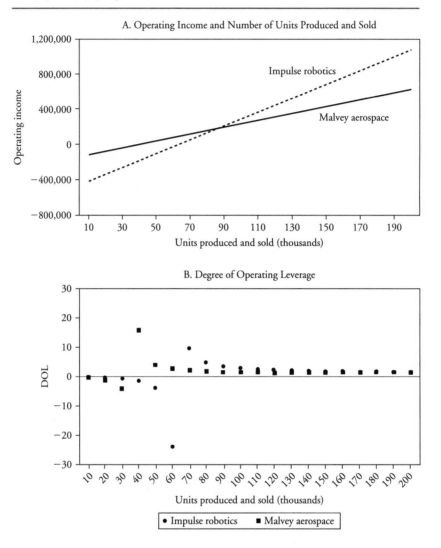

of Exhibit 4-7 shows, the degrees of operating leverage are similar for the two companies for
larger numbers of units produced and sold.

Both sales risk and operating risk influence a company's business risk. And both sales
risk and operating risk are determined in large part by the type of business the company is in.
But management has more opportunity to manage and control operating risk than sales risk.

Suppose a company is deciding which equipment to buy to produce a particular product. The sales risk is the same no matter what equipment is chosen to produce the product.
But the available equipment may differ in terms of the fixed and variable operating costs of
producing the product. Financial analysts need to consider how the operating cost structure
of a company affects the company's risk.

EXAMPLE 4-1   Calculating the Degree of Operating Leverage

Arnaud Kenigswald is analyzing the potential impact of an improving economy on earnings at Global Auto, one of the world's largest car manufacturers. Global is headquartered in Berlin. Two Global Auto divisions manufacture passenger cars and produce combined revenues of €93 billion. Kenigswald projects that sales will improve by 10 percent due to increased demand for cars. He wants to see how Global's earnings might respond given that level of increase in sales. He first looks at the degree of leverage at Global, starting with operating leverage.

Global sold 6 million passenger cars in 2003. The average price per car was €24,000, fixed costs associated with passenger car production total €15 billion per year, and variable costs per car are €14,000. What is the degree of operating leverage of Global Auto?

Solution

$$\frac{\text{DOL @}}{\text{6 million units}} = \frac{6 \, \text{million} \, (\text{€}24{,}000 - \text{€}14{,}000)}{6 \, \text{million} \, (\text{€}24{,}000 - \text{€}14{,}000) - \text{€}15 \, \text{billion}}$$

$$= 1.333$$

For a 10 percent increase in cars sold, operating income increases by $1.333 \times 10\%$ = 13.33%.

Industries that tend to have high operating leverage are those that invest up front to produce a product but spend relatively little on making and distributing it. Software developers and pharmaceutical companies fit this description. Alternatively, retailers have low operating leverage because much of the cost of goods sold is variable.

Because most companies produce more than one product, the ratio of variable to fixed costs is difficult to obtain. We can get an idea of the operating leverage of a company by looking at the change in operating income in relation to changes in sales for the entire company. Although this approach does not provide a precise measure of operating risk, it can help provide a general idea of the sensitivity of operating earnings. For example, compare the relation between operating earnings and revenues for Abbott Laboratories, a pharmaceutical company, and Wal-Mart Stores, a discount retailer, as shown in Exhibit 4-8. Not only is the slope of a least-squares regression line greater for Abbott, but also note the higher volatility of observations around the regression.[4] We can see that operating earnings are more sensitive to changes in revenues for the higher-operating-leveraged Abbott as compared to the lower-operating-leveraged Wal-Mart Stores.

---

[4] A least-squares regression is a procedure for finding the best-fitting line through a set of data points by minimizing the squared deviations from the line.

EXHIBIT 4-8   Relation Between Operating Earnings and Revenues

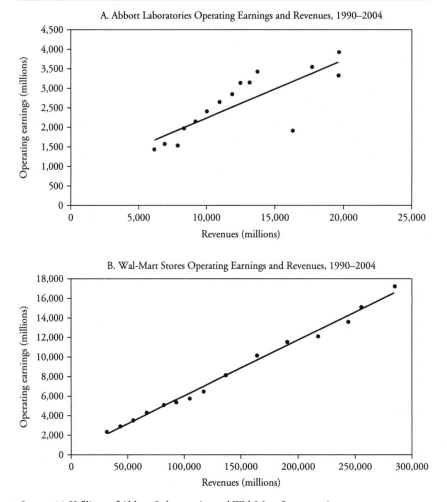

A. Abbott Laboratories Operating Earnings and Revenues, 1990–2004

B. Wal-Mart Stores Operating Earnings and Revenues, 1990–2004

Sources: 10-K filings of Abbott Laboratories and Wal-Mart Stores, various years.

3.4. Financial Risk

We can expand on the concept of risk to accommodate the perspective of owning a security. A security represents a claim on the income and assets of a business; therefore, the risk of the security goes beyond the variability of operating earnings to include how the cash flows from those earnings are distributed among the claimants—the creditors and owners of the business. The risk of a security is therefore affected by both business risk and financial risk.

Financial risk is the risk associated with how a company finances its operations. If a company finances with debt, it is legally obligated to pay the amounts that make up its debts when due. By taking on fixed obligations, such as debt and long-term leases, the company increases its financial risk. If a company finances its business with equity, generated either from operations (retained earnings) or from issuing new equity, it does not incur fixed obligations. The more fixed-cost obligations (e.g., debt) the company incurs, the greater its financial risk will be.

We can quantify this risk in the same way we did for operating risk, looking at the sensitivity of the cash flows available to owners when operating income changes. This sensitivity, which we refer to as the **degree of financial leverage (DFL)**, is

$$DFL = \frac{\text{Percentage change in net income}}{\text{Percentage change in operating income}} \qquad (4\text{-}3)$$

Net income is equal to operating income, less interest and taxes.[5] If operating income changes, how does net income change? Consider Impulse Robotics. Suppose the interest payments are $100,000 and, for simplicity and wishful thinking, the tax rate is 0 percent: If operating income changes from $300,000 to $360,000, net income changes from $200,000 to $260,000 (see Exhibit 4-9).

A 20 percent increase in operating income increases net income by $60,000, or 30 percent. What if, instead, the fixed financial costs are $150,000? A 20 percent change in operating income results in a 40 percent change in the net income, from $150,000 to $210,000 (see Exhibit 4-10).

Using more debt financing, which results in higher fixed costs, increases the sensitivity of owners' income. We can represent the sensitivity of owners' cash flows to a change in operating income, continuing the notation from before and including the fixed financial cost, C, and the tax rate, t, as

$$\begin{aligned} DFL &= \frac{[Q(P - V) - F](1 - t)}{[Q(P - V) - F - C](1 - t)} \qquad (4\text{-}4) \\[6pt] &= \frac{[Q(P - V) - F]}{[Q(P - V) - F - C]} \end{aligned}$$

As you can see in Equation 4-4, the factor that adjusts for taxes, $(1 - t)$, cancels out of the equation. In other words, the DFL is not affected by the tax rate.

EXHIBIT 4-9   Financial Risk of Impulse Robotics (1)

	Operating Income of $300,000 ($)	Operating Income of $360,000 ($)	Percentage Change (%)
Operating income	300,000	360,000	+20
less interest	100,000	100,000	0
Net income	200,000	260,000	+30

---

[5]More complex entities than we have been using for our examples may also need to account for other income (losses) and extraordinary income (losses), together with operating income as the basis for earnings before interest and taxes.

EXHIBIT 4-10   Financial Risk of Impulse Robotics (2)

	Operating Income of $300,000 ($)	Operating Income of $360,000 ($)	Percentage Change
Operating income	300,000	360,000	+20
Less interest	150,000	150,000	0
Net income	150,000	210,000	+40

In the case in which operating income is $300,000 and fixed financing costs are $100,000, the degree of financial leverage is

$$\underset{\$300,000 \text{ operating income}}{\text{DFL} @} = \frac{\$300,000}{\$300,000 - \$100,000}$$
$$= 1.5$$

If, instead, fixed financial costs are $150,000, the DFL is equal to 2.0:

$$\underset{\$300,000 \text{ operating income}}{\text{DFL} @} = \frac{\$300,000}{\$300,000 - \$150,000}$$
$$= 2.0$$

Again, we need to qualify our degree of leverage by the level of operating income because DFL is different at different levels of operating income.

The greater the use of financing sources that require fixed obligations, such as interest, the greater the sensitivity of net income to changes in operating income will be.

EXAMPLE 4-2   Calculating the Degree of Financial Leverage

Global Auto also employs debt financing. If Global can borrow at 8 percent, the interest cost is €40 billion. What is the degree of financial leverage of Global Auto if 6 million cars are produced and sold?

Solution

At 6 million cars produced and sold, operating income = €45 billion. Therefore:

$$\underset{€45 \text{ billion operating income}}{\text{DFL} @} = \frac{€45 \text{ billion}}{€45 \text{ billion} - €40 \text{ billion}}$$
$$= 9.0$$

For every 1 percent change in operating income, net income changes 9 percent due to financial leverage.

Unlike operating leverage, the degree of financial leverage is most often a choice by the company's management. Whereas operating costs are very similar among companies in the same industry, competitors may decide on differing capital structures.

Companies with a higher ratio of tangible assets to total assets may have higher degrees of financial leverage because lenders may feel more secure that their claims would be satisfied in the event of a downturn. In general, "old economy" businesses with plants, land, and equipment use more financial leverage than "new economy" businesses in technology and pharmaceuticals.

3.5. Total Leverage

The degree of operating leverage gives us an idea of the sensitivity of operating income to changes in revenues. And the degree of financial leverage gives us an idea of the sensitivity of owners' income to changes in operating income. But often we are concerned about the combined effect of both operating leverage and financial leverage. Owners are concerned about the combined effect because both factors contribute to the risk associated with their future cash flows. And financial managers, making decisions intended to maximize owners' wealth, need to be concerned with how investment decisions (which affect the operating cost structure) and financing decisions (which affect the capital structure) affect lenders' and owners' risk.

Let's look again at Impulse Robotics. The sensitivity of owners' cash flow to a given change in units sold is affected by both operating and financial leverage. Consider using 100,000 units as the base number produced and sold. A 10 percent increase in units sold results in a 27 percent increase in operating income and a 40 percent increase in net income; a like decrease in units sold results in a similar decrease in operating income and net income (see Exhibit 4-11).

Combining a company's degree of operating leverage with its degree of financial leverage results in the **degree of total leverage** (**DTL**), a measure of the sensitivity of the cash flows to owners to changes in the number of units produced and sold. Once again making the simplifying assumption that a company sells all that it produces in the same period,

$$\text{DTL} = \frac{\text{Percentage change in net income}}{\text{Percentage change in the number of units sold}} \qquad (4\text{-}5)$$

EXHIBIT 4-11   Total Leverage of Impulse Robotics

	Units Produced and Sold		
	90,000	100,000	110,000
Revenues	$900,000	$1,000,000	$1,100,000
Less variable costs	180,000	200,000	220,000
Less fixed costs	500,000	500,000	500,000
Operating income	$220,000	$300,000	$380,000
Less interest	100,000	100,000	100,000
Net income	$120,000	$200,000	$280,000
Relative to 100,000 units produced and sold			
Percentage change in units sold	−10%		+10%
Percentage change in operating profit	−27%		+27%
Percentage change in net income	−40%		+40%

or

$$\begin{aligned} \text{DTL} &= \frac{Q(P-V)}{Q(P-V)-F} \times \frac{[Q(P-V)-F](1-t)}{[Q(P-V)-F-C](1-t)} \\ &= \frac{Q(P-V)}{Q(P-V)-F-C} \\ &= \text{DOL} \times \text{DFL} \end{aligned} \qquad (4\text{-}6)$$

Suppose

Number of units sold (Q) = 100,000

Price per unit (P) = \$10

Variable cost per unit (V) = \$2

Fixed operating cost (F) = \$500,000

Fixed financing cost (C) = \$100,000

Then

$$\begin{aligned} \text{DTL} &= \frac{100,000(\$10-\$2)}{100,000(\$10-\$2)-\$500,000-\$100,000} \\ &= 4.0 \end{aligned}$$

which we could also have determined by multiplying the DOL, 2.67, by the DFL, 1.5. This means that a 1 percent increase in units sold results in a 4 percent increase in net income; a 50 percent increase in units produced and sold results in a 200 percent increase in net income; a 5 percent decline in units sold results in a 20 percent decline in income to owners; and so on.

Because the DOL is relative to the base number of units produced and sold and the DFL is relative to the base operating earnings, DTL is different depending on the number of units produced and sold. We can see the DOL, DFL, and DTL for Impulse Robotics for different numbers of units produced and sold, beginning at the number of units for which the degrees are positive, in Exhibit 4-12.

EXHIBIT 4-12   DOL, DFL, and DTL for Different Numbers of Units
Produced and Sold (P = \$10, V = \$2, F = \$500,000, C = \$100,000)

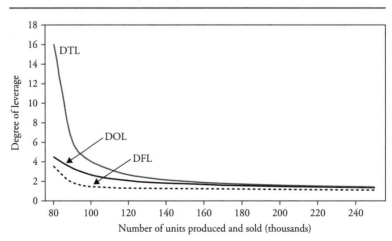

In the case of operating leverage, the fixed operating costs act as a fulcrum. The greater the proportion of fixed operating costs, the more sensitive operating income is to changes in sales. In the case of financial leverage, the fixed financial costs, such as interest, act as a fulcrum. The greater the proportion of financing with fixed cost sources, such as debt, the more sensitive cash flows available to owners are to changes in operating income. Combining the effects of both types of leverage, we see that fixed operating and financial costs together increase the sensitivity of earnings to owners.

EXAMPLE 4-3   Calculating the Degree of Total Leverage

Continuing from Example 4-2, Global Auto's total leverage is

$$\begin{matrix} \text{DTL@} \\ \text{6 million units} \end{matrix} = \left(\begin{matrix} \text{DOL@} \\ \text{6 million units} \end{matrix} \right) \times \left(\begin{matrix} \text{DFL@} \\ \text{€45 million operating income} \end{matrix} \right)$$

$$= \frac{6 \text{ million } (€24{,}000 - €14{,}000)}{6 \text{ million } (€24{,}000 - €14{,}000) - €15 \text{ billion}}$$

$$\times \frac{€45 \text{ billion}}{€45 \text{ billion} - €40 \text{ billion}}$$

$$= 1.333 \times 9.0$$

$$= 12$$

Given Global Auto's operating and capital structures, a 1 percent change in unit sales changes net income by 12 percent.

3.6. Breakeven Rates and Expected Return

Looking back at Exhibit 4-3, we see that there is a number of units at which the company goes from being unprofitable to being profitable—that is, the number of units at which the net income is 0. This number is referred to as the breakeven point. The **breakeven point** is the number of units produced and sold at which the company's net income is 0, the point at which revenues are equal to costs.

Plotting revenues and total costs against the number of units produced and sold, as in Exhibit 4-13, indicates that the breakeven is at 75,000 units. At this number of units produced and sold, revenues are equal to costs and hence profit is 0.

We can calculate this breakeven point for Impulse Robotics and Malvey Aerospace. Consider that net income is 0 when the revenues are equal to the expenses. We can represent this equality of revenues and costs as the following:

$$PQ = VQ + F + C$$

where

P = price per unit

Q = number of units produced and sold

V = variable cost per unit

F = fixed operating costs

C = fixed financial cost

EXHIBIT 4-13   Impulse Robotics Breakeven

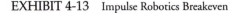

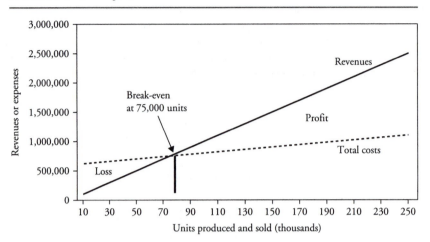

Therefore,

$$PQ_{BE} = VQ_{BE} + F + C$$

and the breakeven number of units, Q_{BE}, is[6]

$$Q_{BE} = \frac{F + C}{P - V} \tag{4-7}$$

In the case of Impulse Robotics and Malvey Aerospace, Impulse Robotics has a higher breakeven point:

Impulse Robotics: $Q_{BE} = \dfrac{\$500,000 + \$100,000}{\$10 - \$2} = 75,000 \text{ units}$

Malvey Aerospace: $Q_{BE} = \dfrac{\$150,000 + \$50,000}{\$10 - \$6} = 50,000 \text{ units}$

This means that Impulse Robotics must produce and sell more units to achieve a profit. So, while the higher-leveraged Impulse Robotics has a greater breakeven point relative to Malvey Aerospace, the profit that Impulse Robotics generates beyond this breakeven point is greater than that of Malvey Aerospace. Therefore, leverage has its rewards in terms of potentially greater profit, but it also increases risk.

We can also specify the breakeven in terms of the operating profit, which we refer to as the **operating breakeven**, Q_{OBE}. In this case, the equality is set for revenues and operating costs and the breakeven number of units, Q_{OBE}, is

$$PQ_{OBE} = VQ_{OBE} + F$$
$$Q_{OBE} = \frac{F}{P - V}$$

---

[6]You will notice that we did not consider taxes in our calculation of the breakeven point. This is because, at the point of breakeven, taxable income is 0.

For the two companies in our example, Impulse Robotics and Malvey Aerospace, the operating breakevens are 62,500 and 37,500 units, respectively:

$$\text{Impulse Robotics:} \quad Q_{OBE} = \frac{\$500,000}{\$10 - \$2} = 62,500 \text{ units}$$

$$\text{Malvey Aerospace:} \quad Q_{OBE} = \frac{\$150,000}{\$10 - \$6} = 37,500 \text{ units}$$

Again, Impulse Robotics has a higher breakeven point in terms of the number of units produced and sold.

EXAMPLE 4-4   Calculating the Breakeven Point

Continuing with his analysis, Kenigswald considers the effect of a possible downturn on Global Auto's earnings. He divides the fixed costs of €15 billion by the per unit contribution margin:

$$Q_{OBE} = \frac{€15 \text{ billion}}{€24,000 - €14,000}$$
$$= 1,500,000 \text{ cars}$$

The operating breakeven for Global is 1,500,000 cars, or €36 billion in revenues. We calculate the total breakeven by dividing fixed operating costs, plus interest costs, by the contribution margin:

$$Q_{BE} = \frac{€15 \text{ billion} + €40 \text{ billion}}{€24,000 - €14,000}$$
$$= \frac{€55 \text{ billion}}{€10,000}$$
$$= 5,500,000 \text{ cars}$$

Considering the degree of total leverage, Global's total breakeven is 5.5 million cars, or revenues of €132 billion.

We can verify these calculations by constructing an income statement for the breakeven sales (in € billions):

	1,500,000 Cars	5,500,000 Cars
Revenues	36	132
Variable operating costs	21	77
Fixed operating costs	15	15
Operating income	0	40
Fixed financial costs	40	40
Net income	−40	0

As business expands or contracts beyond or below breakeven points, fixed costs do not change. The breakeven points for companies with low operating and financial leverage are less important than those for companies with high leverage. Companies with greater total leverage must generate more revenue to cover fixed operating and financing costs. The farther unit sales are from the breakeven point for high-leverage companies, the greater the magnifying effect of this leverage.

EXAMPLE 4-5   The Leveraging Role of Debt

Consider the Capital Company, which is expected to generate $1.5 million in revenues and $0.5 million in operating earnings next year. Currently, the Capital Company does not use debt financing and has assets of $2 million.

Suppose Capital were to change its capital structure, buying back $1 million of stock and issuing $1 million in debt. If we assume that interest on debt is 5 percent and income is taxed at a rate of 30 percent, what is the effect of debt financing on Capital's net income and return on equity if operating earnings may vary as much as 40 percent from expected earnings (see Exhibit 4-14)?

EXHIBIT 4-14   Return on Equity of Capital Company

No Debt, Shareholders' Equity = $2 million	Expected Operating Earnings, Less 40%	Expected Operating Earnings	Expected Operating Earnings, Plus 40%
Earnings before interest and taxes	$300,000	$500,000	$700,000
Interest expense	0	0	0
Income before taxes	$300,000	$500,000	$700,000
Taxes	90,000	150,000	210,000
Net income	$210,000	$350,000	$490,000
Return on equity[7]	10.5%	17.5%	24.5%

Debt to Total Assets = 50% Shareholders' Equity = $1 million	Expected Operating Earnings, Less 40%	Expected Operating Earnings	Expected Operating Earnings, Plus 40%
Earnings before interest and taxes	$300,000	$500,000	$700,000
Interest expense	50,000	50,000	50,000
Income before taxes	$250,000	$450,000	$650,000
Taxes	75,000	135,000	195,000
Net income	$175,000	$315,000	$455,000
Return on equity	17.5%	31.5%	45.5%

[7]Recall that ROE is calculated as Net income/Shareholders' equity.

Depicting a broader array of capital structures and operating earnings, ranging from an operating loss of $500,000 to operating earnings of $2 million, Exhibit 4-15 shows the effect of leverage on the return on equity for Capital Company:

EXHIBIT 4-15   Return on Equity of Capital Corporation for Different Levels of Operating Earnings and Different Financing Choices

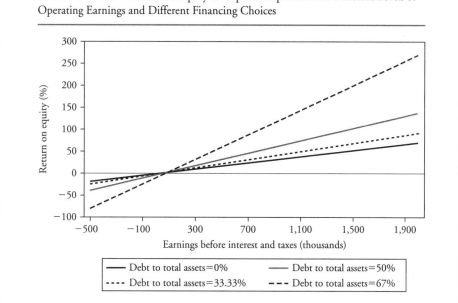

Business is generally an uncertain venture. Changes in the macroeconomic and competitive environments that influence sales and profitability are typically hard to discern and forecast. The larger the proportion of debt in the financing mix of a business, the greater is the likelihood that it will face default. Similarly, the greater the proportion of debt in the capital structure, the more earnings are magnified upward in improving economic times. The bottom line? The greater the leverage, the greater the risk of ownership for equity holders.

3.7. The Risks of Creditors and Owners

As discussed earlier, "business risk" refers to the effect of economic conditions as well as to the level of operating leverage. Uncertainty about demand, output prices, and costs is among the many factors that affect business risk. When conditions change for any of these factors, companies with higher business risk experience more volatile earnings. Financial risk is the additional risk that results from the use of debt and preferred stock. The degree of financial risk grows with greater use of debt. Who bears this risk?

The risk for providers of equity and debt capital differs because of the relative rights and responsibilities associated with the use of borrowed money in a business. Lenders have priority claims on assets, so they have greater security. In return for lending money to a business, lenders require the payment of interest and principal when due. These contractual payments to lenders must be made regardless of the profitability of the business. A business must satisfy these claims in a timely fashion or face the pain of bankruptcy should it default. In return for their higher priority in claims, lenders get predefined yet limited returns.

In contrast, equity providers claim whatever is left over after all expenses, including debt service, have been paid. So, unlike the fixed and known commitments to the lenders, what is left over for the owners may be a great deal or may be nothing. In exchange for this risk, providers of equity capital exercise the decision-making power over the business, including the right to hire, guide, and, if necessary, fire managers. Equity holders also have the right to declare what portion of the business earnings they will take out as dividends. In public companies, ownership rights are usually exercised through an elected board of directors.

Legal codes in most countries provide for these rights, as well as conditions for companies to file for bankruptcy. Most bankruptcy codes provide in some form for two categories of bankruptcies. One form provides for a temporary protection from creditors so that a viable business may reorganize. In the United States, the U.S. Bankruptcy Code sets the terms for the form of negotiated **reorganization** of a company's capital structure that allows it to remain a going concern in Chapter 11.[8] For businesses that are not viable, the second form of bankruptcy process allows for the orderly satisfaction of the creditors' claims. In the United States, this form of bankruptcy is referred to as **liquidation**.[9] Whereas both types of bankruptcy lead to major dislocations in the rights and privileges of owners, lenders, employees, and managers, it is in this latter category of bankruptcy that the original business ceases to exist.

The difference between a company that reorganizes and emerges from bankruptcy and one that is liquidated is often the difference between operating and financial leverage. Companies with high operating leverage have less flexibility in making changes, and bankruptcy protection does little to help reduce operating costs. Companies with high financial leverage use bankruptcy laws and protection to change their capital structure and, once the restructuring is complete, can emerge as ongoing concerns. Examples 4-6 and 4-7 are real-world examples of a Chapter 11 reorganization and a Chapter 7 liquidation.

EXAMPLE 4-6   Chapter 11 Reorganization and Owens Corning

The world's largest manufacturer of glass fiber insulation, Owens Corning Corporation of Toledo, Ohio, filed for Chapter 11 bankruptcy on October 5, 2000, because it faced growing asbestos liability claims. With revenues exceeding $6 billion per year, Owens Corning was one of the largest corporations ever afforded bankruptcy protection by the U.S. courts.

From 1952 to 1972, Owens Corning produced an asbestos-containing high-temperature pipe coating called Kaylo, and, at the time of its bankruptcy filing, it had received more than 460,000 asbestos personal injury claims and had paid or agreed to pay more than $5 billion for asbestos-related awards and settlements, legal expenses, and claims processing fees. While the company had assets of $7 billion and liabilities of $5.7 billion, the trust fund it set aside to pay those claims appeared inadequate.

The company's stock traded at between $15 and $25 per share in the year prior to the announcement; the price fell to $1 per share when Owens Corning declared bankruptcy and admitted that it had been overwhelmed by the asbestos liabilities.

---

[8]U.S. Code, Title 11—Bankruptcy, Chapter 11—Reorganization. Companies filing for bankruptcy under this code are referred to as having filed for Chapter 11 bankruptcy.

[9]U.S. Code, Title 11—Bankruptcy, Chapter 7—Liquidation.

EXAMPLE 4-7   Chapter 7 and Webvan Do Not Deliver

Since the peak of the NASDAQ in March of 2000, many technology companies have found either that they cannot raise enough capital to implement their business plans or that they have an untenable business plan. Some have simply shut their doors and gone out of business, while others have filed for bankruptcy. Either way, these companies have left many unsatisfied creditors.

For example, Webvan.com was a start-up company in the late 1990s that raised over $1.2 billion in equity, $375 million of which came from an IPO in November 1999. It had very ambitious business plans to build a series of warehouses and to deliver groceries to fulfill customer orders placed over the Internet. Webvan.com, however, faced a number of challenges, including a downturn in the economy, and quickly ran through its capital.

Webvan.com filed for Chapter 11 bankruptcy protection in July 1999 and reported that it owed $106 million to creditors. By the time it began liquidation under Chapter 7 in January 2002, it reported that the value of its liquidated assets totaled only $25 million, leaving its creditors to receive pennies on the dollar and its investors to receive little or nothing for their $1.2 billion investment in the company.

Whereas the ability to file for bankruptcy is important to the economy, the goal of the analyst is to avoid ownership of companies that are heading toward this extreme step, as well as to be able to evaluate opportunities among companies already in bankruptcy. Under both Chapter 7 and Chapter 11, providers of equity capital generally lose all value during the bankruptcy. On the other hand, debt holders typically receive at least a portion of their capital, but the payments of principal and interest are delayed during the period of bankruptcy protection.

4. THE CAPITAL STRUCTURE DECISION

A company's **capital structure** is the mix of debt and equity that a company uses to finance its business. The goal of a company's capital structure decision is to determine the financial leverage or capital structure that maximizes the value of the company by minimizing the average cost of capital. The weighted average cost of capital (WACC) is given by the average of the marginal costs of financing for each type of financing used. For a company with both debt and equity in its capital structure for which interest expense is tax deductible at a rate t, the WACC is

$$\text{WACC} = \left(\frac{D}{V}\right) r_d (1 - t) + \left(\frac{E}{V}\right) r_e$$

where

r_e = cost of equity

r_d = before-tax cost of debt

t = marginal tax rate[10]

---

[10]For simplicity, this discussion ignores preferred stock. Additionally, (D/V) and (E/V) have been substituted for w_d and w_e, respectively.

Variables E and D denote the market value of the shareholders' equity and the outstanding debt, respectively, and the value of the company is given by $V = D + E$. You will notice that we use the term "marginal" with respect to both the cost of capital and the tax rate. The cost of capital is a marginal cost: what it costs the company to raise additional capital. Therefore, the cost of equity, the cost of debt, and the tax rate that we use throughout the remainder of this chapter are marginal: the cost or tax rate for additional capital.

In this section, we first consider the theoretical relationship between leverage and a company's value. We then examine the practical relationship between leverage and company value in equal depth.

4.1. Proposition I Without Taxes: Capital Structure Irrelevance

In now classic papers, Nobel Prize–winning economists Franco Modigliani and Merton Miller argued the important theory that, given certain assumptions, a company's choice of capital structure does not affect its value.[11] The assumptions relate to expectations and markets:

1. Investors agree on the expected cash flow from a given investment.[12]
2. Bonds and shares of stock are traded in a perfect capital market.[13]

Implicit in the perfect market assumption is that bankruptcy has no costs.

Consider the capital of a company to be a pie you can split any number of ways, but the size of the pie remains the same. Likewise, Modigliani and Miller reason, the amount and risk of the aggregate returns to debt holders and equity holders of a company do not change with changes in capital structure. They use the concept of arbitrage to demonstrate their point: If the value of an unlevered company—that is, a company without any debt—is not equal to that of a levered company, investors could make an arbitrage profit and this profit taking would force the values to be equivalent.

The importance of the Modigliani and Miller theory is that it demonstrates that managers cannot create value simply by changing the company's capital structure. Consider why this might be true. The operating earnings of a business are available to the providers of its capital. In an all-equity company (that is, a company with no debt), all of the operating earnings are available to the equity holders and the value of the company is the present value of these operating earnings. If, on the other hand, a company is partially financed by debt, these operating earnings are split between the providers of capital: the equity holders and the debt holders. Under market equilibrium, the sum of the values of debt and equity in such a case should equal the value of the all-equity company. In other words, the value of a company is determined solely by its cash flows, not by the relative reliance on debt and equity capital.

This principle does not change the fact of the relative risks of leverage to debt holders versus equity holders. Adding leverage does increase the risk faced by the equity holders. In

---

[11]Modigliani and Miller (1958, 1963).

[12]All investors have the same expectations with respect to the cash flows from an investment in bonds or stocks. In other words, expectations are homogeneous.

[13]A perfect capital market is one in which any two investments with identical cash flow streams must trade for the same price.

such a case, equity holders are compensated for this extra risk by receiving a larger proportion of the operating earnings, with the debt holders receiving a smaller portion, because they face less risk. Indeed, in equilibrium, the increase in equity returns is exactly offset by increases in the risk and by the associated increase in the required rate of return on equity, so that there is no change in the value of the company.

Modigliani and Miller (MM) first illustrated the capital structure irrelevance proposition under the condition of no taxes.

MM Proposition I:

The market value of a company is not affected by the capital structure of the company.

In other words, the value of the company levered (V_L) is equal to the value unlevered (V_U), or $V_L = V_U$.

To understand this proposition, we can think about two companies with the same expected perpetual cash flows and uncertainty and hence the same discount rate applied to value these cash flows. Even if the companies have different capital structures, these two companies must have the same present value using discounted cash flow models. If capital structure changes were to have any effect on a company's value, there would exist an arbitrage opportunity to make endless profits.

In a perfect market, investors can substitute their own leverage for a company's leverage by borrowing or lending appropriate amounts in addition to holding shares of the company. Because this process is costless for investors (remember, we assumed no transaction costs), a company's financial leverage should have no impact on its value. Therefore, a company's capital structure is irrelevant in perfect markets if taxes are ignored.

4.2. Proposition II Without Taxes: Higher Financial Leverage Raises the Cost of Equity

Modigliani and Miller's second proposition focuses on the cost of capital of the company.

MM Proposition II:

The cost of equity is a linear function of the company's debt to equity ratio.

Assuming that financial distress has no costs and that debt holders have prior claim to assets and income relative to equity holders, the cost of debt is less than the cost of equity. According to this proposition, as the company increases its use of debt financing, the cost of equity rises. The net effect of the increased use of a cheaper source of capital and the rising cost of equity is that there is *no* change in the company's overall cost of capital. Again, Modigliani and Miller argue that the relative amount of debt versus equity does not affect the overall value of the company. This is because, despite the low cost of using debt financing, the more debt there is in the capital structure, relative to equity, the riskier the equity capital will be.

The risk of the equity depends on two factors: the risk of the company's operations (business risk) and the degree of financial leverage (financial risk). Business risk determines the cost of capital, whereas the capital structure determines financial risk.

The weighted average cost of capital (WACC), *ignoring taxes*, is

$$r_a = \left(\frac{D}{V}\right)r_d + \left(\frac{E}{V}\right)r_e$$

where

r_a = weighted average cost of capital of the company

r_d = before-tax marginal cost of debt capital

r_e = marginal cost of equity capital

D = value of debt

E = value of equity

V = value of the company, which is equal to $D + E$

We can rearrange the weighted average cost of capital to solve for the cost of equity:

$$r_e = r_a + (r_a - r_d)\left(\frac{D}{E}\right)$$

More than four decades later, the MM theory still provides the foundation for discussions about company value as it relates to capital structure. Higher leverage does not create value. As shown in the preceding equation, as the debt-to-equity ratio increases, the cost of equity capital also increases.

Just as we can express the beta of any investment portfolio as a market-value weighted average of the betas of the investments in that portfolio, we can express the systematic risk of each of the sources of a company's capital in a similar manner.[14] In other words, we can represent the systematic risk of the assets of the entire company as a weighted average of the systematic risk of the company's debt and equity:

$$\beta_a = \left(\frac{D}{V}\right)\beta_d + \left(\frac{E}{V}\right)\beta_e$$

where

β_a = asset's systematic risk, or **asset beta**

β_d = beta of debt

β_e = equity beta

The asset beta represents the amount of the risk that cannot be diversified away by investing in assets that are not perfectly correlated with one another.

According to Modigliani and Miller, the company's cost of capital does not depend on its capital structure but rather is determined by the business risk of the company. On the other hand, as the level of debt rises, the risk of the company's defaulting on its debt increases. These costs are borne by the equity holders. So, as the proportionate use of debt rises, the equity's beta, β_e, also rises. By reordering the formula of β_a to solve for β_e, we get

$$\beta_e = \beta_a + (\beta_a - \beta_d)\left(\frac{D}{E}\right)$$

In the next section, we look at the decision to use debt financing given the taxes and market imperfections found in the real world.

---

[14]Hamada (1972).

4.3.   Taxes, the Cost of Capital, and the Value of the Company

Taxes are the first practical consideration in modifying the results of the MM propositions. Because interest is deductible from income for tax purposes in most countries, the use of debt provides a tax shield that translates into savings that in turn enhance the value of a company. Indeed, ignoring other practical realities of costs of financial distress and bankruptcy, the value of the company increases with increasing levels of debt. In effect, by making the interest costs deductible for income taxes, the government subsidizes companies' use of debt. The actual cost of debt is reduced by the level of the company's tax benefit:

After-tax cost of debt = Before-tax cost of debt × (1 − Marginal tax rate)

Or, representing the after-tax cost of debt as r_d^*,

$$r_d^* = r_d(1 - t)$$

where t is the marginal tax rate. By introducing corporate tax, we adjust the weighted average cost of capital formula to reflect the impact of the tax benefit:

$$r_a = \left(\frac{D}{V}\right) r_d \, (1 - t) + \left(\frac{E}{V}\right) r_e$$

or

$$r_a = \left(\frac{D}{V}\right) r_d^* + \left(\frac{E}{V}\right) r_e$$

We can rearrange this equation to solve for the cost of equity:

$$r_e = r_a + (r_a - r_d^*)\left(\frac{D}{E}\right)$$

Therefore, the cost of equity is equal to the return on the company as a whole, plus an adjustment for financial leverage.

This tax shield afforded by debt financing adds value to a company. In fact, the value of a levered company is the value of an unlevered (i.e., all-equity) company plus the value of the tax shield, td:[15]

$$V_{\mathrm{L}} = V_{\mathrm{U}} + td$$

Therefore, if taxes are considered but financial distress and bankruptcy costs are not, debt financing is highly advantageous, and, in the extreme, a company's optimal capital structure is all debt.

We can see the effect of taxes on the cost of capital in Exhibit 4-16. If there are no taxes, as shown in Panel B, the cost of capital is constant at r_a. If, on the other hand, interest is tax deductible, the cost of capital declines for ever increasing use of debt financing, as shown in Panel C.

---

[15]Note that the annual tax saving is $r_d \cdot td$. Expressing its present value in the form of an annuity, we get PV(tax saving) = $r_d \cdot td / r_d = td$.

EXHIBIT 4-16   Modigliani and Miller Propositions

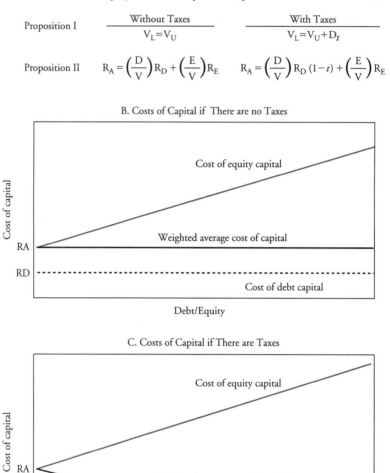

A. Value of the Company and Cost of Capital for Propositions Without and With Taxes

Proposition I $\quad \dfrac{\text{Without Taxes}}{V_L = V_U} \qquad \dfrac{\text{With Taxes}}{V_L = V_U + D_t}$

Proposition II $\quad R_A = \left(\dfrac{D}{V}\right)R_D + \left(\dfrac{E}{V}\right)R_E \qquad R_A = \left(\dfrac{D}{V}\right)R_D\,(1-t) + \left(\dfrac{E}{V}\right)R_E$

B. Costs of Capital if There are no Taxes

Cost of equity capital

Weighted average cost of capital

RA

RD

Cost of debt capital

Debt/Equity

C. Costs of Capital if There are Taxes

Cost of equity capital

RA

Weighted average cost of capital

RD

Cost of debt capital

Debt/Equity

EXAMPLE 4-8   The After-Tax Cost of Debt

Payment People, a provider of temporary accounting workers, is considering an $85 million acquisition. The company could raise capital by selling either debt or equity. If the company finances the acquisition with debt at 8 percent interest, what is the after-tax cost of issuing debt if the company's marginal tax rate is 34 percent?

Solution

Annual interest expense on $85 million at 8 percent is $6.8 million. The $6.8 million is deducted from income, saving $2,312,000 in taxes. The after-tax interest cost is $6.8 million − $2.312 million = $4.488 million. The before-tax cost of debt is 8 percent; the after-tax cost of debt is

$$\text{After-tax cost of debt} = \$4.488\text{ million}/\$85\text{ million} = 5.28\%$$

or

$$0.08(1 - 0.34) = 0.0528, \text{ or } 5.28\%.$$

EXAMPLE 4-9   The Cost of Equity

Hotel chain Hostales Vacaciones finances land purchases for new hotels through debt financing. The company is opening in ten locations for a total cost of 500 million pesos. The company is considering the cost of equity versus debt for its financing needs. The company has a cost of capital of 13 percent, a debt-to-equity ratio of 0.5, debt costs of 9 percent, and a tax rate of 32 percent. What is the company's cost of equity with and without the consideration of taxes?

Solution Without Taxes

$$r_e = r_a + (r_a - r_d)\left(\frac{D}{E}\right)$$

$$= 13\% + \left[(13\% - 9\%)(0.5)\right]$$

$$= 0.15, \text{ or } 15\%$$

Solution With Taxes

$$r_e = r_a + (r_a - r_d^*)\left(\frac{D}{E}\right)$$

$$= 13\% + \left[(13\% - 6.12\%)(0.5)\right]$$

$$= 0.1644, \text{ or } 16.44\%$$

Miller (1977) introduced another aspect into the benefit from tax deductibility of interest on debt. He argued that if investors face different tax rates on dividend and interest income for their personal taxes, this situation may reduce the advantage of debt financing somewhat. If investors face a higher rate of tax on income from debt investments relative to stock investments, they will demand a higher return on debt—and hence a higher cost of debt—than if there were no differential personal taxes in order to compensate for the personal tax on the income from the bond investment.[16]

From these examples with taxes, we can see that the more a company borrows, the greater the company's value will be. In practice, however, the value of a levered company is affected by more than the interest due on the debt. Things get more complicated once we introduce factors such as the cost of financial distress, agency costs, and asymmetric information. We address these additional factors next.

4.4. Costs of Financial Distress

The downside of operating and financial leverage is that earnings are magnified downward during economic slowdowns. Lower or negative earnings put companies under stress, and this **financial distress** adds costs—both explicit and implicit costs—to a company. Even before taking the drastic step of filing for bankruptcy, companies under stress may lose customers, creditors, suppliers, and valuable employees to more secure competitors.

EXAMPLE 4-10   Costs of Financial Distress

Enron Corporation is an extreme example of the loss of value due to financial distress. Until its demise in 2001, Enron was a large player in the natural gas industry. Events leading up to the eventual bankruptcy protection filing caused investors to flee the common stock as creditors refused new lending. Enron went from a favored to a disdained company in record time.

According to a company presentation made ten days after its December 2, 2001 bankruptcy filing, the company's common stock price plunged from $80 per share to $1 per share prior to the bankruptcy announcement, losing $25 billion in market value.[17] This loss in value was due to a number of factors, including

- Investors' and creditors' loss of confidence;
- Financial market reaction from a lack of access to capital markets;
- Current maturities greatly exceeding operating cash flow because of the inability to refinance debt;
- Nervous trade creditors;
- Dynegy pulling out of the merger on November 28, 2001; and
- The bond ratings downgrade on November 28, 2001.

Cash bankruptcy expenses listed in the bankruptcy filing documents totaled $17.3 million, though the bankruptcy costs including accountants', advisors', and lawyers' fees were over $500 million by November 2003.[18]

---

[16]It can be argued that there is a higher personal tax on debt income because debt instruments typically provide investors with taxable interest periodically, whereas taxable income from stock investments could conceivably be lower because the tax consequences of investing in nondividend-paying stocks are deferred until the stock is sold.

[17]Enron Corporation Organizational Meeting, December 12, 2001.

[18]*Houston Business Journal* (November 19, 2003).

The expected cost of financial distress is composed of two key ingredients: (1) the costs of financial distress and bankruptcy and (2) the likelihood of financial distress. We can classify the costs of financial distress into direct and indirect costs. Direct costs of financial distress include the actual cash expenses associated with the bankruptcy process, such as legal and administrative fees. Indirect costs of financial distress include forgone investment opportunities, impaired ability to conduct business, and agency costs associated with the debt during periods in which the company is near or in bankruptcy.

Companies whose assets have a ready secondary market have lower costs associated with financial distress. Companies with safe, tangible assets, such as airlines, shipping companies, and steel manufacturers, incur lower costs from financial distress because such assets are usually more readily marketable. On the other hand, companies with few tangible assets, such as high-tech growth companies, pharmaceutical companies, information technology companies, and others in the service industry, have less to liquidate and therefore have a higher cost associated with financial distress.

The probability of bankruptcy increases as the degree of leverage increases. The probability of bankruptcy for a given company depends on how the fixed costs of debt service interact with the instability of the business environment and the reserves available to the company to delay bankruptcy. In other words, the probability of bankruptcy depends, in part, on the company's business risk. Other factors that affect the likelihood of bankruptcy include the company's corporate governance structure and the management of the company.

4.5. Agency Costs

Agency costs are the costs associated with the fact that all public companies and the larger private companies are managed by nonowners. Agency costs are the incremental costs arising from conflicts of interest when an agent makes decisions for a principal. In the context of a corporation, agency costs arise from conflicts of interest among managers, shareholders, and bondholders.

The smaller the stake that managers have in the company, the less is their share in bearing the cost of excessive perquisite consumption or not giving their best efforts in running the company. This conflict has been called the **agency costs of equity**. Given that outside shareholders are aware of this conflict, they will take actions to minimize the loss, such as requiring audited financial statements. The net agency costs of equity therefore have three components:[19]

1. **Monitoring costs**: These are the costs borne by owners to monitor the management of the company, and they include the expenses of the annual report, board of director expenses, and the cost of the annual meeting.
2. **Bonding costs**: These are the costs borne by management to assure owners that they are working in the owners' best interest. These include the implicit cost of noncompete employment contracts and the explicit cost of insurance to guarantee performance.
3. **Residual loss**: This consists of the costs incurred even when there is sufficient monitoring and bonding, because monitoring and bonding mechanisms are not perfect.

The better a company is governed, the lower the agency costs will be. Good governance practices translate into higher shareholder value, reflecting the fact that managers' interests are better aligned with those of shareholders. Additionally, agency theory posits that a reduction

---

[19]Jensen and Meckling (1976) provide this breakdown of agency costs.

in net agency costs of equity results from an increase in the use of debt versus equity. That is, there is an agency cost savings associated with the use of debt. Similarly, the more financially leveraged a company is, the less freedom managers have to either take on more debt or untowardly spend cash. This is the foundation of Michael Jensen's **free cash flow hypothesis**.[20] According to Jensen's hypothesis, higher debt levels discipline managers by forcing them to make fixed debt service payments and by reducing the company's free cash flow.[21]

4.6. Costs of Asymmetric Information

Asymmetric information arises from the fact that managers have more information about a company's performance and prospects (and future investment opportunities) than do outsiders such as owners and creditors. Whereas all companies have a certain level of insider information, companies with comparatively high asymmetry in information are those with complex products like high-tech companies, companies with little transparency in financial accounting information, or companies with lower levels of institutional ownership. Providers of both debt and equity capital demand higher returns from companies with higher asymmetry in information because there is a greater likelihood of agency costs in companies with higher asymmetry in information.

Some degree of asymmetric information always exists because investors never know as much as managers and other insiders. Consequently, investors often closely watch manager behavior for insight into insider opinions on the company's future prospects. Being aware of this scrutiny, managers take into account how their actions might be interpreted by outsiders. The signaling model of capital structure suggests a pecking order to financing decisions. When a company is presented with a new investment opportunity, management must choose the best way to pay for the project. Management wants to optimize return on the investment at the lowest risk.

The **pecking order theory**, developed by Myers and Majluf, suggests that managers choose methods of financing that range from the least visible signals up the scale to the most visible—public offerings of equity.[22] The least visible form of financing is no external financing at all—that is, internally generated funds. If internal financing is insufficient, managers next prefer debt and finally equity. Another implication of the work of Myers and Majluf is that financial managers tend to issue equity when they believe the stock is overvalued but are reluctant to issue equity if they believe the stock is undervalued. Hence, the issuance of stock is interpreted by investors as a negative signal.

We can read the signals that managers provide in their choice of financing method. For example, commitments to fixed payments, such as dividends and debt service payments, may be interpreted as the company's management having confidence in the company's future prospects of making payments. Such signals are considered too costly for poorly performing companies to afford. Alternatively, the signal of raising money at the top of the pecking order and issuing equity at the bottom of the pecking order holds other clues. If, for instance, the company's cost of capital increases after an equity issuance, we may interpret this effect as an indication that management needed capital beyond what comes cheaply; in other words, this is a negative signal regarding the company's future prospects.

---

[20]Jensen (1986).

[21]Harvey, Lins, and Roper (2004) observe that this discipline is especially important in emerging markets, in which there is a tendency to overinvest.

[22]Myers and Majluf (1984).

4.7.   The Optimal Capital Structure According to the Static Trade-Off Theory

Companies make decisions about financial leverage that weigh the value-enhancing effects of leverage from the tax deductibility of interest against the value-reducing impact of the costs of financial distress or bankruptcy, agency costs, and asymmetric information. Putting together all the pieces of the theory of Modigliani and Miller, along with the taxes, costs of financial distress, agency costs, and asymmetric information, we see that, as financial leverage is increased, there comes a point beyond which further increases in value from value-enhancing effects are offset completely by value-reducing effects. This point is known as the **optimal capital structure**. In other words, the optimal capital structure is the capital structure at which the value of the company is maximized.

Considering only the tax shield provided by debt and the costs of financial distress, the expression for the value of a leveraged company becomes

$$V_{L} = V_{U} + td - PV(\text{Costs of financial distress}) \tag{4-8}$$

Equation 4-8 represents the **static trade-off theory of capital structure**. It results in an optimal capital structure such that debt composes less than 100 percent of a company's capital structure. We diagram this optimum in Exhibit 4-17 on page 204.

The static trade-off theory of capital structure is based on balancing the expected costs from financial distress against the tax benefits of debt service payments, as shown in Panel A of Exhibit 4-17. Unlike the Modigliani and Miller proposition of no optimal capital structure, or a structure with almost all debt when the tax shield is considered, static trade-off theory puts forth an optimal capital structure with an optimal proportion of debt. Optimal debt usage is found at the point where any additional debt would cause the costs of financial distress to increase by a greater amount than the benefit of the additional tax shield.

We cannot say precisely at which level of debt financing a company reaches its optimal capital structure. The optimal capital structure depends on the company's business risk, combined with its tax situation, corporate governance, and financial accounting information transparency, among other factors. However, what we can say, based on this theory, is that a company should consider a number of factors, including its business risk and the possible costs of financial distress, in determining its capital structure.

A company's management uses these tools to decide the level of debt appropriate for the company. The tax benefit from the deductibility of the interest expense on debt must be balanced against the risk associated with the use of debt. The extent of financial leverage used should thus depend on owners' and management's appetites for risk, as well as the stability of the company's business environment. Indeed, as we show in Panel B of Exhibit 4-17, as the proportion of debt in a business rises, the costs of both debt and equity are likely to rise to offset the higher risks associated with higher levels of debt. These cost increases reduce or even negate the cost savings due to the greater use of debt, the cheaper source of financing. The result is a U-shaped weighted average cost of capital curve.

When the company does indeed recognize that it has a most appropriate or best capital structure, it may adopt this as its **target capital structure**. Because management may exploit short-term opportunities in one or another financing source and because market-value fluctuations continuously affect the company's capital structure, a company's capital structure at any point in time may differ from the target. Nevertheless, so long as the assumptions of the analysis and the target are unchanged, analysts and management should focus on the target capital structure.

EXHIBIT 4-17   Trade-off Theory with Taxes and Cost of Financial Distress

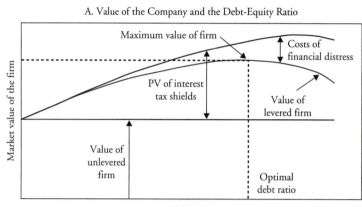

A. Value of the Company and the Debt-Equity Ratio

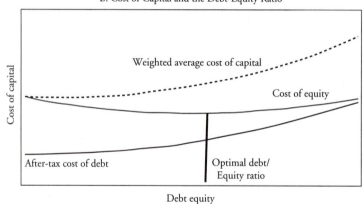

B. Cost of Capital and the Debt-Equity Ratio

EXAMPLE 4-11   Financial Leverage and the Cost of Capital

The Chuang Ho Company provides copper-wired components for cellular telephone manufacturers globally. Chuang Ho is going to establish a subsidiary that would require assets of 3 billion SGD, and it wants to select a capital structure that would minimize its cost of capital for the subsidiary. Alex Ahn, the company's CFO, wants to evaluate a target leverage structure and uses a scenario approach to evaluate the cost of capital for the present 0 percent debt and possible 50 percent debt or 80 percent debt. Chuang Ho's marginal tax rate is 35 percent. Ahn has gathered the following information regarding costs of capital:

• The cost of equity rises with increased levels of debt from 15 percent to 18 percent to 24 percent.

- The company can borrow at 12 percent on 50 percent debt or at 16 percent on 80 percent debt.

Which capital structure is expected to have the lowest cost of capital?

Solution

First, calculate the cost of capital under the three scenarios (see Exhibit 4-18).

EXHIBIT 4-18   Chuang Ho Subsidiary

	Leverage		
	No Debt	50% Debt	80% Debt
Assets	$3,000,000,000	$3,000,000,000	$3,000,000,000
Debt	$0	$1,500,000,000	$2,400,000,000
Equity	$3,000,000,000	$1,500,000,000	$600,000,000
Debt-to-equity ratio	0	1	4
Proportion of debt	0%	50%	80%
Proportion of equity	100%	50%	20%
Before-tax cost of debt	—	12%	16%
Cost of equity	15%	18%	24%
After-tax cost of debt	—	7.8%	10.4%
Weighted average cost of capital	15.0%	12.9%	13.1%

Of the three capital structures that we are evaluating, the cost of capital is lowest for 50 percent debt.

5. PRACTICAL ISSUES IN CAPITAL STRUCTURE POLICY

5.1. Debt Ratings

Debt ratings are an important consideration in the practical management of leverage. As leverage rises, rating agencies tend to lower the ratings of the company's debt to reflect the higher credit risk resulting from the increasing leverage. Lower ratings signify higher risk to both equity and debt capital providers, who therefore demand higher returns.

Most large companies pay one or more rating services to rate their bonds. Debt issues are rated for creditworthiness by public rating agencies. The rating agencies include Moody's, Standard & Poor's, and Fitch. Rating agencies perform a financial analysis of the company's ability to pay the promised cash flows, as well as an analysis of the bond's indenture, the set of complex legal documents associated with the issuance of debt instruments (see Exhibit 4-19).

These agencies evaluate the wealth of information about the issuer and the bond, including the bond's characteristics and indenture, and provide investors with an assessment of the

EXHIBIT 4-19   Bond Ratings by Moody's, Standard & Poor's, and Fitch

	Moody's	Standard & Poor's	Fitch	
Highest quality	Aaa	AAA	AAA	
High quality	Aa	AA	AA	Investment grade
Upper medium grade	A	A	A	
Medium grade	Baa	BBB	BBB	
Speculative	Ba	BB	BB	
Highly speculative	B	B	B	
Substantial risk	Caa	CCC	CCC	Speculative grade
Extremely speculative	Ca			
Possibly in default	C			
Default		D	DDD-D	

company's ability to pay the interest and principal on the bond as promised. We provide the bond rating classifications in Exhibit 4-19. Though there is significant agreement in ratings among the three major services, some disagreements do occur. For example, Standard & Poor's reduced the credit rating of General Motors to speculative grade in early May 2005, but Moody's did not do so until late August 2005.

In practice, most managers consider the company's debt rating in their policies regarding capital structure. Managers must be mindful of their company's bond ratings because the cost of capital is tied closely to bond ratings. Consider the difference in the yields on Aaa- and Baa-rated corporate bonds, as shown in Exhibit 4-20. Typically, a difference of 100 basis points exists between the yields of Aaa and Baa bonds, though this spread widens in economic recessions.[23] The cost of debt increases significantly when a bond's rating drops from investment grade to speculative. For example, when the rating of General Motors' unsecured 7.2 percent bond maturing in 2011 was changed by Moody's from Baa to Ba, the bond's price fell by over 7.5 percent and its yield rose from 7.541 percent to 9.364 percent.

5.2. Evaluating Capital Structure Policy

In evaluating a company's capital structure, the financial analyst must look at the capital structure of the company over time, the capital structure of competitors that have similar business risk, and company-specific factors, such as the quality of corporate governance, that may affect agency costs, among other factors.[24] The financial analyst is not privy to the company's target capital structure but rather can evaluate the company's ability to handle its financial obligations and the potential role of costs of financial distress in determining how much financial leverage a company can handle.

---

[23]The Board of Governors of the Federal Reserve System H.15 series of Aaa and Baa corporate yields shows an average spread of 119 basis points between Aaa- and Baa-rated bonds, on average, from 1919 to mid-2005. The largest spread occurred in 1932, with 565 basis points, and the lowest spread occurred in 1966, with a 32-basis-point difference.

[24]Good corporate governance should lower the net agency costs of equity.

EXHIBIT 4-20   Yields on Aaa- and Baa-Rated Corporate Bonds (1984–2005)

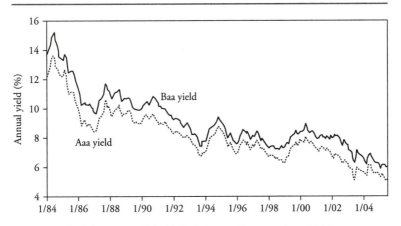

Source: Board of Governors of the Federal Reserve System, release H.15.

A common goal of capital structure decisions is to finance at the lowest cost of capital. Analysts can use a scenario approach to assess this point for a particular company, starting with the current cost of capital for a company and considering various changes to answer the following questions:

1. What happens to the cost of capital as the debt ratio is changed?
2. At what debt ratio is the cost of capital minimized and company value maximized?
3. What will happen to the company value and stock price if the company moves toward its optimal capital structure?

5.3. Leverage in an International Setting

Despite the fact that Modigliani and Miller tell us that under several conditions the market value of a company is independent of its capital structure, we know that a company's capital structure is indeed relevant in the real world due to the effects of taxation, the costs of financial distress, and agency costs. The static trade-off theory suggests that the optimal level of leverage should be the level at which the value of the company is maximized; this is the level of debt financing at which any additional debt increases the costs of financial distress by an amount greater than the benefit from interest deductibility.

A company's capital structure largely depends on company-specific factors such as the probability of bankruptcy, profitability, quality and structure of assets, and growth opportunities. Beyond these factors, the company's industry affiliation, as well as the characteristics of the country where the company operates, can account for differences in capital structure also.

The general business environment differs from one country to another, and researchers show that country-specific factors have explanatory power that is similar to or even greater than that of the company's industry affiliation in determining a company's capital structure.[25]

---

[25]See, for example, Fan, Titman, and Twite (2004).

Drawing conclusions from the comparison of financial leverage indicators of a U.S.-based energy company and a Japanese energy company is not meaningful if we do not take country-specific differences into account. Tradition, tax policy, and regulation may largely explain the different degrees of leverage in the two countries.

In examining the capital structure and debt maturity structure of corporations in an international context, researchers generally find that differences in the capital structures exist between developed and emerging markets, as well as across the developed countries. Moreover, the debt maturity structure—another important capital structure decision—also tends to vary across the international setting. Therefore, when analysts focus on the capital structure of companies in an international setting, they must consider both the relative use of debt and the maturity structure of debt. In fact, short-term and long-term debt ratios follow very different patterns in an international comparison:

- Taking total debt into account, companies in France, Italy, and Japan tend to be more highly leveraged than companies in the United States and the United Kingdom.
- Focusing on the use of long-term debt, on the other hand, a different picture emerges: North American companies tend to use more long-term debt than do Japanese companies.
- Companies in developed markets typically use more long-term debt and tend to have higher long-term debt to total debt ratios compared to their emerging market peers.

Beyond the pure comparison of the capital structures, it is equally or even more important to identify and understand the country-specific factors that explain the cross-country differences.[26] Three major types of factors may be used to explain most capital structure differences in an international comparison:

1. *Institutional and legal environment.* These factors represent the legal and regulatory environment in which companies operate, as well as the requirements related to financial reporting. These institutional factors—including taxation, accounting standards, and even the presence or lack of corruption—may affect a company's optimal capital structure.
2. *Financial markets and banking sector.* These factors include characteristics of the banking sector, as well as the size and activity of the financial markets. Financial institutions are crucial for companies' access to financing.
3. *Macroeconomic environment.* These factors capture the general economic and business environment, addressing the influence of economic growth and inflation on the capital structure.

5.3.1. Institutional and Legal Environment

Taxation, financial legislation, the content of laws (e.g., bankruptcy law), and the quality of their enforcement all differ from one country to another. These differences may influence the capital structures of companies and explain many of the differences that we observe across countries.

The apparent conflict of interest between the companies' management and outside investors has already been addressed as the agency problem. This problem is, in fact, one of the key determinants of a company's ability to obtain capital; hence, agency costs are one of the major factors determining the capital structure. This conflict may be mitigated by

---

[26]We should note, however, that the conclusions drawn in different studies are not always consistent with each other. The results of empirical studies, in fact, may depend on several factors, such as the set of countries and companies taken into the data sample, the analyzed historical period, the hypotheses that the researchers intended to test, and even the definition of leverage that they considered.

carefully prepared contracts. The quality of investors' legal protections depends on both the content and the enforcement of the contracts and laws. As a result, we expect to see higher financial leverage in countries that have weaker legal systems. Further, in countries with weaker legal systems, we expect a greater use of short-term debt financing versus long-term debt financing. Researchers find that companies operating in countries with an efficient legal system tend to use more long-term debt than short-term debt and exhibit lower leverage than comparable companies in countries with weaker legal systems.

Some researchers assume that legal systems based on common law offer external capital providers (both equity and debt providers) with better protection compared to the legal systems of civil law countries. Common law originated in England and is also followed in other countries, such as the United States, Canada, Australia, New Zealand, Singapore, India, and Malaysia. Civil law, on the other hand, has origins going back to ancient Rome; the countries of continental Europe and most of the rest of the world have legal systems based on this tradition. Researchers find mixed and limited evidence that companies operating in common law countries tend to have longer debt maturity structures compared to their peers in civil law countries and use less debt and more equity in their capital structure.

Similar to the rationale described in the case of legal system efficiency, a high level of information asymmetry between insiders and outsiders encourages a greater use of debt relative to equity, as well as a greater reliance on short-term debt than on long-term debt in the capital structure. This is likely due to the fact that enforcing the debt contract is easier than enforcing the less clearly contracted shareholders' rights. Auditors and financial analysts can help in reducing information asymmetries and increase the level of transparency.[27] Researchers confirm that the presence of auditors and analysts is associated with lower financial leverage. The importance of auditors is usually strongest in emerging markets, whereas the presence of analysts is more important in developed markets.

As discussed earlier, taxes affect the capital structure decision by lowering the cost of debt financing to the issuer in those jurisdictions in which interest expense is tax deductible. In the absence of agency and bankruptcy costs, the benefit from the tax deductibility of interest encourages companies to use debt financing instead of equity financing. However, if dividend income is taxed at lower rates than interest income, some of the advantage of debt versus equity financing may be reduced from the corporate perspective because the price at which equity can be sold should reflect that advantage. Taxes are an important factor in a company's capital structure decision.

Researchers find mixed results on the effect of the corporate tax rate on capital structures, but they find that personal tax rates do matter. Because the tax treatment of dividends differs across countries, researchers can examine the importance of different tax treatments of dividend income.[28] They find that companies in countries that have lower tax rates on dividend income also have less debt in their capital structures.[29]

5.3.2. Financial Markets and Banking Sector

The size, activity, and liquidity of capital markets are crucial for corporations' access to capital. Several researchers have analyzed the impact of capital markets' characteristics on companies' capital structures. Some find that

---

[27]Fan et al. (2004).

[28]Fan et al. (2004).

[29]A lower dividend tax burden can be achieved in countries that apply dividend tax relief (e.g., Austria, Belgium, Thailand, and Turkey) or dividend imputation (e.g., Canada, France, Germany, Italy, United Kingdom, and Mexico).

liquid and active capital markets affect companies' debt maturity structure. Specifically, they find that companies in countries with liquid and active capital markets tend to use more long-term debt with longer debt maturity. Researchers attribute this finding to the heightened external monitoring of companies by market participants in active markets.[30]

The banking sector is one of the primary sources of funds for the corporate sector in many countries, and its role is especially significant in countries that do not have a corporate bond market. The importance of the banking sector relative to the capital markets can vary from one country to another, however. Countries with a common law tradition, where the shareholders' rights are stronger, tend to be more market based, whereas civil law countries tend to be more bank based. Because the relationship between a bank and a company is stronger and closer than that between a company and a bondholder, banks can handle information asymmetries more efficiently. This effect may partly explain why civil law countries are more bank oriented.

However, researchers' findings are mixed regarding the effect of the banking system. Some researchers claim that banks have no effect on companies' financial leverage and that the difference between the bank-oriented and market-oriented countries is more reflected by the relative importance of public financing (i.e., stock and bonds) and private financing (i.e., bank loans).[31] On the other hand, some researchers find that companies in bank-based countries exhibit higher financial leverage compared to those that operate in market-based countries.[32]

The presence of institutional investors may also affect the companies' capital structure choice. Some institutional investors may have preferred habitats, and this preference may affect companies' debt maturity structure. Insurance companies and pension plans, for example, may prefer investing in long-term debt securities in order to match the interest rate risk of their long-term liabilities. Researchers find limited results regarding the influence of preferred habitats; companies in countries that have more institutional investors in their markets tend to have less short-term and more long-term debt and somewhat lower debt-to-equity ratios.[33]

5.3.3. Macroeconomic Environment

Inflation is a widely recognized macroeconomic indicator. High inflation has a negative impact on both the level of the debt financing and the desired debt maturity.[34] Companies in higher-inflation countries usually exhibit lower levels of financial leverage, rely more on equity financing, and have a shorter debt maturity structure compared to their peers in lower-inflation countries.

Researchers have also found that the growth in gross domestic product is associated with longer debt maturity in developed markets. In addition, researchers focusing on developing countries find that companies in countries with high growth rely more on equity financing.[35]

5.3.4. Conclusions

Financial analysts must consider country-specific factors when analyzing and comparing companies that operate in different countries. We have summarized these factors in Exhibit 4-21.

These factors include the differences in the business and legal environments in other countries, taxes, and macroeconomic factors, among others. Companies' optimal capital structures may differ simply as a consequence of these many country-specific differences. In addition to presenting challenges for international financial and credit analysis, international

---

[30]See Demirguc-Kunt and Maksimovic (1998).
[31]Rajan and Zingales (1995).
[32]See, for example, Claessens, Djankov, and Nevova (2001).
[33]See, for example, Fan et al. and Domowitz, Glen, and Madhavan (2000).
[34]See, for example, Demirguc-Kunt and Maksimovic (1999), Domowitz et al., and Fan et al.
[35]See Domowitz et al.

EXHIBIT 4-21   Country-Specific Factors and Their Assumed Impacts on the Companies'
Capital Structure

Country-Specific Factor	If a Country	. . . Then D/E Ratio Is Potentially	. . . and Debt Maturity Is Potentially
Institutional framework			
Legal system efficiency	Is more efficient	Lower	Longer
Legal system origin	Has common law as opposed to civil law	Lower	Longer
Information intermediaries	Has auditors and analysts	Lower	Longer
Taxation	Has taxes that favor equity	Lower	
Banking system, financial markets			
Equity and bond markets	Has active bond and stock markets		Longer
Bank-based or market-based country	Has a bank-based financial system	Higher	
Investors	Has large institutional investors	Lower	Longer
Macroeconomic environment			
Inflation	Has high inflation	Lower	Shorter
Growth	Has high GDP growth		Longer

differences in debt ratios present some challenges in developing debt policies for the foreign
subsidiaries of multinational companies. Theory provides little guidance, and corporate practices in this area seem to vary widely.

6. SUMMARY

In this chapter, we have reviewed the fundamentals of business risk, financial risk, and selection
of sources of financing.

- Leverage is the use of fixed costs in a company's cost structure. Business risk is the risk
  associated with operating earnings, including sales risk (uncertainty with respect to the price
  and quantity of sales) and operating risk (the risk related to the use of fixed costs in operations). Financial risk is the risk associated with how a company finances its operations.
- The degree of operating leverage (DOL) is the ratio of the percentage change in operating
  income to the percentage change in units sold. We can use the following formula to measure the degree of operating leverage:

$$DOL = \frac{Q(P - V)}{Q(P - V) - F}$$

- The degree of financial leverage (DFL) is the percentage change in net income for a given percentage change in operating income. We can use the following formula to measure the degree of financial leverage:

$$
\begin{aligned}
\text{DFL} &= \frac{\left[Q(P-V)-F\right](1-t)}{\left[Q(P-V)-F-C\right](1-t)} \\
&= \frac{\left[Q(P-V)-F\right]}{\left[Q(P-V)-F-C\right]}
\end{aligned}
$$

- The degree of total leverage (DTL) is a measure of the sensitivity of the cash flows to owners to changes in unit sales, which is equivalent to DTL = DOL × DFL.
- The breakeven point, Q_{BE}, is the number of units produced and sold at which the company's net income is 0, which we calculate as

$$
Q_{BE} = \frac{F+C}{P-V}
$$

- A high debt ratio increases the risk of bankruptcy where debt holders' claims have priority over equity holders' claims.
- The goal of the capital structure decision is to determine the financial leverage that maximizes the value of the company (or minimizes the weighted average cost of capital).
- The deductibility of interest lowers the cost of debt and the cost of capital for the company as a whole. Adding the tax shield provided by debt to the Modigliani and Miller framework suggests that the optimal capital structure is nearly all debt.
- In the Modigliani and Miller propositions with and without taxes, increasing a company's relative use of debt in the capital structure increases the risk for equity providers and hence the cost of equity capital.
- Using more debt in a company's capital structure reduces the net agency costs of equity.
- The costs of asymmetric information increase as more equity is used versus debt, suggesting the pecking order theory of leverage, in which new equity issuance is the least preferred method of raising capital.
- According to the static trade-off theory of capital structure, in choosing a capital structure, a company balances the value of the tax benefit from deductibility of interest with the present value of the costs of financial distress. At the optimal target capital structure, the incremental tax shield benefit is exactly matched by the incremental costs of financial distress.
- A company may identify its target capital structure, but its capital structure at any point in time may not be equal to its target for many reasons, including that management may exploit tactical opportunities in financing sources, market value fluctuations in its securities, and the uncertainty regarding future retained earnings.
- Many companies have goals for maintaining a certain credit rating, and these goals are influenced by the relative costs of debt financing among the different rating classes.
- In evaluating a company's capital structure, the financial analyst must look at the capital structure of the company over time, the capital structure of competitors that have similar

business risk, and company-specific factors, such as the quality of corporate governance, that may affect agency costs, among other factors.

• Good corporate governance and accounting transparency should lower the net agency costs of equity.

• When comparing capital structures of companies in different countries, an analyst must consider a variety of characteristics that might differ and affect both the typical capital structure and the debt maturity structure. The major characteristics fall into three categories: institutional and legal environment, financial markets and banking sector, and macroeconomic environment.

PRACTICE PROBLEMS

1. If two companies have identical operating risk, they also have identical
   A. Business risk.
   B. Sales risk.
   C. Total leverage.
   D. Sensitivity of operating earnings to changes in the number of units produced and sold.

2. Operating leverage is a measure of the
   A. Sensitivity of net earnings to changes in operating earnings.
   B. Sensitivity of net earnings to changes in sales.
   C. Sensitivity of fixed operating costs to changes in variable costs.
   D. Sensitivity of earnings before interest and taxes to changes in the number of units produced and sold.

3. The Fulcrum Company produces decorative swivel platforms for home televisions. If Fulcrum produces 40 million units, it estimates that it can sell them for $100 each. The variable production costs are $65 per unit, whereas the fixed production costs are $1.05 billion. Which of the following statements is true?
   A. The Fulcrum Company produces a positive operating income if it produces and sells more than 25 million swivel platforms.
   B. The Fulcrum Company's degree of operating leverage is 1.333.
   C. If the Fulcrum Company increases production and sales by 5 percent, its operating earnings are expected to increase by 20 percent.
   D. Increasing the fixed production costs by 10 percent will result in a lower sensitivity of operating earnings to changes in the units produced and sold.

4. Increases and decreases in the level of sales are due to business risk. The business risk of a particular company is characterized by
   A. The ratio of debt to equity in the capital structure.
   B. The level of risk assumed by the debt providers.
   C. Operating leverage and uncertainty about demand, output prices, and competition.
   D. Uncertainty about credit ratings, government debt, interest rates, and the demand for the domestic currency.

5. Consider two companies that operate in the same line of business and that have the same degree of operating leverage: the Basic Company and the Grundlegend Company. The Basic Company has no debt in its capital structure, but the Grundlegend Company has a capital structure that consists of 50 percent debt. Which of the following statements is true?
   A. The Grundlegend Company has a degree of total leverage that exceeds that of the Basic Company by 50 percent.
   B. The Grundlegend Company has the same sensitivity of net earnings to changes in earnings before interest and taxes as the Basic Company.
   C. The Grundlegend Company has the same sensitivity of earnings before interest and taxes to changes in sales as the Basic Company.
   D. The Grundlegend Company has the same sensitivity of net earnings to changes in sales as the Basic Company.

6. Myundia Motors now sells 1 million units at ¥3,529 per unit. Fixed operating costs are ¥1,290 million and variable operating costs are ¥1,500 per unit. If the company pays ¥410 million in interest, the levels of sales at the operating and total breakeven points are, respectively,

	Operating	Total
A.	¥1,500,000,000	¥2,257,612,900.
B.	¥2,243,671,760	¥2,956,776,737.
C.	¥2,975,148,800	¥3,529,000,000.
D.	¥2,257,612,900	¥3,529,000,000.

7. Juan Alavanca is evaluating the risk of two companies in the machinery industry: The Gearing Company and Hebelkraft, Inc. Alavanca used the latest fiscal year's financial statement and interviews with managers of the respective companies to gather the following information:

	The Gearing Company	Hebelkraft, Inc.
Number of units produced and sold	1 million	1.5 million
Sales price per unit	$200	$200
Variable cost per unit	$120	$100
Fixed operating cost	$40 million	$90 million
Fixed financing expense	$20 million	$20 million

   Based on this information, the total breakeven points for The Gearing Company and Hebelkraft, Inc. are
   A. 0.75 million and 1.1 million units, respectively.
   B. 1 million and 1.5 million units, respectively.
   C. 1.5 million and 0.75 million units, respectively.
   D. 1.0 million units for both companies.

8. If there are homogeneous expectations, an efficient market, and no taxes, transactions costs, or bankruptcy costs, the Modigliani and Miller Proposition I states that
   A. Bankruptcy risk rises with more leverage.
   B. Managers cannot increase the value of the company by adding debt.
   C. The value of a company is the product of leverage, taxes, and imperfect markets.
   D. Managers cannot add value by employing tax-saving strategies.

9. If managers justified a choice of optimal capital structure using Modigliani and Miller's Proposition II without taxes, they would contend that
   A. Taxes increase the value of debt.
   B. Taxes increase the value of equity.
   C. Debt is riskier than equity and therefore more costly.
   D. The cost of equity increases with increasing proportionate use of debt in the capital structure.

10. Suppose the cost of capital of the Gadget Company is 10 percent. If Gadget has a capital structure that is 50 percent debt and 50 percent equity, its before-tax cost of debt is 5 percent, and its marginal tax rate is 20 percent, then its cost of equity capital is closest to
    A. 10 percent.
    B. 12 percent.
    C. 14 percent.
    D. 16 percent.

11. The current weighted average cost of capital for Van der Welde, a South African mining company, is 10 percent. The company announced a debt offering that raises the marginal cost of capital to 13 percent. The company is *most likely* signaling that
    A. Debt financing is cheaper than equity.
    B. Equity financing is cheaper than debt.
    C. The company's debt-to-equity ratio has moved beyond the optimal range.
    D. The company's prospects are improving.

12. The financial literature generally finds that
    A. Companies in the United States and United Kingdom tend to have higher financial leverage ratios (taking total debt into account) compared to their peers in Japan, France, or Italy.
    B. Companies in the United States tend to use long-term financing more intensively than their peers in Japan.
    C. Companies in emerging markets tend to use long-term financing more intensively than their peers in the developed markets.
    D. Country-specific factors have no explanatory power regarding companies' financing structures.

13. The corporate debt maturity structure is typically longer in countries where
    A. The legal system is weak.
    B. Capital markets are passive and illiquid.
    C. Inflation is low.
    D. Economic growth is low.

14. Financial leverage ratios tend to be higher in countries where
    A. The legal system is inefficient.
    B. The presence of information intermediaries (e.g., auditors) is significant.
    C. The tax burden on dividends is low.
    D. Inflation is high.

15. According to the pecking order theory,
    A. New debt is preferable to new equity.
    B. New equity is preferable to internally generated funds.
    C. New debt is preferable to internally generated funds.
    D. New equity is always preferable to other sources of capital.

16. According to the static trade-off theory,
    A. The amount of debt a company has is irrelevant.
    B. Debt should be used only as a last resort.
    C. Debt will not be used if a company's tax rate is high.
    D. Companies have an optimal level of debt.

The following information relates to Questions 17 through 22.

Barbara Andrade is a generalist in equity analysis for Greengable Capital Partners, a major global asset manager. The investment committee relies on her input for a variety of equity recommendations. Because she has a background as an analyst in the finance department of an entertainment company, she is often asked to evaluate a variety of issues relating to that industry.

Greengable owns a significant position with a large gain in Mosely Broadcast Group. On a regular quarterly conference call, Brian Hunsaker, Greengable's growth portfolio manager, feels that Mosely's CFO may adjust the company's capital structure to include more debt. Concerned that any changes in the capital structure will impact the value of Greengable's holdings, Hunsaker asks Andrade to evaluate the impact of such a change.

To begin the analysis, Andrade first compiles the following current information relating to Mosely:

Yield to maturity on debt	8.00%
Market value of debt	$100 million
Number of shares of common stock	10 million
Price per share of common stock	$30
Weighted average cost of capital	10.82%
Marginal tax rate	35%

Additionally, Andrade determines that increased levels of debt will result in higher costs of both debt and equity to reflect increased credit risk and more financial leverage. Based on comparisons with similar companies in the industry, Andrade estimates that for the following debt-to-total capital ratios, the corresponding costs of debt and cost of equity will be:

Debt-to-total-capital Ratio (%)	Cost of Debt (%)	Cost of Equity (%)
20	7.7	12.5
30	8.4	13.0
40	9.3	14.0
50	10.4	16.0

17. The current after-tax cost of debt for Mosely is *closest* to
    A. 2.80%.
    B. 5.20%.
    C. 7.65%.
    D. 10.80%.

18. With consideration of taxes, Mosely's current cost of equity capital is *closest* to
    A. 8.25%.
    B. 10.05%.
    C. 11.76%.
    D. 12.69%.

19. Based on the given information, what debt-to-total-capital ratio would minimize Mosely's weighted average cost of capital?
    A. 20%.
    B. 30%.
    C. 40%.
    D. 50%.

20. An increase in the marginal tax rate to 40 percent would
    A. Result in a lower cost of debt capital.
    B. Result in a higher cost of debt capital.
    C. Not affect the company's cost of capital.
    D. Increase both the cost of Mosely's equity capital and the cost of its debt capital.

21. According to the static trade-off theory of capital structure, an increase in Mosely's debt ratio
    A. Would result in a lower market value of the company.
    B. Would result in a higher market value of the company.
    C. Would have no impact on the market value of the company.
    D. Could cause either an increase or decrease in the market value of the company.

22. According to the pecking order theory, Mosely would use the following ranking in raising capital:

	First Choice	Last Choice
A.	Debt	Internally generated funds
B.	Internally generated funds	Debt
C.	Internally generated funds	A new public equity issue
D.	A new public equity issue	Internally generated funds

CHAPTER 5

DIVIDENDS AND DIVIDEND POLICY

George H. Troughton, CFA
Professor Emeritus; California State University, Chico
Chico, California

Catherine E. Clark, CFA
Berkshire Research
Great Barrington, Massachusetts

LEARNING OUTCOMES

After completing this chapter, you will be able to do the following:

- Review cash dividends, stock dividends, stock splits, and reverse stock splits and calculate and discuss their impact on a shareholder.
- Compare the impact on shareholder wealth of a share repurchase and a cash dividend of equal amount.
- Calculate the earnings per share effect of a share repurchase when the repurchase is made with borrowed funds and the company's after-tax cost of debt is greater (less) than its earnings yield.
- Calculate the book value effect of a share repurchase when the market value of a share is greater (less) than book value per share.
- Compare and contrast share repurchase methods.
- Review dividend payment chronology including declaration, holder-of-record, ex-dividend, and payment dates and indicate when the share price will most likely be affected by the dividend.
- Summarize the factors affecting dividend payout policy.
- Calculate the effective tax rate on a dollar of corporate earnings distributed as a dividend using the double-taxation, split rate, and tax imputation systems.

- Discuss the types of information that dividend initiations, increases, decreases, and omissions may convey, and cross-country differences in the signaling content of dividends.
- Discuss the rationales for the residual dividend approach, and illustrate its mechanism given information about a company's earning, capital structure, and capital projects.
- Compare and contrast the following approaches to dividend policy: residual dividend, longer-term residual dividend, dividend stability, and target payout ratio.
- Calculate a company's expected dividend using the variables in the target payout approach.
- Discuss the rationales for share repurchases and explain the signals that share repurchases may generate.
- Discuss observed dividend policies and their evolution over time.
- Compare and contrast the dividend irrelevance, "bird-in the-hand," and tax aversion theories and explain the implications of each theory concerning the effect of dividends on shareholder value.
- Demonstrate how the initiation of a regular dividend payment may lead to a higher price-to-earnings ratio.
- Calculate the expected dividend in a residual dividend approach given information about a company's earnings, capital structure, and capital projects.

1. INTRODUCTION

One of the longest running and most debated issues in corporate finance is whether a company's decision about the level of its dividends has an impact on the value of its equity. Essentially, a company has three choices with respect to its earnings in any given year:

1. It could reinvest the earnings in the business.
2. It could pay the earnings out to the shareholders in the form of dividends.
3. It could repurchase outstanding shares.

In reality, most large companies do some combination of the three. For example, in recent decades, large companies in Germany, Great Britain, and the United States paid out dividends that often ranged from 20 percent to 60 percent of their earnings. Japan and some other developing nations had significantly lower dividend payout ratios.

We emphasize in this chapter that the overriding consideration in determining a company's dividend payout policy is whether it has positive net present value (NPV) reinvestment opportunities. In addition, a country's income taxes on corporate profits, shareholder income, and capital gains play an important role. Furthermore, traditions, transaction costs for new share issues, and shareholder preferences enter the picture. Finally, dividends are often read in the marketplace as sending a signal regarding the company's short- and long-term prospects.

This chapter is organized as follows: In Section 2, we discuss how cash and stock dividends are paid and how shares are repurchased. In Section 3, we present the chronology of dividend payment procedures, including record date, ex-dividend date, and payment date. In Section 4, we discuss the factors affecting a company's payout policy, including taxation, flotation costs, debt covenants and other institutional restrictions, the clientele effect, and the information content of dividends. This leads to a discussion in Section 5 of alternative dividend policies once a company is committed to paying a dividend. We look at the residual, stable, and target cash dividend approaches, as well as whether companies appear to be changing dividend policies. In Section 6, we explore the question of whether dividends matter or are irrelevant, and in Section 7 we touch briefly on the valuation implications of dividends. Section 8 summarizes the chapter.

2. FORMS OF DIVIDENDS

Companies can pay dividends in a number of ways. Cash dividends can be distributed to shareholders through regular, extra, special, or liquidating dividends. Other forms include stock dividends, stock splits, and share repurchases. In this section, we explore the different forms that dividends can take and their impact on both the shareholder and the issuing company.

2.1. Regular Dividends

Many companies choose to distribute dividends on a regular schedule. Most U.S. and Canadian companies pay quarterly dividends. Some non–North American companies, such as Samsung (Korea), Bayer AG (Germany), and Sony (Japan) distribute regular dividends either semiannually or annually. In each case, the intention is to distribute among shareholders a portion of a company's profits on a regular basis.

Most companies that pay regular dividends strive to maintain—or, better yet, increase—their dividends on a regular basis. A record of consistent dividends over a very long period of time is important to many companies and many shareholders. The higher standard of consistently increasing dividends is a goal that a substantial number of companies seek to attain and a significant portion of shareholders value.

Regular dividends, and especially increasing regular dividends, also signal to investors that their company is growing and willing to share the gains with their shareholders. Perhaps more importantly, management can use dividend announcements to communicate confidence in the future. An increase in the regular dividend (especially if it is unexpected) will likely have a more positive effect on the share price than could be explained by the increased monetary value of the dividend.

However, some interpret rising dividends or the payment of any dividends as a tacit sign of lack of sufficient growth opportunities, that is, as a sign that the company is unable to profitably reinvest all its earnings. In general, though, failing to increase a regular dividend over a long period of time—or, worse yet, cutting it—is often an indication that all is not well at the company.

2.1.1. Dividend Reinvestment Plans (DRIPs)
Some companies have in place a system that allows shareholders to automatically reinvest their dividends into the purchase of additional company shares. Shareholders must register to sign up for the dividend reinvestment plan. The advantages for the company are numerous: It retains the cash otherwise sent out to the shareholders; it reduces the transaction costs of making the payments; and it accumulates more equity capital while saving the underwriting costs of a new share issue. The advantages to the shareholders are twofold: It allows the accumulation of shares using cost averaging, and shareholders' additional investments are in a company they have already deemed a good investment. The additional shares are purchased with no transaction costs, and some companies offer the additional benefit of purchasing shares at a discount (usually 3–5 percent) to the market price.

A disadvantage to the shareholder is the extra bookkeeping involved in jurisdictions in which capital gains are taxed. Shares purchased through a dividend reinvestment plan change the average cost basis for capital gains tax purposes. If the share price is higher (lower) than the original purchase price, it increases (decreases) the average cost basis. Either way, the average shareholder is left with an accounting situation that is complicated. A further perceived disadvantage to the shareholder is that the cash dividend is fully taxed in the year received even when reinvested, which means the shareholder is paying tax on cash not actually received.

2.2. Extra (or Special) Dividends

Extra (or special) dividends occur when a company does not have a regular dividend policy or rate or when it wants to make a one-time extra payment.[1] Extra dividends are generally viewed as nonrecurring payments to shareholders brought about by special circumstances. Typically, companies in more cyclical industries are likely to use this form of dividend payment. When times are bad and earnings are down, cash that would otherwise have gone to dividends can be conserved. But when times are good and earnings are up, the companies can "share the wealth" with their shareholders by issuing a special dividend. Some companies in cyclical industries choose to declare a small regular dividend and then, when circumstances warrant, declare an extra dividend at the end of the year. While the word "extra" implies that this dividend is in addition to a more regular base of dividends, extra dividend, irregular dividend, and special dividend are terms used interchangeably. In the past, certain automobile companies were among those that regularly used the extra dividend. Ford and GM declared moderate regular quarterly dividends and used the extra dividend at the end of the year to reflect particularly good earnings.

2.3. Liquidating Dividends

A liquidating dividend occurs when a company dissolves its business and distributes the proceeds to its shareholders. Alternatively, a liquidating dividend could refer to the sale of part of a company's business for cash that is distributed to the shareholders. In either case, the distribution would be treated as a capital gain for tax purposes.

2.4. Stock Dividends

Another form of dividend used by some companies is the stock dividend. Here the company does not send cash to its shareholders, but distributes a certain percentage (typically 2–10 percent) of additional shares to each shareholder. The shareholders' total cost basis remains the same but the cost per share held is reduced. For example, if a shareholder owns 100 shares at a price of $10 per share, the total cost base would be $1,000. After a 5 percent stock dividend, the total cost basis would be the same $1,000, but the cost basis per share would become (approximately) $9.52 on the 105 shares now held ($9.52 = $1,000/105).

Superficially, the stock dividend might seem an improvement on the cash dividend from both the shareholders' and the company's points of view. Each shareholder ends up with more

---

[1]In *The Wall Street Journal's* Dividend News Section, extra or special dividends are referred to as "irregular dividends."

shares, which didn't have to be paid for, and the company didn't have to spend any actual money issuing a dividend. Furthermore, the shareholder postpones any tax due until the stock is ultimately sold. However, the stock dividend does nothing to change the value of each shareholder's ownership position in the company since, along with shares outstanding, earnings per share (and other per share data) are also adjusted. For example, a company with a billion-dollar market capitalization before issuing a stock dividend is still a company with a billion-dollar market capitalization after the stock dividend: The decrease in the share price should be exactly offset by the increase in the number of shares outstanding.

Exhibit 5-1 shows the impact of a 3 percent stock dividend to a shareholder who owns 10 percent of a company with a market value of $20 million.[2] As one can see, the market value of the shareholder's wealth does not change, assuming an unchanged price-to-earnings (P/E) ratio. In addition, a stock dividend and, as we will see shortly, a stock split do not alter a company's asset base or earning power.

In contrast to financial theorists, companies that regularly pay stock dividends see some advantages to this form of dividend payment. From the company's point of view, more shares outstanding broaden the shareholder base. With more shares outstanding, there is a higher probability that more individual shareholders will own the stock, almost always a plus for companies. Market folklore has it that a lower stock price attracts more investors, all else equal. U.S. companies often view the optimal share price as $20 to $80. Assuming a growing company, a systematic stock dividend is more likely to keep the stock in the "optimal" range. For example, Tootsie Roll Industries has issued a 3 percent dividend every year since 1966 in addition to its regular quarterly dividend. When the company pays the same dividend rate on the new shares as they did on the old shares, a shareholder's dividend income has increased.

A stock dividend has no effect on a company's capital structure (its mix of sources of financing) because it leaves the market values of equity and debt unchanged. This is a difference between cash and stock dividends. Cash dividends transfer assets from the company to shareholders, thereby reducing the assets of the company and the market value of its equity. As a result, cash dividends increase leverage (i.e., the proportion of financing provided by debt) from what it was before the payment of the dividend. An increase in leverage could

EXHIBIT 5-1   Illustration of the Effect of a Stock Dividend

	Before Dividend	After Dividend
Shares outstanding	1,000,000	1,030,000
Earnings per share	$1.00	$0.97 (1/1.03)
Stock price	$20.00	$19.4175 (20 × 0.9709)
P/E	20	20
Total market value	$20 million	$20 million (1,030,000 × $19.4175)
Shares owned	100,000 (10% × 1,000,000)	103,000 (10% × 1,030,000)
Ownership value	$2,000,000 (100,000 × $20)	$2,000,000 (103,000 × $19.4175)

---

[2]The table rounds intermediate calculations to only four decimal places. Final results ignore rounding errors.

decrease the market value of existing bonds, and bondholders usually seek to protect their position through certain restrictions on the payment of cash dividends, as discussed in more detail in Section 4.3.

Another difference between a cash dividend and a stock dividend is its accounting treatment on the books of the corporation. By shifting retained earnings (equal to the market value of the additional stock being distributed) to the capital account, a stock dividend merely reclassifies certain amounts of shareholders' equity on the balance sheet, whereas a cash dividend represents a cash outflow and a reduction in shareholders' equity.

2.5. Stock Splits

Stock splits are similar to stock dividends, in that each shareholder ends up with more shares but no change in his or her percentage ownership of the company. For example, if a company announces a three-for-one stock split, each shareholder is issued two additional shares for each share owned, so that the end result is three shares for each one share previously owned. In the process, though, earnings and dividends (and all other per share data) decline by two-thirds, leaving the P/E, dividend yield, and market value all unchanged. While two-for-one and three-for-one stock splits are the most common, unusual splits such as five-for-four or seven-for-three are not unheard of. It is important for shareholders to recognize that their wealth is unchanged by the stock split (just as it was for a stock dividend, all else equal). Exhibit 5-2 is an example of a six-for-five split and its impact on stock price, earnings per share, dividends per share, dividend yield, P/E, and market value.

As one can see, a six-for-five stock split is basically the same as a 20 percent stock dividend, since all per-share data have been reduced by 20 percent. The only difference is in the accounting treatment on the books of the company: Stock splits are accounted for as a reduction in the par value of the shares, whereas stock dividends are a transfer from retained earnings to equity capital.

A company may announce a stock split at any time. Typically it is after a period in which the stock has risen either for reasons specific to that company or, just as likely, during a general rise in the stock market in which the company's stock has done well. Investor folklore has it that an announcement of a stock split is viewed as a positive sign for future stock gains by

EXHIBIT 5-2   Before and After a Six-for-Five Stock Split

	Before Split	After Split
Number of shares outstanding	4 million	4.8 million
Stock price	$40.00	$33.33 [$40/(6/5)]
Earnings per share	$1.50	$1.25 [$1.50/(6/5)]
Dividends per share	$0.50	$0.4167 [$0.50/(6/5)]
Dividend yield	1.25%	1.25% ($0.4167/$33.33)
P/E	26.7	26.7 ($33.33/$1.25)
Market value of company	$160 million	$160 million

some investors. However, announced stock splits more often merely recognize that the stock has risen enough to justify a stock split, and return the stock price to the "optimal" range of $20 to $80 per share.

In mid-1999 when its stock was selling for about $90 per share, Enron announced a two-for-one stock split. Over the next year the stock doubled before the company plunged into bankruptcy in 2001. Ameritrade had two stock splits in 1999, a two-for-one in March and a three-for-one in August. The stock commenced to fall from over $60 per share (adjusted) to less than $3 per share in 2002. Even two of the largest companies in the world (as measured by market value), General Electric and Microsoft, saw their stocks decline significantly during the three years after their 1999 stock splits. In each of these cases, the stock was split after a significant rise but was not, in and of itself, a meaningful predictor of future price action.

Much less common than stock splits are reverse stock splits. A **reverse stock split** increases share price and reduces the number of shares outstanding—again, with no change to the underlying fundamentals. Just as a rising stock price might indicate an upcoming stock split, so, too, a dramatically falling stock price might signal a forthcoming reverse stock split. Reverse stock splits are typically one-for-a-much-larger number, with the objective of getting the stock closer (this time *up*) to the optimal $20 to $80 range. Reverse stock splits are perhaps most common for companies coming out of bankruptcy (for which a one-for-thirty or one-for-fifty reverse stock split are not unusual) or when the share price declines to a low value (for example, in the United States many institutional investors do not regard stocks selling below $5 per share as investment grade). AT&T Corporation had a one-for-five reverse split in November 2002 that brought its stock price up from approximately $5 (adjusting for a liquidating dividend paid on the same date) to about $28.

2.6. Share Repurchases

A **share repurchase** (or buyback) is a transaction in which a company buys back its own shares. Unlike stock dividends and stock splits, share repurchases use corporate cash. Hence, share repurchases can be viewed as an alternative to cash dividends. Shares that have been issued and subsequently repurchased become **treasury shares** (**treasury stock**), which are not considered for dividends, voting, or computing earnings per share. Treasury shares may be reissued later, typically for employee stock options. When used for stock options, repurchased shares reduce or prevent earnings per share dilution but do not increase earnings per share.

Share repurchases have been around for a long time, but only in the last twenty years have they been used extensively. In the early 1980s, cash dividends were approximately five times greater than the market value of share repurchases. For a number of years in the bull market of the late 1990s, the total value of share repurchases was greater than that of cash dividends in the United States.

A share repurchase should be equivalent to the payment of cash dividends of equal amount in their effect on shareholders' wealth, all other things being equal. "All other things being equal" in this context is shorthand for assumptions that the taxation and information content of cash dividends and share repurchases do not differ. (We shall discuss the information content of dividends in a subsequent section.) Understanding this baseline equivalence result permits more advanced analysis to explore the result's sensitivity to various modifications to the "all other things being equal" assumption. For example, in Section 5.4 we discuss the advantage share repurchases may have over cash dividends when the tax rate on dividend income is higher than that on capital gains. Example 5-1 demonstrates the claim of equivalence in the "all other things being equal" case.

EXAMPLE 5-1   The Equivalence of Share Repurchases and Cash Dividends

---

Waynesboro Chemical Industries, Inc. (WCII) has 10 million shares outstanding with a current market value of $20 per share. WCII's board of directors is considering two ways of distributing WCII's current $50 million free cash flow to equity. The first method involves paying a cash dividend of $50 million/10 million = $5 per share. The second method involves repurchasing $50 million worth of shares. For simplicity, we make the assumptions that dividends are received when the shares go ex-dividend and that any quantity of shares can be bought at the market price of $20 per share. We also assume that the taxation and information content of cash dividends and share repurchases do not differ. How would the wealth of a shareholder be affected by WCII's choice of method in distributing the $50 million?

Cash dividend: After the shares go ex-dividend, a shareholder of a single share would have $5 in cash (the dividend) and a share worth $20 − $5 = $15. The ex-dividend value of $15 can be demonstrated as the market value of equity after the distribution of $50 million, divided by the number shares outstanding after the dividend payment, or [(10 million)($20) − $50 million]/10 million = $150 million/10 million = $15. (The payment of a cash dividend, of course, has no effect on the number of shares outstanding.) Total wealth from ownership of one share is therefore $5 + $15 = $20.

Share repurchase: With $50 million, WCII could repurchase $50 million/$20 = 2.5 million shares. The postrepurchase share price would be unchanged at $20, which can be calculated as the market value of equity after the $50 million share repurchase, divided by the shares outstanding after the share repurchase, or [(10 million)($20) − $50 million]/(10 million − 2.5 million) = $150 million/7.5 million = $20. Total wealth from ownership of one share is therefore $20, exactly the same as in the case of a cash dividend.

So it is irrelevant for a shareholder's wealth whether the shareholder actually sold the share back to the WCII in the share repurchase: If the one share was sold, $20 in cash would be realized; if the share was not sold, its market value of $20 would count equally toward the shareholder's wealth.

The assumption made in Example 5-1 that the company repurchases shares at the market price is an important one. Example 5-2 illustrates that if a company repurchases shares from an individual shareholder at a negotiated price representing a premium over the market price, the remaining shareholders' wealth is reduced.

EXAMPLE 5-2   A Share Repurchase That Transfers Wealth

While considering the choice between cash dividends and a share repurchase at the market price of $20 per share, WCII becomes aware that Kirk Parent recently purchased a major position in its outstanding shares with the intention of influencing the business operations of WCII in ways the current board does not endorse. An advisor to the board has suggested approaching Parent privately with an offer to buy back $50 million worth of shares from him at $25 per share, which is a $5 premium over the current market price. The board of WCII declines to do so because of the effect of such a repurchase on its other shareholders. Determine the effect of the proposed share repurchase on the wealth of shareholders other than Parent.

Solution

With $50 million, WCII could repurchase $50 million/$25 = 2 million shares from Parent. The postrepurchase share price would be $18.75, which can be calculated as the market value of equity after the $50 million share repurchase divided by the shares outstanding after the share repurchase, or [(10 million)($20) − $50 million]/(10 million − 2 million) = $150 million/8 million = $18.75. Shareholders other than Parent would lose $20 − $18.75 = $1.25 for each share owned. Although this share repurchase would conserve total wealth (including Parent's), it effectively transfers wealth to Parent from the other shareholders.

The theme of Example 5-1 was that, as the baseline result, a company should not expect to create or destroy shareholder wealth merely by its choice of method in distributing money to shareholders. In Example 5-1, the market price per share of $20 was not affected by the share repurchase. We can interpret $20 as the product of expected earnings per share (EPS) and a forward price-to-earnings ratio, or as the product of book value per share and the price-to-book ratio. A share repurchase may affect the terms in these products (e.g., EPS and price-to-earnings) but, if it does, Example 5-1 suggests that the changes should be offsetting. Examples 5-3 and 5-4 illustrate the types of analysis we can conduct on the effect of share repurchases on EPS and book value per share (BVPS).

EXAMPLE 5-3   Share Repurchases Using Borrowed Funds: The Effect on EPS When the After-tax Cost of Borrowing Equals Earnings Yield (E/P)

Jensen Industries plans to borrow $12 million, which it will use to repurchase shares. The following information is given:

- Share price at time of buyback $60
- EPS before buyback $3
- Earnings yield (E/P) $3/$60 = 5%
- After-tax cost of borrowing   5%

- Shares outstanding   2.2 million
- Planned buyback   200,000 shares

Calculate the EPS after the buyback.

Solution

$$\text{EPS after buyback} = \frac{\text{Earnings} - \text{After-tax cost of funds}}{\text{Shares outstanding after buyback}}$$

$$= \frac{\$6.6 \text{ million} - (200,000 \text{ shares} \times \$60 \times 0.05)}{2 \text{ million shares}}$$

$$= \frac{\$6.6 \text{ million} - \$0.6 \text{ million}}{2 \text{ million shares}}$$

$$= \frac{\$6.0 \text{ million}}{2 \text{ million shares}}$$

$$= \$3.00$$

With the after-tax cost of borrowing equal to the earnings yield (E/P) of the shares, the share repurchase has no effect on the company's EPS.

In Example 5-3, the share repurchase produced no change in EPS because the shares' earnings yield of 5 percent equaled its after-tax cost of borrowing. We can also see that, if the after-tax cost of borrowing were greater than 5 percent, earnings after the buyback would be less than $6 million, so that EPS after the buyback would be less than $3.00. On the other hand, the after-tax cost of borrowing less than 5 percent would increase EPS to a level above $3.00. In summary, a share repurchase may increase, not affect, or reduce EPS, depending on whether the after-tax cost of the funds used to accomplish the repurchase is less than, equal to, or greater than the earnings yield of the shares before the repurchase.

A share repurchase may cause the price-to-earnings ratio to change as well. For example, if a share repurchase causes a company's financial leverage to change, the financial risk of the company's earnings stream changes and the price-to-earnings ratio postrepurchase may change from its prerepurchase level to reflect the change in risk.

EXAMPLE 5-4 The Effect of Share Repurchase on Book Value per Share

Company A and Company B stocks sell at $20 a share, and each company has 10 million shares outstanding. Both companies have announced a $5 million buyback. The only difference is that Company A has a market price per share greater than its book value per share, while Company B has a market price per share less than its book value per share:

- Company A has book value of equity of $100 million and BVPS of $100 million/ 10 million shares = $10. *The market price per share of $20 is greater than BVPS of $10.*

- Company B has a book value of equity of $300 million and BVPS of $300 million/ 10 million shares = $30. *The market price per share of $20 is less than BVPS of $30.*
- Both companies buy back 250,000 shares at the market price per share ($5 million buyback/$20 per share = 250,000).
- Both companies are left with 9.75 million shares outstanding (10 million prebuy-back shares − 0.25 million repurchased = 9.75 million shares).

After the share repurchase:

- Company A's shareholders' equity at book value falls to $95 million ($100 million − $5 million), and its *book value per share decreases* from $10 to $9.74 (shareholders' equity/shares outstanding = $95 million/9.75 million shares = $9.74).
- Company B's shareholders' equity at book value falls to $295 million ($300 million − $5 million), and its *book value per share increases* from $30 to $30.26 (shareholders' equity/shares outstanding = $295 million/9.75 million = $30.26).

Example 5-4 shows that book value per share either increases or decreases depending on whether share price is higher or lower than BVPS. When share price is greater than BVPS, BVPS decreases after a share repurchase; when share price is less than BVPS, BVPS increases after a share repurchase. Still worth underscoring is that, if shares are repurchased at market price, we would not expect the balance sheet effect just illustrated to affect shareholders' wealth, all other things being equal.

2.7. Repurchase Methods

Companies repurchase shares in three main ways:

1. *Buy in the open market:* This is the most common method of repurchase, with the company buying from time to time, as conditions warrant in the open market. This gives the company optimum flexibility and, in many shareholders' minds, acts to set a floor on the price of the shares. The latter is not always the case, but all other things being equal, an outstanding authorized share repurchase probably does function as a support for the share price.
2. *Buy back a fixed number of shares at a fixed price:* Sometimes a company makes a *tender offer* to repurchase a specific number of shares, typically at a premium to the current market. Shareholders may subscribe to the offer, agreeing to sell their shares at the predetermined price. If more shares are subscribed to than the total repurchase, the company typically buys back a pro rata amount from each shareholder.
3. *Repurchase by direct negotiation:* On occasion a company negotiates with a major shareholder to buy back its shares, often at a premium to the market price. Example 5-2 illustrated this practice. The company may do this to keep a large block of shares from overhanging the market (and thus acting to dampen the share price). In some of the more infamous cases, unsuccessful takeover attempts have ended with the company buying back the would-be suitor's shares in what is referred to as a greenmail transaction, often to the detriment of remaining shareholders.[3]

---

[3]**Greenmail** is the purchase of the accumulated shares of a hostile investor by a company that is targeted for takeover by that investor, usually at a substantial premium over market price.

2.8. Dividend Forms Outside the United States

To provide a perspective on dividends, our discussion thus far has been limited to the United States. Laws, customs, and other considerations, all of which can vary from country to country, influence the forms that dividends take. Legal restrictions affect some forms of dividends. Stock repurchases, so common in recent years in the United States, are discouraged or even prohibited in some countries. Repurchases in the open market could be viewed as an attempt at company manipulation of its own stock. In fact, the U.S. Securities and Exchange Commission (SEC) held such a view until it adopted a safe harbor for company repurchases in 1982.

Companies may also consider their competitive environment when contemplating dividends and the form that a prospective dividend might take. In smaller-capitalization markets, a company may feel that returning cash to its shareholders is not in its best interest. Some managements worry that a shareholder would take the cash (from either a cash dividend or repurchased shares) and invest it in a competitor of the company, thus possibly hurting the company's competitive position.

3. DIVIDEND PAYMENT CHRONOLOGY

In the previous section, we saw that dividends can take several forms. Once a company's board of directors votes a dividend, a fairly standard dividend chronology is set in motion. In this section we provide an explanation of dividend payment chronology in the United States. Since the payment chronology is determined by rules set by exchanges in various countries, there are some country-to-country differences; but declaration dates, ex-dividend dates, and record dates are common on most exchanges. Furthermore, the shares of most large non-U.S. companies trade on the New York Stock Exchange (NYSE) and thus must meet the chronology described here. For example, the five largest publicly held non-U.S. companies, BP (UK), DaimlerChrysler (Germany), Toyota (Japan), Royal Dutch (Netherlands/UK) and Total (France), as well as 354 other global companies, trade on the NYSE as American Depository Securities (ADS). Canadian companies such as Royal Bank of Canada, Alcan, Nortel Networks, EnCana, and Canadian National Railway trade like U.S. shares on the NYSE.

3.1. Declaration Date

The first date on the time line is the **declaration date**, the day that the corporation issues a statement declaring a specific dividend. Whether it is a regular, irregular, special, liquidating, or stock dividend, chronology begins with a company's board of directors authorizing its payment. In Japan and several European countries, the company's shareholders must approve the payment. At the time of the declaration, the company states the holder-of-record date and the payment date. Typically, business publications list dividends declared during the previous day (for daily publications) or week (for weekly publications) under the heading "Dividends Reported," including the period for which the dividend applies (e.g., monthly, quarterly, special), the dollar amount of the dividend (to six decimal points if applicable), the payable date, and the record date.

3.2. Ex-dividend Date

After the declaration date, the next pertinent date is the **ex-dividend date** (also referred to as the **ex-date**). This is the first date that a share trades without (i.e., "ex") the dividend.

For a share traded on the ex-dividend date, the buyer does not receive the dividend. To have a claim on the dividend, the share must be bought no later than the last business day *before* the ex-dividend date. This is the last day a share trades *cum dividend*, or with the dividend, and the last day that the buyer of the share will receive the dividend. For example, in the United States, if the ex-date is Tuesday, December 26, shares must be bought by Friday, December 22, to receive the dividend (markets are closed on Christmas Day, Monday, December 25, and are not open on Saturday and Sunday). Trading **ex-dividend** refers to shares that no longer carry the right to the next dividend payment. This trading day is often designated in the share price tables of business publications with an *x* in the volume column. This indicates that the money value of the upcoming dividend has been subtracted from the previous day's closing price. For example, if a share closed at $20 on the day before the ex-date and the upcoming dividend is $0.25, then on the ex-date (all other things being equal) the shares will start the trading day at $19.75. If it closes at $20 for that day, it will show a gain of $0.25 for the day, even though the closing price is the same as it was the day before.

3.3.   Holder-of-Record Date

The **holder-of-record date** (also called the owner-of-record date, shareholder-of-record date, record date, or date of record) is two business days after the ex-dividend date. This is the date that a shareholder listed on the corporation's books is deemed to have ownership of the shares for purposes of receiving the upcoming dividend. While the shareholder-of-record date is determined by the corporation, the ex-date is determined by the exchange on which the shares trade. Currently, the ex-date is two business days before the record date. In our example, if the ex-date were Tuesday, December 26, the record date would be Thursday December 28. Not too many years ago, there were four or five business days between the ex- and the record dates. The shorter time frame no doubt is due to technological improvements in handling share transactions and mirrors the fewer number of days stipulated between trade and settlement dates for share transactions.

3.4.   Payment Date

The final pertinent date on the dividend chronology is the **payment date** (also called the payable date). This is the day that the company actually mails out (or, more recently, electronically transfers) the dividend payment. As discussed earlier, the company typically states the payment date when the dividend declaration is made. Unlike other pertinent dates, such as the ex-date and record date which are only on business days, the payment date is just as likely to be on a weekend or holiday as not. For example, a company may list its payment dates as March 15, June 15, September 15, and December 15 even though some of those dates will inevitably fall on a Saturday, Sunday, or holiday.

3.5.   Interval Between Key Dates in the Dividend Payment Chronology

The time between the ex-date and the record date is fixed (currently at two days), but the time between the other pertinent dates is determined by each company and can vary substantially. For example, record dates are typically anywhere from a week to a month after the declaration date for most normal dividends but can be much longer for less commonly occurring dividends such as irregular dividends, special dividends, liquidating dividends, and stock dividends. Likewise, the time between the record date and the payment date is typically

EXHIBIT 5-3   Typical Timeline for Dividend Chronology

Declaration date	Ex-date	Holder-of-record date	Payment date
Feb 24	March 15	March 17	March 30

2005

anywhere from a few days to a month or more. However, most companies follow a fairly set routine for their dividends, especially for regular quarterly dividends. Some business publications such as *Value Line* include in their individual company reports the approximate dates of a company's next dividend meeting, its ex-date, and payment date. Exhibit 5-3 portrays a typical timeline for dividend chronology.

3.5.1. Impact on Indirect Shareholders   For those who own shares through open-end, closed-end, and exchange-traded funds (ETFs), the dividend chronology is generally the same as for those who own shares directly. That is, on the ex-dividend date for any shares in the fund portfolio, the price of those shares nominally fall by the value of the dividend, and on the payment date the company sends an electronic transfer for the value of the dividend to the fund. However, most funds only declare their dividends (the total dividends and interest received by the portfolio less management fees and expenses) to fund owners on a periodic basis. No doubt, this is for logistical purposes, because accounting for each fund's shareholder payments on a frequent pro rata basis would not be cost-effective. Therefore, equity funds typically distribute dividend income on a periodic basis, usually quarterly or annually. For example, for the Vanguard funds, those with a relatively higher dividend yield (the Wellington Balanced Fund, Index 500, and Value Index Fund) generally distribute dividends quarterly, while funds with a relatively lower dividend yield (the small cap, growth, and international funds) generally distribute dividends once a year, usually in December. Paralleling the ex-dividend concept, on the dividend distribution date, the price of the fund is decreased by the value of the dividends being distributed. The fund owner can then either receive the dividends in cash or reinvest them in additional shares of the fund. For example, if a fund has a net asset value of $20 on January 15 and is distributing $1 in dividends on January 16, the net asset value of the fund drops $1 to $19 (all other things being equal) on January 16. The total value to each fund shareholder is still $20 ($19 in share value and $1 in dividends), although the dividend distribution is a taxable event to the fund shareholder. Under U.S. tax law, regulated investment companies are not taxed on fund income as long as 90 percent of such income (after fees) is passed on to the fund shareholder.

4. FACTORS AFFECTING DIVIDEND PAYOUT POLICY

In this section we explore six factors affecting a company's decision to pay dividends: its **dividend payout policy**. Some factors are external to the company, such as taxation, while other factors are more company-specific, such as possible restrictions on dividend payments and flotation costs. Shareholder preference for current income versus capital gains and the so-called clientele effect are also discussed. We also look at the information content of dividends: how dividends can be used as a signaling device by management.

4.1. Taxation of Dividends

Taxation is an important factor in all investment decisions, because it is the after-tax return that is most relevant to investors. Different countries tax corporate dividends in a wide variety of ways, and even within a single country taxation can be quite complex. In addition, because taxation is a major fiscal policy tool that is subject to politics, governments have a tendency to "readdress" tax issues, sometimes with great frequency, thereby complicating the issue even more. As with other aspects of taxation, governments use the taxation of dividends to address a variety of goals: either to encourage or discourage the retention or distribution of corporate earnings; to redistribute income; or to address other political, social, and/or investment goals.

Most developed markets tax shareholder investment income. Some tax both capital gains and dividend income. Others tax dividends but not capital gains. Hong Kong is an exception in that it levies no tax on either dividends or capital gains.

For the global investor, foreign taxes can be just as important as domestic taxes. Foreign tax credits in the investor's home country also may figure importantly into the overall taxation issue. For example, GlaxoSmithKline PLC (GSK) is a giant pharmaceutical company based in the United Kingdom. In 2003, the United Kingdom withheld approximately 5 percent of GSK's dividend, but U.S. shareholders were generally able to claim a tax credit for the amount withheld by the United Kingdom on their U.S. tax returns.

4.1.1. Taxation Methods We will look at three main systems of taxation that impact dividends: the **double taxation**, **split rate**, and **imputation** tax systems. Other tax systems can be a combination of these.

The United States is often described as an example of a *double taxation* system. Corporate earnings are taxed regardless of whether they will be distributed as dividends or retained at the corporate level, and dividends are taxed again at the individual shareholder level. (In fact, for many U.S. investors, there is triple taxation of dividends because many states also levy a tax on dividend income.) In 2003, taxes on the shareholders' dividends were lowered from a maximum of 39.6 percent (the highest marginal income tax rate) to a maximum of 15 percent. At the same time, the tax on long-term capital gains was also reduced to the same 15 percent (from a 20 percent maximum rate). Exhibit 5-4 depicts the double taxation system using the highest marginal rate on dividends in the United States both before and after the 2003 tax law change.[4]

EXHIBIT 5-4   Double Taxation of Dividends at Different Personal Tax Rates (per $100)

	39.6%	15%
Net income before taxes	$100	$100
Corporate tax rate	35%	35%
Net income after tax	$65	$65
Dividend assuming 100% payout	$65	$65
Shareholder tax	$25.74	$9.75
Net dividend to Shareholder	$39.26	$55.25
Double tax rate per $ of dividend	60.7%	44.8%

---

[4]Under current U.S. tax law, both dividend and capital gains tax rates are scheduled to return to pre-2003 levels in 2009.

Although there is still double taxation of dividends in the example, the net tax rate on a dollar of income distributed in dividends has declined from 61 percent to 45 percent, a decline of about 26 percent. Though U.S. investors clearly prefer the lower preferential tax rate for dividends, it is not clear whether they would prefer a higher or lower payout, because the current tax rate is the same on both dividends and long-term capital gains for most shareholders. Later we discuss a company's decision with respect to the dividend payout ratio.

Other countries, such as Germany, have a *split rate* system of corporate taxes. A split rate system taxes earnings to be distributed as dividends at a different rate than earnings to be retained. Corporate profits distributed as dividends are taxed at a lower rate than those retained in the business. This offsets the higher taxation of dividends at the individual level compared with taxation of capital gains. Exhibit 5-5 depicts this split rate tax system for dividends.

The split rate tax system would lead shareholders in a low tax bracket to prefer a higher payout, since distributed income is taxed less. Alternatively, shareholders in higher brackets would prefer a lower payout, with more funds retained, since capital gains receive a preferential tax treatment. Canada and Japan have a tax credit system that has a similar effect.

A third major taxation system is the *imputation* tax system, which imputes, or attributes, taxes at only one level of taxation. The United Kingdom, New Zealand, and Australia have a form of the imputation system. For countries using an imputation tax system, taxes on dividends are effectively levied only at the shareholder rate. Taxes are paid at the corporate level but they are *attributed* to the shareholder. Shareholders deduct from their tax bill their portion of taxes paid by the company. If the shareholder's tax bracket were lower than the company's, the shareholder would receive a tax credit equal to the difference between the two rates. If the shareholder's tax bracket is higher than the company's, the shareholder pays the difference between the two rates. Exhibit 5-6 depicts the taxation of dividends based on the tax imputation system for both a low-marginal-rate shareholder and a high-marginal-rate shareholder.

Here, as with the split rate system, shareholders in lower tax brackets would prefer higher payouts, because they actually receive a tax credit for the difference between the corporate rate and their individual rate.

4.1.2. Shareholder Preference for Current Income Versus Capital Gains   All other things being equal, one could expect that the lower the tax rate on dividends, the higher the level of dividends will be. But other tax issues impinge on this issue. As mentioned

EXHIBIT 5-5   Taxation of Dividends Based on Split Rate System (per €100)

Pretax earnings	€200
Pretax earnings retained	100
35% tax on retained earnings	35
Pretax earnings allocated to dividends	100
20% tax on earnings allocated to dividends	20
Dividends distributed	80
Shareholder tax rate	35%
After-tax dividend to shareholder	$[(1-0.35) \times 80] = 52$
Effective tax rate on dividend	$[20\% + (80 \times 0.35)] = 48\%$

EXHIBIT 5-6   Taxation of Dividends Based on Tax Imputation System ($Australian)

	Marginal Shareholder Tax Rate	
	15%	47%
Pretax income	$100	$100
Taxes at 30% corporate tax rate	30	30
Net income after tax	70	70
Dividend assuming 100% payout	70	70
Shareholder taxes	15	47
Less tax credit for corporate payment	30	30
Tax due from shareholder	(15)	17
Effective tax rate on dividend	15/100	47/100
	= 15%	= 47%

earlier, the trade-off between taxes on dividends and taxes on capital gains is an important part of the equation. Even if dividends were to be taxed at a lower rate than capital gains, it is not clear that shareholders would necessarily prefer higher dividends. After all, capital gains taxes don't have to be paid until the shares are sold, whereas taxes on dividends must be paid in the year received, even if reinvested. In addition, in some countries such as the United States, shares held at the time of death benefit from a *step-up* valuation to the death date. Finally, tax-exempt institutions such as pension funds and endowment funds are major shareholders in most industrial countries. Such institutions are typically exempt from both taxes on dividends and taxes on capital gains. Hence, all other things being equal, they are indifferent as to whether their return comes in the form of current dividends or capital gains.

4.2. Flotation Costs on New Issues Versus Retaining Earnings

Another factor affecting a company's decision to pay dividends is the flotation costs on new issues versus retained earnings. **Flotation cost** is the percentage cost of new common share issuance and reflects the fees paid to investment bankers as well as other costs of share issuance. It is typically higher for smaller companies and smaller share issues. Because of flotation costs, the cost of new equity capital is always higher than the cost of retained earnings. Therefore, many companies do not pay a dividend when issuing new shares to fund projects with positive NPVs. Issuing shares to fund the payment of dividends would be unprofitable.

EXAMPLE 5-5   A Company That Needs to Reinvest All Profits

Boar's Head Spirits Ltd., based in the United Kingdom, has estimated profits of £500 million. The company's financial analyst has calculated its cost of capital as 12 percent. The same analyst has evaluated modernization and expansion projects with a positive NPV that would require £800 million. The cost of positive NPV projects exceeds estimated profits by £300 million (£800 million − £500 million). Boar's Head does not want to increase its long-term debt in the next year. Hence, in this simplified example, the company would not pay dividends because free cash flow is not positive.

Because the company has unfunded positive NPV projects, it should consider issuing new shares incurring flotation costs of perhaps 5–7 percent of the new issue. The company would not, however, issue shares to fund the payment of dividends.

4.3. Restrictions on Dividend Payments

The ability of a company even to consider paying a dividend is often affected by restrictions, both formal and informal. In some countries there is a legal restriction, known as the **impairment of capital rule**, which states that dividends cannot exceed retained earnings. More typical are formal restrictions resulting from debt covenants, which can be anything that the company and the lender agree to. Here, certain minimum figures are set for such constraints as interest coverage, current ratio, and net worth, before any dividend payments may be considered.

Informal restrictions can also figure into a company's decision to pay dividends. Cash flow is an important one. Some companies continue to pay a regularly scheduled dividend even when earnings are down and the payout ratio exceeds the company's target payout ratio. It is also not unusual for a company's dividend to exceed its earnings for a brief period. But most companies are loath to pay out dividends that exceed their cash flow from operations unless the company is in a liquidation mode.

Industry life cycle may also act as an implicit restriction on dividend payments. Many companies in the technology-related industries have negative net income, although positive EBITDA (earnings before interest, taxes, depreciation, and amortization). Even profitable biotechnology companies, or any company with an assumed high growth rate, might well be viewed negatively for instituting a dividend, because shareholders could interpret a dividend as a lack of investment opportunities for the company. Banks, on the other hand, typically have a dividend yield that exceeds that of the overall market. For example, in late 2004 the shares of Barclay's Bank (U.K.), Citigroup (U.S.), and UBS (Switzerland) yielded 4.3 percent, 3.4 percent, and 2.8 percent, respectively.

4.4. Clientele Effect

Another factor affecting a company's decision to pay dividends is the **clientele effect**, which is the preference some investors have for shares that exhibit certain characteristics. For example, investors with low or no tax exposure are assumed to be attracted to companies with high or relatively high dividend yields. Retired investors typically have a preference for higher current income; they usually prefer to hold stocks with a higher dividend yield. On the other hand, other investor groups, such as younger workers with a long time horizon, might favor industries and companies that reinvest a high proportion of their earnings for long-term capital growth and therefore prefer stocks with little or no dividends.

The tax status of the investor is an important component of this clientele effect. As discussed earlier, tax-exempt entities such as pension funds, university endowments, or charitable foundations would reasonably have a higher preference for current income (and therefore dividends) than would higher-taxed individuals who would rather defer tax payments through capital gains.

Institutional investors, including certain mutual funds, banks, and insurance companies, will only invest in companies that pay at least some dividend. Some even require (either officially or unofficially) a specific minimum dividend yield. As dividend yields fell during the bull market of the 1990s, this requirement was often altered to accept stocks with dividend yields in the top quartile (or half) of their stock universe. Trusts and foundations may be under a restriction stipulating that only income (i.e., interest and dividends) may be distributed to beneficiaries.

Some individual investors use a self-control device of "only spending the dividends, not the principal" to preserve their capital.[5] Furthermore, in some jurisdictions, there are *legal lists* or *approved lists of equity investments* for institutions such as insurance companies and trusts for individuals. Such legal lists typically mandate that permissible investments consist only of companies that pay dividends. Often, such restrictive lists are intended to serve as a proxy discouraging high-risk stocks. All of this suggests that a clientele effect does exist and that a preference for dividends is one way in which the equity market can be segmented.

The question of whether different industries attract different investors can be partially addressed by looking at the dividend yield of major industry groups. Exhibit 5-7 shows the dividend yield for five of the S&P 500 industry groups: Utilities, Financial, Energy, Health Care, and Information Technology. As is evident, there is a dramatic difference in dividend yields for these five industries, with Utilities having the highest yield and Technology having a miniscule one. The clientele effect would suggest that certain investors might be drawn to certain industry groups because of the dividend yield.

4.5. Signaling Effect: The Information Content of Dividends

A final factor affecting dividend payout policy is the information content of dividends. The implication is that a company's board of directors and/or management uses its dividend policy to signal investors about how the company is *really* doing. Empirical studies support

EXHIBIT 5-7   Dividend Yield of Major Standard & Poor's Industry Groups; September 2004 (%)

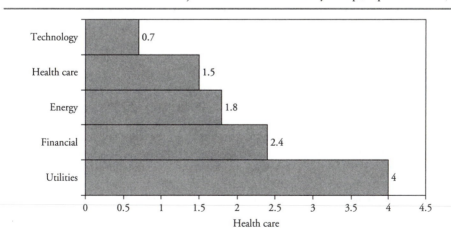

_____
[5]See Shefrin and Statman (1984).

the thesis that dividend initiation or increases are associated with future earnings growth, and a dividend omission or reduction are associated with future earnings problems.[6] Members of both the board and management are, after all, the ultimate insiders, and it is likely that no other group has better information about future earnings and cash flow. A dividend declaration can help resolve some of the information asymmetry between insiders and outsiders. Therefore, a company's decision to initiate, maintain, increase, or cut a dividend can often convey much more information than could words alone.

Good examples of this are companies that regularly increase their dividend. Many companies take pride in their record of consistently increasing dividends on a regular basis over a long period of time. It is an important tool to let shareholders know that the future is good and that the company has a desire to share its increasing fortunes with its shareholders. For example, ExxonMobil has consistently increased its dividend on a yearly basis over the past two decades. While the company's earnings, cash flow, payout, and yield have fluctuated over this time, dividends have continued to increase each year, signaling to the market that the company's long-term outlook is intact. Unlike other companies in its peer group whose dividends have more closely reflected current movements in the fortunes of the oil industry, if ExxonMobil were to cut dividends, or even fail to increase the yearly dividend, it would send a meaningful (and negative) signal to investors about the future of the company. Anecdotal evidence for a signaling effect is also found on the Standard & Poor's Web site. As of September 2004, S&P found 58 companies in the S&P 500 Index that are "Dividend Aristocrats" in that they have increased their dividend for 25 consecutive years. These companies span various industries and include General Electric, Pfizer, Procter & Gamble, and Wal-Mart. Mergent has established a list of Canadian and European companies that are called Dividend Achievers. These companies include Novartis (Switzerland), Barclays (U.K.), Unilever (Netherlands), Imperial Oil (Canada), and Thomson (Canada).[7] Companies that consistently increase their dividends seem to share certain characteristics:

- Dominant or niche positions in their industry (in Michael Porter's terms, they have a competitive advantage).
- Global operations.
- Relatively high returns on assets.
- Relatively low debt ratios (they're unlikely to be affected by debt covenants).

Dividend cuts or omissions present a powerful signaling component. For many companies under financial or operating stress, the dividend declaration date is viewed with more than usual interest. Will they cut the dividend? Will they omit the dividend altogether? In these instances, merely holding the dividend or not cutting it as much as expected is viewed as good news, although in retrospect there are plenty of instances when the dividend should have been cut or omitted and was not. Some companies hang in to the bitter end and omit the dividend only as they file for bankruptcy, sending what turned out to be a most erroneous signal to the market.

In some instances, though, management can attempt to send a positive signal by cutting the dividend (this, admittedly, is more difficult). In 1993, IBM, long the giant of mainframe computers and having maintained an enviable record of dividend increases over the years,

---

[6]For example, see DeAngelo, DeAngelo, and Skinner (1986).

[7]*Barron's*, November 1, 2004, p. 37.

announced a more than 50 percent cut in its dividend, explaining that their intention was to shift its business by strongly investing in nonmainframe technology and consulting services to improve future returns. While the message was met with varying reactions, it was, in retrospect, a positive signal, and those who paid attention were richly rewarded. Likewise, in 2003 Schering-Plough, a leading U.S.-based pharmaceutical company, suffered a triple blow to its worldwide position including loss of patent on its leading drug (Claritin), a U.S. Food and Drug Administration (FDA) consent degree, and legal actions by government prosecutors related to sales and marketing. In April 2003 Fred Hassan was appointed chairman and CEO. Mr. Hassan is generally credited with the turnaround in Pharmacia that was later merged in Pfizer. He announced a six- to eight-year plan to transform Schering-Plough that included a 68 percent cut in the quarterly dividend.

Another even more complicated example of the signaling content of dividends can be found in Microsoft's initial dividend declaration. As we saw from Exhibit 5-7, technology companies have among the lowest dividend yields. This makes sense. By their very nature (most would argue), technology companies are on the cutting edge; they have high R&D requirements, and those that are profitable have high returns on assets. All of this would suggest low (or no) dividend payments, because funds would much better be spent on investing in new product development that will maintain high returns. But in the mid-1990s, as Microsoft's phenomenal growth and dominance of its industry continued, net cash grew to tens of billions of dollars, and many wondered whether the company could effectively use its cash "hoard" and whether it was time for Microsoft to pay a dividend.

In late 2003, Microsoft declared its first annual dividend of $0.06 per share, equaling about 7 percent of its yearly cash flow, less than 2 percent of its net cash position, and representing a yield of 0.3 percent. Then, in the summer of 2004, the company increased its annual dividend to $0.32 per share and announced a special year-end dividend of $3.00 a share. Clearly, the signaling effect was more important than the actual cash impact on either the company or its investors. The stock market viewed these declarations with mixed feelings. Some viewed that Microsoft was signaling an interest in broadening its investor focus and in sharing its wealth with shareholders. The clientele effect, discussed earlier, would suggest that Microsoft's dividend opened up a whole new group of potential shareholders, possibly increasing demand for the company's shares. On the other hand, others viewed the dividend declaration as an admission that it was becoming a mature company—that it could no longer reap the high returns from reinvesting. The future growth prospects for the stock, they would argue, had been diminished. In any event, few could argue that the 2003–2004 dividend declarations by Microsoft were not signals of some importance. It is interesting to speculate that taxes had some impact on Microsoft's dividend decision. Bill Gates and other Microsoft insiders were among those who had their tax rate on dividend income reduced from 39.6 percent in 2002 to 15 percent in 2003 and 2004.

4.5.1. Cross-Country Differences in Signaling Content
It should be noted that there is often a cultural or country-specific element to the signaling aspect of dividends. For example, whereas U.S. investors often infer significant signals in long-term expectations from even minute changes in a dividend, Japanese investors are much less likely to regard even large changes in dividend policy as a message from management about future prospects. U.S. companies are typically reluctant to reduce a regular dividend, because it almost always gives a signal that "all is not well." However, in some Asian markets, a dividend cut is not necessarily viewed as an unfavorable sign and therefore companies are freer to raise and lower their dividends depending on circumstances.

EXHIBIT 5-8   Gross Dividend Yield on Selected FTSE Index Funds (October 2004)

Regions	
FTSE Global Large-Cap	2.1%
FTSE North America Large-Cap	1.9%
FTSE Developed Europe Large-Cap	2.8%
FTSE Asia Pacific Large-Cap (ex-Japan)	2.9%
FTSE All Emerging Large-Cap	2.7%
Specific Countries	
FTSE U.K. All-Cap	3.1%
FTSE U.S.A. All-Cap	1.7%
FTSE Japan (Large-/Mid-Cap)	0.9%

Source: Financial Times, October 12, 2004, p. 30.

Furthermore, dividends are larger and considered more important in some markets than in others. When investing in the global marketplace, investors find that the contribution of dividends to total return varies considerably. As discussed earlier in this chapter, most of the world's largest companies trade on the New York Stock Exchange either as American depository shares (ADS) or as ordinary shares. For example, the five largest non-U.S. companies had the following dividend yields (in US$) in October 2004: BP (UK), 2.9 percent; DaimlerChrysler (Germany), 4.3 percent; Toyota (Japan), 1.5 percent; Royal Dutch (Holland/UK), 4.0 percent; and Total (France), 2.7 percent. Canadian companies trade as ordinary shares. Representative Canadian dividend yields (in U.S. dollars) were Bank of Nova Scotia, 3.7 percent; Thomson, 2.2 percent; and EnCana, 0.8 percent.

An investor who wanted to gain some insight into the relative importance of dividends around the world might look at the gross dividend yield on the FTSE Global Equity Indexes (see Exhibit 5-8).

4.6. Conclusion

Several factors affect a company's decision to pay dividends. We have examined some of them in this section, but it is not possible to argue that one is more dominant than another. Indeed, it is more likely that multiple factors affect dividend policy, with customs, laws, taxes, shareholder preferences, and management signaling interacting to affect a given company's actions.

5. DIVIDEND POLICIES

In the last section, we considered factors affecting a company's decision to pay dividends or not. In this section we look more closely at how the amount of the dividend is actually determined. **Dividend payout policy** is the strategy that companies follow in determining the amount and timing of dividend payments over time to shareholders. Our starting point is the residual dividend approach, one of the gold standards of corporate finance theory. Next we consider a dividend policy that results in a more stable dividend over time. The target payout ratio is next examined as an approach to dividend policy. We then discuss share repurchase as an alternative to the payment of dividends.

5.1. Residual Dividend Approach

The **residual dividend approach,** perhaps the most logical and intuitively appealing of all possible dividend policies, can be defined as the payment of dividends resulting from earnings less funds necessary to finance the equity portion company's capital budget.

Recall that the NPV for any potential investment project is the net present value of all cash inflows minus the net present value of all cash outflows. When the NPV is positive, the investment should be undertaken, and when the NPV is negative, the project should be rejected. The company uses its weighted average cost of capital (WACC) as its discount rate. The company's optimal capital budget includes all positive NPV projects. The company then finances the equity portion of these projects with retained earnings. What is left over—the residual—is distributed to shareholders as a dividend. In essence, a company should reinvest earnings only when it can earn a higher rate of return on shareholders' money than shareholders could earn on their own by investing in equivalent-risk assets. If the company cannot earn such a return, the company should pay the earnings out in the form of dividends.

Exhibit 5-9 depicts how the residual dividend approach might work. We look at the implied residual dividend given a company with earnings of $100 million, a target debt-to-equity (D/E) ratio of 30/70, and three prospective capital spending plans of $50 million, $100 million, and $150 million.

It should be pointed out that, under the residual dividend approach, the only retained earnings the company has available are from the current year's operations, because all previous years' earnings have been either spent on capital projects or paid out as dividends to shareholders. Also, it can be noted that, in the final column of Exhibit 5-9, the $150 million in capital spending requires $105 million in equity ($150 million × 0.70), which is greater

EXHIBIT 5-9   Residual Dividend Approach for a Target Debt-to-Equity Ratio of 30/70 ($ millions)

	$50 in Capital Spending	$100 in Capital Spending	$150 in Capital Spending
Earnings	$100	$100	$100
Target D/E	30/70	30/70	30/70
Capital spending	$50	$100	$150
Financed from new debt	0.3 × 50 = $15	0.3 × 100 = $30	0.3 × 150 = $45
Financed from retained earnings	0.7 × 50 = $35	0.7 × 100 = $70	(0.7 × 150 > 100) = $100
Financed from new equity	$0	$0	$5
Residual cash flow	$100–$35	$100–$70	$100–$100
Equals residual dividend	= $65	= $30	= $0
Implied payout ratio	65/100 = 65%	30/100 = 30%	0/100 = 0%

than the total earnings of \$100 million. Therefore, financing from new equity would be required. If the target debt-to-equity ratio were maintained, new equity issues would incur flotation costs. The cost of capital would be higher, and potentially fewer projects would have a positive NPV.

As can be seen from the exhibit, various capital spending plans result in dramatically different implied dividend payments. Payout ratios, too, range from a zero payment of dividends under the highest capital spending plan, to a 65 percent payout ratio under the lowest capital spending plan.

EXAMPLE 5-6   Determining Dividends Using the Residual Dividend Approach

Acree Products uses the residual dividend approach in determining its dividend policy. The following information is available:

- Earnings are \$1.6 million.
- Debt is \$20 million.
- The capital budget is \$1 million.
- The optimal capital structure is 25/75 debt/equity.

Calculate the expected dividend.

Solution

Expected dividend = Earnings − (Capital budget × Equity percentage)

                     = 1.6 million − (1.0 million × 0.75)

                     = \$850,000

The residual dividend approach definitely has advantages to the company. It is intuitively appealing to use funds generated to profitably maintain and grow the business and to return only what is left over—the residual—to the owners of the company. The residual dividend approach also allows the company to more freely determine attractive investments independent of dividend considerations.

A major disadvantage of the residual dividend approach is that it results in widely fluctuating dividends. Not only do earnings vary with the economic cycle and innumerable company-specific events, but also the optimal capital budget fluctuates with interest rates, investment opportunities, and a plethora of other investment inputs. This uncertainty about future dividend levels implies a higher level of perceived risk by the investor, thereby increasing the investor's required rate of return (k) and lowering the expected value of the stock, as can be seen in the following familiar constant growth dividend discount model equation:

$$V = \frac{D_1}{(k - g)}$$

where

> $V =$ the value of a share of common stock today
>
> $D_1 =$ the expected dividend per share for year 1, assumed to be paid at the end of the year
>
> $k =$ the required rate of return on the stock
>
> $g =$ the expected growth rate of dividends

The implication is that, if future annual dividends are uncertain, as they would be under the residual dividend approach, then the value of the share (V) might decline (all other things being equal) as k increases.

To take advantage of the benefits of the residual approach while reducing its negative implications, many companies forecast their optimal capital budget for the coming 5 or 10 years. The residual from that process is allocated to dividends and paid out on a steadier, more even basis over the same period. A relatively new approach over the last 20 years is for companies to use this **longer-term residual approach** to allocate all funds designated for shareholders—including both cash dividends and share repurchases—paying out a more stable cash dividend to shareholders and allocating a more flexible amount to share repurchases.

5.2. Stable Dividend Policy

In many instances, both management and shareholders prefer more stability in their stream of dividends than strict adherence to the residual dividend approach allows. Companies that employ a stable dividend approach are likely to look more toward a forecast of their long-run sustainable earnings in determining their dividend policy. In addition, over the last three decades when inflation has become a more important consideration, dividend stability has come to mean stability *in the rate of increase* in dividends.

Many companies pride themselves on a long record of gradually and consistently rising dividends. For example, Exhibit 5-10 on page 244 shows the earnings and dividend record of La-Z-Boy Inc. since 1993. As one can see from the exhibit, dividends over this period increased at a fairly consistent, real rate, even while earnings experienced considerable variability. Unless earnings improve, the company may be challenged to maintain its dividend payout.

5.3. Target Payout Ratio

Many companies have a target payout ratio as the basis for their dividend policy. A **payout ratio** is the percentage of total earnings paid out in dividends in any given year (dividends per share/earnings per share, or DPS/EPS). A **target payout ratio** is a strategic corporate goal representing the long-term proportion of earnings that the company intends to distribute to shareholders as dividends.

Companies may, on occasion, state publicly their target payout ratio. What is more likely is that the company will use its dividend policy to move toward a dividend payout target.

In a classic study on this subject in the mid-1950s, John Lintner[8] drew three basic conclusions: (1) Companies have a target payout ratio, based on long run, sustainable earnings; (2) they prefer to move toward this goal in small, incremental steps; and (3) cutting or eliminating a dividend should be done only in extreme circumstances or as a last resort.

---

[8]Lintner (1956).

EXHIBIT 5-10   Earnings and Dividends of La-Z-Boy Inc. (1993–2004)

	Earnings Per share	Change in Earnings	Dividends Per share	Change in Dividends
1993	$0.63	26%	$0.21	5%
1994	$0.67	6%	$0.23	10%
1995	$0.71	6%	$0.25	9%
1996	$0.83	17%	$0.26	4%
1997	$0.91	10%	$0.28	8%
1998	$1.24	36%	$0.30	7%
1999	$1.60	29%	$0.32	7%
2000	$1.19	(26%)	$0.35	9%
2001	$1.23	3%	$0.36	3%
2002	$1.67	36%	$0.39	8%
2003	$1.09	(35%)	$0.40	3%
2004	$0.88	(19%)	$0.43	7%
2005	$0.47	(47%)	$0.44	2%
2006	$0.31	(34%)	$0.48	9%
2007E	$0.51	65%	$0.48	0%

Source: Value Line.

Although the resulting Lintner regression model has many variables, a simplified version can be used to show how a company in certain circumstances could incrementally move toward its target payout ratio.[9] When the payout ratio is below the target payout ratio and earnings are expected to increase, the product of the increase in earnings, the target payout ratio, and the adjustment factor (1 divided by the number of years over which the adjustment in dividends should take place) results in an estimated increase in the dividend. For example, given a current dividend of $0.40, a target payout ratio of 50 percent, an adjustment factor of 0.2 (i.e., the adjustment is to occur over five years), and an earnings increase from $1.00 to $1.50, the expected increase in dividends would be

= Increase in earnings × Target payment ratio × Adjustment factor

= $0.50 × 0.5 × 0.2

= $0.05 increase in dividends

Therefore, even though earnings increased 50 percent from $1.00 to $1.50, the dividend would only incrementally increase by about 13 percent from $0.40 to $0.45.

Using this example, it can be noted that, if in the following year earnings fell from $1.50 to $1.00, the dividend might well be increased by up to $0.05 per share, as the implied new dividend of $0.50 would still be moving the company toward its target payout ratio of 50 percent. Even if earnings were to fall further or even experience a loss, the company would be reluctant to cut or eliminate the dividend (unless its estimate of sustainable earnings or

---

[9]Lease, et al. (2000).

EXAMPLE 5-7   Determining Dividend Using a Target Payout Adjustment Approach

Last year Luna Inc. had earnings of $2.00 per share and paid a regular dividend of $0.40. For the current year, the company anticipates earnings of $2.80. It has a 30 percent target payout ratio and uses a five-year period to adjust the dividend. Compute the expected dividend for the current year.

Solution

$$\text{Expected dividend} = \text{Last dividend} + (\text{Expected increase in earnings} \times \text{Target payout} \\ \text{ratio} \times \text{Adjustment factor})$$

$$= \$0.40 + [(\$2.80 - \$2.00) \times 0.3 \times (1/5)]$$

$$= \$0.40 + (\$0.80 \times 0.3 \times 0.2)$$

$$= \$0.45$$

Thus, while earnings are expected to increase by 40 percent, the increase in the dividend would be 12.5 percent.

target payout ratio were lowered), opting rather to maintain the current dividend until future earnings increases justified an increase in the dividend.

5.4. Share Repurchase

Earlier in this chapter we discussed the mechanics of share repurchase and showed that share repurchases were equivalent to cash dividends of an equal amount in their effect on shareholders' wealth, all other things being equal. For some companies, share repurchase is intended to prevent the earnings per share dilution that would result from the exercise of employee stock options. Whether stated or not, many companies endeavor to buy back at least as many shares as were issued in the exercise of stock options, even though the options are exercised at lower prices than the repurchase price. Otherwise, share repurchase can be considered part of a company's dividend policy. In this section we consider the advantages and disadvantages of substituting a share repurchase program for the payment of a regular or extra cash dividend.

The main advantage of share repurchase over cash dividend occurs in jurisdictions that tax shareholder dividends at higher rates than shareholder capital gains. This argument is now much less powerful in the United States because its tax code now taxes shareholder dividends and capital gains at the same rate. Furthermore, the U.S. tax code prohibits "routine" repurchase, because it could be tax avoidance. Other countries tax share repurchases at the same rate as dividends. Some jurisdictions have actually prohibited company share repurchase. An analyst should evaluate a company's share repurchase policy based on the tax circumstances of the company's home country as well as the investor's home country.

In principle, share repurchase sends the same signal to shareholders as does a cash dividend: Your company does not have sufficient reinvestment opportunities for the amount of cash flow generated. Shareholders have to consider why a company is shrinking its equity base. An alternative view is that management thinks its company's shares are undervalued.

5.4.1. Reasons for Share Repurchase   A company may decide to repurchase its shares for a variety of reasons. Perhaps the best reason is that the company views its own shares as an excellent investment. While the company's stock market judgment can be just as good or bad as any other market participant, there is no question that the company has more information about itself than does any other entity, and it is therefore the ultimate insider. For many years, the oil industry has been a large purchaser of its own shares, because investment returns in their current operations (through a share purchase) were an attractive alternative to drilling for new sources of oil. In one five-year period, ExxonMobil spent more than $30 billion in repurchasing its own shares while it has also paid out $30 billion in cash dividends.

Another closely related reason for announcing a share repurchase is to signal to the investment community that the outlook for the company is good, even if the share price is declining. Management has confidence in the company's future and believes that its stock is undervalued. An unexpected announcement of a meaningful buyback can often have the same positive impact on share price as would a better-than-expected earnings report or other similarly encouraging event. In the days following the global stock market crash of October 1987, a number of prominent companies announced huge buybacks in an effort to halt the slide in the price of their shares and show confidence in the future. It may have been an important aspect in the relatively quick stock market rebound. As indicated earlier, some investment analysts take issue with the notion that share repurchase sends positive signals.

EXAMPLE 5-8   Share Repurchase to Increase Financial Leverage

Canadian Holdings Inc. (CHI) is evaluating the impact of a buyback of $C7 million or 10 percent of the market value of its common stock. The estimated impact on CHI's capital structure depends on whether it has the cash on hand to make the buyback or if it has to borrow to finance the purchase (see Exhibit 5-11):

EXHIBIT 5-11   Estimated Impact on Capital Structure

| | Before Buyback | | After Buyback | | | |
| | | | All Cash | | All Debt | |
	$C millions	%	$C millions	%	$C millions	%
Debt	$30	30	$30	32	$37	37
Equity (at market)	$70	70	$63	68	$63	63
Total Capitalization	$100	100	$93	100	$100	100

Canadian Holdings' beginning debt-to-equity ratio was 30/70. If Canadian Holdings uses borrowed funds to repurchase equity, the debt-to-equity ratio at market will increase to 37/63, which is significantly more than if it used excess cash (32/68).

A third reason for buying back shares is to alter the company's capital structure by decreasing the equity component. Borrowing money to buy back shares intensifies this shift.

Finally, a company could use both a regular cash dividend and a periodic share repurchase policy as a supplement to cash dividends. This policy is particularly apt in years when there are large and extraordinary increases in cash flow that are not expected to continue in future years. In this way, share repurchase becomes a substitute for an extra cash dividend. Such a policy could smooth out dividends similar to the target payout policy. Grullon and Michaely found that U.S. companies used repurchases as a substitute for cash dividends and that companies often initiate payouts through repurchases rather than cash dividends.[10] Share buybacks are more flexible than cash dividends, because repurchases are not a long-term commitment.

While all of the preceding can be the stated or unstated reasons for share repurchases, in general, buybacks are larger when the economy is strong and companies have more cash. During recessions, when company coffers are not as full, buybacks typically fall. This is perhaps the biggest disadvantage of share repurchases: They occur in the greatest number when times are good and, concurrently, when share prices are relatively high. Were shareholders' interests best served in 2000–2001 when high-technology companies bought back their shares when the NASDAQ was at 5000? To carry this one step further, some companies may actually endanger their future viability by embarking on a highly leveraged repurchase endeavor. This is most likely for companies that have been threatened with large holdings by "aggressive" shareholders. More than one company has been eased into bankruptcy by increasing its debt burden to repurchase the shares of a potential hostile takeover suitor.

Example 5-9, in which a company initiates a cash dividend, integrates a number of themes related to cash dividends, stock dividends, and share repurchases.

EXAMPLE 5-9   Scottsville Instruments' Dividend Policy Decision

Scottsville Instruments, Inc., (SCII) is a U.S.-based emerging leader in providing medical testing equipment to the pharmaceutical and biotechnology industries. SCII's primary markets are growing, and the company is spending $100 million a year on research and development to enhance its competitive position. SCII is highly profitable and has substantial positive free cash flow after funding positive NPV projects. During the past three years, SCII has made significant share repurchases. Subsequent to the reduction in the tax rate on cash dividends to 15 percent in the United States, SCII management has begun to consider the initiation of an annual dividend of $0.40 per share. Based on estimated earnings per share of $3.20, this dividend would represent a payout ratio (DPS/EPS) of 0.125 or 12.5 percent. The proposal that will be brought before the board is the following:

Proposed: Scottsville Instruments, Inc. will institute a $0.40 per share annual dividend to be paid quarterly beginning in the next fiscal year.

---

[10]Grullon and Michaely (2002).

The company's board of directors will formally consider the dividend proposal at its next meeting in one month's time. Although some directors favor the dividend initiation proposal, other directors, led by William Marshall, are skeptical of it. Marshall has stated:

> The initiation of a cash dividend will suggest to investors that SCII is no longer a growth company.

As a counterproposal, Marshall has offered his support for the initiation of an annual 2 percent stock dividend. Elise Tashman, a director who is neutral to both the cash and stock dividend ideas, has told Marshall the following:

> The initiation of a cash dividend will have no effect on the value of the firm to shareholders. Likewise, a 2 percent stock dividend should also be value neutral to our shareholders.

Exhibit 5-12 presents selected pro forma financials of SCII, if the directors approve the initiation of a cash dividend.

EXHIBIT 5-12   Scottsville Instruments, Inc. Pro Forma Financial Data Assuming Cash Dividend (in millions, except for ratios and percentages)

Income Statement		Statement of Cash Flows	
Sales	$1,200	Cash flow from operations	$135
Earnings before taxes	140	Cash flow from investing activities	(84)
Taxes	35	Cash flow from financing activities:	
Net income	105	Debt repayment	(4)
		Share repurchase	(32)
		Proposed dividend	(15)
		Estimated change in cash	0
Ratios		Five Year Forecasts	
Current ratio	2.1	Sales growth	8% annually
Debt-to-equity (at market)	0.27	Earnings growth	11% annually
Interest coverage	10.8x	Projected cost of capital	10%
ROA	10.0%		
ROE	19.3%		
P/E	20x		
E/P	5.0%		

Using the preceding information, address the following.

1. Critique Marshall's statement.
2. Justify Tashman's statement concerning stock dividends.

3. Identify and explain the dividend policy approach that the proposed $0.40/share cash dividend reflects.

Solution to 1

The following points argue against the thesis of Marshall's statement:

- As discussed in the text, dividend initiations and increases are on average associated with higher future earnings growth.
- Forecasted sales and earnings growth are relatively high.
- SCII still has considerable positive NPV projects available to it, as shown by the cash flow from investing activities of negative $84 million. This fact is consistent with a company with substantial current growth opportunities.
- For several years SCII has been making share repurchases; so investors are already cognizant that management is distributing cash to shareholders. The initiation of a dividend as a continuation of that policy is less likely to be interpreted as an information signaling event.

Solution to 2

A stock dividend has no effect on shareholder wealth. A shareholder owns the same percentage of the company and its earnings as before the stock dividend. All other things being equal, the price of a stock will decline to reflect the stock dividend, but the decline will be exactly offset by the greater number of shares owned.

Solution to 3

As shown in the statement of cash flows, the $0.40 annual dividend reflects a total amount of $15 million, fully using SCII's free cash flow after acceptance of positive NPV projects. This reflects a residual dividend policy approach.

5.5.   Are Dividend Policies Changing?

In the late 1990s, some financial analysts claimed that the historical role of dividends was "disappearing." This was in a period characterized by its enthusiasts as the New Era Economy and by its critics as Irrational Exuberance. It was highlighted in most of the developed world by several years of rising share prices, particularly in the more speculative industries. Companies that were barely profitable (and sometimes unprofitable) obtained larger market capitalizations than very profitable companies in unglamorous industries. At its peak, almost 40 percent of the S&P Index's market value was composed of companies in the technology and telecommunications sectors. This phenomenon was not limited to the United States, as Nortel Networks had the highest market capitalization in Canada in 2000 and companies such as Nokia in Finland and SAP in Germany were market leaders.

Proponents of New Era investing argued that dividends were a trivial, if not an unwelcome, component of total return for investors more interested in capital gains. Investor preference for or aversion to dividends is a mercurial argument. The more interesting issue is

EXHIBIT 5-13   Net Dividends as Percentages of Corporate Profits After Tax
for U.S. Corporations (1979–2003)

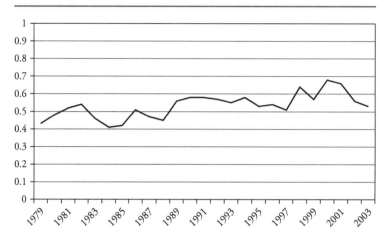

whether corporations were changing their dividend policies. Fama and French[11] investigated the case for disappearing dividends. They found a large decline in the number of U.S.-based industrial companies that paid dividends from 1978 to 1998. But the aggregate payout ratio in the 1990s was about 40 percent—within the 40–60 percent range typical of the 1960–1998 period. Fama and French argued that the decline in dividends was related to the large number of relatively unprofitable companies that were assuming prominence in the stock market. Exhibit 5-13 shows the relatively stable dividend payout range for all U.S. corporations from 1979 to 2003. In fact, the graph would seem to argue that companies follow the target payout approach.

DeAngelo, DeAngelo, and Skinner[12] enhanced Fama and French's argument by showing that, even though fewer corporations were paying dividends, the largest 100 companies in the United States increased their inflation-adjusted dividends by 23 percent from1978 to 2000. What appears to be happening is that there are two tiers of companies. The first tier is composed of approximately 100 large, extremely profitable companies that have a fairly stable payout ratio of around 42 percent. The second tier is composed of two types of nondividend payers: financially troubled marginally profitable or money-losing companies and/or companies related to technology, where companies typically use share repurchase as a substitute for dividends.

In the period following the severe developed-country stock market decline in the early 2000s, investors began to question reported earnings, balance sheets, and cash flows as corporate scandals revealed management shenanigans to overinflate revenues, use accruals to understate expenses, and hide liabilities off-balance sheet. An argument can be made that dividends are more important than ever because it is the one number that a shareholder can trust. Earnings per share and even cash flow per share can be manipulated by management, but dividend checks can be cashed.

---

[11]Fama and French (2001).
[12]DeAngelo, DeAngelo, and Skinner (2004).

6. THE DIVIDEND CONTROVERSY: DO DIVIDENDS MATTER?

For the last forty years, leading financial theorists have argued over whether dividends and dividend policy matter to a company's shareholders. The first school of thought is that dividends are irrelevant. The second school says that dividends do matter because investors prefer them and higher dividend payouts are likely to increase the value of a company's shares. The third school says that dividends do matter, but a company's high dividend payout ratio will lead to a lower share price because dividend income is often taxed at a higher rate than capital gains.

6.1. Dividends Are Irrelevant

In a 1961 paper, Miller and Modigliani (MM) argued that, in a world without taxes and transaction costs, a company's dividend policy would have no impact on its cost of capital or shareholder wealth.[13] Their argument begins by assuming a company has a given capital budget (e.g., it accepts all projects with a positive NPV) and that its current capital structure and debt ratio are optimal. Hence, if the company decided to pay out all its earnings in dividends, it would have to issue new shares of common stock to finance its capital budget. The value of the newly issued shares would exactly offset the value of the dividend. So, if the company paid out a dividend that represented a 5 percent dividend yield (dividend per share/price per share), its share price would drop 5 percent to represent the dilution resulting from the new shares. If a common stock in Australia were priced at A\$20 before an A\$1 dividend, the implied new price would be A\$19. Shareholders have assets worth A\$20 if the dividend is not paid, and assets worth A\$20 if the stock drops to A\$19 and a A\$1 dividend is paid.

Further embellishing MM's theory is the concept of a "homemade" dividend. If a shareholder really wanted or needed income, he or she could construct their own dividend policy by selling sufficient shares to create their own dividend. Using the Australian example above, assume the company did not pay the A\$1 dividend and the stock remained at A\$20. A holder of 1000 shares who desired A\$1000 in income could sell 50 shares at A\$20 reducing his/her holdings to 950 shares.

In the real world, there are market imperfections that create some problems for MM's dividend irrelevance propositions. First, there are transaction costs because a company issuing new shares would incur flotation costs (typically 4 percent to 10 percent of the capital raised, depending on the size of the company and the size of the issue). Second, a shareholder selling shares to create a homemade dividend would incur transaction costs and, in some countries, capital gains taxes (of course, the shareholder would also incur taxes on cash dividends in most countries). Furthermore, selling shares on a periodic basis to create a stream of dividends over time can be problematic when equities are volatile. Some shareholders are reluctant to create a dividend when share price is low because they would have to sell off more shares.

6.2. Dividends Matter: Investors Prefer Dividends

Traditionalists such as Myron Gordon,[14] John Lintner,[15] and Benjamin Graham argued that investors prefer a dollar of dividends to a dollar of reinvested earnings. Graham's viewpoint was

---

[13]Miller and Modigliani (1961).
[14]Gordon (1963).
[15]Lintner (1962).

that ". . . the typical dollar of reinvestment has less economic value to the shareholder than a dollar paid in dividends."[16] Gordon, Lintner, and Graham's argument is similar to the "bird in the hand" analogy. Because a dollar of dividends is more certain than a dollar of capital gains, a company that pays dividends has a lower cost of equity capital. As indicated in the section on the residual dividend approach, in the constant growth dividend discount model, investors often use a lower discount rate for a company that pays dividends than for a company that does not pay dividends.

EXAMPLE 5-10   Dividends and P/Es

Splashco Inc. is an international oil service company headquartered in Calgary, Alberta, Canada. It has a good record of earnings growth over the last 20 years, albeit subject to the ups and downs of oil and gas production. It has never paid dividends but has used its considerable cash flow to repurchase shares. Institutional investors in both Canada and the United States have indicated that they think Splashco would sell at a price/earnings multiple more similar to its competitors if it instituted regular dividend payments. John Petrowitz, CFA, of Splashco's treasurer's office, has been asked to present the case for a dividend to the company's board of directors. He starts his analysis with the fact that Splashco typically sells at a P/E of 12–15x current earnings per share as compared to 17–20x for its competitors. He decides to use the constant growth dividend discount model to make his case.[17]

$$P = \frac{D_1}{(k - g)}$$

where

P = share price (at fair value)

D_1 = expected dividend for year 1

k = required rate of return on the stock

g = expected growth rate of dividends

Dividing both sides of the equation by E_1, where E_1 = next year's estimated earnings per share, the result is

$$\frac{P}{E_1} = \frac{(D_1/E_1)}{(k - g)}$$

Constant growth is estimated at 8 percent. The implied required rate of return for Splashco has been 12 percent, but Petrowitz thinks the initiation of a dividend would lower the required rate of return to 11 percent, close to the average of its competitors. If Splashco had a target payout ratio of 50 percent and next year's earnings were C\$2.00, the P/E_1 would be

---

[16]Graham, Dodd, et al. (1962).
[17]Reilly and Brown (2003).

$$\frac{P}{E_1} = \frac{(1.00/2.00)}{(0.11 - 0.08)}$$

$$= \frac{0.50}{0.03}$$

$$= 16.7\text{x}$$

Petrowitz concludes that, if Splashco initiated a C$1.00 dividend, it might alleviate some investor concern about what the company would do with its earnings and its P/E might increase from 12–15x to 16–17x.

Real-world market imperfections also bolster the "higher payouts lead to higher share prices" argument. There appear to be specific clienteles who desire to live off their wealth, but selling off shares periodically to produce homemade dividends is cumbersome and a taxable event. In some jurisdictions, trusts and institutions are precluded from spending principal. Miller and Modigliani rebut this argument by saying that different dividend policies attract different clienteles and that, assuming both types of clients are active in the marketplace, the value of the company is unaffected by dividend policy.

6.3. Dividends Matter: Investors Are Tax Averse to Dividends

In the United States and several other countries, dividend income has traditionally been taxed at higher rates than capital gains. In the 1970s, tax rates on dividend income in the United States were as high as 70 percent while the long-term capital gains rate was 35 percent. Even as recently as 2002, U.S. tax rates were as high as 39.1 percent on dividends and 20 percent on long-term capital gains. A good argument could be that in a high-dividend-tax country, investors prefer companies that pay low dividends and reinvest earnings in growth opportunities. Presumably, any growth in earnings would translate into a higher P/E. If a company lacked growth opportunities sufficient to consume its annual retained earnings, it should repurchase shares. Taken to its extreme, this school of thought would advocate a *zero* payout ratio. Here again some real-world market imperfections muddy the waters, because tax law often precludes companies from the accumulation of excess earnings and restricts share repurchase if it appears to be an ongoing event such as in lieu of payment of dividends.

As already discussed, effective in 2003 the playing field between dividends and long-term capital gains in the United States was leveled, with both dividends and long-term capital gains being taxed at 15 percent. This neutralized tax environment should provide financial researchers with a fertile laboratory to clarify some of the dividend controversy.

7. VALUATION IMPLICATIONS OF DIVIDENDS

In a world without market imperfections, Miller and Modigliani describe a market where both corporations and shareholders would be unconcerned with dividend policies. In an MM world, there are no valuation implications of dividends. Shareholder value is created by investing in profitable projects, not by manipulating the debt-to-equity ratio on the balance sheet or by financing dividend payments with new equity issues. But looking at the real world, this chapter has established the existence of market imperfections. In addition, some investors are led, by logic or custom, to prefer dividends. When valuing equities in various countries, investors should factor both market imperfections and market preferences into the valuation process.[18]

First and foremost on the list of market imperfections is taxation and in particular any differential in the way dividends are taxed as compared to capital gains. Almost all countries tax corporate profits, and some tax them twice when profits are paid out in dividends. If a government taxes dividends at high rates, it encourages low payouts. At the limit, a 100 percent tax on dividends would lead to a zero payout ratio. The United States reduced the highest tax rate on dividends from 39.1 percent to 15 percent and equalized the tax rate on dividends and long-term capital gains. Researchers are already finding evidence that more companies have initiated dividend payments, and existing dividend payers have increased dividends more than would be associated with a typical period of profit recovery.[19]

In some countries, there are restrictions on the payment of dividends and de facto requirements to pay dividends in order to obtain admission to institutional legal lists or screens. Some investors become part of a clientele for dividend-paying shares, while others have no preference for dividends.

We discussed the information content of dividends (signaling effect). Boards of directors and management send important information about the future prospects of their company by increasing and decreasing the dividend. In a world where the quality of accounting information is suspect, investors would do well to heed management's signals.

Finally, ownership structure and ensuing agency problems provide a possible explanation of country differences in dividend policy.[20] Dividends assume a larger role in the valuation process in certain jurisdictions. Dividend payments are higher in Canada, Great Britain, the United States, and some parts of Europe. They are lower in Japan and in developing countries. There may be more than tradition to explain these differences. For example, ownership of public corporations in the United States, Canada, and Great Britain tends to be diffuse rather than concentrated; corporations finance operations through capital markets. Companies in Asia and developing markets often have large family shareholder control and finance operations using banks and insurance companies rather than through capital markets. There is a natural conflict of interest between owners and management in countries that have dispersed ownership. This agency cost can be alleviated by the payment of dividends. Payment of dividends restricts management's ability to reinvest earnings in negative NPV projects just to build empires. Dividends thus discipline management to be more careful with shareholders' money. In countries where founding families still control large blocks of shares and there are close links between financial institutions and industrial corporations, there is less need of discipline because the "insiders" are less likely to act imprudently with their own money.

So what can we conclude about the link between dividends and valuation? Unfortunately, the evidence is contradictory as shown by a myriad of studies over the years. It is difficult to show an exact relationship between dividends and value because there are so many variables affecting value. In this section we have presented factors that would seem to explain why some companies put emphasis on dividends and others do not. Financial theory proclaims that reinvestment opportunities should be the dominant factor. Indeed, no matter where

---

[18]For practical application of how analysts use dividends and dividend policy in equity valuation, see Stowe, Robinson, Pinto, and McLeavey (2002).
[19]Chetty and Saez (2004).
[20]Megginson (1997).

they are located in the world, smaller, fast-growing companies pay out little or none of their earnings. Regardless of jurisdiction, more mature companies with fewer reinvestment opportunities tend to pay dividends. For these mature companies, taxes, laws, tradition, signaling, ownership structure, and attempts to reconcile agency conflicts all seem to play a role in determining the dividend payout ratio. At a minimum, in looking at a company, an analyst should evaluate whether a given company's dividend policy matches its reinvestment opportunities, clientele preferences, and legal/financial environment.

8. SUMMARY

The dividend policy of a company affects the form in which shareholders receive the return on their investment and is a prominent decision of a company's board of directors. This chapter has made the following points:

- Dividends can take the form of regular or special cash payments, stock dividends, or stock splits. Only cash dividends are payments to shareholders. Stock dividends and splits merely carve equity into smaller pieces.
- A share repurchase is equivalent to the payment of a cash dividend of equal amount in its effect on shareholders' wealth, all other things being equal.
- If a company has to fund a share repurchase with debt and its after-tax cost of debt is greater than the earning yield, earnings per share decline. If the buyback market price is greater than the book value, the book value will decline.
- Share repurchases can be accomplished in the open market, through a tender offer to all shareholders, or by a direct negotiation with a major shareholder. The latter is not likely to affect share price positively.
- The key dates for a cash dividend are the declaration date, the ex-date, the holder-of-record date, and the payment date. All else being equal, the share price is reduced by the amount of the dividend on the ex-date.
- Under double taxation systems, dividends are taxed at both the corporate and shareholder level. Under split rate taxation systems, corporate profits are taxed at different rates depending on whether the profits are retained or paid out in dividends. Under tax imputation systems, a shareholder receives a credit on dividends for the tax paid on corporate profits.
- Companies with debt outstanding often are restricted in the amount of dividends they can pay because of debt covenants, and because of formal and informal traditions in industries and countries. Some institutions require that a company pay a dividend to be on their "approved" list. If a company funds capital expenditures by borrowing while paying earnings out in dividends, it incurs flotation costs on new issues.
- The clientele effect assumes that different classes of investors have differing preferences for dividend income. Those who prefer dividends tend to invest in higher-yielding shares.
- The signaling effect assumes that the declaration of dividends provides information to current and prospective shareholders as to the prospects of the company. Initiating a dividend or increasing a dividend sends a positive signal, while cutting a dividend or omitting a dividend sends a negative signal.
- Using a residual dividend approach, a company first compares its capital expenditure requirements to its net income, and whatever is left is paid out to shareholders in the form of cash dividends. An advantage of the residual approach is that all positive NPV opportunities have the first priority.

- In a strict residual approach, the amount of the annual dividend is equal to annual earnings minus the capital budget times the percentage of the capital budget to be financed through retained earnings.
- Using a stable dividend approach, a company tries to align its dividend growth rate to the company's long-term earnings growth rate. Dividends may increase even in years when earnings decline, and dividends increase at a lower rate than earnings in boom years. A longer-term residual approach is a combination of residual and stable policies, where the company maintains the dividend at some level and increases the dividend periodically. With a target approach, the company has a goal of maintaining the dividend payout within a range; the dividend increases with the company's long-term sustainable growth rate, but the increase is in incremental steps.
- In the target payout adjustment approach, the expected dividend is equal to last year's dividend per share, plus (This year's expected increase in earnings per share) × (The target payout ratio) × (An annual adjustment factor).
- Companies can repurchase shares in lieu of increasing cash dividends. This policy is often justified in jurisdictions where dividends are taxed at higher rates than capital gains. Companies can also pay regular cash dividends supplemented by share repurchases. In years of extraordinary increases in earnings, share repurchase becomes a substitute for increasing dividends, smoothing out potentially volatile payout ratios.
- Share repurchases can signal that company officials think their shares are undervalued. On the other hand, share repurchases could send a negative signal that the company has few positive NPV opportunities. Share repurchases can also lower debt ratings.
- Considering aggregate corporate dividend payout ratios, dividend policy has remained within historical levels in recent years. A large number of companies with little or no earnings and/or questionable financials make it appear that dividends are "disappearing."
- There are three general theories on investor preference for dividends. The first, MM, argues that, in a no-tax, no-market world, dividends are irrelevant. The "bird in the hand" theory contends that investors value a dollar of dividends today more than uncertain capital gains in the future. The third theory argues that investors are tax averse to cash dividends and would prefer companies buy back shares, especially when the tax rate on dividends is greater than the tax rate on capital gains.
- Miller and Modigliani demonstrate that shareholders who want dividends could create their own homemade dividends by periodically selling off part of their holdings.
- According to those who argue that dividends do matter, a company could increase its price/earnings ratio by initiating a cash dividend. The initiation of a dividend results in a higher P/E by reducing the spread between the company's required rate of return and its expected growth rate using a constant growth dividend discount model.

PRACTICE PROBLEMS

1. Would a cash dividend, compared to a stock dividend, *most likely* result in a higher

	Debt-to-equity Ratio?	Current Ratio?
A.	No	No
B.	No	Yes
C.	Yes	No
D.	Yes	Yes

2. In a recent presentation, Doug Pearce made two statements about dividends:

   (1) "A stock dividend should increase share price, all other things being equal."
   (2) "One practical concern with a stock split is that it will reduce the firm's price/earnings ratio."

   Are Pearce's comments about the effects of the stock dividend and stock split correct or incorrect?

	Stock Dividend	*Stock Split*
A.	Correct	Correct
B.	Correct	Incorrect
C.	Incorrect	Correct
D.	Incorrect	Incorrect

3. Devon Ltd. common shares sell at $40 a share and its estimated price/earnings ratio (P/E) is 32 x. If Devon borrows funds to repurchase shares at its cost of capital of 5 percent, its EPS will

   A. Increase.
   B. Decrease.
   C. Remain the same.
   D. Increase initially, but decline in future years.

4. Following are descriptions of potentially significant dates (in random order) in a typical dividend chronology:

   A. Holder-of-record date.
   B. Declaration date.
   C. Payment date.
   D. Not a significant date.
   E. Ex-date.
   F. Last day shares trade cum dividend.

   Match these descriptions with the corresponding calendar dates by placing the letter of the description in the appropriate space in the template.

Calendar Date	Dividend Chronology Description
Friday, June 10	
Thursday, June 23	
Friday, June 24	
Sunday, June 26	
Tuesday, June 28	
Sunday, July 10	

5. Assume that a company is based in a country that has no taxes on dividends and capital gains. The company is considering either paying a special dividend or repurchasing its own shares. Shareholders of the company would have

   A. Greater wealth if the company paid a special cash dividend.
   B. Greater wealth if the company repurchased its shares.
   C. The same wealth under either a cash dividend or share repurchase program.
   D. Less wealth under either a cash dividend or a share repurchase program.

6. Aiken Instruments (AIK) has recently declared a regular quarterly dividend of $0.50, payable on November 12, to holders of record on November 1. October 28 is the ex-date. Which of the following dates is the last day an investor purchasing AIK shares would receive the quarterly dividend?
   A. October 27.
   B. October 28.
   C. November 1.
   D. November 12.

7. WL Corporation is located in a jurisdiction that has a 40 percent corporate tax rate on pretax income and a 30 percent personal tax rate on dividends. WL distributes all its after-tax income to shareholders. What is the effective tax rate on WL pretax income distributed in dividends?
   A. 42 percent.
   B. 52 percent.
   C. 58 percent.
   D. 70 percent.

8. What does the clientele effect imply?
   A. High-tax-bracket investors are indifferent to dividends.
   B. Investors prefer high-dividend-paying shares.
   C. Investors have varying preferences regarding dividends.
   D. Low-tax-bracket investors are indifferent to dividends.

9. Which of the following factors would *not* tend to be associated with a company having a low dividend payout ratio?
   A. Restrictive debt covenants.
   B. High flotation costs on new equity issues
   C. High tax rates on dividends.
   D. Low growth prospects.

10. Which of the following is *most likely* to signal negative information concerning a firm?
    A. Share repurchase.
    B. Increase in the payout ratio
    C. Decrease in the quarterly dividend rate.
    D. A two-for-one stock split.

11. Berkshire Gardens Inc. uses a target payout adjustment approach in paying its annual dividend. Last year Berkshire had earnings per share of $3.00 and paid a dividend of $0.60 a share. This year it estimates earnings at $4.00 a share. Find its dividend per share for this year if it has a 25 percent target payout ratio and uses a five-year period to adjust its dividend.
    A. $0.65.
    B. $0.72.
    C. $0.80.
    D. $0.85.

12. When may investors prefer companies that repurchase their shares instead of paying a cash dividend?
    A. When capital gains are taxed at higher rates than dividends.
    B. When capital gains are taxed at lower rates than dividends.
    C. When capital gains are taxed at the same rate as dividends.
    D. When the company needs more equity to finance capital expenditures.

13. Sophie Chan owns 100,000 shares of PAT Company. PAT is selling for €40 per share, so her investment is worth €4,000,000. Chan reinvests the gross amount of all dividends received to purchase additional shares. If PAT pays a €1.50 dividend, Chan's new share ownership after reinvesting dividends at the ex-dividend price is closest to
    A. 103,450.
    B. 103,600.
    C. 103,750.
    D. 103,900.

14. Mary Young intends to take a position in Megasoft Industries once Megasoft begins paying regular dividends with a special dividend of C$4 on December 2. The ex-date for the dividend is November 10, and the holder-of-record date is November 12. What is the last possible date for Young to purchase her shares if she wants to receive the dividend?
    A. November 9.
    B. November 10.
    C. November 11.
    D. November 12.

15. The Apex Corp. has a target debt-to-equity ratio of 40/60. Its capital budget for next year is estimated at $40 million. Estimated net income is $30 million. Find its dividend using the residual dividend approach.
    A. $6 million.
    B. $12 million.
    C. $14 million.
    D. $18 million.

16. Which of the following scenarios best reflects a stable dividend policy?
    A. Maintaining a constant dividend payout ratio of 40 percent to 50 percent.
    B. Maintaining the dividend at $1.00 a share for several years.
    C. Increasing the dividend at the company's long-term earnings growth rate of 5 percent.
    D. Paying special dividends when earnings are abnormally high.

17. Match the phrases in Column A with the corresponding dividend theory in Column B. Note that you may use the answers in Column B more than once.

Column A	*Column B*
A. Bird in the hand	(1) Dividends matter.
B. Homemade dividends	(2) Dividends are irrelevant.
C. High tax rates on dividends	
D. No transaction costs	

18. Which of the following assumptions is *not* required for Miller and Modigliani's (MM) dividend theory?
   A. Shareholders have no transaction costs when buying and selling shares.
   B. There are no taxes.
   C. There are no flotation costs on new issues.
   D. Markets are inefficient.

The following information relates to Questions 19 through 25.

Janet Wu is treasurer of Wilson Paper Company, a manufacturer of paper products for the office and school markets. Wilson Paper is selling one of its divisions for $70 million cash. Wu is considering whether to recommend a special dividend of $70 million or a repurchase of 2 million shares of Wilson common stock in the open market. She is reviewing some possible effects of the buyback with the company's financial analyst. Wilson has a long-term record of gradually increasing earnings and dividends. Wilson's board has also approved capital spending of $15 million to be entirely funded out of this year's earnings.

Book value of equity	$750 million ($30 a share)
Shares outstanding	25 million
Twelve-month trading range	$25–$35
Current share price	$35
After-tax cost of borrowing	7 percent
Estimated full-year earnings	$25 million
Last year's dividends	$9 million
Target debt-to-equity (market value)	35/65

19. Assume that Wilson Paper could buy back its shares at the current market price. A $70 million buyback would result in a book value per share that
   A. Increases.
   B. Decreases.
   C. Remains unchanged.
   D. May remain unchanged or increase.

20. In investor's minds, Wilson's share buyback could be a signal that
   A. The company is decreasing its financial leverage.
   B. The company has more investment opportunities than it could fund internally.
   C. The company lacks good investment opportunities.
   D. The company's share price is too high.

21. Assume that Wilson Paper funds its capital spending out of its estimated full-year earnings. Using the residual dividend approach, determine Wilson's implied dividend payout ratio.
   A. 36 percent.
   B. 40 percent.
   C. 60 percent.
   D. 72 percent.

22. Suppose the sale of the division did not occur and Wilson Paper had to raise $70 million in new funds at the company's after-tax cost of borrowing in order to fund the buyback. The expected earnings per share following the share repurchase is *closest* to
    A. $0.80.
    B. $0.87.
    C. $1.09.
    D. $1.15.

23. Wilson's buyback is *most likely* to be dilutive to earnings per share if
    A. The after-tax cost of borrowing is lower than the earnings yield.
    B. The after-tax cost of borrowing is higher than the earnings yield.
    C. Book value is less than market value.
    D. Book value is higher than the buyback price.

24. If a company borrows to finance a share repurchase, what is the *likely* result?
    A. An increase in the market value of the company.
    B. An increase in the market value of debt offset by a decrease in the market value of equity.
    C. An increase in the market value of equity offset by a decrease in the market value of debt.
    D. No change in the market value or debt-to-equity ratio

25. The *most likely* tax environment in which Wilson Paper's shareholders would prefer that Wilson repurchase its shares (share buybacks) instead of paying dividends is when
    A. There is no tax on shareholder dividends or capital gains.
    B. The tax rate on capital gains and dividends is the same.
    C. Capital gains tax rates are higher than dividend income tax rates.
    D. Capital gains tax rates are lower than dividend income tax rates.

CHAPTER 6

WORKING CAPITAL MANAGEMENT

Edgar A. Norton, Jr., CFA
Illinois State University
Normal, Illinois

Kenneth L. Parkinson
Treasury Information Services
New York

Pamela Peterson Drake, CFA
James Madison University
Harrisonburg, Virginia

LEARNING OUTCOMES

After completing this chapter, you will be able to do the following:

- Calculate and interpret liquidity measures using selected financial ratios for a company and compare them with ratios for peer companies.
- Evaluate the overall working capital effectiveness of a company, using the operating and cash conversion cycles, and compare its effectiveness with other peer companies.
- Classify the components of a cash forecast and prepare a cash forecast, given estimates of revenues, expenses, and other items.
- Identify and evaluate the necessary tools to use in managing a company's net daily cash position.
- Compute comparable yields on various securities and compare portfolio returns against a standard benchmark and evaluate a company's short-term investment policy guidelines.

- Assess the performance of a company's accounts receivable, inventory management, and accounts payable functions against historical figures and comparable peer company values.
- Evaluate the choices of short-term funding available to a company and recommend a financing method.

1. INTRODUCTION

The focus of this chapter is on the short-term aspects of corporate finance activities, collectively referred to as **working capital management**. The goal of effective working capital management is to ensure that a company has adequate ready access to the funds necessary for day-to-day operating expenses, at the same time making sure that the company's assets are invested in the most productive way. Achieving this goal requires a balancing of concerns. Insufficient access to cash could ultimately lead to severe restructuring of a company by selling off assets, reorganization via bankruptcy proceedings, or final liquidation of the company. On the other hand, excessive investment in cash and liquid assets may not be the best use of company resources.

Effective working capital management encompasses several aspects of short-term finance: maintaining adequate levels of cash, converting short-term assets (i.e., accounts receivable and inventory) into cash, and controlling outgoing payments to vendors, employees, and others. To do this successfully, companies invest short-term funds in working capital portfolios of short-dated, highly liquid securities, or they maintain credit reserves in the form of bank lines of credit or access to financing by issuing commercial paper or other money market instruments.

Working capital management is a broad-based function. Effective execution requires managing and coordinating several tasks within the company, including managing short-term investments, granting credit to customers and collecting on this credit, managing inventory, and managing payables. Effective working capital management also requires reliable cash forecasts, as well as current and accurate information on transactions and bank balances.

Both internal and external factors influence working capital needs; we summarize them in Exhibit 6-1.

The scope of working capital management includes transactions, relations, analyses, and focus:

- *Transactions* include payments for trade, financing, and investment.
- *Relations* with financial institutions and trading partners must be maintained to ensure that the transactions work effectively.

EXHIBIT 6-1   Internal and External Factors That Affect Working Capital Needs

Internal Factors	External Factors
Company size and growth rates	Banking services
Organizational structure	Interest rates
Sophistication of working capital management	New technologies and new products
Borrowing and investing positions, activities, and capacities	The economy
	Competitors

- *Analyses* of working capital management activities are required so that appropriate strategies can be formulated and implemented.
- *Focus* requires that organizations of all sizes today must have a global viewpoint with strong emphasis on liquidity.

In this chapter, we examine the different types of working capital and the management issues associated with each. We also look at methods of evaluating the effectiveness of working capital management.

2. MANAGING AND MEASURING LIQUIDITY

Liquidity is the extent to which a company is able to meet its short-term obligations using assets that can be readily transformed into cash. When we evaluate the liquidity of an asset, we focus on two dimensions: the type of asset and the speed at which the asset can be converted to cash, by either sale or financing. Unlike many aspects of corporate finance, corporate liquidity management does not involve a great deal of theory or generally accepted principles. For companies that have the luxury of large excesses of cash, liquidity is typically taken for granted, and the focus is on putting the excess liquidity to its most productive use. On the other hand, when a company faces tight financial situations, it is important to have effective liquidity management to ensure solvency. Unfortunately, this recognition comes too late for some companies, with bankruptcy and possible liquidation representing the company's final choice.

2.1. Defining Liquidity Management

Liquidity management refers to the ability of an organization to generate cash when and where it is needed. Liquidity refers to the resources available for an entity to tap into cash balances and to convert other assets or extend other liabilities into cash for use in keeping the entity solvent (i.e., being able to pay bills and stay in operation). For the most part, we associate liquidity with short-term assets and liabilities, yet longer-term assets can be converted into cash to provide liquidity. In addition, longer-term liabilities can also be renegotiated to reduce the drain on cash, thereby providing liquidity by preserving the limited supply of cash. Of course, the last two methods may come at a price because they tend to reduce the company's overall financial strength.

The challenges of managing liquidity include developing, implementing, and maintaining a liquidity policy. To do this effectively, a company must manage all of its key sources of liquidity efficiently. These key sources may vary from company to company, but they generally include the primary sources of liquidity, such as cash balances, and secondary sources of liquidity, such as selling assets.

2.1.1. **Primary Sources of Liquidity**   Primary sources of liquidity represent the most readily accessible resources available. They may be held as cash or as near-cash securities. Primary sources include

- *Ready cash balances,* which are cash balances available in bank accounts resulting from payment collections, investment income, liquidation of near-cash securities (i.e., those with maturities of fewer than 90 days), and other cash flows;

- *Short-term funds,* which may include items such as trade credit, bank lines of credit, and short-term investment portfolios; and
- *Cash flow management,* which is the company's effectiveness in its cash management system and practices, and the degree of decentralization of the collections or payments processes. The more decentralized the system of collections is, for example, the more likely the company will be to have cash tied up in the system and not available for use.

These sources represent liquidity that is typical for most companies. They represent funds that are readily accessible at relatively low cost.

2.1.2. Secondary Sources of Liquidity

The main difference between the primary and secondary sources of liquidity is that using a primary source is not likely to affect the normal operations of the company, whereas using a secondary source may result in a change in the company's financial and operating positions. Secondary sources include

- *Negotiating debt contracts,* relieving pressures from high interest payments or principal repayments;
- *Liquidating assets,* which depends on the degree to which short-term and/or long-term assets can be liquidated and converted into cash without substantial loss in value; and
- *Filing for bankruptcy protection and reorganization.*

Use of secondary sources may signal a company's deteriorating financial health and provide liquidity at a high price—the cost of giving up a company asset to produce emergency cash. The last source, reorganization through bankruptcy, may also be considered a liquidity tool because a company under bankruptcy protection that generates operating cash will be liquid and generally able to continue business operations until a restructuring has been devised and approved.

2.1.3. Drags and Pulls on Liquidity

Cash flow transactions—that is, cash receipts and disbursements—have significant effects on a company's liquidity position. We refer to these effects as drags and pulls on liquidity. A **drag on liquidity** is when receipts lag, creating pressure from the decreased available funds; a **pull on liquidity** is when disbursements are paid too quickly or trade credit availability is limited, requiring companies to expend funds before they receive revenues from sales that could cover the liability.

Major drags on receipts involve pressures from credit management and deterioration in other assets, and include the following:

- *Uncollected receivables:* The longer these are outstanding, the greater the risk that they will not be collected at all. They are indicated by the large number of days of receivables and high levels of bad debt expenses. Just as the drags on receipts may cause increased pressures on working capital, pulls on outgoing payments may have similar effects.
- *Obsolete inventory:* If inventory stands unused for long periods, it may be an indication that it is no longer usable. Slow inventory turnover ratios can also indicate obsolete inventory. Once identified, obsolete inventory should be attended to as soon as possible to minimize storage and other costs.
- *Tight credit:* When economic conditions make capital scarcer, short-term debt becomes more expensive to arrange and use. Attempting to smooth out peak borrowings can help blunt the impact of tight credit, as can improving the company's collections.

In many cases, drags may be alleviated by stricter enforcement of credit and collection practices.[1]

However, managing the cash outflows may be as important as managing the inflows. If suppliers and other vendors who offer credit terms perceive a weakened financial position or are unfamiliar with a company, they may restrict payment terms so much that the company's liquidity reserves are stretched thin. Major pulls on payments include the following:

- *Making payments early:* By paying vendors, employees, or others before the due dates, companies forgo the use of funds. Effective payment management means not making early payments. Payables managers typically hold payments until they can be made by the due date.
- *Reduced credit limits:* If a company has a history of making late payments, suppliers may cut the amount of credit they will allow to be outstanding at any time, which can squeeze the company's liquidity. Some companies try to extend payment periods as long as possible, disregarding the possible impact of reduced credit limits.
- *Limits on short-term lines of credit:* If a company's bank reduces the line of credit it offers the company, a liquidity squeeze may result. Credit line restrictions may be government-mandated, market-related, or simply company-specific. Many companies try to avert this situation by establishing credit lines far in excess of what they are likely to need. This "over-banking" approach is often commonplace in emerging economies or even in more developed countries where the banking system is not sound and the economy is shaky.
- *Low liquidity positions:* Many companies face chronic liquidity shortages, often because of their particular industry or from their weaker financial position. The major remedy for this situation is, of course, to improve the company's financial position, or else the company will be heavily affected by interest rates and credit availability. Most companies facing this situation have to deal with secured borrowing to obtain any working capital funds. Therefore, it is important for these companies to identify assets that can be used to help support the company's short-term borrowing activities.

It is critical that these drags and pulls be identified as soon as possible, preferably when they have not yet happened or have just arisen.

2.2. Measuring Liquidity

Liquidity contributes to a company's creditworthiness. **Creditworthiness** is the perceived ability of the borrower to pay what is owed on the borrowing in a timely manner and represents the ability of a company to withstand adverse impacts on its cash flows. Creditworthiness allows the company to obtain lower borrowing costs and better terms for trade credit and contributes to the company's investment flexibility, enabling it to exploit profitable opportunities.

The less liquid the company, the greater the risk that it will suffer financial distress or, in the extreme case, insolvency or bankruptcy. Because debt obligations are paid with cash, the company's cash flows ultimately determine solvency. The immediate source of funds for paying bills is cash on hand, proceeds from the sale of marketable securities, or the collection of

---

[1]In a recent survey of CFOs, results show that companies have become more efficient in working capital management, with U.S. companies in 2005 reducing their investment in working capital by 2.5 percent from 2004 levels and European companies reducing their investment by 3.3 percent (The Hackett Group, REL 2005 CFO Survey, http://careers.cfo.com/article.cfm/4315504/c_9459232).

accounts receivable. Additional liquidity also comes from inventory that can be sold and thus converted into cash, either directly through cash sales or indirectly through credit sales (i.e., accounts receivable).

There is, however, some point at which a company may have too much invested in low- and nonearning assets. Cash, marketable securities, accounts receivable, and inventory represent a company's liquidity. However, these investments are low-earning relative to the long-term, capital investment opportunities that companies may have available.

Various financial ratios can be used to assess a company's liquidity as well as its management of assets over time. Here we look at some of these ratios in a little more detail.

We calculate **liquidity ratios** to measure a company's ability to meet short-term obligations to creditors as they mature or come due. This form of liquidity analysis focuses on the relationship between current assets and current liabilities and the rapidity with which receivables and inventory can be converted into cash during normal business operations.

In short-term financial management, a great deal of emphasis is placed on the levels of and changes in current assets and liabilities. The two most common measurements are the current ratio and the quick ratio. The **current ratio** is the ratio of current assets to current liabilities:

$$\text{Current ratio} = \frac{\text{Current assets}}{\text{Current liabilities}}$$

The **quick ratio** (also known as the acid-test ratio) is the ratio of the quick assets to current liabilities. **Quick assets** are the assets that can be most readily converted to cash. In most situations, the least liquid of the current assets is inventory. Hence, we typically exclude inventory when calculating the quick ratio:

$$\text{Quick ratio} = \frac{\text{Cash} + \text{Short-term marketable investments} + \text{Receivables}}{\text{Current liabilities}}$$

The greater the current ratio or the quick ratio (that is, the greater the potential ability to cover current liabilities), the higher a company's liquidity will be. Whether a given current or quick ratio is good or bad, however, depends on a number of factors, including the trend in these ratios, the comparability of these ratios with competitors, and the available opportunities in more profitable, long-lived, capital investments.

In addition to looking at the relations among these balance sheet accounts, we can also form ratios that measure how well key current assets are managed over time. The key ratios for asset management are turnover ratios. For example, the **accounts receivable turnover** is the ratio of sales on credit to the average balance in accounts receivable:[2]

$$\text{Accounts receivable turnover} = \frac{\text{Credit sales}}{\text{Average receivables}}$$

---

[2]You will notice that we use credit sales instead of total revenue; the difference lies in the context. In the context of working capital management, the corporate financial analyst has access to details regarding the company's credit versus cash sales. For some companies, sales may be for cash or be some combination of cash sales and credit sales. For the analyst who is looking at the company without benefit of internal information regarding how much of sales is in the form of credit sales, an approximation is generally based on industry norms for credit practices.

This ratio is a measure of how many times, on average, accounts receivable are created by credit sales and collected on during the fiscal period.

As another example, the inventory turnover is the ratio of the cost of goods sold to the balance in inventory:

$$\text{Inventory turnover} = \frac{\text{Cost of goods sold}}{\text{Average inventory}}$$

This ratio is a measure of how many times, on average, inventory is created or acquired and sold during the fiscal period.

Another perspective on the activity in the current accounts is to estimate the number of days that the current asset or liability is on hand. For example, the **number of days of receivables**, also referred to as the days sales outstanding and days in receivables, gives us an idea of the management of the extension and collection of credit to customers:

$$\text{Number of days of receivables} = \frac{\text{Accounts receivable}}{\text{Average days sales on credit}} = \frac{\text{Accounts receivable}}{\text{Sales on credit}/365}$$

For example, a number of days of 35.5 tells us that it takes, on average, 35.5 days to collect on the credit accounts. Whether this is good or bad depends on credit terms that are offered to customers and the relation between sales and the extension of credit, which is often dictated by industry customs and competitive pressures.

The **number of days of inventory** gives us an indication of how well the inventory acquisition, process, and distribution is managed:

$$\text{Number of days of inventory} = \frac{\text{Inventory}}{\text{Average days cost of goods sold}} = \frac{\text{Inventory}}{\text{Cost of goods sold}/365}$$

The number of days of inventory, also known as the average inventory period, days sales in ending inventory, and the inventory holding period, is the length of time, on average, that the inventory remains within the company during the fiscal period. We expect variation in the number of days of inventory among industries because of differences in production cycles of different types of inventory. For example, we expect a grocery store to have a lower number of days inventory than, say, an aircraft manufacturer.

We can also look at the disbursement side of cash flows with the **number of days of payables**, which provides a measure of how long it takes the company to pay its own suppliers:

$$\text{Number of days of payables} = \frac{\text{Accounts payable}}{\text{Average days purchases}} = \frac{\text{Accounts payable}}{\text{Purchases}/365}$$

The number of days of payables is also referred to as the days payables outstanding and the average days payable. Purchases are not an item on published financial statements; so if you are evaluating a company's payables, you can estimate the purchases by using what you know about the company's cost of goods sold and beginning and ending balances in inventory.[3]

Each of these turnover ratios and numbers of days helps tell a story of how the company is managing its liquid assets. Like all ratios, the numbers themselves do not indicate much, but when we put these together with trends, information on the company's profitability, and information about competitors, we develop a good understanding of a company's performance.[4]

EXHIBIT 6-2   Liquidity Analysis of Wal-Mart Stores

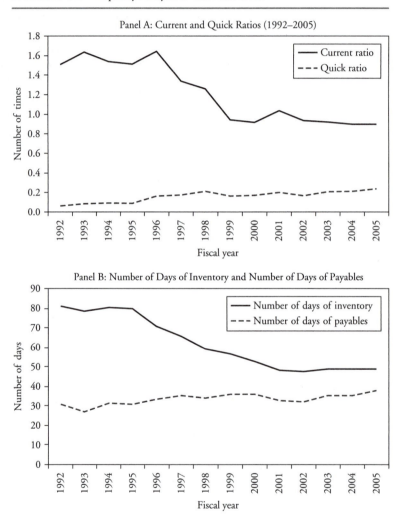

---

[3]We know that Beginning inventory + Purchases − Cost of good sold = Ending inventory. Therefore, if we know the inventory balances (from the balance sheet) and the cost of goods sold (from the income statement), we can determine the purchases: Purchases = Cost of goods sold + Ending inventory − Beginning inventory.

[4]For example, if we see a small number of days of inventory, it could mean that the company is managing its production very efficiently or that the company is at significant risk of a shortage of inventory. We don't know more until we look at what is needed or usual for companies in the industry, trends in turnover for the company, and the company's profitability in relation to the number of days of inventory.

Some of the major applications of this type of analysis include performance evaluation, monitoring, creditworthiness, and financial projections. But ratios are useful only when they can be compared. The comparison should be done in two ways: (1) over time for the same company and (2) over time for the company compared with its peer group. Peer groups can include competitors from the same industries as the company as well as other companies with comparable size and financial situations.

Consider Wal-Mart Stores, Inc. We can see the change in the current ratio and quick ratio over the fiscal years 1992 through 2005 in Exhibit 6-2, Panel A. Here, we see that the current ratio has declined, yet the quick ratio has increased slightly. We can see what is driving these trends in Panel B of the exhibit. One driver is the efficiency in the management of inventory, which results in holding onto inventory for fewer days, as indicated by the downward trend in the number of days of inventory. Putting it in perspective, this trend may be because of, in part, the product shift when Wal-Mart Stores increased its presence in the grocery line of business. Another driver is the increasing number of days of payables, which means that company is taking longer to pay what it owes suppliers.

Comparing Wal-Mart with Target Inc. and Kohl's in the 2005 fiscal year, as shown in Exhibit 6-3 (page 272), we see differences among the three competitors. These differences may be explained, in part, by the different product mixes (e.g., Wal-Mart has more sales from grocery lines than the others), as well as different inventory management systems and different inventory suppliers. The different need for liquidity may also be explained, in part, by the different operating cycles of the companies.

EXAMPLE 6-1   Measuring Liquidity.

Given the following ratios, how well has the company been managing its liquidity for the past two years?

Ratio	Current Year		Past Year	
	Company	Industry	Company	Industry
Current ratio	1.9	2.5	1.1	2.3
Quick ratio	0.7	1.0	0.4	0.9
Number of days of receivables	39.0	34.0	44.0	32.5
Number of days of inventory	41.0	30.3	45.0	27.4
Number of days of payables	34.3	36.0	29.4	35.5

Solution

The ratios should be compared in two ways: over time (there would typically be more than two years' worth of data) and against the industry averages. In all ratios shown here, the current year shows improvement over the previous year in terms of increased liquidity. In each case, however, the company remains behind the industry average in terms of liquidity. A brief snapshot such as this example could be the starting point to initiate or encourage more improvements with the goal of reaching or beating the industry standards.

EXHIBIT 6-3   Liquidity Ratios Among Discount Retailers

	Company		
Ratio for 2005 fiscal year	Wal-Mart	Target	Kohl's
Current ratio	0.9	1.5	2.4
Quick ratio	0.2	0.9	1.2
Number of days of inventory	48.9	61.0	94.5
Number of days of payables	38.1	64.7	33.9

Source: Wal-Mart, Kohl's, and Target's 10-K filings with the Securities and Exchange Commission for fiscal year 2005.

We can combine the number of days of inventory, number of days of receivables, and number of days of payables to get a sense of the company's operating cycle and net operating cycle. The **operating cycle** is a measure of the time needed to convert raw materials into cash from a sale. It consists of the number of days of inventory and the number of days of receivables:

$$\text{Operating cycle} = \frac{\text{Number of days}}{\text{of inventory}} + \frac{\text{Number of days}}{\text{of receivables}}$$

The operating cycle does not take everything into account, however, because the available cash flow is increased by deferring payment to suppliers. This deferral is considered in the **net operating cycle**, also called the cash conversion cycle. The net operating cycle is a measure of the time from paying suppliers for materials to collecting cash from the subsequent sale of goods produced from these supplies. It consists of the operating cycle minus the number of days of payables:

$$\text{Net operating cycle} = \frac{\text{Number of days}}{\text{of inventory}} + \frac{\text{Number of days}}{\text{of receivables}} - \frac{\text{Number of days}}{\text{of payables}}$$

In general, the shorter these cycles are, the greater a company's cash-generating ability will be and the less it will need liquid assets or outside finance. For many companies, the cash conversion cycle represents a period of time that requires financing; that is, the company offsets some of the financing need by deferring payments through payables terms, but the remainder must be financed.

3. MANAGING THE CASH POSITION

Although the mix or magnitude of data items may change from day to day, the goal is the same: ensuring that the net cash position is not negative. Ideally, the company's daily cash inflows and outflows are equal, but this is rarely the case. Without the reliability of matching these flows, companies must take other steps to ensure that the flows net out each day. Most companies try to avoid negative balances because the cost of garnering daily funds by issuing debt or by drawing on bank overdraft facilities is very costly, although the cost of maintaining a small short-term investment portfolio, in terms of an opportunity cost, is regarded as an acceptable cost of doing business.

In addition, it is difficult to borrow the exact amount needed; so many companies borrow a little extra to be safe and invest any small excesses overnight at lower rates than if they could invest them earlier or in securities with higher rates. To manage the cash position effectively, the treasury function, which is usually responsible for this activity, must gather information from various sources at all times during the day, making decisions based on the latest information.

Several critical factors help determine how a company can establish an efficient cash flow system. In most cases, the central treasury function may not be able to dictate how the company collects from customers or pays its vendors. What it can do, however, is use the best services and techniques associated with the company's payment configuration.

As an example of a typical cycle of cash management information that occurs daily, consider the process outlined in Exhibit 6-4. This hypothetical schedule shows how important it is to have an efficient, smoothly flowing information system that can meet the time requirements.

3.1. Forecasting Short-Term Cash Flows

Forecasting cash flows is necessary to allow for the effective management of working capital accounts. For cash forecasting to be effective, it has to be relatively precise. However, a forecast that is precise may not be *accurate*. Many factors are outside of the company's control,

EXHIBIT 6-4   Example of the Daily Cycle of Cash Management

Information from bank reporting systems is gathered and analyzed.	Morning
⇩	
The cash manager receives information from company sources.	
⇩	
The cash manager receives updates from the company's bank(s) on current-day transactions.	
⇩	
The cash management staff is arranging short-term investments and/or loans, as necessary, through broker–dealers from their banks or investment banks.	
⇩	
The cash management staff makes funds transfers.	Midday
⇩	
The cash movements for the day are completed or are scheduled for completion, and the company's cash position is finalized.	
⇩	
Necessary paperwork for all transactions is completed. Also, the running cash worksheet is updated and set for the next business day.	Close of the business day

such as the general economy, unexpected raw material shortages, and changing interest rates. The uncertainty in forecasting encourages companies to maintain some minimum level of cash on hand as a buffer.

3.1.1. Minimum Cash Balances Most companies want a cash buffer as protection from unexpected cash needs or to provide the financial flexibility to take advantage of attractive opportunities, such as procuring raw material inventory at a discount. This buffer is often expressed as a minimum desired cash balance. The size of this buffer depends on several influences, including the variation in the levels of the company's cash inflows and outflows, the company's ability to access other liquidity sources, and the company's ability to access borrowing facilities with little lead time.

3.1.2. Identifying Typical Cash Flows Having an accurate forecast can help a financial manager make better use of the company's financial history. Many product lines, especially those that are not in high-growth stages but rather are in steadier, mature stages, have similar cash flows from year to year or from season to season. If an extensive database has been established, it will be possible to draw reasonable projections for the current period or longer.

Even in cases of heavy growth through mergers and acquisitions, companies should try to transfer the acquired company's cash flow history to be used as a starting point for consolidating the new operation into the rest of the company. The cash manager must identify cash flow elements to build a reliable forecast. These elements are not difficult to identify in general terms, but it is much harder to define them specifically enough to be able to collect data regularly.

The cash elements that comprise a total forecast vary from company to company. However, it is good practice to identify the elements that pertain to any one individual company. Exhibit 6-5 shows typical elements arranged as inflows and outflows. It may be more useful to try to arrange the elements in this manner—i.e., show matching elements by the direction of their flow (in or out). In most cases, a company's data elements can be arranged this way to facilitate data gathering, reviewing variances, and presenting final reports to management and other cash users or providers.

These elements should reflect real cash flows, excluding such items as depreciation or accruals that are paid at a later date (these should be included when they are to be paid).

3.1.3. Cash Forecasting Systems Cash forecasting should be structured as a system to be effective, and, to do this, several aspects of the forecast must be considered. We provide

EXHIBIT 6-5 Examples of Cash Inflows and Outflows

Inflows:	Outflows:
• Receipts from operations, broken down by operating unit, departments, etc.	• Payables and payroll disbursements, broken down by operating unit, departments, etc.
• Funds transfers from subsidiaries, joint ventures, third parties.	• Funds transfers to subsidiaries.
• Maturing investments.	• Investments made.
• Debt proceeds (short- and long-term).	• Debt repayments.
• Other income items (interest, etc.).	• Interest and dividend payments.
• Tax refunds.	• Tax payments.

EXHIBIT 6-6   Examples of Cash Forecasting Aspects over Different Forecast Horizons

	Short Term	Medium Term	Long Term
Data frequency	Daily/weekly for 4–6 weeks	Monthly for one year	Annually for 3–5 years
Format	Receipts and disbursements	Receipts and disbursements	Projected financial statements
Techniques	Simple projections	Projection models and averages	Statistical models
Accuracy	Very high	Moderate	Lowest
Reliability	Very high	Fairly high	Not as high
Uses	Daily cash management	Planning financial transactions	Long-range financial position

some examples of these aspects in Exhibit 6-6, which highlights each aspect for three different forecast horizons. In some cases, one aspect may be more important than others. For instance, if daily cash is being handled fairly easily, it may be critical to spend time and resources to assure that the medium-term forecasting part of the overall system is functioning at the highest levels of reliability. In addition, some factors, such as format or time horizon, should not be changed arbitrarily because change may affect their accuracy and reliability levels.

3.2. Monitoring Cash Uses and Levels

Another facet of cash forecasting is monitoring and control. Managing the cash position essentially means keeping a running score on daily cash flows. Monitoring daily cash flows is a key aspect of a company's cash forecasting system in that the financial manager in charge of managing the cash position must know the company's cash balance in the bank on virtually a real-time basis. However, it really is not *forecasting* as such because most of the transactions are actually known; the challenge lies in the collection of this known information in time to do something with that information. For example, receiving information about a deposit too late to transfer the funds renders the information valueless.

To receive the appropriate information on a timely basis, information should be gathered from principal users and providers of cash, supplemented by short-term cash projections in days or even throughout the current day. The minimum level of cash available is estimated in advance, adjusted for known funds transfers, seasonality, or other factors, and is used as a **target balance** figure for each bank. Note that most companies use one major bank as their lead bank (or concentration bank) and control the balances for the bank through one main concentration account, with the target balance applied to the main account. For larger companies, more than one concentration bank is possible, but managing the cash positions in multiple concentration banks quickly makes the system complex and requires an efficient information processing system.

For most companies, it is necessary to manage a cash position with the assistance of short-term investments and borrowings. These short-term liquidity sources help counter the excesses and deficits that typically occur in a company's cash flow. The short-term investments are usually kept in a portfolio that is very liquid, with short maturities. In this way, funds are available whenever they are needed, but the company gives up the extra yield that might have been earned if the investments were made for longer periods of time or with securities with less liquidity. Short-term borrowing is for very short periods of time, but a borrower may find more economies in borrowing for regular periods, such as 30 days, to reduce the number of transactions and associated paperwork. Also, by extending the borrowing period, companies can usually obtain better rates and availabilities of funds than if they continually borrow very short maturities.

Many companies face predictable peaks and valleys in their business throughout the year. For instance, manufacturers of consumer electronics products achieve the bulk of their sales during the holiday shopping season (from late November through the end of the year), which means that they have a buildup of products that are shipped well before they receive payment. Thus, they have to finance this inventory rollout before they receive any cash. During this period, they are likely to use up most or all of the temporary excess funds they set aside or to tap into the credit lines they arranged for this purpose. When sales roll in during the busy shopping season, they use the proceeds to pay down the borrowing and then invest any excess.

Other influencing factors on a company's cash needs may be associated with nonoperating activities, such as major capital expenditure programs, mergers and acquisitions, sales or disposition of company assets, and the timing of long-term financial transactions, such as bond issues, private placements of debt or equity, and equity issues.

Predicting the peak need caused by seasonality of other nonoperating activities is important if the company is going to have to borrow funds to cover the need. If a company sets aside too much, it incurs excess costs that are unjustified. If it sets aside too little, it has to pay a penalty to raise funds quickly. Either case is a costly error. A reliable forecast can help avoid this situation.

4. INVESTING SHORT-TERM FUNDS

Short-term investments represent a temporary store of funds that are not necessarily needed in a company's daily transactions. If a substantial portion of a company's working capital portfolio is not needed for short-term transactions, it should be separated from a working capital portfolio and placed in a longer-term portfolio. Such longer-term portfolios are often handled by another area or are handled by an outside money manager under the company's supervision. In this way, the risks, maturities, and portfolio management of longer-term portfolios can be managed independently of the working capital portfolio.

Short-term working capital portfolios consist of securities that are highly liquid, less risky, and shorter in maturity than other types of investment portfolios. Thus, a company's working capital portfolio may consist of short-term debt securities, such as short-term U.S. government securities and short-term bank and corporate obligations. This type of portfolio changes almost constantly, as cash is needed or more excess cash is available for investments.

4.1. Short-term Investment Instruments

We describe examples of the major instruments for short-term investments in Exhibit 6-7. The relative amounts of each security can vary from one company to another, depending on the company's risk tolerance and how quickly the invested funds are needed.

EXHIBIT 6-7 Examples of Short-term Investment Instruments

Instruments	Typical Maturities	Features	Risks
U.S. Treasury bills (T-bills)	13, 26, 52 weeks	• Obligations of U.S. government (guaranteed), issued at a discount • Active secondary market • Lowest rates for traded securities	Virtually no risk
Federal agency securities	5–30 days	• Obligations of U.S. federal agencies (e.g., Fannie Mae, Federal Home Loan Board) issued as interest-bearing • Slightly higher yields than T-bills	Slight liquidity risk; insignificant credit risk
Bank certificates of deposit (CDs)	14–365 days	• Bank obligations, issued interest-bearing in $100,000 increments	Credit and liquidity risk (depending on bank's credit)
Banker's acceptances (BAs)	30–180 days	• Bank obligations for trade transactions (usually foreign), issued at a discount • Investor protected by underlying company and trade flow itself • Small secondary market	Credit and liquidity risk (depending on bank's credit)
Offshore or foreign time deposits	1–180 days	• Time deposit with bank in a foreign country • Can be CD or straight time deposit (TD) • Interest-bearing investment • Small secondary market for CDs, but not TDs	Credit risk (depending on bank); very high liquidity risk for TDs
Bank sweep services	1 day	• Service offered by banks that essentially provides interest on checking account balance (usually over a minimum level) • Large number of sweeps for overnight	Credit and liquidity risk (depending on bank)

(Continued)

EXHIBIT 6-7 (continued)

Instruments	Typical Maturities	Features	Risks
Repurchase agreements (repos)	1 day +	• Sale of securities with the agreement of the dealer (seller) to buy them back at a future time • Typically overcollateralized at 102 percent • Often done for very short maturities (less than 1 week)	Credit and liquidity risk (depending on dealer)
Commercial paper (CP)	1–270 days	• Unsecured obligations of corporations and financial institutions, issued at discount • Secondary market for large issuers • CP issuers obtain short-term credit ratings	Credit and liquidity risk (depending on credit rating)
Mutual funds and money market mutual funds	Varies	• Money market mutual funds commonly used by smaller businesses • Low yields but high liquidity for money market funds; mutual fund liquidity dependent on underlying securities in fund • Can be linked with bank sweep arrangement	Credit and liquidity risk (depending on fund manager)
Tax-advantaged securities	7, 28, 35, 49, 90 days	• Preferred stock in many forms, including adjustable rate preferred stocks (ARPs), auction rate preferred stocks (AURPs), and convertible adjustable preferred stocks (CAPs) • Dutch auction often used to set rate • Offer higher yields	Credit and liquidity risk (depending on issuer's credit)

278

4.1.1. Computing Yields on Short-Term Investments   Some securities, such as T-bills and banker's acceptances, are issued at a discount. Thus, the investor invests less than the face value of the security and receives the face value back at maturity. For instance, a $1 million security that pays 5 percent in interest with one month remaining to maturity would be purchased at $995,833.33.

$$\text{Purchase price} = \$1,000,000 - \big[(0.05)(1/12)(\$1,000,000)\big] = \$995,833.33$$
$$\text{Proceeds (face value)} = \$1,000,000$$

The difference between the purchase price and the face value, $4,166.67, is the **discount interest**.

Interest-bearing securities differ from discounted securities in that the investor pays the face amount and gets back that same face amount plus the interest on the security. For example, a 5 percent, 30-day, $1 million security would return $1 million face value plus interest earned:

$$\text{Purchase price (face value)} = \$1,000,000$$
$$\text{Proceeds} = \$1,000,000 + \big[(0.05)(1/12)(\$1,000,000)\big] = \$1,004,166.67$$

Rates on securities may be quoted as nominal rates or as yields. A **nominal rate** is a rate of interest based on the security's face value. In the previous two examples, the nominal rate in each instance was 5 percent. A **yield**, on the other hand, is the actual return on the investment if it is held to maturity. For example, if you buy the discount security for $995,833.33 and hold it for one month until it matures for $1 million, your yield on this investment is

$$\text{Yield} = \left(\frac{\$1,000,000 - 995,833.33}{995,833.33}\right)(12) = (0.004184)(12) = 5.0209\%$$

where the second factor, 12, annualizes the monthly yield of 0.4184 percent. The factor that is used to annualize the yield depends on the type of security and the traditions for quoting yields. For example, the **money market yield** is typically annualized using the ratio of 360 to the number of days to maturity:

$$\text{Money market yield} = \left(\frac{\text{Face value} - \text{Purchase price}}{\text{Purchase price}}\right)\left(\frac{360}{\text{Number of days to maturity}}\right)$$

On the other hand, the **bond equivalent yield** is typically annualized using the ratio of 365 to the number of days to maturity:

$$\text{Bond equivalent yield} = \left(\frac{\text{Face value} - \text{Purchase price}}{\text{Purchase price}}\right)\left(\frac{365}{\text{Number of days to maturity}}\right)$$

One source of confusion is that the yield on U.S. T-bills may be quoted on the basis of the discount basis or the bond equivalent basis (also referred to as the **investment yield basis**).

The yield on a T-bill using the discount basis is calculated using the face value as the basis for the yield and then using a 360-day year:

$$\text{Discount-basis yield} = \left(\frac{\text{Face value} - \text{Purchase price}}{\text{Face value}} \right) \left(\frac{360}{\text{Number of days to maturity}} \right)$$

Although the relevant yield for investment decision purposes is the bond equivalent yield, it is important to understand the discount basis because it is often quoted in the context of these securities.

EXAMPLE 6-2   Computing Investment Yields

For a 91-day $100,000 U.S. T-bill sold at a discounted rate of 7.91 percent, calculate the following:

1. Money market yield.
2. Bond equivalent yield.

   Purchase price = $100,000 − [(0.0791)(91/360)($100,000)] = $98,000.53

Solution to 1

   Money market yield = [1,999.47/98,000.53] × [360/91] = 8.07 percent

Solution to 2

   Bond equivalent yield = [1,999.47/98,000.53] × [365/91] = 8.18 percent

---

4.1.2. Investment Risks   Investors face several types of risks. We list a number of these in Exhibit 6-8. In this exhibit, we list the types of risk—credit, market, liquidity, and foreign exchange—and the attributes and safety measures associated with each type. The attributes describe the conditions that contribute to the type of risk, and the safety measures describe the steps that investors usually take to prevent losses from the risk. With the exception of foreign exchange risk, the key safety measures taken are to shift to "safety" (i.e., government securities, such as U.S. T-bills) or to shorten maturities so that securities mature sooner, allowing an investor to shift funds to a safer type of security.

4.2. Strategies

Short-term investment strategies are fairly simple because the securities in a working capital portfolio are limited in type and are much shorter in maturity than a longer-term portfolio. Most short-term investors seek "reasonable" returns and do not want to take on substantial

EXHIBIT 6-8   Types of Investment Risks and Safety Measures

Type of Risk	Key Attributes	Safety Measures
Credit (or default)	• Issuer may default. • Issuer could be adversely affected by economy or market. • There is little secondary market.	• Minimize amount. • Keep maturities short. • Watch for "questionable" names. • Emphasize government securities.
Market (or interest rate)	• Price or rate changes may adversely affect return. • There is no market to sell the maturity to, or there is only a small secondary market.	• Keep maturities short. • Keep portfolio diverse in terms of maturity and issuers.
Liquidity	• Security is difficult or impossible to (re)sell. • Security must be held to maturity and cannot be liquidated until then.	• Stick with government securities. • Look for good secondary market. • Keep maturities short.
Foreign exchange	• Adverse general market movement against your currency.	• Hedge regularly. • Keep most in your currency and domestic market (avoid foreign exchange).

risk. Short-term investment strategies can be grouped into two types: passive and active. A **passive strategy** is characterized by one or two decision rules for making daily investments, whereas an **active strategy** involves constant monitoring and may involve matching, mismatching, or laddering strategies.

Passive strategies are less aggressive than active ones and place top priority on safety and liquidity. Yet passive strategies do not have to offer poor returns, especially if companies have reliable cash forecasts. Often, companies with good cash forecasts can combine a passive strategy with an active matching strategy to enhance the yield of a working capital portfolio without taking on substantially greater risks.

The major problem associated with passive strategies is complacency, which can cause the company to roll over the portfolio mechanically, with little attention paid to yields and more focus on simply reinvesting funds as they mature. Passive strategies must be monitored, and the yield from investment portfolios should be benchmarked regularly against a suitable standard, such as a T-bill with comparable maturity.

Active strategies require more daily involvement and possibly a wider choice of investments. Although investments are rolled over with an active strategy, just as they are with a passive strategy, this type of strategy calls for more shopping around, better forecasts, and a more flexible investment policy or guideline.

Active strategies can include intentional matching or mismatching the timing of cash outflows with investment maturities. A **matching strategy** is the more conservative of the two and uses many of the same investment types as are used with passive strategies. A **mismatching strategy** is riskier and requires very accurate and reliable cash forecasts. These strategies usually use securities that are more liquid, such as T-bills, so that securities can be liquidated if adverse market conditions arise. Mismatching strategies may also be accomplished using derivatives, which may pose additional risks to a company unaccustomed to buying and selling derivatives.

A **laddering strategy** is another form of active strategy, which entails scheduling maturities on a systematic basis within the investment portfolio so that investments are spread out equally over the term of the ladder. A laddering strategy falls somewhere between a matching and a passive strategy. Laddering strategies have been used effectively in managing longer-term investment portfolios, but laddering should also be an effective short-term strategy.

Managing a working capital portfolio involves handling and safeguarding assets of the company. Accordingly, companies with investment portfolios should have a formal, written policy or guideline that protects the company and the investment managers. Investment policies and guidelines should not be very lengthy, especially because they must be understood by the company's investment managers and communicated to the company's investment dealers.

Although the investment policy or guideline should be customized for an individual company, the basic structure of such a policy is provided in Exhibit 6-9.

EXHIBIT 6-9   Sample Format of an Investment Policy

Purpose	List and explain the reasons that the portfolio exists and also describe the general attributes of the portfolio, such as a summary of the strategy that will be used and the general types of securities that are acceptable investments.
Authorities	Identify the executives who oversee the portfolio managers making the investments that compose the portfolio and the outside managers who could be used and how they would be managed. Also describe procedures that must be performed if the policy is not followed.
Limitations and/or restrictions	Describe, in general terms, the types of investments that should be considered for inclusion in the portfolio. The list should not consist of specific securities; it should describe the general *types* of securities, such as commercial paper, U.S. T-bills, or bank CDs. In this manner, the policy retains more flexibility than if specific issuers or securities are listed. In the latter case, the policy would require change every time an issuer was no longer issuing any securities. This section should also include any restrictions as to the relative amount of each security that is allowable in the overall portfolio. This section may also include procedures when a maximum has been exceeded or must be exceeded under special circumstances, such as when the portfolio is temporarily inflated prior to using the funds for an acquisition or other long-term use.
Quality	Quality may be in a separate section or included with the previous one. Investments with working capital funds must be safe; so many companies include credit standards for potential investments in their policy statements. Reference may be made to long-term ratings or, more frequently, to short-term credit ratings. The ratings cited are usually those from the major rating agencies: Standard & Poor's and Moody's.
Other items	Other items are sometimes included in a policy or guideline, such as statements that require the portfolio to be included in the financial audit or that regular reports will be generated by the investment manager. Some companies also define the types of securities that are "eligible," but this does not seem necessary if the policy is well written.

EXAMPLE 6-3   Evaluating an Investment Policy

A sample investment policy follows. Review the client's investment policy, considering the basic investment policy structure shown in Exhibit 6-9. The average portfolio size is $100 million, with no significant peaks or valleys throughout the year. After reviewing the policy, answer the following questions:

1. Is the policy an effective one?
2. What shortcomings or potential problem areas, if any, does it have?
3. How would you change this policy, if at all?

Working Capital Portfolio Investment Policy/Guidelines

- *Purpose:* This is a working capital portfolio with emphasis on safety and liquidity. We will sacrifice return for either of these two goals.
- *Authorities:* The treasurer, with agreement from the CFO, will be in charge of managing short-term investments. Authority and control to execute can be delegated by the treasurer or CFO to another treasury manager if the delegation is documented.
- *Maximum maturity:* Securities may not be made for longer than three (3) years.
- Types/amounts of investments permitted: no more than 10 percent of the portfolio or $50 million with any issuer, subject to the credit limitation that any eligible issuer must be rated A-1, P-1 by Standard & Poor's and Moody's.
- *Repurchase agreements:* Agreements must be equal or to or preferably exceed the PSA Standard Investment Agreement, which requires 102 percent collateral for repurchases.
- All investments must be held in safekeeping by XYZ Bank.
- The investment manager can execute exception transactions but must document them in writing.

Solution to 1

The policy is fairly effective in that it tries to provide simple, understandable rules. It calls for credit quality, limits the possible position with any single issuer, accepts market standards (such as the PSA), and calls for safekeeping. It also has a straightforward exception procedure.

Solution to 2

The credit ratings may be too restrictive. Many investment securities may not be rated by both S&P and Moody's, which is implied, if not stated, in the policy. Also, the 10 percent limitation apparently is to be applied to all securities. However, most investment managers do not consider securities issued by governmental agencies or the government itself to be so risky that a limitation needs to be applied.

Solution to 3

The words "or equivalent" should be added to the credit quality of the types of investments. Also, there should be no limitation to highly rated governmental securities, such as U.S. Treasury bills and the equivalent from the major developed countries. A credit rating reference could be applied to determine eligible governmental securities.

EXHIBIT 6-10   Short-Term Investment Portfolio Report

Security/Loan	Dealer/Bank	€ Amt (000)	Weight (%)	Yield (%)	Maturity (days)
U.S. T-bills	ABC Bank	23,575	39.8	3.50	90
Finco CP	XYZ Co.	20,084	33.9	4.65	45
Megabank CD	Megabank	15,560	26.3	5.05	30
Weighted average yield from investments				4.30	
Short-term benchmark rate*				4.25	

*Benchmark rate = independent source, such as synthetic portfolio maintained independently or rate provided by third party, such as a money manager or other empirical source (e.g., a financial institution, trade association, or central bank).

4.3. Evaluating Short-Term Funds Management

Tracking tools can range from simple spreadsheets to more expensive treasury workstations. If portfolios are not too large or diversified, a spreadsheet may be sufficient to compare effective yields and borrowing costs on an ongoing basis and to generate periodic performance reports.

Investment returns should be expressed as bond equivalent yields, to allow comparability among investment alternatives. In addition, the overall portfolio return should be weighted according to the currency size of the investment. We provide an abbreviated example of a portfolio report in Exhibit 6-10. The report provides the weighted average returns of the different investments. The yields are all calculated on a bond equivalent yield basis.

5. MANAGING ACCOUNTS RECEIVABLE

Credit accounts vary by type of customer and the industry, and granting credit involves a trade-off between increasing sales and uncollectible accounts. There are three primary activities in accounts receivable management: (1) granting credit and processing transactions, (2) monitoring credit balances, and (3) measuring performance of the credit function.

Processing accounts receivable transactions requires recording credit sales to create a record and posting customer payments—or at least monitoring the posting—to the accounts receivable account by applying the payment against the customer's outstanding credit balance. Monitoring the outstanding accounts receivable requires a regular reporting of outstanding receivable balances and notifying the collection managers of past due situations. Monitoring is an ongoing activity. Measuring the performance of the credit functions entails preparing and distributing key performance measurement reports, including an accounts receivable aging schedule and day's sales outstanding reports.

Essentially, the accounts receivable management function is a go-between for the credit manager, treasury manager, and accounting manager. This role is an important one because it can slow up the recording of payments, which may, in turn, prevent customers from purchasing more of the company's products or, worse yet, prevent the treasury manager from depositing the check and converting the check to available funds.

The accounts receivable management function is also considered to be a derivative activity from credit granting because it helps in providing information needed by the credit management function. It depends on the source of the sale for its records, on the credit manager for additional information on the status of the accounts receivable record, and possibly on the treasury manager to establish an efficient system of getting the payment information to the accounts receivable manager for cash application (e.g., from a bank lockbox).

The goals for the accounts receivable management system include

- Efficient processing and maintaining accurate, up-to-date records that are available to credit managers and other interested parties as soon as possible after payments have been received;
- Control of accounts receivable and assuring that accounts receivable records are current and that no unauthorized entry into the accounts receivable file has occurred;
- Collection on accounts and coordination with the treasury management function;
- Frequent coordination with and notification to the credit managers; and
- Preparation of regular performance measurement reports.

Companies may achieve scale economies by centralizing the accounts receivable function by using a captive finance subsidiary.[5] A **captive finance subsidiary** is a wholly-owned subsidiary of the company that is established to provide financing of the sales of the parent company.

One of the challenges in accounts receivable management is monitoring receivables and collecting on accounts. Many companies resort to outsourcing the accounts receivable function, primarily to increase the collection on accounts, provide credit evaluation services, and to apply the most recent technology.[6] Also, some companies may invest in credit insurance, which reduces the risk of bad debts and shifts some of the evaluation of creditworthiness to the insurer.

5.1. Key Elements of the Trade Credit-Granting Process

Credit management is an integral part of the collection process. It sets the framework for sales in that it can restrict sales by rejecting credit or expand it by loosening acceptance criteria. It also links the collection and cash application processes and has a profound effect on the method of collection as well. In addition, credit management techniques incorporate fundamental financial analysis methods in setting credit policy, granting credit, and managing existing credit customers.

A weak, ineffective credit management function may enhance sales, but many of those sales may become bad debts. On the other hand, a strong, active credit management function can work in tandem with sales and marketing on one side and with accounting and treasury on the other. To establish an effective credit management function, a company must have a well conceived strategy customized to the company's needs and reflecting the company's goals.

Credit management policies are usually established as a set of basic guidelines to be used by credit managers. A company's credit policy sets the boundaries for the credit management function. It lays out procedures as part of the policy and offers guidance for each typical

---

[5]As pointed out by Mian and Smith (1992), companies that have highly variable accounts receivable (for example, from seasonality) may find the use of a captive finance subsidiary attractive because it may allow the subsidiary's debt indentures to differ from those of the parent company.
[6]Hall (2003).

situation. The policy shows the steps in the granting process and provides decision rules for specific situations. The policy can also influence the sales level by making it easy or difficult for customers to buy on credit.

Customers may start out with one type of credit account that is restrictive, such as cash on delivery, and may eventually demonstrate that they are regular payers and can be given open book credit accounts.

The major types of credit accounts include

- *Open book,* which is the most common for company to company transactions;
- *Documentary,* with or without lines of credit, the most common for cross-border transactions;
- *Installment credit,* with regular timed payments; and
- *Revolving credit.*

The types of credit terms offered vary by type of customer, relative financial strength by the customer, and the type of credit terms the competition is offering. The different forms of terms of credit other than cash, which generally implies 7 to 10 days, include the following:

- *Ordinary terms:* Terms are set forth in a standard format—*net t* or *d/t₁ net t₂*, where t in the first example refers to the length of time a customer has to pay the invoice before becoming past due. In the second example, t_1 is the time period for taking discounts, and t_2 is the same as t in the first example. For example, "net 60" means that the full amount of the invoice is due in 60 days. Most trade credit customers will take the full 60 days. Terms of "1/10 net 30" mean that the customer can take a 1 percent discount if the invoice is paid in 10 days or else pay the full amount of the invoice by 30 days from the invoice date.
- *Cash before delivery (CBD):* These terms require that the amount of the invoice must be paid in advance before delivery is scheduled. Checks must clear before any shipment is made.
- *Cash on delivery (COD):* These terms require that payment must be made (usually in the form of a bank check) when the product is delivered; otherwise, no delivery is made.
- *Bill-to-bill:* These terms require that each prior bill must be paid before new shipments are possible.
- *Monthly billing:* These terms require payment monthly. They have a different format; for example, *2/10th Prox net 30th* means that the customer can take a 2 percent discount if it pays in the first 10 days of the next month or else it must pay the full amount of the invoice by the thirtieth day of the next month.

Credit managers may evaluate customers' creditworthiness using a credit scoring model. A **credit scoring model** is a statistical model used to classify borrowers according to creditworthiness. These models were first designed for assisting in making consumer credit decisions. Major credit card issuers needed a tool they could use to make mass credit decisions. It was also used for small business loans after many larger banks discovered that their costs of reviewing and deciding whether to grant loans were such that they could not efficiently make loans of the smaller sizes required by smaller businesses. To overcome this problem, they adopted credit scoring models.

Credit scoring models offer an opportunity for a company to make fast decisions on the basis of simple data, not requiring a great deal of paperwork. The scoring models give greater weight to such factors as

- Ready cash (e.g., high checking account balances);
- Organization type, with corporations rated higher than sole proprietorships or partnership;
- Being current in supplier payments, as indicated by financial services such as Dun & Bradstreet.

The models penalize the potential borrower for the following:

- *Prior late payment behavior or defaults:* Payment patterns are habitual.
- *Heavy use of personal credit cards:* No reserves or reduced reserves are available.
- *Previous personal bankruptcy or tax liens:* This carries over from person to company.
- *High-risk categories:* Food services and hospitality industries are examples.

Credit scoring can also be used to predict late payers.

5.2. Managing Customers' Receipts

Cash collections systems are a function of the types of customers a company has and the methods of payment that the customers use. For instance, if a company's sales are made at retail locations, it cannot take advantage of the benefits offered by bank lockbox services. Instead, it must deal with organizing and controlling local deposits and concentrating these deposits efficiently and economically. On the other hand, if a company manufactures and sells products to other businesses, it can use a bank lockbox service to expedite processing and clearing of check payments.

We illustrate a typical network for a company with both electronic and check payments in Exhibit 6-11. Checks from one type of customer are directed to a bank lockbox, while electronic payments from another type of customer are transmitted via **electronic funds transfer** (EFT) through one of the available networks, such as the **Automated Clearing House** (ACH) system or the **Giro system**. The ACH system is an electronic payment network available to businesses, individuals, and financial institutions in the United States, U.S. territories, and Canada. The Giro systems are postal-based systems in Europe and elsewhere.

EXHIBIT 6-11   Cash Collections and Concentrations

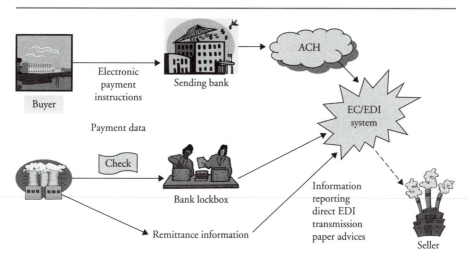

In most cases, the best practice for collections involves the establishment of a system that accelerates payments as well as their information content, such as the customer's name and identification number and which invoices are being paid. From the collecting company's point of view, the way to achieve this best practice is to establish an electronic collection network. This can apply to either retail or wholesale companies.

Retail payments can be made by credit or debit cards or by electronic checks, which are converted to electronic debits or digitized images, or by direct debit. These payments clear electronically, possibly facilitated through **point of sale** (POS) systems, which are systems that capture the transaction data at the physical location in which the sale is made. A **direct debit program** is an arrangement whereby the customer authorizes a debit to a demand account; such a system is used by companies—such as utilities, telecommunications service providers, cable companies, insurance companies, and credit card companies—to collect routine payments for services.

If payments cannot be converted to electronic payments, the next best practice is to use a bank lockbox service. A **lockbox system** is coordinated with the banking institution in which customer payments are mailed to a post office box and the banking institution retrieves and deposits these payments several times a day, enabling the company to have use of the funds sooner than in a centralized system in which customer payments are sent to the company. An acceptable bank lockbox arrangement is one in which the checks deposited today are available tomorrow or the next business day. This one-day availability lays the groundwork for best practices in cash concentration.

A good performance measure for check deposits is a calculated **float factor**. The **float** in this context is the amount of money that is in transit between payments made by customers and the funds that are usable by the company. We compute the float factor by dividing the average daily deposit in dollars into the average daily float:[7]

$$\text{Float factor} = \frac{\text{Average daily float}}{\text{Average daily deposit}} = \frac{\text{Average daily float}}{\text{Total amount of checks deposited}/\text{Number of days}}$$

This calculation gives the average number of days it takes deposited checks to clear. If the float factor is very small (e.g., less than 1.0), it is probably worthwhile to investigate further to determine whether same-day wire transfers from the depository account are warranted, assuming the depository account is with a bank other than the company's lead bank. The float factor measures only how long it takes for checks to clear, not how long it takes to receive the checks, deposit them, and then have them clear. However, it is still very useful and can be computed easily for any depository accounts.

EXAMPLE 6-4   Calculating Float Factors

Given the following data, compute a float factor for this company bank account.

Total deposits for the month	$3,360,900
Number of days in month	30 days
Average daily float	$154,040

---

[7]We determine the average daily float from an analysis of cash accounts.

Solution

$$\text{Average daily deposit} = \frac{(\$3,360,900)}{30}$$

$$= \$112,030$$

$$\text{Float factor} = \frac{\text{Average daily float}}{\text{Average daily deposit}}$$

$$= \frac{\$154,040}{\$112,030}$$

$$= 1.375$$

Cash concentration involves two major activities: consolidating deposits and moving funds between company accounts or to outside points. The best practice for cash concentration may be different for concentration than for moving funds, depending on the timing required and the availability of the funds being transferred.

For bank lockbox concentration, assuming that the checks clear in one business day (on average), the concentration technique of choice is the electronic funds transfer method. In this method, bank lockbox personnel call in the deposit via a reporting service or directly to the concentration bank. The concentration bank creates an electronic funds transfer debit that clears overnight, giving the company available funds in its concentration account. This system can be set up to run with or without intervention by the company's cash manager. In most cases, the best practice does not involve any intervention.

Electronic funds transfers offer distinct advantages to companies that use them for concentration of funds. First, they are substantially cheaper than the alternative, the wire transfer. In addition, they are reliable in that the transfer can be made part of a routine that can be performed daily without exception. Even small payments that would not be economical to transfer out by wire can be transferred economically by electronic funds transfer.

5.3.   Evaluating Accounts Receivable Management

There are numerous ways of measuring accounts receivable performance. Most of them deal with how effectively outstanding accounts receivable items can be converted into cash. Measures can be derived from general financial reports as well as from more detailed internal financial records.

Many measures, such as number of days of receivables, can be calculated easily from financial statements. The standard number of days of receivables evaluates the total receivables outstanding but does not consider the age distribution within this outstanding balance.

5.3.1.   Accounts Receivable Aging Schedule   One key report that accounts receivable managers should use is the **aging schedule**, which is a breakdown of the accounts into categories of days outstanding. We provide an example of an aging schedule in Exhibit 6-12, Panel A. As you can see in this example, the report shows the total sales and receivables for each reporting period (typically 30 days). It is handier to convert the aging schedule to percentages, as we show in this exhibit. Note that in the exhibit, it is easy to spot a change in April's aging.

EXHIBIT 6-12   An Accounts Receivable Aging Schedule

Panel A: The Aging Schedule

($ millions)	January	February	March	April
Sales	530	450	560	680
Total accounts receivable	600	560	650	720
Current (1–30 days old)	330	290	360	280
1–30 days past due	90	120	160	250
31–60 days past due	80	60	60	110
61–90 days past due	70	50	40	50
>90 days past due	30	40	30	30
Aging (%)	January	February	March	April
Current (1–30 days old)	55.0	51.8	55.4	38.9
1–30 days past due	15.0	21.4	24.6	34.7
31–60 days past due	13.3	10.7	9.2	15.3
61–90 days past due	11.7	8.9	6.2	6.9
>90 days past due	5.0	7.1	4.6	4.2

Panel B: Calculation of the Weighted Average Collection Period

	March			April		
Aging Group	Collection Days[1]	Weight[2] (%)	Weighted Days[3]	Collection Days	Weight (%)	Weighted Days
Current (1–30 days)	20	55.4	11.1	29	38.9	11.3
31–60 days	48	24.6	11.8	55	34.7	19.1
61–90 days	80	9.2	7.4	88	15.3	13.5
91–120 days	110	6.2	6.8	115	6.9	7.9
121 + days	130	4.6	6.0	145	4.2	6.1
Weighted average collection days[4]			43.0			57.9

Notes:
1. The average days for collecting receivables in each grouping.
2. The weighting from the aging schedule.
3. This figure, expressed in days, is the product of the previous two columns.
4. The sum of each grouping's product equals the overall days.

Accounts receivable have not been collected and converted to cash as rapidly as in previous months. In this case, the April change should be scrutinized. For example, the extension of credit terms may have been increased as part of a special program. This change could also signal a change in payments by the company's customers.

5.3.2. The Number of Days of Receivables   The number of days of receivables gives us the overall picture of accounts receivable collection. We can compare the number of days with the credit policy to give us an idea of how well the company is collecting on its accounts, relative to the terms that it grants credit. But we can take this a step further by calculating a weighted average of the collection period, or weighted average day's sales outstanding. By focusing on the time it takes to collect receivables, the weighted average collection period is a good measure of how long it is taking to collect from the company's customers regardless of the sales level or the changes in sales.

The calculation of the weighted average collection period requires data on the number of days it takes to collect accounts of each age grouping. For example, we could group receivables in regular increments, such as 30-day periods, and then weight the collection period in each group by the monetary amount of accounts in the group.

Using the data provided in Exhibit 12, Panel A, it is possible to compute the number of days of receivables for March and April, as shown in Panel B of this exhibit. As you can see in this example, we can get a better idea of why the number of days of receivables changed from one month to the next. The weighted average collection days increased from March to April, primarily because of the large representation in receivable accounts in the 31–60 and 61–90 day ranges, which made up only 24.6 percent + 9.2 percent = 33.8 percent of accounts in March, but 50 percent of accounts in April.

The primary drawback to this measure is that it requires more information than the number of days of receivables, and this information is not readily available, especially for comparisons among companies.

6. MANAGING INVENTORY

The primary goal for an inventory system is to maintain the level of inventory so that production management and sales management can make and sell the company's products without investing more than necessary in the asset. Like cash and accounts receivable management, inventory management involves balancing: having sufficient inventory, but not too much.

Inventory is a current asset that is created by purchasing, paid by accounts payable, and funded by the treasury. The investment in inventory does not produce cash until it is sold or otherwise disposed of. Excessive levels of inventory can possibly overstate the value of inventory because the more that is on hand, the greater the potential is for obsolete inventory, which can be sold off, but at a discount. Shortages of inventory result in lost sales.

The amount of inventory that a company holds or feels it has to hold creates a financial requirement for the company. If the company's product lines are more diverse or if its production processes are more involved in using inventory to make final products and then store the products, the company may have a significant financial investment in inventory.

The investment in inventory has been staggering for many companies, which has caused them to look for new inventory management techniques. New techniques in inventory control, aided by improved technology, have enabled substantial reduction of the inventory levels a company must maintain and still be able to make products and have them available for sale as needed. For instance, newer just-in-time approaches to inventory management have lowered required inventory balances and cemented major trading partner relationships.

The motives for holding inventory, which dictate how much inventory is held and, in turn, how much working capital is tied up in inventory, are very similar to the need for holding cash. The major motives include the transactions motive, the precautionary motives, and the speculative motive.

The **transactions motive** reflects the need for inventory as part of the routine production–sales cycle. Inventory need is equal to the planned manufacturing activity, and the approach to inventory is dictated by the manufacturing plan.

Precautionary stocks also may be desirable to avoid any **stock-out losses**, which are profits lost from not having sufficient inventory on hand to satisfy demand. Managing inventory well means keeping extra inventory, especially if it could become obsolete quickly, at a minimum. To do this, a company must have a reliable forecast and a flexible inventory approach. In addition, many companies that do not have a reliable forecast maintain a reserve as a precaution for shortfalls in the plan. Of course, how much stock is determined by the lead time for additional inventory purchases, the length of time it takes to deliver final products to the market, and how much can be spent on extra inventory.

In certain industries, managers may acquire inventory for speculative reasons, such as ensuring the availability and pricing of inventory. Inventory managers working together with purchasing managers can benefit from out-of-the-ordinary purchases. For instance, if a publisher is certain that paper costs will be increasing for the next year, it can buy more paper in the current year and store it for future use. This decision assumes that the storage costs are not greater than the savings.

Companies usually attempt to strike a balance in managing their inventory levels. Overinvestment can result in liquidity squeezes or related problems with an increase in debt without an increase in cash. Overinvestment can also lead to the misuse of facilities as more storage is required for the built-up inventory. Having large amounts of inventory on hand can result in losses from shrinkage, spoilage, and so on. Finally, overinvestment can reduce the company's competitiveness because it may not be able to match pricing due to its large inventory costs.

On the other hand, underinvestment in inventory can create problems from losing customers who could not purchase a product or from gaining their ill will from long delays in delivery. Plant shutdowns and expensive special runs can also be costly. Finally, a risk with underinvestment is the company's inability to avoid price increases by suppliers.

6.1. Approaches to Managing Levels of Inventory

To control inventory costs, a company should adopt the appropriate approach for its inventory. The two basic approaches are the economic order quantity and just-in-time.

Many companies use the classical approach, **economic order quantity–reorder point** (EOQ–ROP), at least for some portion of their inventory. This method is based on expected demand and the predictability of demand, and it requires determining the level of inventory at which new inventory is ordered. This ordering point is determined based on the costs of ordering and carrying inventory, such that the total cost associated with inventory is minimized. The demand and lead times determine the inventory level. For EOQ–ROP to work well, there must be a reliable short-term forecast. Often, a company may use EOQ–ROP for smaller items that have low unit costs.

EXHIBIT 6-13   EOQ-ROP Inventory Method

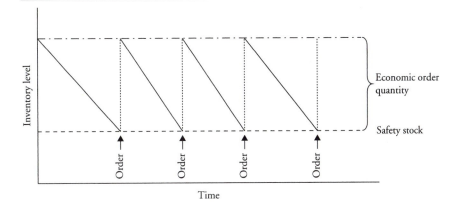

Use of the EOQ–ROP method may involve safety stocks and anticipation stocks. A **safety stock** is a level of inventory beyond anticipated needs that provides a cushion in the event that it takes longer to replenish inventory than expected or in the case of greater-than-expected demand. A company may consider the number of days of inventory on hand and the lead time in replenishing stock in determining the appropriate level of the safety stock. An **anticipation stock** is inventory in excess of that needed for anticipated demand, which may fluctuate with the company's sales or production seasonality. We illustrate the EOQ–ROP method in Exhibit 6-13.

The **just-in-time (JIT) method** is a system that minimizes in-process inventory stocks—raw materials and in production—by evaluating the entire system of the delivery of materials and production. Materials are ordered, for example, at a point at which current stocks of material reach a reorder point, a point determined primarily by historical demand. **Materials or manufacturing resource planning** (**MRP**) systems incorporate production planning into inventory management. The analysis of production and materials needed for production are incorporated into an analysis that provides both a materials acquisition schedule and a production schedule. Combining the JIT and MRP methods can provide a broader base for integrating inventory into the company's supply chain management and effectively reduce inventory levels.[8]

In most instances, companies have several types of inventory that can be managed effectively using one or more of these approaches. Obviously, a company should select the method that allows the most cost-beneficial investment in inventory.

6.2. Inventory Costs

There are several component costs of inventory. Some components represent opportunity costs, whereas others may be real costs. The component costs include the following:

---

[8]More recent innovations have integrated cash management and inventory management. For example, the moment a customer orders and pays for a computer with Dell Corporation, the production process begins. This efficiency results in a negative operating cycle; that is, Dell Corporation is collecting on accounts as it invests in the inventory production. Because it uses trade credit for its supplies, it has little need for working capital.

- *Ordering:* Procurement or replenishment costs, both of which may be fixed or variable. These costs depend on number of orders placed. Examples are freight, labor and handling, paperwork, machine setup.
- *Carrying:* Financing and holding costs, which are opportunity or real costs. These costs depend on average inventory levels and the type of goods. Examples are storage, capital costs, obsolescence, insurance, and taxes.
- *Stock-out:* Opportunity or real costs, which are affected by level of inventory, item mix, processing time versus term of sale. These costs might vary greatly depending on how they are estimated. Examples are lost sales, back-order costs, substitution costs.
- *Policy:* Costs of gathering data and general operating costs, which may be real costs or "soft" costs. These costs depend on inventory mix and complexity. Examples are data processing, labor charges, overtime, training.

6.3. Evaluating Inventory Management

The most common way to measure the company's investment in inventory and evaluate its inventory management is to compute the inventory turnover ratio and the number of days of inventory. The inventory turnover is a rough measure, but it is simple to calculate and compare with other standards or past history. Inventory turnover varies among industries, as you can see in Exhibit 6-14, which provides a calculated inventory turnover and number of days of inventory for various industries.

Further, the inventory turnover may differ among companies in an industry because of different product mixes. For example, in fiscal year 2005, Wal-Mart Stores had an inventory turnover of 7.5 times compared with Target's 5.7 times. This difference may be because of Wal-Mart's greater foothold in the higher-turnover grocery business, as compared with Target.

EXHIBIT 6-14   Inventory Turnover and Number of Days of Inventory for U.S. Corporations in Different Industries (2002)

Industry	Inventory Turnover (times)	Number of Days of Inventory
Apparel manufacturing	4.9	74.0
Chemical manufacturing	5.7	64.4
Electronics and appliances stores	7.3	50.2
Food manufacturing	8.1	44.9
Food, beverage, and liquor stores	11.2	32.7
Machinery manufacturing	5.6	65.2
Mining	10.4	35.2
Motor vehicle dealers and parts dealers	5.6	65.2
Paper manufacturing	6.8	53.8
Transportation equipment manufacturing	9.7	37.7

Source: Data from *Statistics of Income, 2002,* Corporation Returns with Net Income, Table 7, www.irs.gov.

Although the analysis of trends is important, care should be taken when interpreting changes. For example, a decrease in the inventory turnover may mean that more inventory is on hand and is not moving through manufacturing and being sold. On the other hand, a decrease in inventory turnover may indicate a change in the company's product mix, or it may mean that the company is reducing its risk of inventory stock-outs.

EXAMPLE 6-5   Financial Impact of Inventory Methods

If a company's inventory turnover ratio is 6.1 times (annually) and the industry average number of days of inventory is 52 days, how does the company compare with the industry average?

Solution

Convert the turnover ratio to a number of days of inventory:

$$\text{Number of days of inventory} = 365/\text{Inventory turnover}$$
$$= 365/6.1$$
$$= 59.84 \text{ days}$$

Comparing this answer with the industry average, 52.0 days, it appears that the company's inventory turnover is slower than the industry average.

---

7. MANAGING ACCOUNTS PAYABLE

Accounts payable are amounts due to suppliers of goods and services that have not been paid. They arise from **trade credit**, which is a spontaneous form of credit in which a purchaser of the goods or service is effectively financing its purchase by delaying the date on which payment is made. Trade credit may involve a delay of payment, with a discount for early payment. The terms of the latter form of credit are generally stated in the discount form: A discount from the purchase price is allowed if payment is received within a specified number of days, otherwise the full amount is due by a specified date. For example, the terms "2/10, net 30" indicate that a 2 percent discount is available if the account is paid in 10 days; otherwise the full amount is due by the thirtieth day. The terms differ among industries, influenced by tradition in the industry, terms of competitors, and current interest rates.

A key working capital link is the purchasing–inventory–payables process. This process is concerned with the procurement of goods—finished or not—that become the company's items for sale. Handled efficiently, the process minimizes excess funds "in the pipeline." Handled inefficiently, the process can create a severe drain on a company's liquidity, tying up funds and reducing the company's financial reserves.

Inefficiencies may arise in managing purchasing, inventory, and payables. Each area has to be organized and efficiently linked with the other areas. Purchasing can often influence how payments are to be made and the terms of credit. Here again, purchasing management needs to be kept informed as to the types of payment mechanisms the company can handle to avoid agreeing with suppliers to make payments in a medium that the company does not yet support.

The effective management of accounts payable is an important working capital management activity because inefficient payables management may result in opportunity costs from payments made too early, lost opportunities to take advantage of trade discounts, and failure to use the benefits of technologies offered by e-commerce and other Web-based activities.

Accounts payable is the final step in the procurement cycle because it combines the paperwork, approvals, and disbursements of funds. An effective accounts payable function helps integrate the components of the cycle and does not require the uneconomical outlay of the company's funds until the outlay is due.

A company may not believe that it needs a formal guideline or policy to manage the function well. However, there must be some method to assure that payables practices are organized, consistent, and cost-effective. For example, if payables management is decentralized and more than one operating entity deals with the same supplier, the credit terms offered to each entity should be the same unless there are special circumstances, such as volume constraints, that warrant different terms. To handle payables effectively, a company needs rules to ensure that company assets are not being depleted unnecessarily.

A company should consider several factors as guidelines for effectively managing its accounts payable, including the following:

- *Financial organization's centralization:* The degree to which the company's core financial function is centralized or decentralized affects how tightly payables can be controlled.
- *Number, size, and location of vendors:* The composition of the company's supply chain and how dependent the company is on its trading partners (and vice versa) determines how sophisticated a payables system it needs.
- *Trade credit and cost of borrowing or alternative cost:* The importance of credit to the company and its ability to evaluate trade credit opportunities, such as trade discounts, encourage standardized payables procedures and enhanced information management throughout the company.
- *Control of disbursement float:* Many companies still pay suppliers by check and create disbursement float—the amount of time between check issuance and a check's clearing back against the company's account. This float has value to many companies because it allows them to use their funds longer than if they had to fund their checking account on the day the checks were mailed.
- *Inventory management:* Newer inventory control techniques, such as MRP and JIT, increase the number of payments that must be processed by accounts payable. Many older systems cannot accommodate this extra volume; so newer management techniques and systems are required.
- *E-commerce and electronic data interchange (EDI:)* Global developments to use the Internet and other direct connections between customer and supplier are revolutionizing the supply chain for many companies. Because payments for many of these activities should be considered as part of the overall process, many companies have determined that paying electronically offers a more efficient, cost-effective alternative to checks, which are more valuable only when the disbursement float value is large and interest rates (which provide value to float) are also high.

Stretching payables, also known as pushing on payables when it stretches beyond the due date, is sometimes done by corporate cash managers and other financial managers.[9] Stretching payables is taking advantage of vendor grace periods. The evaluation of payables stretching opportunities is fairly straightforward. The number of additional days that payments can be extended or stretched is determined and valued by applying the company's opportunity cost for the additional days times the amount of the payable.

For example, if a payable that averaged $100,000 can be stretched for an additional seven days, the company gains an additional seven days' use of the funds. This opportunity can be valued by multiplying the amount, $100,000, by the company's opportunity cost for short-term funds. For example, if the company's estimated cost for short-term funds is 8 percent annually (0.02191 percent daily), then the value of stretching a $100,000 payment for seven days is $153.42. The values for each opportunity (throughout a year's activity) can be valued in this way to determine the overall benefit, which can then be weighed against the costs (both financial and nonfinancial).

There are basically two countering forces: (1) Paying too early is costly unless the company can take advantage of discounts, and (2) paying late affects the company's perceived creditworthiness.

7.1.   The Economics of Taking a Trade Discount

One key activity that companies should review from time to time is the evaluation of trade discounts. Trade discounts should be evaluated using the following formula, which computes the implicit rate (of return) represented by the trade discount offer; that is, it is the equivalent return to the customer of an alternative investment. The implicit rate is calculated as follows:

$$\text{Cost of trade credit} = \left(1 + \frac{\text{Discount}}{1 - \text{Discount}}\right)^{\left(\frac{365}{\text{Number of days beyond discount period}}\right)} - 1$$

The cost of funds during the discount period is 0 percent; so it is beneficial for the customer to pay close to the end of the discount period. Once the discount period ends, the cost of the credit to the customer jumps up and then declines as the net day is approached. For example, if the terms are 2/10, net 30, which means that there is a 2 percent discount for paying within 10 days and the net amount is due by the thirtieth day, the cost of trade credit is 109 percent if the credit is paid on the twentieth day, but it is only 44.6 percent if paid on the thirtieth day.

If the customer's cost of funds or short-term investment rate is less than the calculated rate, the discount offers a better return or incremental return over the company's short-term borrowing rate.

---

[9]Keep in mind that stretching payments beyond their due dates might be considered unethical and may draw retaliation from suppliers in the form of tighter credit terms in the future.

EXAMPLE 6-6   Evaluating Trade Discounts

Compute the cost of trade credit if terms are 1/10, net 30 and the account is paid on

- The twentieth day.
- The thirtieth day.

Solution

$$\text{Cost of trade credit if paid on day 20} = \left(1 + \frac{0.01}{1 - 0.01}\right)^{\left(365/10\right)} - 1$$

$$= 44.32 \text{ percent}$$

$$\text{Cost of trade credit if paid on day 30} = \left(1 + \frac{0.01}{1 - 0.01}\right)^{\left(365/20\right)} - 1$$

$$= 20.13 \text{ percent}$$

As you can see, the cost of the credit is much lower when the company pays on the net day than any day prior to the net day.

7.2. Managing Cash Disbursements

Handling cash disbursements effectively is a common goal for most companies. To accomplish this, companies use best practices that include the ability to delay funding bank accounts until the day checks clear, to erect safeguards against check fraud, to pay electronically when it is cost-effective to do so, and to manage bank charges for disbursement services. Best practices in cash disbursements, like check collections, depend on the nature of the payments—i.e., whether they are made electronically or by check.

Banks offer controlled disbursement services to optimize the funding of checks on the same day they clear against the company's account. When combined with a positive pay service, which provides a filter against check fraud, this method provides the best practice in handling paper-based (check) disbursements.

7.3. Evaluating Accounts Payable Management

The number of days of payables, which is also referred to as the average age of payables, is a useful measure in evaluating a company's credit extension and collection.

If the accounts payable balance from the company's balance sheet is €450 million and the amount of purchases is €4,100 million, the number of days of payables is

$$\text{Number of days of payables} = \frac{\text{Accounts payable}}{\text{Average days purchases}}$$

$$= \frac{450}{4100/365} = 40.06 \text{ days}$$

Comparing the number of days of payables with the credit terms under which credit was granted to the company is important. Paying sooner than necessary is costly in terms of the cost of credit, and paying later than the net day is costly in terms of relations with suppliers.

In some cases, treasurers manage the company's payables closely, comparing the number of days of payables with the number of days of inventory because in some industries these two numbers of days are similar to one another.

8. MANAGING SHORT-TERM FINANCING

An overall short-term financial strategy should focus on assuring that the company maintains a sound liquidity position. It should also reflect the degree of risk the company believes can be managed without affecting the company's stability. It is common to consider short-term financial strategies as applying mostly to investments. However, they should include other financial activities as well. In many cases, a company is only an investor or borrower, but it is common for large multinational corporations to have both short-term investments and short-term borrowing.

A short-term policy should include guidelines for managing investment, borrowing, foreign exchange, and risk management activities, and it should encompass all the company's operations, including foreign subsidiaries and other domestic subsidiaries that are self-financing. These guidelines accomplish several things.

Too often companies do not explore their options sufficiently, and, as a result, they do not take advantage of cost savings that some forms of borrowing offer. This lack of awareness usually indicates that a company's treasurer may not be familiar with the common forms of short-term borrowing and has not factored them into an effective borrowing strategy.

8.1. Sources of Short-Term Financing

The main types of short-term borrowing alternatives that borrowers should consider include bank sources as well as money market sources. The main types of bank short-term borrowing include uncommitted and committed bank lines of credit and revolving credit agreements ("revolvers"). The latter two types can be unsecured or secured, depending on the company's financial strength and the general credit situation, which may vary from country to country. Two of these types—uncommitted lines and revolvers—are more common in the United States, whereas regular lines are more common in other parts of the world. We provide examples of several types of short-term borrowing options in Exhibit 6-15 on page 300, with bank sources in Panel A of this exhibit and nonbank sources in Panel B. In this exhibit, we provide the primary features for each type of borrowing, including the typical users, source(s) for the alternative, the base rate for computing interest, type of compensation required, and any other comments.

Uncommitted lines of credit are, as the name suggests, the weakest form of bank borrowing. A bank may offer an uncommitted line of credit for an extended period of time, but it reserves the right to refuse to honor any request for use of the line. In other words, an uncommitted line is very unstable and is only as good as the bank's desire to offer it. Therefore, companies should not rely very much on uncommitted lines. In fact, banks do not officially acknowledge that an uncommitted line is usable, which means that uncommitted lines cannot be shown as a financial reserve in a footnote to the company's financial statements.

EXHIBIT 6-15   Short-Term Financing Instruments

Panel A: Bank Sources

Source/Type	Users	Rate Base	Compensation	Other
Uncommitted line	Large corporations	Prime (U.S.) or base rate (other countries), money market, LIBOR+	None	Mainly in U.S.; limited reliability
Regular line	All sizes		Commitment fee	Common everywhere
Overdraft line	All sizes		Commitment fee	Mainly outside U.S.
Revolving credit agreement	Larger corporations		Commitment fee + extra fees	Strongest form (primarily in U.S.)
Collateralized loan	Small, weak borrowers	Base+	Collateral	Common everywhere
Discounted receivables	Large companies	Varies	Extra fees	More overseas, but some in U.S.
Banker's acceptances	International companies	Spread over commercial paper	None	Small volume
Factoring	Smaller	Prime++	Service fees	Special industries

Panel B: Nonbank Sources

Source/Type	Users	Rate Base	Compensation	Other
Nonbank finance companies	Small, weak borrowers	Prime+++	Service fees	Weak credits
Commercial paper	Largest corporations	Money market sets rate	Backup line of credit, commissions+	Lowest rates for short-term funds

The primary attraction of uncommitted lines is that they do not require any compensation other than interest.

Committed lines of credit are the form of bank line of credit that most companies refer to as regular lines of credit. They are stronger than uncommitted because of the bank's formal commitment, which can be verified through an acknowledgment letter as part of the annual financial audit and can be footnoted in the company's annual report. These lines of credit are in effect for 364 days (one day short of a full year). This effectively makes sure that they are short-term liabilities, usually classified as notes payable or the equivalent, on the financial statements.

Regular lines are unsecured and are prepayable without any penalties. The borrowing rate is a negotiated item. The most common interest rates negotiated are borrowing at the bank's prime rate or at a money market rate plus a spread. The most common money market rate is an offshore rate—the London Interbank Offered Rate (LIBOR), which is a Eurodollar rate—plus a spread. The spread varies depending on the borrower's creditworthiness. Regular lines, unlike uncommitted lines, require compensation, usually in the form of a commitment fee. The fee is typically a fractional percentage (e.g., ½ percent) of the full amount or the unused amount of the line, depending on bank–company negotiations.

Revolving credit agreements, which are often referred to as revolvers, are the strongest form of short-term bank borrowing facilities. They have formal legal agreements that define the aspects of the agreement. These agreements are similar to regular lines with respect to borrowing rates, compensation, and being unsecured. Revolvers differ in that they are in effect for multiple years (e.g., 3–5 years) and may have optional medium-term loan features. In addition, they are often done for much larger amounts than a regular line, and these larger amounts are spread out among more than one bank.

For companies with weak financial positions, such as those facing financial distress or with deteriorated profitability, and for many smaller companies that do not have sufficient capital, banks or other lenders (see nonbank sources in Exhibit 6-15) require that the company (or individual for much smaller companies) provide collateral in the form of an asset, such as a fixed asset that the company owns or high-quality receivables and inventory. These assets are pledged against the loans, and banks or other lenders file a lien against them with the state in which the loan is made. This lien becomes part of the borrower's financial record and is shown on its credit report.

8.2.   Short-Term Borrowing Approaches

Given the various forms of short-term borrowing, it is essential that a borrower have a planned strategy before getting stuck in an uneconomical situation. Many borrowing companies spend too little time establishing a sound strategy for their short-term borrowing beyond making sure that they are able to borrow at all from any source.

The major objectives of a short-term borrowing strategy include

- Assuring that there is sufficient capacity to handle peak cash needs;
- Maintaining sufficient sources of credit to be able to fund ongoing cash needs; and
- Assuring that rates obtained are cost-effective and do not substantially exceed market averages.

In addition, borrowers should consider several factors as part of their short-term borrowing strategies, including the following:

- *Size and creditworthiness:* There is no doubt that the size of the borrower dictates the options available. Larger companies can take advantage of economies of scale to access commercial paper, banker's acceptances, and so on. The size of the borrower often reflects a manufacturing company's need for short-term financing. The size of lender is also an important criterion because large banks have heightened house or legal lending limits. The creditworthiness of the borrower determines the rate, compensation, or even whether the loan will be made at all.
- *Sufficient access:* Borrowers should diversify to have adequate alternatives and not be too reliant on one lender or form of lending if the amount of their lending is very large. Even so, it is typical for borrowers to use one alternative primarily, but often with more than one provider. Borrowers should be ready to go to other sources and know how to. Borrowers should not stay too long with just one source or with the lowest rates. Many borrowers are usually prepared to trade off rates (somewhat) for certainty.
- *Flexibility of borrowing options:* "Flexibility" means the ability to manage maturities efficiently; that is, there should not be any "big" days, when significant amounts of loans mature. To do this successfully, borrowers need active maturity management, awareness of the market conditions (e.g., knowing when the market or certain maturities should be avoided), and the ability to prepay loans when unexpected cash receipts happen.

Borrowing strategies, like investment strategies, can be either passive or active. Passive strategies usually involve minimal activity with one source or type of borrowing and with little (if any) planning. This "take what you can get" strategy is often reactive in responding to immediate needs or "panic attacks." Passive strategies are characterized by steady, often routine rollovers of borrowings for the same amount of funds each time, without much comparison shopping. Passive strategies may also arise when borrowing is restricted, such as instances where borrowers are limited to one or two lenders by agreement (e.g., in a secured loan arrangement).

Active strategies are usually more flexible, reflecting planning, reliable forecasting, and seeking the best deal. With active strategies, borrowers are more in control and do not fall into the rollover "trap" that is possible with passive strategies.

Many active strategies are matching strategies. Matching borrowing strategies function in a manner similar to matching investment strategies; loans are scheduled to mature when large cash receipts are expected. These receipts can pay back the loan; so the company does not have to invest the funds at potentially lower rates than the borrowing cost, thereby creating unnecessary costs.

8.3. Asset-Based Loans

Many companies that do not have the credit quality sufficient to qualify for unsecured bank loans may borrow from financial institutions by arranging for a secured loan, where the loan is secured using assets of the company. These secured loans are often referred to as **asset-based loans**. Often the assets used in short-term secured loans are the current assets of receivables and inventory. Unlike the collateral that may be used in longer-term borrowing, asset-based loans secured by accounts receivable and inventory present a challenge for the lender because the cash flows from accounts receivable depend on the amount and timing of collections and are influenced by the business risk of the company and its customers.

Lenders of these short-term asset-based loans are protected by the existence of the collateral and by provisions in the law that may provide them with a blanket lien on current and future assets of the company. The downside of a blanket lien is that even if the asset-based loan is secured by, say, accounts receivable, the lender may have a legal interest in other assets of the company until the loan is repaid.

Besides using working capital as the security for a loan, a company can use other means to generate cash flow from these working capital accounts. For example, a company can use its accounts receivable to generate cash flow through the **assignment of accounts receivable**, which is the use of these receivables as collateral for a loan, or a company can factor its accounts receivable, which is selling the receivables to the factor. In an assignment arrangement, the company remains responsible for the collection of the accounts, whereas in a factoring arrangement the company is shifting the credit granting and collection process to the factor. The cost of this credit depends on the credit quality of the accounts and the costs of collection.

Like accounts receivables, inventory may be a source of cash flow through the use of the inventory as collateral, with different types of arrangements possible:

• An **inventory blanket lien**, in which the lender has a claim on some or all of the company's inventory, but the company can sell the inventory in the ordinary course of business.

- A **trust receipt arrangement**, in which the lender requires the company to certify that the goods are segregated and held in trust, with proceeds of any sale remitted to the lender immediately.
- A **warehouse receipt arrangement**, similar to the trust receipt arrangement, but a third party (i.e., a warehouse company) supervises the inventory.

The cost of asset-based loans security by inventory depends on the length of time it takes to sell the goods.

8.4. Computing the Costs of Borrowing

In carrying out a sound short-term borrowing strategy, one of the key decisions is selecting the most cost-effective form of short-term loan. However, this selection is often not a simple task, because each of the major forms has to be adjusted to be on a common basis for comparability. The fundamental rule is to compute the total cost of the form of borrowing and divide that number by the total amount of loan you received (i.e., net proceeds), adjusted for any discounting or compensating balances.

For example, in the case of a line of credit that requires a commitment fee,[10] the cost of the line of credit is

$$\text{Cost} = \frac{\text{Interest} + \text{Commitment fee}}{\text{Loan amount}}$$

On the other hand, if the interest rate is stated as "all-inclusive" such that the amount borrowed includes the interest, as may be the case in a banker's acceptance, the interest is compared with the net proceeds when determining the cost:

$$\text{Cost} = \frac{\text{Interest}}{\text{Net proceeds}}$$
$$= \frac{\text{Interest}}{\text{Loan amount} - \text{Interest}}$$

If there are dealer's fees and other fees, the cost must consider the expenses beyond the interest. For example, if a borrowing involves a dealer's fee and a backup fee and is quoted as all-inclusive, the cost is

$$\text{Cost} = \frac{\text{Interest} + \text{Dealer's commission} + \text{Backup costs}}{\text{Loan amount} - \text{Interest}}$$

The key is to compare the interest and fees paid with the net proceeds of the loan. If the loan is for a period less than a year, then we annualize accordingly.

---

[10]A commitment fee is a fee paid to the lender in return for the legal commitment to lend funds in the future.

EXAMPLE 6-7   Computing the Effective Cost of Short-Term Borrowing Alternatives

You are asked to select one of the following choices as the best offer for borrowing $5 million for one month:

1. Drawing down on a line of credit at 6.5 percent with a 1/2 percent commitment fee on the full amount.
2. A banker's acceptance at 6.75 percent, an all-inclusive rate.
3. Commercial paper at 6.15 percent with a dealer's commission of 1/8 percent and a backup line cost of 1/4 percent, both of which would be assessed on the $5 million of commercial paper issued.

Solution

Line of credit cost:

$$\text{Line cost} = \frac{\text{Interest} + \text{commitment fee}}{\text{Usable loan amount}} \times 12$$

$$= \frac{\left(0.065 \times \$5,000,000 \times \frac{1}{12}\right) + \left(0.005 \times \$5,000,000 \times \frac{1}{12}\right)}{\$5,000,000} \times 12$$

$$= \frac{\$27,083.33 + 2,083.33}{\$5,000,000} \times 12$$

$$= 0.07 \text{ or } 7 \text{ percent}$$

Banker's acceptance cost:

$$\text{BA cost} = \frac{\text{Interest}}{\text{Net proceeds}} \times 12$$

$$= \frac{0.0675 \times \$5,000,000 \times \frac{1}{12}}{\$5,000,000 - \left(0.0675 \times \$5,000,000 \times \frac{1}{12}\right)} \times 12$$

$$= \frac{\$28,125}{\$4,971,875} \times 12$$

$$= 0.0679 \text{ or } 6.79 \text{ percent}$$

Commercial paper cost (quoted as nominal rate at a discount):

$$\text{CP cost} = \frac{\text{Interest} + \text{Dealer's commission} + \text{Back-up costs}}{\text{Net proceeds}} \times 12$$

$$= \frac{\left(0.0615 \times \$5,000,000 \times \frac{1}{12}\right) + \left(0.00125 \times \$5,000,000 \times \frac{1}{12}\right) + \left(0.0025 \times \$5,000,000 \times \frac{1}{12}\right)}{\$5,000,000 - \left(0.0615 \times \$5,000,000 \times \frac{1}{12}\right)} \times 12$$

$$= \frac{\$25,625 + 520.83 + 1041.67}{\$5,000,000 - 25,625} \times 12$$

$$= 0.0656 \text{ or } 6.56 \text{ percent}$$

We have simplified this cost analysis by assuming a loan for one month, using a factor of one-twelfth to determine the interest and a factor of 12 to annualize. For specific arrangements for which the cost is determined using a 365-day or 360-day year, the appropriate adjustment is required.

As the results show, the commercial paper alternative comes out with the lowest effective cost, and the line of credit has the highest effective cost. The commitment fee that was payable on the full line added more costs than the additional fees and discounting effects added in the other two options.

Line cost	7.00 percent
Banker's acceptance cost	6.79 percent
Commercial paper cost	6.56 percent

9. SUMMARY

In this chapter, we considered a key aspect of financial management: the management of a company's working capital. This aspect of finance is a critical one in that it ensures, if done effectively, that the company will stay solvent and remain in business. If done improperly, the results can be disastrous for the company.

Working capital management covers a wide range of activities, most of which are focused on or involve the company's cash levels. Competing uses for the company's cash, which is often a scarce resource, create the need for an efficient method of handling the short-term financing of company activities.

Major points that were covered in this chapter:

- Understanding how to evaluate a company's liquidity position.
- Calculating and interpreting operating and cash conversion cycles.
- Evaluating overall working capital effectiveness of a company and comparing it with other peer companies.

- Identifying the components of a cash forecast to be able to prepare a short-term (i.e., up to one year) cash forecast.
- Understanding the common types of short-term investments and computing comparable yields on securities.
- Measuring the performance of a company's accounts receivable function.
- Measuring the financial performance of a company's inventory management function.
- Measuring the performance of a company's accounts payable function.
- Evaluating the short-term financing choices available to a company and recommending a financing method.

Working capital management is an integral part of the financial management of a company because many short-term activities have effects on long-term financial decisions. Having an effective short-term financial strategy, for example, allows a company to plan ahead with the confidence that its short-term concerns are being handled properly. Perhaps unlike other areas of finance, short-term finance has more qualitative features, making each company's case somewhat different from another's. This unique nature, combined with the short time frame associated with this aspect of finance, makes short-term finance a dynamic, challenging activity.

PRACTICE PROBLEMS

1. Suppose a company has a current ratio of 2.5x and a quick ratio of 1.5x. If the company's current liabilities are €100 million, the amount of inventory is closest to
   A. €50 million.
   B. €100 million.
   C. €150 million.
   D. €200 million.

2. Given the following financial statement data, calculate the operating cycle for this company.

	($ millions)
Credit sales	25,000
Cost of goods sold	20,000
Accounts receivable	2,500
Inventory—beginning balance	2,000
Inventory—ending balance	2,300
Accounts payable	1,700

The operating cycle for this company is *closest* to
A. 36.5 days.
B. 42.0 days.
C. 47.9 days.
D. 78.5 days.

3. Given the following financial statement data, calculate the net operating cycle for this company.

	($ millions)
Credit sales	40,000
Cost of goods sold	30,000
Accounts receivable	3,000
Inventory—beginning balance	1,500
Inventory—ending balance	2,000
Accounts payable	4,000

The net operating cycle of this company is *closest* to
A. 3.8 days.
B. 24.3 days.
C. 27.4 days.
D. 51.7 days.

4. The bond equivalent yield for a 182-day U.S. Treasury bill that has a price of $9,725 per $10,000 face value is *closest* to
A. 5.41%.
B. 5.53%.
C. 5.67%.
D. 5.79%.

5. A company increasing its credit terms for customers from 1/10, net 30 to 1/10, net 60 will likely experience
A. An increase in cash on hand.
B. An increase in the average collection period.
C. Higher net income.
D. A higher level of uncollectible accounts.

6. Suppose a company uses trade credit with the terms of 2/10, net 50. If the company pays its account on the fiftieth day, the effective borrowing cost of skipping the discount on day 10 is *closest* to
A. 14.6%.
B. 14.9%.
C. 15.0%.
D. 20.2%.

7. William Jones is evaluating three possible means of borrowing $1 million for one month:
   - Drawing down on a *line of credit* at 7.2 percent with a ½ percent commitment fee on the full amount with no compensating balances.
   - A *banker's acceptance* at 7.1 percent, an all-inclusive rate.
   - *Commercial paper* at 6.9 percent with a dealer's commission of 1/4 percent and a backup line cost of 1/3 percent, both of these would be assessed on the $1 million of commercial paper issued.

Which of these forms of borrowing results in the lowest cost of credit?
A. Line of credit.
B. Banker's acceptance.
C. Commercial paper.
D. All three forms have identical costs of borrowing.

The following information relates to Problems 8 through 12.

Mary Gonzales is evaluating companies in the office supply industry and has compiled the following information:

Company	20X1 ($ million)		20X2 ($ million)	
	Credit Sales	Average Receivables Balance	Credit Sales	Average Receivables Balance
A	5.0	1.0	6.0	1.2
B	3.0	1.2	4.0	1.5
C	2.5	0.8	3.0	1.0
D	0.5	0.1	0.6	0.2
Industry	25.0	5.0	28.0	5.4

8. Which of the companies had the highest number of days of receivables for the year 20X1?
A. Company A.
B. Company B.
C. Company C.
D. Company D.

9. Which of the companies has the lowest accounts receivable turnover in the year 20X2?
A. Company A.
B. Company B.
C. Company C.
D. Company D.

10. The industry average receivables collection period
A. Increased from 20X1 to 20X2.
B. Decreased from 20X1 to 20X2.
C. Did not change from 20X1 to 20X2.
D. Increased, along with the increase in the industry accounts receivable turnover.

11. Which of the companies reduced the average time it took to collect on accounts receivable from 20X1 to 20X2?
A. Company A.
B. Company B.
C. Company C.
D. Company D.

12. Gonzales determined that Company A had an operating cycle of 100 days in 20X2, whereas Company D had an operating cycle of 145 days for the same fiscal year. This means that

    A. Company D's inventory turnover is less than that of Company A.
    B. Company D's inventory turnover is greater than that of Company A.
    C. Company D's cash conversion cycle is shorter than that of Company A.
    D. Company D's cash conversion cycle is longer than that of Company A.

CHAPTER 7

FINANCIAL STATEMENT ANALYSIS

Pamela Peterson Drake, CFA

James Madison University
Harrisonburg, Virginia

LEARNING OUTCOMES

After completing this chapter, you will be able to do the following:

- Interpret common-size balance sheets and common-size income statements, discuss the circumstances under which the use of common-size financial statements is appropriate, and demonstrate their use by applying either vertical analysis or horizontal analysis.
- Calculate, interpret, and discuss measures of a company's operating efficiency, internal liquidity (liquidity ratios), solvency, and profitability, and demonstrate the use of these measures in company analysis.
- Calculate, interpret, and discuss variations of the DuPont expression and demonstrate use of the DuPont approach in corporate analysis.
- Calculate, interpret, and contrast basic earnings per share and diluted earnings per share.
- Calculate, interpret, and discuss book value of equity per share, price-to-earnings ratio, dividends per share, dividend payout ratio, and plowback ratio.
- Demonstrate the use of pro forma income and balance sheet statements.

1. INTRODUCTION

The **financial analysis** of a company is a process of selecting, evaluating, and interpreting financial data, along with other pertinent information, in order to formulate an assessment of the company's present and future financial condition and performance. We can use financial analysis to evaluate the efficiency of a company's operations, its ability to manage expenses, the effectiveness of its credit policies, and its creditworthiness, among other things.

The analyst draws the data needed in financial analysis from many sources. The primary source of these data is the company itself, through its annual and quarterly reports and other required disclosures. The annual report comprises the income statement, the balance sheet, the statement of cash flows, and the statement of shareholders' equity, as well as footnotes to these statements and management's discussion and analysis.

In addition to information that companies are required to disclose through financial statements, we can find other useful information quite readily, including the market prices of securities of publicly traded corporations and industry statistics. Another source of information is economic data, such as the gross domestic product (GDP), the producer price index (PPI), and the consumer price index (CPI), which we can use in assessing the recent performance or future prospects of a company or industry.[1]

Suppose you are evaluating a company that owns a chain of retail outlets. What information do you need to judge the company's performance and financial condition? You need financial data, but those data do not tell the whole story. You also need information on consumer spending, producer prices, consumer prices, and competition. These are economic data that are readily available from government and private sources. We are often concerned about how a company performs in different economic climates; so we would want to make sure to evaluate the company through at least one full economic cycle.[2]

In addition to financial statement data, market data, and economic data, we also need to examine events that may help explain the company's present condition and may have a bearing on its future prospects. For example, did the company recently close production facilities? Is the company developing a new product or acquiring another company? Current events can provide information that may be incorporated into financial analysis, both to explain recent performance and to help predict future performance.

The financial analyst must select the pertinent information, analyze it, and interpret the analysis, offering judgments on the current and future financial condition and operating performance of the company. This chapter introduces you to the tools of financial analysis. These tools include common-size analysis, financial ratio analysis, and pro forma analysis.

In common-size analysis, we restate financial statements in a form that helps the analyst detect significant changes and trends. The approach requires us to use a reference point—either an account in a given financial statement or a prior year's entire statement—to scale the financial statement data. This approach allows us to compare a company with itself over time or to compare companies of different sizes.

In financial ratio analysis, we select relevant information—primarily from the financial statement data—and evaluate it in the context of other financial data, as well as over time and in comparison with other companies or the industry. We show how to incorporate market data and economic data into the analysis and interpretation of financial ratios.

In pro forma analysis, we use what we have learned through common-size and financial ratio analyses to forecast the company's financial condition and performance. We can then use these pro forma statements to perform sensitivity analyses for future periods.

---

[1]In the United States, for example, the GDP is calculated by the U.S. Department of Commerce, Bureau of Economic Analysis, and the PPI and CPI are produced by the U.S. Department of Labor, Bureau of Labor Statistics.

[2]An economic cycle is generally viewed as the period over which we can observe expansion, a peak, recession, and a trough in economic activity.

2. COMMON-SIZE ANALYSIS

If we examine financial statements over time for a company, it is fairly difficult to spot changes in relationships because the scale of the company's accounts changes over time due to inflation, growth, and acquisitions and divestitures. It is also challenging to compare financial statements of companies of different sizes. A technique that we can use to control for the scale effect is common-size analysis.

Common-size analysis is the restatement of financial statement items using a common denominator or reference item that allows us to identify trends and major differences. There are two types of common-size analysis. The most common is **vertical common-size analysis**, in which we compare the accounts in a given period to a benchmark item in that same year.

- For the income statement, the benchmark is revenues. For a given period, each item in the income statement is restated as a percentage of revenues.
- For the balance sheet, the benchmark is total assets. For a given point in time, each item in the balance sheet is restated as a percentage of total assets.

The analyst can then compare these proportions across time and across the company's industry:

- Comparing the same company in different years allows us to focus on changes in the composition of accounts or expenses over time.
- Comparison with competitors' vertical common-size statements for the same year allows us to examine differences in the makeup of accounts for similar companies.
- Comparison of the company's vertical common-size statements with competitors' common-size statements over time allows the analyst to compare shifts in accounts over time.

Another form of common-size analysis is **horizontal common-size analysis**, in which we use the accounts in a given period as the benchmark or base period and restate every account in

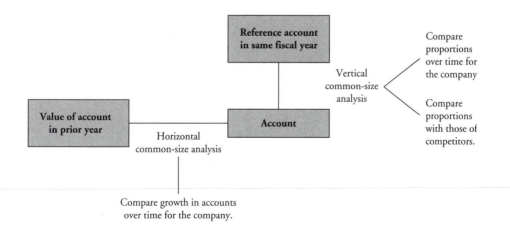

subsequent periods as a percentage of the base period's same account. Horizontal common-size analysis is a time-series analysis and is useful for identifying trends and growth in accounts over time. Whereas each account in a vertical common-size analysis is restated each year as a proportion of the reference account (e.g., revenues or total assets), each account in a horizontal common-size analysis is instead compared with the value of that same account in a benchmark year.

2.1. Vertical Common-Size Analysis

We use vertical common-size analysis to analyze patterns in profitability (using common-size income statements) and patterns in investments and financing (using common-size balance sheets). Because we scale each account by the reference account, we can also use the resulting percentages to make comparisons across companies. For example, we can get a sense of how profit margins have changed over time by examining gross profit as a percentage of revenues over successive periods. Additionally, we can examine this percentage relative to the company's competitors. We can also see how a company's reliance on debt financing has changed over time by focusing on liabilities as a percentage of assets. Moreover, we can represent this information in graphical form, which allows us to more readily visualize trends in these components over time.

To see how this approach works, consider The Procter & Gamble Company's financial statements for 2003 and 2004, summarized below. The reported financial data from the "Amount" columns have been converted into percentages of revenues (i.e., common-size statements), shown in the "Common-Size Statement" columns:

	Amount ($ millions)		Common-Size Statement (% of revenues)	
Fiscal year ending June 30	**2003**	**2004**	**2003**	**2004**
Revenues	43,377	51,407	100.0	100.0
Cost of goods sold	22,141	25,076	51.0	48.8
Gross profit	21,236	26,331	49.0	51.2
Selling, general, and administrative expenses	13,383	16,504	30.9	32.1
Operating income	7,853	9,827	18.1	19.1
Interest expense	561	629	1.3	1.2
Other nonoperating income, net	238	152	0.5	0.3
Earnings before income taxes	7,530	9,350	17.4	18.2
Income tax	2,344	2,869	5.4	5.6
Net income	5,186	6,481	12.0	12.6

Preparing these statements over several periods allows us to spot trends and interruptions in trends. For example, we can examine changes in profitability by comparing various expenses and net income as percentages of revenues, as in Exhibit 7-1. Panel A shows the dollar amounts of income and expenses, whereas Panel B shows the common-size income statement. In Panel B, in which everything has been scaled relative to revenues, it is easier to see the proportions of income and expenses and how those proportions changed over the years. In Panel B, we see that Procter & Gamble's net income has increased over time as a percentage of sales and that this increase is concurrent with a gradual decrease in the cost of sales.

EXHIBIT 7-1   Procter & Gamble Company Income Statements (1995–2004)

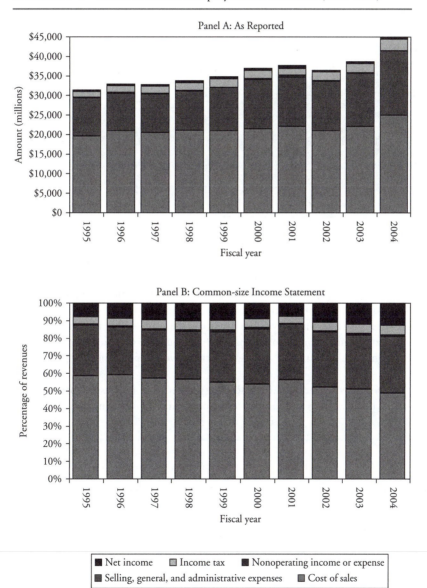

Source: Data from the Procter & Gamble Company annual reports, various years.

As we did for the income statement, we can restate Procter & Gamble's reported balance sheet items in terms of a percentage of total assets:

	Amount ($ millions)		Common-Size Statement (% of assets)	
Fiscal year ending June 30	**2003**	**2004**	**2003**	**2004**
Cash, cash equivalents, and marketable securities	5,912	5,469	13.5	9.6
Investment securities	300	423	0.7	0.7
Accounts receivable	3,038	4,062	7.0	7.1
Inventories	3,640	4,400	8.3	7.7
Deferred income taxes	843	958	1.9	1.7
Prepaid expenses and other receivables	1,487	1,803	3.4	3.2
Total current assets	15,220	17,115	34.8	30.0
Net property, plant, and equipment	13,104	14,108	30.0	24.7
Intangible assets	13,507	23,900	30.9	41.9
Other assets	1,875	1,925	4.3	3.4
Total assets	43,706	57,048	100.0	100.0

As with the income statement, it is also helpful to represent common-size balance sheet accounts over several successive periods, as in Exhibit 7-2, to gauge how the company's investments have changed over time. From an examination of these proportions over time, we can see how the company's investments in working capital accounts, fixed assets, and intangible assets have changed over the years. In the case of Procter & Gamble, there is an increase in the investment in intangibles, attributable to goodwill and other intangibles through acquisitions, and a lower relative investment in net property, plant, and equipment.

We can similarly restate liabilities and equity in terms of total assets, providing a look at patterns and changes in the composition of the company's capital structure.

	Amount ($ millions)		Common-Size Statement (% of assets)	
Fiscal year ending June 30	**2003**	**2004**	**2003**	**2004**
Accounts payable	2,795	3,617	6.4	6.3
Accrued and other liabilities	5,512	7,689	12.6	13.5
Taxes payable	1,879	2,554	4.3	4.5
Debt due in one year	2,172	8,287	5.0	14.5
Total current liabilities	12,358	22,147	28.3	38.8

	Amount ($ millions)		Common-Size Statement (% of assets)	
Long-term debt	11,475	12,554	26.3	22.0
Deferred income taxes	1,396	2,261	3.2	4.0
Other noncurrent liabilities	2,291	2,808	5.2	4.9
Total liabilities	27,520	39,770	63.0	69.7
Convertible Class A preferred stock	1,580	1,526	3.6	2.7
Common shareholders' equity	14,606	15,752	33.4	27.6
Total shareholders' equity	16,186	17,278	37.0	30.3
Total liabilities and shareholders' equity	43,706	57,048	100.0	100.0

The common-size liabilities and equity for the years 1995–2004 are provided in Exhibit 7-3. As we can see in this exhibit, Procter & Gamble has increased its relative use of debt in its capital structure over time, most notably following 1999, which coincides with its major restructuring in the 1999–2001 period.

2.2. Horizontal Common-Size Analysis

In horizontal common-size analysis, we use a base year as the benchmark and then restate all subsequent years relative to that base. In the case of Procter & Gamble, if we choose

EXHIBIT 7-2   Common-Size Assets of Procter & Gamble, 1995–2004

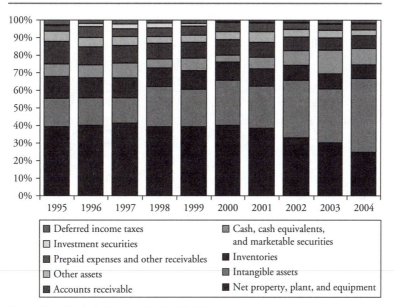

Source: Data from the Procter & Gamble Company annual reports, various years.

EXHIBIT 7-3   Common-Size Liabilities and Equity for Procter & Gamble, 1995–2004

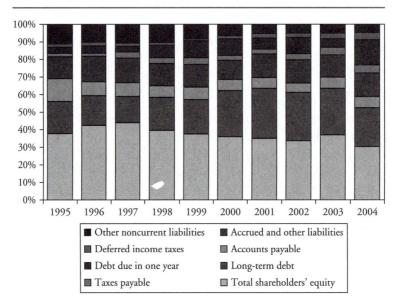

Source: Data from the Procter & Gamble Company annual reports, various years.

2003 as the base, we would then calculate the common-size income statement for 2004 as follows:[3]

	Amount ($ millions)		Common-Size Statement (% of 2003 value)	
Fiscal year ending June 30	**2003**	**2004**	**2003**	**2004**
Revenues	43,377	51,407	100.0	118.5
Cost of goods sold	22,141	25,076	100.0	113.3
Gross profit	21,236	26,331	100.0	124.0
Selling, general, and administrative expenses	13,383	16,504	100.0	123.3
Operating income	7,853	9,827	100.0	125.1
Interest expense	561	629	100.0	112.1
Other nonoperating income, net	238	152	100.0	63.9
Earnings before income taxes	7,530	9,350	100.0	124.2
Income tax	2,344	2,869	100.0	122.4
Net income	5,186	6,481	100.0	125.0

[3]Horizontal common-size analysis, as in this example, is often also referred to as "common-base-year analysis." Note that for illustrative purposes we are examining the difference between two years. In practice, however, an analyst would typically examine trends over several years.

We can see that the growth in net income is traceable largely to the slower growth of cost of goods sold and interest expense relative to revenue growth.

Calculating Procter & Gamble's common-size assets for 2004 relative to 2003, we see that much of the growth in assets is attributable to the growth in intangible assets:

	Amount ($ millions)		Common-Size statement (% of 2003 value)	
Fiscal year ending June 30	**2003**	**2004**	**2003**	**2004**
Cash, cash equivalents, and marketable securities	5,912	5,469	100.0	92.5
Investment securities	300	423	100.0	141.0
Accounts receivable	3,038	4,062	100.0	133.7
Inventories	3,640	4,400	100.0	120.9
Deferred income taxes	843	958	100.0	113.6
Prepaid expenses and other receivables	1,487	1,803	100.0	121.3
Total current assets	15,220	17,115	100.0	112.5
Net property, plant, and equipment	13,104	14,108	100.0	107.7
Intangible assets	13,507	23,900	100.0	176.9
Other assets	1,875	1,925	100.0	102.7
Total assets	43,706	57,048	100.0	130.5

Procter & Gamble's common-size liabilities for 2004 relative to 2003 indicate that much of the growth in assets was financed by debt rather than equity:

	Amount ($ millions)		Common-Size Statement (% of 2003 value)	
Fiscal year ending June 30	**2003**	**2004**	**2003**	**2004**
Accounts payable	2,795	3,617	100.0	129.4
Accrued and other liabilities	5,512	7,689	100.0	139.5
Taxes payable	1,879	2,554	100.0	135.9
Debt due in one year	2,172	8,287	100.0	381.5
Total current liabilities	12,358	22,147	100.0	179.2
Long-term debt	11,475	$12,554	100.0	109.4
Deferred income taxes	1,396	2,261	100.0	162.0
Other noncurrent liabilities	2,291	2,808	100.0	122.6
Total liabilities	27,520	39,770	100.0	144.5
Convertible Class A preferred stock	1,580	1,526	100.0	96.6
Common shareholders' equity	14,606	15,752	100.0	107.8
Total shareholders' equity	16,186	17,278	100.0	106.7
Total liabilities and shareholders' equity	43,706	57,048	100.0	130.5

In the case of Procter & Gamble, total liabilities rose 44.5 percent from 2003 to 2004, whereas shareholders' equity increased by only 6.7 percent. We can also see that the increase in current liabilities is primarily attributable to the increase in debt due in one year.

As you can see in our example of Procter & Gamble, common-size analysis is useful for comparing different periods because we have scaled all the accounts either to a reference point within the statement (vertical common-size analysis) or to a reference point in time (horizontal common-size analysis). We can also use common-size analysis to aid in our comparisons of companies of different sizes. For example, to compare Procter & Gamble with Clorox, a much smaller company, we can apply vertical common-size analysis to scale the assets in the balance sheet for each company:

	2004 Amounts ($ millions)		Common-Size Statement (% of total assets)	
Fiscal year ending June 30	**Clorox**	**P&G**	**Clorox**	**P&G**
Cash, cash equivalents, and marketable securities	232	5,469	6.1	9.6
Investment securities	0	423	0.0	0.7
Accounts receivable	460	4,062	12.0	7.1
Inventories	306	4,400	8.0	7.7
Other current assets	45	2,761	1.2	4.8
Total current assets	1,043	17,115	27.2	30.0
Net property, plant, and equipment	1,052	14,108	27.4	24.7
Intangible assets	1,375	23,900	35.9	41.9
Other assets	364	1,925	9.5	3.4
Total assets	3,834	57,048	100.0	100.0

We can see from this comparison that Clorox has a heavier investment in accounts receivable than Procter & Gamble, less invested in intangible assets, and less in cash and cash equivalents.

3. FINANCIAL RATIO ANALYSIS

Financial ratio analysis is the use of financial accounting and other information to assess a company's financial performance and financial condition. Specifically, financial ratio analysis uses comparisons of financial data in the form of ratios to assess a company's financial health and profitability.

Hundreds of ratios can be formed using available financial data. One of the challenges in financial analysis is determining which ratios are the most appropriate for the company in question. In the analysis of a retail store, for example, ratios that relate to inventory, collections on credit, and comparative sales on a per-store basis are informative in assessing financial performance. However, in assessing the success of an airline, ratios such as seats sold versus capacity, costs per passenger or flight mile, and efficiency in using the investment in aircraft would be important, whereas ratios related to inventory or collections on credit might be less useful.

Another challenge is selecting ratios that are the most appropriate for the purpose at hand. For example, if the purpose of the analysis is to understand a company's profitability, the ratios that relate to returns, which include profit margins and asset utilization, are important. If we want to understand a company's effectiveness in its credit policies and collections, we focus on ratios involving its accounts receivable. To evaluate a company's creditworthiness, an analyst might instead focus on ratios related to the company's debts and its ability to satisfy those obligations.

Financial ratios are calculated using a company's financial statement and market data, yet the interpretation of these ratios should also consider company-specific events and the general economic cycle. For example, if a company acquires another company that is in a different line of business, a noticeable shift in some ratios may accompany that acquisition. Such shifts may simply reflect the different balance in accounts and margins of the acquired business. Further, changes in ratios may be in response to changes in general economic conditions; for example, a cyclical company will likely experience a change in profitability as economic conditions change.

Though this chapter demonstrates the calculation of financial ratios, in practice, many analysts rely on financial ratios that have been calculated and provided by a vendor. In these instances, care must be taken to understand how the ratio is calculated by the vendor for several reasons. First, some ratios do not have a unique calculation. For example, the return on assets may be calculated by comparing operating profit to total assets by one financial service but calculated as the ratio of net profit to total assets by another. Second, a ratio may be calculated by one vendor using end-of-period values and by another using average values over the period. For example, one vendor may calculate the return on assets using the net profit for the fiscal year and the end-of-period balance in total assets, whereas another vendor may calculate the return on assets using the net profit for the fiscal year and the average of the total assets over the same year. Third, with the large number of possible financial ratios that can be calculated, many ratios do not have a unique name. For example, the plowback ratio, which is the proportion of earnings reinvested in the company, may also be referred to as the retention ratio.

We can classify ratios into several types, based on the dimension of the company's performance and condition:

- We use *activity ratios* to evaluate a company's effectiveness in putting its asset investment to good use.
- We use *liquidity ratios* to measure a company's ability to meet its short-term, immediate obligations.
- We look at a company's *solvency ratios* to gauge its ability to meets its debt obligations.
- We use *profitability ratios* to analyze a company's ability to manage its expenses to generate profits from its sales.

A thorough financial analysis of a company requires the use of ratios from more than one of these classifications, along with other information about the company.

3.1.   Activity Ratios

We often want to evaluate how well a company does in putting its investments to use. We can use **activity ratios** as measures of how well assets are used. Activity ratios can help us evaluate the benefits produced by specific assets, such as inventory or accounts receivable.

Or they can be used to evaluate the benefits produced by all of a company's assets collectively. There are two types of activity measures: turnover ratios and numbers of days. With turnover ratios, we measure how many times during the period the company has effectively used its assets to produce a benefit. With number of days measures, we arrive at an approximation of how long it takes to recoup the company's investment. As you will see, there is a direct relationship between turnover ratios and the numbers of days.

3.1.1. Turnover Ratios   We use turnover ratios to gauge the company's efficiency in the use of its assets. A turnover ratio compares a measure of output to the investment used to generate that output. The most common turnover ratios are the inventory turnover, the total asset turnover, and the receivables turnover. **Inventory turnover** is the ratio of cost of goods sold to inventory. This ratio is an indication of the resources tied up in inventory relative to the speed at which inventory is sold during the period:

$$\text{Inventory turnover} = \frac{\text{Cost of goods sold}}{\text{Average inventory}}$$

Though it is possible to construct such a ratio with account balances as of the most recent financial statements, for account balances drawn from the balance sheet, it is ideal to use average balances over multiple periods. Many companies exhibit seasonality in their revenues. Additionally, many companies choose fiscal year-ends that coincide with the lowest points in their operating cycles. Consequently, inventory and other balance sheet items that are drawn from a company's annual financial statements may not be representative of the typical account balances that are carried throughout the year.

In the case of Procter & Gamble, we can see that there is seasonality in both revenues and inventory, as shown in Exhibit 7-4 with quarterly revenues and inventory over a four-year

EXHIBIT 7-4   Quarterly Revenues and Inventory for Procter & Gamble, March 2001 through December 2004

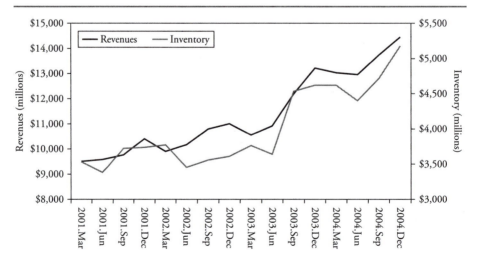

Source: Data from the Procter & Gamble Company quarterly reports, various years.

period. Procter & Gamble's revenues and inventory levels are lowest in the quarter ending in June of each year, its fiscal year-end. Therefore, in the calculation of the inventory turnover ratio, we would want to use an average inventory amount if it differs significantly from the year-end inventory.[4]

There is no particular number for an inventory turnover ratio that is inherently good or bad. An appropriate turnover ratio may vary among companies and even among product lines in the same company. What is important is the interaction of turnover and profitability, which then influences the returns on the company's or owners' investment.

Receivables turnover is the ratio of total revenue to average accounts receivable. This ratio provides an indication of the resources tied up in accounts receivable and the speed at which receivables are collected during the period:

$$\text{Receivables turnover} = \frac{\text{Total revenue}}{\text{Average receivables}}$$

The receivables turnover is a measure of the number of times accounts receivables have been created through the sale of goods on credit and extinguished through customer payments during the period. In other words, this estimate helps us gauge how long it takes customers to pay, on average, during the period. If the turnover is, say, 12 times, we know that it takes customers approximately 30 days to pay on their accounts. The longer customers take to pay on their accounts, all else being equal, the higher the investment in working capital that will be required by the company. This ratio is therefore quite useful in assessing a company's credit policy.

Total asset turnover is the ratio of revenues to total assets. This ratio indicates the extent to which the investment in total assets results in revenues.

$$\text{Total asset turnover} = \frac{\text{Total revenue}}{\text{Average total assets}}$$

The resultant number is a multiplier of the revenues that are generated for the investment in total assets. For example, if assets are £100 million and revenues are £125 million, the total asset turnover is 1.25, meaning that £1.25 of revenues are generated per £1 of asset investment.

Still another turnover measure that may be useful in assessing a company's efficiency is working capital turnover. **Working capital** is the difference between current assets and current liabilities.[5] With the **working capital turnover**, we compare revenues with working capital to produce a measure that shows how efficiently working capital is employed:

$$\text{Working capital turnover} = \frac{\text{Total revenue}}{\text{Average working capital}}$$

---

[4]This is the case for any ratio that involves the balance in an account that is seasonal, such as inventory and accounts receivable. However, when we are on the outside looking in, as is often the case in financial analysis, we must use annual amounts or the average of the quarterly amounts to estimate this turnover ratio.

[5]The difference between current assets and current liabilities is sometimes also referred to as the net current assets.

As with any other ratio, turnover ratios cannot be judged in isolation but rather must be considered in conjunction with other dimensions of the company's condition and performance, the trends of the ratios over time, and industry norms.

Consider that a turnover ratio may be constructed to evaluate the use of any set of assets by comparing the gross benefit—usually revenues—to the employed assets. For example, if you wish to focus on a company's fixed assets, you can construct a fixed asset turnover as the ratio of revenues to net plant and equipment.

EXAMPLE 7-1   Turnover Ratios for Procter & Gamble (2004)

Given the 2004 financial results for Procter & Gamble provided in Section 2, calculate the inventory turnover, receivables turnover, and total asset turnover ratios for Procter & Gamble.

$$\text{Inventory turnover} = \frac{\$25,076}{\$4,400} = 5.70 \text{ times}$$

$$\text{Receivables turnover} = \frac{\$51,407}{\$4,062} = 12.66 \text{ times}$$

$$\text{Total asset turnover} = \frac{\$51,407}{\$57,048} = 0.90 \text{ times}$$

Notes:
1. Working capital turnover is not meaningful for Procter & Gamble for 2004 because working capital is negative.
2. Preferably, we would use the average of several quarterly balance sheets in calculating these ratios. But for the sake of brevity, in these examples, the calculations are based on the 2004 balance sheet.

3.1.2. The Operating Cycle and Its Components   Turnover ratios help us measure how efficiently a company's management puts various assets to use. Another way of looking at efficiency is to examine the company's operating cycle—in other words, to "follow the money." The **operating cycle** is the duration between the time a company makes an investment in goods and services—for example, to purchase inventory—and the time that investment produces cash. For example, a company that produces and sells goods has an operating cycle comprising four events:

1. The company purchases raw materials from suppliers and produces goods, investing in inventory.
2. The company sells goods, generating revenues, which may or may not be cash.

3. The company extends credit to customers, creating accounts receivable.
4. The company collects accounts receivable from customers, generating cash.

The operating cycle is therefore the length of time it takes to convert an investment of cash in inventory back into cash through collection of accounts.

Just as a company might extend credit to customers and create accounts receivable, not all investments in inventory and other purchases a company makes are paid for immediately with cash. The **net operating cycle** is the length of time it takes to convert an investment of cash in inventory back into cash considering that the company makes some purchases on credit (see Exhibit 7-5).[6]

The number of days a company ties up funds in inventory is determined by the total amount of money represented in inventory and the average day's cost of goods sold. The current investment in inventory—that is, the money "tied up" in inventory—is the ending balance of inventory on the balance sheet. The average day's cost of goods sold is the cost of goods sold on an average day in the year, which can be estimated by dividing the cost of goods sold found on the income statement by the number of days in the year.

We compute the **number of days of inventory** by calculating the ratio of the amount of inventory on hand to the average day's cost of goods sold:

$$\text{Number of days of inventory} = \frac{\text{Inventory}}{\text{Average day's cost of goods sold}}$$

$$= \frac{\text{Inventory}}{(\text{Cost of goods sold}/365)}$$

We can extend the same logic from the inventory turnover to estimate the **number of days of receivables**, which is the length of time between a sale—when an account receivable

EXHIBIT 7-5   Operating Cycle and Net Operating Cycle

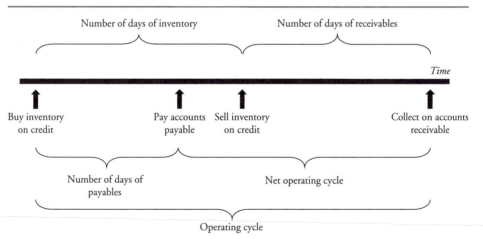

---

[6]The net operating cycle is also known as the cash conversion cycle.

is created—and the collection of the account receivable in cash. If the balance of receivables at the end of the year is representative of the receivables on any day throughout the year, then it takes, on average, approximately the number of days of receivables to collect the accounts receivable:

$$\text{Number of days of receivables} = \frac{\text{Accounts receivable}}{\text{Average day's revenue}} = \frac{\text{Accounts receivable}}{(\text{Revenue}/365)}$$

We also need to look at the liabilities on the balance sheet to see how long it takes a company to pay its short-term obligations. We can apply the same logic to accounts payable as to accounts receivable and inventories, calculating the **number of days of payables**. How long does it take a company, on average, to go from creating a payable (buying on credit) to paying for it in cash?

$$\text{Number of days of payables} = \frac{\text{Accounts payable}}{\text{Average day's purchases}} = \frac{\text{Accounts payable}}{(\text{Purchases}/365)}$$

First, we need to determine the amount of an average day's purchases on credit. If we assume all purchases are made on credit, the total purchases for the year would be the cost of goods sold (COGS) less any amounts included in this cost of goods sold that are not purchases, such as depreciation. An analyst outside the company would not have access to detailed purchasing data but could use the following accounting relationship to estimate purchases:

$$\text{Purchases} = \text{COGS} + \text{Ending inventory} - \text{Beginning inventory}$$

The operating cycle is a measure of how long it takes to convert an investment in cash in inventory back into cash through collection of accounts receivable:

$$\text{Operating cycle} = \text{Number of days of inventory} + \text{Number of days of receivables}$$

The number of days of payables tells us how long it takes the company to pay for purchases made to create the inventory. If we put these two pieces of information together, we can see how long, net, the company ties up cash. The difference between the operating cycle and the number of days of payables is the net operating cycle:

$$\text{Net operating cycle} = \text{Operating cycle} - \text{Number of days of payables}$$

or, substituting for the operating cycle,

$$\text{Net operating cycle} = \text{Number of days of inventory} + \text{Number of days of receivables} - \text{Number of days of payables}$$

The net operating cycle is an estimate of how long it takes for the company to get cash back from its investment in inventory and accounts receivable, considering that purchases may be made on credit. By not paying for purchases immediately (that is, by using trade credit), the company reduces its liquidity needs.

EXAMPLE 7-2   The Net Operating Cycle Components for Procter & Gamble (2004)

$$\text{Number of days of inventory} = \frac{\$4,400}{(\$25,076/365)} = \frac{4,400}{68.70} = 64.05 \text{ days}$$

$$\text{Number of days of receivables} = \frac{\$4,062}{(\$51,407/365)} = \frac{4,062}{140.84} = 28.84 \text{ days}$$

$$\text{Number of days of payables}^* = \frac{\$3,617}{(\$25,836/365)} = \frac{3,617}{70.78} = 51.10 \text{ days}$$

*Purchases estimated as COGS + Ending inventory − Beginning inventory = \$25,076 + \$4,400 − \$3,640 = \$25,836.
Operating cycle = 92.89 days.
Net operating cycle = 41.79 days.

3.1.3. Turnover and the Numbers of Days   As you can see, there is a relationship between the turnover ratios and the numbers of days. Dividing 365 by inventory turnover produces the number of days of inventory. Likewise, dividing 365 by the number of days of inventory produces the inventory turnover. For example, suppose a company has a cost of goods sold of \$100 and an average inventory of \$20. Then, the inventory turnover is found as \$100/\$20 = 5 times. The number of days of inventory can be found as either 20/(100/365) = 73 or 365/5 = 73. The same relationship exists with other turnover and corresponding number of days ratios, such as receivables turnover and number of days of receivables.

The operating cycle connects the level of the company's activity with its liquidity. For example, the lower the turnover of its inventory, the longer its operating cycle will be and hence the more investment in current assets will be needed (relative to current liabilities) because it takes longer to convert inventory into cash. In other words, the longer the operating cycle, the more working capital will be required.

3.2. Liquidity Analysis

In the context of financial analysis, we refer to **liquidity** as the company's ability to satisfy its short-term obligations using assets that are most readily converted into cash. We refer to the assets that may be converted into cash in a short period of time as the company's **liquid assets**. These assets are listed in financial statements as **current assets**.[7]

---

[7]Current assets are often referred to as "working capital" because they represent the resources needed for the day-to-day operations of the company. However, we use the term "working capital" in this chapter to mean the difference between current assets and current liabilities.

We assume that current assets are used to satisfy short-term obligations, or **current liabilities**. Current liabilities include accounts payable, wages payable, and accrued liabilities. The amount by which current assets exceed current liabilities is referred to as the company's **working capital**.

3.2.1. Measures of Liquidity   **Liquidity ratios** provide a measure of a company's ability to generate cash to meet its immediate needs. We can construct several such ratios to assess a company's liquidity. We will look at three of these ratios: the current ratio, the quick ratio, and the cash ratio.

The **current ratio** is the ratio of current assets to current liabilities. This ratio is a measure of a company's ability to satisfy its current liabilities with its current assets:

$$\text{Current ratio} = \frac{\text{Current assets}}{\text{Current liabilities}}$$

A more stringent measure of liquidity is the **quick ratio**. This ratio indicates a company's ability to satisfy current liabilities with its most liquid assets:

$$\text{Quick ratio} = \frac{\text{Cash} + \text{Short-term marketable investments} + \text{Receivables}}{\text{Current liabilities}}$$

The quick ratio is also referred to as the acid test ratio. We can provide an even more stringent test with the **cash ratio**, which is a measure of the company's ability to meet its current obligations with just the cash and cash equivalents on hand:

$$\text{Cash ratio} = \frac{\text{Cash} + \text{Short-term marketable investments}}{\text{Current liabilities}}$$

In this ratio, we are not considering less liquid assets, such as accounts receivable, in the coverage of current liabilities. Rather, we are considering whether the company can pay off its immediate obligations without selling inventory or collecting on its accounts.

Generally, the larger these liquidity ratios are, the better the ability of the company to satisfy its immediate obligations. Is there a magic number that defines good or bad? Not really. Consider the current ratio. A large amount of current assets relative to current liabilities provides assurance that the company will be able to satisfy its immediate obligations. However, if the company has more current assets than it needs to provide this assurance, the company may be investing too heavily in these non- or low-earning assets and therefore not putting its assets to the most productive use. A more thorough interpretation of this liquidity ratio requires taking a look at the profitability of the company, trends in liquidity, and industry norms. As mentioned earlier, another consideration is the operating cycle. A company with a long operating cycle may have more need for liquid assets than a company with a short operating cycle.[8]

---

[8]We should note that there may be a specific requirement—say, to comply with a bond covenant—that the current ratio be at least a specified number. In this case, the ratio is indeed "good" or "bad" only as it relates to compliance with the bond indenture.

EXAMPLE 7-3   Liquidity Ratios for Procter & Gamble (2004)

$$\text{Current ratio} = \frac{\$17,115}{\$22,147} = 0.77$$

$$\text{Quick ratio}^* = \frac{(\$5,469 + \$423 + \$4,062)}{\$22,147} = 0.45$$

$$\text{Cash ratio}^* = \frac{(\$5,469 + \$423)}{\$22,147} = 0.27$$

*We have assumed that investment securities are short-term marketable investments. However, we would need to investigate this assumption further when interpreting this ratio.

3.3. Solvency Analysis

A company can finance its assets with equity, debt, or some combination of the two. Financing with debt involves risk because debt legally obligates the company to pay interest and to repay the principal as promised. Equity financing does not obligate the company to pay anything; dividends are paid at the discretion of the board of directors. There is always some risk, which we refer to as **business risk**, inherent in any operating segment of a business. But how a company chooses to finance its operations—the particular mix of debt and equity—may add **financial risk** on top of business risk. Financial risk is the risk arising from the company's obligation to meet required payments under its financing agreements, such as the payment of promised interest and principal repayment on a bond issue.[9]

We use solvency ratios to assess a company's level of financial risk. There are two types of solvency ratios: component percentages and coverage ratios. Component percentages typically compare a company's debt level with either its total assets or its equity capital.[10] Coverage ratios reflect a company's ability to satisfy the obligations that arise out of debt financing, such as interest, principal repayment, and lease payments.

3.3.1. Component-Percentage Solvency Ratios

We use component-percentage solvency ratios to gauge how reliant a company is on debt financing. Solvency ratios that compare debt with either equity or total assets are also commonly referred to as financial leverage ratios and gearing ratios. We construct these ratios by comparing the amount of debt either to the total capital of the company or to the equity capital. The amount of debt can be measured in several ways. Short-term debt includes obligations due in less than a year as well as the portion of longer-term obligations that is due in less than a year. The calculation for long-term debt includes obligations with a maturity of more than a year. These obligations may be in the form of interest-bearing debt, such as bonds, or other long-term liabilities, such as deferred income

---

[9]Business risk and financial risk are discussed in greater detail in Chapter 4, Capital Structure and Leverage.

[10]Recall that total assets are equivalent to a company's total capital because of the following accounting relationship: Assets = Liabilities + Shareholders' equity.

taxes. In calculating total debt, analysts commonly disregard short-term liabilities that arise from the company's typical day-to-day operations, such as accounts payable, accrued current liabilities, and taxes payable.

The debt-to-assets ratio is a measure of the proportion of assets that is financed with debt (both short-term and long-term debt):

$$\text{Debt-to-assets ratio} = \frac{\text{Total debt}}{\text{Total assets}}$$

The long-term debt-to-assets ratio is the proportion of the company's assets that is financed with long-term debt:

$$\text{Long-term debt-to-assets ratio} = \frac{\text{Long-term debt}}{\text{Total assets}}$$

With the debt-to-equity ratio, we compare the uses of debt and equity as sources of capital to finance the company's assets, evaluated using book values of the capital sources, which are provided on the balance sheet:

$$\text{Debt-to-equity ratio} = \frac{\text{Total debt}}{\text{Total shareholders' equity}}$$

Still another ratio in this category is the financial leverage ratio, also called the equity multiplier. The significance of this ratio will become apparent in the sections covering return-on-investment ratios and DuPont analysis.

$$\text{Financial leverage} = \frac{\text{Total assets}}{\text{Total shareholders' equity}}$$

Though we compute these financial leverage ratios using different comparisons, they share a common characteristic: The greater the use of debt relative to equity in financing the company, the greater the financial leverage ratio will be.

One problem with looking at risk through a financial ratio that uses the book value of equity—for example, the debt-to-equity ratio—is that most often there is little relation between the book value of equity and its market value. The book value of equity consists of

- The proceeds to the company of all the stock issued since it was first incorporated, less any treasury stock (stock repurchased by the company); and
- The accumulation of all the earnings of the company, less any dividends, since it was first incorporated.

Consider the following example of book value versus market value of equity. Procter & Gamble was incorporated in 1890. Its book value of equity represents the sum of all its stock issued and all its earnings, less all dividends paid, *since 1890*. As of the end of June 2004, Procter & Gamble's book value of equity was approximately $15.8 billion, and its market value of equity was approximately $140.5 billion. The book value understates the market value by nearly $125 billion. The book value generally does not give a true picture of the investment of shareholders in the company because

- Earnings are recorded according to accounting principles, which may not reflect the true economics of transactions; and
- Due to inflation, the dollars from earnings and proceeds from stock issued in the past do not reflect today's values.

The market value, on the other hand, is the value of equity as perceived by investors. So why bother with the book value of equity? First, many financial services and rating services report ratios using the book value rather than the market value, and it is important to understand the construction of these ratios. Second, many bond covenants are written in terms of the book value of accounts rather than the market value.

Incorporating the market value of equity into these ratios is straightforward: Replace the book value of shareholders' equity with the market value of equity (which is the current number of shares outstanding times the current market price per share of stock).[11]

3.3.2. Coverage Ratios   In addition to the component-percentage solvency ratios, which use information about how debt is related to either assets or equity, a number of ratios capture the company's ability to satisfy its debt obligations. Many ratios accomplish this end, but the two most common are the interest coverage ratio and the fixed-charge coverage ratio.

The interest coverage ratio, also referred to as the times-interest-earned ratio, compares the earnings available to meet the interest obligation with the interest obligation:

$$\text{Interest coverage ratio} = \frac{\text{Earnings before interest and taxes}}{\text{Interest payments}}$$

The assessment of the coverage of financial obligations may be expanded to include other obligations; for example, a fixed-charge coverage ratio can be constructed to include any fixed charges, such as lease payments and preferred dividends.[12] For example, to gauge a company's ability to cover its interest and lease payments, you could use the following ratio:

$$\text{Fixed-charge coverage ratio} = \frac{\text{Earnings before interest and taxes} + \text{Lease payments}}{\text{Interest payments} + \text{Lease payments}}$$

Because earnings may not fully reflect available funds, we often look at the coverage of interest using the cash flow coverage ratio. This ratio is similar to the interest and fixed-charge coverage ratios, yet we substitute cash flow from operations plus interest and taxes in the numerator to reflect the funds available to satisfy interest:

$$\text{Cash flow coverage ratio} = \frac{\dfrac{\text{Cash flow from}}{\text{operations}} + \dfrac{\text{Interest}}{\text{payments}} + \dfrac{\text{Tax}}{\text{payments}}}{\text{Interest payments}}$$

---

[11]It is much less common to replace the book value of debt with the market value of debt in component-percentage solvency ratios. Doing so can lead to contradictory results. For example, if the market value of a company's debt falls dramatically because of a ratings downgrade, using the market value of the company's debt would lead to a decline in the debt-to-assets ratio, which would make the company appear better off instead of worse off following the downgrade.

[12]When you plan to include an obligation that is paid out of after-tax earnings, such as preferred stock dividends, you must first gross up the obligation to place it on a pretax basis. This is accomplished by dividing the obligation by a factor equal to one minus the tax rate.

Because we use cash flow instead of earnings to indicate available funds, we get a truer picture of the company's ability to satisfy its debt obligations.

Another measure of debt coverage is the cash-flow-to-debt ratio:

$$\text{Cash-flow-to-debt ratio} = \frac{\text{Cash flow from operations}}{\text{Total debt}}$$

With this ratio, we can estimate the length of time it would take for the company to repay its debt if it were to apply all of its cash flow from operations toward debt repayment. For example, if the cash-flow-to-debt ratio is 0.25, the company could pay off one-quarter of its debt obligation with its current cash flow. This figure also means that, if cash flows continue at the current level and there are no changes in the debt obligation, the company could pay off its debt obligation in $1/0.25 = 4$ years. Therefore, the greater the cash-flow-to-debt ratio, the greater the company's ability to repay its obligations and take on additional obligations if necessary.[13]

An alternative formulation of the cash-flow-to-debt ratio uses earnings before interest, taxes, depreciation, and amortization (EBITDA) in the numerator. Though widely used in some applications, this form of the ratio relies on EBITDA as a measure of cash flow. In some applications, the EBITDA-to-debt ratio is similar to the cash-flow-to-debt ratio and provides an indication of the ability of a company to meet its obligations that is similar to that of the interest coverage ratio. However, unlike cash flow from operations, EBITDA does not consider changes in working capital that could affect a company's ability to meet its obligations. A company with significant growth in investments in its receivables and inventory may have difficulty meeting its debt obligations because of the cash tied up in current assets, but this situation may not be apparent when EBITDA is compared with total debt.

EXAMPLE 7-4   Solvency Ratios for Procter & Gamble (2004)

$$\text{Debt-to-assets}^* = \frac{\$25,910}{\$57,048} = 45.4 \text{ percent}$$

$$\text{Long-term debt-to-assets} = \frac{\$17,623}{\$57,048} = 30.9 \text{ percent}$$

$$\text{Debt-to-equity} = \frac{\$25,910}{\$17,278} = 1.50$$

$$\text{Financial leverage} = \frac{\$57,048}{\$17,278} = 3.30$$

---

[13]The use of cash flow from operations in the numerator assumes that the company's cash flows can be devoted to the repayment of debt. Though depreciation and amortization are noncash expenses, they represent expenditures that the company may eventually have to make for replacement of existing depreciable assets.

$$\text{Interest coverage} \quad = \quad \frac{\$9,827}{\$629} \quad = 15.62$$

$$\text{Cash flow coverage}^{**} = \frac{\$9,362 + \$629 + \$2,869}{\$629} = 20.45$$

$$\text{Cash-flow-to-debt} \quad = \quad \frac{\$9,362}{\$25,910} \quad = 36.1 \text{ percent}$$

*Total debt was calculated as $8,287 + $12,554 + $2,261 + $2,808 = $25,910.
**Cash flow from operations can be found on the company's statement of cash flows.

Coverage ratios are often used in debt covenants to help protect creditors because these ratios require that interest be "covered" along with a cushion. For example, a requirement to maintain an interest coverage ratio of 2.0 times results in a cushion equal to the interest commitment.

3.4. Profitability Analysis

An analyst can instantly tell whether a company is profitable based on whether net income is positive. Of course, net income alone does nothing to describe the efficiency with which profit was generated or the level of investment required to generate that profit. To conduct a more thorough analysis of profitability, analysts examine various margins and return-on-investment ratios.

3.4.1. Margins
We use *margins* (also referred to as profit margin ratios and return-on-sales ratios) to compare components of income with revenues—calculations that we saw earlier with the vertical common-size analysis of the income statement. These ratios give us an idea of what makes up a company's income and are usually expressed as a portion of each dollar of revenues. The profit margin ratios discussed here differ only in the numerator. It's in the numerator that we reflect and thus evaluate performance for different aspects of the business.

The **gross profit margin** is the ratio of gross profit to revenues. Gross profit is the difference between revenues and the cost of goods sold. We use this ratio to see how much of every dollar of revenues is left after the cost of goods sold:

$$\text{Gross profit margin} = \frac{\text{Gross profit}}{\text{Total revenue}}$$

The **operating profit margin** is the ratio of operating income (i.e., income before interest and taxes) to revenues. This ratio indicates how much of each dollar of revenues is left over after both cost of goods sold and operating expenses are considered:

$$\text{Operating profit margin} = \frac{\text{Operating income}}{\text{Total revenue}}$$

The **net profit margin** is the ratio of net income (a.k.a. net profit) to revenues and indicates how much of each dollar of revenues is left over after all costs and expenses:

$$\text{Net profit margin} = \frac{\text{Net income}}{\text{Total revenue}}$$

A further refinement in margins is to look at the company's profit margin before tax, or **pretax profit margin**, which allows us to isolate the effects of taxes on the company's profitability:

$$\text{Pretax profit margin} = \frac{\text{Earnings before taxes}}{\text{Total revenue}}$$

Profit margins alone do not tell us much about the company's performance or its ability to generate profits in the future. Additional information that we would need includes the trends in these profit margins over time, the company's turnover ratios and the trends in these ratios, and the industry norms for these ratios.

EXAMPLE 7-5   Profit Margins for Procter & Gamble (2004)

$$\text{Gross profit margin} = \frac{\$26,331}{\$51,407} = 51.2 \text{ percent}$$

$$\text{Operating profit margin} = \frac{\$9,827}{\$51,407} = 19.1 \text{ percent}$$

$$\text{Net profit margin} = \frac{\$6,481}{\$51,407} = 12.6 \text{ percent}$$

$$\text{Pretax profit margin} = \frac{\$9,350}{\$51,407} = 18.2 \text{ percent}$$

3.4.2. Return-on-Investment Ratios   We use **return-on-investment** ratios, also commonly called return-on-assets ratios, to compare benefits generated from investments. We represent the benefit in the numerator and the resources affecting that benefit, such as the total assets of the company, in the denominator.[14]

The **operating return on assets** is the ratio of operating earnings to assets:[15]

$$\text{Operating return on assets} = \frac{\text{Operating income}}{\text{Average total assets}}$$

This ratio is a measure of the operating income resulting from the company's investment in total assets and is useful in comparing companies that are in the same line of business.

---

[14]What distinguishes return-on-investment ratios from the activity ratios (such as inventory turnover and receivables turnover) is that the numerator is the net benefit, rather than the gross benefit, from an activity.
[15]This ratio is also referred to as the "basic earning power ratio."

The **return on assets** is the ratio of net income to assets and indicates the company's net profit generated per dollar invested in total assets:

$$\text{Return on assets} = \frac{\text{Net income}}{\text{Average total assets}}$$

This ratio is a measure of what the company receives, as a whole, from the investment it has made in assets. We can be more specific and focus on the return to the investments made by both creditors and shareholders by calculating a **return on total capital**:

$$\text{Return on total capital} = \frac{\text{Net income}}{\text{Total capital}}$$

$$= \frac{\text{Net income}}{\text{Average interest-bearing debt} + \text{Average total equity}}$$

The capital of the company consists of the interest-bearing debt and the equity—both preferred and common—of the company.

The **return on equity** is more specifically directed to the return to shareholders and is the ratio of net income to shareholders' equity. This return represents the profit generated per dollar of shareholders' investment:

$$\text{Return on equity} = \frac{\text{Net income}}{\text{Average shareholders' equity}}$$

The difference between the return-on-assets ratio and the return-on-equity ratio is the investment that is considered; the return on equity is affected by the financial leverage of the company:

$$\text{Return on equity} = \frac{\text{Net income}}{\text{Average shareholders' equity}}$$

$$= \frac{\text{Net income}}{\text{Average total assets}} \times \frac{\text{Average total assets}}{\text{Average shareholders' equity}}$$

We can also be more specific in terms of the type of equity. For example, we can construct a **return on common equity**, which is the ratio of net income available to common shareholders to common shareholders' equity. This return is the profit generated per dollar of common shareholders' investment:

$$\text{Return on common equity} = \frac{\text{Net income} - \text{Preferred dividends}}{\text{Average common shareholders' equity}}$$

EXAMPLE 7-6 Return-on-Investment Ratios for Procter & Gamble (2004)

$$\text{Operating return on assets} = \frac{\$9,827}{\$57,048} = 17.23 \text{ percent}$$

$$\text{Return on assets} = \frac{\$6,481}{\$57,048} = 11.36 \text{ percent}$$

$$\text{Return on total capital} = \frac{\$6,481}{\$12,554 + \$8,287 + \$17,278} = 17.00 \text{ percent}$$

$$\text{Return on equity} = \frac{\$6,481}{\$17,278} = 37.51 \text{ percent}$$

$$\text{Return on common equity}^* = \frac{\$6,481 - \$131}{\$17,278 - \$1,526} = 40.31 \text{ percent}$$

*Preferred stock dividends were $131 million in 2004.

3.4.3. DuPont Analysis   DuPont analysis was developed by E. I. du Pont de Nemours in 1919 as a way to better understand return ratios and why they change over time.[16] The bases for this approach are the linkages made through financial ratios between the balance sheet and the income statement. We can better understand a company's returns over time or its returns in comparison with its competitors by breaking returns into their components. This approach began as an analysis of the elements in the return on assets. For example,

$$\text{Return on assets} = \frac{\text{Net income}}{\text{Average total assets}} = \frac{\text{Net income}}{\text{Revenues}} \times \frac{\text{Revenues}}{\text{Average total assets}}$$

or

$$\text{Return on assets} = \text{Net profit margin} \times \text{Total asset turnover}$$

This breakdown of a return on assets into a two-component model is the simplest form of the DuPont approach.[17] This approach to breaking down return ratios was originally depicted as the DuPont Triangle, shown in Exhibit 7-6, with the return on assets at the top of the triangle and the profit margin and total asset turnover at the bottom.

For example, using the financial data found in Exhibit 7-7, we can calculate that for the fiscal year 2004, Office Depot, Inc., had a return on assets of 4.95 percent. We can use the DuPont approach to look at the components of this return, with dollar amounts in millions:[18]

$$\text{Return on assets} = \frac{\text{Net income}}{\text{Revenues}} \times \frac{\text{Revenues}}{\text{Average total assets}}$$

$$\frac{\$335}{\$6,767} = \frac{\$335}{\$13,565} \times \frac{\$13,565}{\$6,767}$$

$$4.95 \text{ percent} = 2.47 \text{ percent} \times 2.00$$

---

[16]American Management Association (1960). This system is consistent with the logic set forth by Alfred Marshall (1892), book 2, chapter 12, sections 3 and 4.

[17]An easy way to remember the DuPont system is to keep in mind that cross-cancellation of terms produces the desired return. For example,

$$\text{Return on assets} = \frac{\text{Net income}}{\text{Average total assets}} = \frac{\text{Net income}}{\cancel{\text{Revenues}}} \times \frac{\cancel{\text{Revenues}}}{\text{Average total assets}}$$

[18]Source of financial data: Office Depot, 2004 annual report for fiscal year ending December 25, 2004.

EXHIBIT 7-6   The DuPont Triangle

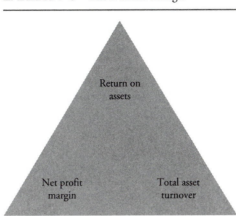

EXHIBIT 7-7   Financial Data for Office Depot, Inc.

Office Depot, Inc.

Consolidated Balance Sheet

Fiscal Year Ending December 25 ($ millions)

Assets	2003	2004
Cash and cash equivalents	791	794
Investment securities	100	161
Accounts receivable	1,112	1,304
Inventories	1,336	1,409
Deferred income taxes	170	133
Prepaid expenses and other current assets	68	115
Total current assets	3,577	3,916
Net property, plant, and equipment	1,294	1,463
Goodwill	1,004	1,050
Other assets	320	338
Total Assets	6,195	6,767
Liabilities and Shareholders' Equity		
Accounts payable	1,323	1,650
Accrued and other liabilities	814	820
Taxes payable	129	133
Current maturities of long-term debt	13	15
Total current liabilities	2,279	2,618

EXHIBIT 7-7   (Continued)

Deferred income taxes	340	342
Long-term debt	829	584
Total liabilities	3,448	3,544
Common shareholders' equity	489	630
Retained earnings	2,258	2,593
Total shareholders' equity	2,747	3,223
Total liabilities and shareholders' equity	6,195	6,767

Office Depot, Inc.

Consolidated Statement of Earnings

Fiscal Year Ending December 25 ($ millions)

	2003	2004
Sales	12,359	13,565
Cost of sales	8,484	9,309
Gross profit	3,875	4,256
Selling, general, and administrative expenses	3,409	3,726
Operating income	466	530
Interest expense and other nonoperating expenses	25	69
Earnings before income taxes	441	461
Income tax	142	126
Earnings after income taxes	299	335
Cumulative effect of accounting change	(26)	0
Net earnings	273	335

Source: Data from the Office Depot, Inc. 10-K filings.

Using the two-component breakdown, we can also use the DuPont approach to compare Office Depot's return on assets for 2003 and 2004 and examine why the return changed from 4.41 percent in 2003 to 4.95 percent in 2004:

$$\text{Return on assets} = \frac{\text{Net income}}{\text{Revenues}} \times \frac{\text{Revenues}}{\text{Average total assets}}$$

$$\frac{\$273}{\$6,195} = \frac{\$273}{\$12,359} \times \frac{\$12,359}{\$6,195}$$

$$4.41 \text{ percent} = 2.21 \text{ percent} \times 1.99$$

Comparing the breakdowns from 2003, we see that we can attribute the increase in the return on assets to the increase in the net profit margin from 2.21 percent to 2.47 percent.

EXHIBIT 7-8   Return on Assets for Office Depot for Fiscal Years 1991–2004

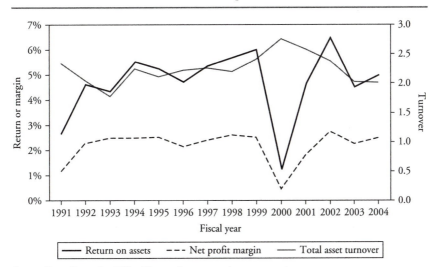

Source: Data from the Office Depot, Inc., annual reports, various years.

Taking a look over a longer span of time, 1991–2004, as shown in Exhibit 7-8, we see that the primary driver of Office Depot's return on assets over time is its net profit margin. In 2000, for example, the return on assets declined, along with the net profit margin, despite an increasing total asset turnover. This observation tells us that to understand changes in return, we need to better understand what drives Office Depot's net profit margin.

We can also compare one company with another using the DuPont approach. Consider Office Depot's competitor Staples, Inc. In 2004, Staples had revenues of $14,448 million, net income of $708 million, and total assets of $7,071 million. Its return on assets for 2004 is higher than Office Depot's—10.01 percent versus 4.95 percent—due to its higher net profit margin:

$$\text{Return on assets} = \frac{\text{Net income}}{\text{Revenues}} \times \frac{\text{Revenues}}{\text{Average total assets}}$$

$$\frac{\$708}{\$7,071} = \frac{\$708}{\$14,448} \times \frac{\$14,448}{\$7,071}$$

$$10.01\% = 4.90\% \times 2.04$$

The key to understanding Office Depot's return on assets, both in comparison with itself over time and in comparison with competitors, is the net profit margin. We can gain a better understanding of the net profit margin by breaking this ratio into three components: the operating profit margin, the effect of nonoperating expenses (or nonoperating income), and the tax effect. Exhibit 7-9 shows this finer breakdown, with return on assets broken down into the four components of total asset turnover, the operating profit margin, the effect of nonoperating items, and the tax effect in Panel A. Panel B of this exhibit provides the two-component and four-component DuPont models for Office Depot's return on assets for 2004.

The effect of nonoperating items reflects everything in the company's income statement between its operating income and its earnings before taxes. If the company has net nonoperating expense, the ratio of income before tax to operating income is less than 1.0; on the other hand, if the company has net nonoperating income, this ratio is greater than 1.0.

EXHIBIT 7-9   Two-Component and Four-Component DuPont Models of the Return on Assets

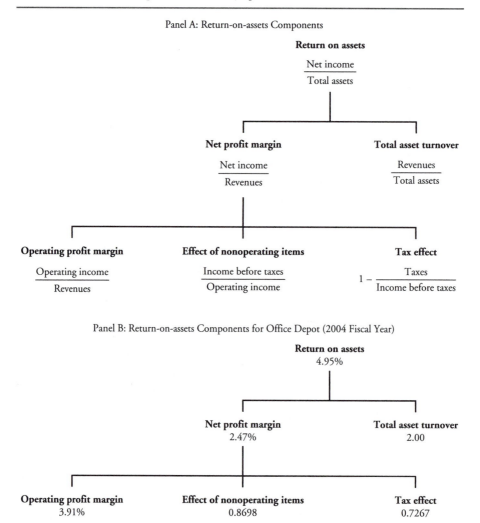

Panel A: Return-on-assets Components

Panel B: Return-on-assets Components for Office Depot (2004 Fiscal Year)

The effect of nonoperating items is often referred to as the *interest effect* or *interest burden* because for many companies the interest expense is the primary nonoperating expense. Companies with higher interest expense have lower ratios of income before taxes to operating income, whereas companies with larger nonoperating income have higher ratios of income before taxes to operating income. In the case of Office Depot in 2004, its nonoperating net expenses are 13.02 percent of its operating income.

The tax effect is one minus the ratio of taxes to income before taxes [1 − (Taxes/Income before taxes)]. The complement of the tax effect is the average *tax burden*, which is the ratio of taxes to income before taxes. For Office Depot, the tax effect ratio is 0.7267; therefore, its average tax rate for 2004 is 1 − 0.7267 = 27.33 percent.

So far, we have seen how the return on assets can be broken down into two or four components. Similarly, we can represent the return on shareholders' equity as a three-component DuPont model:

$$\text{Return on equity} = \frac{\text{Net income}}{\text{Average shareholders' equity}}$$

$$= \frac{\text{Net income}}{\text{Revenues}} \times \frac{\text{Revenues}}{\text{Average total assets}} \times \frac{\text{Average total assets}}{\text{Average shareholders' equity}}$$

Extending this model to include the net profit margin in components as we did previously, we can produce a five-component DuPont model, as illustrated in the corresponding expanded DuPont Triangle in Exhibit 7-10. For example, we can use the five-component DuPont model for Office Depot's return on equity, as Panel A of Exhibit 7-11 shows. Using the breakdown in Panel A, we can show that the product of the five components is the return on equity:

$$\begin{aligned}\frac{\text{Return}}{\text{on equity}} &= \frac{\text{Operating}}{\text{income}} \times \frac{\text{Income}}{\text{before}} \times \left[1 - \frac{\text{Taxes}}{\text{Income}}\right] \times \frac{\text{Revenues}}{\text{Average}} \times \frac{\text{Average}}{\text{total}} \\ &\quad \frac{}{\text{Revenues}} \quad \frac{}{\text{Operating}} \quad \quad \frac{}{\text{before}} \quad \frac{}{\text{total}} \quad \frac{}{\text{shareholders}} \\ &\quad \quad \quad \quad \text{income} \quad \quad \quad \text{taxes} \quad \quad \text{assets} \quad \quad \text{equity}\end{aligned}$$

$$10.39\% = \frac{\$530}{\$13,565} \times \frac{\$461}{\$530} \times \left[1 - \frac{\$126}{\$461}\right] \times \frac{\$13,565}{\$6,767} \times \frac{\$6,767}{\$3,223}$$

$$10.39\% = 0.0391 \times 0.8698 \times 0.7267 \times 2.0046 \times 2.0996$$

EXHIBIT 7-10   The Five-Component DuPont Triangle

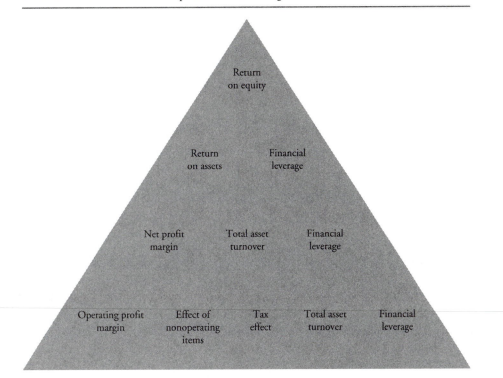

EXHIBIT 7-11   Five Component DuPont Model

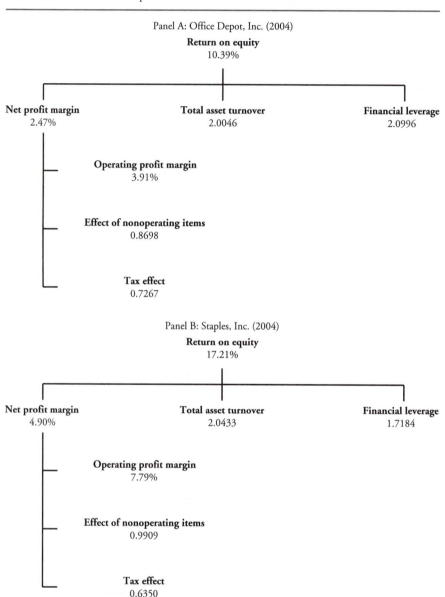

Panel A: Office Depot, Inc. (2004)

Return on equity
10.39%

Net profit margin
2.47%

Total asset turnover
2.0046

Financial leverage
2.0996

Operating profit margin
3.91%

Effect of nonoperating items
0.8698

Tax effect
0.7267

Panel B: Staples, Inc. (2004)

Return on equity
17.21%

Net profit margin
4.90%

Total asset turnover
2.0433

Financial leverage
1.7184

Operating profit margin
7.79%

Effect of nonoperating items
0.9909

Tax effect
0.6350

We can also compare these components with competitors' components to understand the differences among the companies' financial condition and performance that produce different returns on equity. For example, Staples in 2004 has a higher return on equity than Office Depot, 17.21 percent versus 10.39 percent. We can take a closer look at the differences by comparing Office Depot's five-component DuPont model with Staples' five-component model, as shown in Panel B of Exhibit 7-11. Here we see that, although the total asset turnover is similar for the two companies, the companies differ primarily in two ways:

1. The management of operating costs, as reflected in the operating profit margin, with Staples able to generate greater operating profits per dollar of revenues; and
2. The financing decisions, with Office Depot slightly more reliant on debt financing. This reliance affects not only the financial leverage but also the interest expense that influences the net profit margin.

Another use of DuPont analysis is to diagnose the source of change in returns on equity over time. Consider Kmart during the years leading up to and including its bankruptcy filing in January 2002. What was the source of Kmart's woes? A company's financial difficulties usually have more than one source, but the DuPont approach allows us to get some idea of what led to Kmart's challenges.

We can see in Panel A of Exhibit 7-12 that Kmart's return on equity was negative in several years and that Kmart was unable to provide consistent, positive returns to its shareholders. Looking more closely at the components of the return on equity, we get a clearer picture of the elements that led toward Kmart's bankruptcy. In Panel B, we see that the financial leverage ratio is relatively consistent, with the exception of the year ending around the bankruptcy filing. We can see that Kmart had total assets that were twice its equity throughout the 1990–2000 period. In other words, its debt-to-equity ratio was around 1.0 and its use of debt financing did not change much in the 10 years leading up to bankruptcy. Looking at Kmart's total asset turnover in Panel C, we see that the turnover in fact rose slightly over the 10 years leading up to bankruptcy. The company's net profit margin, as shown in Panel D, is evidently the source of the problem. The changing net profit margin—and hence Kmart's inability to manage its expenses—appears to have been a strong influence on Kmart's return on equity.

EXHIBIT 7-12   DuPont Analysis of Kmart's Return on Assets Leading Up to Bankruptcy in 2002

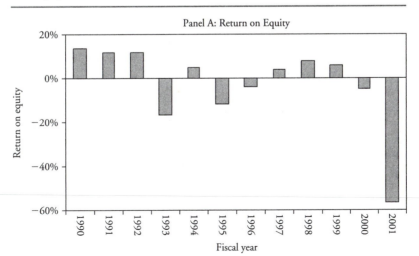

EXHIBIT 7-12   (Continued)

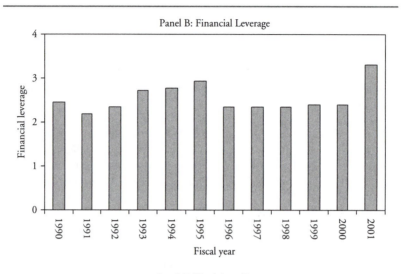

Panel B: Financial Leverage

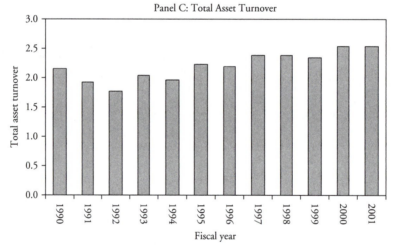

Panel C: Total Asset Turnover

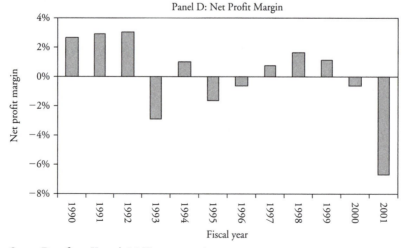

Panel D: Net Profit Margin

Source: Data from Kmart's 10-K reports, various years.

What does this all mean? What we surmise from this analysis is that Kmart's difficulties are related to the management of expenses, rather than the deployment and use of its assets or its assumption of financial risk. If we wanted a more detailed picture, we would

- Break the net profit margin into its components—the operation profit margin, the interest burden, and the tax burden—as we did for Office Depot and Staples, to see why the net profit margin changed over time; and
- Compare the trends in these components with those of Kmart's major competitors during this period, namely, Wal-Mart Stores and Target Corporation.

3.5. Other Ratios

The ratios discussed thus far deal with the company's performance and financial condition. These ratios provide information for managers (who are interested in evaluating the company's performance) and for creditors (who are interested in the company's ability to pay its obligations). We now take a look at ratios that focus on the interests of the owners: shareholder ratios. These ratios translate the overall results of operations so that they can be compared in terms of a share of stock.

Earnings per share (EPS) is the amount of income earned during a period per share of common stock:

$$\text{Earnings per share} = \frac{\text{Net income available to common shareholders}}{\text{Number of common shares outstanding}}$$

Companies provide information on earnings per share in their annual and quarterly financial statements, as well as in their periodic press releases. There are two numbers of earnings per share currently disclosed in financial reports: basic and diluted earnings per share. These numbers differ with respect to the definition of available net income and the number of shares outstanding.

Basic earnings per share is net income, minus preferred dividends, divided by the average number of common shares outstanding. *Diluted* earnings per share is net income, minus preferred dividends, divided by the number of shares outstanding considering all dilutive securities (e.g., convertible debt and options).[19] Diluted earnings per share gives the shareholder information about the *potential* dilution of earnings. For companies with a large number of dilutive securities (e.g., stock options, convertible preferred stock, or convertible bonds), there can be a significant difference between basic and diluted EPS.

Book value equity per share is the amount of the book value (also called carrying value) of common equity per share of common stock, calculated by dividing the book value of shareholders' equity by the number of shares of common stock outstanding. As we saw earlier, the book value of equity may differ from the market value of equity. The market value per share, if available, is a much better indicator of the investment of shareholders in the company.

The price-to-earnings ratio (P/E, or PE ratio) is the ratio of the price per share of common stock to the earnings per share:

$$\text{Price-to-earnings ratio} = \frac{\text{Market price per share}}{\text{Earnings per share}}$$

---

[19]If dilutive securities have obligations that affect the earnings available to shareholders (e.g., interest), these obligations are added back to the numerator in the diluted EPS calculation.

The earnings per share typically used in the denominator is the sum of the earnings per share for the last four quarters. In this case, the P/E is often referred to as the *trailing P/E*. In contrast, the *leading P/E* is typically calculated using an estimate or forecast for earnings per share over the next four quarters.

The P/E is sometimes used as a proxy for investors' assessment of the company's ability to generate cash flows in the future. If the company has zero or negative earnings, the P/E that we calculate is meaningless.

A financial analyst is often interested in how much of a company's earnings is paid out to investors. Two common measures address this issue: dividends per share and the dividend payout ratio. **Dividends per share** (DPS) is the dollar amount of cash dividends paid during a period per share of common stock:

$$\text{Dividends per share} = \frac{\text{Dividends paid to shareholders}}{\text{Weighted average number of ordinary shares outstanding}}$$

This measure represents the amount paid out in cash during a given period but does not reflect noncash distributions, such as stock dividends.

The **dividend payout ratio** is the ratio of cash dividends paid to earnings for a period:

$$\text{Dividend payout ratio} = \frac{\text{Dividends paid to common shareholders}}{\text{Net income attributable to common shares}}$$

The dividend payout ratio is the complement of the **plowback ratio**, which is the proportion of earnings that is reinvested in the company.[20]

$$\text{Plowback ratio} = \frac{\dfrac{\text{Net income attributable}}{\text{to common shares}} - \text{Common share dividends}}{\text{Net income attributable to common shares}}$$

$$= 1 - \left[\frac{\text{Dividends}}{\text{Net income attributable to common shares}} \right]$$

Some companies' dividends appear to follow a pattern of constant or constantly growing dividends per share, while a smaller number of companies' dividends appear to be a constant percentage of earnings. Panel A of Exhibit 7-13 shows Procter & Gamble's dividend payout ratio, and Panel B shows its dividends per share. We can see in these charts that Procter & Gamble tends to pay dividends that increase by a relatively constant amount each year.

EXAMPLE 7-7   Other Ratios for Procter & Gamble (2004)

$$\text{Basic earnings per share}^* = \frac{(\$6{,}481 - \$131)}{2{,}580.1} = \$2.46$$

$$\text{Diluted earnings per share}^* = \frac{(\$6{,}481 - \$4)}{2{,}790.1} = \$2.32$$

$$\text{Market price per share} = \quad \$54.44$$

---

[20]The plowback ratio is also commonly referred to as the "retention ratio" or "retention rate."

$$\text{Book value per share } = \frac{\$17,278 - \$1,526}{2,580.1} = \$6.11$$

$$\text{Dividends per share } = \frac{\$2,408}{2,580.1} = \$0.93$$

$$\text{Dividend payout ratio } = \frac{\$2,408}{\$6,481 - \$131} = 37.92\%$$

$$\text{Plowback ratio } = \frac{\$3,942}{\$6,350} = 62.08\%$$

*Average number of common shares outstanding and the effects of dilutive securities were found in Procter & Gamble's 2004 10-K filing.

EXHIBIT 7-13   Procter & Gamble Dividends, 1996–2004

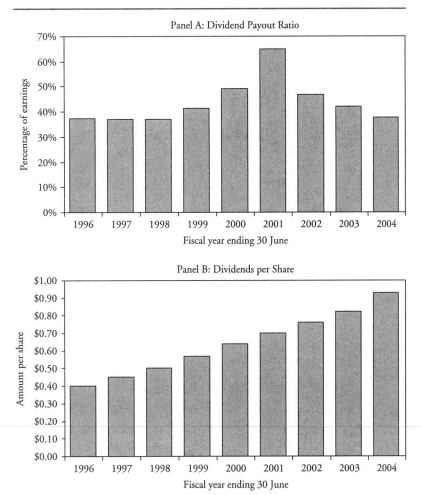

Source: Data from the Procter & Gamble Company annual reports, various years.

3.6.   Effective Use of Ratio Analysis

Financial analysis requires pulling together many pieces of information. The analysis of a company requires gathering such information as

- A description of the company, including its line(s) of business, and major corporate events, such as acquisitions and divestitures;
- Information on the industry or industries in which the company operates and its major competitors;
- Major factors (e.g., economic, competitive, and legal) that have affected the company in the recent past and may affect the company in the future; and
- Relevant financial ratios for at least the past five years, but preferably extending over at least one complete economic cycle.

   A thorough analysis of a company requires more space than can be allowed here, but we can look at the basic financial ratio analysis. We will take Procter & Gamble as an example, using published annual financial data for fiscal years June 30, 1995 through June 30, 2004.

   One of the important lessons of financial ratio analysis is that there is no value for a particular ratio that is good or bad. The interpretation of a financial ratio depends on how that ratio fits into the broader scheme of the company's overall financial condition and performance. For example, a company that has 65 percent of its assets financed with debt may be worrisome to its creditors and owners if it has a high degree of business risk, but the situation may be less troubling in cases where the company has a lower degree of business risk. As another example, consider a company that has a high rate of inventory turnover. High turnover may be good, indicating that the company is managing its inventory very efficiently. On the other hand, high turnover may be bad, indicating that the company has a high risk of stock-outs. How do we resolve whether this situation is good or bad? We look at other dimensions of the company. In the case of the inventory turnover, for example, we also look at the company's profitability to see whether the high turnover is a problem.

   With respect to trends over time, we generally look at the company's ratios over a period of at least five years, but preferably over enough years to see how the company performs at different points in an economic cycle (i.e., peaks and troughs). Additionally, we must consider major company events that may explain changes over time. For example, a major acquisition or divestiture will affect any trends.

   Also, consider whether there were significant changes in accounting principles that may affect the observed trend. For example, consider goodwill, an intangible balance sheet account. In 2001, goodwill was changed so that it is no longer amortized. Instead, goodwill is now reviewed annually to see whether its value is impaired. Consequently, financial statements after 2001 show a slight upward bias in the company's net income because goodwill amortization is no longer charged against earnings. For companies that choose to write off a portion of this goodwill (e.g., because it is found to be impaired), the financial picture is distorted because

- the company takes a large, one-time expense when the goodwill is written off; and
- returns on assets are enhanced from a lower asset base following the write-off.[21]

---

[21]For example, Therma-Wave, Inc., a manufacturer of systems used in semiconductor manufacturing, wrote off $68 million of goodwill for its year ending March 2003, which was 34 percent of its total assets.

Therefore, it is important to consider the impact of accounting changes on the comparability of financial results over time.

3.6.1. Company Description, Industry, and Major Factors

The Procter & Gamble Company is a consumer products producer with a wide range of household and personal care products. Procter & Gamble is the largest consumer products company, with approximately 50 percent of the market share and revenues over $51 billion in 2004. Its major U.S. competitors are Kimberly-Clark Corporation and Colgate-Palmolive Company.

The consumer and household products industry is a noncyclical industry, which means that the revenues and earnings are not affected by the health of the general economy. As we saw earlier, there is seasonality in Procter and Gamble's revenues, with the peak in the December-ending quarter of each year and the trough in the June-ending quarter. Procter & Gamble is the leading U.S. company in its industry and is continuing to grow, partly through acquisitions.

In this example, we are using financial data for the past 10 years to analyze the financial condition and performance of this company to assess how the company is likely to perform in the future. In doing so, we need to understand the major influences on the past 10 years' performance so that we can include this information in our analysis of trends. Factors occurring in the past 10 years that affect the financial data that we are using in this analysis include

- Changes in accounting, including accounting for derivatives and hedging (Statement of Financial Accounting Standards [SFAS] Nos. 133 and 149), accounting for business combinations and goodwill (SFAS Nos. 141 and 142), and accounting for asset retirement obligations (SFAS No. 143);
- Changes in the product mix, including the divestiture of Hawaiian Punch in 1999 and the acquisition of Tambrands in 1997, Iams in 1999, Clairol in 2001, and Wella in 2003; and
- A restructuring program during the years 1999–2000.

The changes in the product mix, the changes in the accounting, and the restructuring should be kept in mind when looking at the trends in financial ratios over the 10-year period.

3.6.2. Activity

Exhibit 7-14 shows the turnover ratios for Procter & Gamble over the period 1995–2004. The turnover ratios provide information on the effectiveness with which a company puts its assets to use. In the case of Procter & Gamble, we see that inventory turnover declined slightly over time, with a significant increase in the 1999–2000 restructuring period, and that accounts receivable turnover remained relatively stable throughout the 1995–2004 period.

3.6.3. Liquidity

Exhibit 7-15 provides a chart of the current and quick ratios of Procter & Gamble for the 1995–2004 fiscal years. These ratios follow similar trends over these years, with a drop in the restructuring years, 1999–2000. You will notice a change in the physical distance between these two trend lines in this exhibit. The difference between the quick and current ratios is in the numerator, where the quick ratio excludes inventory. The tightening of these two lines indicates that inventory has declined relative to the other current assets over time. This decline may reflect changes in the management of inventory but also may reflect changes in the product mix from acquisitions and divestitures.

EXHIBIT 7-14   Turnover Ratios, Procter & Gamble, 1995–2004

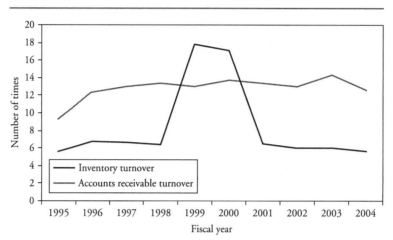

Source: Data from the Procter & Gamble Company annual reports, various years

EXHIBIT 7-15   Liquidity Ratios, Procter & Gamble, 1995–2004

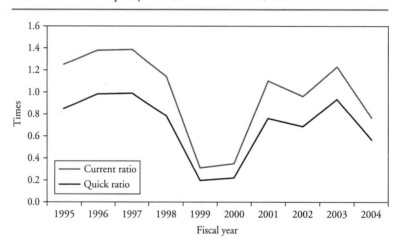

Source: Data from the Procter & Gamble Company annual reports, various years.

3.6.4. Solvency   Exhibit 7-16 provides both the total debt-to-assets and the long-term debt-to-assets ratios for Procter & Gamble over the 1995–2004 fiscal years. Procter & Gamble increased its financial leverage overall from 1995 to 2004. However, the change in the leverage in the latter part of this period is due to a greater reliance on short-term liabilities, as indicated by the divergence of the two debt ratios.

3.6.5. Profitability   The profit margins of Procter & Gamble are shown in Exhibit 7-17. These profit margins have increased over time, with the noticeable exception of the 1999 and 2000 fiscal years. A look at the management's discussion of the financial results in that period indicates that this fall in margins is attributable to spending on acquisitions and lower earnings in those years due to restructuring expenses.

EXHIBIT 7-16   Solvency Ratios, Procter & Gamble, 1995–2004

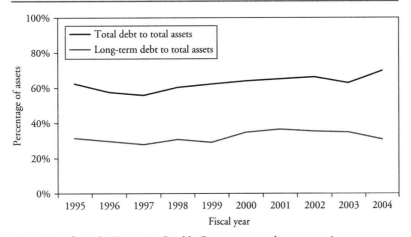

Source: Data from the Procter & Gamble Company annual reports, various years.

EXHIBIT 7-17   Profit Margins, Procter & Gamble, 1995–2004

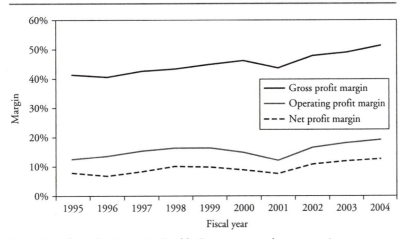

Source: Data from the Procter & Gamble Company annual reports, various years.

3.6.6. Returns   Exhibit 7-18 provides a graph of the return on assets and the return on equity for Procter & Gamble for the period 1995–2004. The return on assets is flat during the 1995–2004 period, whereas the return on equity trends upward. This situation is attributed to Procter & Gamble's increased use of short-term debt financing, which is consistent with what we saw in Exhibit 7-16.

The return on equity trended upward during this 10-year period, though there was a drop-off in 2001, which is consistent with the lower profit margins in 2001.

The breakdown of the return on equity into the three components of net profit margin, total asset turnover, and financial leverage, as shown in Exhibit 7-19, indicates that the upward

EXHIBIT 7-18   Return on Investment, Procter & Gamble, 1995–2004

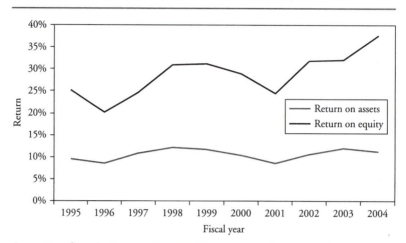

Source: Data from the Procter & Gamble Company annual reports, various years.

EXHIBIT 7-19   DuPont Components, Procter & Gamble, 1995–2004

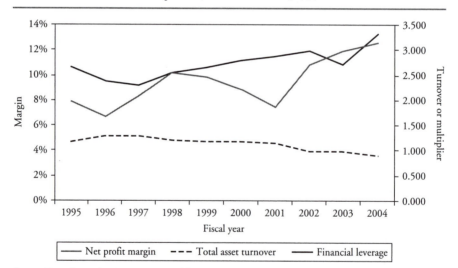

Source: Data from the Procter & Gamble Company annual reports, various years.

trend in the return on equity is attributable to the increased ability to manage expenses and the increased use of debt. The downward trend in the turnover, which puts downward pressure on returns, likely reflects the change in product mix due to divestures and joint ventures.

One interpretation of the data represented in Exhibits 7-18 and 7-19 is that the primary driver for the change in return on equity is the change in the net profit margin. A secondary driver is the change in debt, specifically the short-term debt.

3.6.7. Other Analysis and Factors   To this point, we have focused on a few ratios that depict the condition and performance of Procter & Gamble over a limited period of time. Additional information that we would want to consider includes the condition and performance of competitors and forecasts of the economy.

3.6.8. Comparables   In assessing the financial health of a company, we often compare the financial ratios of a company with those of its major competitors or of the industry as a whole. The challenge is often found in identifying the appropriate competitors or industry to use as a basis for comparison. With respect to competitors, we want to compare the company with competitors that have similar lines of business in similar proportions.

It may be difficult in some cases to find competitors that are truly comparable. Consider the comparison of Procter & Gamble (PG) with Colgate-Palmolive (CL). Though both companies are in the consumer products industry, their participation in the industry differs, as we can see from the business segment data from their respective 10-K filings for 2004:

Procter & Gamble	Revenues ($billions)
P&G beauty	19.483
Health care	7.786
Baby care and family care	11.890
Fabric care and Home care	15.262
Snacks and coffee	3.140
Colgate-Palmolive	Revenues ($billions)
Oral, personal, and home care	8.587
Pet nutrition	1.316

The competitor dimension of the analysis is an important aspect to explore in order to gauge the normal or typical ratio level for businesses with similar product lines and to understand the ability of competitors to affect the market in the future. For example, as Procter & Gamble incorporates its newest acquisition, Gillette, and perhaps embarks on additional products, how financially nimble are its competitors and how fast might they be able to introduce competing products?

Suppose we wish to use an industry average instead of comparing a company with one or two competitors. This approach would give us a broader picture of the condition and performance of the industry. One issue that becomes important, especially in industries that include companies of different sizes, is how to compute the average. Suppose we are calculating an industry average of the return on assets for the consumer products industry. And suppose we want to calculate an average that includes Procter & Gamble's major competitors: Kimberly-Clark, Colgate-Palmolive, Newell Rubbermaid, and Clorox.[22] These companies are of different sizes, so just how we compute the average affects the conclusions we draw.

---

[22]It is important for analysts to carefully consider the benchmark that is desired. Is it of interest to consider all the companies in the industry? A drawback to this approach is that we are including results for both the leaders and the laggards in the industry. Another issue is identifying the appropriate competitors. For example, some analysts consider Johnson & Johnson to be in the consumer products industry, whereas other analysts classify this company in the health care sector.

We can calculate an equal-weighted industry average, in which each company has the same weight in the average, or a value-weighted industry average, in which each company's ratio is included in proportion to its size.[23] Procter & Gamble's major competitors range in size from Kimberly-Clark, with total assets of over $17 billion, to Clorox, which has assets of just over $3.6 billion. Therefore, the weighting may make a difference in what is considered "average" for these competitors.

Another consideration in looking at an industry average is that, no matter how it is calculated, it is less volatile than a given company's ratio because of the portfolio effect; the ups and downs of an individual company are smoothed by the ups and downs of the other companies that are not perfectly in synch with one another.

A thorough analysis of Procter & Gamble requires examining each dimension of its financial condition and performance—activity, liquidity, solvency, and profitability—and comparing these dimensions over time and against major competitors and the industry as a whole. In addition, a thorough analysis requires an examination of the company's common-size statements in conjunction with those of the major competitors. Further, company-specific information (e.g., the expected length of time for incorporating its newest acquisition) must be incorporated into any projections made of future condition and performance based on the analysis of financial statements.

4. PRO FORMA ANALYSIS

We use common-size statements and financial ratios to gauge the company's financial condition and performance over recent fiscal periods. These analyses are useful in the assessment of what the company has done in the past and what trends and patterns may continue into the future. We can get an even stronger sense of a company's future by constructing pro forma statements, based both on relationships that existed in the recent past and on anticipated events and changes.[24] Pro forma statements are income statements and balance sheets based on projections. We often make these projections by using relations that we estimate from the recent past, forecasting revenues, and then using these forecasted revenues in conjunction with the past relations to develop a picture of the company's future.

If we simply take a company's current balance sheet and income statement and make the bold assumptions that all elements vary with sales and that the company will continue to grow at a rate similar to its most recent past growth rate, we can generate pro forma income statements and balance sheets quite easily. For example, using Procter & Gamble and

---

[23]An equal-weighted industry average includes each company with an equal weight; so the calculation is simple: Sum the returns on assets and divide by the number of companies in the average. A value-weighted industry average, on the other hand, allows larger companies to play a larger role. Computing a value-weighted average requires summing the components and then calculating the ratio. For the value-weighted industry average return on assets, for example, we sum the net income for all companies and divide this result by the sum of the total assets of the companies.

[24]Pro forma statements should not be confused with pro forma financial information released by companies in disclosures regarding financial performance. In the former use of the term "pro forma," we are referring to projections or predictions of future results and conditions; in the latter case, the term "pro forma" is used to indicate reported results that are not calculated in conformity with generally accepted accounting principles.

assuming the same growth in revenues in 2005 as in 2004, the pro forma income statement for 2005 is as follows:

Fiscal Year Ending June 30	Actual 2004 ($ millions)	Projected Percentage of Sales	Pro Forma 2005 ($ millions)
Sales	51,407	100.0	60,924
Cost of sales	25,076	48.8	29,718
Gross profit	26,331	51.2	31,206
Selling, general, and administrative expenses	16,504	32.1	19,559
Operating income	9,827	19.1	11,647
Interest expense	629	1.2	745
Other nonoperating income, net	152	0.3	180
Earnings before income taxes	9,350	18.2	11,082
Income tax	2,869	5.6	3,400
Net income	6,481	12.6	7,682

How far did we miss in our projections? We predicted $7.682 billion in net income, yet the actual net income for 2005 was $7.257 billion. As you can see, we were off by approximately $425 million:

Fiscal Year Ending June 30	Projected Percentage of Sales	Pro Forma 2005 ($ millions)	Actual Percentage of Sales	Actual 2005 ($ millions)
Sales	100.0	60,924	100.0	56,741
Cost of sales	48.8	29,718	49.0	27,804
Gross profit	51.2	31,206	51.0	28,937
Selling, general, and administrative expenses	32.1	19,559	31.7	18,010
Operating income	19.1	11,647	19.3	10,927
Interest expense	1.2	745	1.5	834
Other nonoperating income, net	0.3	180	0.6	346
Earnings before income taxes	18.2	11,082	18.4	10,439
Income tax	5.6	3,400	5.6	3,182
Net income	12.6	7,682	12.8	7,257

Why did we miss the mark? The projected percentages of sales were actually quite close to the actual percentages of sales, with the primary exception being "other nonoperating income, net," which is difficult to predict for most companies. We also missed slightly in terms of revenue growth. Using 2004 revenue growth of 18.5 percent, we predicted sales of roughly $60.9 billion. Actual revenue growth was lower, at 10.4 percent.

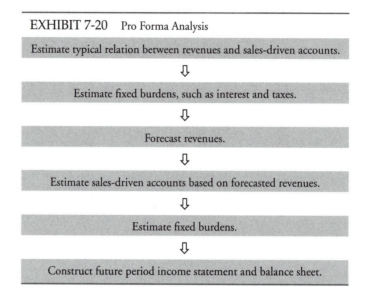

EXHIBIT 7-20   Pro Forma Analysis

Estimate typical relation between revenues and sales-driven accounts.

⇩

Estimate fixed burdens, such as interest and taxes.

⇩

Forecast revenues.

⇩

Estimate sales-driven accounts based on forecasted revenues.

⇩

Estimate fixed burdens.

⇩

Construct future period income statement and balance sheet.

As you can see in this example, it is important to produce a good prediction of revenue growth, as well as refinement in terms of how other income and expenses vary with sales. We can develop more accurate forecasts by determining which accounts in the income statement and balance sheet tend to vary with revenues and which do not. For example, interest expense and nonoperating income and expenses do not tend to vary with revenues but rather are driven by other factors. Exhibit 7-20 outlines the process of considering both sales-driven and nonsales-driven accounts in the development of pro forma statements.

For purposes of demonstrating this process, we use the statements for Imaginaire, a fictitious company:[25]

Imaginaire Company Income Statement, Year 0 (€ millions)		Imaginaire Company Balance Sheet, End of Year 0 (€ millions)	
Sales revenues	1,000.0	Current assets	600.0
Cost of goods sold	600.0	Net plant and equipment	1,000.0
Gross profit	400.0	Total assets	1,600.0
Selling, general, and administrative expenses	100.0		
Operating income	300.0	Current liabilities	250.0
Interest expense	32.0	Long-term debt	400.0
Earnings before taxes	268.0	Common stock and paid-in capital	25.0
Taxes	93.8	Retained earnings	925.0
Net income	174.2	Total liabilities and equity	1,600.0
Dividends	87.1		

---

[25]Note that, at various points throughout our Imaginaire example, the calculations may vary slightly due to rounding. For this example, calculations were completed with a spreadsheet.

4.1. Estimating the Sales-Driven Relations

Several accounts tend to vary with the revenues of a business. In other words, the relation between these accounts and revenues is relatively fixed over time. In general, these sales-driven accounts include the cost of goods sold; selling, general, and administrative expenses; and the working capital accounts included in current assets and current liabilities.

In the case of Imaginaire, we calculate the following:

Cost of goods sold as a percentage of sales	60%
Operating expenses as a percentage of sales	10%
Current assets as a percentage of sales	60%
Current liabilities as a percentage of sales	25%

As a real-world example, Exhibit 7-21 shows the sales-driven relations for Wal-Mart Stores. The cost of goods sold as a percentage of sales has been rather constant at about 79 percent during the past 15 years. Operating expenses, including selling, general, and administrative expenses, have been approximately 16 percent of sales. When making projections involving Wal-Mart Stores, we can be fairly confident that the sales-driven costs of sales and operations are relatively constant.

If we look at Wal-Mart's current assets and current liabilities, we see that, while these may be sales-driven, there is some variability in the percentages. The current assets range from 12.5 percent to 19 percent of sales, whereas the current liabilities range from 10.4 percent to 15.6 percent of sales. However, the last five years' percentages are rather constant for both accounts, providing a reasonable estimation of current assets of approximately 13.5 percent of sales and current liabilities of approximately 15 percent of sales.

4.2. Estimating the Fixed Burdens

The fixed burdens are primarily interest and taxes. If we make the assumption that tax rates will not change in the near future, we can look at the company's recent experience with taxes to assess the tax burden. In the case of the Imaginaire Company, the tax rate is 35 percent. In most cases, the tax burden is constant unless a change occurs in the federal corporate tax structure. We can see this constancy in the income tax burden of Procter & Gamble in Exhibit 7-1. If tax rates are expected to change, this estimate can be adjusted accordingly. Also, if we project that a company will, say, generate losses instead of gains, we will want to adjust the tax burden to reflect this change.[26]

The interest burden is a function of the company's capital structure. In making our forecasts, we must make an assumption about the company's capital structure in the future and work from there to determine the interest burden. If we assume that the capital structure will not change, we look at the interest burden in the past to make our projections for the future.

In the case of Procter & Gamble, we can see in Exhibit 7-3 that the capital structure has changed over time, with more financial leverage in the more recent years. In making our predictions, we may want to focus on the more recent years (say, 2000–2004), which reflect the capital structure most likely to continue in the future.

---

[26]In the case of Kmart, for example, the losses generated tax-loss carryovers and actually produced a tax benefit instead of a burden in the years leading up to bankruptcy in 2002.

EXHIBIT 7-21   Sales-Driven Accounts for Wal-Mart Stores, 1990–2004

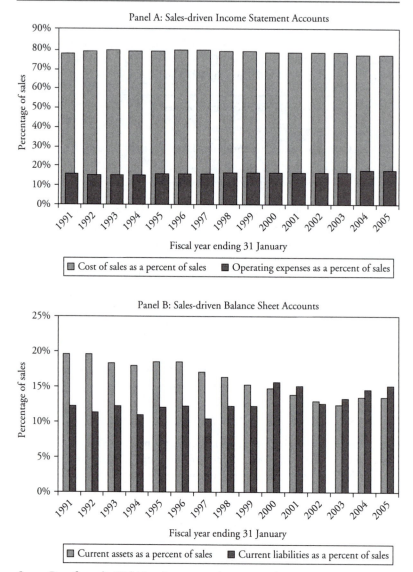

Source: Data from the Wal-Mart Stores annual reports, various years.

4.3. Forecasting Revenues

We can forecast future revenues a number of ways. We already saw that, if we simply use the most recent year's revenue growth for Procter & Gamble, we wind up with a significant forecast error for 2005. If we forecast revenues into the future using the average growth rate of 5.43 percent over the period 1994–2004, we predict revenues of $54,198 million for the fiscal year ending June 30, 2005.[27] On the other hand, if we use a time-series linear regression

---

[27]The growth rate of revenues varied widely between 1994 and 2004, from −1.77 percent in 2001 to 18.51 percent in 2004.

to forecast revenues, we predict revenues of $47,841 million in 2005.[28] The actual revenues for 2005 were $56,741 million. In other words, whether relying on the average growth rate to continue for the following year or extrapolating a linear trend, we would have underforecasted revenues. Why are we off?

Strictly using forecasts from prior periods does not take into account the other factors that affect revenues. In the case of Procter & Gamble, recent acquisitions and divestitures changed the product mix, affecting the predictability of the different segments' revenues.

In predicting revenues, we want to consider not only the path that revenues have taken in the past but also company-specific, market-related, and economic events that may affect future revenues. If the company provides consistent segment data, we can often track trends in these segments to develop the forecasts for the company as a whole.

4.4. Constructing Pro Forma Statements

We construct the financial statements based on the sales-driven estimates and the interest and tax burdens. If all accounts vary with sales, the projections that we provide in the pro forma statements are simple: We extrapolate forward in time using the percentages, typically using the components we determined in our common-size analysis. But not all accounts vary with sales, so we will encounter a residual that we need to resolve.

When we make predictions for both the sales-driven accounts and the fixed burdens, we inevitably encounter either a financing deficiency or a surplus. We must then make an assumption regarding how we expect the company to deal with this residual. Will the company finance expansion with debt? Equity? Both? When funds are available in excess of operating needs, will they be used to pay down debt? Repurchase stock? Both? In other words, we need to make an assumption about the company's capital structure decisions. To see how this question plays out, we will forecast one year ahead for the Imaginaire Company. If we assume that revenues will grow at 5 percent, the predicted net income one year ahead, assuming no changes in financing, is €184 million:

	Imaginaire Company Income Statement (€ millions)		
	Year 0	One Year Ahead	
Sales revenues	1,000.0	1,050.0	⇐ Growth at 5%
Cost of goods sold	600.0	630.0	⇐ 60% of revenues
Gross profit	400.0	420.0	⇐ Sales revenues less cost of goods sold
Selling, general, and administrative expenses	100.0	105.0	⇐ 10% of revenues
Operating income	300.0	315.0	⇐ Gross profit less operating expenses
Interest expense	32.0	32.0	⇐ 8% of long-term debt
Earnings before taxes	268.0	283.0	⇐ Operating income less interest expense
Taxes	93.8	99.1	⇐ 35% of earnings before taxes
Net income	174.2	184.0	⇐ Earnings before taxes less taxes
Dividends	87.1	92.0	⇐ Assume dividend payout ratio of 50%

---

[28]We estimate the linear regression based on the 11 years of revenues, 1994 through 2004, against time, forecasting the following year's revenues as $29,301 + $1,545(12) = $47,841.

We then carry the income statement information into our forecast for the next year's balance sheet:

Imaginaire Company
Balance Sheet
End of Year (€ millions)

	Year 0	One Year Ahead	
Current assets	600.0	630.0	⇐ 60% of revenues
Net plant and equipment	1,000.0	1,050.0	⇐ 100% of revenues
Total assets	1,600.0	1,680.0	
Current liabilities	250.0	262.5	⇐ 25% of revenues
Long-term debt	400.0	400.0	⇐ Assume no change
Common stock and paid-in capital	25.0	25.0	⇐ Assume no change
Retained earnings	925.0	1,017.0	⇐ Retained earnings in year 0, plus net income, less dividends
Total shareholders' equity	950.0	1,042.0	
Total financing	1,600.0	1,704.5	⇐ Sum of projected liabilities and equity
Total assets		1,680.0	
Financing surplus (or deficiency)		24.5	⇐ Difference between financing and assets

Whenever we make projections with a combination of percentages of sales and fixed burdens, we are likely to need a "plug" item to balance the accounts. In this case, we see that there is a financing surplus of €24.5 million, which means that the company can pay down debt, repurchase equity, or increase dividends by €24.5 million. If we assume that the company's capital structure does not change, we assume that the €24.5 million is spread proportionately between debt and equity. But now we have another issue: If debt changes, there are consequences for the interest expense, taxes, net income, and equity. In other words, the adjustment is not a simple one but rather one that requires iterations until the appropriate solution is determined.

For example, if we assume that Imaginaire will make adjustments only in debt, then the pro forma financial statements are as follows:

Imaginaire Company
Income Statement (€ millions)

	Year 0	One Year Ahead	
Sales revenues	1,000.0	1,050.0	⇐ Growth at 5%
Cost of goods sold	600.0	630.0	⇐ 60% of revenues
Gross profit	400.0	420.0	⇐ Sales revenues less cost of goods sold
Selling, general, and administrative expenses	100.0	105.0	⇐ 10% of revenues

	Year 0	One Year Ahead	
Operating income	300.0	315.0	⇐ Gross profit less operating expenses
Interest expense	32.0	30.0	⇐ 8% of long-term debt (originally €400 million, now €375.5 million)
Earnings before taxes	268.0	285.0	⇐ Operating income less interest expense
Taxes	93.8	99.7	⇐ 35% of earnings before taxes
Net income	174.2	185.2	⇐ Earnings before taxes less taxes
Dividends	87.1	92.6	⇐ Assume dividend payout ratio of 50%

Imaginaire Company
Balance Sheet
End of Year (€ millions)

	Year 0	One Year Ahead	
Current assets	600.0	630.0	⇐ 60% of revenues
Net plant and equipment	1,000.0	1,050.0	⇐ 100% of revenues
Total assets	1,600.0	1,680.0	
Current liabilities	250.0	262.5	⇐ 25% of revenues
Long-term debt	400.0	375.5	⇐ Financing surplus applied toward debt
Common stock and paid-in capital	25.0	25.0	⇐ Assume no change
Retained earnings	925.0	1,017.6	⇐ Retained earnings in year 0, plus net income, less dividends
Total liabilities and equity	1,600.0	1,680.6	

With one iteration, we have reduced the financing surplus to €0.6 million. Additional iterations would eventually reduce the surplus (or deficit) to the point where it would be small enough to eliminate through rounding. For example, a second iteration would reduce long-term debt to €374.9 million and reduce the surplus to €328.00.

If we were instead to make the assumption that the company will maintain its current relation between total debt and equity, the pro forma statements would be slightly different:

Imaginaire Company
Income Statement
(€ millions)

	Year 0	One Year Ahead	
Sales revenues	1,000.0	1,050.0	⇐ Growth at 5%
Cost of goods sold	600.0	630.0	⇐ 60% of revenues
Gross profit	400.0	420.0	⇐ Sales revenues less cost of goods sold
Selling, general, and administrative expenses	100.0	105.0	⇐ 10% of revenues

	Year 0	One Year Ahead	
Operating income	300.0	315.0	⇐ Gross profit less operating expenses
Interest expense	32.0	33.6	⇐ 8% of long-term debt (now € 420.0 million)
Earnings before taxes	268.0	281.4	⇐ Operating income less interest expense
Taxes	93.8	98.5	⇐ 35% of earnings before taxes
Net income	174.2	182.9	⇐ Earnings before taxes less taxes
Dividends	87.1	91.5	⇐ Assume dividend payout ratio of 50%

Imaginaire Company
Balance Sheet
End of Year (€ millions)

	Year 0	One Year Ahead	
Current assets	600.0	630.0	⇐ 60% of revenues
Net plant and equipment	1,000.0	1,050.0	⇐ 100% of revenues
Total assets	1,600.0	1,680.0	
Current liabilities	250.0	262.5	⇐ 25% of revenues
Long-term debt	400.0	420.0	⇐ Debt increased by € 20 million to maintain the same capital structure
Common stock and paid-in capital	25.0	25.0	⇐ Assume no change
Treasury stock		(44.0)	⇐ Repurchased shares
Retained earnings	925.0	1,016.5	⇐ Retained earnings in year 0, plus net income, less dividends
Total liabilities and equity	1,600.0	1,680.0	

Retained earnings for one year ahead were found by adding net income less dividends to retained earnings in year 0. If the common stock and paid-in capital account remains at €25.0 million, then a treasury stock purchase of €44.0 million is required to eliminate the financing surplus. A repurchase of shares creates a treasury stock contra-equity account, which results in a reduction of the company's reported equity.

As you can see, generating pro forma statements requires a reliance on assumptions about the growth in revenues, which items in the balance sheet and income statement tend to vary with revenues, and how the company will deal with financing shortfalls or surpluses. Divergences from these assumptions can have a dramatic impact on overall results. Thus, great care should be taken to ensure that pro forma assumptions are as realistic as possible.

5. SUMMARY

A challenge that we face in financial analysis is making sense of the wealth of information that is available about a company and the industry in which it operates. Companies provide shareholders and investors with quarterly and annual financial statements, as well as numerous other financial releases. Financial ratio analysis and common-size analysis help us gauge the financial performance and condition of a company through an examination of relationships among these many financial items.

A thorough financial analysis of a company requires examining its efficiency in putting its assets to work, its liquidity position, its solvency, and its profitability. We can use the tools of common-size analysis and financial ratio analysis, including the DuPont model, to help understand where a company has been. We then apply these relationships in pro forma analysis, forecasting the company's income statements and balance sheets for future periods, to see how the company's performance is likely to evolve.

PRACTICE PROBLEMS

Use the information in the following tables to answer Problems 1 through 3.

Tab, Inc. Income Statements Fiscal Years 2003, 2004, and 2005

	Amount ($ millions)		
	2005	**2004**	**2003**
Revenues	25,000	22,000	21,000
Cost of sales	20,000	18,000	17,000
Gross profit	5,000	4,000	4,000
Selling, general, and administrative expenses	500	500	800
Operating income	4,500	3,500	3,200
Interest and other nonoperating expense	200	250	250
Earnings before income taxes	4,300	3,250	2,950
Income tax	1,410	975	885
Net income	2,890	2,275	2,065

Tab, Inc. Balance Sheets End of Fiscal Years 2003, 2004, and 2005

	Amount ($ millions)		
	2005	**2004**	**2003**
Cash, cash equivalents, and marketable securities	200	150	100
Accounts receivable	1,800	1,350	900
Inventories	8,000	7,500	7,000
Total current assets	10,000	9,000	8,000
Net property, plant, and equipment	20,000	19,000	19,000
Intangible assets	1,000	1,000	1,000
Total assets	31,000	29,000	28,000
Accounts payable	500	790	615
Debt due in one year	1,000	1,000	1,000
Long-term debt	12,000	13,000	14,000
Shareholders' equity	17,500	14,210	12,385
Total liabilities and equity	31,000	29,000	28,000

1. Using vertical common-size analysis and restating the balance sheets using total assets as the benchmark to analyze changes at Tab between fiscal year 2003 and fiscal year 2005, an analyst would correctly conclude that Tab
   A. Reduced its relative investment in inventory.
   B. Incurred a greater relative burden of accounts payable.
   C. Increased the role of intangible assets in its investments.
   D. Decreased its reliance on debt financing relative to equity financing.

2. Using vertical common-size analysis of the income statement of Tab for 2005, the cost of sales relative to the benchmark is *closest* to
   A. 75 percent.
   B. 80 percent.
   C. 85 percent.
   D. 90 percent.

3. Using horizontal common-size analysis of the income statement of Tab for 2005, the cost of sales relative to the benchmark of 2003 is *closest* to
   A. 95 percent.
   B. 112 percent.
   C. 118 percent.
   D. 123 percent.

4. Common-size analysis is used in financial analysis to
   A. Evaluate changes in a company's operating cycle over time.
   B. Predict changes in a company's capital structure using regression analysis.
   C. Compare companies of different sizes or compare a company with itself over time.
   D. Restate each element in a company's financial statement as a proportion of the similar account for another company in the same industry.

5. The TBI Company has a number of days of inventory of 50. Therefore, the TBI Company's inventory turnover is *closest* to
   A. 4.8 times.
   B. 7.3 times.
   C. 8.4 times.
   D. 9.6 times.

6. The difference between a company's operating cycle and its net operating cycle is
   A. The number of days that it takes, on average, for the company to sell its inventory.
   B. The number of days that it takes the company to pay on the accounts due its suppliers.
   C. The number of days that it takes for the company to collect on its accounts receivable.
   D. The number of days that it takes for the company's cash investment in inventory to result in cash collections from customers.

7. The net operating cycle is
   A. Inversely related to a company's need for liquidity.
   B. The sum of the number of days of inventory and the number of days of receivables.
   C. The length of time it takes for an investment in inventory to be returned from collected accounts.
   D. The sum of the number of days of inventory and the number of days of receivables, less the number of days of payables.

8. A measure of the extent to which a company is able to satisfy its short-term obligations is referred to as a
   A. Liquidity ratio.
   B. Activity ratio.
   C. Profitability ratio.
   D. Financial leverage ratio.

9. Which of the following *best* describes the relationship between the current ratio and the cash ratio?
   A. The cash ratio is equal to the current ratio.
   B. The current ratio and the cash ratio should not bear any relation to one another.
   C. The current ratio is at least equal to the cash ratio but may be larger than the cash ratio.
   D. The cash ratio is at least equal to the current ratio but may be larger than the current ratio.

10. Suppose a company has earnings before taxes of $20 billion and its income tax is 35 percent of its earnings before taxes. If the company has an interest expense of $2 billion, its interest coverage ratio is closest to
    A. 6.5 times.
    B. 10.0 times.
    C. 11.0 times.
    D. 13.0 times.

11. If a company has a net profit margin of 12 percent and a tax rate of 40 percent, the before-tax profit margin is closest to
    A. 7.2 percent.
    B. 12.4 percent.
    C. 16.8 percent.
    D. 20.0 percent.

12. If a company's operating profit margin is 4 percent and its total asset turnover is 1.5 times, its operating return on assets is
    A. 2.7 percent.
    B. 6.0 percent.
    C. 7.3 percent.
    D. 8.0 percent.

13. DuPont analysis involves breaking return-on-assets ratios into their
    A. Profit components.
    B. Marginal and average components.
    C. Operating and financing components.
    D. Profit margin and turnover components.

14. The DuPont system allows us to break down the return on equity into
    A. Return on assets and the financial leverage ratio.
    B. Profit margin, the tax retention ratio, and inventory turnover.
    C. Operating return on assets, the tax burden, and the interest burden.
    D. Gross profit margin, total asset turnover, and the debt-to-equity ratio.

15. If a company's net profit margin is –5 percent, its total asset turnover is 1.5 times, and its financial leverage ratio is 1.2 times, its return on equity is *closest* to
    A. –9.0 percent.
    B. –7.5 percent.
    C. –3.2 percent.
    D. 1.8 percent.

Use the information in the following table to answer Problems 16 and 17.

LaPearla Company Income Statement Year 2005 (€ millions)		LaPearla Company Balance Sheet End of Year 2005 (€ millions)	
Revenues	10,000	Current assets	2,000
Cost of goods sold	5,500	Net plant and equipment	18,000
Gross profit	4,500	Total assets	20,000
Selling, general, and administrative expenses	800		
Operating income	3,700	Current liabilities	1,000
Interest expense	500	Long-term debt	5,000
Earnings before taxes	3,200	Common stock and paid-in capital	500
Taxes	960	Retained earnings	13,500
Net income	2,240	Total liabilities and equity	20,000

16. Suppose that LaPearla's revenues are expected to grow at a rate of 10 percent and all elements of the income statement and balance sheet are sales-driven except for the tax burden, which remains at 30 percent. LaPearla's pro forma net income for 2006 is *closest* to
    A. €2.2 billion.
    B. €2.5 billion.
    C. €2.8 billion.
    D. €3.0 billion.

17. If LaPearla's long-term debt and paid-in capital accounts remain at their 2005 levels, the tax rate remains at the 2005 rate, and all other income statement and balance sheet accounts are sales-driven with an expected growth rate of revenues of 10 percent, in 2006 LaPearla will have a financing
    A. Deficiency if it pays no dividends.
    B. Surplus if it pays out all income in dividends.
    C. Surplus if it pays out 50 percent of its net income in dividends.
    D. Deficiency if it pays out 50 percent of its net income in dividends.

CHAPTER 8

MERGERS AND ACQUISITIONS

Rosita P. Chang, PhD, CFA
University of Hawaii
Honolulu, Hawaii

Keith M. Moore, PhD, CFA
Jupiter Capital Partners, LP
Greenlawn, New York

LEARNING OUTCOMES

After completing this chapter, you will be able to do the following:

- Distinguish between an acquisition and a merger and explain the classification of mergers by the form of integration.
- Contrast horizontal and vertical mergers.
- Explain the common motivations behind merger and acquisition (M&A) activity.
- Illustrate how earnings per share (EPS) bootstrapping works and calculate a company's post-merger EPS.
- Discuss the relationship among merger motivations and types of mergers relative to industry life cycles.
- Contrast merger transaction characteristics by form of acquisition, method of payment, and mind-set of target management.
- Distinguish between and describe pre-offer and post-offer takeover defense mechanisms.
- Summarize antitrust regulatory oversight.
- Calculate the Herfindahl–Hirschman Index (HHI) and evaluate the likelihood of an antitrust challenge for a given business combination.
- Compare and contrast the three primary techniques for valuing a target company, noting the advantages and disadvantages of each.
- Calculate free cash flows for a target company and estimate the company's intrinsic value based on discounted cash flow analysis.

- Estimate the intrinsic value of a company using comparable company analysis.
- Estimate the intrinsic value of a company using comparable transaction analysis.
- Evaluate a merger bid, calculate the estimated post-merger value of an acquirer, and calculate the gains accrued to both the target shareholders and the acquirer shareholders.
- Explain the effects of price and payment method on the distribution of risks and benefits in a merger transaction.
- Describe the empirical evidence regarding the distribution of benefits in a merger.
- Discuss the major reasons for divestitures.
- Define, compare, and contrast divestitures, equity carve-outs, spin-offs, split-offs, and liquidations.

1. INTRODUCTION

Companies enter into merger and acquisition activities for a variety of reasons. Many companies use mergers as a means to achieve growth. Others seek to diversify their businesses. In all cases, it is important for corporate executives and analysts to understand both the motives for mergers and their financial and operational consequences.

Merger and acquisition (M&A) activities involve a variety of complexities and risks. For the case described in Example 8-1, corporate managers, investors, regulators, and a bevy of advisers—including investment bankers, financial analysts, lawyers, and accountants—each evaluated the various offers from a variety of perspectives.

EXAMPLE 8-1   Guidant–Boston Scientific Merger

On December 15, 2004, Guidant Corporation (GDT), a manufacturer of heart defibrillators and other specialized medical equipment, agreed to merge with Johnson & Johnson (JNJ), a large multinational producer of medical products and equipment. Guidant shareholders were to receive $30.40 in cash and $45.60 in JNJ stock (subject to conditions) per share of Guidant stock held. Although a merger such as the combination between GDT and JNJ normally would take about fours months to complete, unanticipated events caused the planned merger transaction to become a year-long saga.

While the companies worked to obtain the required regulatory clearances, a number of investigative articles exposing problems with GDT's defibrillators appeared in *The New York Times* in the spring of 2005. The company issued notices to physicians who prescribed the company's products, warning them of potential problems with various defibrillator models. During the summer of 2005, GDT removed some defibrillators from the market as it tried to correct the technical problems. Meanwhile, numerous liability suits were filed against the company, and GDT subsequently lost a significant portion of its sales. Because of these negative developments, JNJ sought to renegotiate the terms of the transaction claiming that the "material adverse change" clause in the merger agreement had been violated.[1]

---

[1]Many merger and acquisition agreements include provisions for renegotiation or cancellation following events that have a significant negative effect on the company's value or business operations.

GDT held that the loss of business did not violate the "material adverse change" clause. After initially filing a lawsuit in the U.S. District Court in an attempt to force JNJ to adhere to the original agreement, GDT later decided to enter into negotiations with JNJ to see if the two companies could agree on an acceptable modified agreement. In November 2005, the two companies agreed to modify the consideration that JNJ would pay GDT shareholders. In the new agreement, GDT shareholders were to receive $33.25 in cash and 0.493 shares of JNJ stock for each share of GDT held. With JNJ stock trading at a price of about $62.00 in November 2005, the total value of the deal to GDT shareholders was about $63.82 per share of GDT held, which was a significantly lower merger price than in the original agreement.

Shortly after the modified merger agreement was announced, the chairman of another medical device manufacturer, Boston Scientific Corporation (BSX), contacted the chairman of GDT and indicated an interest in pursuing a business combination as an alternative to the JNJ merger. Because of the existing GDT–JNJ merger agreement, Guidant's legal advisers reminded the company's managers that they were prevented from entering into any competing merger discussions unless there was a merger proposal that could be deemed "superior" to the JNJ offer. As a result, on December 5, 2005, BSX communicated an offer to acquire GDT for $36 in cash and $36 in BSX common stock (subject to various conditions).

Although JNJ had fought for many months to acquire GDT at a reduced price, within a month, it improved the price it was willing to pay for GDT. A bidding war was under way. On January 11, 2006, JNJ's offer was for $37.25 in cash and 0.493 shares of JNJ stock—an increase of $4 in cash. The following day, BSX responded by increasing its offer to a total of $73—$36.50 in cash and $36.50 in stock plus $0.012 interest per day for every day after April 1 that the merger was not completed. By offering compensation for any delay past April 1, BSX sought to reassure any shareholders who might otherwise decline the offer out of concerns that antitrust objections might delay completion of the merger.

JNJ responded the next day, on January 13, by increasing its offer to $40.52 in cash and 0.493 shares of JNJ stock. Although some believed that the auction was over, BSX was not done. On January 15, 2006 BSX increased its offer to $42 in cash and $38 in BSX stock for a total of $80. The two companies entered into a definitive merger agreement, the agreement with JNJ was terminated, and the GDT–BSX merger was ultimately completed in April 2006.

Despite all the legal issues and product liability problems, a competitive bidding war resulted in a more lucrative merger consideration for Guidant shareholders, who ultimately received $4.00 more than they would have with the original JNJ merger proposal.

This chapter discusses many of the issues brought forth in Example 8-1, such as the forms of payment in a merger, legal and contractual issues, and the necessity for regulatory approval. More importantly, this chapter aims to equip you with the basic tools for analyzing M&A deals and the companies behind them. In subsequent sections, we discuss the motives behind business combinations, various transaction characteristics of M&A deals, the regulations governing M&A activity, and how to evaluate a target company and a proposed merger. Section 2 discusses the basic types of mergers. Section 3 examines the common motives that drive merger activities. In Section 4, we consider various transaction characteristics and their impact on different facets of M&A deals. Section 5 focuses on takeovers and the common defenses used to defeat unwelcome takeover attempts. In Section 6, we outline the various regulations that apply to M&A activity. Section 7 explores methods for analyzing a target company and provides a framework for analyzing merger bids. In Section 8, we review the empirical evidence related to the distribution of gains in mergers. Section 9 provides a brief introduction to corporate restructuring activities, and Section 10 summarizes the chapter.

2. MERGERS AND ACQUISITIONS: DEFINITIONS AND CLASSIFICATIONS

Business combinations come in different forms. A distinction can be made between acquisitions and mergers. In the context of M&A, an **acquisition** is the purchase of some portion of one company by another. An acquisition might refer to the purchase of assets from another company, the purchase of a definable segment of another entity, such as a subsidiary, or the purchase of an entire company, in which case the acquisition would be known as a merger. A **merger** represents the absorption of one company by another. That is, one of the companies remains and the other ceases to exist as a separate entity. Typically, the smaller of the two entities is merged into the larger, but that is not always the case.

Mergers can be classified by the form of integration. In a **statutory merger**, one of the companies ceases to exist as an identifiable entity and all its assets and liabilities become part of the purchasing company. In a **subsidiary merger**, the company being purchased becomes a subsidiary of the purchaser, which is often done when the company being purchased has a strong brand or good image among consumers that the acquiring company wants to retain. A **consolidation** is similar to a statutory merger except that, in a consolidation, *both* companies terminate their previous legal existence and become part of a newly formed company. A consolidation is common in mergers where both companies are approximately the same size.

The parties to a merger are often identified as the target company and the acquiring company. The company that is being acquired is the **target company**, or simply the **target**. The company acquiring the target is called the **acquiring company**, or the **acquirer**. We will use this terminology throughout the chapter.

In practice, many of the terms used to describe various types of transactions are used loosely such that the distinctions between them are blurred. For example, the term "consolidation" is often applied to transactions where the entities are about the same size, even if the transaction is technically a statutory merger. Similarly, mergers are often described more generally as **takeovers**, although that term is often reserved to describe **hostile transactions**, which are attempts to acquire a company against the wishes of its managers and board of directors. A **friendly transaction**, in contrast, describes a potential business combination that is endorsed by the managers of both companies, although that is certainly no guarantee that the merger will ultimately occur.

An additional way that mergers are classified is based on the relatedness of the merging companies' business activities. Considered this way, there are three basic types of mergers: horizontal, vertical, and conglomerate.

A **horizontal merger** is one in which the merging companies are in the same kind of business, usually as competitors. The Vodafone AirTouch acquisition of telecommunications competitor Mannesmann AG in 2000 is one example of a horizontal merger. Another example is the merger of Mobil and Exxon in 1999. One of the great motivators behind horizontal mergers is the pursuit of **economies of scale**, which are savings achieved through the consolidation of operations and the elimination of duplicate resources. Another common reason for horizontal mergers is to increase market power, because the merger results in a reduction of the number of industry competitors and an increase in the size of the acquiring company.

In a **vertical merger**, the acquirer buys another company in the same production chain, for example, a supplier or a distributor. In addition to cost savings, a vertical merger may provide greater control over the production process in terms of quality or procurement of resources or greater control over the distribution of the acquirer's finished goods. If the acquirer purchases a target that is ahead of it in the value chain (a supplier), it is called **backward integration**. An example of backward integration is if a steel manufacturer purchases an iron ore mining company. When an acquirer purchases a company that is further down the value chain (a distributor), it is called **forward integration**. An example of forward integration is Merck & Co.'s 1993 acquisition of Medco Containment Services, a marketer of discount prescription medicines. The merger brought together the production and distribution of pharmaceuticals into one integrated company.

When an acquirer purchases another company that is unrelated to its core business, it may be called a **conglomerate merger**. General Electric is an example of a conglomerate, having purchased companies in a wide range of industries, including media, finance, home appliances, aircraft parts, and medical equipment. Conglomerate mergers were particularly popular from the 1960s through the 1980s. The concept of company-level diversification was commonly used as a rationale for interindustry mergers during this period. By investing in companies from a variety of industries, companies hoped to reduce the volatility of the conglomerate's total cash flows. As we will discuss in the section on merger motivations, company-level diversification is not necessarily in the shareholders' best interests.

EXAMPLE 8-2   History of U.S. Merger Activity

The history of merger activity in the United States illustrates the various types of M&A combinations. Merger and acquisition activities have historically come in waves. The predominant types of mergers and the structures of merger deals have varied with each wave, typically as a result of differences in the regulatory environment. Similarly, the industries involved tend to vary by wave. Merger activity is apt to be concentrated in a relatively small number of industries, usually those going through dramatic changes, such as deregulation or rapid technological advancement.

First Wave (1897–1904)

At the close of the 1800s, growth in the railroads linked regional markets and created an environment conducive to large companies that could capitalize on the emerging national U.S. economy, particularly in the mining and manufacturing industries. A relatively lax regulatory environment contributed to the situation, and many horizontal mergers resulted in nearly monopolistic conditions in several industries. The wave ended in 1904 as a result of a landmark decision by the U.S. Supreme Court limiting horizontal mergers among large competitors.

Second Wave (1916–1929)

In the 1920s, motor vehicles and radio, coupled with improved railroad infrastructure, further bolstered the U.S. economy. Like the previous wave, the second wave was accompanied by a sharp increase in stock prices. This time, however, the regulatory environment was less friendly to horizontal combinations and more sensitive to market power. Because market power was already concentrated among a few companies and further horizontal integration was difficult, companies sought to integrate backward into supply and forward into distribution through vertical mergers. Consequently, business combinations in this wave tended to create oligopolies. This second wave came to a conclusion with the 1929 stock market crash.

Third Wave (1965–1969)

The third wave occurred in a regulatory environment that strongly discouraged any merger—horizontal or vertical—that would reduce competition in an industry. Companies seeking to expand thus looked outside their own industries and began forming conglomerates. Many of the conglomerates created during this period subsequently underperformed the market. The third merger wave ended in 1969 as antitrust enforcement curtailed the rise of conglomerates.

Fourth Wave (1981–1989)

The regulatory environment in the 1980s was friendlier to both horizontal and vertical mergers than it had been in the 1960s, but what really fueled business combinations during this period was the development of the high-yield bond market, which benefited as falling interest rates and rising stock prices created an environment conducive to the greater use of leverage.

Although hostile takeovers were nothing new, increased ability to tap the high-yield bond market put the capacity to finance a takeover in the hands of people and companies that otherwise might not have had access to the necessary capital. This period was marked by the rise of the corporate raider and increasingly sophisticated takeover attempts (and defenses). A **corporate raider** is a person or organization seeking to profit by acquiring a company and reselling it.[2] As the 1980s came to a close, the stock market and economy softened, bringing the fourth wave to its conclusion.

Fifth Wave (1992–2001)

Following the 1990–1991 recession, merger activity increased in 1992 and intensified throughout the decade. A strong and long-running bull market created many companies with high market valuations, which were then more easily able to use their equity

---

[2]As we will point out later in the section on takeover defenses, in some circumstances a corporate raider can profit from an unsuccessful takeover attempt. It was common during this merger wave for companies to pay raiders a premium in exchange for the raider terminating the attempted takeover, a tactic commonly referred to as "greenmail." Indeed, many raiders initiated takeover attempts without expecting to complete the acquisition.

to purchase other companies; thus, stock-swap mergers became more common during this wave. Additionally, during the latter half of the 1990s, U.S. regulators were more open to industry consolidation as merger waves in Europe and Asia created larger international competitors. Deregulation and technological advancement further fueled merger activity, particularly in banking, health care, defense, and telecommunications. The fifth wave ended with a dramatic decline in transactions in 2001 as the market and the economy waned following the end of the Internet bubble of the late 1990s.

Sixth Wave (2003–Present)

Based on M&A industry statistics, such as M&A deal volume, it appears that we are in the midst of a sixth wave that began in 2003. After a sharp decline in the number of M&A deals directly following the conclusion of the fifth wave in 2001, the market began to pick up again in 2003 and strengthened rapidly through 2004. The number of transactions increased again in 2005 and surpassed the transaction volume records set at the height of the Internet bubble to reach a new all-time high. As in the fifth wave, there has been much industry consolidation in the sixth wave, which is producing larger companies that are better able to compete globally.

3. MOTIVES FOR MERGER

In the previous section, we mentioned some of the basic motives behind mergers, such as the search for economies of scale (in a horizontal merger) or cost savings through integration (in a vertical merger). In this section, we expand on this topic and survey some of the reasons companies merge—the motives or rationales for merger.

The topic is important because, in assessing a proposed combination, investors and analysts need to carefully evaluate the rationale behind the merger. Does the stated rationale make sense? Is the merger likely to create value? What is the probability that each of the stated goals for the merger will be attained? Keep in mind that many motives are interrelated and that there are typically several motives, both acknowledged and tacit, behind any merger.

3.1. Synergy

Among the most common motivations for a merger is the creation of synergy, in which the whole of the combined company will be worth more than the sum of its parts. Generally speaking, synergies created through a merger will either reduce costs or enhance revenues. Cost synergies are typically achieved through economies of scale in research and development, procurement, manufacturing, sales and marketing, distribution, and administration. Revenue synergies are created through the cross-selling of products, expanded market share, or higher prices arising from reduced competition. For example, a bank that acquires its competitors can both increase its market share and realize operating efficiencies by closing duplicate branches and integrating back-office operations.

3.2. Growth

Corporate managers are under constant pressure to grow their companies' revenues, and they often turn to M&A activity to achieve that growth. Companies can grow either by making investments internally (i.e., **organic growth**) or by buying the necessary resources externally (i.e., **external growth**). It is typically faster for companies to grow externally. Growth through M&A activity is common when a company is in a mature industry. For example, the global oil industry is a mature industry, and BP, Exxon Mobil, and Chevron Corporation have increased their reserves and output by acquiring smaller competitors.

External growth can also mitigate risk. It is considered less risky to merge with an existing company than to enter an unfamiliar market and establish the resources internally. The last several years of the fifth merger wave in the 1990s were characterized by a surge in cross-border M&A transactions, many of which were motivated by the desire to establish footholds in international markets.

3.3. Increasing Market Power

In industries where there are few competitors or where market share is sufficiently concentrated, horizontal integration may be a means by which to increase market power. When a company increases its market power through horizontal mergers, it may have a greater ability to influence market prices. Taken to an extreme, horizontal integration results in a monopoly.

Vertical integration may also result in increased market power. Vertical mergers can lock in a company's sources of critical supplies or create captive markets for its products. Imagine, for example, an industry in which one company supplies raw materials to two separate manufacturing companies. If one of the manufacturers were to acquire the raw materials provider, the acquirer would be in a position to influence industry output and ultimately prices. As we discuss further in the section on antitrust regulation, government regulators routinely block both horizontal and vertical mergers that reduce competition in an industry and concentrate market power in the hands of too few companies.

3.4. Acquiring Unique Capabilities and Resources

Many companies undertake a merger or an acquisition either to pursue competitive advantages or to shore up lacking resources. When a company cannot cost-effectively create internally the capabilities needed to sustain its future success, it may seek to acquire them elsewhere. For example, a company may engage in M&A activity to acquire specific competencies or resources it lacks, such as a strong research department, nimble sales force, intellectual capital, or creative talent.

3.5. Diversification

Companies sometimes cite diversification as one of the motives behind a merger. Indeed, this was an especially popular motive for conglomerates during the third merger wave. The idea behind company-level diversification is that the company can be treated as a portfolio of investments in other companies. If a conglomerate invests in companies from a variety of industries, then the variability of the conglomerate's total cash flows should be reduced, at least to the extent that the industries are uncorrelated.

Although this may seem like a rational motive, typically it is not in the best interests of the conglomerate's shareholders. In a well functioning capital market, investors can diversify their own portfolios more easily and at less expense. Additionally, the desire to diversify has led some companies to lose sight of their major competitive strengths and to expand into businesses where they lack comparative advantages.

3.6. Bootstrapping Earnings

Even when there are no reasons to believe that synergies or growth would result from a merger, it is possible to create the illusion of synergies or growth. When a company's earnings increase as a consequence of the merger transaction itself (rather than because of resulting economic benefits of the combination), it is referred to as the "bootstrap effect" or "bootstrapping earnings." The bootstrap effect occurs when the shares of the acquirer trade at a higher price-to-earnings ratio (P/E) than those of the target and the acquirer's P/E does not decline following the merger.

EXAMPLE 8-3   Bootstrapping Earnings

Assume two companies are planning a merger. Company A is the acquirer, Company T is the target, and Company A* is the post-merger combination of the two companies. The companies' stock prices and earnings per share follow. Note that the acquirer has a P/E of 25.0 and the target has a P/E of 20.0:

	A	T	A*
Stock price	$100.00	$50.00	
EPS	$4.00	$2.50	$4.20
P/E	25.0	20.0	
Total shares outstanding	100,000	50,000	125,000
Total earnings	$400,000	$125,000	$525,000
Market value of equity	$10,000,000	$2,500,000	

Given its stock price, the acquirer can issue 25,000 of its own shares and use the proceeds to buy the target company. This amount is determined by dividing the target's market value by the acquirer's stock price ($2,500,000/$100 = 25,000). The total shares outstanding of the merged company will be 125,000—the acquirer's initial 100,000 shares plus the 25,000 shares that the acquirer issued to purchase the target. After the merger, the company's combined earnings are divided by the number of shares outstanding to determine the new EPS ($525,000/125,000 = $4.20), which is $0.20 higher per share than the acquirer would have reported without the merger.

If the acquirer's pre-merger stock price had been $80 instead of $100, then A's pre-merger P/E would have been 20.0 ($80/$4.00). In that scenario, the acquirer would have issued 31,250 shares to purchase the target. The EPS of the merged company would then have been $525,000/131,250 = $4.00, thus illustrating that, for bootstrapping to work, the acquirer's P/E must be higher than the target's P/E.

If the market is efficient, the post-merger P/E should adjust to the weighted average of the two companies' contributions to the merged company's earnings. In the previous example, the P/E of the merged company would be about 23.8, which implies that the acquirer's stock price would remain at $100. If, however, the acquiring company's P/E is higher than the target's and management can convince investors to value the merged company using the acquirer's pre-merger P/E, then the stock price of the new company should rise. If the acquirer bootstraps earnings to $4.20 per share, as shown in the example, then the share price should increase to $105 if investors apply the pre-merger P/E of 25.0 times earnings ($4.20 × 25.0 = $105). When there are no expected gains from synergy or other factors, such share price increases are not expected.

The market usually recognizes the bootstrapping effect, and post-merger P/Es adjust accordingly. But there have been periods when bootstrapping seemed to pay off for managers, at least in the short run. During the third merger wave, many conglomerates benefited from bootstrapping as investors grappled with how to value these diversified corporate behemoths. Likewise, during the Internet bubble of the late 1990s, many high P/E companies bootstrapped their earnings and showed continuous EPS growth through a constant string of mergers with lower P/E companies.

3.7. Managers' Personal Incentives

Various managerial-related theories for mergers have been developed over the years based on evidence of agency problems. **Managerialism theories** posit that, because executive compensation is highly correlated with company size, corporate executives are motivated to engage in mergers to maximize the size of their company rather than shareholder value. Additionally, corporate executives may be motivated by self-aggrandizement. For example, being the senior executive of a large company conveys greater power and more prestige.

3.8. Tax Considerations

It is possible for a profitable acquirer to benefit from merging with a target that has accumulated large tax losses. Instead of carrying the tax losses forward, the merged company uses the tax losses to immediately lower its tax liability. In many countries, the taxing authority disallows an offset when the primary reason for the merger is tax avoidance. Mergers are typically conducted for a variety of reasons, however, and it is difficult for regulatory authorities to prove that tax considerations are a primary motivator.

3.9. Unlocking Hidden Value

A potential target company may be uncompetitive over a sustained period for a host of reasons, including poor management, lack of resources, high legacy costs, or poor organizational structure. In those instances, when a potential target is underperforming, an acquirer may believe it can acquire the company cheaply and then unlock hidden value through reorganization, better management, or synergy. If the target has been underperforming significantly, the acquirer may even believe it can obtain the company for less than its breakup value. A company's **breakup value** is the value that can be achieved if a company's assets are divided and sold separately.

Sometimes mergers are conducted because the acquirer believes that it is purchasing assets for below their replacement cost. For example, a pharmaceutical company may believe it can acquire another company's research more cheaply than to undergo a lengthy development process of its own. Or an oil company may believe it is less expensive to acquire another oil company's assets than to find and develop additional reserves of its own.

3.10.   Cross-Border Motivations

The growth of cross-border deals was high during the 1990s, and foreign M&A became a popular strategic tool for multinational companies seeking to extend their market reach, acquire new manufacturing facilities, develop new sources of raw materials, and tap into the capital markets. Given the increasing international privatization trends, reduction in cumbersome industry regulations and bureaucracy, and development of uniform accounting standards, cross-border mergers and acquisitions will likely intensify in the future. In addition to the various factors that drive domestic mergers, cross-border mergers can provide an efficient way of achieving other international business goals.

3.10.1.   Exploiting Market Imperfections   Cross-border transactions can enable companies to more fully exploit market imperfections. For example, to take advantage of differences in the relative cost of labor, a manufacturer may purchase a company in a country where the relative cost of labor is lower.

3.10.2.   Overcoming Adverse Government Policy   Cross-border mergers can be a means by which to overcome disadvantageous government policy, for example, to circumvent protective tariffs, quotas, or other barriers to free trade.

3.10.3.   Technology Transfer   Companies that possess a new or superior technology may make acquisitions abroad to open new markets or otherwise more fully exploit their business advantage. Conversely, it is common for a company to purchase a foreign company that possesses a new or superior technology to enhance the acquirer's competitive position both at home and abroad.

3.10.4.   Product Differentiation   Companies often purchase foreign companies to exploit the advantages of having a highly differentiated line of products. Similarly, buying certain intangibles, such as a good reputation, helps to ensure success in the global market. Lenovo's (China) acquisition of IBM's (United States) personal computer line is one example of this strategy.

3.10.5.   Following Clients   Companies may engage in a cross-border merger to follow and support domestic clients more effectively. As an example, many German banks have established cross-border presences to provide services abroad to their domestic clients.

EXAMPLE 8-4   Mergers and the Industry Life Cycle

The types of mergers (e.g., horizontal, vertical, or conglomerate) occurring in an industry and the motivations behind those mergers vary over time as an industry proceeds through its life cycle. The stages in an industry life cycle are normally categorized by their rates of growth in sales; growth stages can vary in length.

Mergers and Industry Life Cycle

Industry Life Cycle Stage	Industry Description	Motives for Merger	Types of Mergers
Pioneering development	Industry exhibits substantial development costs and has low, but slowly increasing, sales growth.	Younger, smaller companies may sell themselves to larger companies in mature or declining industries and look for ways to enter into a new growth industry. Young companies may look to merge with companies that allow them to pool management and capital resources.	Conglomerate Horizontal
Rapid accelerating growth	Industry exhibits high profit margins caused by few participants in the market.	Explosive growth in sales may require large capital requirements to expand existing capacity.	Conglomerate Horizontal
Mature growth	Industry experiences a drop in the entry of new competitors, but growth potential remains.	Mergers may be undertaken to achieve economies of scale, savings, and operational efficiencies.	Horizontal Vertical
Stabilization and market maturity	Industry faces increasing competition and capacity constraints.	Mergers may be undertaken to achieve economies of scale in research, production, and marketing to match the low cost and price performance of other companies (domestic and foreign). Large companies may acquire smaller companies to improve management and provide a broader financial base.	Horizontal
Deceleration of growth and decline	Industry faces overcapacity and eroding profit margins.	Horizontal mergers may be undertaken to ensure survival. Vertical mergers may be carried out to increase efficiency and profit margins. Companies in related industries may merge to exploit synergy. Companies in this industry may acquire companies in young industries.	Horizontal Vertical Conglomerate

Source: Adapted from Weston, Chung, and Hoag (1990, 102) and Solnik and McLeavey (2004, 264–265).

4. TRANSACTION CHARACTERISTICS

The specifics of M&A transactions can vary along many dimensions, including the form of acquisition, financing, timing, control and governance, accounting choices, and numerous details ranging from the post-merger board composition to the location of the new headquarters. In this section, we focus on the form of acquisition, method of payment, and mindset of target management. These three characteristics play large roles in determining how the transaction will occur, which regulatory rules might apply, how the transaction will be valued, and how it will be taxed.

4.1. Form of Acquisition

There are two basic forms of acquisition: An acquirer can decide to purchase the target's stock or its assets. The decision has several consequences, as summarized in Exhibit 8-1.

Stock purchases are the most common form of acquisition. A **stock purchase** occurs when the acquirer gives the target company's shareholders some combination of cash and securities in exchange for shares of the target company's stock. For a stock purchase to proceed, it must be approved by at least 50 percent of the target company's shareholders and sometimes more depending on the legal jurisdiction. Although it can be difficult and time-consuming to win shareholder approval, it also stands as an opportunity to circumvent the target company's management in cases where management opposes the merger.

In an **asset purchase**, the acquirer purchases the target company's assets and payment is made directly to the target company. One advantage of this type of transaction is that it can be conducted more quickly and easily than a stock purchase because shareholder approval is not normally required unless a substantial proportion of the assets are being sold, usually more than 50 percent. Another advantage is that an acquirer can focus on buying the parts of a company of particular interest, such as a specific division, rather than the entire company.

Some of the more dramatic consequences of the decision to pursue one form of acquisition over another concern taxation. In a stock purchase, the target company's shareholders exchange their shares for compensation and must pay tax on their gains, but there are no tax

EXHIBIT 8-1 Major Differences of Stock versus Asset Purchases

	Stock Purchase	Asset Purchase
Payment	Target shareholders receive compensation in exchange for their shares.	Payment is made to the selling company rather than directly to the shareholders.
Approval	Shareholder approval is required.	Shareholder approval might not be required.
Corporate tax	There are no corporate-level taxes.	The target company pays taxes on any capital gains.
Shareholder tax	The target company's shareholders are taxed on their capital gain.	There are no direct tax consequence for target company's shareholders.
Liabilities	The acquirer assumes the target's liabilities.	The acquirer generally avoids the assumption of liabilities.

consequences at the corporate level.[3] For an asset purchase, in contrast, there are no direct tax consequences for the target company's shareholders but the target company itself may be subject to corporate taxes.

In addition to shifting the basic tax burden, the form-of-acquisition decision plays a role in determining how tax rules are applied in accounting for the merger. For example, the use of a target's accumulated tax losses is allowable in the United States for stock purchases, but not for asset purchases.

Another key difference between stock and asset purchases relates to the assumption of liabilities. In stock purchases, the acquiring company assumes the target company's liabilities. Acquiring companies must thus be on guard to avoid assuming unexpected or undisclosed liabilities. With asset purchases, acquiring companies generally avoid assuming the target's liabilities. However, purchasing substantially all of a company's assets instead of conducting a stock purchase so as to specifically avoid assuming liabilities is fraught with legal risk because courts have tended to hold acquirers responsible for the liabilities in these cases.

4.2. Method of Payment

The acquirer can pay for the merger with cash, securities, or some combination of the two in what is called a **mixed offering**. In a **cash offering**, the cash might come from the acquiring company's existing assets or from a debt issue. In the most general case of a **securities offering**, the target shareholders receive shares of the acquirer's common stock as compensation.[4] Instead of common stock, however, the acquirer might offer other securities, such as preferred shares or even debt securities.

In a stock offering, the **exchange ratio** determines the number of shares that stockholders in the target company receive in exchange for each of their shares in the target company. Because share prices are constantly fluctuating, exchange ratios are typically negotiated in advance for a range of stock prices. The acquirer's cost is the product of the exchange ratio, the number of outstanding shares of the target company, and the value of the stock given to target shareholders. Each shareholder of the target company receives new shares based on the number of target shares he or she owns multiplied by the exchange ratio.

EXAMPLE 8-5   Stock Offering

Discount Books, a Canadian bookseller, has announced its intended acquisition of Premier Marketing Corporation, a small marketing company specializing in print media. In a press release, Discount Books outlines the terms of the merger, which specify that Premier Marketing's shareholders will each receive 0.90 shares of Discount Books for every share of Premier Marketing owned. Premier Marketing has 1 million

---

[3]Keep in mind throughout this discussion of taxation that we are speaking in generalities and that the complexity of M&A deals, coupled with the complexity and variability of tax laws in different jurisdictions, can generate a host of exceptions.

[4]In the case of a consolidation, the target company's shareholders may receive new shares in the surviving entity.

shares outstanding. On the day of the merger announcement, Discount Books' stock closes at C$20.00 and Premier Marketing's stock closes at C$15.00. Catherine Willis is an individual investor who owns 500 shares of Premier Marketing, currently worth C$7,500 (500 × C$15.00).

1. Based on the current share prices, what is the cost of the acquisition for Discount Books?
2. How many shares of Discount Books will Catherine Willis receive, and what is the value of those shares (based on current share prices)?

Solution to 1

Because there are 1 million shares of Premier Marketing outstanding and the exchange ratio is 0.90 shares, Discount Books will need to issue 0.90 × 1 million = 900,000 shares of Discount Books stock to complete the transaction. Because the cost per share of Discount Books stock is currently C$20.00, the cost of the transaction to Discount Books will be C$20.00 × 900,000 = C$18 million.

Solution to 2

Catherine Willis will turn over her 500 shares of Premier Marketing stock. As compensation, she will receive 0.90 × 500 = 450 shares of stock in Discount Books. With each share of Discount Books being worth C$20.00, the value of those shares to Catherine is C$9,000.

Note that the value of Willis' Premier Marketing shares was C$7,500. The C$1,500 difference in value is a premium paid by Discount Books for control of Premier Marketing. The pre-merger value of Premier Marketing was C$15 million, but Discount Books' total cost to purchase the company was C$18 million. The 20 percent, or C$3 million, difference is the total-control premium paid by Discount Books.

A variety of factors influence a company's decision to negotiate for one method of payment over another. As we shall explore in more detail later, the form of payment has an impact on the distribution of risk and reward between acquirer and target shareholders. In a stock offering, target company shareholders assume a portion of the reward as well as a portion of the risk related to the estimated synergies and the target company's value. Consequently, when an acquiring company's management is highly confident both in their ability to complete the merger and in the value to be created by the merger, they are more inclined to negotiate for a cash offering rather than for a stock offering.

Another factor in the decision relates to the relative valuations of the companies involved in the transaction. When an acquirer's shares are considered overvalued by the market relative to the target company's shares, stock financing is more appropriate. In effect, the shares are more valuable as a currency. In fact, investors sometimes interpret an acquirer's stock offering as a signal that the company's shares may be overvalued. This effect is similar to the negative market reaction observed in seasoned equity offerings. Indeed, during the stock market bubble in the late 1990s, stock financing of mergers was quite popular.

Another important consideration when deciding on the payment method is the accompanying change in capital structure. The costs and benefits of different payment structures reflect how the offer will affect the acquirer's capital structure. For instance, on the one hand, borrowing to raise funds for a cash offering increases the acquirer's financial leverage and risk. On the other hand, issuing a significant number of new common shares for a stock offering can dilute the ownership interests of existing shareholders.

Preferences in the use of cash versus stock vary over time, but the proportions in 2005 are characteristic of the past several years. According to *Mergerstat Review 2006*, cash payment accounted for 54 percent of merger transactions in 2005, pure stock exchanges accounted for about 19 percent, and mixed offerings represented 25 percent.[5] A very small portion of deals, about 2 percent, were completed with other securities, such as debt, options, or warrants.

4.3. Mind-Set of Target Management

Mergers are referred to as either "friendly" or "hostile" depending on how the target company's senior managers and board of directors view the offer. The distinction is not trivial because an enormous amount of time and resources can be expended by both acquirer and target when the takeover is hostile. Whether a merger is friendly or hostile has an impact on how it is completed, what regulations must be followed, how long the transaction takes, and possibly how much value is created (or destroyed) as a result of the combination.

4.3.1. Friendly Mergers   Unless there is cause to think the target will be hostile to a merger, the acquirer generally starts the process by approaching target management directly. The target could approach the acquirer, although this method is much less common. If both management teams are amenable to a potential deal, then the two companies enter into merger discussions. The negotiations revolve around the consideration to be received by the target company's shareholders and the terms of the transaction as well as other aspects, such as the post-merger management structure.

Before negotiations can culminate in a formal deal, each of the parties examines the others' books and records in a process called "due diligence." The purpose of due diligence is to protect the companies' respective shareholders by attempting to confirm the accuracy of representations made during negotiations. For example, an acquirer would want to ensure that the target's assets exist and are worth approximately what was claimed by the target. Likewise, a target might want to examine an acquirer's financial records to gauge the likelihood that the acquirer has the capacity to pay for the acquisition as outlined in negotiations. Any deficiencies or problems uncovered during the due diligence process could have an impact on negotiations, resulting in adjustments to the terms or price of the deal. If the issue is large enough, the business combination might be called off entirely.

Once due diligence and negotiations have been completed, the companies enter into a definitive merger agreement. The **definitive merger agreement** is a contract written by both companies' attorneys and is ultimately signed by each party to the transaction. The agreement contains the details of the transaction, including the terms, warranties, conditions, termination details, and the rights of all parties.

---

[5]FactSet Mergerstat, LLC, *Mergerstat Review 2006* (www.mergerstat.com).

Common industry practice has evolved such that companies typically discuss potential transactions in private and maintain secrecy until the definitive merger agreement is reached. This trend may have been influenced by shifts in securities laws toward more stringent rules related to the disclosure of material developments to the public. Additionally, news of a merger can cause dramatic changes in the stock prices of the parties to the transaction. Premature announcement of a deal can cause volatile swings in the stock prices of the companies as they proceed through negotiations.

After the definitive merger agreement has been signed, the transaction is generally announced to the public through a joint press release by the companies. In a friendly merger, the target company's management endorses the merger and recommends that its stockholders approve the transaction. When a shareholder vote is needed, whether it is the target shareholders approving the stock purchase or the acquirer shareholders approving the issuance of a significant number of new shares, the material facts are provided to the appropriate shareholders in a public document called a **proxy statement**, which is given to shareholders in anticipation of their vote.

After all the necessary approvals have been obtained—from shareholders as well as any other parties, such as regulatory bodies—the attorneys file the required documentation with securities regulators and the merger is officially completed. Target shareholders receive the consideration agreed upon under the terms of the transaction, and the companies are officially and legally combined.

4.3.2. Hostile Mergers   In a hostile merger, which is a merger that is opposed by the target company's management, the acquirer may decide to circumvent the target management's objections by submitting a merger proposal directly to the target company's board of directors and bypassing the CEO. This tactic is known as a **bear hug**.

Because bear hugs are not formal offers and have not been mutually agreed upon, there are no standard procedures in these cases. If the offer is high enough to warrant serious consideration, the board may appoint a special committee to negotiate a sale of the target.

Although unlikely in practice, it is possible that target management will capitulate after a bear hug and enter into negotiations, which may ultimately lead to a friendly merger. If the bear hug is not successful, then the hopeful acquirer attempts to appeal more directly to the target company's shareholders.

One method for taking a merger appeal directly to shareholders is through a **tender offer**, whereby the acquirer invites target shareholders to submit ("tender") their shares in return for the proposed payment.[6] It is up to the individual shareholders to physically tender shares to the acquiring company's agent to receive payment. A tender offer can be made with cash, shares of the acquirer's own stock, other securities, or some combination of securities and cash. Because a cash tender offer can be completed in less time than a cash merger, some acquiring companies use this type of transaction to gain control of a target company quickly.

Another method of taking over a target company involves the use of a proxy fight. In a **proxy fight**, a company or individual seeks to take control of a company through a shareholder vote. Proxy solicitation is approved by regulators and then mailed directly to target

---

[6]Tender offers are often associated with hostile mergers, but they also occur in a friendly context. Tender offers are considered hostile only when the offer is opposed by the target company's management and board of directors.

company shareholders. The shareholders are asked to vote for the acquirer's proposed slate of directors. If the acquirer's slate is elected to the target's board, then it is able to replace the target company's management. At this point, the transaction may evolve into a friendly merger.

Regardless of how an acquirer seeks to establish control, target managers have a variety of alternatives available for defending the company against unwanted overtures. In these cases, the target usually retains the services of law firms and investment bankers to design a defense against the unwanted takeover attempt. As we discuss in the next section, target company managers may use a variety of legal and financial defensive maneuvers to ward off a takeover attempt.

5. TAKEOVERS

When a target company is faced with a hostile tender offer (takeover) attempt, the target managers and board of directors face a basic choice. They can decide to negotiate and sell the company, either to the hostile bidder or a third party, or they can attempt to remain independent. Aside from the strength of the company's defenses and target management's resolve to stay independent, the premium over the market price offered by the acquirer for the target company's shares is the major driving factor in the decision to support or resist any given takeover.

If the target management decides to resist the unwanted overture, they have a variety of takeover defense mechanisms at their disposal. Once the decision has been reached, the target company generally seeks the counsel of investment bankers and lawyers to explore the fairness of the hostile offer and to advise the board of the alternatives.

A target might use defensive measures to delay, negotiate a better deal for shareholders, or attempt to keep the company independent. Defensive measures can be implemented either before or after a takeover attempt has begun. Most law firms specializing in takeovers recommend that defenses be set up before a company receives or expects any takeover activity.

5.1. Pre-Offer Takeover Defense Mechanisms

In the United States, most hostile takeover attempts result in litigation. The courts generally bless legal pre-offer defense mechanisms but tend to scrutinize post-offer defenses very closely. The target usually assumes the burden of proof in showing that the recently enacted defenses are not simply intended to perpetuate management's tenure at the target company. It is for this reason that most attorneys recommend that target companies put defenses in place prior to any takeover action. Following this policy gives the target more flexibility when defending against a takeover bid.

With different twists in takeover strategy come new innovations and variations in takeover defenses. Given the many possible variations, the following is not an exhaustive list but an overview of the more well-known antitakeover strategies. The two broad varieties of pre-offer defenses are rights-based defenses, such as poison pills and poison puts, and a variety of changes to the corporate charter (e.g., staggered boards of directors and supermajority provisions) that are sometimes collectively referred to as **shark repellents**.

5.1.1. Poison Pills   The **poison pill** is a legal device that makes it prohibitively costly for an acquirer to take control of a target without the prior approval of the target's board of directors. Most poison pills make the target company less attractive by creating rights that allow for the issuance of shares of the target company's stock at a substantial discount to market value.

There are two basic types of poison pills: the **flip-in pill** and the **flip-over pill**. When the common shareholder of the target company has the right to buy its shares at a discount, the pill is known as a flip-in. The pill is triggered when a specific level of ownership is exceeded. Because the acquiring company is generally prohibited from participating in the purchase through the pill, the acquirer is subject to a significant level of dilution. Most plans give the target's board of directors the right to redeem the pill prior to any triggering event. If the takeover becomes friendly, the board generally exercises this waiver.

In the case of a flip-over pill, the target company's common shareholders receive the right to purchase shares of the acquiring company at a significant discount from the market price, which has the effect of causing dilution to all existing acquiring company shareholders. Again, the board of the target generally retains the right to redeem the pill should the transaction become friendly.

Another possible aspect of the poison pill is the **dead-hand provision**. This provision allows the board of the target to redeem or cancel the poison pill only by a vote of the continuing directors. Because continuing directors are generally defined as directors who were on the target company's board prior to the takeover attempt, this provision has the effect of making it much more difficult to take over a target without prior board approval.

5.1.2. Poison Puts   Whereas poison pills grant common shareholders certain rights in a hostile takeover attempt, **poison puts** give rights to the target company's bondholders. In the event of a takeover, poison puts allow bondholders to put the bonds to the company. In other words, if the provision is triggered by a hostile takeover attempt, then bondholders have the right to sell their bonds back to the target at a redemption price that is pre-specified in the bond indenture, typically at or above par value. The effect of a poison put defense is to require that an acquirer be prepared to refinance the target's debt immediately after the takeover. This defense increases the need for cash and raises the cost of the acquisition.

5.1.3. Incorporation in a State with Restrictive Takeover Laws (United States)   In the United States, many states have adopted laws that specifically address unfriendly takeover attempts. These laws are designed to provide target companies with flexibility in dealing with unwanted suitors. Some states have designed their laws to give the company maximum protection and leeway in defending against an offer. As a result, companies that anticipate the possibility of a hostile takeover attempt may find it attractive to reincorporate in a jurisdiction that has enacted strict antitakeover laws. Ohio and Pennsylvania are examples of two U.S. states that have been regarded historically as "target-friendly" states; their state laws tend to give target companies the most power in defending against hostile takeover attempts.[7]

---

[7]Delaware has historically been the most popular state for corporations to domicile their legal entities. To protect this status, the state has found it necessary to toughen its laws regarding takeover attempts. In the past, as some states adopted strict takeover laws, some corporations left Delaware and reincorporated in these "friendly" states. To compete, Delaware has changed its own laws to make it more difficult to take over a Delaware corporation on a hostile basis.

5.1.4. Staggered Board of Directors   Instead of electing the entire board of directors each year at the company's annual meeting, a company may arrange to stagger the terms for board members so that only a portion of the board seats are due for election each year. For example, if the company has a board consisting of nine directors, members could be elected for three-year terms with only three directors coming up for election each year. The effect of this staggered board is that it would take at least two years to elect enough directors to take control of the board.

5.1.5. Restricted Voting Rights   Some target companies adopt a mechanism that restricts stockholders who have recently acquired large blocks of stock from voting their shares. Usually, there is a trigger stockholding level, such as 15 or 20 percent. Shareholders who meet or exceed this trigger point are no longer able to exercise their voting rights without the target company's board releasing the shareholder from the constraint. The possibility of owning a controlling position in the target without being able to vote the shares serves as a deterrent.

5.1.6. Supermajority Voting Provisions   Many target companies change their charter and bylaws to provide for a higher percentage approval by shareholders for mergers than normally is required. A typical provision might require a vote of 80 percent of the outstanding shares of the target company (as opposed to a simple 51 percent majority). This supermajority requirement is triggered by a hostile takeover attempt and is frequently accompanied by a provision that prevents the hostile acquirer from voting its shares. Thus, even if an acquirer is able to accumulate a substantial portion of the target's shares, it may have great difficulty accumulating enough votes to approve a merger.

5.1.7. Fair Price Amendments   Fair price amendments are changes to the corporate charter and bylaws that disallow mergers for which the offer is below some threshold. For example, a fair price amendment might require an acquirer to pay at least as much as the highest stock price at which the target has traded in the public market over a specified period. Fair price amendments protect targets against temporary declines in their share prices by setting a floor value bid. Additionally, fair price amendments protect against two-tiered tender offers where the acquirer offers a higher bid in a first step tender offer with the threat of a lower bid in a second step tender offer for those who do not tender right away.

5.1.8. Golden Parachutes   Golden parachutes are compensation agreements between the target company and its senior managers. These employment contracts allow the executives to receive lucrative payouts, usually several years worth of salary, if they leave the target company following a change in corporate control. In practice, golden parachutes do not offer much deterrent, especially for large deals where the managers' compensation is small relative to the overall takeover price. One reason they persist is that they help alleviate target management's concerns about job loss. Golden parachutes may encourage key executives to stay with the target as the takeover progresses and the target explores all options to generate shareholder value. Without a golden parachute, some contend that target company executives might be quicker to seek employment offers from other companies to secure their financial future. Whether this is actually the case and whether golden parachutes are fair and in the best interest of shareholders is the subject of considerable debate among shareholder rights activists and senior managers.

5.2. Post-Offer Takeover Defense Mechanisms

A target also has several defensive mechanisms that can be used once a takeover has already been initiated. Because they may not be as successful when used in isolation and because they have historically been subject to greater scrutiny by the courts, post-offer defenses are typically used in conjunction with pre-offer defenses.

5.2.1. "Just Say No" Defense Probably the simplest place for a target company to start when confronted with a hostile takeover bid is to rely on pre-takeover defenses and to decline the offer. If the acquirer attempts a bear hug or tender offer, then target management typically lobbies the board of directors and shareholders to decline and build a case for why the offering price is inadequate or why the offer is otherwise not in the shareholders' best interests. This strategy forces the hopeful acquirer to adjust its bid or further reveal its own strategy to advance the takeover attempt.

5.2.2. Litigation A popular technique used by many target companies is to file a lawsuit against the acquiring company based on alleged violations of securities or antitrust laws. In the United States, these suits may be filed in either state or federal courts. Unless there is a serious antitrust violation, these suits rarely stop a takeover bid. Instead, lawsuits often serve as a delaying tactic to create additional time for target management to develop other responses to the unwanted offer. Generally, any securities law violations, even if upheld, can be corrected with additional public disclosures. In the United States, most antitrust claims that eventually prevent takeover attempts are initiated by either antitrust or securities regulators rather than by the target company.

5.2.3. Greenmail This technique involves an agreement allowing the target to repurchase its own shares back from the acquiring company, usually at a premium to the market price. Greenmail is usually accompanied by an agreement that the acquirer will not pursue another hostile takeover attempt of the target for a set period. In effect, greenmail is the termination of a hostile takeover through a payoff to the acquirer. The shareholders of the target company do not receive any compensation for their shares. Greenmail was popular in the United States during the 1980s, but its use has been extremely restricted since 1986 when the U.S. Internal Revenue Code was amended to add a 50 percent tax on profits realized by acquirers through greenmail.

5.2.4. Share Repurchase Rather than repurchasing only the shares held by the acquiring company, as in greenmail, a target might use a share repurchase to acquire shares from any shareholder. For example, a target may initiate a cash tender offer for its own outstanding shares. An effective repurchase can increase the potential cost for an acquirer by either increasing the stock's price outright or by causing the acquirer to increase its bid to remain competitive with the target company's tender offer for its own shares. Additionally, a share repurchase often has the effect of increasing the target company's use of leverage because borrowing is typically required to purchase the shares. This additional debt makes the target less attractive as a takeover candidate.

In some cases, a target company buys all of its shares and converts to a privately held company in a transaction called a leveraged buyout. In a **leveraged buyout (LBO)**, the management team generally partners with a private equity firm that specializes in buyouts. The new entity borrows a high proportion of the overall purchase price, the financial firm contributes a certain amount of capital, and the management team provides the management expertise to run the business. In exchange for their expertise, management generally receives a payout percentage based on the profitability and success of the company after the LBO is completed. This strategy may allow the target to defend against a hostile bid provided that the LBO provides target shareholders with a level of value that exceeds the would-be acquirer's offer.

5.2.5. Leveraged Recapitalization   A technique somewhat related to the leveraged buyout is the leveraged recapitalization. A **leveraged recapitalization** involves the assumption of a large amount of debt, which is then used to finance share repurchases (but in contrast to a leveraged buyout, in a recapitalization, some shares remain in public hands). The effect is to dramatically change the company's capital structure while attempting to deliver a value to target shareholders in excess of the hostile bid.

5.2.6. "Crown Jewel" Defense   After a hostile takeover is announced, a target may decide to sell off a subsidiary or asset to a third party. If the acquisition of this subsidiary or asset was one of the acquirer's major motivations for the proposed merger, then this strategy could cause the acquirer to abandon its takeover effort. When a target initiates such a sale after a hostile takeover bid is announced, there is a good chance that the courts will declare this strategy illegal.

5.2.7. "Pac-Man" Defense   The target can defend itself by making a counteroffer to acquire the hostile bidder. This technique is rarely used because, in most cases, it means that a smaller company (the target) is making a bid for a larger entity. Additionally, once a target uses a Pac-Man defense, it forgoes the ability to use a number of other defensive strategies. For instance, after making a counteroffer, a target cannot very well take the acquirer to court claiming an antitrust violation.

5.2.8. White Knight Defense   Often the best outcome for target shareholders is for the target company's board to seek a third party to purchase the company in lieu of the hostile bidder. This third party is called a **white knight** because it is coming to the aid of the target. A target usually initiates this technique by seeking out another company that has a strategic fit with the target. Based on a good strategic fit, the third party can often justify a higher price for the target than what the hostile bidder is offering.

Once a white knight bid is made public, it may elicit an additional higher bid from the hostile bidder. This can help kick off a competitive bidding situation. In some cases, because of the competitive nature of the bidders, the winner's curse can prevail and the target company shareholders may receive a very good deal. **Winner's curse** is the tendency for the winner in certain competitive bidding situations to overpay, whether because of overestimation of intrinsic value, emotion, or information asymmetries.[8]

5.2.9. White Squire Defense   In the **white squire** defense, the target seeks a friendly party to buy enough of a minority stake in the target to block the hostile takeover without

---

[8]The winner's curse is most likely to occur when the target company has roughly the same value to all bidders but the target's true value is hard to ascertain. The average bid in such cases may represent the best estimate of the target's intrinsic value, and the high (winning), an overestimate of its intrinsic value.

selling the entire company. Although the white squire may pay a significant premium for a substantial number of the target's shares, these shares may be purchased directly from the target company and the target shareholders may not receive any of the proceeds.[9]

The use of the white squire defense may carry a high litigation risk depending on the details of the transaction and local regulations. Additionally, stock exchange listing requirements sometimes require that target shareholders vote to approve these types of transactions, and shareholders may not endorse any transaction that does not provide an adequate premium to them directly.

EXAMPLE 8-6   Engelhard Takeover Defenses

On December 14, 2005, BASF, a worldwide producer of chemicals and high-performance products, offered to acquire Engelhard Corporation for $37 cash per share. Engelhard, a manufacturer and developer of value-added technologies, determined that the $37 offer was inadequate and decided to defend itself against the unwanted takeover attempt.

Prior to the BASF takeover offer, Engelhard had participating preferred stock purchase rights in place.[10] These rights acted as a poison pill by allowing Engelhard to issue shares at a discount if triggered by a takeover that was unsupported by Engelhard's board of directors. Additionally, in advance of the takeover attempt, Engelhard restated its certificate of incorporation to include a supermajority provision. It stated that business combinations with a holder of more than 5 percent of Engelhard's outstanding shares would require an affirmative vote of both the holders of 80 percent of the outstanding shares and at least 50 percent of the outstanding shares not held by the acquirer unless the board of directors approved the business combination.

After the tender offer was commenced by BASF, Engelhard also pursued a recapitalization plan that involved the repurchase of approximately 20 percent of Engelhard's outstanding shares through a tender offer at $45 per share, a price superior to BASF's tender offer. Together these pre- and post-offer defenses made it very difficult for BASF to succeed with its $37 cash tender offer.

Although Engelhard did not complete the tender for its own shares, the recapitalization plan was incentive enough for BASF to increase its offer. Takeover targets frequently use their takeover defenses to negotiate a better deal for their shareholders. After much negotiation, BASF increased its tender offer and Engelhard withdrew all takeover defenses. On May 30, 2006, the companies announced a definitive merger agreement under which BASF would acquire all outstanding shares of Engelhard for $39 per share in cash.

---

[9]For example, the white squire may purchase shares of convertible preferred stock instead of common stock.

[10]Shares of participating preferred stock offer the possibility of a higher dividend when the dividend on common shares reaches a pre-specified threshold.

6. REGULATION

Even when a merger has been accepted by the target company's senior managers, the board of directors, and shareholders, the combination must still be approved by regulatory authorities. Additionally, companies must follow a variety of rules when initiating and completing the merger transaction itself. This section provides an overview of the key rules and issues that arise from M&A activity.

The two major bodies of jurisprudence relating to mergers are antitrust law and securities law. Antitrust laws are intended to ensure that markets remain competitive; the securities laws we discuss are concerned largely with maintaining both fairness in merger activities and confidence in the financial markets.

6.1. Antitrust

Most countries have antitrust laws, which prohibit mergers and acquisitions that impede competition. Antitrust legislation began in the United States with the Sherman Antitrust Act of 1890, which made contracts, combinations, and conspiracies in restraint of trade or attempts to monopolize an industry illegal. The Sherman Antitrust Act was not effective at deterring antirust activity partly because the U.S. Department of Justice at the time lacked the resources necessary to enforce the law rigorously. Within a few years of its passage, the law was challenged in the courts and rendered unenforceable because of ambiguous aspects of its wording.

To resurrect antitrust law, the U.S. Congress passed the Clayton Antitrust Act in 1914, which clarified and strengthened the Sherman Antitrust Act by detailing the specific business practices that the U.S. Congress wished to outlaw. To ensure that the law could be effectively enforced, the legislature also passed the Federal Trade Commission Act of 1914, which established the Federal Trade Commission (FTC) as a regulatory agency to work in tandem with the Department of Justice to enforce antitrust law.

During the ensuing years, additional weaknesses and loopholes in antitrust legislation became apparent. For instance, the Clayton Act regulated only the acquisition of shares of stock, not the acquisition of assets. The Celler–Kefauver Act was passed in 1950 to close this loophole; the law also addressed vertical and conglomerate mergers, whereas previous legislation had focused primarily on horizontal combinations.

The last major piece of U.S. antitrust legislation was the Hart–Scott–Rodino Antitrust Improvements Act of 1976, which required that the FTC and Department of Justice have the opportunity to review and approve mergers in advance. A key benefit of the Hart–Scott–Rodino Act is that it gives regulators an opportunity to halt a merger prior to its completion rather than having to disassemble a company after a merger is later deemed to be anticompetitive.

Just as U.S. transactions are reviewed by the FTC and the Department of Justice, the European Commission (EC) has the authority to review the antitrust implications of transactions among companies that generate significant revenues within the European Union. Although the European Commission's member states have jurisdiction on mergers within their respective national borders, mergers with significant cross-border effects are subject to EC review. Similar to the requirements in the United States, pre-merger notification is required.

In addition to regulatory watchdogs, such as the FTC and the European Commission, approval may be needed from other regulatory agencies. For example, in the United States, a merger involving banks requires approvals from state banking authorities as well as the Federal Reserve Bank and possibly the Federal Deposit Insurance Corporation (FDIC). Insurance mergers require the approval of state insurance commissioners. In some cases where one of the company's businesses is deemed to be of strategic national interest, additional government approvals may be necessary. Each merger must be analyzed by legal experts to determine the specific regulatory approvals required to comply with the relevant rules and laws. This is a very specialized area and can cause significant delays in the closing of some transactions.

The situation can become further complicated when the merging companies have a global presence that falls within multiple jurisdictions of regulatory control. For example, a large trans-Atlantic merger would require approval of both the United States regulatory bodies and the European Commission. Global companies often face dozens of regulatory agencies with different standards and filing requirements. For example, Coca-Cola Company's 1999 acquisition of the Cadbury Schweppes beverage brands involved sales and production in more than 160 countries, requiring antitrust approval in more than 40 jurisdictions around the world.

Prior to 1982, the FTC and Department of Justice used market share as a measure of market power when determining potential antitrust violations among peer competitors in an industry. Using a simple measure of industry concentration and the market shares of the acquirer and the target, companies contemplating a horizontal merger could determine in advance whether the combination would likely be challenged. The transparency and predictability of the measure was advantageous, but the approach proved to be too simplistic and rigid in practice.

In 1982, the agencies shifted toward using a new measure of market power called the **Herfindahl–Hirschman Index** (HHI). By summing the squares of the market shares for each company in an industry, the HHI does a better job of modeling market concentration while remaining relatively easy to calculate and interpret. To calculate the HHI, the market shares for competing companies are squared and then summed:

$$\text{HHI} = \sum_{i}^{n} \left(\frac{\text{Sales or output of firm } i}{\text{Total sales or output of market}} \times 100 \right)^2 \tag{8-1}$$

Regulators initially calculate the HHI based on *post-merger* market shares. If post-merger market shares result in an HHI of less than 1,000, the market is not considered to be concentrated and a challenge is unlikely unless other anticompetitive issues arise. A moderately concentrated HHI measure of between 1,000 and 1,800, or a highly concentrated measure of more than 1,800, requires a comparison of post-merger and pre-merger HHIs. A merger resulting in an increase of 100 points in a moderately concentrated market or 50 points in a highly concentrated market is likely to evoke antitrust concerns; smaller increases are less likely to pose a problem.[11] Exhibit 8-2 on page 393 summarizes HHI ranges and the corresponding probability for regulatory action.

---

[11]See the U.S. Department of Justice and the Federal Trade Commission's Horizontal Merger Guidelines, issued April 2, 1992 and revised April 8, 1997.

EXAMPLE 8-7   Herfindahl–Hirschman Index

Given an industry with 10 competitors and the following market shares, calculate the pre-merger HHI. How would the HHI change if Companies 2 and 3 merged? How would it change if Companies 9 and 10 merged instead? Would either set of mergers be likely to evoke an antitrust challenge?

Company	1	2	3	4	5	6	7	8	9	10
Market share (%)	25	20	10	10	10	5	5	5	5	5

Solution

To calculate the pre-merger HHI, first square the market share for each company. Then add together the squared market shares to obtain an HHI of 1,450, which indicates that this is a moderately concentrated industry. If Companies 2 and 3 were to merge, the HHI would jump 400 points to 1,850. The large change in the HHI, combined with the high post-merger HHI value, indicates that this merger would likely evoke antitrust objections. If Companies 9 and 10 were to merge instead of Companies 2 and 3, the HHI would climb only 50 points to 1,500. Although the post-merger HHI indicates a moderately concentrated industry, the combination is unlikely to raise antitrust concerns because the post-merger HHI is only 50 points higher than the pre-merger HHI.

Pre-Merger			Post-Merger: Companies 2 and 3			Post-Merger: Companies 9 and 10		
Company	Market Share (%)	Market Share Squared	Company	Market Share (%)	Market Share Squared	Company	Market Share (%)	Market Share Squared
1	25	625	1	25	625	1	25	625
2	20	400	2 + 3	30	900	2	20	400
3	10	100	4	10	100	3	10	100
4	10	100	5	10	100	4	10	100
5	10	100	6	5	25	5	10	100
6	5	25	7	5	25	6	5	25
7	5	25	8	5	25	7	5	25
8	5	25	9	5	25	8	5	25
9	5	25	10	5	25	9 + 10	10	100
10	5	25						
	HHI:	1,450		HHI:	1,850		HHI:	1,500
				HHI Change:	400		HHI Change:	50

EXHIBIT 8-2   HHI Concentration Levels and Possible Government Action

Post-Merger HHI	Concentration	Change in HHI	Government Action
Less than 1,000	Not concentrated	Any amount	No action
Between 1,000 and 1,800	Moderately concentrated	100 or more	Possible challenge
More than 1,800	Highly concentrated	50 or more	Challenge

Although the introduction of the Herfindahl–Hirschman Index was an improvement, regulators still found it to be too mechanical and inflexible. Thus, by 1984, the Department of Justice sought to increase the flexibility of its policies through the inclusion of additional information, such as market power measured by the responsiveness of consumers to price changes, as well as qualitative information, such as the efficiency of companies in the industry, the financial viability of potential merger candidates, and the ability of U.S. companies to compete in foreign markets.[12]

When reviewing quantitative and qualitative data, one should note that merger guidelines are just that—guidelines. It is possible that under unusual circumstances the government may not challenge one merger that does violate the guidelines and may challenge another merger that does not. Each transaction must be analyzed carefully to fully explore all potential antitrust issues.

When conflicts between companies and regulators arise, it is often because of disagreements about how the markets are defined. Regulators must consider the market in terms of both geography and product. When considering the industry's geography, regulators must decide whether the relevant competitors are global, national, regional, or local. When considering product offerings, there may be one or multiple relevant product market overlaps. In some cases the overlap may be clear, and in other transactions it may not be obvious.

Parties to the transaction are usually counseled by attorneys who have relevant experience in the antitrust area. Most companies try to complete their analyses prior to signing a merger agreement to avoid entering into a long period of uncertainty while the government decides whether to challenge the transaction. Not only do delays increase costs, but they may also cause the companies to lose other important strategic opportunities.

6.2. Securities Laws

As we discussed in the section covering pre-offer takeover defense mechanisms, in the United States individual states regulate M&A activities to varying degrees. But companies must also comply with federal U.S. securities regulations. In the United States, the cornerstone of securities legislation regulating merger and acquisition activities is the Williams Amendment to the Securities Exchange Act of 1934 (also known as the Williams Act), which was passed in 1968 near the end of the third merger wave.

During the 1960s, tender offers became a popular means to execute hostile takeovers. Acquirers often announced tender offers that expired in short time frames or that threatened

---

[12]Gaughan (2002, 95).

lower bids and less desirable terms for those shareholders who waited to tender. In addition to giving shareholders little time to evaluate the fairness of an offer, it gave target management little time to respond. The Williams Act sought to remedy these problems in two keys ways: disclosure requirements and a formal process for tender offers.

Section 13(d) of the Williams Act requires public disclosure whenever a party acquires 5 percent or more of a target's outstanding common stock. As part of this disclosure, the company acquiring the stake must provide a variety of details, including self-identification, the purpose of the transaction, and the source of the funds used to finance the stock purchases. This disclosure requirement calls target managers' and shareholders' attention to large share purchases, which keeps acquirers from gaining too large a toehold before the target is aware of the acquirer's interest.

Section 14 of the Williams Act creates a tender offer process by setting forth various rules and restrictions that companies must observe. For example, as part of initiating a tender offer, an acquirer must file a public statement that contains the details of the offer and information about the acquirer. Target management must then respond through a formal statement containing their opinion and advice to accept or reject the offer; target management can abstain from offering an opinion as long as they provide the reasons for doing so.

Other important provisions of Section 14 are that the tender offer period be at least 20 business days, that the acquirer must accept all shares tendered, that all tendered shares must receive the same price, and that target shareholders can withdraw tendered shares during the offer period. These provisions ensure that target shareholders receive equitable treatment and that they have adequate time to investigate and evaluate a tender offer without the risk of receiving a lower price. Section 14 also gives target management the time and opportunity to adequately respond to a hostile tender offer.

7. MERGER ANALYSIS

In this section, we examine the analysis of merger activity from two perspectives. First, we discuss valuation of the target company, something of key importance for analysts on both sides of the deal as well as for shareholders as they all grapple to determine the fairness and adequacy of an offer. Then, we discuss the analysis of the bid. Analysts can estimate the distribution of benefits in a merger based on expected synergies relative to the premium paid for the target in excess of its intrinsic value.

7.1. Target Company Valuation

The three basic valuation techniques that companies and their advisers use to value companies in an M&A context are (1) discounted cash flow analysis, (2) comparable company analysis, and (3) comparable transaction analysis. An analyst is likely to use some combination of these primary techniques and possibly others when gauging a company's fair value.

7.1.1. Discounted Cash Flow Analysis   **Discounted cash flow (DCF) analysis**, as it is generally applied in this context, discounts the company's expected future free cash flows to the present to derive an estimate for the value of the company. **Free cash flow (FCF)** is the relevant measure in this context because it represents the actual cash that would be

available to the company's investors after making all investments necessary to maintain the company as an ongoing enterprise.[13] Free cash flows are the internally generated funds that can be distributed to the company's investors (e.g., shareholders and bondholders) without impairing the value of the company.

An analyst might use several variations to the models to estimate and discount free cash flows. In the following, we develop an approximation to free cash flow and illustrate its use in valuation using a two-stage model.[14] Estimating a company's free cash flows begins with the creation of pro forma financial statements. The first step is to select an appropriate time horizon for the first stage. The first stage should include only the years over which the analyst feels capable of generating reasonably accurate estimates of the company's free cash flows. These free cash flow estimates are then discounted to their present value.

To incorporate value deriving from years beyond the first stage, the analyst estimates the value of expected second-stage free cash flows as of the end of the first stage. The result is the so-called terminal value (or continuing value) of the company. The analyst then discounts the terminal value back to the present. The sum of the two pieces (the present value of first-stage expected free cash flows plus the present value of the company's terminal value) is the estimated value of the company.

There is no standard approach for creating pro forma financial statements. The art of financial analysis involves an ability to use the appropriate tools and to exercise good judgment in order to produce the best possible estimates for each financial statement item. In the process, analysts make adjustments to their prior projections based on proposed synergies and the announced plans for the merged company. For example, duplicated resources might result in the sale of one of the target's divisions. Or the operating costs might be adjusted downward in anticipation of economies of scale. These adjustments are easier to estimate in friendly mergers where the analyst has access to detailed financial data about the target than in hostile mergers. But even in a hostile merger scenario, an analyst with experience in the appropriate industry can still make reasonably good estimates.

Once pro forma financial statements have been generated, the analyst can begin the conversion from pro forma net income to pro forma free cash flow for each year of the first stage. To demonstrate this process, we will use the pro forma financial statements and FCF calculations provided in Exhibit 8-3 (page 396). The perspective is that of a valuation being done at the beginning of 2007.

The calculation of FCF involves first making adjustments to net income to convert it to **net operating profit less adjusted taxes (NOPLAT)**. This adjustment is made so that the resulting estimate of FCF represents the after-tax cash flows available to all providers of capital to the company. The first step in this process is to add net interest after tax to net income. This step removes the tax shield from interest payments and puts the cash flows on common footing with other cash flows that are available to all capital providers of the company.[15] This

---

[13]Free cash flow as used in this context is also called **free cash flow to the firm,** particularly when a distinction is being made between free cash flows accruing to all providers of capital and those accruing only to equity holders (**free cash flow to equity**).

[14]See Stowe, Robinson, Pinto, and McLeavey (2002) for details of estimating free cash flow (free cash flow to the firm) more precisely.

[15]The tax deductibility of interest will be accounted for later in the calculation when we discount free cash flows by the weighted average cost of capital (WACC).

EXHIBIT 8-3   Sample Pro Forma Financial Statements and FCF Calculations

	Historical	Pro Forma				
	2006	2007	2008	2009	2010	2011
Income Statement ($ 000s)						
Revenues	14,451	15,752	17,327	19,060	20,966	23,063
Cost of goods sold	7,948	8,664	9,530	10,483	11,531	12,685
Gross profit	6,503	7,088	7,797	8,577	9,435	10,378
Selling, general, and administrative expenses	2,168	2,363	2,599	2,859	3,145	3,459
Depreciation	506	551	606	667	734	807
Earnings before interest and taxes	3,829	4,174	4,592	5,051	5,556	6,112
Net interest expense	674	642	616	583	543	495
Earnings before taxes	3,155	3,532	3,976	4,468	5,013	5,617
Income tax	1,104	1,236	1,392	1,564	1,755	1,966
Net income	2,051	2,296	2,584	2,904	3,258	3,651
Balance Sheet ($ 000s)						
Current assets	8,671	9,451	10,396	11,436	12,580	13,838
Net property, plant, and equipment	10,116	11,026	12,129	13,342	14,676	16,144
Total assets	18,787	20,477	22,525	24,778	27,256	29,982
Current liabilities	3,613	3,938	4,332	4,765	5,242	5,766
Deferred income taxes	92	111	132	155	181	209
Long-term debt	7,924	7,548	7,243	6,862	6,394	5,830
Total liabilities	11,629	11,597	11,707	11,782	11,817	11,805
Common stock and paid-in capital	1,200	1,200	1,200	1,200	1,200	1,200
Retained earnings	5,958	7,680	9,618	11,796	14,239	16,977
Shareholders' equity	7,158	8,880	10,818	12,996	15,439	18,177
Total liabilities and shareholders' equity	18,787	20,477	22,525	24,778	27,256	29,982
Selected Pro Forma Cash Flow Data ($ 000s)						
Change in net working capital		455	551	607	667	734
Capital expenditures		1,461	1,709	1,880	2,068	2,275

EXHIBIT 8-3   (*Continued*)

FCF Calculations	Pro Forma				
	2007	2008	2009	2010	2011
Net income	2,296	2,584	2,904	3,258	3,651
Plus: Net interest after tax	417	400	379	353	322
Unlevered net income	2,713	2,984	3,283	3,611	3,973
Plus: Change in deferred taxes	19	21	23	26	28
Net op profit less adj. taxes (NOPLAT)	2,732	3,005	3,306	3,637	4,001
Plus: Depreciation	551	606	667	734	807
Less: Change in net working capital	455	551	607	667	734
Less: Capital expenditures	1,461	1,709	1,880	2,068	2,275
Free cash flow	1,367	1,351	1,486	1,636	1,799
Valuation Calculations					
WACC	9.41%				
PV of FCF		5,802			
Terminal growth rate	6.0%				
Terminal value, 2011	55,922				
Terminal value, 2006		35,670			
Enterprise Value, 2006		41,471			

is referred to as unlevered net income.[16] For the year 2007 in Exhibit 8-3, pro forma net income for the year is $2.296 million. There is no reported interest income, so net interest expense is simply $642,000. The company's estimated tax rate is 35 percent, found by dividing the previous year's income tax by the company's earnings before tax.

Step 1:

Unlevered net income = Net income + Net interest after tax

Net interest after tax = (Interest expense − Interest income) × (1 − tax rate)   (8-2)

---

[16]It is also possible to calculate unlevered net income as earnings before interest and taxes (EBIT) × (1 − tax rate).

For 2007

$$\text{Unlevered net income} = \$2,296 + 642(1 - 0.35)$$
$$= \$2,713$$
$$= \$2.713 \text{ million}$$

To convert unlevered net income to NOPLAT, we must account for differences in depreciation for financial reporting purposes versus depreciation for tax purposes, which has an impact on cash flows. Companies typically report depreciation for property, plant, and equipment at a faster rate for tax purposes (higher depreciation shields more income from taxes) than for financial reporting purposes (lower depreciation results in higher net income). The differences in depreciation result in different taxes. This difference is accounted for as a liability on the balance sheet: deferred income taxes. To account for this impact on cash flow, we add the change in deferred taxes to unlevered net income (an increase in deferred taxes increases cash flow; a decrease in deferred taxes reduces cash flow).[17]

Step 2:

$$\text{NOPLAT} = \text{Unlevered net income} + \text{Change in deferred taxes} \qquad (8\text{-}3)$$

For 2007

$$\text{NOPLAT} = \$2,713 + (111 - 92)$$
$$= \$2,732$$
$$= \$2.732 \text{ million}$$

At this point, NOPLAT is adjusted to add back net noncash charges (NCC), which prominently include depreciation (of tangible assets) and amortization and impairment (of intangible assets); noncash charges affect net income but do not represent cash expenditures. To estimate free cash flow, we then subtract the value of necessary or otherwise planned investments in working capital and property, plant, and equipment.[18] They are recorded as the change in net working capital and capital expenditures (capex), respectively.

Step 3:

$$\text{FCF} = \text{NOPLAT} + \text{NCC} - \text{Change in net working capital} - \text{Capex} \qquad (8\text{-}4)$$

For 2007

$$\text{FCF} = \$2,732 + 551 - 455 - 1,461$$
$$= \$1,367$$
$$= \$1.367 \text{ million}$$

(The only NCC in this example is depreciation.)

---

[17]Some analysts also estimate and subtract the value of after-tax nonoperating income to obtain an estimate more closely reflecting operating results only. See Copeland, Koller, and Murrin (2000), Chapter 9, for more details on NOPLAT.

[18]Working capital is defined in this use as current assets (excluding cash and equivalents) minus current liabilities (excluding short-term debt).

Summarizing, FCF is approximated by:

	Net income
+	Net interest after tax
	Unlevered net income
+	Change in deferred taxes
	Net operating profit less adjusted taxes (NOPLAT)
+	Net noncash charges
−	Change in net working capital
−	Capital expenditures (capex)
	Free cash flow (FCF)

Once free cash flow has been estimated for each year in the first stage (2007–2011 in Exhibit 8-3), the free cash flows are discounted back to present at the company's weighted average cost of capital (WACC).[19] When evaluating the target from a noncontrol perspective, we would use the target's WACC, which reflects that company's existing business risk and operating environment. In anticipation of a merger, however, we would adjust that WACC to reflect any anticipated changes in the target's risk from such actions as a redeployment of assets or change in capital structure.

For the company in Exhibit 8-3, we assume that the appropriate discount rate is 9.41 percent. Discounting free cash flow for the years 2007 through 2011 at 9.41 percent results in a present value of $5.802 million. That is the portion of the company's current value that can be attributed to the free cash flows that occur over the first stage. Next, we must determine the portion of the present value attributable to the company's terminal value, which arises from those cash flows occurring from the end of the first stage to perpetuity.

There are two standard methods for calculating a terminal value. The first method makes use of the constant growth formula. To apply the constant growth formula, an analyst must select a terminal growth rate, which is the long-term equilibrium growth rate that the company can expect to achieve in perpetuity, accounting for both inflation and real growth. The terminal growth rate is often lower than the growth rate applied during the first stage because any advantages from synergies, new opportunities, or cost reductions are transitory as competitors adjust and the industry evolves over time. The constant growth formula can be applied whenever the terminal growth rate is less than the WACC.

$$\text{Terminal value}_T = \frac{\text{FCF}_T(1 + g)}{(\text{WACC} - g)} \tag{8-5}$$

where

FCF$_T$ = free cash flow produced during the final year of the first stage

g = terminal growth rate

---

[19]For details on the estimation of WACC, see Chapter 3, Cost of Capital.

For the company in Exhibit 8-3, we assume a terminal growth rate of 6.0 percent:

$$\text{Terminal value}_{2011} = \frac{\$1,799(1 + 0.06)}{(0.0941 - 0.06)}$$
$$= \$55,922$$
$$= \$55.922 \text{ million}$$

A second method for estimating the terminal value involves applying a multiple at which the analyst expects the average company to sell at the end of the first stage. The analyst might use a free cash flow or other multiple that reflects the expected risk, growth, and economic conditions in the terminal year. Market multiples are rules of thumb applied by analysts, investment bankers, and venture capitalists to produce rough estimates of a company's value. Multiples tend to vary by industry. They can be based on anything applicable to the industry and correlated with market prices. Some service industries tend to be priced as multiples of EBITDA (earnings before interest, taxes, depreciation, and amortization). In contrast, retail stores in some industries might be priced based on multiples applied to floor space. In these cases, the respective multiples can be used directly to produce a terminal value, or they can be incorporated into a pro forma analysis to convert the multiple into a consistent value for free cash flow.

If the company in Exhibit 8-3 is in an industry where the typical company sells for about 20 times its free cash flow, then the company's terminal value estimate would be:

$$\text{Terminal value}_{2011} = 20 \times \$1,799$$
$$= \$35,980$$
$$= \$35.980 \text{ million}$$

Having established an estimate for the terminal value, the analyst must discount it back from the end of the estimate horizon to the present. The discount rate used is the same WACC estimate that was previously applied to discount the free cash flows. If we decide that the terminal value found using the constant growth method is more accurate than a market multiple, we would discount that value back five years (2011 back to the present):

$$\text{Terminal value}_{2006} = \frac{\$55,922}{(1 + 0.0941)^5}$$
$$= \$35,670$$
$$= \$35.670 \text{ million}$$

Adding the present value of the free cash flows ($5.802 million) to the present value of the terminal value ($35.670 million), we can estimate the value of the company to be $41.471 million.[20] Note that a large proportion of the company's value is attributable to its terminal value (more than 85 percent in our example). The assumed terminal growth rate and WACC estimate can have a dramatic impact on the terminal value calculation: The final estimate of the company's value is only as accurate as the estimates used in the model.

---

[20]The estimate differs slightly from the sum due to rounding.

Advantages of Using Discounted Cash Flow Analysis

- Expected changes in the target company's cash flows (e.g., from operating synergies and cost structure changes) can be readily modeled.
- An estimate of intrinsic value based on forecast fundamentals is provided by the model.
- Changes in assumptions and estimates can be incorporated by customizing and modifying the model.

Disadvantages of Using Discounted Cash Flow Analysis

- It is difficult to apply when free cash flows do not align with profitability in the first stage. For example, a rapidly expanding company may be profitable but have negative free cash flows because of heavy capital expenditures to the horizon that can be forecast with confidence. The free cash flow value of the company then derives from a later and harder to estimate period when free cash flow turns positive.
- Estimating cash flows and earnings far into the future is not an exact science. There is a great deal of uncertainty in estimates, even for the following year, much less in perpetuity.
- Estimates of discount rates can change over time because of capital market developments or changes that specifically affect the companies in question. These changes can also significantly affect acquisition estimates.
- Terminal value estimates often subject the acquisition value calculations to a disproportionate degree of estimate error. The estimate of terminal value can differ depending on the specific technique used. Additionally, the range of estimates can be affected dramatically by small changes in the assumed growth and WACC estimates.

7.1.2. Comparable Company Analysis   A second approach that investment bankers use to estimate acquisition values is called "comparable company analysis." In this approach, the analyst first defines a set of other companies that are similar to the target company under review. This set may include companies in the target's primary industry as well as companies in similar industries. The sample should be formed to include as many companies as possible that have similar size and capital structure to the target.

Once a set of comparable companies is defined, the next step is to calculate various relative value measures based on the current market prices of the comparable companies in the sample. Such valuation is often based on enterprise multiples. A company's enterprise value is the market value of its debt and equity minus the value of its cash and investments. Examples include enterprise value to free cash flow, enterprise value to EBITDA, enterprise value to EBIT, and enterprise value to sales. Because the denominator in such ratios is pre-interest, they may be preferred when the companies being compared have differences in leverage. The equity can also be valued directly using equity multiples, such as price to cash flow per share (P/CF), price to sales per share (P/S), price to earnings per share (P/E), and price to book value per share (P/BV).

The specific ratios that the analyst selects are determined by the industry under observation. Often, in addition to common market multiples, analysts include industry-specific multiples. For instance, in the oil and gas industry, in addition to looking at price paid to earnings and cash flow ratios, many analysts evaluate the price paid per barrel of oil or per thousand cubic feet of natural gas reserves.

Analysts typically review the mean, median, and range for whichever metrics are chosen, and then they apply those values to corresponding estimates for the target to develop an estimated company value. This is quite similar to the approach we discussed earlier for using multiples to produce a terminal value estimate. In this case, however, we are calculating various relative value metrics rather than using an industry rule of thumb.

Each metric (P/E, P/CF, etc.) is likely to produce a different estimate for the target's value. Analysts hope that these values converge because that increases confidence in the overall estimate. To the extent that they diverge, analysts must apply judgment and experience to decide which estimates are producing the most accurate market values.

It should be noted that the value determined up to this point in the process yields an estimate of where the target company should trade as a stock in the marketplace relative to the companies in the sample. To calculate an acquisition value, the analyst must also estimate a takeover premium. The **takeover premium** is the amount by which the takeover price for each share of stock must exceed the current stock price to entice shareholders to relinquish control of the company to an acquirer. This premium is usually expressed as a percentage of the stock price and is calculated as

$$PRM = \frac{(DP - SP)}{SP} \tag{8-6}$$

where

PRM = takeover premium (as a percentage of stock price)

DP = deal price per share of the target company

SP = stock price of the target company[21]

To calculate the relevant takeover premium for a transaction, analysts usually compile a list of the takeover premiums paid for companies similar to the target. Preferably, the calculations are from the recent past because acquisition values and premiums tend to vary over time and economic cycles.

EXAMPLE 8-8   Comparable Company Analysis

Sam Jones, an investment banker, has been retained by the Big Box Company to estimate the price that should be paid to acquire New Life Books Inc. Jones decides to use comparable company analysis to find a fair value for New Life, and has gathered the following information about three comparable companies:

Valuation Variables	Company 1	Company 2	Company 3
Current stock price ($)	20.00	32.00	16.00
Earnings per share ($)	1.00	1.82	0.93
Cash flow per share ($)	2.55	3.90	2.25
Book value per share ($)	6.87	12.80	5.35
Sales per share ($)	12.62	18.82	7.62

---

[21]The analyst must be careful to note any pre-deal jump in the price that may have occurred because of takeover speculation in the market. In these cases, the analyst should apply the takeover premium to a selected representative price from before any speculative influences on the stock price.

First, Jones calculates valuation metrics using the data he gathered. For each metric, he also calculates the mean.

Relative Valuation Ratio	Company 1	Company 2	Company 3	Mean
P/E	20.00	17.58	17.20	18.26
P/CF	7.84	8.21	7.11	7.72
P/BV	2.91	2.50	2.99	2.80
P/S	1.58	1.70	2.10	1.79

Jones then applies the mean relative valuation ratios to the corresponding data for New Life Books to estimate the comparable *stock* price. Because the four valuation metrics produce estimates that are all relatively close, he decides he is comfortable using an average of the four estimates to produce the estimated stock value.

Target Company Valuation Variables	Target Company (a)	Comparable Companies' Valuation Variables	Mean Multiples for Comparable Companies (b)	Estimated Stock Value Based on Comparables (a × b)
Earnings per share	1.95	P/E	18.26	$35.61
Cash flow per share	4.12	P/CF	7.72	$31.81
Book value per share	12.15	P/BV	2.80	$34.02
Sales per share	18.11	P/S	1.79	$32.42
Estimated stock value				Mean: $33.47

To determine the proper acquisition or takeover value, Jones must now estimate the relevant takeover premium. Using five of the most recent takeovers of companies that are similar to the target, he has compiled the following estimates:

Target Company	Stock Price Prior to Takeover ($)	Takeover Price ($)	Takeover Premium (%)
Target 1	23.00	28.50	23.9
Target 2	17.25	22.65	31.3
Target 3	86.75	102.00	17.6
Target 4	45.00	53.75	19.4
Target 5	36.75	45.00	22.4
Mean premium			22.9

After examining the data, Jones decides that the mean estimated premium is reasonable. His next step is to apply the takeover premium to his mean estimate of the stock price for New Life Books:

Target's estimated stock value	$33.47
Estimated takeover premium	22.9%
Estimated takeover price of target	$33.47(1.229) = $41.14

From these calculations and estimates, Jones concludes that a fair takeover price for the Big Box Company to pay for each share of New Life Books would be $41.14.[22]

Advantages of Using Comparable Company Analysis

- This method provides a reasonable approximation of a target company's value relative to similar companies in the market. This assumes that like assets should be valued on a similar basis in the market.
- With this method, most of the required data are readily available.
- The estimates of value are derived directly from the market. This is unlike the discounted cash flow method where the takeover value is determined based on many assumptions and estimates.

Disadvantages of Using Comparable Company Analysis

- The method is sensitive to market mispricing. To illustrate the issue, suppose that the comparable companies are overvalued. A valuation relative to those companies may suggest a value that is too high in the sense that values would be revised downward when the market corrects.
- Using this approach yields a market-estimated fair *stock* price for the target company. To estimate a fair *takeover* price, analysts must additionally estimate a fair takeover premium and use that information to adjust the estimated stock price.
- The analysis may be inaccurate because it is difficult for the analyst to incorporate any specific plans for the target (e.g., changing capital structure or eliminating duplicate resources) in the analysis.
- The data available for past premiums may not be timely or accurate for the particular target company under consideration.

7.1.3. Comparable Transaction Analysis   A third common approach to value target companies is known as "comparable transaction analysis." This approach is closely related to comparable company analysis except that the analyst uses details from recent takeover transactions for comparable companies to make direct estimates of the target company's takeover value.

---

[22]As we shall discuss in the section covering bid evaluation, the analysis in Example 8-8 is not quite complete because the acquirer must evaluate the estimated takeover price relative to any expected synergies.

The first step in comparable transaction analysis is to collect a relevant sample of recent takeover transactions. The sample should be as broad as possible but limited to companies in the same industry as the target or at least to closely related ones. Once the transactions are identified, the analyst can look at the same types of relative value multiples that were used in comparable company analysis (P/E, P/CF, other industry-specific multiples, etc.). In this case, however, we are not comparing the target against market multiples. For this approach we compare the multiples actually paid for similar companies in other M&A deals. As before, analysts typically look at descriptive statistics, such as the mean, median, and range for the multiples, and they apply judgment and experience when applying that information to estimate the target's value.

EXAMPLE 8-9   Comparable Transaction Analysis

Joel Hofer, an analyst with an investment banking firm, has been asked to estimate a fair price for the General Health Company's proposed acquisition of Medical Services Inc. He has already taken the initial step and assembled a sample containing companies involved in acquisitions in the same industry in which Medical Services operates. These companies have all been acquired in the past two years. Details on the acquisition prices and relevant pricing variables follow:

Valuation Variables	Acquired Company 1	Acquired Company 2	Acquired Company 3
Acquisition share price ($)	35.00	16.50	87.00
Earnings per share ($)	2.12	0.89	4.37
Cash flow per share ($)	3.06	1.98	7.95
Book value per share ($)	9.62	4.90	21.62
Sales per share ($)	15.26	7.61	32.66

The next step in the process is for Hofer to calculate the multiples at which each company was acquired:

Relative Valuation Ratio	Comparable Company 1	Comparable Company 2	Comparable Company 3	Mean
P/E	16.5	18.5	19.9	18.3
P/CF	11.4	8.3	10.9	10.2
P/BV	3.6	3.4	4.0	3.7
P/S	2.3	2.2	2.7	2.4

After reviewing the distribution of the various values around their respective means, Hofer is confident about using the mean value for each ratio because the range in values above and below the mean is reasonably small. Based on his experience with this particular industry, Hofer believes that cash flows are a particularly important predictor of value for these types of companies. Consequently, instead of finding an equally weighted average, Hofer has decided to apply the following weights for calculating a weighted average estimated price.

Target Company Valuation Variables	Target Company (a)	Comparable Companies' Valuation Multiples	Mean Multiple Paid for Comparable Companies (b)	Estimated Takeover Value Based on Comparables (c = a × b)	Weight (d)	Weighted Estimates (e = c × d)
Earnings per share	$2.62	P/E	18.3	$47.95	20%	$9.59
Cash flow per share	$4.33	P/CF	10.2	$44.17	40%	$17.67
Book value per share	$12.65	P/BV	3.7	$46.81	20%	$9.36
Sales per share	$22.98	P/S	2.4	$55.15	20%	$11.03
Weighted average estimate						$47.65

In sum, Hofer multiplied each valuation multiple by the corresponding variable for the target company to produce an estimated takeover value based on each comparable. He then decided to overweight cash flow per share and calculated a weighted average to determine an overall takeover value estimate of $47.65 per share for Medical Services Inc. The same procedure could be repeated using the median, high, and low valuations for each of the valuation variables. This would generate a range of takeover values for Medical Services Inc.

Advantages of Comparable Transaction Approach

- It is not necessary to separately estimate a takeover premium. The takeover premium is derived directly from the comparable transactions.
- The takeover value estimates come directly from values that were recently established in the market. This is unlike the discounted cash flow method where the takeover value is determined based on many assumptions and estimates.
- The use of prices established through other recent transactions reduces litigation risk for both companies' board of directors and managers regarding the merger transaction's pricing.

Disadvantages of Comparable Transaction Approach

- Because the value estimates assume that the M&A market has properly determined the intrinsic value of the target companies, there is a risk that the real takeover values in past transactions were not accurate. If true, these inaccurate takeover values are imputed in the estimates based on them.

- There may not be any, or an adequate number of, comparable transactions to use for calculating the takeover value. In these cases, analysts may try to use data from related industries. These derived values may not be accurate for the specific industry under study.
- The analysis may be inaccurate because it is difficult for the analyst to incorporate any specific plans for the target (e.g., changing capital structure or eliminating duplicate resources) in the analysis.

7.2. Bid Evaluation

Assessing the target's value is important, but it is insufficient for an assessment of the deal. Even if both the acquirer and the target separately agree on the target company's underlying value, the acquirer obviously wants to pay the lowest price possible while the target negotiates for the highest price possible. Both the price and form of payment in a merger determine the distribution of risks and benefits between the counterparties to the deal.

Acquirers must typically pay a premium to induce the owners of the target company to relinquish control. In an M&A transaction, the premium is the portion of the compensation received by the target company's shareholders that is in excess of the pre-merger market value of their shares. The target company's managers attempt to negotiate the highest possible premium relative to the value of the target company.[23]

$$\text{Target shareholders' gain} = \text{Premium} = P_T - V_T \tag{8-7}$$

where

P_T = price paid for the target company

V_T = pre-merger value of the target company

The acquirer is willing to pay in excess of the target company's value in anticipation of reaping its own gains. The acquirer's gains are derived from the synergies generated by the transaction—usually from some combination of cost reductions and revenue enhancements. All else constant, synergies increase the value of the acquiring company by the value of the synergies minus the premium paid to target shareholders:

$$\text{Acquirer's gain} = \text{Synergies} - \text{Premium} = S - (P_T - V_T) \tag{8-8}$$

where

S = synergies created by the business combination

---

[23]A burst of speculative stock activity typically accompanies merger negotiations. This activity typically results in a higher share price for the target company in anticipation of a takeover premium. When conducting a bid evaluation, the analyst should use some combination of an assessment of the company's intrinsic value and a representative stock price from before any merger speculation.

The post-merger value of the combined company is a function of the pre-merger values of the two companies, the synergies created by the merger, and any cash paid to the target shareholders as part of the transaction:

$$V_{A^*} = V_A + V_T + S - C \qquad (8\text{-}9)$$

where

V_{A^*} = post-merger value of the combined companies

V_A = pre-merger value of the acquirer

C = cash paid to target shareholders

When evaluating a bid, the pre-merger value of the target company is the absolute minimum bid that target shareholders should accept. Individual shareholders could sell their shares in the open market for that much instead of tendering their shares for a lower bid. At the other extreme, unless there are mitigating circumstances or other economic justifications, the acquirer's shareholders would not want to pay more than the pre-merger value of the target company plus the value of any expected synergies. If the acquirer were to pay more than that, then the acquirer's post-merger value would be lower than its pre-merger value—therefore, a reduction in shareholder value.

Bidding should thus generally be confined to a range dictated by the synergies expected from the transaction, with each side of the transaction negotiating to capture as much of the synergies as possible. Consequently, analysis of a merger depends not only on an assessment of the target company's value but also on estimates of the value of any synergies that the merged company is expected to attain.

Confidence in synergy estimates has implications not only for the bid price but also for the method of payment. The reason for this is that different methods of payment for the merger—cash offer, stock offer, or mixed offer—inherently provide varying degrees of risk shifting with respect to misestimating the value of merger synergies. To see why this is the case, we will first walk through the evaluation of an offer for each method of payment.

EXAMPLE 8-10   Adagio Software Offer

Adagio Software Inc. and Tantalus Software Solutions Inc. are negotiating a friendly acquisition of Tantalus by Adagio. The management teams at both companies have informally agreed on a transaction value of about €12.00 per share of Tantalus Software Solutions stock but are presently negotiating alternative forms of payment. Sunil Agrawal, CFA, works for Tantalus Software Solutions' investment banking team and is evaluating three alternative offers presented by Adagio Software:

1. *Cash offer:* Adagio will pay €12.00 per share of Tantalus stock.

2. *Stock offer:* Adagio will give Tantalus shareholders 0.80 shares of Adagio stock per share of Tantalus stock.

3. *Mixed offer:* Adagio will pay €6.00 plus 0.40 shares of Adagio stock per share of Tantalus stock.

Agrawal estimates that the merger of the two companies will result in economies of scale with a net present value of €90 million. To aid in the analysis, Agrawal has also compiled the following data:

	Adagio	Tantalus
Pre-merger stock price (€)	15.00	10.00
Number of shares outstanding (millions)	75	30
Pre-merger market value (€ millions)	1,125	300

Based only on the information given, which of the three offers should Agrawal recommend to the Tantalus Software Solutions management team?

Solution

Alternative 1: Cash offer of €12.00 per share of Tantalus stock

A cash offer is the most straightforward and easiest to evaluate. The price paid for the target company, P_T, is equal to cash price per share times the number of target shares: €12.00 × 30 million = €360 million. Because Tantalus' value, V_T, is €300 million, the premium is the difference between the two: €360 million − €300 million = €60 million.

Adagio's gain in this transaction is €30 million, which equals the value of the synergies minus the premium paid to Tantalus shareholders. A longer way to get to the same conclusion is to remember that the value of the post-merger combined company equals the pre-merger values of both companies plus the value of created synergies, less the cash paid to target shareholders:

$$V_{A^*} = V_A + V_T + S - C$$
$$= €1,125 + €300 + €90 - €360$$
$$= €1,155 \text{ million}$$

Adagio's pre-merger market value was €1,125 million, and Adagio's gain from the transaction is thus €1,155 − 1,125 = €30 million. Agrawal can divide the post-merger market value of €1,155 by the number of shares outstanding to determine Adagio's post-merger stock price. Under a cash offer, Adagio will not issue additional shares of stock; so Agrawal divides €1,155 by 75 million shares to see that, all else constant, Adagio's stock price after the merger should rise to €15.40.

In an all-cash offer, Tantalus shareholders receive €60 million—the premium. Adagio's gain from the transaction equals the expected synergies (€90 million) less the premium paid to Tantalus shareholders (€60 million), which equals €30 million.

Alternative 2: Stock offer of 0.80 shares of Adagio stock per share of Tantalus stock

A stock offer of 0.80 shares might seem at first glance to be equivalent to a cash offer of €12.00 because Adagio's share price is €15.00 (0.80 × €15 = €12). The results are actually slightly different, however, because Agrawal must account for the dilution that occurs when Adagio issues new shares to Tantalus stockholders. Because 30 million shares of the target are outstanding, Adagio must issue 24 million shares (30 million × 0.80).

To calculate the price paid for Tantalus, Agrawal starts by ascertaining the post-merger value of the combined company. Agrawal uses the same formula as before while using a value of 0 for C because this is a stock offer and no cash is changing hands:

$$V_{A*} = V_A + V_T + S - C$$
$$= €1,125 + €300 + €90 - €0$$
$$= €1,515 \text{ million}$$

Next, Agrawal divides Adagio's post-merger value by the post-merger number of shares outstanding. Because Adagio issued 24 million shares to complete the transaction, Agrawal adds 24 million to the original 75 million shares outstanding to arrive at 99 million. Dividing the post-merger market value by the post-merger number of shares outstanding, Agrawal determines that the value of each share given to Tantalus shareholders is actually worth €1,515 million/99 million = €15.30 and that the total value paid to Tantalus shareholders is €15.30 × 24 million = €367 million.

The premium is thus €367 − 300 = €67 million, which is €7 million higher than it was for the cash offer. Because the target shareholders receive €7 million more than in the cash offer, the acquirer's gain is correspondingly less. Because the synergies are valued at €90 million and the premium is €67 million, the acquirer's gain under a stock transaction with these terms is €23 million.

Alternative 3: Mixed offer of €6.00 plus 0.40 shares of Adagio stock per share of Tantalus stock

A mixed offer still results in some dilution, although not as much as a pure stock offer. Agrawal begins by calculating Adagio's post-merger value. Agrawal inserts €180 million for C because the company is paying €6 per share for 30 million shares:

$$V_{A*} = V_A + V_T + S - C$$
$$= €1,125 + €300 + €90 - €180$$
$$= €1,335 \text{ million}$$

Next, Agrawal determines that Adagio must issue 12 million shares to complete the transaction: 0.40 × 30 million = 12 million. Combined with the original 75 million shares outstanding, Adagio's post-merger number of shares outstanding will be 87 million. Agrawal divides €1,335 million by 87 million and finds that each share given to the Tantalus shareholders is worth €15.35.

The total value paid to Tantalus shareholders includes a cash component, €6.00 × 30 million = €180 million, and a stock component, 12 million shares issued with a value of €15.35 each, equaling €184 million. When these are added, the total value is €180 + 184 = €364 million, and the premium is therefore €364 million − 300 million = €64 million. The acquirer's gain is $26 million.

Conclusion

Agrawal should recommend that the Tantalus Software Solutions management team opt for the all stock offer because that alternative provides Tantalus shareholders the most value (the highest premium).

In Example 8-10, Adagio's gain ranged from €30 million in the pure cash offer to €26 million in the mixed offer and €23 million in the pure stock offer. If the dilution of a stock offer reduces the acquirer's gains from the transaction, why would an acquirer ever pay stock in a merger? The answer brings us back to the beginning of the section where we pointed out that the price and form of payment in a merger determine the distribution of risks and benefits. The choice of payment method is influenced by both parties' confidence in the estimated synergies and the relative value of the acquirer's shares.

The more confident the managers are that the estimated synergies will be realized, the more the acquiring managers will prefer to pay with cash and the more the target managers will prefer to receive stock. And the more the merger is paid for with the acquirer's stock, the more that the risks and benefits of realizing synergies will be passed on to the target shareholders. For example, in the cash offer we analyzed in Example 8-10, if the synergies later turned out to be worth €60 million rather than the originally estimated €90 million, then the Tantalus shareholders' premium would be unaffected but Adagio's gain would completely evaporate. In contrast, if the synergies were greater than estimated, then Tantalus shareholders' premium would still be unchanged but Adagio's gain would increase.

When stock is used as payment, the target shareholders become part owners of the acquiring company. In the Adagio stock offer, Tantalus shareholders would receive 24 million shares and thus own 24/99(24.2 percent) of the post-merger acquirer. Thus, Tantalus shareholders would participate by that proportion in any deviation of synergies from pre-merger estimates. If synergies were worth only €60 million, Adagio would lose its €23 million gain and Tantalus shareholders' gain from the transaction would fall by €7 million.

The other factor affecting the method of payment decision relates to the counterparties' confidence in the companies' relative values. The more confident managers are in estimates of the target company's value, the more the acquirer would prefer cash and the more the target would prefer stock. For example, what if Adagio estimates that Tantalus is worth more than €10 per share and consequently offers €12.50 per share in cash instead of €12.00? In that case, Tantalus shareholders would receive a premium that is €15 million higher and Adagio's gain from the transaction would be reduced by €15 million to €15 million.

If Adagio and Tantalus had agreed on a stock offer, then Adagio would have shifted some of the cost of its error to Tantalus shareholders. Suppose Adagio still overestimates the value of Tantalus, but instead of a cash offer the company makes a stock offer of 0.83 shares (instead of the 0.80 shares that were offered in Example 8-10). In that case, Tantalus shareholders' gain increases by nearly €12 million to €78.8 million. Conversely, Adagio's gain falls by the same amount to €11.3 million, making the company slightly better off than it would have been in the cash offer where its gain was reduced by €15 million.

8. WHO BENEFITS FROM MERGERS?

What does the empirical evidence say about who actually gains in business combinations? Studies on the performance of mergers fall into two categories: short-term performance studies, which examine stock returns surrounding merger announcement dates, and long-term performance studies of post-merger companies. The empirical evidence suggests that merger transactions create value for target company shareholders in the short run. On average, target shareholders reap 30 percent premiums over the stock's pre-announcement market price, and the acquirer's stock price falls, on average, between 1 and 3 percent.[24] Moreover, on average, both the acquirer and target tend to see higher stock returns surrounding cash acquisition offers than around share offers.[25]

The high average premiums paid to target shareholders may be attributed, at least partly, to the winner's curse—the tendency for competitive bidding to result in overpayment. Even if the average bidding company accurately estimates the target company's value, some bidders overestimate the target's value and other potential buyers underestimate its value. Unless the winner can exploit some strong synergies that are not available to other bidders, the winning bidder is likely to be the one who most overestimates the value.

Roll argues that high takeover bids may stem from hubris, from "the overbearing presumption of bidders that their valuations are correct."[26] Implied in this behavior is that these executives are somehow smarter than everyone else and can see value where others cannot. Even if there were no synergies from a merger, managerial hubris would still lead to higher-than-market bids and a transfer of wealth from the acquiring company's shareholders to the target's shareholders. The empirical evidence is consistent with Roll's hubris hypothesis.

When examining a longer period, empirical evidence shows that acquirers tend to underperform comparable companies during the three years following an acquisition. This implies a general post-merger operational failure to capture synergies. Average returns to acquiring companies subsequent to merger transactions are negative 4.3 percent with about 61 percent of acquirers lagging their industry peers.[27] This finding suggests that financial analysts are well served to thoroughly scrutinize estimates of synergy and post-merger value creation.

Analysts must attempt to distinguish between deals that create value and those that do not. Too often, companies with surplus cash but few new investment opportunities are prone to make acquisitions rather than distribute excess cash to shareholders. When distinguishing value-creating deals, analysts must examine the operational strengths possessed by the acquirer and the target to discern the likelihood that post-merger synergies will be achieved.

---

[24]Weston and Weaver (2001, 93–116).
[25]Bruner (2005, 33).
[26]Roll (1986, 176–216).
[27]Koller, Goedhart, and Wessels (2005, 439, footnotes 3 and 4).

Based on past empirical results, the following are characteristics of M&A deals that create value[28]:

- *The buyer is strong.* Acquirers whose earnings and share prices grow at a rate above the industry average for three years before the acquisition earn statistically significant positive returns upon announcement.
- *The transaction premiums are relatively low.* Acquirers earn negative returns upon announcement when paying a high premium.
- *The number of bidders is low.* Acquirer stock returns are negatively related to the number of bidders.
- *The initial market reaction is favorable.* Initial market reaction is an important barometer for the value investors place on the gains from merging as well as an indication of future returns. If the acquiring company's stock price falls when the deal is announced, investors are sending a message that the merger benefits are doubtful or that the acquirer is paying too much.

9. CORPORATE RESTRUCTURING

Just as mergers and acquisitions are a means by which companies get bigger, a corporate restructuring is usually used in reference to ways that companies get smaller—by selling, splitting off, or otherwise shedding operating assets. When a company decides to sell, liquidate, or spin off a division or a subsidiary, it is referred to as a **divestiture.**

Given, as we have discussed, that many companies have great difficulty actually achieving the planned synergies of a business combination, it is not surprising that many companies seek to undo previous mergers. Indeed, periods of intense merger activity are often followed by periods of heightened restructuring activity. Of course, previous mergers that did not work out as planned are not the only reason companies may choose to divest assets. Some of the common reasons for restructuring follow:

- *Change in strategic focus:* Through either acquisitions or other investments over time, companies often become engaged in multiple markets. Management may hope to improve performance by eliminating divisions or subsidiaries that are outside the company's core strategic focus.
- *Poor fit:* Sometimes a company decides that a particular division is a poor fit within the overall company. For example, the company many not have the expertise or resources to fully exploit opportunities pursued by the division and may decide to sell the segment to another company that does have the necessary resources. Or the division might simply not be profitable enough to justify continued investment based on the company's cost of capital.
- *Reverse synergy:* Managers may feel that a segment of the company is undervalued by the market, sometimes because of poor performance of the overall company or because the division is not a good strategic fit. In these cases, it is possible that the division and the company are worth more separately than combined.
- *Financial or cash flow needs:* If times are tough, managers may decide to sell off portions of the company as a means by which to raise cash or cut expenses.

---

[28]Weston and Weaver (2001, Chapter 5).

Restructuring can take many forms, but the three basic ways that a company divests assets are by (1) a sale to another company, (2) a spin-off to shareholders, or (3) liquidation. As part of a sale to another company, a company might offer to sell the assets of a division or may offer an equity carve-out. An **equity carve-out** involves the creation of a new legal entity and sales of equity in it to outsiders.

In a **spin-off**, shareholders of the parent company receive a proportional number of shares in a new, separate entity. Whereas the sale of a division results in an inflow of cash to the parent company, a spin-off does not. A spin-off simply results in shareholders owning stock in two different companies where there used to be one. A similar type of transaction is called a **split-off**, where some of the parent company's shareholders are given shares in a newly created entity in exchange for their shares of the parent company. **Liquidation** involves breaking up a company, division, or subsidiary and selling off its assets piecemeal. For a company, liquidation is typically associated with bankruptcy.

10. SUMMARY

Mergers and acquisitions are complex transactions. The process often involves not only the acquiring and target companies but also a variety of other stakeholders, including securities antitrust regulatory agencies. To fully evaluate a merger, analysts must ask two fundamental questions: First, will the transaction create value? Second, does the acquisition price outweigh the potential benefit? This chapter has made the following important points:

- An acquisition is the purchase of some portion of one company by another. A merger represents the absorption of one company by another such that only one entity survives following the transaction.
- Mergers can be categorized by the form of integration. In a statutory merger, one company is merged into another; in a subsidiary merger, the target becomes a subsidiary of the acquirer; and in a consolidation, both the acquirer and target become part of a newly formed company.
- Horizontal mergers occur among peer companies engaged in the same kind of business. Vertical mergers occur among companies along a given value chain. Conglomerates are formed by companies in unrelated businesses.
- Merger activity has historically occurred in waves. These waves have typically coincided with a strong economy and buoyant stock market activity. Merger activity tends to be concentrated in a few industries, usually those undergoing changes, such as deregulation or technological advancement.
- The motives for M&A activity include synergy, growth, market power, the acquisition of unique capabilities and resources, diversification, increased earnings, management's personal incentives, tax considerations, and the possibilities of uncovering hidden value. Cross-border motivations may involve technology transfer, product differentiation, government policy, and the opportunities to serve existing clients abroad.
- A merger transaction may take the form of a stock purchase (when the acquirer gives the target company's shareholders some combination of cash or securities in exchange for shares of the target company's stock) or an asset purchase (when the acquirer purchases the target company's assets and payment is made directly to the target company). The decision of which approach to take affects other aspects of the transaction, such as how approval is

obtained, which laws apply, how the liabilities are treated, and how the shareholders and the company are taxed.

- The method of payment for a merger can be cash, securities, or a mixed offering of both. The exchange ratio in a stock or mixed offering determines the number of shares that stockholders in the target company receive in exchange for each of their shares in the target company.

- Hostile transactions are those opposed by target managers, whereas friendly transactions are endorsed by the target company's managers. A target can use a variety of pre- and post-offer defenses to ward off an unwanted takeover bid.

- Examples of pre-offer defense mechanisms include poison pills and puts, incorporation in a jurisdiction with restrictive takeover laws, staggered boards of directors, restricted voting rights, supermajority voting provisions, fair price amendments, and golden parachutes.

- Examples of post-offer defenses include a "just say no" defense, litigation, greenmail, share repurchases, leveraged recapitalization, a "crown jewel" defense, a "Pac-Man" defense, or finding a white knight or white squire.

- Antitrust legislation prohibits mergers and acquisitions that impede competition. Major U.S. antitrust legislation includes the Sherman Antitrust Act, the Clayton Act, the Celler–Kefauver Act, and the Hart–Scott–Rodino Act.

- The Federal Trade Commission and Department of Justice review mergers for antitrust concerns in the United States. The European Commission reviews transactions in the European Union.

- The Herfindahl–Hirschman Index (HHI) is a measure of market power based on the sum of the squared market shares for each company in an industry. High index values or combinations that result in a large jump in the index are more likely to meet regulatory challenges.

- The Williams Act is the cornerstone of securities legislation for M&A activities in the United States. The Williams Act ensures a fair tender offer process through the establishment of disclosure requirements and formal tender offer procedures.

- Three major tools for valuing a target company are discounted cash flow analysis (which involves discounting free cash flows estimated with pro forma financial statements), comparable company analysis (which estimates a company's intrinsic value based on relative valuation metrics for similar companies), and comparable transaction analysis (which derives valuation from details of recent takeover transactions for comparable companies).

- In a merger bid, the gain to target shareholders is measured as the control premium, which equals the price paid for the target company in excess of its value. The acquirer gains equal the value of any synergies created by the merger minus the premium paid to target shareholders. Together, the bid and the method of payment determine the distribution of risks and returns among acquirer and target shareholders with regard to the realization of synergies as well as the correct estimation of the target company's value.

- The empirical evidence suggests that merger transactions create value for target company shareholders. Acquirers, in contrast, tend to accrue value in the years following a merger. This finding suggests that synergies are often overestimated or difficult to achieve.

- When a company decides to sell, liquidate, or spin off a division or a subsidiary, it is referred to as a divestiture. Companies may divest assets for a variety of reasons, including a change in strategic focus, poor fit of the asset within the corporation, reverse synergy, or cash flow needs.

- The three basic ways that a company divests assets are a sale to another company, a spin-off to shareholders, and liquidation.

PRACTICE PROBLEMS

The following information relates to Questions 1 through 6.

Modern Auto, an automobile parts supplier, has made an offer to acquire Sky Systems, creator of software for the airline industry. The offer is to pay Sky Systems' shareholders the current market value of their stock in Modern Auto's stock. The relevant information it used in those calculations follows:

	Modern Auto	Sky Systems
Share price	$40	$25
Number of outstanding shares (millions)	40	15
Earnings (millions)	$100	$30

Although the total earnings of the combined company will not increase and are estimated to be $130 million, Charles Wilhelm (treasurer of Modern Auto) argues that there are two attractive reasons to merge. First, Wilhelm says, "The merger of Modern Auto and Sky Systems will result in lower risk for our shareholders because of the diversification effect." Second, Wilhelm also says, "If our EPS increases, our stock price will increase in line with the EPS increase because our P/E will stay the same."

Sky Systems managers are not interested in the offer by Modern Auto. The managers, instead, approach HiFly, Inc., which is in the same industry as Sky Systems, to see if it would be interested in acquiring Sky Systems. HiFly is interested, and both companies believe there will be synergies from this acquisition. If HiFly were to acquire Sky Systems, it would do so by paying $400 million in cash.

HiFly is somewhat concerned whether antitrust regulators would consider the acquisition of Sky Systems an antitrust violation. The market in which the two companies operate consists of eight competitors. The largest company has a 25 percent market share. HiFly has the second largest market share of 20 percent. Five companies, including Sky Systems, each have a market share of 10 percent. The smallest company has a 5 percent market share.

1. The acquisition of Sky Systems by Modern Auto and the acquisition of Sky Systems by HiFly, respectively, would be examples of a
   A. Horizontal merger and a vertical merger.
   B. Vertical merger and a horizontal merger.
   C. Conglomerate merger and a vertical merger.
   D. Conglomerate merger and a horizontal merger.

2. If Sky Systems were to be acquired by Modern Auto under the terms of the original offer, the post-merger EPS of the new company would be *closest* to
   A. $2.00.
   B. $2.32.
   C. $2.63.
   D. $3.25.

3. Are Wilhelm's two statements about his shareholders benefiting from the diversification effect of the merger and about the increase in the stock price, respectively, correct?

	The merger will result in lower risk for shareholders.	The stock price will increase in line with the EPS increase.
A.	No	No
B.	No	Yes
C.	Yes	No
D.	Yes	Yes

4. Which of the following defenses *best* describes the role of HiFly in the acquisition scenario?
   A. Crown jewel.
   B. Pac-Man.
   C. White knight.
   D. White squire.

5. Suppose HiFly acquires Sky Systems for the stated terms. The gain to Sky Systems' shareholders resulting from the merger transaction would be *closest* to
   A. $25 million.
   B. $160 million.
   C. $375 million.
   D. $400 million.

6. If HiFly and Sky Systems attempt to merge, the increase in the Herfindahl–Hirschman Index (HHI) and the probable action by the Department of Justice and the FTC, respectively, in response to the merger announcement are

	Increase in the HHI	Probable Response of Department of Justice and FTC
A.	290	Challenge the merger
B.	290	Investigate the merger
C.	400	Challenge the merger
D.	400	Investigate the merger

The following information relates to Questions 7 through 12.

Kinetic Corporation is considering acquiring High Tech Systems. Jim Smith, the vice president of finance at Kinetic, has been assigned the task of estimating a fair acquisition price for High Tech. Smith is aware of several approaches that could be used for this purpose. He plans to estimate the acquisition price based on each of these approaches and has collected or estimated the necessary financial data.

High Tech has 10 million shares of common stock outstanding and no debt. Smith has estimated that the post-merger free cash flows from High Tech, in millions of dollars, would be 15, 17, 20, and 23 at the end of the following four years. After year 4, he projects the free cash flow to grow at a constant rate of 6.5 percent a year. He determines that the appropriate rate for discounting these estimated cash flows is 11 percent. He also estimates that after four years High Tech would be worth 23 times its free cash flow in the fourth year.

Smith has determined that three companies—Alpha, Neutron, and Techno—are comparable to High Tech. He has also identified three recent takeover transactions—Quadrant, ProTech, and Automator—that are similar to the takeover of High Tech under consideration. He believes that the price-to-earnings, price-to-sales, and price-to-book-value-per-share ratios of these companies could be used to estimate the value of High Tech. The relevant data for the three comparable companies and for High Tech follow:

Valuation Variables	Alpha	Neutron	Techno	High Tech
Current stock price ($)	44.00	23.00	51.00	31.00
Earnings per share ($)	3.01	1.68	2.52	1.98
Sales per share ($)	20.16	14.22	18.15	17.23
Book value per share ($)	15.16	7.18	11.15	10.02

The relevant data for the three recently acquired companies follow:

Valuation Variables	Quadrant	ProTech	Automator
Stock price pre-takeover ($)	24.90	43.20	29.00
Acquisition stock price ($)	28.00	52.00	34.50
Earnings per share ($)	1.40	2.10	2.35
Sales per share ($)	10.58	20.41	15.93
Book value per share ($)	8.29	10.14	9.17

While discussing his analysis with a colleague, Smith makes two comments:

1. "If there were a pre-announcement run-up in Quadrant's price because of speculation, the takeover premium should be computed based on the price prior to the run-up."

2. "Because the comparable transaction approach is based on the acquisition price, the takeover premium is implicitly recognized in this approach."

7. What is the present value per share of High Tech stock using the discounted cash flow approach if the terminal value of High Tech is based on using the constant growth model to determine terminal value?
   A. $35.22.
   B. $39.38.
   C. $40.56.
   D. $41.57.

8. What is the value per share of High Tech stock using the discounted cash flow approach if the terminal value of High Tech is based on using the cash flow multiple method to determine terminal value?
   A. $35.22.
   B. $40.56.
   C. $41.57.
   D. $58.61.

9. The average stock price of High Tech for the three relative valuation ratios (if it is traded at the mean of the three valuations) is *closest* to
   A. $35.21.
   B. $39.38.
   C. $40.56.
   D. $41.57.

10. Taking into account the mean takeover premium on recent comparable takeovers, what is the estimate of the fair acquisition price of High Tech based on the comparable company approach?
    A. $35.22.
    B. $40.83.
    C. $41.29.
    D. $52.48.

11. The fair acquisition price of High Tech using the comparable transaction approach is *closest* to
    A. $35.22.
    B. $40.86.
    C. $41.31.
    D. $52.48.

12. Are Smith's two comments about his analysis correct?
    A. Both of his comments are correct.
    B. Both of his comments are incorrect.
    C. His first comment is correct, and his second comment is incorrect.
    D. His first comment is incorrect, and his second comment is correct.

GLOSSARY

Abandonment option   The ability to terminate a project at some future time if the financial results are disappointing.

Accounts receivable turnover   Ratio of sales on credit to the average balance in accounts receivable.

Acid test ratio   *See* Quick ratio

Acquirer   *See* Acquiring company

Acquiring company (acquirer)   The company in a merger or acquisition that is acquiring the target.

Acquisition   The purchase of some portion of one company by another; the purchase may be for assets, a definable segment of another entity, or the purchase of an entire company.

Active strategy   In reference to short-term cash management, an investment strategy characterized by monitoring and attempting to capitalize on market conditions to optimize the risk-and-return relationship of short-term investments.

Agency costs   Costs associated with the conflict of interest present when a company is managed by nonowners. Agency costs result from the inherent conflicts of interest between managers and equity owners.

Agency costs of equity   The smaller the stake that managers have in the company, the less is their share in bearing the cost of excessive perquisite consumption or not giving their best efforts in running the company.

Agency problem (principal-agent problem)   A conflict of interest that arises when the agent in an agency relationship has goals and incentives that differ from those of the principal to whom the agent owes a fiduciary duty.

Agency relationships   An arrangement whereby someone, an agent, acts on behalf of another person, the principal.

Aging schedule   A breakdown of accounts into categories of days outstanding.

Anticipation stock   Excess inventory that is held in anticipation of increased demand, often because of seasonal patterns of demand.

Asset-based loan   A loan that is secured with company assets.

Asset beta   The unlevered beta; reflects the business risk of the assets; the asset's systematic risk.

Asset purchase   An acquisition in which the acquirer purchases the target company's assets and payment is made directly to the target company.

Assignment of accounts receivable   The use of accounts receivable as collateral for a loan.

Asymmetric information   The differential of information between corporate insiders and outsiders regarding the company's performance and prospects. Managers typically have more information about the company's performance and prospects than owners and creditors.

Automated Clearing House   An electronic payment network available to businesses, individuals, and financial institutions in the United States, U.S. territories, and Canada.

Backward integration   A merger involving the purchase of a target ahead of the acquirer in the value or production chain; for example, the acquisition of a supplier.

Bear hug   A tactic used by acquirers to circumvent target management's objections to a proposed merger by submitting the proposal directly to the target company's board of directors.

Bond equivalent yield   A calculation of yield that is annualized using the ratio of 365 to the number of days to maturity. Bond equivalent yield allows for the restatement and comparison of securities with different compounding periods.

Bonding costs   Costs borne by management to assure owners that they are working in the owners' best interest (e.g., implicit cost of noncompete agreements).

Bond yield plus risk premium approach   An estimate of the cost of common equity that is produced by summing the before-tax cost of debt and a risk premium that captures the additional yield on a company's stock relative to its bonds. The additional yield is often estimated using historical spreads between bond yields and stock yields.

Book value equity per share   The amount of book value (also called carrying value) of common equity per share of common stock, calculated by dividing the book value of shareholders' equity by the number of shares of common stock outstanding.

Bootstrapping earnings   An increase in a company's earnings that results as a consequence of the idiosyncrasies of a merger transaction itself rather than because of resulting economic benefits of the combination.

Breakeven point   The number of units produced and sold at which the company's net income is zero (revenues = total costs).

Break point   In the context of the weighted average cost of capital (WACC), the amount of capital at which the cost of one or more of the sources of capital changes, leading to a change in the WACC.

Breakup value   The value that can be achieved if a company's assets are divided and sold separately.

Business risk   The risk associated with operating earnings. Operating earnings are uncertain because total revenues and many of the expenditures contributed to produce those revenues are uncertain.

Cannibalization   Cannibalization occurs when an investment takes customers and sales away from another part of the company.

Capital rationing   An environment assuming that the company has a fixed amount of funds to invest.

Capital structure   The mix of debt and equity that a company uses to finance its business.

Captive finance subsidiary   A wholly-owned subsidiary of a company that is established to provide financing of the sales of the parent company.

Cash offering   A merger or acquisition that is to be paid for with cash; the cash for the merger might come from the acquiring company's existing assets or from a debt issue.

Cash ratio   A measure of a company's ability to meet its current obligations with just the cash and cash equivalents on hand.

Clientele effect   The preference some investors have for shares that exhibit certain characteristics.

Committed lines of credit   A bank commitment to extend credit up to a prespecified amount; the commitment is considered a short-term liability and is usually in effect for 364 days (one day short of a full year).

Common-size analysis   The restatement of financial statement items using a common denominator or reference item that allows one to identify trends and major differences.

Comparable company   A company that has similar business risk; usually in the same industry and preferably with a single line of business.

Component cost of capital   The rate of return required by suppliers of capital for an individual source of a company's funding, such as debt or equity.

Conglomerate merger   A merger involving companies that are in unrelated businesses.

Consolidation   A merger in which both companies terminate their previous legal existence and become part of a newly formed company.

Contribution margin   The amount available for fixed costs and profit after paying variable costs; revenue minus variable costs.

Conventional cash flow   A cash flow pattern with an initial outflow followed by a series of inflows.

Corporate governance   The system of principles, policies, procedures, and clearly defined responsibilities and accountabilities used by stakeholders to overcome the conflicts of interest inherent in the corporate form.

Corporate raider   A person or organization seeking to profit by acquiring a company and reselling it, or by seeking to profit from the takeover attempt itself (e.g., greenmail).

Corporation   A legal entity with rights similar to those of a person. The chief officers, executives, or top managers act as agents for the firm and are legally entitled to authorize corporate activities and to enter into contracts on behalf of the business.

Cost of capital   The rate of return that suppliers of capital require as compensation for their contribution of capital.

Cost of debt   The cost of debt financing to a company, such as when it issues a bond or takes out a bank loan.

Cost of preferred stock   The dividend yield that a company commits to pay preferred stockholders.

Cost structure   The mix of a company's variable costs and fixed costs.

Credit scoring model   A statistical model used to classify borrowers according to creditworthiness.

Creditworthiness   The perceived ability of the borrower to pay what is owed on the borrowing in a timely manner; it represents the ability of a company to withstand adverse impacts on its cash flows.

Current assets (liquid assets)   Assets that may be converted into cash in a short period of time.

Current liabilities   Short-term obligations, such as accounts payable, wages payable, or accrued liabilities.

Current ratio   The ratio of current assets to current liabilities.

Dead-hand provision   A poison pill provision that allows for the redemption or cancellation of a poison pill provision only by a vote of continuing directors (generally directors who were on the target company's board prior to the takeover attempt).

Debt incurrence test   A financial covenant made in conjunction with existing debt that restricts a company's ability to incur additional debt at the same seniority based on one or more financial tests or conditions.

Debt rating approach   A method for estimating a company's before-tax cost of debt based on the yield on comparably rated bonds for maturities that closely match that of the company's existing debt.

Debt ratings   An objective measure of the quality and safety of a company's debt based on an analysis of the company's ability to pay the promised cash flows, as well as an analysis of any indentures.

Debt-to-assets ratio   A measure of the proportion of assets that is financed with debt.

Declaration date   The day that the corporation issues a statement declaring a specific dividend.

Definitive merger agreement   A contract signed by both parties to a merger that clarifies the details of the transaction, including the terms, warranties, conditions, termination details, and the rights of all parties.

Degree of financial leverage (DFL)   The ratio of the percentage change in net income to the percentage change in operating income; the sensitivity of the cash flows available to owners when operating income changes.

Degree of operating leverage (DOL)   The ratio of the percentage change in operating income to the percentage change in units sold; the sensitivity of operating income to changes in units sold.

Degree of total leverage   The ratio of the percentage change in net income to the percentage change in units sold; the sensitivity of the cash flows to owners to changes in the number of units produced and sold.

DFL   *See* Degree of financial leverage

Direct debit program   An arrangement whereby a customer authorizes a debit to a demand account; typically used by companies to collect routine payments for services.

Disbursement float   The amount of time between check issuance and a check's clearing back against the company's account.

Discounted cash flow analysis   In the context of merger analysis, it is an estimate of a target company's value found by discounting the company's expected future free cash flows to the present.

Discount interest   The implicit interest provided by discount securities; the difference between the purchase price and the face value.

Divestiture   The sale, liquidation, or spin-off of a division or subsidiary.

Dividend discount model based approach   An approach for estimating an equity risk premium. The market rate of return is estimated as the sum of the dividend yield and the growth rate in dividends for a market index. Subtracting the risk-free rate of return from the estimated market return produces an estimate for the equity risk premium.

Dividend payout policy   The strategy a company follows with regard to the amount and timing of dividend payments.

Dividend payout ratio   The ratio of cash dividends paid to earnings for a period.

Dividends per share   The dollar amount of cash dividends paid during a period per share of common stock.

DOL   *See* Degree of operating leverage

Double taxation   Corporate earnings are taxed twice when paid out as dividends. First, corporate earnings are taxed regardless of whether they will be distributed as dividends or retained at the corporate level, and second, dividends are taxed again at the individual shareholder level.

Drag on liquidity   When receipts lag, creating pressure from the decreased available funds.

Earnings per share   The amount of income earned during a period per share of common stock.

Economic order quantity-reorder point   An approach to managing inventory based on expected demand and the predictability of demand; the ordering point for new inventory is determined based on the costs of ordering and carrying inventory, such that the total cost associated with inventory is minimized.

Economies of scale   In reference to mergers, the savings achieved through the consolidation of operations and elimination of duplicate resources.

Elasticity   A measure of sensitivity; the incremental change in one variable with respect to an incremental change in another variable.

Electronic funds transfer   The use of computer networks to conduct financial transactions electronically.

Equity carve-out   A form of restructuring that involves the creation of a new legal entity and the sale of equity in it to outsiders.

Equity risk premium   The expected return on equities minus the risk-free rate; the premium that investors demand for investing in equities.

Exchange ratio   The number of shares that target stockholders are to receive in exchange for each of their shares in the target company.

Ex-dividend   Term referring to shares that no longer carry the right to the next dividend payment.

Ex-dividend date   The first date that a share trades without (i.e., "ex") the dividend.

External growth   Company growth in output or sales that is achieved by buying the necessary resources externally (i.e., achieved through mergers and acquisitions).

Externality   The effect of an investment on other things besides the investment itself.

Financial analysis   The process of selecting, evaluating, and interpreting financial data in order to formulate an assessment of a company's present and future financial condition and performance.

Financial distress   Heightened uncertainty regarding a company's ability to meet its various obligations because of lower or negative earnings.

Financial risk   The risk arising from a company's obligation to meet required payments under its financing agreements; the risk that environmental, social, or governance risk factors will result in significant costs or other losses to a company and its shareholders.

Fixed costs   Costs that remain at the same level regardless of a company's level of production and sales.

Fixed rate perpetual preferred stock   Nonconvertible, noncallable preferred stock that has a fixed dividend rate and no maturity date.

Flip-in pill   A poison pill takeover defense that dilutes an acquirer's ownership in a target by giving other existing target company shareholders the right to buy additional target company shares at a discount.

Flip-over pill   A poison pill takeover defense that gives target company shareholders the right to purchase shares of the acquirer at a significant discount to the market price, which has the effect of causing dilution to all existing acquiring company shareholders.

Float   In the context of customer receipts, the amount of money that is in transit between payments made by customers and the funds that are usable by the company.

Float factor   An estimate of the average number of days it takes deposited checks to clear; average daily float divided by average daily deposit.

Flotation cost   Fees charged to companies by investment bankers and other costs associated with raising new capital.

Forward integration A merger involving the purchase of a target that is farther along the value or production chain; for example, the acquisition of a distributor.

Free cash flow hypothesis The hypothesis that high debt levels discipline managers by forcing them to make fixed debt service payments and by reducing the company's free cash flow.

Free cash flow to equity The cash flow available to a company's common shareholders after all operating expenses, interest, and principal payments have been made, and the necessary investments in working and fixed capital have been made.

Free cash flow to the firm The cash flow available to the company's suppliers of capital after all operating expenses have been paid and necessary investments in working capital and fixed capital have been made.

Friendly transaction A potential business combination that is endorsed by the managers of both companies.

Giro system An electronic payment system used widely in Europe and Japan.

Greenmail The purchase of the accumulated shares of a hostile investor by a company that is targeted for takeover by that investor, usually at a substantial premium over market price.

Gross profit margin The ratio of gross profit to revenues.

Growth option (expansion option) The ability to make additional investments in a project at some future time if the financial results are strong.

Herfindahl–Hirschman Index (HHI) A measure of market concentration that is calculated by summing the squared market shares for competing companies in an industry; high HHI readings or mergers that would result in large HHI increases are more likely to result in regulatory challenges.

HHI *See* Herfindahl–Hirschman Index

Historical equity risk premium approach An estimate of a country's equity risk premium that is based on the historical averages of the risk-free rate and the rate of return on the market portfolio.

Holder-of-record date The date that a shareholder listed on the corporation's books is deemed to have ownership of the shares for purposes of receiving an upcoming dividend; two business days after the ex-dividend date.

Horizontal common-size analysis A form of common-size analysis in which the accounts in a given period are used as the benchmark or base period, and every account is restated in subsequent periods as a percentage of the base period's same account.

Horizontal merger A merger involving companies in the same line of business, usually as competitors.

Hostile transaction An attempt to acquire a company against the wishes of the target's managers.

Impairment of capital rule A legal restriction that dividends cannot exceed retained earnings.

Imputation In reference to corporate taxes, a system that imputes, or attributes, taxes at only one level of taxation. For countries using an imputation tax system, taxes on dividends are effectively levied only at the shareholder rate. Taxes are paid at the corporate level but they are *attributed* to the shareholder. Shareholders deduct from their tax bill their portion of taxes paid by the company.

Incremental cash flow The cash flow that is realized because of a decision; the cash flow with a decision minus the cash flow without that decision.

Independent projects Independent projects are projects whose cash flows are independent of each other.

Inventory blanket lien The use of inventory as collateral for a loan. Though the lender has claim to some or all of the company's inventory, the company may still sell or use the inventory in the ordinary course of business.

Inventory turnover The ratio of cost of goods sold to inventory.

Investment opportunity schedule A graphical depiction of a company's investment opportunities, ordered from highest to lowest expected return. A company's optimal capital budget is found where the investment opportunity schedule intersects with the company's marginal cost of capital.

Just-in-time method Method of managing inventory that minimizes in-process inventory stocks.

Laddering strategy A form of active strategy that entails scheduling maturities on a systematic basis within the investment portfolio such that investments are spread out equally over the term of the ladder.

LBO   *See* Leveraged buyout

Legal risk   The risk that failures by company managers to effectively manage a company's environmental, social, and governance risk exposures will lead to lawsuits and other judicial remedies, resulting in potentially catastrophic losses for the company.

Legislative and regulatory risk   The risk that governmental laws and regulations directly or indirectly affecting a company's operations will change with potentially severe adverse effects on the company's continued profitability and even its long-term sustainability.

Leverage   In the context of corporate finance, the use of fixed costs within a company's cost structure. Fixed costs that are operating costs (such as depreciation or rent) create operating leverage. Fixed costs that are financial costs (such as interest expense) create financial leverage.

Leveraged buyout (LBO)   A transaction whereby the target company management team converts the target to a privately held company by using heavy borrowing to finance the purchase of the target company's outstanding shares.

Leveraged recapitalization   A postoffer takeover defense mechanism that involves the assumption of a large amount of debt that is then used to finance share repurchases; the effect is to dramatically change the company's capital structure while attempting to deliver a value to target shareholders in excess of a hostile bid.

Liquid assets   *See* Current assets

Liquidation   To sell the assets of a company, division, or subsidiary piecemeal, typically because of bankruptcy; the form of bankruptcy that allows for the orderly satisfaction of creditors' claims, after which the company ceases to exist.

Liquidity   A company's ability to satisfy its short-term obligations using assets that are the most readily converted into cash.

Liquidity ratios   A form of liquidity analysis that focuses on the relationship between current assets and current liabilities and on the rapidity with which receivables and inventory can be converted into cash during normal business operations.

Lockbox system   A payment system in which customer payments are mailed to a post office box and the banking institution retrieves and deposits these payments several times a day, enabling the company to have use of the funds sooner than in a centralized system in which customer payments are sent to the company.

Long-term debt-to-assets ratio   The proportion of a company's assets that is financed with long-term debt.

Managerialism theories   Theories positing that corporate executives are motivated to engage in mergers to maximize the size of their company rather than shareholder value.

Manufacturing resource planning (MRP)   The incorporation of production planning into inventory management. An MRP analysis provides both a materials acquisition schedule and a production schedule.

Matching strategy   An active investment strategy that includes intentional matching of the timing of cash outflows with investment maturities.

Matrix pricing   In the fixed income markets, pricing a security on the basis of valuation-relevant characteristics (e.g., debt-rating approach).

Merger   The absorption of one company by another; that is, two companies become one entity and one or both of the pre-merger companies cease to exist as separate entities.

Mismatching strategy   An active investment strategy whereby the timing of cash outflows is not matched with investment maturities.

Mixed offering   A merger or acquisition that is to be paid for with cash, securities, or some combination of the two.

Money market yield   Yield on short-term debt securities; typically annualized using the ratio of 360 to the number of days to maturity.

Monitoring costs   Costs borne by owners to monitor the management of the company (e.g., board of director expenses).

MRP   *See* Manufacturing resource planning

Mutually exclusive projects   Mutually exclusive projects compete directly with each other. For example, if Projects A and B are mutually exclusive, you can choose A or B, but you cannot choose both.

Net operating cycle   An estimate of the average time that elapses between paying suppliers for materials and collecting cash from the subsequent sale of goods produced.

Net operating profit less adjusted taxes (NOPLAT)   A company's operating profit with adjustments to normalize the effects of capital structure.

Net present value   For a project, the present value of the project inflows minus the present value of the project outflows.

Net profit margin   The ratio of net income to revenues; indicates how much of each dollar of revenues is left after all costs and expenses.

Nominal rate   A rate of interest based on the security's face value.

Nonconventional cash flow   In a nonconventional cash flow pattern, the initial outflow is not followed by inflows only, but the cash flows can flip from positive (inflows) to negative (outflows) again (or even change signs several times).

NOPLAT   *See* Net operating profit less adjusted taxes

Number of days of inventory   The average length of time that inventory remains within the company.

Number of days of payables   Estimate of the average number of days it takes the company to pay its own suppliers.

Number of days of receivables   Estimate of the average number of days it takes to collect on credit accounts.

Operating breakeven   The number of units produced and sold at which the company's operating profit is zero (revenues = operating costs).

Operating cycle   A measure of the time needed to convert raw materials into cash from a sale; it consists of the number of days of inventory and the number of days of receivables.

Operating profit margin   The ratio of operating income (i.e., income before interest and taxes) to revenues.

Operating return on assets   The ratio of operating earnings to assets.

Operating risk   The risk attributed to the operating cost structure, in particular the use of fixed costs in operations; the risk arising from the mix of fixed and variable costs; the risk that a company's operations may be severely affected by environmental, social, and governance risk factors.

Operational risk   The risk of loss from failures in a company's systems and procedures or from external events.

Opportunity cost   What a resource is worth in its next-best use.

Optimal capital structure   The capital structure at which the value of the company is maximized.

Organic growth   Company growth in output or sales that is achieved by making investments internally (i.e., excludes growth achieved through mergers and acquisitions).

Partnership   A business owned and operated by more than one individual.

Passive strategy   In reference to short-term cash management, an investment strategy characterized by simple decision rules for making daily investments.

Payment date   The day that the company actually mails out (or electronically transfers) a dividend payment.

Payout ratio   The percentage of total earnings paid out in dividends in any given year (in per-share terms, DPS/EPS).

Pecking order theory   The theory that managers take into account how their actions might be interpreted by outsiders and thus order their preferences for various forms of corporate financing. Forms of financing that are least visible to outsiders (e.g., internally generated funds) are most preferable to managers and those that are most visible (e.g., equity) are least preferable.

Per-unit contribution margin   The amount that each unit sold contributes to covering fixed costs—that is, the difference between the price per unit and the variable cost per unit.

Pet projects   Projects in which influential managers want the corporation to invest. Often, unfortunately, pet projects are selected without undergoing normal capital budgeting analysis.

Point of sale   Systems that capture transaction data at the physical location in which the sale is made.

Poison pill   A preoffer takeover defense mechanism that makes it prohibitively costly for an acquirer to take control of a target without the prior approval of the target's board of directors.

Poison puts   A preoffer takeover defense mechanism that gives target company bond holders the right to sell their bonds back to the target at a prespecified redemption price, typically at or above par value; this defense increases the need for cash and raises the cost of the acquisition.

Precautionary stocks   A level of inventory beyond anticipated needs that provides a cushion in the event that it takes longer to replenish inventory than expected or in the case of greater-than-expected demand.

Priced risk   Risk for which investors demand compensation for bearing (e.g., equity risk, company-specific factors, macroeconomic factors).

Price-setting option   The operational flexibility to adjust prices when demand varies from forecast. For example, when demand exceeds capacity, the company could benefit from the excess demand by increasing prices.

Principal-agent problem   *See* Agency problem

Production-flexibility   The operational flexibility to alter production when demand varies from forecast. For example, if demand is strong, a company may profit from employees working overtime or from adding additional shifts.

Project sequencing   To defer the decision to invest in a future project until the outcome of some or all of a current project is known. Projects are sequenced through time so that investing in a project creates the option to invest in future projects.

Proxy fight   An attempt to take control of a company through a shareholder vote.

Proxy statement   A public document that provides the material facts concerning matters on which shareholders will vote.

Pull on liquidity   When disbursements are paid too quickly or trade credit availability is limited, requiring companies to expend funds before they receive funds from sales that could cover the liability.

Pure-play method   A method for estimating the beta for a company or project; it requires using a comparable company's beta and adjusting it for financial leverage differences.

Quick assets   Assets that can be most readily converted to cash (e.g., cash, short-term marketable investments, receivables).

Quick ratio (acid test ratio)   A stringent measure of liquidity that indicates a company's ability to satisfy current liabilities with its most liquid assets.

Receivables turnover   The ratio of total revenue to average accounts receivable.

Reorganization   Agreements made by a company in bankruptcy under which a company's capital structure is altered and/or alternative arrangements are made for debt repayment; U.S. Chapter 11 bankruptcy. The company emerges from bankruptcy as a going concern.

Reputational risk   The risk that a company will suffer an extended diminution in market value relative to other companies in the same industry due to a demonstrated lack of concern for environmental, social, and governance risk factors.

Residual dividend approach   A dividend payout policy under which earnings in excess of the funds necessary to finance the equity portion of company's capital budget are paid out in dividends.

Residual loss   Agency costs that are incurred despite adequate monitoring and bonding of management.

Return on assets   The ratio of net income to assets; indicates a company's net profit generated per dollar invested in total assets.

Return on common equity   The ratio of net income available to common shareholders to common shareholders' equity; the profit generated per dollar of common shareholders' investment.

Return on equity   The ratio of net income to shareholders' equity; represents the profit generated per dollar of shareholders' investment.

Reverse stock split   A reduction in the number of shares outstanding with a corresponding increase in share price, but no change to the company's underlying fundamentals.

Revolving credit agreements   The strongest form of short-term bank borrowing facilities; they are in effect for multiple years (e.g., three to five years) and may have optional medium-term loan features.

Safety stock A level of inventory beyond anticipated needs that provides a cushion in the event that it takes longer to replenish inventory than expected or in the case of greater-than-expected demand.

Sales risk Uncertainty with respect to the quantity of goods and services that a company is able to sell and the price it is able to achieve; the risk related to the uncertainty of revenues.

Securities offering A merger or acquisition in which target shareholders are to receive shares of the acquirer's common stock as compensation.

Share repurchase A transaction in which a company buys back its own shares. Unlike stock dividends and stock splits, share repurchases use corporate cash.

Shark repellents A preoffer takeover defense mechanism involving the corporate charter (e.g., staggered boards of directors and supermajority provisions).

Sole proprietorship A business owned and operated by a single person.

Sovereign yield spread An estimate of the country spread (country equity premium) for a developing nation that is based on a comparison of bond yields in the country being analyzed and a developed country. The sovereign yield spread is the difference between a government bond yield in the country being analyzed, denominated in the currency of the developed country, and the Treasury bond yield on a similar maturity bond in the developed country.

Spin-off A form of restructuring in which shareholders of the parent company receive a proportional number of shares in a new, separate entity; shareholders end up owning stock in two different companies where there used to be one.

Split-off A form of restructuring in which shareholders of the parent company are given shares in a newly created entity in exchange for their shares of the parent company.

Split-rate In reference to corporate taxes, a tax system that taxes earnings to be distributed as dividends at a different rate than earnings to be retained. Corporate profits distributed as dividends are taxed at a lower rate than those retained in the business.

Static trade-off theory of capital structure A theory pertaining to a company's optimal capital structure; the optimal level of debt is found at the point where additional debt would cause the costs of financial distress to increase by a greater amount than the benefit of the additional tax shield.

Statutory merger A merger in which one company ceases to exist as an identifiable entity and all its assets and liabilities become part of a purchasing company.

Stock-out losses Profits lost from not having sufficient inventory on hand to satisfy demand.

Stock purchase An acquisition in which the acquirer gives the target company's shareholders some combination of cash and securities in exchange for shares of the target company's stock.

Subsidiary merger A merger in which the company being purchased becomes a subsidiary of the purchaser.

Sunk cost A cost that has already been incurred.

Survey approach An estimate of the equity risk premium that is based on estimates provided by a panel of finance experts.

Sustainable growth rate The rate of dividend (and earnings) growth that can be sustained over time for a given level of return on equity, keeping the capital structure constant and without issuing additional common stock.

Takeover A merger; the term may be applied to any transaction but is often used in reference to hostile transactions.

Takeover premium The amount by which the takeover price for each share of stock must exceed the current stock price in order to entice shareholders to relinquish control of the company to an acquirer.

Target balance A minimum level of cash to be held available—estimated in advance and adjusted for known funds transfers, seasonality, or other factors.

Target capital structure A company's chosen proportions of debt and equity.

Target company (target) The company in a merger or acquisition that is being acquired.

Target payout ratio A strategic corporate goal representing the long-term proportion of earnings that the company intends to distribute to shareholders as dividends.

Tender offer A public offer whereby the acquirer invites target shareholders to submit (tender) their shares in return for the proposed payment.

Total asset turnover   The ratio of revenues to total assets.

Trade credit   A spontaneous form of credit in which a purchaser of the goods or service is financing its purchase by delaying the date on which payment is made.

Transactions motive   In the context of inventory management, the need for inventory as part of the routine production–sales cycle.

Treasury shares   Shares that were issued and subsequently repurchased by the company.

Trust receipt arrangement   The use of inventory as collateral for a loan. The inventory is segregated and held in trust, and the proceeds of any sale must be remitted to the lender immediately.

Unlimited funds   An unlimited funds environment assumes that the company can raise the funds it wants for all profitable projects simply by paying the required rate of return.

Variable costs   Costs that fluctuate with the level of production and sales.

Vertical common-size analysis   The most common type of common-size analysis, in which the accounts in a given period are compared to a benchmark item in that same year.

Vertical merger   A merger involving companies at different positions of the same production chain; for example, a supplier and a distributor.

Warehouse receipt arrangement   The use of inventory as collateral for a loan; similar to a trust receipt arrangement except there is a third party (i.e., a warehouse company) that supervises the inventory.

Weighted average cost of capital   The required rate of return that investors demand for the average-risk investment of a company and the cost that a company incurs for additional capital. It is found as the average of the company's component costs of capital, weighted by their proportions in the company's capital structure.

White knight   A third party that is sought out by the target company's board to purchase the target in lieu of a hostile bidder.

White squire   A third party that is sought out by the target company's board to purchase enough of a minority stake in the target to block a hostile takeover without selling the entire company.

Winner's curse   The tendency for the winner in certain competitive bidding situations to overpay, whether because of overestimation of the intrinsic value, emotion, or information asymmetries.

Working capital   The difference between current assets and current liabilities.

Working capital management   Corporate finance activities that ensure a company has adequate ready access to the funds necessary for day-to-day operating expenses, at the same time making sure that the company's assets are invested in the most productive way.

Working capital turnover   A comparison of revenues with working capital to produce a measure that shows how efficiently working capital is employed.

Yield   The actual return on a debt security if it is held to maturity.

Yield to maturity   The annual return that an investor earns on a bond if the investor purchases the bond today and holds it until maturity.

REFERENCES

Amendments to Rules Governing the Investment Company Act of 1940, 17 CFR Part 270, July 2004.

American Management Association. 1960. "Executive Committee Control Charts."*AMA Management Bulletin,* No. 6: 22.

Anderson, Miranda, and David Gardiner. 2006. *Climate Risk and Energy in the Auto Sector: Guidance for Investors and Analysts on Key Off-balance Sheet Drivers.* Ceres, Inc.

Armitage, Seth. 2000. "The Direct Costs of UK Rights Issues and Open Offers." *European Financial Management,* Vol. 6, No. 1: 57–68.

Bancel, Franck, and Usha Mittoo. 2004. "The Determinants of Capital Structure Choice: A Survey of European Firms." *Financial Management,* Vol. 44, No. 4.

Bauer, Rod, and Nadja Guenster. 2003. "Good Corporate Governance Pays Off!: Well-Governed Companies Perform Better on the Stock Market." Working paper.

Blume, Marshall. 1971. "On the Assessment of Risk." *Journal of Finance,* Vol. 26, No. 1: 1–10.

Brounen, Dirk, Abe de Jong, and Kees Koedijk. 2004. "Corporate Finance in Europe: Confronting Theory with Practice." *Financial Management,* Vol. 33, No. 4: 71–101.

Brown, Lawrence D., and Marcus Caylor. 2004. "Corporate Governance Study: The Correlation Between Corporate Governance and Company Performance." Institutional Shareholder Services, available at http://www.tkyd.org/files/downloads/corporate_governance_study_104.pdf, accessed February 1, 2008.

Bruner, Robert F. 2005. *Deals from Hell: M&A Lessons That Rise Above the Ashes.* Hoboken, NJ: Wiley.

Bruner, Robert F., Robert M. Conroy, Wei Li, Elizabeth O'Halloran, and Miquel Palacios Lleras. 2003. *Investing in Emerging Markets.* Charlottesville, VA: AIMR Research Foundation.

Bühner, Thomas, and Christoph Kaserer. 2002. "External Financing Costs and Economies of Scale in Investment Banking: The Case of Seasoned Equity Offerings in Germany." *European Financial Management,* Vol. 9, No. 2: 249–253.

Chance, Don M. 2003. *Analysis of Derivatives for the CFA® Program.* Charlottesville, VA: Association for Investment Management and Research.

Chetty, Raj, and Emmanuel Saez. 2004. "Do Dividends Respond to Taxes? Preliminary Evidence from the 2003 Dividend Tax Cut." National Bureau of Economic Research Working Paper 10572.

Claessens, Stijn, Simeon Djankov, and Titiana Nenova. 2001. "Corporate Risk Around the World." In *Financial Crises in Emerging Markets.* Edited by Reuven Glick, Ramon Moreno, and Mark Speigel. New York: Cambridge University Press.

Copeland, Tom, Tim Koller, and Jack Murrin. 2000. *Valuation: Measuring and Managing the Value of Companies,* 3rd ed. Hoboken, NJ: Wiley.

Corporate Governance of Listed Companies: A Manual for Investors. 2005. Charlottesville, VA: CFA Institute Centre for Financial Market Integrity.

Damodaran, Aswath. 1999. "Estimating Equity Risk Premiums." New York University working paper.

Damodaran, Aswath. 2003. "Measuring Company Exposure to Country Risk: Theory and Practice." New York University working paper.

Daves, Phillip R., Michael C. Ehrhardt, and Robert A. Kunkel. 2000. "Estimating Systematic Risk: The Choice of Return Interval and Estimation Period." *Journal of Financial and Strategic Decisions,* Vol. 13, No. 1: 7–13.

DeAngelo, Harry, Linda DeAngelo, and Douglas Skinner. 1986. "Reversal of Fortune: Dividend Signals and the Disappearance of Sustained Earnings Growth." *Journal of Financial Economics,* Vol. 40, No. 3: 341–371.

DeAngelo, Harry, Linda DeAngelo, and Douglas Skinner. 2004. "Are Dividends Disappearing? Dividend Concentration and the Consolidation of Earnings." *Journal of Financial Economics,* Vol. 72, No. 3: 425–456.

Demirguc-Kunt, Asli, and Voljislav Maksimovic. 1998. "Law, Finance, and Company Growth." *Journal of Finance,* Vol. 53, No. 6: 2107–2137.

Demirguc-Kunt, Asli, and Voljislav Maksimovic. 1999. "Institutions, Financial Markets, and Company Debt Maturity." *Journal of Financial Economics,* Vol. 54, No. 3: 295–336.

Dimson, Elroy, Paul Marsh, and Mike Staunton. 2003. "Global Evidence on the Equity Risk Premium." *Journal of Applied Corporate Finance* (Fall): 27–38.

Domowitz, Ian, Jack Glen, and Ananth Madhavan. 2000. "International Evidence on Aggregate Corporate Financing Decisions." Pennsylvania State University working paper.

Edmondson, Gail. 2004. "How Parmalat Went Sour." *Business Week* (July 12).

Edwards, Edgar O., and Philip W. Bell. 1961. *The Theory and Measurement of Business Income.* Berkeley: University of California Press.

Erb, Claude, Campbell R. Harvey, and Tadas Viskanta. 1996. "Expected Returns and Volatility in 135 Countries." *Journal of Portfolio Management.*

Ezzell, John R., and R. Burr Porter. 1976. "Flotation Costs and the Weighted Average Cost of Capital." *Journal of Financial and Quantitative Analysis,* Vol. 11, No. 3: 403–413.

Fabozzi, Frank. 2004. *Fixed Income Analysis for the Chartered Financial Analyst® Program,* 2nd ed. Charlottesville, VA: CFA Institute.

Fama, Eugene, and Kenneth French. 1992. "The Cross-Section of Expected Stock Returns." *Journal of Finance,* Vol. 47, No. 2: 427–465.

Fama, Eugene, and Kenneth French. 2001. "Disappearing Dividends: Changing firm Characteristics or Lower Propensity to Pay?" *Journal of Financial Economics,* Vol. 60, No. 1: 3–43.

Fama, Eugene, and Kenneth French. 2004. "The Capital Asset Pricing Model: Theory and Evidence." *Journal of Economic Perspectives,* Vol. 18, No. 3: 25–46.

Fan, J.P.H., Sheridan Titman, and Garry J. Twite. 2004. "An International Comparison of Capital Structure and Debt Maturity Choices." European Finance Association 2003 Annual Conference Paper No. 769.

Fisher, Irving. 1930. *The Theory of Interest.* New York: Macmillan.

Gaughan, Patrick A. 2002. *Mergers, Acquisitions,, and Corporate Restructurings,* 3rd ed.Hoboken, NJ: Wiley.

Gill, Amar. 2001. "Corporate Governance in Emerging Markets—Saints and Sinners: Who's Got Religion?" CLSA Emerging Markets, *CG Watch research report* (April).

Gitman, Lawrence, and V. Mercurio. 1982. "Cost of Capital Techniques Used by Major U.S. Firms: Survey and Analysis of Fortune's 1000." *Financial Management,* Vol. 14, No. 4.

Gompers, Paul A., Joy L. Ishii, and Andrew Metrick. 2003. "Corporate Governance and Equity Prices." *Quarterly Journal of Economics,* Vol. 118, No. 1: 107–155.

Gordon, Myron J. 1962. *The Investment, Financing, and Valuation of the Corporation.* Homewood, IL: Irwin.

Gordon, Myron. 1963. "Optimal Investment and Financing Policy." *Journal of Finance,* Vol. 18, No. 2: 264–272.

Graham, Benjamin, David Dodd, et al. 1962. *Security Analysis,* 4th ed. New York: McGraw-Hill.

Graham, John R., and Campbell R. Harvey. 2001. "The Theory and Practice of Corporate Finance: Evidence from the Field." *Journal of Financial Economics,* Vol. 60, Nos. 2–3: 187–243.

Graham, John R., and Campbell Harvey. 2002. "How Do CFOs Make Capital Budgeting and Capital Structure Decisions?" *Journal of Applied Corporate Finance,* Vol. 15, No. 1: 8–22.

Grullon, Gustavo, and Roni Michaely. 2002. "Dividends, Share Repurchases, and the Substitution Hypothesis." *Journal of Finance,* Vol. 57, No. 4: 1649–1684.

Hall, Martin. 2003. "A/R Outsourcing: Coming of Age in the New Millennium." *Business Credit* (February): 1–2.

Hamada, Robert. 1972. "The Effect of the Firm's Capital Structure on the Systematic Risk of Common Stocks." *Journal of Finance,* Vol. 27, No. 2: 435–452.

Harvey, Campbell R. 2001. "The International Cost of Capital and Risk Calculator." Duke University working paper.

Harvey, Campbell R., Karl V. Lins, and Andrew H. Roper. 2004. "The Effect of Capital Structure When Expected Agency Costs Are Extreme." *Journal of Financial Economics,* Vol. 74, No. 1: 3–30.

Hirschleifer, Jack. 1958. "On the Theory of Optimal Investment Decisions." *Journal of Political Economy,* Vol. 66, No. 4: 329–352.

Ibbotson, Roger G., Paul D., Kaplan, and James D. Peterson. 1997. "Estimates of Small Stock Betas Are Much Too Low." *Journal of Portfolio Management,* Vol. 23, No. 4: 104–111.

Jensen, Michael C. 1969. "The Performance of Mutual Funds in the Period 1945–1964." *Journal of Finance.* Vol. 23, No. 2: 390–416.

Jensen, Michael C. 1986. "Agency Costs of Free Cash Flow, Corporate Finance, and Takeovers." *American Economic Review,* Vol. 76, No. 2: 323–329.

Jensen, Michael C., and William H. Meckling. 1976. "Theory of the Company: Managerial Behavior, Agency Costs, and Ownership Structure." *Journal of Financial Economics,* Vol. 3, No. 4: 305–360.

Kaserer, Christoph, and Fabian Steiner. 2004. "The Cost of Raising Capital—New Evidence from Seasoned Equity Offerings in Switzerland." Technische Universität München working paper (February).

Koller, T., M. Goedhart, and D. Wessels. 2005. *Valuation: Measuring and Managing the Value of Companies,* 4th ed. Hoboken, NJ: Wiley.

Lease, Ronald, et al. 2000. *Dividend Policy Its Impact on Firm Value.* Boston: Harvard Business School Press.

Lee, Inmoo, Scott Lochhead, Jay R. Ritter, and Quanshui Zhao. 1996. "The Costs of Raising Capital." *Journal of Financial Research,* Vol. 19, No. 1: 59–74.

Lintner, John. 1956. "Distribution of Incomes of Corporations Among Dividends, Retained Earnings, and Taxes." *American Economic Review,* Vol. 46: 97–113.

Lintner, John. 1962. "Dividends, Earnings, Leverage, Stock Prices and the Supply of Capital to Corporations."*Review of Economics and Statistics,* Vol. 44, No. 3: 243–269.

Maremont, Mark, and Laurie Cohen. 2002. "How Tyco's CEO Enriched Himself." *The Wall Street Journal* (August 7).

Mariscal, Jorge O., and Rafaelina M. Lee. 1993. "The Valuation of Mexican Stocks: An Extension of the Capital Asset Pricing Model." New York: Goldman Sachs.

Markon, Jerry, and Robert Frank. 2002. "Five Adelphia Officials Arrested on Fraud Charges." *The Wall Street Journal* (July 25): A3.

Marshall, Alfred. 1892. *Elements of Economics of Industry,* Book 2, Chapter 12, Sections 3 and 4. New York: Macmillan.

Megginson, William J. 1997. *Corporate Finance Theory.* Reading, MA: Addison-Wesley.

Mian, Shehzad L., and Clifford W. Smith. 1992. "Accounts Receivable Management Policy: Theory and Evidence." *Journal of Finance,* Vol. 47, No. 1: 169–200.

Miles, James A., and John R. Ezzell. 1980. "The Weighted Average Cost of Capital, Perfect Capital Markets, and Project Life: A Clarification."*Journal of Financial and Quantitative Analysis,* Vol. 15, No. 3: 719–730.

Miller, Merton H. 1977. "Debt and Taxes." *Journal of Finance,* Vol. 32, No. 2: 261–275.

Miller, Merton, and Franco Modigliani. 1961. "Dividend Policy, Growth, and the Valuation of Shares." *Journal of Business,* Vol. 34, No. 4: 411–433.

Modigliani, Franco, and Merton H. Miller. 1958. "The Cost of Capital, Corporation Finance, and the Theory of Investment."*American Economic Review,* Vol. 48, No. 3: 261–297.

Modigliani, Franco, and Merton H. Miller. 1963. "Corporate Income Taxes and the Cost of Capital: A Correction." *American Economic Review,* Vol. 54, No. 3: 433–443.

Myers, Stewart, and Nicholas S. Majluf. 1984. "Corporate Financing and Investment Decisions When Firms Have Information That Investors Do Not Have." *Journal of Financial Economics,* Vol. 13, No. 2: 187–221.

New York Society of Securities Analysts. 2003. *Corporate Governance Handbook.* New York City.

Nofsinger, John, and Kenneth Kim. 2003. *Infectious Greed.* Upper Saddle River, NJ: Prentice Hall Financial Times.

Peterson, Pamela P., and David R. Peterson. 1996. *Company Performance and Measures of Value Added.* Charlottesville, VA: The Research Foundation of the ICFA.

Powers, William C. Jr., Raymond S. Troubh, and Herbert S. Winokur, Jr. 2002. Report of Investigation by the Special Investigative Committee of the Board of Directors of Enron Corp. (February 1). Collingdale, PA: Diane Pub. Co.

Rajan, Raghuram G., and Luigi Zingales. 1995. "What Do We Know About Capital Structure? Some Evidence from International Data." *Journal of Finance*, Vol. 50, No. 5: 1421–1460.

Reilly, Frank, and Keith Brown. 2003. *Investment Analysis and Portfolio Management*, 7th ed. Mason, OH: South-Western.

Roll, Richard. 1986. "The Hubris Hypothesis on Corporate Takeovers." *Journal of Business*, Vol. 59, No. 2: 176–216.

Shefrin, Hersh and Meir Statman. 1984. "Explaining Investor Preference for Cash Dividends." *Journal of Financial Economics*, Vol. 13, No. 2: 253–282.

Siegel, Jeremy J. 2005. "Perspectives on the Equity Risk Premium." *Financial Analysts Journal*, Vol. 61, No. 6: 61–71.

Solnik, Bruno, and Dennis McLeavey. 2004. *International Investments,* 5th ed. Reading, MA: Addison-Wesley).

Stewart, G. Bennett. 1991. *The Quest for Value.* New York: HarperCollins.

Stowe, John D., Thomas R. Robinson, Jerald E. Pinto, and Dennis W. McLeavey. 2002. *Analysis of Equity Investments: Valuation.* Charlottesville, VA: Association for Investment Management and Research.

Materiality of Social, Environmental and Corporate Governance Issues to Equity Pricing: 11 Sector Studies by Brokerage House Analysts. 2004. New York: United Nations Environmental Programme Finance Initiative (UNEP FI), Asset Management Working Group.

Thomas, Landon Jr. 2004a. "Regulators Said to Be Focusing on Board's Vote for Grasso Pay." *The New York Times* (March 26).

Thomas, Landon Jr. 2004b. "Saying Grasso Duped Big Board, Suit Seeks Return of $100 Million." *The New York Times* (May 25).

Weston, J. Fred, and Samuel C. Weaver. 2001. *Mergers & Acquisitions.* New York: McGraw-Hill.

Weston, J. Fred, Kwang S. Chung, and Susan E. Hoag. 1990. *Mergers, Restructuring, and Corporate Control.* Upper Sadde River, NJ: Prentice Hall.

White, Gerald I., Ashwinpaul C. Sondhi, and Dov Fried. 2003. *The Analysis and Use of Financial Statements,* 3rd ed. Hoboken, NJ: Wiley.

ABOUT THE AUTHORS

Raj Aggarwal, CFA, is the Frank C. Sullivan Professor of International Business and Finance and the dean of the College of Business Administration at the University of Akron in Ohio. Prior to his current position, he was the Firestone Chair in Corporate Finance at Kent State University and the Mellen Chair in Finance at John Carroll University. He has also taught at Harvard University, the University of Michigan, and the University of South Carolina. He serves as a director of Ancora Mutual Funds, Manco/Henkel AC, and the Financial Executives Research Foundation, a division of Financial Executives International.

An author of texts and widely cited scholarly books and papers, he is ranked highly in studies of academic contributions in finance and international business. He has been an officer of professional associations such as the Financial Management Association and is a graduate of Leadership Cleveland and a member of the Union Club.

Catherine Clark, CFA, was a vice president at Bankers Trust and Reich & Tang, where she was a securities analyst and portfolio manager. Ms. Clark received her BA degree in economics from the University of Washington in 1972 and MBA degree from New York University in 1975. She has been a CFA charterholder since 1979 and has been an active volunteer with CFA Institute for more than twenty years.

Rosita P. Chang, PhD, CFA, is professor of finance and the codirector of the Asia Pacific Financial Markets (FIMA) Research Center at the Shidler College of Business, University of Hawaii at Manoa. Her research has appeared in the *Journal of Finance, Journal of International Business Studies, Journal of Financial Services Research,* and the *Pacific Basin Finance Journal,* among others. In addition, she has conducted commissioned studies for international institutions such as the Organisation for Economic Cooperation and Development (OECD), United Nations Industrial Development Organization, Securities & Futures Commission of Hong Kong, and several Asian stock exchanges. Her current research interests include issues related to Chinese capital markets, financial services industry, and market microstructure.

Dr. Chang received her BA from Mills College and her MBA and PhD from the University of Pittsburgh. She has been a CFA charterholder since 1984, and served as an independent trustee for Zurich Scudder Investments, Inc. from 1995 to 2001.

Michelle R. Clayman, CFA, is the founder, managing partner, and chief investment officer of New Amsterdam Partners LLC, an institutional money management firm in New York. Ms. Clayman received a degree in philosophy, politics, and economics from Oxford University in England, and an MBA from Stanford University, California. She has been a CFA charterholder since 1983. Ms. Clayman sits on the boards of the Society of Quantitative Analysts (of which she is a past president) and the Institute for Quantitative Research in Finance.

Yves Courtois, CFA, is a corporate finance director with 11 years of experience in the KPMG network advising European, American, Middle Eastern, and Asian firms. He has extensive cross-border work experience in Europe and in the United States. He is currently head of the valuation and alternative investments advisory groups in Luxembourg and is an accredited valuer within the KPMG global corporate finance network. His other key areas of expertise include M&A, due diligence, financial risk management, and structuring. He is a frequent speaker at alternative investment funds industry forums on private equity, hedge funds, and valuation. He has worked on a wide range of projects with CFA Institute, including a webcast and CFA curriculum development. He received his BSBA degree from Solvay Business School in Brussels in 1995 and an MS degree in accountancy from Katholieke Universiteit Leuven in Belgium in 1996.

Martin S. Fridson, CFA, is CEO of FridsonVision, LLC in New York. He is "perhaps the most well-known figure in the high yield world," according to *Investment Dealers' Digest*. Over a 25-year span with brokerage firms including Salomon Brothers, Morgan Stanley, and Merrill Lynch, he became known for his innovative work in credit analysis and investment strategy. He has served as president of the Fixed Income Analysts Society, governor of the Association for Investment Management and Research (now CFA Institute), and director of the New York Society of Security Analysts. In 2000, *The Green Magazine* called Fridson's *Financial Statement Analysis* "one of the most useful investment books ever." The Financial Management Association International named Fridson the Financial Executive of the Year in 2002. In 2000, he became the youngest person ever inducted into the Fixed Income Analysts Society Hall of Fame. Fridson received his BA cum laude in history from Harvard College and his MBA from Harvard Business School.

Jacques R. Gagné, CFA, is director of asset and risk management at La société de l'assurance automobile du Québec in Quebec City. He also teaches corporate finance to actuarial students at Laval University. Previously, he had been vice president at the Quebec Pension Board and director of financial planning at the Quebec Ministry of Finance. He also has 10 years of experience as a pension consulting actuary. Mr. Gagné received his BSc degree (mathematics) from McGill University in 1966, became a fellow of the Society of Actuaries and of the Canadian Institute of Actuaries in 1975, and has been a CFA charterholder since 1995.

Cynthia Harrington, CFA, is a business and investment writer focusing on investment theory and accounting practices. She is a contributing editor for *Accounting Today* and has written over 450 articles that appear in national publications, including *Bloomberg Wealth Manager, Entrepreneur Magazine, Fraud Magazine, CFA Magazine, Journal of Accountancy,* and *Financial Engineering News.* She is a coauthor of the "Financial Statement Fraud" course for the Association of Certified Fraud Examiners. Prior to her writing career in 1999, she was president/owner/CIO of Harrington Capital Management, Ltd., a value-style asset management company catering to high-net-worth individuals and small institutions. She holds a BA from St. Olaf College. She is a certified fraud examiner (CFE) and a member of the ACFE. Ms. Harrington has been a CFA charterholder since 1993 and serves on the board of trustees of the CFALA Charitable Foundation and on the board of the Applied Behavioral Finance Group.

Kenneth Kim, PhD, is an associate professor of finance at the State University of New York at Buffalo. At SUNY-Buffalo, Dr. Kim teaches corporate finance and international corporate finance to MBA students. During 1998 and 1999, Dr. Kim worked as a senior financial economist at the U.S. Securities and Exchange Commission in Washington, D.C., where he worked on a wide variety of corporate finance and governance issues, including mergers and acquisitions regulations. His primary research interests include corporate finance and corporate governance. He has been published in the *Journal of Finance, Journal of Business, Journal of Corporate Finance,* and *Journal of Banking and Finance,* among other leading journals. Dr. Kim is also a coauthor of *Infectious Greed* and the textbooks *Corporate Governance* and *Global Corporate Finance.* Dr. Kim has also won numerous awards for teaching.

Adam Kobor, PhD, CFA, is a principal investment officer at the World Bank Treasury. Mr. Kobor is responsible for strategic asset allocation and active risk budgeting recommendations for several internal and external clients of the World Bank Group. He also advises central banks and other institutions on topics related to investment policy, asset allocation, and risk management. Prior to joining the World Bank in 2001, he worked for the National Bank of Hungary as a risk analyst. His main responsibilities covered the preparation and periodic revision of the investment policy, as well as the development of several risk analytics for the foreign exchange reserves portfolio. Mr. Kobor has been a CFA charterholder since 2002 and received his PhD in business administration from the Budapest University of Economic Sciences in 2003. He is author and coauthor of several publications, and he speaks at conferences.

Gene C. Lai is Safeco Distinguished Professor of Insurance and chair of the Department of Finance, Insurance, and Real Estate at Washington State University. Professor Lai received his bachelor's degree in economics from National Chengchi University in Taiwan, his master's degree in decision science from Georgia State University in 1981, and his doctorate degree in risk management and insurance and finance from the University of Texas at Austin in 1987. His publications have appeared in *The Journal of Risk and Insurance* and *Journal of Banking and Finance* among others. Dr. Lai serves as a coeditor for the *Journal of Insurance Issues* and associate editor for many journals, including *The Journal of Risk and Insurance.* He is a board member of the American Risk and Insurance Association and past president of the Western Risk and Insurance Association, and he was a board member of the Asia-Pacific Risk and Insurance Association.

Rebecca T. McEnally, PhD, CFA, is senior policy analyst with the Capital Markets Policy Group for the CFA Centre for Financial Market Integrity, where she is responsible for financial reporting and capital markets advocacy efforts of the CFA Centre. She has appeared on behalf of the members of CFA Institute before regulatory authorities, legislative bodies, professional associations, and the general public in both the United States and abroad to further the CFA Institute mandate to improve corporate financial reporting and disclosure. Prior to joining CFA Institute, Dr. McEnally taught financial reporting and financial statement analysis at various universities, including the University of North Carolina at Chapel Hill, the Stern School of Business at New York University, and the School of Management at Boston University. She has published a number of articles, monographs, and books, and she has served as a consultant on accounting and finance to financial institutions in the United States, Europe, and Asia.

Keith M. Moore, CFA, is managing partner of Jupiter Capital LLC, a hedge fund specializing in risk arbitrage. Prior to founding Jupiter Capital, he was a partner at Neuberger Berman, in charge of that firm's merger arbitrage and convertible arbitrage activities and a senior vice president in charge of merger arbitrage at Donaldson, Lufkin & Jenrette. Mr. Moore is also an adjunct professor of finance at New York University's Stern School of Business and an adjunct member of the faculty at the University of Rhode Island. He has been a CFA charterholder since 1982.

Edgar A. Norton, PhD, CFA, is professor of finance at the College of Business at Illinois State University. He has authored or coauthored more than 30 papers that have been published in journals and conference proceedings, as well as presented at international, national, and regional conferences. He is coauthor of several textbooks, including *Investments; Finance: An Introduction to Institutions, Investments, and Management; Foundations of Financial Management;* and *Economic Justice in Perspective: A Book of Readings.* Mr. Norton has served on the board of directors and as president of the Midwest Finance Association and on the board of the Financial Planning Association of Illinois. Mr. Norton has served CFA Institute for many years in a number of capacities.

Kenneth L. Parkinson is managing director of Treasury Information Services, a consulting and publishing firm. He is a visiting and adjunct associate professor at Stern Graduate School of Business at New York University, where he teaches courses in working capital management, corporate finance, and corporate treasury practices. Mr. Parkinson actively consults with corporations of all sizes on treasury management projects and is a frequent speaker at major industry conferences and seminars. He is the author or coauthor of several texts and a frequent author of articles in trade magazines. Previously, Mr. Parkinson was director of treasury operations at RCA Corporation, managing treasury and banking activities worldwide. He holds a BS from Penn State and an MBA from Wharton Graduate School, and he is a permanently certified cash manager (CCM).

Pamela Peterson Drake, PhD, CFA, is department head and J. Gray Ferguson Professor of Finance at James Madison University. Professor Peterson Drake received her PhD from the University of North Carolina at Chapel Hill, and taught at Florida State University and Florida Atlantic University before joining James Madison University. She has been a CFA charterholder since 1992. Professor Peterson Drake is author and coauthor of a number of books, including *The Complete CFO: From Accounting to Accountability,* with Frank J. Fabozzi and Ralph S. Polimeni; *Analysis of Financial Statements* and *Financial Management and Analysis,* both with Frank J. Fabozzi; and *Real Options* (AIMR Research Foundation), with Don Chance. She has published numerous articles in academic and practitioner journals.

John D. Stowe, PhD, CFA, is head of Curriculum Development at CFA Institute. He is coauthor of *Analysis of Equity Investments: Valuation* and *Corporate Financial Management* and author of 25 professional and academic journal articles in finance. He received his BA degree from Centenary College and his PhD from University of Houston. Prior to joining CFA Institute in 2003, he was finance professor, department head, and associate dean at the University of Missouri. He became a CFA charterholder in 1995 and has served the CFA Program in a number of capacities.

George H. Troughton, PhD, CFA, is professor emeritus of finance at California State University, Chico. He holds an AB degree from Brown, an MBA from Columbia, and a PhD from the University of Massachusetts, Amherst. He began his career as an investment analyst at Lehman Brothers and Scudder, Stevens & Clark in New York. He was professor of finance at Babson College before moving to Chico, California. Mr. Troughton has been an active participant in the CFA Program for more than 20 years. At CFA Institute, he was awarded the C. Stewart Sheppard Award in 1999 and the Donald L. Tuttle Award in 2004. He occasionally teaches a corporate finance course at California State, Chico.

ABOUT THE
CFA PROGRAM

The Chartered Financial Analyst® designation (CFA®) is a globally recognized standard of excellence for measuring the competence and integrity of investment professionals. To earn the CFA charter, candidates must successfully pass through the CFA Program, a global graduate-level self-study program that combines a broad curriculum with professional conduct requirements as preparation for a wide range of investment specialties.

Anchored by a practice-based curriculum, the CFA Program is focused on the knowledge identified by professionals as essential to the investment decision-making process. This body of knowledge maintains current relevance through a regular, extensive survey of practicing CFA charterholders across the globe. The curriculum covers 10 general topic areas ranging from equity and fixed-income analysis to portfolio management to corporate finance, all with a heavy emphasis on the application of ethics in professional practice. Known for its rigor and breadth, the CFA Program curriculum highlights principles common to every market so that professionals who earn the CFA designation have a thoroughly global investment perspective and a profound understanding of the global marketplace.

www.cfainstitute.org

INDEX

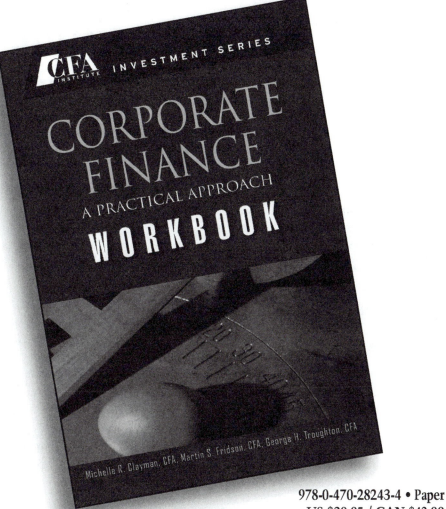

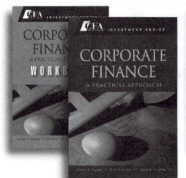
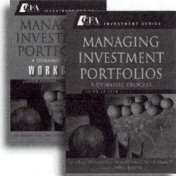

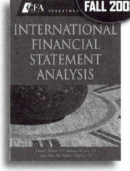